Islam and Rationality

Islamic Philosophy, Theology and Science

TEXTS AND STUDIES

Edited by

Hans Daiber
Anna Akasoy
Emilie Savage-Smith

VOLUME 94

The titles published in this series are listed at *brill.com/ipts*

Islam and Rationality

The Impact of al-Ghazālī

Papers Collected on His 900th Anniversary

VOLUME 1

Edited by

Georges Tamer

BRILL

LEIDEN | BOSTON

Cover illustration by Georges Tamer and Allen Tuazon.

Library of Congress Cataloging-in-Publication Data

Islam and rationality : the impact of al-Ghazali : papers collected on his 900th anniversary / edited by Georges Tamer.
volumes cm. — (Islamic philosophy, theology and science ; v. 94)
Includes bibliographical references and index.
ISBN 978-90-04-29094-5 (hardback : alk. paper) — ISBN 978-90-04-29095-2 (e-book) 1. Ghazzali, 1058-1111. 2. Faith and reason—Islam. 3. Practical reason. 4. Rationalism. I. Tamer, Georges.

B753.G34I78 2015
297.2092—dc23

2015014839

This publication has been typeset in the multilingual "Brill" typeface. With over 5,100 characters covering Latin, IPA, Greek, and Cyrillic, this typeface is especially suitable for use in the humanities.
For more information, please see www.brill.com/brill-typeface.

ISSN 0169-8729
ISBN 978-90-04-29094-5 (hardback)
ISBN 978-90-04-29095-2 (e-book)

This book is printed on acid-free paper.

Allen Tuazon
(25th November 1980–22nd November 2014)
In Memoriam

Contents

Preface IX
Notes on Contributors XX

1 **God versus Causality**
Al-Ghazālī's Solution and its Historical Background 1
Hans Daiber

2 **Al-Ghazālī's Changing Attitude to Philosophy** 23
Wilferd Madelung

3 **Al-Ghazālī and the Rationalization of Sufism** 35
Binyamin Abrahamov

4 **Revelation, Sciences and Symbolism**
Al-Ghazālī's **Jawāhir al-Qur'ān** 49
Georges Tamer

5 **Al-Ghazālī at His Most Rationalist**
The Universal Rule for Allegorically Interpreting Revelation (al-Qānūn al-Kullī fī t-Ta'wīl) 89
Frank Griffel

6 **The Comedy of Reason**
Strategies of Humour in al-Ghazālī 121
Eric Ormsby

7 **Al-Ghazālī on the Emotions** 138
Taneli Kukkonen

8 **Sex, Marriage and the Family in Al-Ghazālī's Thought**
Some Preliminary Notes 165
Avner Giladi

9 **The Duties of the Teacher**
Al-Iṣfahānī's **Dharī'a** *as a Source of Inspiration for al-Ghazālī's* **Mīzān al-'Amal** 186
Yasien Mohamed

10 Revisiting al-Ghazālī's Crisis through His *Scale for Action* (*Mizān al-ʿAmal*) 207
Kenneth Garden

11 Al-Ghazālī on Knowledge (*ʿilm*) and Certainty (*yaqīn*) in *al-Munqidh min aḍ-Ḍalāl* and in *al-Qisṭās al-Mustaqīm* 229
Luis Xavier López-Farjeat

12 Ghazālī's Hermeneutics and Their Reception in Jewish Tradition *Mishkāt al-Anwār* (*The Niche of Lights*) and Maimonides' *Shemonah Peraqim* (*Eight Chapters*) 253
Scott Michael Girdner

13 Al-Ghazālī, Averroes and Moshe Narboni *Conflict and Conflation* 275
Alfred L. Ivry

14 The Changing Image of al-Ghazālī in Medieval Jewish Thought 288
Steven Harvey

15 The Influence of al-Ghazālī on the Juridical, Theological and Philosophical Works of Barhebraeus 303
Hidemi Takahashi

16 R. Marti and His References to al-Ghazālī 326
Jules Janssens

17 Al-Ghazālī's Esotericism According to Ibn Taymiyya's *Bughyat al-Murtād* 345
Yahya M. Michot

18 Arbitrating between al-Ghazālī and the Philosophers *The* Tahāfut *Commentaries in the Ottoman Intellectual Context* 375
M. Sait Özervarlı

Bibliography 399
Index of Works by al-Ghazālī 440
Index of Authors 442
Index of Subjects 452

Preface

The studies included in this volume will discuss important topics of al-Ghazālī's work, which demonstrate rational aspects of his interpretation of Islamic theology and spirituality, as rooted in the Qur'ān. In the Qur'ān, the root *ʿ-Q-L* – meaning at its core, "reason/reasoning" and "understanding" – occurs fifty-nine times; the verbs are not exclusively meant to imply rational activities. In almost all occurrences, these verbs are semantically related to the senses, and in several instances connote a conversion to the proclaimed religion as a result of the perception of natural phenomena.[1] Rationality as presented throughout the Qur'ān is clearly a cognitive activity in which a sensual perception is involved that in turn leads man to believe in God. In reverse, to not believe in God means that man eliminates his rational faculty. Remarkably, this conception of a 'towards-faith-oriented-rationality' corresponds with the Qur'ānic characterization of Arabia's pre-Islamic era as a period of ignorance, the *jāhiliyya*.[2]

While the faculty of reasoning – that is, the intellect – does not appear in the scripture of Islam, it is nevertheless declared in a statement attributed to the Prophet Muhammad as the noblest ability created by God. The first act the newly created *ʿaql* performs is the requirement of total submission to God's obedience: God commanded the intellect to first approach Him, and then conversely to get away from Him, and each time the intellect obeyed God's command. Furthermore, the intellect serves within this *ḥadīth* as a reminder of God's reward and punishment of humans.[3] The beginning of the statement might be interpreted in two different ways, however. According to one interpretation (*awwalu mā khalaqa Allāhu l-ʿaqlu*) the intellect is the very first

1 See for example: Q 2:164, 242; 3:118; 16:12; 23:80; 30:28; 37:138; 59:14; 67:10.

2 Q 3:154; 5:50; 48:26. In his MA-Thesis, Allen Tuazon provided a semantic study of the root ʿ-Q-L in the Qur'ān: " 'Understanding' in Revelation: the root ʿ-Q-L in the Qur'ān," 2011: https://etd.ohiolink.edu/!etd.send_file?accession=osu1306868259&disposition=inline.

3 "*Awwal mā khalaqa Allāhu l-ʿaql qāla lahu: aqbil fa-aqbal. Thumma qāla lahu: adbir fa-adbar. Thumma qāl: wa-ʿizzatī wa-jalālī mā khalaqtu khalqan akrama ʿalayya minka, bika ākhudhu wa-bika uʿṭī wa-bika uthību wa-bika uʿāqib.*" This is the wording of the *ḥadīth* as it is quoted by al-Ghazālī (s. below n. 10). The *ḥadīth* is weak without reliable authorities of transmission. It is not mentioned in the canonical collections. In aṭ-Ṭabarānī, *Al-Muʿjam al-awsaṭ*, Ed. Ṭāriq b. ʿAwaḍ Allāh b. Muḥammad and ʿAbdalmuḥin b. Ibrāhīm al-Ḥusaynī, 10 Vols., Cairo: Dār al-Ḥramayn 1415/1996, No. 1845 (Vol. 2, p. 235f.) and No. 7241 (Vol. 7, p. 190f.), the *ḥadīth* begins with a temporal assertion: "*Lammā khalaqa Allāhu* [...]," "When God created [...]."

being created by God and thus holds a primary position amongst all beings.[4] Another version begins with a more temporal genesis (*awwala mā khalaqa Allāhu l-ʿaqla*), and states merely that the first thing that happened to the intellect upon its creation was that it immediately received God's command, and consequently submitted itself accordingly.[5] The former version corresponds to the cosmologies of the philosophers who ascribe to the intellect primacy in the chain of beings.[6] By contrast, theologians who accept only the latter version indicate an accidental nature to the intellect.[7] As confirmed by Ibn Taymiyya, this *ḥadīth* has been persistently subjected to extensive controversy within theological and philosophical circles, although its authenticity remains in doubt.[8]

Both the scriptural evidence as well as the contradictory versions of the above-mentioned prophetic statement demonstrates the strained position that rationality occupies in relation to religion in pre-modern Islamic intellectual discourses.[9] Yet, the history of the Arab-Islamic civilization shows brilliant articulations of rational thought throughout different fields of scholarship.

---

4 *"Awwalu mā khalaqa Allāhu l-ʿaqlu qāla lahu: aqbil fa-aqbal. Thumma qāla lahu: adbir fa-adbar. Thumma qāl: wa-ʿizzatī wa-jalālī mā khalaqtu khalqan akrama ʿalayya minka, bika ākhudhu wa-bika uʿṭī wa-bika uthību wa-bika uʿāqib."*

"The first thing which God created was the intellect. On creating it He said to it: 'Come forth!' and it came forth. He then said to it 'Return!' and it returned. Thereupon He said: 'By my power and glory! I have not created anything which is more reverent to me than you. Through you I take and through you I give; through you I reward and through you I punish.' "

5 *"Awwala mā khalaqa Allāhu l-ʿaqla qāla lahu: aqbil fa-aqbal. Thumma qāla lahu: adbir fa-adbar. Thumma qāl: wa-ʿizzatī wa-jalālī mā khalaqtu khalqan akrama ʿalayya minka, bika ākhudhu wa-bika uʿṭī wa-bika uthību wa-bika uʿāqib."*

"At first, when God created the intellect, He said to it: 'Come forth!' and it came forth. He then said to it 'Return!' and it returned. Thereupon He said: 'By my power and glory! I have not created anything which is more reverent to me than you. Through you I take and through you I give; through you I reward and through you I punish.' "

6 See for instance *Al-Fārābī on the Perfect State*: Abū Naṣr al-Fārābī's *Mabādiʾ ārāʾ ahl al-madīna al-fāḍila*. A revised text with introduction, translation, and commentary by Richard Walzer, Oxford: Clarendon Press, 1985, Ch. 3, p. 100; Ibn Sīnā, *Ash-Shifāʾ. Al-Ilāhiyyāt*, Ed. G. C. Anawati and S. Zayed, Rev. I. Madkour, Beirut: n.p., n.d., IX, 4, pp. 402–409.

7 See for instance Taqī d-Dīn Ibn Taymiyya, *Majmūʿ fatāwā Ibn Taymiyya*, 37 Volumes, Mujammaʿ al-Malik Fahd, Riad 1416/1995. Vol. 18, pp. 336–338.

8 Ibid. See above n. 3.

9 It should be mentioned in this context that the subordination of the human intellectual faculty to God's power is also substantial in the Scriptures of Judaism and Christianity. See for instance: Proverbs 1:7, where the fear of God precedes wisdom; St. Paul, 1 Cor. 1: 18–21, declares that through Christ's crucifixion God made foolish the wisdom of the world.

In particular, the works of the great philosophers (*al-falāsifa*) and scientists of the Abbasid period are brilliant testimony to their creativity in respect of achievements of rationality. Certainly one major area of Arab-Islamic philosophy is that which addresses religious phenomena, such as the prophecies and hermeneutics of the Qur'ān. Here, Muslim philosophers such as al-Fārābī, Ibn Sīnā and Ibn Rushd were able to make important contributions of lasting relevance for the philosophical interpretation of religion. In addition, some *mutakallimūn* like the Muʿtazilites and the Ashʿarites developed rational approaches to complicated theological questions. It is in this philosophical and theological context that al-Ghazālī undertook his theological education and developed his rational and balanced Sufism.

In accordance with the philosophers and the *Ikhwān aṣ-Ṣafā'*, al-Ghazālī advocated the reading of the above-mentioned *ḥadīth*, which presented the intellect, *ʿaql*, as the very first substance that God created.[10] Taking rationality as the criterion, modern scholarship presents two contradictory images of al-Ghazālī, however. For generations of scholars in both the East and the West al-Ghazālī was considered to be disdainful of rationality due to his mystical worldview, and to a large extent allegedly contributed to a decline of philosophy in Islam that, its proponents argue, continues to the present.[11] This view predominates in Arabic scholarship, particularly among adherents of Averroes.[12] For others, al-Ghazālī is a rational jurist and theologian who created a symbiosis of philosophy and theology and infused rationality into Sufism.[13]

---

10 Al-Ghazālī, who is known for depending on prophetic statements with weak transmission (*isnād*), refers to this statement several times. See for instance: *Iḥyā' ʿulūm ad-dīn*, ed. ʿAbd al-Muʿṭī Amīn Qalʿajī, 2nd Ed., Beirut: Dār Ṣādir, 2004, 5 volumes, Book 1: *Kitāb al-ʿIlm*, Vol. 1, p. 117; Book 21: *Kitāb Sharḥ ʿajā'ib al-qalb*, Vol. 3, p. 5.

11 See e.g. Arnaldez, Roger, "Falsafa," in: *EI*², ii, Leiden: Brill 1965, 769–775; Watt, William Montgomery, "al-Ghazālī," in: *EI*², ii, Leiden: Brill 1965, 1038–1041.

12 Eminent scholars like Muḥammad ʿĀbid al-Jābirī, Ḥassan Ḥanafī and Naṣr Ḥāmid Abū Zayd represent this classical position ascribing to al-Ghazālī an anti-rational attitude and accusing him of launching the destruction of rational thought in Islam. See for instance: Muḥammad ʿĀbid al-Jābirī, *Naqd al-ʿaql al-ʿarabī*, 3 Volumes: 1: *Takwīn al-ʿaql al-ʿarabī*, Beirut: Markaz Dirāsāt al-Waḥda al-ʿArabiyya 1982; 2: *Bunyat al-ʿaql al-ʿarabī*, Beirut: Markaz Dirāsāt al-Waḥda al-ʿArabiyya 1986; 3: *al-ʿAql as-siyāsī l-ʿarabī*, Beirut: Markaz Dirāsāt al-Waḥda l-ʿArabiyya 1990; Naṣr Ḥāmid Abū Zayd, *Mafhūm an-naṣṣ. Dirāsa fī ʿulūm al-Qur'ān*, 3rd Ed., Beirut: Al-Markaz ath-Thaqāfī l-ʿArabī, 1996, pp. 243–311; id., *An-Naṣṣ, as-sulṭa, al-ḥaqīqa*, Beirut: Al-Markaz ath-Thaqāfī l-ʿArabī, 1997; Ḥassan Ḥanafī, *Min al-fanā' ilā l-baqā'. Muḥāwala li-iʿādat binā' ʿulūm at-taṣawwuf*, 2 Volumes, Beirut: Dār al-Madār al-Islāmī 2009.

13 The pioneer work of this interpretation is Richard M. Frank's study *Al-Ghazālī and the Ashʿarite School*, Durham: Duke University Press, 1994. In the same line: Frank Griffel,

In fact, al-Ghazālī himself attacked early Greek and Muslim philosophers with accusations of apostasy since they believed in the eternity of the world, rejected God's knowledge of particular objects, and negated physical resurrection. At the same time, however, al-Ghazālī made full use of Aristotelian logic in his books on jurisprudence, ethics, and dogmatic theology. A true adherent of skepsis, he developed a concept of religious spirituality based upon rationality in his *magnum opus, Iḥyāʾ ʿulūm ad-dīn* (Revival of Religious Knowledge).

Al-Ghazālī considered himself a reformer of Islam. He based his reformation on a balance between rationality and spirituality. His project which was not unencumbered by inconsistencies included an infusion of logical methods and criteria into jurisprudence, the liberation of theology from blind imitation (*taqlīd*) for it to become more critical, and the rationalization of Sufism to free itself of excessiveness. Al-Ghazālī's aim was to design a way of life for his fellow Muslims, combining knowledge and action (*al-ʿilm wa-l-ʿamal*), and centered around the knowledge required to qualify an individual soul to enjoy eternal life in the Hereafter (*ʿilm ṭarīq al-ākhira*). It is for this reason that he wrote his *Iḥyāʾ*. This voluminous work presents a system of Islamic orthodoxy and orthopraxy intertwined. Rationality is an integral part of this system: it is the power that balances various and sometimes-conflicting forces and traditions. Al-Ghazālī does not consider rationality itself the highest form of knowledge. He ascribes this position to the ability of spiritual 'tasting' (*dhawq*) that goes beyond the limits of human rationality in order to obtain knowledge of spiritual realities. Nevertheless, rationality is actively present in this conception as a factor of stabilization and protection against radicalism and excessiveness. Despite his critique of the philosophers (*falāsifa*) and his decision to follow the path of Sufism, al-Ghazālī did not cease to be a rational Muslim scholar; he continued to utilize rational ideas and critical methods adopted from the philosophers (mainly Ibn Sīnā) and incorporated into his epistemological system.

Based on this understanding of al-Ghazālī and his legacy, the present and subsequent volumes will be dedicated to examining al-Ghazālī's lifelong aspiration to combine Islam and rationality.[14] This volume includes papers presented at the international conference "Islam and Rationality: The Impact of al-Ghazālī," which I organized at The Ohio State University in Columbus, Ohio,

---

Al-Ghazālī's Philosophical Theology, Oxford: Oxford University Press 2009; Alexander Treiger, *Inspired Knowledge in Islamic Thought. Al-Ghazālī's theory of mystical cognition and its Avicennian foundation*, Routledge, 2012, and several studies by Jules Janssens.

14 The forthcoming second volume of "Islam and Rationality: The Impact of al-Ghazālī," edited by Frank Griffel, includes papers presented on the workshop "Al-Ghazālī and His Influence," held at Yale University, New Haven, on December 9–10, 2011.

from 10–12 November 2011, on the occasion of Abū Ḥāmid's 900th anniversary. The majority of the papers herein deal with various aspects of al-Ghazālī's ambitious aims to bring rationality and Islamic religiosity into an enduring symbiosis, and some contributions address how al-Ghazālī's intellectual endeavors were later received by scholars who had the same concern of reconciling religion and rationality within and beyond the sphere of Islam.

The conflicting discussions in early Islam on divine determinism, and the attempts of certain circles to replace God by matter as a cause of change, resulted in a concept of causality that rationality was the essence within nature that shaped the world. As an example of reconciling God's creationist power with the role of natural causes, the Muʿtazilite an-Naẓẓām (d. ca. 230/845) stated that God intrinsically provided the stone with a nature that meant it would roll if someone pushed it. Hans Daiber's contribution shows how subsequent discussions by Islamic theologians and philosophers culminated in the seemingly contradictory solution provided by al-Ghazālī, when he proposed that God is the first cause, and yet at the same time, causality then followed strict rules of cause and effect. The paper argues that Neoplatonists had postulated a similarity between the transcendent divine cause and the effects that resulted from intermediate causes. The hierarchy of cause and effects was actually the background of Ibn Sīnā's concept of different modes of existence as regards priority and posteriority, self-sufficiency and need, necessity and possibility. Conditioning causes are thus superior to the conditioned effects. Due to the multitude of intermediate causes, the ultimate divine cause makes possible many similar effects, which in turn marks the beginning of a certain separation between natural sciences and theology. For al-Ghazālī, it was not necessary to finalize this separation; he developed Ibn Sīnā's Neoplatonic hierarchy of cause and effect, later criticized by al-Ghazālī's adversary Ibn Rushd.

In the next paper, Wilferd Madelung traces al-Ghazālī's changing attitude to philosophy, subsequent to his famous refutation of the philosophers in *Tahāfut al-falāsifa*. The title of the book may suggest that al-Ghazālī intended to point out contradictions and inconsistencies in philosophical thought. Al-Ghazālī was in fact more concerned with a demonstration of the incompatibility of philosophical thought with the Sunnī Muslim creed. In particular he maintained that three points of Ibn Sīnā's teaching constituted unbelief (*kufr*) in Islam: the thesis of the eternity of the world; God's knowledge only of universals; and the denial of the physical resurrection. On the other hand, al-Ghazālī's *Maqāṣid al-falāsifa*, which he composed shortly before the *Tahāfut*, demonstrates his admiration for the rational achievement of Ibn Sīnā. In later life, al-Ghaẓālī wrote several treatises he reserved for his elite students, in which he seemed to fully adopt the philosophical thought of Ibn Sīnā – even in the arguments he had described as unbelief in his *Tahāfut*. It seems evident that al-Ghazālī no longer considered Ibn Sīnā a rationalist philosopher, but rather, an inspired Sufi. There are indications, however, that al-Ghazālī ultimately remained undecided on whether the philosophers or the theologians were in possession of the truth about God and the world.

Philosophy penetrated not only into the spheres of cosmology, cosmogony, and causality of al-Ghazālī's thought, but also into his Sufism. This is demonstrated in the contribution of Binyamin Abrahamov, particularly through his close observation of the concept of *tafakkur*, meaning the syllogistic procedure that brings together two parts of knowledge in order to conclude from them a third. Al-Ghazālī did not limit the process of attaining knowledge only to the discussion of metaphysical issues; he also recognized it as the principle that helps the Sufi to master the stations (*maqāmāt*) of the Sufi path, which are each composed of knowledge, states, and acts. Knowledge is the fruit of *tafakkur*, and produces states that subsequently cause one's actions. The paper shows that, for al-Ghazālī, *tafakkur* is the key to all good things, and that syllogistic thinking stands at the root of all mystical Sufi aspirations.

Through an in-depth investigation of al-Ghazālī's *Jawāhir al-Qurʾān wa-duraruhu* (The Jewels of the Qurʾān and its Pearls), Georges Tamer demonstrates how, in this treatise, al-Ghazālī applied rationality to the highly symbolic hermeneutics of the Qurʾān. As a result of this hermeneutical approach, the Qurʾān appears as a stimulus for the believer, in not only the acquisition of religious knowledge, but also the scientific. The paper presents distinctive features of al-Ghazālī's reasoning as formulated in *The Jewels*, including what appears to be al-Ghazālī's ultimate response to Ibn Sīnā's division of rational sciences.

Similarly, the contribution by Frank Griffel reveals striking rational features of al-Ghazālī's theory of the interpretation of sacred texts. This study deals with al-Ghazālī's short text *al-Qānūn al-kullī fī t-taʾwīl* (The Universal Rule of Interpreting Revelation), initially a letter addressed to his student Abū Bakr ibn al-ʿArabī (d. 543/1148), and written in response to a number of questions pertaining to certain *aḥādīth*. Chief amongst them was the *ḥadīth*, "Satan runs in the blood vessels of one of you." Al-Ghazālī's clarification of the word "satan" as a cipher for bad temptations and whisperings from the active intellect is clearly inspired by certain teachings of Ibn Sīnā. Furthermore, the concept regarding the relationship between reason and revelation displayed in this letter is distinct from al-Ghazālī's writings elsewhere. Instead, here he exposes a radical rationalism that clearly challenges the Ashʿarite school traditions.

Eric Ormsby's study explores some of the ways in which al-Ghazālī employed humor in his works in order to finalize his arguments. His methods ranged from rhetorical devices as *reductio ad absurdum*, hyperbole and irony, to outright satire, caricature and parody, seen through examples drawn mainly from *Iḥyāʾ ʿulūm ad-dīn* and *Tahāfut al-falāsifa*. The author argues that the importance of such considerations is twofold: firstly, they demonstrate that al-Ghazālī, in his use of such devices, was firmly positioned within the classic tradition of *adab*; and secondly, they allow certain aspects of tone and style exhibited within his prose to be explored. The suspect reputation which al-Ghazālī encountered amongst various detractors – for example, recurrent accusations of insincerity or inconsistency – may be explained, at least in part, by his employment of such stylistic strategies. Ormsby's paper demonstrates that al-Ghazālī's irony was too often taken quite literally.

Taneli Kukkonen's contribution discusses al-Ghazālī's rational assessment as to how virtues are cultivated, an area of thought that has received surprisingly little philosophical attention to date. It is a commonplace argument that al-Ghazālī's later works addressed practical concerns, as these are often considered the works of a religious reformer and moral preacher rather than of a theorist. Even if the overall characterization of al-Ghazālī's later works as ethical treatises were accurate, one might yet wonder whether an intellectual such as al-Ghazālī could have left the domain of philosophical reflection untouched by his own preconceptions – particularly as the inner reform of Islam and the unification of knowledge and practice stood at the center of his intellectual project. According to the author, it turns out that al-Ghazālī's exposition of moral psychology represents a reasonably sophisticated and well thought-out interpretation of Aristotelian virtue ethics. In order to demonstrate this, the focus of the paper rests upon specific problems that arise from a need to balance habituation and practical reasoning as resources for virtuous action.

Thereafter, Avner Giladi examines al-Ghazālī's attitudes towards sex, marriage, and family. As a jurist loyal to a comprehensive and total legal system, al-Ghazālī did not hesitate to address the most intimate aspects of the Islamic way of life – including marriage and procreation as encouraged by the *Sharīʿa*. For Sufis, on the other hand, the option of seclusion and withdrawal from sex, although probably not frequently applied, seemed legitimate. In his efforts to harmonize these two religious approaches, al-Ghazālī offered an extremely interesting discussion, rich not only in sophisticated legal, theological and ethical arguments, but also because they reveal his own psychological insights. Sex, marriage, and family and their place and context within the *Iḥyāʾ*, as well as the manner of how they are interwoven into the greater plan, are a few of the specific topics discussed in this chapter.

For his part, Yasien Mohamed provides a new discussion of the question of whether al-Ghazālī's ethics of teaching was inspired by ar-Rāghib al-Iṣfahānī's (d. 452/1060) educational thinking. With a focus on al-Iṣfahānī's *adh-Dharīʿa ilā makārim ash-sharīʿa* and al-Ghazālī's *Mīzān al-ʿamal*, the study offers a detailed analysis of the content, style, and differences between these two works. The paper also pays particular attention to the duties of the teacher, which form a major part of any discussion surrounding the ethics of education.

Al-Ghazālī's ethical work *Mīzān al-ʿamal* (The Criterion for Action) is examined in Ken Garden's contribution that offers a new evaluation of al-Ghazālī's famous personal crisis of 488/1095. This resulted in al-Ghazālī's well-known transformation: his acceptance of the practice of Sufism, his relinquishment of a prestigious post at the Niẓāmiyya madrassa in Baghdad, and his renunciation of any officially sponsored teaching position for the next eleven years. The crisis also led al-Ghazālī to openly promote a radical plan found within the *Iḥyāʾ*. By comparing the *Revival* to *The Criterion*, the paper seeks to identify continuities and changes in al-Ghazālī's ethical thought before and after 488/1095. Garden focuses upon the question of the respective roles of philosophy and Sufism, and thereafter his ethical thought and agenda, which emanated from al-Ghazālī's crisis.

Intrinsically related to al-Ghazālī's famous crisis is his conception of *ʿilm* (knowledge) and *yaqīn* (certainty). In his autobiographical treatise *al-Munqidh min aḍ-ḍalal*, al-Ghazālī carefully evaluated the different means and methods of the seekers of truth, i.e., theologians, philosophers, authoritarians, and mystics. These seekers differ regarding the various ways and methods to be used in order to attain truth and avoid error. Al-Ghazālī addressed certain epistemological difficulties on the sources of knowledge and their connections to certainty when searching for the correct method for the attainment of truth. This methodology could be brought into contemporary discussions, specifically the epistemic controversies related to skepticism, foundationalism, and fallibilism. Examining al-Ghazālī's explanation of the different methods of knowledge, Luis Xavier López-Farjeat presents al-Ghazālī as a foundationalist who adopted skepticism as a starting point of his epistemology. López-Farjeat discusses al-Ghazālī's intent to show that the only alternative to avoid skepticism was to defend the view that the first principles or primary truths – wherein knowledge is grounded – must be instinctively understood. This solution, however, is directly connected with the knowledge that God guarantees the ultimate foundations of knowledge. Al-Ghazālī's question on the nature of knowledge is therefore a simultaneous question on the correct way of knowing God – a question that leads to an original understanding of the relationship between reason and revelation.

The next chapters of the present volume deal with the reception of al-Ghazālī's project to harmonize Islam and rationality by Jewish, Christian and Muslim scholars alike. Scott Girdner provides a brief overview of his conception of al-Ghazālī's combination of traditionalist and rationalist scriptural hermeneutics, focusing on the role of the psychology of the philosophers. Concentrating on *Mishkāt al-anwār* (The Niche of Lights), the paper argues that al-Ghazālī adapted Ibn Sīnā's philosophical psychology to assert both the validity of rationalist epistemologies, and the traditionalist hermeneutical principle that the truths of God and the Qur'ān exhaust human comprehension. The author then provides an overview of the reception of al-Ghazālī's philosophical-psychological hermeneutics in the medieval Jewish tradition.

Alfred Ivry, in his paper, investigates the complex relationship between al-Ghazālī and Moses Narboni (d. 1362), a follower of Averroes. Narboni considered *Maqāṣid al-falāsifa* to be al-Ghazālī's confirmation of Avicenna's philosophy; his positive attitude towards al-Ghazālī's book is reflected in the reception it received amongst Jewish readers. Ivry shows, however, that Narboni's acceptance of al-Ghazālī's Avicennianism is limited to its compatibility with Averroes's doctrines.

Steven Harvey then presents the impact of al-Ghazālī on the development of rational discourses in Judaism. Al-Ghazālī was known in twelfth century Andalusia directly to a few Jewish thinkers through some of his Arabic writings, although many more became aware of him through thirteenth- and fourteenth-century Hebrew translations of several of his books. The paper builds upon recent research into al-Ghazālī's influence on Jewish thought, and presents a picture of the changing image of Abū Ḥāmid (as he was known in Hebrew), as seen by Jewish thinkers of the twelfth to fifteenth centuries. Special attention is given to the different ways in which the medieval Jewish reader would have reacted to al-Ghazālī's presentation and critique of Aristotelian philosophy and science.

The chapter by Hidemi Takahashi draws the attention of the reader to al-Ghazālī's influence on the philosophy and theology of the Syrian Orthodox Christian prelate and polymath Gregory Barhebraeus (1225/6–1286). These works seem to have been the result of a new intellectual synthesis of older Syriac literary heritage and the fruits of the contemporary scholarly works that would have been available to him (mostly) in Arabic. One of the Muslim authors Barhebraeus most frequently drew upon, alongside Ibn Sīnā and his older contemporary Naṣīr ad-Dīn aṭ-Ṭūsī (d. 672/1274), was al-Ghazālī, whose influence on Barhebraeus's theology and philosophy is apparent from a reading of several of his books. The paper closely examines Barhebraeus's methodology, and demonstrates where he drew upon a number of al-Ghazālī's works, sometimes altering and 'Christianizing' the contents of the source passages.

Jules Janssens provides an evaluation of the Ghazālīan quotations in Raymundus Marti's *Pugio Fidei*. Marti (d. ca. 1286) had studied Arabic in Toledo in one of the Dominican centers for the study of languages that flourished during his time. Thus it is not completely surprising that in his major work, *Pugio Fidei*, he quotes several passages of al-Ghazālī's different books, otherwise unknown in Europe. The paper shows that Marti was not only familiar with several of al-Ghazālī's works but also made liberal use of some of his ideas. Hence, a particular, though limited, reception of al-Ghazālī's thought in thirteenth century Europe in Latin comes to the fore, which is quite different from the reception limited to the knowledge of his *Maqāṣid*.

Yahya Michot's paper deals with Ibn Taymiyya's (661/1263–728/1328) mapping of the development of al-Ghazālī's esotericism, from the philosophical definitions in *Miʿyār al-ʿilm* (The Standard of Knowledge) to the five degrees of existence, which al-Ghazālī distinguished in his treatise *at-Tafriqa bayn al-īmān wa-z-zandaqa* (The Distinction Between Faith and Free-Thinking). For Ibn Taymiyya, al-Ghazālī was an important milestone on the path of sophistic, Qarmaṭizing, scriptural distortion (*taḥrīf*) that led towards the doctrine of the uniqueness of existence (*waḥdat al-wujūd*). The fact that al-Ghazālī eventually renounced his esoteric ideas did not prevent their propagation: Ibn Taymiyya condemned their pernicious impact on several post-al-Ghazālī Islamic thinkers.

Lastly, M. Sait Özervarlı focuses on Ottoman thinkers' commentaries of al-Ghazālī's *Tahāfut al-falāsifa* to demonstrate classical Ottoman contributions to al-Ghazālī's legacy. The paper examines *Tahāfut* commentaries written by eminent scholars of the classical Ottoman period of the fifteenth century, such as Hocazāde, Ṭūsī, Kemalpaţazāde, and Karabāğī. In keeping with the scholarly traditions of the time, their commentaries were produced in Arabic, and a close examination of the texts demonstrates that Ottoman works were not just mere reiterations but profound examples of new insights using critical analysis.

•••

In closing, I wish to thank my current Graduate Student Assistant Michail Hradek for managing the Bibliography and the Indexes. I am grateful to the anonymous reviewer of the papers for constructive remarks. Finally, I wish to thank Prof. Hans Daiber, Prof. Anna Akasoy and Prof. Emilie Savage-Smith for accepting this volume in the book series, "Islamic Philosophy, Theology and Science." Dr. Kathy van Vliet and Teddi Dols from Brill Academic Publishers were not only competent but also friendly and helpful as they accompanied me throughout the production process of the book. They deserve my gratitude.

It fills my heart with sorrow that Allen Tuazon, M.A., my former Graduate Research Assistant at The Ohio State University, did not live to see this volume printed. A committed and brilliant assistant, Allen diligently and with exemplary dedication assisted me with the organization of the international conference "Islam and Rationality: The Impact of al-Ghazālī," (Ohio State University, 10–12 November 2011). Allen spared no effort to make the conference a memorable event to all participants and guests. He led the Student Assistants Team professionally, provided creative ideas to design the wonderful image on the cover and took care of editing most of the contributions in this book. The volume is deservedly dedicated to his memory. Requiescat in pace!

Georges Tamer
Erlangen, March 2015

Notes on Contributors

Binyamin Abrahamov
is Professor Emeritus of Islamic Theology and Mysticism, and Qur'ānic Studies at Bar-Ilan University. His main publications are *Islamic Theology – Traditionalism and Rationalism* (Edinburgh University Press 1998) and *Divine Love in Islamic Mysticism: The Teachings of al-Ghazālī and al-Dabbāgh* (RoutledgeCurzon Sufi Series 2003). His latest book publication is *Ibn al-Arabi and the Sufis* (Oxford 2014).

Hans Daiber
was until his retirement 2010 holder of the Chair of Oriental Languages at the Johann Wolfgang Goethe-University in Frankfurt am Main. He has published extensively on Islamic philosophy, theology, history of sciences and Greek-Syriac-Arabic-Latin translations. His latest book publication is *Islamic Thought in the Dialogue of Cultures. A Historical and Bibliographical Survey* (Brill 2012).

Kenneth Garden
is Associate Professor in the Department of Religion of Tufts University. He is the author of *The First Islamic Reviver: Abū Ḥāmid al-Ghazālī and his* Revival of the Religious Sciences (Oxford 2014).

Avner Giladi
is Professor of Islamic Studies in the Department of Middle East History at the University of Haifa. His main research interests are the history of education, family and childhood, as well as women and gender in medieval Islamic contexts. His publications include the works *Infants, Parents and Wet Nurses: Islamic Views on Breastfeeding and Their Social Implications* (Brill 1999) and *Muslim Midwives: The Craft of Birthing in the Premodern Middle East* (Cambridge University Press 2014). He is also the co-author of the publication *La famille en Islam d'après les sources arabes* (Les Indes Savantes 2013).

Scott Michael Girdner
is Assistant Professor in the Department of Philosophy and Religious Studies at Old Dominion University, Norfolk, Virginia. His main research interests are in the history of philosophical and mystical scriptural hermeneutics in Islamic, Jewish, and Christian traditions. He has published "Scripture and Doctrine",

in *Islamic Beliefs, Practices, and Cultures*, New York: Marshall Cavendish, 2011. Forthcoming works include a monograph on al-Ghazālī's scriptural hermeneutics in *Mishkāt al-anwār* (The Niche of Lights), and additional studies of the reception of this work in their Hebrew translations.

Frank Griffel
is Professor of Islamic Studies at Yale University. He is the author of many articles on al-Ghazālī, of *Al-Ghazālī's Philosophical Theology* (Oxford University Press 2009) and of *Apostasie und Toleranz im Islam* (Brill 2000). He is also the editor of three collective works, among them the second volume of this collection.

Steven Harvey
is Professor of Philosophy and former Chair of Jewish Philosophy at Bar-Ilan University. He has published extensively on the medieval Jewish and Islamic philosophers, with special focus on medieval Arabic and Hebrew commentaries on Aristotle and on the influence of the Islamic philosophers on Jewish thought. He is the author of *Falaquera's Epistle of the Debate: An Introduction to Jewish Philosophy* (1987) and editor of *The Medieval Hebrew Encyclopedias of Science and Philosophy* (2000) and *Anthology of the Writings of Avicenna* (2009, in Hebrew).

Alfred Ivry
is Professor Emeritus of Jewish and Islamic Philosophy at New York University. His main areas of research concern the philosophy of Maimonides and Averroes. He published Averroes' Middle Commentary on Aristotle's *De anima* in Arabic and Hebrew critical editions.

Jules Janssens
is Associated Member at De Wulf-Mansion Centre for Ancient, Medieval and Renaissance Philosophy at Katholieke Universiteit Leuven and Associated Researcher at the Centre National de la Recherché Scientifique. His research focuses on Avicenna and his reception in the Islamic and the Western world, as well as his impact on al-Ghazālī and Henry of Ghent. He has published numerous articles and books, among them *Ibn Sīnā (Avicenne). Commentaire sur le livre Lambda de la Métaphysique d'Aristote (chapitres 6–10)* (Vrin 2014) and a survey of Thomas's explicit quotations of Avicenna in the *Summa contra Gentiles* (*American Catholic Philosophical Quarterly* 88-2, 2014).

Taneli Kukkonen
is Professor of Philosophy at New York University Abu Dhabi. He works on Arabic philosophy and the Aristotelian commentary tradition. He is the author of *Ibn Tufayl* (Oxford 2014) and over thirty articles and book chapters spanning topics in logic, cosmology, metaphysics, and cognitive and moral psychology. Forthcoming is a monograph on al-Ghazālī's thought.

Luis Xavier López-Farjeat
is Associate Professor at the School of Philosophy at Universidad Panamericana, Mexico City. He has written on Arabic medieval philosophy and is co-editor of the volume *Philosophical Psychology in Arabic Thought and the Latin Aristotelianism of the 13th Century* (Vrin 2013) and of the Routledge Companion to Islamic Philosophy (forthcoming).

Wilferd Madelung
is Emeritus Laudian Professor of Arabic, University of Oxford, and Senior Research Fellow at the Institute of Ismaili Studies in London. His main research area is the political, religious and intellectual history of early and medieval Islam. He is the author of *The Succession to Muhammad: A study of the early caliphate* (Cambridge 1997).

Yahya M. Michot
is Professor of Islamic Thought and Christian-Muslim Relations at Hartford Seminary. His research interests focus on classical Islamic thought, Ottoman puritanism and the role of drugs in Islamic societies. He is author of several works on Avicenna and Ibn Taymiyya, including *Ibn Sīnā: Refutation de l'astrologie* (Dar Albouraq 2006) and *Ibn Taymiyya: Against Extremisms* (Dar Albouraq 2012). He is also co-editor of *The Muslim World* Journal.

Yasien Mohamed
is Professor of Arabic and Islamic Philosophy at the University of the Western Cape, South Africa. His main areas of research are Arabic literature and Islamic philosophical ethics. Among his numerous publications is *The Path to Virtue: The Ethical Philosophy of al-Raghib al-Isfahani* (ISTAC 2006).

Eric Ormsby
was until his retirement Professor and Senior Research Associate at the Institute of Ismaili Studies in London. He is a famous poet and designated connoisseur of al-Ghazālī. His monographs include *Theodicy in Islamic Thought: The Dispute over al-Ghazālī's "Best of All Possible Worlds"* (Princeton 1984),

Ghazali: The Revival of Islam (Oxford 2008) as well as *Love, Longing, Intimacy and Satisfaction* (*Kitāb al-Maḥabba wa'l-shawq wa'l-uns wa'l-riḍā*), Book 36 of the magnum opus *The Revival of Religious Sciences* (*Iḥyā' 'ulūm ad-dīn*) (Islamic Texts Society 2011).

M. Sait Özervarlı
is Professor of Intellectual History at Yıldız Technical University, Istanbul. Most of his research is on Ottoman thought, Islamic philosophy, East-West relations and Turkish modernization. His publications include the monograph *Aspects of Ottoman Intellectual History* (2008) and several articles, book chapters and encyclopedia entries.

Hidemi Takahashi
teaches in the Graduate School of Arts and Sciences at the University of Tokyo. He is a Researcher in Syriac Studies. His publications include *Aristotelian Meteorology in Syriac: Barhebraeus, "Butyrum sapientiae", Books of Mineralogy and Meteorology* (Brill 2003) and *Barhebraeus: A Bio-Bibliography* (Gorgias Press 2005).

Georges Tamer
is holder of the Chair of Oriental Philology and Islamic Studies at the University of Erlangen-Nuremburg. His main research areas are the hermeneutics of the Qur'ān, Islamic theology, Arabic philosophy and its modern reception. He is the author and editor of several works, including *Islamische Philosophie und die Krise der Moderne: Das Verhältnis von Leo Strauss zu Alfarabi, Avicenna und Averroes* (Brill 2001), *The Trias of Maimonides* (Walter de Gruyter 2005), *Zeit und Gott: Hellenistische Zeitvorstellungen in der altarabischen Dichtung und im Koran* (Walter de Gruyter 2008) and *Humor in Arabic Culture* (Walter de Gruyter 2009).

CHAPTER 1

God versus Causality

Al-Ghazālī's Solution and its Historical Background

Hans Daiber

In modern historiography, rationalism means scientific knowledge based on unprejudiced cognition. This idea is basically similar to the ideals exalted by the European Enlightenment (17–19th c.), which sought to replace divine religion with human rationality.[1] Is it possible, in view of this, to discuss al-Ghazālī's impact on the development of rationality in Islam?

I will present the thesis that al-Ghazālī's concept of causality[2] is the result of his philosophical theology, which itself is based on his Qur'ānic-Ash'arite

---

1 Cf. G. Gawlick, "Rationalismus" in *Historisches Wörterbuch der Philosophie* 8, Darmstadt 1992, col. 44–47.

2 Al-Ghazālī's concept of causality has been the subject of a large number of articles and monographs which do not consider the Stoic-Neoplatonic background. See the bibliography in Frank Griffel's monograph (2009; s. below p. ...); the following publications are a reasonable sample: Muhammed Yasin El-Taher Uraibi, *Al-Ghazalis Aporien im Zusammenhang mit dem Kausalproblem*, thesis, University of Bonn, 1972, pp. 250ff.; Kwame Gyekye, "Al-Ghazālī on Causation," in *Second Order* 2/1, Ile-Ife, Nigeria 1973, pp. 31–39; Carol Lucille Bargeron, *The Concept of Causality in Abu Hāmid Muḥammad Al-Ghazālī's Tahāfut Al-Falāsifah*, thesis, University of Wisconsin-Madison, 1978; Mohammed Allal Sinaceur, "Logique et causalité chez Ghazali," in *Un trait d'union entre l'orient et l'occident: Al-Ghazzali et Ibn Maimoun*, Rabat, 1986 (= *Académie du Royaume du Maroc. Publications*. 12), pp. 173–211; Luciano Rubio, *El "Ocasionalismo" de los teologos especulativos del Islam. Su posible influencia en Guillermo de Ockham y en los "ocasionalistas" de la Edad Moderna*, El Escorial, 1987 (on Ghazālī s. pp. 161–198); Abu Yaarub Al-Marzouki, *Le concept de causalité chez Gazali*, Tunis (s.d.); Yusuf Rahman, "Causality and Occasionalism: A Study of the Theories of the Philosophers Al-Ghazālī and Ibn Rushd," in *Hamdard Islamicus* 21/1, 1998, pp. 23–31; Lenn E. Goodman, "Three Enduring Achievements of Islamic Philosophy," in *Mohaghegh Nāma. Collected papers presented to Professor Mehdi Mohaghegh*, ed. by B. Khorramshāhī and J. Jahānbakhsh. II, Tehran, 2001 (pp. 59–89), pp. 79–83, 86f. (Goodman alludes to Neoplatonism, but regretfully does not elaborate on this); Edward Omar Moad, "Al-Ghazali on Power, Causation, and 'Acquisition,'" in *Philosophy East and West* 57, Honolulu, 2007, pp. 1–13; Frank Griffel, "Al-Ghazali," in *Stanford Encyclopedia of Philosophy* (2007), ch. 7; id., "Al-Ghazālī's Appropriation of Ibn Sīnā's Views on Causality and the Development of the Science in Islam," in *Uluslararasi Ibn Sīnā sempozyumu bildiriler*, 22–24 Mayis 2008. II, pp. 105–115; id., *Al-Ghazālī's Philosophical Theology*, Oxford: Oxford University Press, 2009, pp. 147ff., 175ff. and 215ff.

 | DOI 10.1163/9789004290952_002

theology and on his knowledge of Ibn Sīnā, whose Neoplatonism al-Ghazālī criticized and took as a starting point for a more extended attack.[3] Al-Ghazālī modified previous discussions by resuming the Stoic-Neoplatonic concept of causality as formulated by Proclus in *Institutio theologica* (see below, p. 8ff.); with this modification, he dissociated himself from Ibn Sīnā's Aristotelian view and contributed, in a very original manner, to rationality in Islam.

Al-Ghazālī's reflection on causality turns out to be a reaction to the preceding discussions of those who tried to replace God by another cause. It deserves our attention that al-Ghazālī influenced – through his *Tahāfut al-falāsifa* and its refutation by Ibn Rushd, the *Tahāfut at-Tahāfut*[4] – the discussion in medieval Europe, the arguments of Albertus Magnus, Thomas Aquinas, Bernard of Arezzo and of Nicolaus of Autrecourt.[5] His originality has even prompted a

3 Some remarks can be found in Noor Nabi, "Criticism of Al-Ghazali on the Theory of Emanation presented by Plotinus and Ibn Sina," in *Reason and Tradition in Islamic Thought*, ed. Mahmudul Haq, Aligarh, 1992, pp. 116–129.

4 Ed. by Maurice Bouyges, Beirut, 1930. = *Bibliotheca arabica scholasticorum*. Série arabe. III. [3rd edition Beirut 1992]; see also Simon van den Bergh (trans.), *Averroes' Tahafut Al-Tahafut* (*The Incoherence of the Incoherence*), I–II. London, 1969. On Ibn Rushd's concept of causality and his critique of Ghazālī, cf. Barry S. Kogan, *Averroes and the Metaphysics of Causation*, Albany: State University of New York Press, 1985 (review by H. Daiber in *Der Islam* 64, 1987, 310f.). Recently it has been shown that Ibn Rushd's concept of causality shows traces of the Neoplatonic doctrine of intermediaries; cf. Cecilia Martini Bonadeo, "Averroes on the Causality of the First Principle: a Model in Reading 'Metaphysics,'" Lambda 7, 1072b 4–16, in *Wissen über Grenzen. Arabisches Wissen und lateinisches Mittelalter*, ed. Andreas Speer and Lydia Wegener, Berlin-New York, 2006 (*Miscellanea Mediaevalia*. 33), pp. 425–437; cf. Barry S. Kogan, *Averroes and the Metaphysics of Causation*, pp. 248ff. Both do not take into account the role of Proclus's *Institutio theologica*, whose importance I had emphasized in my review of Kogan's monograph in *Der Islam* 64, 1987, p. 311.

5 Cf. Johannes Erich Heyde, *Entwertung der Kausalität?* Stuttgart: Kohlhammer, 1957, pp. 14ff.; Majid Fakhry, *Islamic Occasionalism*, London: Allen & Unwin, 1958; Harry Austryn Wolfson, "Nicolaus of Autrecourt and Ghazālī's Argument Against Causality," in *Speculum* 44, 1969, 234–238 (reprinted in Wolfson, *The Philosophy of the Kalam*, Cambridge, Massachusetts and London: Harvard University Press, 1976, pp. 593–600); R. E. Abu Shanab, "Ghazali and Aquinas on Causation," in *Monist* 58, 1974, 140–150; David Burrell, "Causality and necessity in Islamic thought" in *Routledge Encyclopedia of Philosophy*, ed. Edward Craig, vol. II, London and New York: Routledge, 1998; and Kojiro Nakamura, "Al-Ghazali," ibid. vol. IV, esp. p. 65 col. a; the monograph by Dominik Perler and Ulrich Rudolph, *Occasionalismus. Theorien der Kausalität im arabisch-islamischen und im europäischen Denken*, Göttingen: Vandenhoeck and Ruprecht, 2000 (= *Abhandlungen der Akademie der Wissenschaften in Göttingen – Philologisch-historische Klasse*. Göttingen. 3. Folge. 235); recently, Taneli Kukkonen, "Creation and Causation," in *Cambridge History of Medieval Philosophy*, ed. Robert Pasnau, Cambridge: Cambridge University Press, 2010 (pp. 232–246), pp. 236f. On the Latin transmission of

comparison with similar ideas found in the work of David Hume, an English philosopher active in the 18th century.[6]

At first sight, al-Ghazālī appears to have given a clear answer to those who tried to replace God with another kind of causality; these are variously referred to in early Islamic sources by the name "Dahrites," i.e. "materialists" who may be called "atheists" (to use a term which originated in the 16th–17th centuries in Europe).[7] The term "Dahrites" has its origin in the Qur'ānic concept of *dahr* as we find it in sūra 45, verses 22–24. In the context of the following remark about the unbeliever, I quote the translation of Arthur J. Arberry: "Hast thou seen him who has taken his caprice (*hawāhu*) to be his god, and God has led him astray out of a knowledge... They say, 'There is nothing but our present life; we die, and we live, and nothing but Time (*dahr*) destroys us.' "

Here, we detect the divine cause replaced by the inclination of man (*hawāhu*), who, orienting himself solely towards his life in this world, considers himself to be both perishable and a victim of time.[8] Remarkable in the formulation of the verses quoted is the assessment of individuality as causal factor equal to God. According to Muhammad this is not compatible with his

---

al-Ghazālī's works compare H. Daiber, *Islamic Thought in the Dialogue of Cultures*. A Historical and Bibliographical Survey, Leiden-Boston: Brill, 2012 (= *Themes in Islamic Studies 7*), pp. 132–136.

6 Cf. Abdul Matin, "The Ghazalian and the Humian Critiques of Causality: a comparison," in *The Dacca University Studies*, A. 29, 1978, pp. 29–434.

7 Cf. H.-W. Schütte, "Atheismus" in *Historisches Wörterbuch der Philosophie*, vol. 1, Darmstadt, 1971, col. 595–599. On the history of "atheism," see Georges Minois, *Geschichte des Atheismus. Von den Anfängen bis zur Gegenwart* (Translated from French [*Histoire de l'athéisme. Les incroyants dans le monde occidental à nos jours*] by Eva Moldenhauer), Weimar, 2000. The book includes a short chapter on "the Arabic-Muslim contribution to unbelief" (pp. 68–76). This can be supplemented by a collection of articles ed. by Friedrich Niewöhner and Olaf Pluta under the title: *Atheismus im Mittelalter und in der Renaissance*, Wiesbaden, 1999 (= *Wolfenbütteler Mittelalter-Studien*. 12); on "atheism" in Islam see the contributions by H. Daiber, "Rebellion gegen Gott. Formen atheistischen Denkens im frühen Islam" (23–44); Sarah Stroumsa, "The Religion of the Freethinkers of Medieval Islam" (45–59); Muhammad Abū Al-Fadl Badran: "... denn die Vernunft ist ein Prophet' – Zweifel bei Abū 'l-ʿAlāʾ al-Maʿarrī" (61–84); Dominique Urvoy: "La démystification de la religion dans les textes attribués à Ibn al-Muqaffaʿ" (85–94); and Mohammad Mohammadian: "Der oblique Blick. Zum Verhältnis von Philosophie und Religion in den Robāʿiyāt von Omar Khayyām" (95–114).

8 On the concept of *dahr* cf. here Georges Tamer, *Zeit und Gott: Hellenistische Zeitvorstellungen in der altarabischen Dichtung und im Koran*, Berlin: Walter de Gruyter 2008, pp. 193ff. and 107ff. More details can be found in the following discussion: H. Daiber, "Rationalism in Islam and the Rise of Scientific Thought: The Background of al-Ghazalī's Concept of Causality," in id., *The Struggle for Knowledge in Islam: Some Historical Aspects*, Sarajevo, 2004, pp. 67–86.

new belief in one God, to whom everyone must surrender; as such, these verses are the starting-point of later descriptions of the so-called "Dahrites" who deny God.[9] The famous prose-writer al-Jāḥiẓ, who died in about 254/868, demonstrates in his book on animals that even animals hint at God's existence;[10] his cosmological and teleological proof of God contradicts the denial of God by the Dahrites who, moreover, replace God with the unchangeable movement of stars.[11] Al-Jāḥiẓ refers to discussions of agnostic circles from the 8th/9th century, who, in the tradition of old skeptic-materialistic Sassanian traditions from the 6th century, acknowledge the influence of the stars on the sublunar world.[12] According to al-Jāḥiẓ, the assumption of any astrological influence on creation means the denial of God. He, who asserts the eternal uniformity of the celestial bodies, cannot assume neither generation nor corruption, or the distinction between Creator and created, but solely "eternal matter" (*aṭ-ṭīna al-qadīma*).[13]

This conclusion by al-Jāḥiẓ is not new. It takes up an alleged discussion between the theologian Abū Ḥanīfa and a Dahrite, which is summarized in the 10th century by Abū l-Layth as-Samarqandī in his commentary on the oldest Islamic credo, that is, Abū Ḥanīfa's *Al-Fiqh al-absaṭ*.[14] Although the report seems to be late,[15] we can nevertheless detect old ideas within it. The thesis of the Dahrite and the refutation of it, attributed to Abū Ḥanīfa, contain the argument that contrary qualities like humidity, dryness, cold and heat can only be combined by a superior factor, viz., by God. This line of thought is – among others[16] – also found in the theologian al-Māturīdī, who died in 332/944. In his *Book on the unity of God*, (*Kitāb at-Tawḥīd*),[17] he informs us that he draws his information on the Dahrites from their critic Ibn Shabīb, a pupil of the Muʿtazilite an-Naẓẓām, who died between 220/835 and 230/845.[18] Apparently

9 On the term, cf. D. Gimaret, "Dahrī II (In the Islamic Period)," in *Encyclopedia Iranica* VI, Costa Mesa, California 1993, pp. 588b–590a.

10 Al-Jāḥiẓ, *Kitāb al-Ḥayawān*, 8 vols., ed. ʿAbdassalām Hārūn II, (2nd edition, Cairo, 1965), p. 109,5f.

11 Cf. ibid. VII, (2nd edition, Cairo, 1968), 12,11ff. Compare, in addition, Daiber, "Rebellion," p. 25.

12 For further details see Daiber, "Rebellion," pp. 26f.

13 Al-Jāḥiẓ, *Kitāb al-Ḥayawān*, 12,11ff.

14 Ed. (with commentary) by H. Daiber, *The Islamic Concept of Belief in the 4th/10th Century. Abū l-Laiṯ as-Samarqandī's Commentary on Abū Ḥanīfa (died 150/767), al-Fiqh al-absaṭ*, Tokyo, 1995 (= *Studia culturae islamicae*. 52), ll. 771–784. Compare for further details Daiber, "Rebellion," pp. 28–30.

15 Cf. Daiber, "Rebellion," pp. 29f.

16 For further references ibid., p. 30, n. 27.

17 Ed. Fathallah Kholeif, Beirut, 1970, p. 141ff.

18 On his doctrine cf. J. van Ess, *Theologie*, III p. 367.

Ibn Shabīb was also Māturīdī's source for his own counterarguments and his thesis of the prevailing divine cause.

We know that Ibn Shabīb, like al-Māturīdī, follows an-Naẓẓām, whose critical description of the Dahrite principles is preserved;[19] to combat the Dahrites and dualists, an-Naẓẓām had developed the doctrine that all things, even contrary things, are "mixed" by the intervention of God.[20] Here, God is not a completely transcendent being, totally alienated from creation, but can be reckoned in the reasonable order of creation itself. Moreover, God imposes a nature on all things created by Him; it is this nature which determines their causality. Through nature – created by Him and latent in things – God acts indirectly. An-Naẓẓām adduced the example that "God provided the stone with such a nature that it rolls, if someone pushes it."[21]

An-Naẓẓām's thesis that contrary things are forcibly put together through the intervention of a superior divine cause is likewise not new. He himself might have been inspired by the Christian circles of his time, who themselves ultimately follow the doctrine of the pseudo-Aristotelian treatise *De mundo*, described in chapters five and six of this work.[22] Consequently, causality in an-Naẓẓām remains something determined by God; an-Naẓẓām resumes discussions before him and continues those that were on-going during his time; for example, the Islamic theologian Ḍirār Ibn ʿAmr, who lived between 109/728 and 179/796, opposed the so-called "naturalists" (*aṣḥāb aṭ-ṭabāʾiʿ*) by denying the independent "nature" (*ṭabīʿa*) of things and assuming a connection of things, of "parts" (*ajzāʾ, abʿāḍ*), by God. Even man's action is determined by God: as such, man "acquires" (*iktasaba*) what God has created.[23] A contemporary of Ḍirār, the Shiite Hishām Ibn al-Ḥakam, introduced a new concept, namely the "cause" created by God; this "cause" (*sabab*) "necessarily" "calls forth" the acts of man, provided that man wants them[24] and under the condition that he has the capacity.[25] This deterministic component appears a little later and in a different manner in an-Naẓẓām's theology. An-Naẓẓām replaces the term "cause"

19 Al-Jāḥiẓ, *Kitāb al-Ḥayawān*, p. 40,5ff.; translation van Ess, *Theologie*, VI p. 66.

20 Cf. ibid. III pp. 366f.

21 Al-Ashʿarī, *Maqālāt*, ed. Ritter p. 404,7f.; cf. Daiber, *Muʿammar*, p. 403f.

22 Cf. Davidson, *Proofs*, pp. 150f.; van Ess, *Theologie*, III p. 367; regarding terminology, ibid. Cf. now Daiber, On possible Echoes of De mundo in the Arabic-Islamic World: Christian, Islamic and Jewish Thinkers, in: *Cosmic Order and Divine Power*. Pseudo-Aristotle, *On the Cosmos*. Ed. by J.C. Thom. Tübingen: Mohr Siebeck 2014 (= SAPERE XXIII), pp. 169-180.

23 Cf. van Ess, *Theologie*, III pp. 38, 41f. and 44ff.

24 Cf. al-Ashʿarī, *Maqālāt*, ed. Ritter p. 40, 12ff.; Wolfson, *Philosophy of Kalam*, pp. 672f.; van Ess, *Theologie*, I pp. 369f.

25 Cf. al-Ashʿarī, *Maqālāt*, ed. Ritter p. 42,12ff./English translation W. Montgomery Watt, *Free Will and Predestination in Early Islam*, London 1948, p. 116; cf. van Ess, *Theologie*, I pp. 370f.

with the terms "nature" (*khilqa, ṭabīʿa*) and "coercion" (*ījāb*): According to him, God has created in things and imposed on them their "nature" or "coercion"; man has only the potentiality to give the impulse to a causality, which as such is determined by God and is therefore unavoidable.[26]

His contemporary Muʿammar Ibn ʿAbbād as-Sulamī differed from this. According to him, nature is not something created by God, but a key-term for causality, which is inherent in things. God determines this causality only indirectly. Here, Muʿammar offers a unique solution: according to him, the determinant cause, for its part, is determined indirectly by God, namely through an endless chain of causes of determinant factors (*maʿānī*).[27]

This solution, which reminds us of the Neoplatonic doctrine of emanations as intermediary causes, appears to be a promising step in the direction of the revolutionary thesis of John Philoponus in the 6th century. Based on the Christian axiom that God created the whole world, John Philoponus rejected the heathen thesis of the immanence of gods in the world as well as their immanence in the stars; he defended the doctrine of a transcendent God Who created the universe from nothing[28] and Who thereupon left the universe to its immanent laws.[29]

Here, in John Philoponus, we detect the first beginnings of a separation between natural sciences and theology.[30] This separation could not yet gain a foothold in Islam and was confined primarily to the deprivation of stars and matter of their divinity. God remains active in creation through nature; His activity exists indirectly and its final effect no longer has the identity of cause and effect in the Aristotelian sense. This being so, God remains a transcendent creator of substances; the nature created by God in these substances determines the causality of things coming into being, i.e., the causality of "accidents." Nature has become a causal principle, which is related to the first, divine effective cause, Aristotle's unmoved prime mover, solely via an endless chain of determinant factors, the *maʿānī*.

26 Cf. Daiber, *Muʿammar*, pp. 403f.; van Ess, *Theologie*, III pp. 378f.

27 Cf. Daiber, *Muʿammar*, pp. 222ff.; id., "Muʿammar" in *Encyclopaedia of Islam* VIII (2nd ed. Leiden 1993); van Ess, *Theologie*, III pp. 67ff.

28 On this and its afterlife among Islamic and Jewish thinkers, cf. Davidson, *Proofs*, pp. 86ff.

29 Cf. W. Böhm, *Johannes Philoponus, Grammatikos von Alexandrien (6. Jahrhundert n. Chr.). Ausgewählte Schriften übersetzt, eingeleitet und kommentiert*, München, Paderborn, Wien: Schöningh, 1967, pp. 300ff.

30 On this cf. Sambursky, *The Physical World of Late Antiquity*, London: Routledge and Kegan Paul, 1962, pp. 154ff.

Muʿammar's doctrine reminds us of al-Ghazālī's assumption of a series of intermediate causes and their effects determined by God. This appears, as we have seen, to be a refutation of the ancient Greek thesis of the eternity of matter and of astrologers, who supplanted the divine creator with the influence of stars.

Now, we must give some explanations on the concept of intermediary causes mediating between the first cause, namely God, and the final effect: al-Ghazālī adopted it in a very specific way, which – as I try to show – betrays his thorough knowledge of Neoplatonic theology and its concept of causality. In the generation before al-Ghazālī, already the Andalusian scholar Ibn Ḥazm (d. 456/1064) had developed a doctrine in his critique of al-Kindī's metaphysics,[31] which in some details anticipated al-Ghazālī's explanation of causality and its Neoplatonic background. Ibn Ḥazm criticized al-Kindī, a philosopher from the 9th century, who, in his metaphysics entitled *al-Falsafa al-ūlā*, is said to have been inconsequent with regard to God's transcendence: God cannot be called *ʿilla* (cause), as this is not compatible with the concept of God's unity (*tawḥīd*). Ibn Ḥazm argues, in the footsteps of Proclus' *Institutio theologica* or its Arabic adaptation, *al-Khayr al-maḥḍ* – known in the Middle Ages as *Liber de causis* – that God acts through the mediation of causes, of "natures," whose "name" (*ism*) and "state" (*ḥāl*) depend upon the "decree" (*taqdīr*) of the "almighty and knowing" God (*al-ʿAzīz al-ʿAlīm*).[32] God is not comparable with anything, neither with the cause nor with the effect.[33] Similar to an-Naẓẓām, Ibn Ḥazm asserts that God provided natures with some coercion, which necessitates the effect.[34] Because of God's willing and acting, God's will and action start to exist.[35]

Of course, Ibn Ḥazm could hardly have had any *direct* influence on al-Ghazālī. More likely is the assumption that both follow common Neoplatonic sources, which we shall examine now as the immediate background of Ghazālī's

31 His *Risālat ar-Radd ʿalā l-Kindī al-faylasūf* was edited by Iḥsān ʿAbbās in Ibn Ḥazm, *ar-Radd ʿalā Ibn an-Naghrīla al-Yahūdī wa-rasāʾil-ukhrā*, Cairo, 1960, pp. 187–235; cf. the analysis by Daiber, "Die Kritik des Ibn Ḥazm an Kindīs Metaphysik," in *Der Islam* 63, 1986, pp. 284–302. Here we should be aware that al-Kindī's concept of Neoplatonic causality found some echo in Kindī's text *De radiis*, which, though lost in its Arabic original, reminds us of Plotinus' metaphor of the sun (see here above). cf. Pinella Travaglia, *Magic, Causality and Intentionality: The doctrine of rays in al-Kindī*, Turnhout: Edizioni del Galluzzo, 1999, esp. pp. 20ff.

32 Cf. Daiber, "Kritik," pp. 294f.

33 See ibid. p. 293, n. 109.

34 Cf. ibid. pp. 293f.

35 Cf. ibid. 296f.

doctrine of causality. Plotinus' *Enneads*, at least the Arabic transmission, does not give a clear picture of causality; the Arabic Plotinus, as Ibn Sīnā understood it, considers creation to be something mediated by a series of intellects between the Necessary Being and the sublunar world.[36] Moreover, the Arabic Plotinus contains an echo of *Enneads* VI 8, "On the Free Will and the Will of the One,"[37] a chapter which intends to explain the compatibility of God's free will – that is, the pure cause – and the necessity of His emanations, the caused things. J. M. Rist, in his monograph on Plotinus,[38] in a chapter on "Emanation and Necessity,"[39] gave the following explanation: "emanation is necessary because the One wills it to be so"; "the products of the One, as well as the One itself, are the products of will."[40] In the footsteps of Plato's comparison of the Good with the sun and with the light of the intelligible world, Plotinus[41] explained the emanation from the One with the light of the sun[42] or the heat of the fire;[43] he may[44] have been drawing from the background of

36 Cf. Adamson, *The Arabic Plotinus*, pp. 137ff. Al-Fārābī is a forerunner of Ibn Sīnā in his emphasis of the divine intellect as creative First Cause, based on Proclus and the *Kalām fī maḥḍ al-khayr*; cf. Damien Janos, "The Greek and Arabic Proclus and al-Fārābī's Theory of Celestial Intellection and its Relation to Creation," in *Documenti e studi sulla tradizione filosofica medievale* 21, 2010, pp. 19–44.

37 See Adamson, *The Arabic Plotinus*, pp. 145ff.

38 Cambridge, 1967.

39 Rist, *Plotinus*, pp. 66–83.

40 Ibid. p. 82.

41 *Enneads* 5.1.6; cf. the echo in the Arabic "Dicta sapientis graeci" I, translated by Geoffrey Lewis in *Plotini opera*, II: *Enneads* IV–V, ed. Paul Henry et Hans-Rudolf Schwyzer, Paris-Bruxelles, 1959, p. 275. Regrettably, this Stoic-Neoplatonic tradition is not taken into consideration in the monograph by Klaus Hedwig, *Sphaera lucis. Studien zur Intelligibilität des Seienden im Kontext der mittelalterlichen Lichtspekulation*, Münster: Aschendorff, 1980 (= Beiträge zur Geschichte der Philosophie und Theologie des Mittelalters, N.F. 18), pp. 93ff.

42 In *Enneads* IV 6f. explained as *energeia* of the shining. Proclus took this up: cf. Lucas Siorvanes, *Proclus: Neo-Platonic Philosophy and Science*, New Haven, Connecticut: Yale University Press, 1997, p. 241ff.

43 Cf. Rist, *Plotinus*, p. 68.

44 According to the opinion of A. C. Lloyd (*The Anatomy of Neoplatonism*, Oxford: Clarendon Press, 1998, p. 99), Plotinian emanation does not have a Stoic source but "takes over Aristotle's model of physical causation, transposing it, of course, to non-physical causation." This differs from Aristotle inasmuch as the effect has a lower degree than the cause (cf. Lloyd, *Anatomy*, p. 100 and, here, the following discussion).

the Stoic concept of the sun[45] as *hegēmonikon*, as "the governing part," which is the heat that permeates the dynamic process of interaction[46] which generates the organism of the cosmos. The Stoic Cleanthes described it as *tonos*, as strength-producing "tension";[47] the Stoic Chrysippus describes it as *pneuma*,[48] and it reappears under Stoic influence in Alexander of Aphrodisias' treatises *On Providence* and *On the Principles of the Universe*, which both were translated into Arabic. Both, also, with their assessment of the planets as medium between the divine Providence and the sublunar world, contributed to what has been called "astrologization of the Aristotelian cosmos."[49] The Stoic immanence of the divine dynamic medium, the *pneuma*, is replaced in Neoplatonism by a concept of the divine One, who as divine intellect is both immanent and transcendent; through the subsequent causes, the divine One creates in a secondary causality or activity. Under the condition that there is no hindrance,[50] He creates the multiplicity of things on an ontologically inferior level.[51] The difference of degree in unity led Proclus in his *Institutio theologica* to the more systematized conclusion that there is merely "similarity" (*homoiotes*)

45 According to Sambursky, *The Physical World of Late Antiquity*, p. 112, Plotinus' discourse on light was "obviously" influenced by Alexander of Aphrodisias. Alexander (*De fato*) is, moreover, our source for the Stoic view on causality; cause and effect presuppose the same circumstances – or, as Ghazālī formulated, the same conditions. On the Stoic postulate of causality, which "comes remarkably near to our present notion of causality," cf. S. Sambursky, *Physics of the Stoics*, pp. 54f.

46 Cf., for example, the references in J. Hübner, "Ursache/Wirkung" in *Historisches Wörterbuch der Philosophie* 11, Darmstadt, 2001 (col. 377–384), col. 379f.

47 The term appears, by the way, in Proclus' *Institutio theologica*, proposition 23, in the verb *anateinontai*; the participated substances "are linked by an upward tension to existences not participated."

48 Cf. Rist, *Plotinus*, p. 70 and on the Stoic doctrines, cf. David E. Halm, *The Origins of Stoic Cosmology*, Columbus, Ohio: Ohio State University Press, 1977, pp. 150ff.; Max Pohlenz, *Die Stoa*, 4th ed., Göttingen: Vandenhoeck and Ruprecht, 1970, pp. 101ff. On the interaction between the parts of the cosmos, the *sympatheia* in Posidonius, cf. ib. 217ff., Karl Reinhardt, *Kosmos und Sympathie*, Munich: Beck, 1926 (p. 254, n. 1 mentions a parallel with Stoic *sympatheia* in Plotin, *Enneads* IV 1.4, 32); Siorvanes, *Proclus*, pp. 64f.

49 See Gad Freudenthal, "The Medieval Astrologization of the Aristotelian Cosmos: From Alexander of Aphrodisias to Averroes," in *Mélanges de l'Université Saint-Joseph* 59, 2006, pp. 29–68, esp. 37ff. Freudenthal refers to the Stoic background of Alexander and to echoes in Islamic philosophy; we can now add al-Ghazālī to the list of examples of "astrologization of the cosmos," here inspired by Neoplatonic sources.

50 Cf. Lloyd, *Anatomy*, pp. 100f.

51 Cf. Philipp Rosemann, *Omne agens agit sibi simile: A Repetition of Scholastic Metaphysics*, Leuven University Press, 1996, pp. 67ff.; Lloyd, *Anatomy*, pp. 102ff.

between cause and effect, and that the effect is an image only of the cause.[52] This concept of causal similarity, which replaces the Aristotelian[53] equality of cause and effect in favor of an ontological hierarchy, reappears in Ibn Sīnā, who – in addition to the Aristotelian concept of material and formal causality[54] – distinguished three different modes of "existence" (*wujūd*) of cause and effect: viz., "priority" respectively "posteriority," "self-sufficiency" respectively "need," "necessity" respectively "possibility."[55] Here, Ibn Sīnā appears to follow Proclus' *Institutio theologica*, which explains, in proposition 5, the posteriority of the manifold to the One; likewise, proposition 7 asserts the superiority of the productive cause to the product; proposition 9[56] explains self-sufficiency, which is "in some way akin to the One, the Good," which, however, Proclus considers to be inferior to the "unqualified Good"; proposition 77ff. describes the dependence of potentiality and of its proceeding to actuality on the superior perfect and infinite potency. In addition, Proclus assumes different grades of reality (proposition 14ff., 25ff.) and accordingly a gradation of causes and their potency (proposition 56ff.) according to their remoteness

52 On the details, cf. the differentiating description of Rosemann, *Omne agens*, pp. 92ff., esp. 97ff.; Lloyd, *Anatomy*, pp. 107ff.; Siorvanes, *Proclus*, p. 86ff.

53 Cf. Rosemann, *Omne agens*, pp. 33ff.

54 Cf. Amos Bertolacci, "The Doctrine of Material and Formal Causality in the 'Ilāhiyyāt' of Avicenna's 'Kitāb al-Šifā','" in *Quaestio* 2, 2002, pp. 125–154. On the echo of Ibn Sīnā in Mullā Ṣadrā's concept of causality, cf. the remarks by Rüdiger Arnzen, "The Structure of Mullā Ṣadrā's *al-Ḥikma al-mutaʿāliya fī l-asfār al-ʿAqliyya al-arbaʿa* and his Concepts of First Philosophy and Divine Science," in *Medioevo* 32, 2007 (pp. 199–239), pp. 220f.; and, above all, David B. Burrell, "Mulla Sadra on 'Substantial Motion': A Clarification and a Comparison with Thomas Aquinas," in *Journal of Shiʿa Islamic Studies* 11/4, 2009 (pp. 369–386), pp. 379ff. Burrell correctly mentions the background of Neoplatonic emanation from the first cause, which can explain similarity and difference between creator and creation.

55 Cf. Rosemann, *Omne agens*, pp. 161ff., 171ff.; on "causal self-sufficiency vs. causal productivity" in Ibn Sīnā, cf. Robert Wisnovsky, *Avicenna's Metaphysics in Context*. Ithaca, New York: Cornell University Press, 2003, pp. 181ff. On Ibn Sīnā's concept of the two modes of existence, the possible and the necessary, in their application to the proof of God's existence from contingence, cf. Michael Marmura, "Avicenna's Proof from Contingency for God's Existence in the *Metaphysics* of the *Shifāʾ*," in *Medieval Studies* 42, 1980, pp. 337–352.

56 Cf. also proposition 40ff.; for a discussion of the "self-constituted" and the Arabic *Liber de causis*, see proposition 20 ed./transl. Richard Taylor, *The Liber de causis* (Kalam Fi Mahd Alkhair): A Study of Medieval Neoplatonism, PhD thesis Toronto 1981, p. 317 (transl.). On "self-sufficiency" in Proclus, cf. Siorvanes, *Proclus*, p. 82ff. Siorvanes discusses, in addition, the hierarchy of cause and effect: see pp. 86ff. (causes are greater than effects) and pp. 92ff. (causes are prior to effects).

from the first, the primal Cause.[57] In addition, all things participate in the unparticipated Being, Life and Intelligence (proposition 101).

A comparison with al-Ghazālī immediately shows common features, which urge us to reflect on al-Ghazālī's causality with a background of Neoplatonic concepts in mind. We start with al-Ghazālī's concept of God as it is described in his *al-Maqṣad al-asnā fī sharḥ maʿānī asmāʾ Allāh al-ḥusnā*: besides the Qurʾānic-Ashʿarite divine attributes, sometimes shaped by Ibn Sīnā's Metaphysics,[58] we find the following description of God: God is "an existent necessarily existing in Himself" (*al-mawjūd al-wājib al-wujūd bi-dhātihī*)[59] and has "no need for a cause or an agent" (*istighnāʾ ʿan-i-l-ʿilla wa-l-fāʿil*);[60] He is the "cause of causes" (*musabbib al-asbāb*), which is "above the effect" (*fawqa l-musabbab*);[61] there is a "difference" (*tafāwut*) between "cause and effect" (*al-ʿilla wa-l-maʿlūl*), "perfect and imperfect" (*al-kāmil wa-n-nāqiṣ*).[62] God's decree and predestination (*qaḍāʾ wa-qadar*) and his will (*mashīʾa, murāduhu*) are explained as His "ruling" (*taqdīr*), his "arranging the causes" (*tartīb al-asbāb*), His "setting up universal causes" (*waḍʿ al-asbāb al-kullīya*) and His application of them to their effects, "the movement of the sun, moon, and stars flowing out to effect events on earth."[63] The effects, "whatever enters into existence enters into it by necessity. For it is necessary that it exists: if it is not necessary in itself, it will be necessary by the eternal decree which is irresistible."[64] Things depend on each other, while everything depends on the power (*qudra*) of God."[65] God "is the creator of the action, the creator of the place to receive it and the creator of *the conditions of its reception*" (*khāliq al-fiʿl wa-khāliq al-maḥall al-qābil wa-khāliq*

57 Cf. also the Arabic *The Liber de causis* ed./transl. Taylor, proposition 1 and 19.

58 Cf. al-Ghazālī, *al-Iqtiṣād fī l-iʿtiqād*, ed. Çubukçu/Atay, Ankara 1962, p. 79, 10ff.; ʿAbdu-r-raḥmān Abū Zayd, *al-Ghazali on Divine Predicates and their Properties*, Lahore, 1970 (repr. 1974), introduction pp. VII ff.

59 Al-Ghazālī, *Al-Maqṣad al-asnā fī sharḥ asmāʾ Allāh al-ḥusnā*, Arabic text, ed. Fadlou A. Shehadi, Beirut, 1971, p. 47,12/also *The Ninety-Nine Beautiful Names of God* (*Al-Maqṣad al-asnā fī sharḥ asmāʾ Allāh al-ḥusnā*), trans. David B. Burrell and Nazih Daher, Cambridge: Islamic Texts Society, 1999, p. 35.

60 Ed. Shehadi 50, 7/translation by Burrell/Daher p. 38.

61 Ed. Shehadi p. 116, 11ff./translation by Burrell/Daher p. 103.

62 Ed. Shehadi 115, 19ff./translation by Burrell/Daher p. 102; cf. ed. Shehadi 158, 16ff./translation by Burrell/Daher p. 146.

63 Ed. Shehadi 98ff., esp. 101/translation by Burrell/Daher pp. 86ff., esp. p. 89; ed. Shehadi p. 101, 11ff./translation by Burrell/Daher p. 89.

64 Ed. Shehadi p. 103, 4ff./translation by Burrell/Daher p. 90; cf. also Ghazālī, *Maqāṣid al-falāsifa* II (Fī l-ilāhiyyāt), Cairo, 1936, p. 64, 10ff.

65 Ed. Shehadi 124, 14f./translation by Burrell/Daher p. 111.

sharā'iṭ qubūlihi).[66] In his *Mishkāt al-anwār*, al-Ghazālī concentrates on the Qur'ānic equation of God with the light in sūra 24: 35 and correlates it with the Plotinian equation of the divine cause with the light of the sun; he assumes a hierarchy of lights between the heavenly lights and earthly lights and the existence of angels as mediators between the "Lordly Presence" (*ḥaḍrat ar-rubūbīya*) and the light on earth.[67]

The given examples sufficiently prove the Neoplatonic background of al-Ghazālī's doctrine of attributes with regard to his description of God as cause and with regard to his concept of causality as a descending chain of causes. The gradation of causes within a cosmology inspired by Neoplatonism and the sufism of Abū Ṭālib al-Makkī[68] led al-Ghazālī to the assumption, that

66 Ed. Shehadi 125, 9f./translation by Burrell/Daher p. 111. The term "condition" in the context of causality (cf. also Griffel, *al-Ghazālī's Philosophical Theology*, pp. 222ff., 231ff.) might be inspired by Ibn Sīnā: cf. his *Dānish Nāma-i ʿalā'ī*, translated by Parviz Morewedge, *The Metaphysics of Avicenna (Ibn Sīnā): A critical translation-commentary and analysis of the fundamental arguments in Avicenna's* Metaphysica *in the* Dānish Nāma-i ʿalā'ī (The Book of Scientific Knowledge), London, 1973, pp. 43ff., 83ff. and 90ff. In the generation after al-Ghazālī we find, in Muʿtazilite circles, some reflections on causation under the condition that no hindrance prevents this. The context is an occasionalistic view of God and not natural philosophy; cf. Jan Thiele, *Kausalität in der muʿtazilitischen Kosmologie.* Das *Kitāb al-Mu'aṯṯirāt wa-miftāḥ al-muškilāt* des Zayditen al-Ḥasan ar-Raṣṣāṣ (st. 584/1188). Leiden: Brill, 2011. = *Islamic Philosophy, Theology and Science* 84), index p. 151, *šarṭ*.

67 See Al-Ghazālī, *The Niche of Lights: A parallel English-Arabic text translated, introduced, and annotated by David Buchman*, Provo, Utah: Brigham Young University Press, 1998, pp. 10 and 13f. On the Neoplatonic background of al-Ghazālī's symbolism of light, cf. Have Lazarus-Yafeh, *Studies in al-Ghāzzālī*, Magnes Press of the Hebrew University, 1975, pp. 264ff. The Neoplatonic background is not taken into account in Griffel, *Al-Ghazālī's Philosophical Theology*, pp. 245ff.; against Griffel (pp. 260ff.) it seems to me quite possible that al-Ghazālī – even though or because he was a critic of the Ismāʿīlīs – employed some Ismāʿīlī adaptations of Neoplatonic cosmology in his *Mishkāt*; cf. Hermann Landolt, "Ghazālī and 'Religionswissenschaft,'" in *Asiatische Studien* 45/1, Bern (etc.) 1991, pp. 19–72 and the publications mentioned by Griffel.

68 On the Sufism of al-Ghazālī, cf. Lazarus-Yafeh, *Studies*, pp. 503ff.; Kojiro Nakamura, "Imām Ghazālī's cosmology reconsidered with special reference to the concept of *jabarūt*," in *Studia islamica* 80, 1994, pp. 29–46; id., "Al-Ghazali, Abu Hamid," in *Routledge Encyclopedia of Philosophy* IV, London: Routledge, 1998 (pp. 61–68), 66. The Neoplatonism of Ghazālī's cosmology is doubted by Griffel (*al-Ghazālī's Philosophical Theology*, pp. 283); cf. however al-Ghazālī's *ar-Risāla al-ladunīya*, translated by Che Zarrina Sa'ari in her monograph on *Al-Ghazālī and Intuition: An Analysis, Translation and Text of* al-Risāla al-Laduniyya, Kuala Lumpur, 2007, introduction, ch. 3 (cosmology). The Neoplatonic background of al-Ghazālī's cosmology is confirmed by his *Maḍnūn* corpus, on which see M. Afifi al-Akiti, "The Good, the Bad, and the Ugly of *Falsafa*: Al-Ghazālī's *Maḍnūn, Tahāfut*, and *Maqāṣid*,

God not only creates the subsequent causes through the intermediary causes (including angels) and using the metaphor of the light of the sun, but also creates the conditions.[69] God "puts all the existing causes at the service of man's power" (*hayya'a lahu jamīʿ asbāb al-wujūd li-maqdūrihi*).[70]

Now we shall enter into the details of al-Ghazālī's concept of causality and extract those key-terms whose previous history and presence in al-Ghazālī's theology throws new light on al-Ghazālī's thought. The starting-point for al-Ghazālī is his concept of God as the determining factor against the Aristotelian-Avicennian thesis of the eternity and perpetuity of the world; God created the world from nothing.[71] In the 16th question of his *Tahāfut al-falāsifa*,[72] al-Ghazālī criticizes the Neoplatonic-Avicennian reduction of the movements of the heavens and of the effects of nature to "separate intelligences" through the mediation of celestial causes inasmuch as this doctrine ascribes a determining power to things and not to God. Al-Ghazālī criticizes here the conclusion that every effect is ultimately, via a series of intermediary causes, caused by the "eternal heavenly movement."[73] According to al-Ghazālī, then, God is

with Particular Attention to their *Falsafī* Treatments of God's Knowledge of Temporal Events," in *Avicenna and His Legacy: A Golden Age of Science and Philosophy*, ed. by Y. Tzvi Langermann, Turnhout: Brepols Publishers, 2009, pp. 51–100, the table of contents on pp. 96ff., esp. pp. 97 and 98f.; I refer here to the facsimile edition of the text (with the title *al-Masā'il al-maḍnūn bihā ʿan ghayr ahlihā*) by Pourjavady, *Majmūʿah-ye Falsafī-e Marāghah*, the chapter on celestial bodies p. 72,17ff.; medieval Hebrew translation ed./transl. by H. Malter, *Die Abhandlung des Abu Hâmid al-Gazzâli*, Francfort-on-the-Main: J. Kauffmann, 1896, pp. 20ff. On the Hebrew text cf. Y. Tzvi Langermann, "The 'Hebrew Ajwiba' Ascribed to al-Ghazālī: Corpus, Conspectus and Context," in *The Muslim World* 101/4, 2011, pp. 680–697.

69 Cf. also *al-Maḍnūn*, facsimile edition by Pourjavady, p. 73, 73, 2ff./medieval Hebrew translation, German version by Malter pp. 21f.

70 Ed. Shehadi p. 145, 11/translation Burrell/Daher p. 132. On the Ashʿarite doctrine of God's determining power and man's free will to meet his duties cf. Gimaret, *La doctrine d'al-Ashari*, Paris: Cerf, 1990, pp. 441ff.

71 See al-Ghazālī's *The Incoherence of the Philosophers: Tahāfut al-falāsifa, a Parallel English-Arabic Text*, ed./transl. E. Marmura, Provo, Utah: Brigham Young University Press, pp. 12ff. esp. 31ff.; cf. the analysis of Marmura, *The Conflict over the World's Pre-eternity in the Tahāfuts of Al-Ghazāli and Ibn Rushd*, thesis, University of Michigan 1959, pp. 39ff.

72 Ed./transl. Marmura pp. 156ff.

73 Cf. ibid. pp. 157ff.; Griffel, *Ghazālī's Philosophical Theology*, pp. 147ff. Al-Ghazālī refers to Ibn Sīnā's doctrine as described, for example, in his *Kitāb an-Nadjāt*, ed. Majid Fakhry, Beirut, 1985, pp. 175ff. On Ibn Sīnā's Neoplatonic doctrine of emanation, cf. Louis Gardet, *La pensée religieuse d'Avicenne*, Paris, 1951, pp. 45ff.; Osman Chahine, *Ontologie et théologie chez Avicenne*, Paris, 1962, pp. 121ff.; Mohammed Noor Nabi, "Theory of Emanation in the

denied as the determining factor and is replaced by the causality of nature, the laws of generation and corruption, which laws are ultimately determined by the movement of the heavenly bodies and the volition of the "celestial souls";[74] there would be no place, therefore, for divine miracles.[75]

Here, the notion of necessity implied in this kind of causality[76] is criticized by al-Ghazālī as something based purely on the observation that the effect "occurs *with* the cause, but not (necessarily) *by* it" (*ʿindahu lā bihi*).[77] Although acting factors of nature (e.g., fire) might possess specific qualities which lead to identical effects, it might happen, for example, that through the intervention of God's Will, of a free and omnipotent Agent,[78] or of one of His angels that fire does not lead to combustion.[79] Causes are mere conditions of the conditioned and do not necessarily imply any effect relatable to it. As in Ashʿarite theology,[80] God is the sole agent. He possesses unlimited activity.

Philosophical System of Plotinus and Ibn Sīnā," in *Islamic Culture* 56, 1982, pp. 233–238; Jules Janssens, *Avicenna: tussen neoplatonisme en Islam* (thesis, Catholic University of Leuven, 1984) I pp. 75ff.; id., "Creation and Emanation in Ibn Sīnā," in *Documenti e studi sulla tradizione filosofica medievale* 8, 1997, pp. 455–477 (reprint in id., *Ibn Sīnā and his Influence on the Arabic and Latin World*, Aldershot, Hampshire, 2006; the monograph by Olga Lizzini, *Fluxus* (*fayḍ*): *Indagine sui fondamenti della metafisica e della fisica di Avicenna*, Bari, 2011 (some remarks on the terminology of "emanation" in al-Ghazālī: pp. 553f.). A recently published article by Damien Janos ("Moving the Orbs: Astronomy, Physics, and Metaphysics, and the Problem of Celestial Motion According to Ibn Sīnā" in *Arabic Sciences and Philosophy* 21, 2011, pp. 165–214) casts doubt on the influence of al-Fārābī's Neoplatonic theory of ten separate intellects, though unconvincingly; Janos acknowledges, though, the adoption of the common source of both philosophers, namely Alexander of Aphrodisias' *Principles of the Cosmos*, the *Mabādiʾ al-kull* (s. Janos p. 179, n. 42). Moreover, the Neoplatonic tradition of Ibn Sīnā is mirrored in the terminology of "emanation" (see Janos pp. 207ff.); because "emanation" is a dynamic process according to our explanation in Neoplatonism, it deserves more attention. It should also be considered in connection with Ibn Sīnā's celestial kinematics.

74 Cf. Fakhry, *Islamic Occasionalism*, pp. 58ff.

75 Cf. al-Ghazālī, *Tahāfut*, ed./transl. Marmura pp. 168f.

76 Cf. also Blake D. Dutton, "Al-Ghazālī on Possibility and the Critique of Causality," in *Medieval Philosophy and Theology* 10, 2001, pp. 23–46.

77 Al-Ghazālī, *Tahāfut*, ed./transl. Marmura p. 171; cf. Fakhry, *Islamic Occasionalism*, pp. 61; 63f.; Wolfson, *Philosophy of Kalam*, pp. 543ff.; M. Marmura, "Ghazali and Demonstrative Science," in *Journal of the History of Philosophy* 3, 1965, pp. 183–204.

78 Al-Ghazālī, T*ahāfut*, ed./transl. Marmura p. 77, 15ff.; cf. Fakhry, *Islamic Occasionalism* p. 66. On the Ashʿarite equation of God's will and acting, see Gimaret, *La doctrine*, ch. IV ff.

79 Cf. Al-Ghazālī, *Tahāfut*, 17th discussion, ed./transl. Marmura pp. 170ff.; cf. Fakhry, *Islamic Occasionalism*, p. 69.

80 Cf. Griffel, *al-Ghazālī's Philosophical Theology*, pp. 126ff.

Al-Ghazālī's assumption of God as sole agent and real cause does not exclude a critique of necessitarianism, that is, of the necessary causal connection between cause and effect; as has already been shown by Michael Marmura,[81] al-Ghazālī's critique has a background in the writing of the Ashʿarite al-Bāqillānī, who died in 403/1013. Bāqillānī's theology found some echo already in Ibn Sīnā who, however, did not abandon his concept of necessitarianism.

Al-Ghazālī has modified the Ashʿarite concept of God's all-determining will, which according to the Ashʿarites is God's act[82] that does not proceed from God's essence. In contrast to the Ashʿarites – who denied natural causes and kept to the doctrine that God is the only real cause[83] – and in contrast to Ibn Sīnā, al-Ghazālī combined the necessity of God's causing the effects[84] with the non-necessity (contingency) of natural causality: he introduced his own doctrine of causality. Assuming intermediary causes between the divine First Cause, its "primary planning" (*at-tadbīr al-awwal*) and "ruling" (*al-ḥukm*), and their ultimate final effects, al-Ghazālī ascribes to God's decree (*qaḍāʾ*) and predestination (*qadar*)[85] the arrangement and application of causes to their "numbered and defined effects" (*musabbabātuhā al-maʿdūda al-maḥdūda*) "according to a determined measure which neither increases nor decreases" (*lā yazīdu wa-lā-yanquṣu*). The causes (*asbāb*) are described as "universal, primary, fixed and stable … [they] remain and do not change, like the earth, the seven heavens, the stars and celestial bodies, with their harmonious and constant movements, which neither change nor end."[86]

81 Cf. Michael E. Marmura, "The Metaphysics of Efficient Causality in Avicenna (Ibn Sina)," in *Islamic Theology and Philosophy: Studies in Honor of George F. Hourani*, ed. by M. E. Marmura, New York, 1984 (pp. 172–187), pp. 183ff.

82 Cf. al-Ashʿarī, *Kitāb al-Lumaʿ*, ed. Richard J. McCarthy: *The Theology of Al-Ashʿarī*, Beyrouth, 1953, pp. 24ff. (§§ 49ff.)/ translation pp. 33ff.; cf. above n. 76.

83 Cf. Richard M. Frank, "The Structure of Created Causality according to Al-Ašʿarī. An Analysis of the *Kitāb al-Lumaʿ*," § 82–164, in *Studia Islamica* 25, 1966, pp. 13–75.

84 Cf. Richard M. Frank, *Creation and the Cosmic System: Al-Ghazâlî & Avicenna*, Heidelberg, 1992, pp. 63ff.

85 Cf. Frank, *Creation*, pp. 47ff.: "God's 'Determination' of what must be."

86 Cf. *al-Maqṣad al-asnā*, ed. Shehadi, p. 98, 7ff. esp. l. 10ff./English translation by Burrell/ Daher p. 86. The text is quoted in al-Ghazālī's *Kitāb al-Arbaʿīn fī uṣūl ad-dīn*, Cairo: n.d., p. 13, 6ff. On the interpretation of the text, cf. Abrahamov, "Al-Ghazālī's Theory of Causality," *Studia Islamica* 67 (1988), 75–98, pp. 80–84; Griffel, *al-Ghazālī's Philosophical Theology*, pp. 242ff. On God's creation of the secondary causes in al-Ghazālī, cf. Richard M. Frank, *Al-Ghazālī and the Ashʿarite School*, Duke University Press, 1994, pp. 36ff. On celestial causes in al-Ghazālī, cf. Frank, *Creation*, pp. 38ff.

This description of the causes clearly shows traces of the Aristotelian[87] and Avicennian[88] doctrine of eternal moving celestial spheres and their unmoved Prime Mover. Al-Ghazālī illustrates it with a water clock, in which a hollow vessel swims on water in a hollow cylinder with a small hole in its bottom. If the water flows out of this hole little by little, the hollow vessel swimming on it sinks and draws through the string connected with it a ball in such a manner that the ball falls after every hour into a bowl and rings.[89]

The analogy of the water-clock exemplifies the interaction of divine and natural causality leading to one and the same effect. This co-operation, which reminds us of a similar explanation of causality in Thomas Aquinas,[90] presupposes a chain of causes between the divine First Cause and the effect of causes which derive from God's action, from His will and from the nature of the intermediary causes.

In connection with this theory of intermediary causes between God and final effect al-Ghazālī explicitly warns against the assumption that a thing does *not* come into being through God's power.[91] Here, he gives the explanation that

---

87 Cf. Aristotle, *Metaphysics* XIII 8.

88 Cf. Ibn Sīnā, *Kitāb an-Nadjāt*, ed. Fakhry, p. 300, 15ff.

89 *Al-Maqṣad al-asnā*, ed. Shehadi p. 99/translation by Burrell/Daher pp. 86f. *Kitāb al-Arbaʿīn* (s. prec. n.) pp. 14f.; cf. Griffel, *Al-Ghazālī's Philosophical Theology*, pp. 236ff. This type of water-clock is described in Eilhard Wiedemann, *Aufsätze zur arabischen Wissenschaftsgeschichte*, ed. Wolfdietrich Fischer I, Hildesheim-New York, 1970, p. 366; cf. ibid., *Gesammelte Schriften zur arabisch-islamischen Wissenschaftsgeschichte*, Gesammelt, bearbeitet und mit Indices versehen v. Dorothea Girke u. Dieter Bischoff, III (Frankfurt/M. 1984. = *Veröffentlichungen des Institutes für Geschichte der Arabisch-islamischen Wissenschaften*. Ed. by F. Sezgin. B, 1/3), pp. 1234f.

90 *Summa contra gentiles* ch. 70, 3rd book; cf. Fakhry, *Islamic Occasionalism*, pp. 148ff.

91 Al-Ghazālī, *Iḥyāʾ ʿulūm ad-dīn*, ed. ʿAbdallāh al-Khālidī, IV p. 334,1ff./German translation by Wehr, *Al-Ġazzālī's Buch vom Gottvertrauen*, p. 31; cf. Abrahamov, "Al-Ghazālī's Theory," pp. 89f. On the concept of causality in the *Iḥyāʾ*, cf. Griffel, *al-Ghazālī's Philosophical Theology*, pp. 215ff. For this reason al-Ghazālī cannot be interpreted as maintaining that beings other than God have real causal efficacy; this thesis is elaborated by Frank, *Creation*. With good reason it is criticized by M. Marmura, "Ghazālian Causes and Intermediaries," in *Journal of the American Oriental Society* 115, 1995, pp. 89–100. Here, in the accentuation of God as being the real cause acting through intermediaries, al-Ghazālī appears to be an Ashʿarite and not a philosopher following Ibn Sīnā. This observation does not, of course, exclude the amalgamation of Avicennian rudiments, e.g. the Aristotelian-Avicennian notion of God as prime mover. On the problem of classifying al-Ghazālī as an Ashʿarite, cf. Kojiro Nakamura, "Was Ghazālī an Ashʿarite?" in *Memoirs of the Research Department of the Toyo Bunko* 51, Tokyo 1993, pp. 1–24; Griffel, *al-Ghazālī's Philosophical Theology*, pp. 284f.

each one of the intermediary causes derives from the other "in the same way as a conditioned thing (*mashrūṭ*) derives from another condition."[92] At the same time God's power remains present in the things. This is exemplified by al-Ghazālī with the example of an impure person submerged up to his neck in water: his impurity will only be removed under the condition that he also washes his face. God's eternal power surrounds the determined things in the same way as water surrounds the impure man's body.[93] God's power is actualized under the condition that the man also washes his face; yet, the real cause remains God's eternal power which is actualized under certain conditions. The series of causes or conditions constitute a rule or law, called *sunna* or *ʿāda*.[94] This rule or law – the connection of effects with conditioning causes – can be violated, in the case of miracles, through God's power,[95] which reveal God's wisdom.[96]

The same rule or law of the connection of divine and secondary causality is also valid for the action of man and his free will; al-Ghazālī modifies the

92 Al-Ghazālī, *Iḥyā'*, ed. ʿAbdallāh al-Khālidī IV p. 334,9/translation Wehr, *Al-Ġazzālī's Buch vom Gottvertrauen*, p. 31. The translation by Wehr and Abrahamov, found on p. 90 of Al-Ghazālī's Theory ("some of the determined things ... derive from others") is misleading; this has seduced Abrahamov into assuming that "al-Ghazālī contradicts himself. Above he says that *some* determined things derive from others, whereas here he says that *all* that happens in the world come about through a necessary derivation" (emphasis in original). The Arabic word *baʿḍ* does not mean "some," here, but rather "one," "the other." Consequently, the following discussion by Abrahamov (pp. 90f.) is superfluous.

93 Al-Ghazālī, *Iḥyā'*, ed. ʿAbdallāh al-Khālidī IV p. 334,23ff./German translation by Wehr, *Al-Ġazzālī's Buch vom Gottvertrauen*, pp. 32f. cf. Abrahamov, "Al-Ghazālī's Theory," pp. 91f.

94 This is clarified by Wolfson, *Philosophy of Kalam*, pp. 544f.; on Ibn Rushd's critique, ibid. pp. 551ff. Contrary to Abrahamov's claim ("Al-Ghazālī's Theory," p. 95), there is no difference between *sunna* (as used in al-Ghazālī's *Iḥyā'*) and *ʿāda* (as used in his *Tahāfut*). This is confirmed by al-Ghazālī's statement that miracles occur through God's power (*fī maqdūrāt Allāh*); see al-Ghazālī, *Tahāfut* ed./transl. Marmura p. 176, 1ff. If "in the habitual course of nature" (*bi-ḥukm al-ʿāda*) e.g. the change of earth and other elements into a plant does not occur as usual over a long space of time, but "in a time shorter than has been known" (*Tahāfut* ed./transl. Marmura p. 176,4ff.). On Ghazālī's concept of miracles, cf. Barry S. Kogan, "The Philosophers Al-Ghazālī and Averroes on Necessary Connection and the Problem of the Miraculous," in *Islamic Philosophy and Mysticism*, ed. by Parviz Morewedge, New York: Caravan Books, 1981, pp. 113–132; Edward H. Madden, "Averroes and the Case of the Fiery Furnace," ibid., pp. 133–150; Jalāl al-Ḥaqq, "Al-Ghazālī on Causality, Induction, and Miracles," in *Al-Tawḥīd* III/3, Tehran, 1986, 55–62; Frank, *Al-Ghazālī*, pp. 20f.

95 See the preceding note.

96 Cf. Abrahamov, "Al-Ghazālī's Theory," pp. 80 and 95.

Ash'arite doctrine and develops a differentiating view,[97] in which three kinds of human actions are distinguished:[98] (1) action according to nature (*fiʿl ṭabīʿī*), e.g. when someone stands on water, he breaks through it; (2) action based on his instinct, his "volition" (*fiʿl irādī*), e.g. when one breathes; (3) action based on choice (*fiʿl ikhtiyārī*), e.g. writing. The kinds of action mentioned remain exposed to necessity, compulsion, i.e. the rule or law imposed by God. Like every effect, the previously mentioned types of action are also the result of conditioning causes; breaking through water is conditioned by man's weight; the motion of the throat for breathing is conditioned by man's instinct; volitional action and man's choice or motivation are conditioned by his judgment and knowledge; and, finally, man's motivation, his motives, which with good reason have been compared with Naẓẓām's "inspirative force" (*khāṭir*),[99] are the condition of man's power (*qudra*) to act. All mentioned components of action are ultimately conditioned by the existence of man as a living being, by his life.

Al-Ghazālī's doctrine of man's will and action follows the same scheme of conditioning causes and conditioned effects. Even man's choice is compulsory and ultimately determined by God, insofar as it is conditioned by his life, his knowledge of the necessity of causal connections as repeated connection of two events[100] and his creation by God.[101]

My short description so far has revealed the following elements as cornerstones of al-Ghazālī's doctrine of causality:

1) God as the all-determining cause;
2) Nature implanted by God in the substances, God's creatures. This is the rule of things or the law according to which a chain of causes leads to effects, which appear to be conditioned by a series of causes conditioning each other;

97 For more details, cf. Frank, *al-Ghazālī*, pp. 42ff.; Griffel, *al-Ghazālī's Philosophical Theology*, pp. 217ff.

98 Al-Ghazālī, *Iḥyā'*, ed. ʿAbdallāh al-Khālidī IV p. 332,5ff./German translation by Wehr, *Al-Ġazzālī's Buch vom Gottvertrauen*, pp. 27f.; cf. Abrahamov, Al-Ghazālī's Theory, pp. 86f.

99 Wolfson, *Philosophy of Kalam*, pp. 624–644 ("The Ḫāṭirāni in the Kalam and Ghazālī as Inner Motive Powers of Human Actions"), esp. pp. 639ff.

100 Cf. Griffel, *al-Ghazālī's Philosophical Theology*, pp. 162ff., 175ff. and 211ff.

101 Cf. Abrahamov, "Al-Ghazālī's Theory," pp. 88–90; Thérèse-Anne Druart, "Al-Ghazālī's concept of the Agent in the *Tahāfut* and in the *Iqtiṣād*: Are people really agents?," in *Arabic Theology, Arabic Philosophy: From the Many to the One: Essays in Celebration of Richard M. Frank*, ed. by James E. Montgomery, Peeters: Leuven 2006 (= *Orientalia Lovaniensia Analecta* 152), pp. 425–440.

3) Man's choice and action as a result of conditioning power and cognition;
4) The establishment of primary and unchangeable causes, namely the earth, the seven heavens, the stars, the celestial sphere and their proportional perpetual motions, all of which are created by God's decree (*qaḍāʾ*) and, which, through their proportioned and measured motions, were directed by God to their final effects.[102]

This explanation forms the basis of al-Ghazālī's doctrine of causality: al-Ghazālī uses the terms *ṭabīʿī, sunna* or *ʿāda*[103] to describe causality and specifies this by introducing a series of conditioning causes between God and the final effect: a cause becomes a condition for the caused; the conditioned, the effect. This doctrine continues preceding discussions by Hishām Ibn al-Ḥakam, an-Naẓẓām and Muʿammar in the spirit of Neoplatonic emanationism. According to al-Ghazālī, God's ruling power remains present in the hierarchy of intermediate causes between God and the final effect. As such, God determines whether a cause becomes a condition for the effect or not, and God determines whether the chain of causes can be shortened, thus leading to a miracle.[104] Even man's choice and action are subjected to God's power, which determines their conditions, namely man's cognition and capacity.

Al-Ghazālī's statement about the cognition of man as a condition of his choice preceding his action assumes that man's action causes something, provided the conditions do not prevent it. Moreover, his statement assumes that man can recognize causalities (effects following their causes) if the conditions are fulfilled and if there is no hindrance. This reminds us of modern discussions in the 20th century: a monograph on causality published by the German philosopher Johannes Erich Heyde in 1957 declares that causality means "the being condition for change";[105] it is not dependent on "regularity" or "necessity."[106] Moreover, he explains, man perceives and reflects causality as he perceives himself; his will and action are "causes" of changes which he desires.[107] Against the "positivists" this reflection on causality, on the relation

102 Cf. n. 86.
103 Cf. above, n. 94 and 98.
104 Cf. above n. 75 and 95.
105 Heyde, *Entwertung der Kausalität?* p. 132: "bei 'Kausalität' handelt es sich … um das '*Bedingung sein für Veränderung*' selbst."
106 Heyde, *Entwertung der Kausalität?* pp. 133ff.
107 Heyde, *Entwertung der Kausalität?* p. 145.

between cause and effect, forms the basis for a true understanding of "reality" ("*Wirklichkeit*").[108]

Al-Ghazālī has contributed to this reflection on causality not only in classical Islam[109] but also in European philosophy.[110] He continues to contribute to this reflection in our own age. Our short description of the background of al-Ghazālī's doctrine of causality reveals the correlation of Islam and rationalism. It confirms that religion, as a catalyst of science, shaped the history of science within Islam in a very specific manner.

The relationship between Islam and science is a controversial topic, as we know. On March 29, 1884, at the Sorbonne in Paris, Ernest Renan delivered his famous paper on Islam's natural hostility to science. In a riposte to this paper, Jamāladdīn al-Afghānī described Islamic religion as a moral force and as an inspirer of human fantasy, which enabled Muslims to contribute to science.[111]

As we have seen, however, Islam was not simply a moral force or a mere inspirer of human imagination. The contrast between the "atheistic" view of matter as the only causality and al-Ghazālī's doctrine of divine causality demonstrates the real starting-point of al-Ghazālī's doctrine: he formulated it in the context of contemporary Ashʿarite theology, maintaining, at the same time, a critical attitude towards Ibn Sīnā's mainly Aristotelian philosophy. Finally, al-Ghazālī's doctrine must be understood as a development, within the framework of a theocratic religion, which was the result of discussions in agnostic and Muʿtazilite circles preceding al-Ghazālī. Moreover, it can be described as a reaction to Neoplatonic ideas circulating since the philosopher al-Kindī in the 9th century. Al-Ghazālī's concept of a dynamic causality – whose first cause is only similar to and not identical with the final effect because of its descending chain of intermediary causes – gives an original answer to the problem of the necessity of created beings, as discussed since Ashʿarī: according to Ibn Sīnā[112] they are necessarily existing with respect to their cause; according to al-Ghazālī,

108 Heyde, *Entwertung der Kausalität?* p. 146.

109 Al-Ghazālī was criticized by Ibn Rushd in his *Tahāfut at-Tahāfut*, a Latin translation of which was available since the 14th century: see Daiber, *Islamic Thought in the Dialogue of Cultures*, p. 134; cf. p. 179.

110 Cf. above n. 5 and 6.

111 See H. Daiber, *Islamic Thought in the Dialogue of Cultures*, ch. 1; id., "Science and Technology versus Islam: A Controversy from Renan and Afghānī to Nasr and Needham and its Historical Background," in *Annals of Japan Association for Middle East Studies* 8, 1993, pp. 169–187 (also in *Journal for the History of Arabic Science* 10/1–2, Aleppo, 1992–1994, pp. 119–153).

112 Cf. Griffel, *Al-Ghazālī's Philosophical Theology*, pp. 141ff.

divine determinism appears to be restricted to the "best of all possible worlds."[113] The intermediary causes preserve God's transcendence from any involvement in the visible world, the final effect or their conditions. Nevertheless, God appears to be an all-permeating power, a causal energy or *dynamis* which is not identical with its effect.[114] This has been misunderstood among scholars as a criticism of causality by Ghazālī. In fact, al-Ghazālī's concept of a hierarchical chain of causes ending in the first, the divine, transcendent cause can already be found in Ibn Sīnā and before him in al-Kindī,[115] in al-Fārābī[116] and to some extent in the early Muʿtazilite Muʿammar Ibn ʿAbbād as-Sulamī.[117] Such a doctrine is a naturally consequent conclusion from Neoplatonic emanationism and its doctrine of cause and effect. In contrast to Ibn Sīnā and after him Mullā Ṣadrā – who both emphasized that God, in His transcendence, can only be known in an "ambiguous manner" (*bi-t-tashkīk*)[118] – al-Ghazālī kept to the Ashʿarite theology of divine attributes, modified by Neoplatonic concepts, and added a concept of causality. This concept is dual causality, a combination of divine dynamism and causal conditions, divine cause and secondary causality.[119] As in Neoplatonism, every effect results from a concurrence (*syndromē*) of several contributing causes, which in Neoplatonism act on a

---

113 Cf. E. M. Ormsby, *Theodicy in Islamic Thought. The Dispute over al-Ghazālī's "Best of all Possible Worlds,"* Princeton University Press, 1984; cf. Griffel, *al-Ghazālī's Philosophical Theology*, pp. 225ff.

114 After completing the article I found that Eduard von Hartmann came to a similar conclusion in his *Geschichte der Metaphysik* from the year 1899 (vol. 1, Leipzig; reprinted Darmstadt 1969), p. 222: "Eine Notwendigkeit der Verknüpfung zwischen Ursache und Wirkung, zwischen einem Dinge und einem anderen soll schlechthin ausgeschlossen sein … Diese ganze Auffassung der Kausalität weist auf die Plotinische eines organischen Zusammenhanges lebendiger Kräfte zurück im Gegensatz zu dem unlebendigen Mechanismus einer rein passiven Gesetzmässigkeit."

115 See above n. 31ff.

116 Cf. Griffel, *al-Ghazālī's Philosophical Theology*, pp. 136ff.

117 See above n. 27ff.

118 Cf. H. Daiber, "The Limitations of Knowledge According to Ibn Sīnā. Epistemological and theological aspects and the consequences," in *Erkenntnis und Wissenschaft. Probleme der Epistemologie in der Philosophie des Mittelalters*. Ed. M. Lutz-Bachmann, A. Fidora and P. Antolic. Berlin: Akademie-Verlag, 2004, pp. 25–34.

119 Regarding echoes of this double-agency in creation, the reader is referred to the stimulating collection of articles in *Creation and the God of Abraham*, ed. by David B. Burrell, et al., Cambridge University Press, 2010, esp. the contributions by David B. Burrell (pp. 40–52), Rahim Acar (pp. 77–90: "Creation: Avicenna's metaphysical account"), Ibrahim Kalin (pp. 107–132: "Will, necessity and creation as monistic theophany in the Islamic philosophical tradition"; also in *Ishraq*. Islamic philosophy yearbook 1, Moscow 2010, pp. 345–367),

suitable entity at the appropriate time and the allotted place.[120] For this reason, al-Ghazālī could combine contingent causality and occasionalism.[121] He was not a skeptic.[122] His concept of causality reveals several aspects alluded to in medieval and modern theories. I mention the modern debates about the criteria of causal relatedness, about necessary and sufficient conditions of causality, about probability and regularity, and about causality as transfer of energy.[123]

This actuality of Ghazāli's reflections on causality cannot hide the fact that Ghazālī developed his concept of causality from a religious background and in the context of Ashʿarite theology; God is the First Cause. God's creation, however, can produce causalities on its own, and has conditioned effects. This is, because God remains transcendent and at the same time He is present everywhere, comparably to the ubiquity of the sun's rays and their all-pervading energy.

Simon Oliver (pp. 133–151) and James R. Pambrun (pp. 192–220: "Creatio ex nihilo and dual causality").

120 Cf. Siorvanes, *Proclus*, p. 129ff.

121 On al-Ghazālī's combination of causality and occasionalism, cf. Michael E. Marmura, "al-Ghazālī," in *The Cambridge Companion to Arabic Philosophy*, ed. by P. Adamson and R. C. Taylor, Cambridge: The Cambridge University Press, 2005 (pp. 137–154), pp. 145ff.; Jon McGinnis, "Occasionalism, Natural Causation and Science in al-Ghazālī," in *Arabic Theology, Arabic Philosophy: From the Many to the One: Essays in Celebration of Richard M. Frank*, ed. by James E. Montgomery, Leuven: Peeters, 2006 (= *Orientalia Lovaniensia Analecta* 152), pp. 441–463; Frank Griffel, "al-Ghazali," in *Stanford Encyclopedia of Philosophy* (2007), ch. 7.4: "The Cum-possibility of Occasionalism and Secondary Causality." All explanations suffer from the neglect of the Stoic-Neoplatonic doctrine of causality.

122 According to al-Ghazālī, God has given man the intellect and all his apprehending faculties to attain certitude in religion: cf. Taneli Kukkonen, "Al-Ghazālī's Skepticism Revisited," in *Rethinking the History of Skepticism: the missing medieval background*, ed. by Henrik Lagerlund, Leiden: Brill, 2010 (= *Studien und Texte zur Geistesgeschichte des Mittelalters* 103), pp. 29–59.

123 Cf. John Losee, *Theories of Causality: From Antiquity to the Present*, London: Transaction Publishers, 2011, and the conclusion on pp. 197ff.

CHAPTER 2

Al-Ghazālī's Changing Attitude to Philosophy

Wilferd Madelung

Through his life, al-Ghazālī, a Muslim religious scholar basically educated in Shāfiʿī jurisprudence and Ashʿarī theology and early initiated into Sufi theory and practice, felt profoundly challenged, fascinated, both attracted and repelled by philosophy. The challenge arose primarily from the teaching of Avicenna, who had claimed that the theological knowledge offered by Peripatetic philosophy and by the revelation of Islam was essentially identical, deriving from the same divine source. While the intellectual elite of philosophers could gain knowledge of the highest truths from its divine source through their effort of thought and reasoning, the common people needed an intermediary, a prophet, who would translate the metaphysical truths into images and language which they were able to comprehend. Avicenna and his disciples endeavored in their teaching and writing to demonstrate that their theological views, if correctly understood, agreed with those of the Muslim speculative theologians.

Avicenna's claim obviously was deeply disturbing to Muslim religious scholars. They had been taught that the ultimate truths had been revealed to the Prophet Muhammad in the Qurʾān, the speech of God he alone had been privileged to receive. Could it be that these truths were attainable by others immediately and more clearly by their own effort of thought without an inspired and divinely chosen intermediary? As a young scholar assured of the truths of the Qurʾān, al-Ghazālī was determined to examine Avicenna's claim. Encouraged by his famous teacher Abū l-Maʿālī l-Juwaynī,[1] he studied the philosopher's teaching comprehensively, yet with a critical mind.

Al-Ghazālī's first public venture into the field of philosophy was in his *Book on the Intentions of the Philosophers* (*Kitāb Maqāṣid al-falāsifa*), published early in his teaching career. In it he addressed an anonymous questioner, most likely one of his students, who had asked him to uncover the incoherence and contradictions of the teaching of the philosophers, their concealed deceit, and their seduction. Al-Ghazālī answered that such a refutation first requires an exposition of their teaching and beliefs, since a sound understanding of the

1 See Frank Griffel, *Al-Ghazālī's Philosophical Theology*, Oxford University Press 2009, pp. 30–31.

 | DOI 10.1163/9789004290952_003

falsehood of any doctrine is impossible without discernment of its claims and assertions. He would therefore, in his present book, succinctly recount the intentions of the philosophers in their sciences without distinguishing between truth and falsehood.

The philosophical disciplines, he explained, are four: mathematics, logics, physics and theology. He would not deal with mathematics since nothing of them can be denied or rejected. In contrast, most of the philosophers' theological doctrines are contrary to the truth, and soundness is rare in them. Most of their logic is sound, and the people of the truth, the Muslim religious scholars, differ from them only in terminology and method, not in substance. In their physics, truth is mixed with falsehood, as al-Ghazālī would explain in his future refutation of the philosophers.

Al-Ghazālī's exposition of the teaching of the philosophers was largely copied from the introductory manuals which the philosophers of the school of Avicenna had composed for the basic instruction of their pupils.[2] These manuals were ultimately based on Avicenna's *Dānish-nāma-yi ʿAlāʾī*. Al-Ghazālī was familiar with them from his earlier study of philosophy and could quickly adapt their contents for his own presentation of the intentions of the philosophers. At the end of the book he assured the reader again that he had simply related their doctrines in logic, theology and physics without occupying himself with the distinction between 'the lean and the fat' and that he would next work on his book exposing the incoherence of their thought so that the falsehood of what was false in these views would become apparent.

Al-Ghazālī, it is evident, did not compose his own manual on the philosophical sciences only as a basis for his refutation of Avicennian theology. He wanted to encourage his students and Muslim religious scholars in general to study these sciences and benefit from what was rationally sound in them. While this was most definitely true of Aristotelian logics, it applied also to some extent to physics and even theology, though most of it in his view was false.

Al-Ghazālī's refutation of Avicennian philosophy, his *Incoherence of the Philosophers* (*Tahāfut al-falāsifa*) promised in the *Maqāṣid al-falāsifa*, was probably completed some years after his announcement there. Unlike the *Maqāṣid* and some of his other books produced around this time, it could not quickly be composed by extensive copying from the works of others, but required much critical thought and careful formulation of his own. The refutation turned out to be not just a rational analysis of errors in reasoning; it was

2 See Wilferd Madelung, "Ibn al-Malāḥimī's Refutation of the Philosophers," in Camilla Adang, Sabine Schmidtke, David Sklare (eds.), *A Common Rationality: Muʿtazilism in Islam and Judaism*, Würzburg: Ergon Verlag, 2007, pp. 331–336, p. 334.

introduced by a furious attack on the philosophers themselves. They were a lot of immoral conceited fraudsters, who arrogantly looked down on the Muslim religious scholars and pretended that only their own theories constituted incontrovertible truth built upon apodeictic proof (*burhān*). Their claim that their theology agreed with Islam was sheer deception. In reality they denied God's essential attributes of life, will, power and knowledge recognized by the Muslims and held that the world eternally emanated from His essence by necessity. The God of the philosophers, an involuntary necessary cause of the world, was not the living creator God of Islam. Critically examining Avicennian philosophy, al-Ghazālī charged the Muslim philosophers with infidelity meriting the death penalty on three grounds, their doctrine of the pre-eternity of the world, their denial of God's immediate knowledge of particular events in the sublunar world, and their denial of the bodily Resurrection. On numerous other points he accused them merely of heretical innovation matched by deviant Muslim schools of thought, in particular the Muʿtazila.

In refuting the fraudulent teaching of the philosophers, al-Ghazālī explained, he would not seek to defend any specific theological school doctrine; rather, he would set forth the true doctrine in a future separate work. He evidently meant Ashʿarī school doctrine, which nonetheless distinctly underlies most of his critical argument. There were, however, two major instances where he defended non-Ashʿarī positions, one allowing secondary physical causality and the other admitting the immateriality of a self-subsistent human soul.[3] Although he refuted ten of Avicenna's arguments for the immateriality and immortality of the soul, he affirmed that the existence of a self-subsistent spiritual soul that could survive the human body was not inconsistent with Islam and the dogma of the bodily resurrection. It even had some support in the religious law.

The work in which he, as envisaged in the *Tahāfut*, defended the true theological doctrine, was his *al-Iqtiṣād fī l-iʿtiqād*. Here he distanced himself initially from both the Ḥashwiyya, the Sunnī traditionalists who adhered only to imitation in traditional belief without recourse to rational investigation, and from the philosophers and extremist Muʿtazila, who in their one-sided pursuit of reason ignored conclusive evidence of the revealed religious law. He briefly explained and then employed three methods of logical proof, among them the Aristotelian syllogism. Further on in his book he fully upheld the traditional Ashʿarī position that God's omnipotence attaches directly to everything

3 This is duly noted by Michael Marmura in the Introduction to his translation of the *Tahāfut* (Al-Ghazālī, *The Incoherence of the Philosophers*, trans. by Michael Marmura, Provo, Utah: Brigham Young University Press, 1997), pp. xxiii–xxvi.

possible and that He is the sole agent who creates everything and every event in the world, without admitting any secondary causality. He also reaffirmed the early Ashʿarī doctrine that man is constituted by his material body and that life is merely an accident that inheres in the body. Implicitly rejecting Avicenna's emanationist thesis that restoration (*iʿāda*) of anything lapsed or annihilated as absurd, he affirmed that reason allows for both the human body and the accident life to be restored after their annihilation by God, as He created them in the first instance. It was also possible, he noted, that the dead human body would remain in a decomposed state and that the accident life would be restored to it at the resurrection, or the like of it would be renewed in it. He, al-Ghazālī, had mentioned the possibility that a self-subsistent soul of man might survive the death of the body merely because some Muslim scholars considered restoration of accidents after annihilation to be impossible. This, he now insisted, was not the case, though proof of it fell beyond the scope of his present book.

Soon after the publication of his *Tahāfut al-falāsifa* and *al-Iqtiṣād fī l-iʿtiqād*, al-Ghazālī gave up his prestigious teaching position at the Niẓāmiyya Madrasa in Baghdad in the throes of the famous spiritual crisis of his life. On the surface, the crisis had a political dimension. Al-Ghazālī felt that the patronage of the Seljuq regime and the caliph to which he owed his teaching position was compromising the freedom of his religious conscience and thought.[4] At a deeper level, however, the crisis signified a sharp anti-rationalist turn of his religious thought towards Sufi mysticism as well as Sunnī traditionalism. Al-Ghazālī, to be sure, never had been a genuine rationalist despite his early enthusiasm for Aristotelian logic. The Ashʿarī school of *kalām* theology, in which he grew up, had emerged as a vigorous reaction against the rationalist *kalām* of the Muʿtazila. From a Ḥanbalī traditionalist point of view, all *kalām* could be judged and condemned as rationalist, but this holds true only at a secondary level. Abū l-Ḥasan al-Ashʿarī had in fact proposed to defend Ibn Ḥanbal's traditionalist theology by rational argument against Muʿtazilī rationalist criticism. At the primary level Ashʿarī theology ever was predominantly anti-rationalist.

Although al-Ghazālī never expressly depreciated Aristotelian logic, he rarely appealed to it in his later life; more and more he questioned the competence of human reason in the acquisition of supreme knowledge. His critical examination of the theological doctrine of Avicenna and his followers must have convinced him that the use of logic was of little epistemological benefit in metaphysics. The philosophers' claims of apodeictic proof for their incoherent emanationist scheme had proved to be sham, and al-Ghazālī felt confirmed in

4 See Griffel, *Al-Ghazālī's Philosophical Theology*, pp. 36–44.

his early belief that the ultimate truths could not be discovered by any effort of rational enquiry. True knowledge could only be attained as a gift from God by revelation. This did not mean for him, however, that only prophets could directly obtain it. He was well aware from his youth that Sufi saints also professed a claim of privileged knowledge of the divine, not by rational thought, but by mystical 'taste' or intuition. As the age of prophethood had definitely ended with the Prophet Muhammad, religious knowledge could still be gained or refreshed by Sufi mystical intuition.

As al-Ghazālī emerged from his spiritual crisis, he felt called upon to revitalize the Muslim religion comprehensively and composed his monumental *Revival of the Religious Sciences* (*Iḥyā' ʿulūm ad-dīn*) which has secured him wide recognition as the greatest reformist religious scholar of Islam. The book deals primarily with religious practice, ethical conduct with a view to eternal reward in the hereafter, from a distinctly Sufi perspective. Rational theology, with which al-Ghazālī was concerned in the *Tahāfut* and the *Iqtiṣād*, are hardly touched. It may be noted, however, that al-Ghazālī now fully accepted, against his denial in the *Iqtiṣād*, the existence of a self-subsistent spiritual soul that would survive the death of the human body. He based his view not on rational considerations, but on the *ḥadīth* of the Prophet: "*Man māta fa-qad qāmat qiyāmatuh* (whoever dies, his resurrection is taking place [at that time])." In the *Book of Steadfastness* (*Kitāb aṣ-Ṣabr*) of the *Iḥyā'* he explained that this statement of the Prophet referred to the minor personal resurrection that is experienced by every human being individually immediately after death and in which all the horrors and conditions of the future universal Resurrection are anticipated.[5]

Sufi mysticism, insofar as it claims a privileged supernatural vision of God and the universe, is, to be sure, not necessarily anti-rational. It may view human reason, though inadequate to reach and penetrate the mysteries of that vision, still absolutely reliable as far as it reaches. The sense of superiority of the mystic visionary, however, easily turns into depreciation of rational thought and the conviction that the human intellect is merely a slave of human emotions and passions. Al-Ghazālī's avowed Sufi thought in the *Iḥyā'* is not explicitly anti-rational and quite consistent with a respect for rational argument. It is in works al-Ghazālī composed after the *Iḥyā'* during the last teaching phase of his life that his anti-rationalism becomes fully apparent.

In his late book on methodology of Islamic religious law, the *Kitāb al-Mustaṣfā min ʿilm al-uṣūl*, al-Ghazālī first presents a brief lesson on logic for

5 See W. Madelung, "Al-Ghazālī on Resurrection and the Road to Paradise," forthcoming, in S. Günther and T. Lawson (eds.), *Roads to Paradise*, Brill.

the benefit of Muslim jurists. He then argues against the rationalist doctrine of the Muʿtazila that good and evil are essentially discernible by the human mind. Al-Ghazālī insists that good and evil are known only by the command and prohibition of God transmitted by the prophets. The human intellect by itself neither orders nor prohibits anything. Al-Ghazālī's anti-Muʿtazilī argumentation here is initially based on Avicennian doctrine. Avicenna taught that thanking the benefactor or helping someone in need is not truly good since it is inevitably done for a selfish purpose. Only what is done without any purpose (*gharaḍ*) can be purely good. God is *summum bonum* because He emanates existence without the purpose to do good to any of His creatures.

At this point Avicenna and al-Ghazālī parted company. Avicenna asserted that good and evil are known to the elite of philosophers by reason. The Muʿtazila were mistaken because with their inferior intellects they adhered to mere *mashhūrāt*, widely held unproven beliefs, in asserting that to help the weak and needy is rationally good. In Avicenna's view, the universe and all that is in it was, as a necessary emanation from God, essentially good. The little amount of evil that occurs in the lower world necessarily and unintentionally results from secondary causation and cannot be prevented by God. The reality of this incapacity of God to prevent evil must be concealed from the common people lest they doubt His omnipotence.[6] Avicenna did not hold that God commands and forbids, rewards obedience and punishes transgression. Mankind, when properly understanding good and evil, can make their own laws in their best interest.

From his Ashʿarī perspective, al-Ghazālī could not conceive that the evil in this world might occur by necessity without being willed as such by God. It was firm Ashʿarī dogma that everything and every event in the universe, good or evil, happens according to the eternal and unchangeable divine will. The philosophers' rational argument that all existence emanating from the Supreme Good must also essentially be good was to him equally specious as the assertion of the Muʿtazila that God creates only what is good while evil is produced by mankind. Human acts, al-Ghazālī maintained, are good or bad not intrinsically, but only by arbitrary designation by God, and their quality can thus only be known by His command and prohibition. Good are all actions for which God has promised eternal reward in the hereafter and evil are all actions for which He has threatened punishment. Al-Ghazālī consequently impugns the

---

6 See al-Ghazālī, *Maqāṣid al-falāsifa*, ed. Sulaymān Dunyā, Cairo, 1961, pp. 296–300.

competence of the human mind in judging good and evil with the common anti-rationalist argument that the intellect is ruled by selfish subjectivity.[7]

Kitāb al-Mustaṣfā was composed and published by al-Ghazālī as part of his late public teaching effort, addressed to a wide readership of Muslim religious scholars. Much of his late private teaching, however, was devoted and restricted to a select group of his close and trusted disciples. For them he wrote a number of esoteric works collectively designated as *maḍnūn bihī min ghayri ahlih*, "to be withheld from those not worthy of it." These works were not meant to be published and mostly never became widely known. A major treatise of them has only recently been critically edited and designated as the *Major Maḍnūn*[8] and is to be published soon.

At the beginning of the *Major Maḍnūn* al-Ghazālī promises to set forth "the science of the recognition of God and the science of the Return" (*ʿilm maʿrifat Allāh wa-ʿilm al-maʿād*). By this, he explains, he neither means the creed which the commoners learn by tradition and imitation, nor the methods of the *kalām* theologians who defend this creed by dialectics and disputation. Rather he means "a kind of certain knowledge that is the fruit of a light God casts into a worshipper's heart which has been purified by exertion from abominations and reprehensible morals" (*nawʿ yaqīn huwa thamarat nūr yaqdhifuhu Allāhu fī qalb ʿabd ṭuhhir bi-l-mujāhada ʿan al-khabāʾith wa-l-akhlāq al-madhmūma*). Al-Ghazāli here is describing his book as representing Sufi inspiration rather than rational philosophical thought.

The fruit of Sufi inspiration turns out to be pure Avicennian theology as described by al-Ghazālī in his *Maqāṣid al-falāsifa*. Although he never mentions Avicenna nor refers to his earlier book, the *Major Maḍnūn* is largely excerpted, often literally, from the sections on theology and physics of the *Maqāṣid*. In it, al-Ghazālī unreservedly upholds the truth of what he had condemned in his *Tahāfut* as unbelief requiring the death penalty: the eternity of the world as the necessary emanation from the Necessary Existent and the negation of God's knowledge of particulars except through universals. He describes the hereafter entirely in terms of the survival of the human soul without mention of a physical resurrection. He accepts Avicenna's cosmology with all its superior separate Intellects and Souls, the eternal circular motion of the spheres,

7 For an English translation of the relevant section of al-Ghazālī's *Kitāb al-Mustaṣfā min ʿilm al-uṣūl* see A. Kevin Reinhart, *Before Revelation: The Boundaries of Muslim Moral Thought*, Albany: State University of New York Press, 1995.

8 M. Afifi al-Akiti, *The* Maḍnūn *of al-Ghazālī: A Critical Edition of the Unpublished* Major Maḍnūn *with Discussion of his Restricted, Philosophical Corpus*, D. Phil. thesis, Oxford University, 2007.

and a sublunar sphere of temporary existence and corruption which he had denounced as unproven despite the philosophers' claims of apodeictic proof. He adduces with evident approval the Avicennian proofs for the existence of a self-subsistent immaterial soul he had refuted in the *Tahāfut*. Against his position in *Kitāb al-Mustaṣfā*, he asserts mankind's need for prophets on the grounds of their function as keepers and enforcers of order and justice in this world, not as conveyors of God's promise of reward and warning of punishment in the hereafter.

How is this apparent volte-face in al-Ghazālī's attitude to Avicennian thought to be explained in the context of his spiritual development? Al-Ghazālī evidently saw Avicenna, without naming him, no longer as a rationalist philosopher, but rather as an inspired Sufi visionary. When describing the 'subtle and obscure' way of explaining divine omniscience according to Avicennian theory in spite of the fact that God can know particulars only in a universal way, al-Ghazālī remarks that no philosopher could attain such subtlety (*wa-l-falsafī lā yatanabbah li-hādhihi d-daqīqa*). In his autobiographical *Deliverer from Error* (*al-Munqidh min aḍ-ḍalāl*), al-Ghazālī had already expressed his conviction that whatever is sound in philosophy and philosophical ethics must ultimately be derived from prophetic revelation or the inspiration of saintly ascetics.

On the other hand, al-Ghazālī's formulation that what he would present was 'a kind of certain knowledge' is significant. He did not mean to deny that the traditional creed of the ordinary Muslim or the dialectical apologetics of the *kalām* theologian could not equally provide a kind of certain knowledge. He had come to distinguish between objective truth and subjective certainty. Objective truth evidently was for him the Qur'ān, the very speech of God. The speech of God, however, could be understood differently by humans, and al-Ghazālī by now was convinced that human reason was incapable of deciding the right interpretation with certainty. He knew by his own long teaching experience how easy it was to argue reasonably now for one truth and tomorrow for another. Certainty might be cast by God into the believer's heart, but that was subjective certainty that might mislead others to doubt the objective truth of God's speech. This was the reason why Sufi wisdom, even though inspired by God, must be withheld from those who are not worthy of it.

While al-Ghazālī thus did not accept Avicenna's philosophical system as unquestionable reality, he was now satisfied that it could be interpreted so as to be consistent with the Qur'ān and Islam, as the followers of Avicenna were contending. In another unpublished text of the *Maḍnūn* corpus, the *Masā'il al-Maḍnūn*, he explained to his intimate disciples how the Qur'ānic Resurrection and some of the events and circumstances associated with it in the Muslim creed could be reconciled with the philosophers' view of the eternity of the world.[9] His proposal there of an endless return of similar cycles of existence with the possibility of a sudden revolutionary dissimilar cycle constituting a resurrection manifests an affinity to some Ismāʿīlī speculations about cyclical recurrent *qiyāmas* in an ever ascending salvation history, an affinity he may well have found disturbing. Al-Ghazālī leaves no doubt that he considered the interpretation of the Qurʾānic Resurrection by the *kalām* theologians envisaging a sudden cataclysmic end of this world as equally reasonable.

Al-Ghazālī was now deeply convinced of the impotence of the human intellect. He no longer could rationally prove the incoherence of philosophy as he had asserted in the *Tahāfut*, but he still could denounce the philosophers' arrogant claim that they knew the truth by their own rational thought better than the Muslim scholars and laymen who adhered to their traditional creed derived from the Qurʾān. He could now even envisage the possibility that the world might be eternal and that God knows particulars only in a universal way, but he was probably far from convinced of it. He was, however, certainly convinced now of the reality of a self-subsistent immaterial soul as described by Avicenna. He was well aware that by his age most Jewish and Christian theologians as well as Muslim Sufis upheld the thesis of a spiritual soul that could survive the destruction of the body. Here the traditional Ashʿarī creed he had defended in *al-Iqtiṣād* was clearly mistaken.

In al-Ghazālī's last work, *Iljām al-ʿawāmm ʿan ʿilm al-kalām* (*Restraining the Common People from the Science of Speculative Theology*), completed only days before his death, his progressive anti-rationalism and traditionalism become fully apparent. The book was, al-Ghazālī explains, written in answer to a question, presumably from one of his students, about *ḥadīth* reports suggestive of anthropomorphism and about the theological subjects that ought not be investigated rationally. Such anthropomorphist *ḥādīth* reports were frequently related among the rabble and ignorant Ḥashwiyya and ascribed to the *salaf*, the pious ancestors. Al-Ghazālī answers emphatically that the teaching of the *salaf* is indeed the truth and that the *ḥadīth* transmitted from them must be accepted, believed and exalted unconditionally. Apparently anthropmorphist *ḥadīth*, like the report that God descends to the lowest heavens every night, must not be rejected or explained away, since they are susceptible to various interpretations, and their real meaning cannot be known in this world. It is unshakable belief, faith in the truth of the Qurʾān, rather than knowledge that is required of the ignorant masses on earth. The common people must be

9 See Madelung, "Al-Ghazālī on Resurrection and the Road to Paradise."

restrained from thinking and from examining the sense of the holy texts and must accept them as an impenetrable mystery without further investigation.

What should he do, al-Ghazālī remarks, if someone were to ask him about the case of a common Muslim who was dissatisfied with mere religious beliefs without a rational proof (*dalīl*)? Would al-Ghazālī permit the inquirer to present the proof to the commoner? If al-Ghazālī permitted that, he would in fact allow rational thought and investigation. Al-Ghazālī answers that he would permit the commoner to hear the proof for the recognition of the Creator and His unity, the truthfulness of the Messenger and the certainty of the Last Day, on two conditions: the proof must not go beyond the proofs to be found in the Qur'ān, and the questioner must not question the belief seriously; rather, he must think about it only slightly without any penetrating investigation (*īghāl fī l-baḥth*).[10] Al-Ghazālī here espouses the elitism of the philosophers with an anti-rationalist edge. Further on, he acknowledges that his interlocutor might contend that even firm conviction falls short of the real knowledge which God has imposed on man, since such conviction is mere belief which may be a kind of ignorance incapable of distinguishing between falsehood and truth. Al-Ghazālī counters that this view is erroneous. Rather the happiness (*saʿāda*) of mankind consists in firm belief that something really is as it is believed to be, so that the image that is imprinted in their hearts is in agreement with the real truth, and that when they die and the veil is lifted from them, they will witness that things are really as they imagined.[11] In contrast, the religious elite could receive true knowledge through Sufi inspiration already in this life and were allowed to meditate and think about it in their hearts. Yet the elite must not reveal this knowledge to the ignorant common people and must restrain them from seeking it through *kalām*, rational theological thought.

Strict traditionalist Muslims have ever treasured al-Ghazālī's last work and at times have understood it as an invitation to burn his books on theology and philosophy. A case can be made for such an interpretation, for while al-Ghazālī clearly did not suggest to restrain the elite from meditating about religious questions, he wanted them to do so in their hearts only lest their thought might disturb the firm belief of the simple-minded. Books cannot easily be stopped from falling into the hands of those not qualified to understand them properly. Most likely, however, al-Ghazālī merely wished that these books would in future be classed together with his *Maḍnūn* works as 'to be withheld from the

10 Al-Ghazālī, *Iljām al-ʿawāmm ʿan ʿilm al-kalām*, ed. Muḥammad al-Muʿtaṣim bi-llāh al-Baghdādhī, Beirut, 1406/1985, p. 78.

11 Al-Ghazālī, *Iljām*, p. 116.

unqualified.' Whether he would have wished modern rationalist students of Islamic thought to investigate them is debatable.

Throughout the bulk of his voluminous writings, al-Ghazālī comes across as a highly perceptive, intelligent and resourceful thinker with a broad range of interests and extraordinary power of absorption, critical analysis, as well as constructive imagination. He is justly admired as one of mankind's great teachers of religion and mystical thought far beyond the confines of his Ashʿarī Sunnī background and of Islam. Some of his admirers find it difficult to accept his own confession in his autobiography that he turned away from both philosophy and *kalām* theology at face value. How could the author of *Maqāṣid al-falāsifa*, the most widely read introductory volume to Avicennian philosophy, be denied the title of a philosopher? How can the author of *Tahāfut*, the most widely recognized refutation of Avicenna's system of thought from an at least partly Ashʿarī point of view, be denied the title of both an outstanding theologian and a philosopher? These are obviously valid questions to ask; yet should not al-Ghazālī's own view and wishes be respected? Al-Ghazālī certainly did not wish to be considered a philosopher; his distaste for the perceived rationalist arrogance of the philosophers was clear and pervasive. When he presented Avicennian thought as the fruit of mystical inspiration in his *Major Maḍnūn*, he implicitly turned the philosopher into a Sufi saint. This was not entirely unreasonable, for Avicenna's thought contained a good deal of mystical elements which were criticized by more rationalist thinkers like the philosopher Ibn Rushd and the Muʿtazilī theologian Ibn al-Malāḥimī.[12]

Al-Ghazālī's aversion to *kalām* theology is more complex to explain. His religious creed always remained essentially Ashʿarī, yet he progressively distanced himself from Ashʿarī speculative theology, and in his *Iljām* advocated to curb its public teaching. It seems that in his later life he no longer understood the crucial difference between religions, which humans may choose, trust, and exchange by a 'leap of faith', and theology, a science like other sciences they can and must learn to acquire certain necessary knowledge. The reality of God was in al-Ghazālī's age a matter of knowledge, not merely of faith and belief, for theologians and philosophers alike. They all called God the Necessary Being, *Wājib al-wujūd*, a designation Avicenna popularized but that was used well before him by the rationalist *kalām* theologians. The concept goes much further back among the philosophers, for Aristotle's necessary

12 See Rukn ad-Dīn b. al-Malāḥimī al-Khwārazmī, *Tuḥfat al-mutakallimīn fī r-radd ʿalā l-falāsifa*, ed. Hassan Ansari and Wilferd Madelung, Tehran, 2008. Ibn al-Malāḥimī's rationalist refutation of Avicennian philosophy is far more comprehensive and incisive than al-Ghazālī's.

Unmoved Mover expressed the same idea. Al-Ghazālī himself had adopted the term and concept in his *Tahāfut*. He recognized then that God, unlike much of religion, is a rational necessity. To deny that the One necessarily precedes the many is to deny reason itself. Yet in *Iljām* he suggests that knowledge of the Creator is primarily a question of faith in the truth of the Qurʾān. Any proof of God's reality should not go beyond the word of the Qurʾān. Muslim rational theologians and philosophers had long realized that immature minors and the ignorant must first be taught to think rationally before they can appreciate any truth of the Qurʾān. The popularity of Ghazālī's religious thought, despite the apparent decline of his power of discrimination in his old age, has evidently contributed to the decline of rationalist theology in later Islam.

CHAPTER 3

Al-Ghazālī and the Rationalization of Sufism

Binyamin Abrahamov

By rationalization[1] I mean the cognitive process of making something consistent with or based on reason. In keeping with this definition, the mystic uses his reason to understand the nature of religion and its commandments, norms and secrets; to verify his way and experiences; and even to experience contact or unity with God. The opposite of rationalization is to think of existence or of religious matters in terms of sacred texts, traditions, sayings of the ancestors, mysteries, magic, etc. In al-Ghazālī, rationalization is not pure but mixed with elements of its opposite.

It seems to me that the use of the present title is preferable to "Philosophizing of Sufism," because generally[2] the content of al-Ghazālī's mystical stations and experiences is not philosophical and philosophy cannot account for them.[3] In contrast, for al-Ghazālī, as we shall see, reason exists in the mystical process and even explains or judges it. The word "Intellectualization" could also be placed in the title, because it means to supply a rational structure or meaning for the themes with which we are dealing, however; it seems that in rationalization the element of logic is more prominent, and logic plays an important role in al-Ghazālī's mystical writings.[4]

---

1 In modern times this term was coined by the German sociologist Max Weber (1864–1920); cf. Sung Ho Kim, "Max Weber," The Stanford Encyclopedia of Philosophy (Fall 2008 Edition), ed. Edward N. Zalta, http://plato.stanford.edu/archives/fall2008/entries/weber/ (accessed June 27, 2012).

2 Of course, there are exceptions, such as the love for God.

3 Gideon Freudenthal, "The Philosophical Mysticism of Maimonides and Maimon," in *Maimonides and His Heritage*, ed. Idit Dobbs-Weinstein et al., New York: State University of New York Press, 2009, p. 116. Madkour (*La Place d'Alfarabi dans l'école philosophique musulmane*, Paris, 1934) characterized al-Fārābī's teachings as intellectual mysticism, while Gardet (*La pensée religieuse d'Avicenne*, Paris, 1951) typified Ibn Sīnā's thought as intellectual mysticism; cf. also D. R. Blumenthal, *Philosophic Mysticism: Studies in Rational Religion*, Ramat Gan, Israel: Bar-Ilan University Press, 2006, p. 44. The question of whether philosophy serves as a bridge to mysticism or contains mysticism is a much debated issue; ibid., pp. 21–48.

4 In his book on Ibn al-ʿArabī's exegesis of the Qurʾān, Nettler (*Sufi Metaphysics and Qurʾānic Prophets*, Cambridge: The Islamic Texts Society, 2003, p. 13) speaks of the intellectualization of Sufism. In his introduction to *Philosophic Mysticism: Studies in Rational Religion*, Paul

 | DOI 10.1163/9789004290952_004

The word "Sufism" raises the question of whether al-Ghazālī regarded himself as a Sufi. In his writings he frequently refers to the Sufis as a group without affiliating himself with them; for example, in *Kitāb at-Tawakkul* he counts four groups, ascribing to each a different view with respect to God's unity. The fourth group holds that to see only one entity in existence means to adhere to God's unity: "this is the witness of the righteous and the Sufis call it annihilation in God's unity" (*wa-tusammīhi aṣ-ṣūfiyya al-fanāʾ fī t-tawḥīd*).[5] Had he considered himself a Sufi, al-Ghazālī would not have related to this group in the third person, but would have said, "we call it" instead. If this were the case, instead of Sufism, I would have used the term "Mysticism" in the title. Because there is no clear-cut proof that al-Ghazālī did not affiliate himself with the Sufis, however, and because he refers objectively to Sufis, Sufi conduct, and Sufi sayings, I prefer the present title.

In its early phases, Sufism did not incorporate reason and rational enquiry into its thought and practice.[6] For example, the early mystic al-Muḥāsibī (d. 857/242) wrote a book entitled *Kitāb Māhiyyat al-ʿaql* (*The Book on the Essence of the Intellect*). Though this title seems to promise an investigation into rational discussions of mystical values, in fact, reason plays no role in his mysticism; al-Muḥāsibī's main concern was the improvement of one's morals through psychological considerations. His eloquence seems to stem from his knowledge of the vocabulary used by the Muʿtazila.[7] Moreover, very probably following the Muʿtazila, he regards reason as a device to attain knowledge of God and to know benefit and damage in human acts. He even asserts that adults should accept rational arguments. The perfect knower of God is whoever carries out the commandments, fears God and believes firmly in God's promise and threats.[8] However, all these ideas had no impact on the mystical way as elaborated in his main work, *Kitāb ar-Riʿāya li-ḥuqūq Allāh* (*The Book of Keeping What God Deserves*).

An examination of the Sufi stations (*maqāmāt*) appearing in al-Kharrāz (d. 899 or 900/286–287), as-Sarrāj (d. 988/377), al-Kalābādhī (d. 990/380 or

---

Fenton points out that Georges Vajda applies the concept of intellectual mysticism to Jewish thought; David Blumenthal, *Philosophic Mysticism: Studies in Rational Religion*, Ramat Gan, Israel: Bar-Ilan University Press, 2006, p. 14.

5 Al-Ghazālī, *Iḥyāʾ ʿulūm ad-dīn*, Cairo: Al-Maktaba al-Tijāriyya al-Kubrā, n.d., vol. IV, p. 245.

6 Ali Hassan Abdel-Kader, *The Life, Personality and Writings of al-Junayd*, London: Gibb Memorial Trust, 1976, pp. 96f.

7 Annemarie Schimmel, *Mystical Dimensions of Islam*, Chapel Hill, North Carolina: University of North Carolina Press, 1975, p. 54.

8 Al-Muḥāsibī, *Kitāb Māhiyyat al-ʿaql*, in *Al-ʿAql wa-fahm al-Qurʾān*, ed. Ḥusayn al-Quwwatilī, Beirut, 1982, pp. 202, 206, 218–220.

994/384), al-Makkī (d. 996/386) and al-Qushayrī (d. 1074/466) reveals that the concept of *tafakkur*, whether meaning 'thinking' or 'contemplating in a syllogistic manner,' never occurs.[9] Only later, in al-Anṣārī al-Harawī's (d. 1089/482) *Manāzil as-sā'irīn* does the station of *tafakkur* appear. Here, the main substance of the term is to think about the marvels of God's creation and about one's acts and states. According to al-Anṣārī, and contrary to al-Ghazālī's teaching, *tafakkur* has no impact on the other stations and it is inferior to *tadhakkur* (remembrance). In any case, al-Anṣārī does not define *tafakkur* in terms of logic.[10] This does not, however, exclude the appearance of theological discussions in the style of *kalām* in Sufi manuals; for example, al-Kalābādhī's treatment of the possibility of seeing God in the Hereafter corresponds to al-Ash'arī's.[11] Generally, the main Sufi manuals are stamped by Ash'arite theology; this does not turn their Sufism into a rational system, however, because they accept this theology at face value without rational discourse; furthermore, their Ash'arism does not affect their Sufism.

Until now we have discussed the absence of rationality in Sufism through the argument from silence; that is, rational notions do not appear in early Sufism, neither as a basis of a given theory nor as its explanation. However, there was also a clear opposition to dealing with rationality in Sufism that, on the one hand, pointed out the basis of a theory; on the other, it established a prohibition against dealing with Sufism through rational arguments. This is obviously shown in al-Hujwīrī's (d. ca. 1071/463) *Kashf al-maḥjūb* (*The Revelation of the Veiled*): in chapter 14, which is dedicated to the doctrines of different sects of the Sufis, he writes: "the real essence of Ṣūfism lies amidst the traditions (*akhbār*) of the Shaykhs."[12]

Al-Hujwīrī clearly distinguishes between *'ilm* and *ma'rifa*; the first term means "every knowledge which is stripped of spiritual meaning and devoid of religious practice," while the second is "every knowledge that is allied with (religious) practice and feeling (*ḥāl*), and the knower of which expresses his feeling." In al-Hujwīrī's view, the knower (*'ālim*) relies on himself, while the gnostic (*'ārif*) relies on his Lord.[13] Thus, *'ilm* is repudiated in true Sufism.

---

9 Mohamed Ahmed Sherif, *Al-Ghazālī's Theory of Virtue*, Albany: State University of New York Press, 1975, p. 160.

10 'Abd al-Mu'ṭī al-Laḥmī al-Iskandarī, *Sharḥ manāzil as-sā'irīn*, Cairo 1954, pp. 29–32.

11 Al-Kalābādhī, *Kitāb at-Ta'arruf li-madhhab ahl at-taṣawwuf*, Beirut, 1980, pp. 42f.

12 Al-Hujwīrī, *Kashf al-Maḥjūb of al-Hujwīrī: "The Revelation of the Veiled," An Early Persian Treatise on Sufism*, trans. from the Persian by Reynold A. Nicholson, London: Gibb Memorial Trust, 2000 (rep. of the 1911 edition), p. 176.

13 Ibid., pp. 382f.

Moreover, al-Hujwīrī believes that reason and rational enquiry do not lead to the real knowledge of God. "If reason were the cause of gnosis, it would follow that every reasonable person must know God, and that all who lack reason must be ignorant of Him; which is manifestly absurd."[14] And he adds: "Heretics of all sorts use the demonstrative method, but the majority of them do not know God."[15] Hence, "Reason and the proofs adduced by reason are unable to direct anyone into the right way."[16] He immediately justifies the last statement: "The first step of demonstration is a turning away from God, because demonstration involves the consideration of some other thing, whereas gnosis is a turning away from all that is not God."[17] Al-Hujwīrī notes only one exception to his rule of rejecting reason as a device of Sufism embodied in the Sufis Abū ʿAlī d-Daqqāq (d. 1015/405 or 1021/411) and Abū Sahl aṣ-Ṣuʿlūkī and his father, who held that the beginning of gnosis is demonstrative, but it ends with intuitive (necessary) knowledge. Al-Hujwīrī, however, rejects their stand.[18]

The intellect as a device which helps humans to distinguish between good and evil acts is found in the writings of al-Ḥakīm at-Tirmidhī (d. between 905/292 and 910/297). At-Tirmidhī, who cannot be regarded as a Sufi[19] but rather as a theosophist, also holds that the intellect paves the way for divine illumination.[20]

In sum, al-Hujwīrī essentially expresses a long tradition of rejecting reason as a method for drawing nearer to and knowing God. The few exceptions which we have brought forth prove the Sufis' generally negative attitude toward rational discussion. Al-Ghazālī states that the Sufis did not instigate their colleagues to learn the sciences; their aim, rather, was to achieve the type of true knowledge of the world that transcends mere information.[21]

---

14 Ibid., p. 268.

15 Ibid.

16 Ibid., pp. 268–9.

17 Ibid., p. 269.

18 Ibid., pp. 272f. It is worth noting that in al-Hujwīrī's work the word *ʿaql* (intellect) appears only once (p. 309); likewise *fikra* (thought; p. 239).

19 The name "Sufi" does not occur even once in his writings.

20 At-Tirmidhī, *Al-Masāʾil allatī saʾalahu ahl sarakhs ʿanhā*, in at-Tirmidhī's *Thalāth muṣannafāt*, ed. Bernd Radtke, Beirut 1992. Trans. into German by Bernd Radtke: *Drei Schriften des Theosophen von Tirmid*, Beirut: F. Steiner Verlag, 1996, pp. 142f. Here is not the place to delve into a discussion on at-Tirmidhī, who was an extraordinary figure in Islamic mysticism and whose writings deeply influenced the philosophical mysticism of Ibn al-ʿArabī, some three hundred years after the former's death.

21 *Mīzān al-ʿamal*, ed. Sulayman Dunya, Cairo, 1965, p. 221.

Thus, against the backdrop of his Sufi predecessors' attitude toward reason, al-Ghazālī's approach to reason and to rational inquiry reaches a high degree of eminence. In this article I would like to deal with his approach in the sphere of mysticism rather than in theology and philosophy. There is no doubt now that his theology is philosophical and hence rationalistic. He accepts demonstration (*burhān*) as the exact and true means to deal with theological issues.[22]

First, one should note al-Ghazālī's admiration of and adherence to the intellect (*ʿaql*) as seen throughout his mystical writings. As such, his high estimation of the intellect merits closer examination. I shall then continue by identifying some structural and stylistic features in his oeuvre which show his predilection for reasoning and its result, knowledge. In the third phase the function of reason in his mysticism will be introduced.

In *Mishkāt al-anwār*,[23] a prominent mystical treatise, al-Ghazālī devotes a number of pages to the value of the intellect. He compares the intellect to the eye and finds that the former is better than the latter in that it perceives things which the eye cannot perceive, such as distant things, veiled or hidden things, the essences of things and infinite things. In short, all existents may be the objects of the intellect's investigation. As for the judgment of the intellect, al-Ghazālī asserts that when the intellect is devoid of fantasy and imaginations no error can be made.[24] In my view, the climax of al-Ghazālī's attitude toward the intellect is his statement that the ruling authority of the rational faculty is God's balance on the earth (*sulṭān al-ʿaql alladhī huwa mīzān Allāh fī arḍihi*).[25]

The intellect brings about one's perfection, which is defined as the attainment of the intelligible things as they really are without taking imaginary forms and sense perceptions into consideration. In al-Ghazālī's opinion, the intellect is the specific characteristic of humans and the sake for which humanity was created.[26] Here, al-Ghazālī creates a correspondence between the logical structure of the world – because the intellect is a divine device which lies at

22 Frank Griffel, *Al-Ghazālī's Philosophical Theology*, Oxford University Press, 2009, pp. 7, 120.

23 For an analysis of some parts of the text, its different versions and the possible influences exerted on it, see Hermann Landolt, "Ghazālī and 'Religionswissenschaft,': Some Notes on the *Mishkāt al-Anwār*," *Asiatische Studien* 45 (1991), pp. 19–72.

24 Al-Ghazālī, *Mishkāt al-anwār* (*The Niche of Lights*), *A parallel English-Arabic Text, translated, introduced and annotated by David Buchman*, Provo, Utah: Brigham Young University Press, 1998, pp. 5–9.

25 Ibid., p. 18, l. 4. In other writings of our author, we find that one's pleasure in rational activity never ends: just as one is happy because one has the faculty of reasoning, so even one who lacks such an ability is also happy, thinking himself nevertheless the possessor of it; *Iḥyāʾ*, vol. IV, pp. 101, 124.

26 *Mīzān al- ʿamal*, pp. 196, 210, 331.

the basis of everything – and the structure of the human being. If we can use the argument from silence, it is very interesting to see that our author does not say that humans were created for the purpose of receiving revelation. To account for this absence I suggest that, in al-Ghazālī's view, revelation and unveiling of divine matters pertain only to prophets and saints (*awliyāʾ*), while rational thinking applies to the majority of people. Moreover, he also admonishes the Sufis for their conviction that revelation may come as a result of the Sufi practice alone, without the help of reason.[27] He often refers the reader to his treatise on logic, *Miʿyār al-ʿilm* (*The Standard of Knowledge*), which teaches the demonstrative proofs through which truth is disclosed and whereby certainty is attained.[28] Al-Ghazālī emphatically states that one should not weaken one's favorable attitude toward the sciences because of the Sufi way, for the Sufis do not view the sciences as despicable; their way, rather, refers to prophets and saints.[29]

As mentioned above, reason is the device by which knowledge and the sciences may be attained. When classifying the sciences, al-Ghazālī distinguishes between religious sciences, which are attained through *taqlīd*, and rational sciences. The rational sciences are divided in turn into necessary sciences[30] and acquired sciences; the latter are attained through learning or inspiration and underlying them are included the sciences of this world and the world to come. While the sciences of this world are such as medicine, arithmetic, different kinds of crafts, the sciences of the next world include the practical science (*ʿilm al-muʿāmala*) and the science of revelation (*ʿilm al-mukāshafa*), a metaphysical science dealing with the knowledge of God, His attributes and His names. Indeed, al-Ghazālī states that human beings need both kinds of science just as they need both medicines and food.[31] Moreover, the fact that the mystical sciences – that is, both the practical and the metaphysical – are reckoned among the rational sciences proves the position of reason in his eyes. It is worth noting that even knowledge caused by inspiration (*ilhām*) is considered rational, although its source is external.

---

27 Ibid., pp. 223f.

28 Ibid., pp. 243, 254f. Ibn Ḥazm (d. 1064/456) preceded al-Ghazālī in putting Greek logic at the service of theology and jurisprudence; cf. Anwar G. Chejne, "Ibn Ḥazm of Cordova on Logic," *Journal of the American Oriental Society* 104 (1984), pp. 57–72.

29 *Mīzān al-ʿamal*, p. 361.

30 By necessary sciences (*ʿulūm ḍarūriyya*) al-Ghazālī means necessary knowledge (*ʿilm ḍarūrī*) which one knows without learning. See my "Necessary Knowledge in Islamic Theology," *British Journal of Middle Eastern Studies* 20 (1993), pp. 20–32.

31 Hava Lazarus-Yafeh, *Studies in al-Ghazzālī*, Jerusalem: Magnes Press of the Hebrew University, 1975, pp. 358–363, 396, n. 21.

The importance of knowledge is also attested in the structure of the *Iḥyāʾ*, which, like the structure of *kalām* summae, begins with the Book of Knowledge. Furthermore, many discussions in this voluminous work are imbued with the dialectical character of *kalām* works, which are written in the style of question and response.

Al-Ghazālī's attitude toward rational inquiry as a means of attaining knowledge has already been discussed in scholarship. As I have demonstrated in my article "Al-Ghazālī's Supreme Way to Know God," our author holds two ways to arrive at the knowledge of God: the way of revelation and the way of rational investigation. Contrary to what I wrote in this article, I now think that he espouses both the way of revelation and the way of rational inquiry to attain knowledge of God. However, the fact that in some of his works the rational way heads the list of ways proves that he inclines very strongly to this way.[32] Moreover, the notion that the rational faculty is God's balance reminds one of a view of some scholars, introduced by al-Ghazālī, who claim that one should know the sciences before indulging in the Sufi way in order to know whether that which is revealed to one is true revelation or false imagination. These thinkers regard this system as the nearest and safest device to reach the target.[33] In my article "Al-Ghazālī's Supreme Way to Know God," I proved that this is the view of al-Ghazālī himself as elaborated in *Mīzān al-ʿamal*.

Answering the question concerning the proportional value of the mystical or the intellectual ways, al-Ghazālī states that it is suitable for most people to study in order to know how to carry out devotional acts according to the Sufi system. Only an intelligent person (*dhakī*) who was aware of his intellectual ability in his youth and was taught by a wise person who was not committed to any opinion is ready to exercise both ways. After studying all the demonstrative sciences (*al-ʿulūm al-burhāniyya*) it is unobjectionable that such a person withdraw from the community and become an ascetic and then expect that through this way (of abstinence), what was confused to other followers of this way (the Sufis) may be revealed to him.[34] Thus the supreme way to know God

---

32 Binyamin Abrahamov, "Al-Ghazālī's Supreme Way to Know God," *Studia Islamica* 77 (1993): 141–168, p. 142 (referring to *Iljām al-ʿawāmm ʿan ʿilm al-kalām*). See Martin Whittingham's *Al-Ghazālī and the Qurʾān: One Book, Many Meanings*, London and New York: Routledge, 2007 (i.e., Ch. 6) for a criticism of Davidson's view and mine regarding al-Ghazālī's supreme way to know God.

33 *Iḥyāʾ*, vol. III, p. 20.

34 *Mīzān al-ʿamal*, pp. 221–228 and esp. p. 228.

is a blend of wisdom or philosophical reasoning and asceticism. Abstinence alone as a means of obtaining the truth is rejected.[35]

In *Kitāb al-ʿIlm*, the first book of the *Iḥyāʾ*, the seventh chapter is entitled "On the intellect, its eminence, essence and parts." The intellect is highly estimated, because it is the device leading to knowledge and to happiness in this world and the world to come. According to a tradition, it is the first created entity, the noblest in God's eyes and the means by which God bestows favors, rewards, and punishments.[36] Interestingly, in the section on the essence of the intellect and its parts, al-Ghazālī divides the parts of the rational faculty in keeping with the philosophical division beginning with the material intellect without, however, mentioning the philosophical terms.[37]

In al-Ghazālī's view, knowledge is the human being's aim and the special attribute for which he was created; in pursuit of this, humans attain knowledge only by means of syllogistic reasoning. Knowledge serves as the primary instrument in the attainment of perfect happiness, and as such it is an essential part of one's life.[38] Al-Ghazālī's opinion of knowledge and its attainment accounts for his total rejection of imitative obedience (*taqlīd*), whether of treatises or scholars.[39] His criticism of *taqlīd* is general, applying to traditional scholars, theologians and philosophers.[40]

The intellect also has the function of verifying prophecy; likewise, it demonstrates that prophets are the healers of souls and admits its inability to perceive what prophecy can perceive; in other words, the intellect leads people to prophecy.[41] Revelation cannot verify itself and be the source of its own authority; hence reason is an indispensable tool for this purpose.[42]

Al-Ghazālī's concept of causality also proves his rational approach to the phenomena in the world. In the theory of causality found in his non-philosophical works, al-Ghazālī creates a combination of philosophy and

---

35 Abrahamov, *Studia Islamica* 77 (1993), pp. 151f.

36 *Iḥyāʾ*, vol. I, p. 83.

37 Ibid., p. 85.

38 Ibid., pp. 149f (referring to *Iḥyāʾ*, vol. III, p. 13f.). *Iḥyāʾ*, vol. III, pp. 22, 283; cf. Sherif, *Al-Ghazālī's Theory of Virtue*, p. 12.

39 Hava Lazarus-Yafeh, "Some Notes on the Term 'Taqlīd' in the Writings of Al-Ghazzālī," in *Studies in al-Ghazzālī*, pp. 488–502.

40 Richard M. Frank, "Al-Ghazālī on *Taqlīd*: Scholars, Theologians, and Philosophers," *Zeitschrift Für Geschichte Der Arabisch-Islamischen Wissenschaften* 7 (1991/92), pp. 207–252.

41 *Al-Munqidh min aḍ-ḍalāl*, Dimashq 1934, p. 146. Richard Joseph McCarthy, *Deliverance from Error: An Annotated Translation of al-Munkidh min al-ḍalāl and Other Relevant Works of al-Ghazālī*, Louisville, Kentucky: Fons Vitae, 1980, p. 88.

42 Hourani, *Reason and Tradition in Islamic Ethics*, Cambridge, 1985, ch. 11, p. 166.

religion, claiming that all parts of the world act in a rational way which can be anticipated; consequently, one can attain knowledge of the world. God's predetermination does not mean the absence of rationality. It should be noted that this theory appears in the *Iḥyāʾ*, *Kitāb al-Arbaʿīn fī uṣūl ad-din* (a compendium of the *Iḥyāʾ*), and *Al-Maqṣad al-asnā fī sharḥ asmāʾ Allāh al-ḥusnā*.

As is natural, al-Ghazālī could not enthusiastically embrace Aristotle's logic without being influenced by Aristotle's metaphysics and the teachings of the latter's commentators.[43] This phenomenon is manifest in al-Ghazālī's discussion of divine love:

> Intellectual efforts play an important role in al-Ghazālī's theory of love. In that, he expresses a naturalistic stand which resembles the philosophers'. Advocating the possibility of happiness in this world, he emphasizes, however, that the highest happiness man can achieve is in the world to come. The last happiness takes the form of a continuous love for God which never comes to an end because man's knowledge of God increases forever. In combining love for God in this world and the world to come, al-Ghazālī seems to reconcile the Aristotelian position of mundane happiness and the Neoplatonic position of the happiness of the soul. Al-Ghazālī expresses the *eros* motif in Islamic dress. Man always has to aspire to perfection which is stated in terms of knowledge and spiritual pleasure.[44]

Needless to say, divine love (*maḥabbat Allāh*) is one of the stations in the fourth volume of the *Iḥyāʾ*, and one has to emphasize that this is the ultimate goal of all stations. The other stations serve either as its preliminaries (repentance, forbearance and asceticism) or its results (longing, intimacy and contentment).[45]

The most significant book of the *Iḥyāʾ* relevant to our thesis of the rationalization of Sufism is *The Book of Syllogistic Thinking* (*Kitāb at-Tafakkur*). In the beginning of the section "The explanation of the real meaning of thinking

---

43 Griffel, *Al-Ghazālī's Philosophical Theology*, p. 7. Leor Halevi, "The Theologian's Doubts: Natural Philosophy and the Skeptical Games of Ghazālī," *Journal of the History of Ideas* 63 (2002), p. 20. Ayman Shihadeh, "From al-Ghazālī to al-Rāzī: 6th/12th Century Developments in Muslim Philosophical Theology," *Arabic Sciences and Philosophy* 15 (2005), p. 149, n. 29.

44 Binyamin Abrahamov, *Divine Love in Islamic Mysticism: The Teachings of al-Ghazālī and al-Dabbāgh*, London and New York: RoutledgeCurzon, 2003, pp. 84f.; cf. T. J. Gianotti, *Al-Ghazālī's Unspeakable Doctrine of the Soul: Unveiling the Esoteric Psychology and Eschatology of the* Iḥyāʾ, Leiden: Brill, 2001, pp. 12, 121.

45 Abrahamov, ibid., p. 42.

and its fruit" (*bayān ḥaqīqat al-fikr wa-thamaratihi*), al-Ghazālī plainly defines thinking as bringing together two pieces of knowledge (premises) to conclude from them a third piece of knowledge. This syllogistic procedure is exemplified by the following syllogism: (1) that which is eternal is worthy of being preferred; (2) the world to come is eternal; (3) hence, it is worthy of being preferred. No doubt, this way is better than the way of *taqlīd*, that is, acceptance of the authoritative person's view without rational discussion.[46] Naturally, the third knowledge may serve as the basis of another syllogism and hence the process may advance infinitely. Another significant notion is the way of the occurrence of syllogism; it sometimes occurs through divine light illuminating the heart by means of the inborn trait (*fiṭra*) of the human being. This is the way of the prophets; hence it is very rare. Generally, the process takes place as a product of study. At the end of *Mishkāt al-anwār*, our author introduces Ibrāhīm, the patriarch, as using the gradual way of attaining syllogism and the Prophet Muhammad as doing so in one stroke.[47]

In al-Ghazālī's view, *tafakkur* is the key to and foundation of all good things, because its fruit is knowledge. When knowledge exists in the heart, the state of the heart changes and as a result the acts of the limbs also change. Consequently, al-Ghazālī states that all depends on syllogistic thinking, which is preferable to remembrance (*tadhakkur*); the latter is defined as bringing about only two premises, while syllogism includes remembrance and more than that, that is, the final result. In like manner, remembrance of the heart is better than the acts of the limbs. Hence, *tafakkur* is better than the sum of all acts.[48] Now, since *tafakkur* is the foundation of all good things, it is the basis of all the stations. One should note that every station (*maqām*) is composed of knowledge, state and act (*ʿilm, ḥāl* and *ʿamal*). This is a revolutionary idea which ascribes to syllogistic reasoning the foundation of mysticism both in theory and in practice. Al-Ghazālī plainly expresses this idea.

In the section entitled "The explanation of the application of syllogistic thinking" (*bayān majārī l-fikr*), al-Ghazālī states that this kind of reasoning applies both to matters regarding religion and matters which have no connection with religion. Naturally, he deals with the first part, which concerns the relationship between the human being and God. *Tafakkur* applies to two issues regarding God: (1) His essence, attributes and names; and (2) His acts, rule and

46 *Iḥyāʾ*, vol. IV, p. 425.

47 Ibid., p. 426. Abrahamov, "Al-Ghazālī's Supreme Way," pp. 161–165.

48 *Iḥyāʾ*, vol. IV, pp. 426f.

kingdom and all that is in the heaven and on the earth and in between.[49] In the human being *tafakkur* also applies to two issues: (1) what God loves, that is, good human attributes and acts; and (2) what God detests, that is, evil human attributes and acts. In other words, this thinking applies to the divine commandments and prohibitions and to destructive attributes (*ṣifāt muhlikāt*) and to rescuing attributes (*ṣifāt munjiyāt*).[50] Consequently, one can safely conclude that the whole *Iḥyā'* – composed of *'ibādāt* (acts of devotion), *'ādāt* (manners), *muhlikāt* and *munjiyāt* – is founded on *tafakkur*.[51]

Furthermore, when reading the Qur'ān one should use the device of *tafakkur*, because the Qur'ān contains all stations, all states, and healing for all people; behind every verse lay infinite mysteries (*taḥta kull kalima asrār lā tanḥaṣir*). The same procedure applies to the Tradition.[52] Moreover, syllogism, which is a natural part of the human process of thinking, appears in the Qur'ān, as al-Ghazālī proves in *al-Qisṭās al-mustaqīm*. Hence, two consequences arise: a. the justification for using this device in theology because it is found in the Qur'ān; and b. no contradiction arises between reason and revelation, inasmuch as the Sacred Book contains both. Applying syllogistic methods enables humans to discover hidden meanings contained in the Qur'ānic text, and also syllogistic thought patterns promote spiritual ascent, which in turn brings about closeness to God.[53] Speaking from the standpoint of hermeneutics, in *Fayṣal at-tafriqa bayn al-islām wa-z-zandaqa*, al-Ghazālī mainly uses syllogistic logic as the basis of his arguments.[54] Also, it is important to note that rational considerations, not always syllogistic, which arrive at rational impossibilities in the apparent meaning of a verse (*ẓāhir*), allow deviation from this meaning, thus enabling metaphorical interpretation (*majāz*).[55]

Finally, the highest aim of *tafakkur* is to build the innermost part of the mystic (*'imārat al-bāṭin*) so that he will be worthy of coming close to God and even to the point of being annihilated in Him (*fanā'*). No doubt, al-Ghazālī

---

49 Al-Ghazālī devotes a long chapter (ibid., pp. 435–448) to explaining how to contemplate God's creation (*bayān kayfiyyat at-tafakkur fī khalq Allāh ta'ālā*). This chapter can be subsumed under the title of al-Ghazālī's argument from design.

50 Ibid., pp. 427–430.

51 Cf. Sherif, *Al-Ghazālī's Theory of Virtue*, p. 121.

52 Ibid., p. 431; cf. Griffel, *Al-Ghazālī's Philosophical Theology*, p. 115 and also Nicholas Heer, "Abū Ḥāmid al-Ghazālī's Esoteric Exegesis of the Koran," in *The Heritage of Sufism*, ed. Leonard Lewisohn, vol. 1, Oxford: Oneworld, 1999, p. 244.

53 Whittingham, *Al-Ghazālī and the Qur'ān*, pp. 81–101.

54 Ibid., pp. 16, 26. For the rational impossibility of Qur'ān 16:40, see ibid., pp. 58f.

55 Ibid., pp. 33f. As Whittingham rightly states there are two other meanings of *majāz* (ibid., pp. 34f); however, these are not relevant to our discussion.

sees reason as being the principal means of the mystics. In the context of dealing with the famous dictum "whoever knows his soul (self) knows his Lord," al-Ghazālī obviously connects reason with mystical experience and revelation saying "if you are among the people of reason (or intellect, *baṣīra*),[56] you enter among the people of mystical experience and revelation" (*ahl adh-dhawq wa-l-mushāhada*).[57] He reiterates this notion in *Kitāb al-Imlāʾ fī ishkālāt al-iḥyāʾ* (*The Book of Dictation Regarding the Difficulties in the* Iḥyāʾ), which was written as a response to criticism raised against the *Iḥyāʾ*, saying, "as for the traveling and the way, we mean by them the traveling of the heart through the device of discursive reasoning (*ālat al-fikr*) in the way of the intelligibles (*fī ṭarīq al-maʿqūlāt*)."[58] Al-Ghazālī believes that in comparison to other devices "rational knowledge is capable of giving a better and more objective account of the spiritual experience."[59]

It is clear that this is the way of the elite as shown in *Kitāb ash-Shukr*, in which al-Ghazālī plainly states that there are two ways to know that which God loves. The first is the way based on Qurʾānic verses and traditions and the second rests on reason (*baṣīrat al-qalb*) and is explained in terms of contemplation of creation in order to know God's wisdom and hence His will; knowing His will, one knows that which God loves or hates. The second way is open only to the elite, and therefore God bestows the Sacred Text and the

56 Al-Ghazālī calls the intellect by several names: *qalb* (literally: heart), *rūḥ* (literally: spirit), *nafs* (soul) and *ʿaql* (intellect). Although these four terms have different denotations, they all share one idea, which is the subtle power of perceiving things as they really are. *Iḥyāʾ*, vol. III, pp. 3–5. For the appearance of *baṣīra* in the meaning of intellect see, for example, ibid., vol. I, p. 88; Gianotti, *Al-Ghazālī's Unspeakable Doctrine of the Soul*, p. 125.

57 *Kitāb al-Arbaʿīn fī uṣūl ad-dīn*, Cairo, 1925, pp. 143f.

58 *Iḥyāʾ*, vol. V, p. 15, l. 3 from the bottom. Most of *Kitāb al-Imlāʾ* deals with the beginning of *Kitāb at-Tawḥīd wa-t-tawakkul*, in which al-Ghazālī enumerates the four kinds of people who unify God.

59 Sherif, *Al-Ghazālī's Theory of Virtue*, p. 107. For the reaction of Muslim scholars to al-Ghazālī's rational approach to mysticism see, ibid., n. 4. For example, the greatest mystic of Islam, Muḥyī d-Dīn Ibn al-ʿArabī states in his *al-Futūḥāt al-makkiyya*, Beirut, 1999 (vol. V, p. 116): "The opponents of the Folk of the Real hold that the servant's reason can give him knowledge of some – though not all – of the ways to gain nearness (*qurba*) to God. But there is nothing true in this statement, since no one knows the path which brings about nearness to God and bestows endless felicity upon the servant except him who knows what is in the Self of the Real. And none of God's creatures knows that except through God's giving knowledge of it" (*The Sufi Path of Knowledge: Ibn al-ʿArabi's Metaphysics of Imagination*, trans. by William Chittick, New York: State University of New York Press, 1989, p. 171).

traditions on those who cannot exercise rational thinking.[60] Loyal to his elitism,[61] al-Ghazālī states elsewhere that the stratum of the believers is inferior to that of the knowers, because the name "believer" applies to the one who blindly follows others (*muqallid*). In light of what we have said above, it is thus no wonder that knowledge is the first favor God bestows on the human being for which he should thank Him.[62]

To sum up, there are a variety of positions: there is the idea that reason occupies the first place in al-Ghazālī's mystical teachings; in contrast, one may believe that he espouses two ways in dealing with mystical notions, the traditional and the rational; it is also possible to believe that he vacillates between the two ways, sometimes inclining toward the traditional and other times toward the rational way. Whatever the case, it is obvious that rational thinking, more precisely discursive reasoning, occupies a significant place in his writings in contrast to the position of reason in the writings of the earlier Sufis.

Did al-Ghazālī's approach influence later Sufis? In Ayman Shihadeh's view, there are some similarities, skepticism being among them, between al-Ghazālī's acceptance of Sufism and Fakhr ad-Dīn ar-Rāzī's (d. 1210/606) turning to Sufism at the end of his life.[63] For our purposes, the following is instructive: "In the *Maṭālib*,[64] al-Rāzī indicates that spiritually advanced individuals should seek guidance in rational theology to interpret, contextualize and assess their spiritual experiences critically, which otherwise could lead into serious error."[65] This paragraph is reminiscent of al-Ghazālī's approach to the function of the intellect as indicated above.

Also, ar-Rāzī introduces four kinds of individuals who seek the spiritual way: (a) those who seek the spiritual experience through delving into metaphysical contemplation; (b) those who have an inborn inclination toward mysticism; (c) those who combine a natural tendency with metaphysical discussion; and (d) those who adhere to the mystical way through learning from others.[66] It is very significant that the first seekers are those who engage in rational

60 *Iḥyā'*, vol. IV (*Kitāb ash-Shukr*), pp. 90f.

61 Al-Ghazālī clearly states that God's wisdom is found in prophets, scholars and righteous rulers – all the rest are barbarians who cannot have wisdom; ibid., p. 98.

62 Ibid., p. 99.

63 Ayman Shihadeh, "The Mystic and the Sceptic in Fakhr al-Dīn al-Rāzī," in *Sufism and Theology*, ed. Ayman Shihadeh, Edinburgh University Press, 2007, p. 118.

64 Ar-Rāzī, *Al-Maṭālib al-ʿāliya min al-ʿilm al-ilāhī*, ed. Aḥmad Ḥijāzī as-Saqqā, Beirut, 1987, vol. I, part 1, p. 58.

65 Shihadeh, "The Mystic and the Sceptic in Fakhr al-Dīn al-Rāzī," p. 115.

66 Ar-Rāzī, *Sharḥ al-ishārāt wa-t-tanbihāt*, Cairo, 1907, vol. II, p. 111. Shihadeh, ibid.

thinking. Moreover, in what corresponds to al-Ghazālī's theory of divine love,[67] ar-Rāzī sees knowledge and the love of God connected as a cause and an effect, respectively.[68]

We also encounter some parallels between al-Ghazālī and another eminent scholar: the greatest mystic of Islam, Muḥyī d-Dīn Ibn al-ʿArabī (d. 1240/637).[69] Although Ibn al-ʿArabī censures al-Ghazālī for adhering to the notion that knowledge of the sciences should precede the mystical way,[70] he seems to adopt some of al-Ghazālī's ideas regarding the use of reason. Ibn al-ʿArabī views the cosmos as structured in keeping with rational considerations; hence, in order to know the world, and in order to know God – whose existence, unity and attributes are proven by signs in the cosmos – one should use reason.

Reason also affirms the authority of religion and God's transcendence. Using rational arguments, Ibn al-ʿArabī rejects the Ashʿarite concept of attributes which are added to God's essence, claiming that the attributes are relationships. That God is the necessary existent by virtue of Himself is also proven by rational arguments.[71] In sum, Ibn al-ʿArabī's reliance on reason is very similar to his reliance on revelation, and the two devices, when joined together, produce a full picture of knowledge of the cosmos.

These two examples of possible Ghazālīan impact on later mystics are inconclusive and only point to the probability of finding parallels between al-Ghazālī's teachings and the teachings of others. As for al-Ghazālī himself, he undoubtedly formulated a new kind of mysticism whose ingredients are rational contemplation (including philosophical and theological notions), revelation, and tradition. Al-Ghazālī produces not only a compromise between orthodox Islam and Sufism, but also between Sufism and rational thinking. In so doing, he seems to pave the way for later generations.

---

67 Abrahamov, *Divine Love*, pp. 42–86.

68 Ar-Rāzī, *Sharḥ al-ishārāt wa-t-tanbihāt*, Cairo, 1907, vol. II, pp. 108f. Shihadeh, "The Mystic and the Sceptic in Fakhr al-Dīn al-Rāzī," p. 117.

69 Abrahamov, "Ibn al-ʿArabī's Attitude toward al-Ghazālī," in *Avicenna and His Legacy: A Golden Age of Science and Philosophy*, ed. Y. Tzvi Langermann, Turnhout, Belgium: Brepols Publishers, 2010.

70 Ibid., pp. 113–115.

71 Abrahamov, "Ibn al-ʿArabī's Theory of Knowledge," *Journal of the Muhyiddin Ibn ʿArabī Society* 42 (2007), II, pp. 9–22.

CHAPTER 4

Revelation, Sciences and Symbolism

Al-Ghazālī's Jawāhir al-Qur'ān

Georges Tamer

1 Introduction

It is no surprise that Abū Ḥāmid al-Ghazālī would dedicate remarkable intellectual endeavors to the hermeneutics of the Qur'ān. Held in Islam to be God's speech revealed to the prophet Muhammad in order to lead humans to their well-being, the Qur'ān enjoys a pivotal position in the mind of Muslims throughout ages. Specifically Islamic disciplines, such as *fiqh* (jurisprudence), *kalām* (theology) and *taṣawwuf* (mysticism), are based on the rock of this scripture; extensive works have been authored to analyze its philological phenomena and explain its meanings; and great thinkers of the classical period of Islamic theology and philosophy made considerable intellectual efforts in order to harmonize its anthropomorphic expressions with the requirements of reason. Al-Ghazālī, who introduced Aristotelian logic into jurisprudence and saved no effort to essentially connect rationality, on one side, with mysticism, on the other, vigorously included Qur'ānic statements in his writings, granting, thus, his ideas and arguments Qur'ānic foundation. Qur'ānic authority and rational arguments obviously concurred in his mind. He also delivered his own contribution to the extensive debate regarding the permissibility and limitations of the allegorical interpretation of seemingly irrational statements of the Qur'ān. The dedicated Sufi al-Ghazālī, however, in his late years, was no more primarily concerned with the issue of how Muslims would correctly interpret their Holy Book; his main concern was rather how they would live in accordance with it: Here, the right understanding of the Qur'ān proves as an important prerequisite for a spiritual life in harmony with this scripture. Accordingly, al-Ghazālī's magnum opus *Iḥyā' 'ulūm ad-dīn, The Revival of the Religious Sciences*, can be reckoned as a prolific work of Sufi religious psychology, firmly established on the Qur'ān, illustrating practical dimensions of spiritual life, with the aim of guiding the believer to experience bliss in the afterlife. However, al-Ghazālī's engagement with the Qur'ān is multi-facetted. In some of his later writings, he undertakes Sufi interpretations of Qur'ānic passages the most intriguing of which is included in *Mishkāt al-anwār, The Niche of Lights*, a

 | DOI 10.1163/9789004290952_005

highly speculative, distinctly Neoplatonic analysis of the Light Verse Q. 24:35.[1] In *al-Qisṭās al-mustaqīm, The Just Balance*, he derives – although obviously in an artificial way – logical syllogisms out of the Qurʾānic text.[2]

Among al-Ghazālī's writings which intensively deal with the Qurʾān, the treatise *Jawāhir al-Qurʾān wa-duraruhu, The Jewels of the Qurʾān and its Pearls*, proves unique in its structure, terminology and hermeneutical approach.[3] Its major part consists of Qurʾānic selections. Its language is highly symbolic utilizing alchemistic terms; therein al-Ghazālī divides the Qurʾānic text into ten categories which correlate with several religious sciences, and classifies Qurʾānic passages as more, others as less important. Furthermore, al-Ghazālī unfolds in the present context a mature Sufi view of the Qurʾān in an attempt to bring reason and revelation together. The hermeneutical approach al-Ghazālī presents here is, in my view, the alternative he suggests in reply to the way how both the traditional disciplines of exegesis (*tafsīr*), *kalām*-theology and jurisprudence, on one side, and an esoteric reading of the Qurʾān advocated

1 Abū Ḥāmid al-Ghazālī, *Mishkāt al-anwār wa-miṣfāt al-asrār*, edited, introduced, and annotated by ʿAbd al-ʿAzīz ʿIzz ad-Dīn as-Sayrawān, Beirut: ʿĀlam al-Kutub, 1407/1986; *Al-Ghazzālī's Mishkāt al-Anwār ("The Niche of Lights")*. A Translation with Introduction by W. H. T. Gairdner, London: Royal Asiatic Society, 1924; al-Ghazālī, *The Niche of Lights, Mishkāt al-anwār*. A parallel English-Arabic text translated, introduced, and annotated by David Buchman, Provo, Utah: Brigham Young University Press, 1998. See Scott Gardner's contribution in the present volume.

2 Abū Ḥāmid al-Ghazālī, *al-Qisṭās al-mustaqīm*, edited by Victor Chelhot, Beirut: Imprimerie Catholique, 1959; Al-Ghazali, *The Just Balance*. A Translation with Introduction and Notes by D. P. Brewster, Lahore: Sh. Muhammad Ashraf, 1978.

3 Two editions of the text are used in this study. The primary one is: *Jawāhir al-Qurʾān wa-duraruhu* li-ḥujjat al-Islām Abī Ḥāmid Muḥammad bin Muḥammad al-Ghazālī, edited by Khadīja Muḥammad Kāmil, reviewed by ʿIffat ash-Sharqāwī, Cairo: Dār al-Kutub wa-l-Wathāʾiq al-Qawmiyya, 1432/2011, later indicated to in this article with (K). The text of this edition is compared with: *Jawāhir al-Qurʾān*, edited by Sālim Shams ad-Dīn, Beirut: Al-Maktaba al-ʿAṣriyya, 2006/1427, later indicated to with (S). This edition is identical with an earlier edition of the text: *Jawāhir al-Qurʾān wa-duraruhu*, edited by Lijnat Iḥyāʾ at-Turāth al-ʿArabī, Dār al-Āfāq al-Jadīda, 6. Edition, 1411/1990. If nothing else mentioned, page numbers refer to the Cairo edition.
Two English translations of the work are available: *The Jewels of the Qurʾān*. Al-Ghazālī's Theory. A translation with an introduction and annotation, of al-Ghazālī's *Kitāb Jawāhir al-Qurʾān* by Muhammad Abul Quasem, Kuala Lumpur: University of Malaya Press, 1977, and Al-Ghazzālī, *Jewels of the Quran*, edited by Laleh Bakhtiar, Chicago: Great Books of the Islamic World, 2009. This translation shows, unfortunately, numerous inaccuracies, which renders it unreliable. All quotations are my translation, partially based on Quasem's translation. Numbers following the backslash refer to Quasem's translation.

by the Bāṭinites, on the other side, dealt with the Qur'ān; the intrinsic connection between the Qur'ān and sciences he develops in the *Jewels* in result of this hermeneutics is, finally, his response to the conception of rational sciences in Islamic philosophy.

Despite its unique status in al-Ghazālī's oeuvre, *Jawāhir al-Qur'ān* has not yet been given the scholarly attention it deserves.[4] Therefore, the present study aspires to fill a gap in contemporary scholarship on al-Ghazālī. I am particularly interested in the first part of the *Jawāhir*. Therein, al-Ghazālī employs a highly symbolic language in his treatment of the Qur'ān, establishing, thus, a distinct hermeneutical approach to the scripture which appears, in result, as a stimulus for the believer not only to acquire religious knowledge, but to seek scientific knowledge, as well. After giving an overview on the nature, formal structure and date of authorship of the treatise (2), I will present al-Ghazālī's richly symbolic treatment of the Qur'ān (3); in the following section (4) I will discuss his theory about the emergence of sciences from this scripture. In the fifth section (5) I will display aspects of al-Ghazālī's rationality, as they are manifested in the *Jewels*, and present this book as al-Ghazālī's response to the philosophers', particularly Ibn Sīnā's division of rational sciences. Concluding remarks (6) provide a critical assessment of al-Ghazālī's views in this treatise.

2 Structure and Possible Date of Authorship

In *Jawāhir al-Qur'ān*, al-Ghazālī seems to address a novice, a person who is still at the beginning of his Sufi carrier. It could originally be an epistle written in response to an inquiry sent to al-Ghazālī by this person in a letter.[5] Its clear

4 To my knowledge, it was in recent scholarship solely the famous Egyptian scholar Naṣr Ḥāmid Abū Zayd (1943–2010) who, in the due course of developing his hermeneutical approach to the Qur'ān, subjected *Jawāhir al-Qur'ān* to a critical discussion: Naṣr Ḥāmid Abū Zayd, *Mafhūm an-naṣṣ. Dirāsa fī 'ulūm al-Qur'ān*, 3rd Ed., Beirut: Al-Markaz ath-Thaqāfī l-'Arabī, 1996, pp. 243–311; id., *An-Naṣṣ, as-sulṭa, al-ḥaqīqa*, 2nd Ed., Beirut: Al-Markaz ath-Thaqāfī l-'Arabī, 1997, pp. 194–212. Martin Whittingham, *Al-Ghazālī and the Qur'ān. One book, many meanings*, London and New York: Routledge, 2007, especially pp. 43–48, 67–80, discusses briefly al-Ghazālī's hermeneutical theory and its application in the exegesis of Qur'ānic passages.

5 In chapter 8 of the *Jawāhir*, al-Ghazālī warns his addressee not to attempt to acquire knowledge about the relationship of the world of dominion and the world of perception "by means of correspondence" (*bi-l-mukātaba wa-l-murāsala*), but by means of "spiritual struggle and piety" (*min bāb al-mujāhada wa-t-taqwā*), p. 92/56. It should also be mentioned that verbs in the second person plural are used throughout the text.

structure reflects the educational purpose behind it. The treatise is divided into three parts. The first part deals with "introductory matters and prolegomena" (*al-muqaddimāt wa-s-sawābiq*); it consists of nineteen chapters.[6] In this part, al-Ghazālī develops a hermeneutical approach to the Qur'ān using symbolic expressions and connecting the revealed text to religious and secular sciences. The second part is on "the purposes" (*al-maqāṣid*) of the treatise; it consists of "the pith of the verses of the Qur'ān" (*lubāb āyāt al-Qur'ān*), which are divided into two sections corresponding to "two types" (*namaṭāni*) of verses. The first section includes verses which deal with "the essence of God [...], especially His attributes and acts." This part is on "theoretical knowledge" (*huwa al-qism al-ʿilmī*). It contains 783 selected verses of the Qur'ān beginning with the first Sura 1 and ending with Sura 112. Al-Ghazālī describes the verses included in this section as "jewels" (*jawāhir*). The second section comprises the verses which are "revealed to describe the straight path (*aṣ-ṣirāṭ al-mustaqīm*) and to urge [the people] to follow it. This is the practical part" (*huwa al-qism al-ʿamalī*) of the selection; its contents are called "pearls" (*durar*). It consists of 786 selected verses beginning with the first five verses of Sura 2 and ending with Sura 114.[7] In a short conclusion, al-Ghazālī declares that he limited his selection to only these two categories of verses with the purpose of inciting the awareness of the reader to obtain from the "jewels" the light of theoretical knowledge, and to pursue, based on the "pearls," the straight path of action, due to the fact that "faith is based both on knowledge and action."[8]

---

6 *Jawāhir*, p. 63/15. Nineteen is the number of the hell's guardians according to Q 74:30f. Cf. for further information: Franz Rosenthal, "Nineteen," in: *Analecia Biblica* 12 (1959): 304–318.

7 This amounts to 1569 selected verses, almost 25% of the whole Qur'ān. As the act of selection itself is a hermeneutical act, the investigation of al-Ghazālī's bipartite collection of Qur'ānic verses could shed new light on his Qur'ānic hermeneutics.

8 *Jawāhir*, 111/87. In *al-Mustaṣfā min ʿilm al-uṣūl*, ed. M. S. al-Ashqar, 2 Vols., Beirut: Mu'assasat ar-Risāla, 1417/1997, Vol. I, p. 33, al-Ghazālī mentions *Jawāhir al-Qur'ān* together with *Iḥyā' ʿulūm ad-dīn* and *Kīmiyā' as-saʿāda* as works dedicated to "the science of the path to the hereafter and the knowledge of the inner mysteries of religion" (*ʿilm ṭarīq al-ākhira wa-maʿrifat asrār ad-dīn al-bāṭina*). He classifies these three books according to length stating that the *Iḥyā'* is the most extensive one (*basīṭa*), the *Kīmiyā'* of intermediate length (*wasīṭa*) and the *Jawāhir* is compendious (*wajīza*). Alexander Treiger, "Al-Ghazali's Classifications of the Sciences and Descriptions of the Highest Theoretical Science," in: *Dîvân. Disiplinlerarasi Çalişmalar Dergisi*, cilt 16 sayı 30 (2011/1), XX–XX: 1–32, p. 27, n. 75, observes that these books parallel al-Ghazālī's "trilogy on *fiqh*:" the extensive *Basīṭ*, the intermediate *Wasīṭ*, and the compendious *Wajīz*. He assumes that this "parallel is probably not accidental in a work written for specialists in *fiqh*."

The third major part of the book contains "the appendages" (*al-lawāḥiq*) which determine "the aims" (*al-maqāṣid*) related to the selected verses. Although connected to *Jawāhir al-Qurʾān*, this text is, according to the author's own statement, to be treated as a separate book called *Kitāb al-Arbaʿīn fī uṣūl ad-dīn* (*The Book of Forty on the Principles of Religion*). This is obviously a summary of *Iḥyāʾ ʿulūm ad-dīn*; it consists of four parts, including "the important matters of Qurʾānic sciences" (*al-muhimmāt min ʿulūm al-Qurʾān*). In the first part, forms of knowledge (*al-maʿārif*) are discussed; in the second part, "the outer deeds" (*al-aʿmāl aẓ-ẓāhira*); in the third part, "the discarded ethical attitudes" (*al-akhlāq al-madhmūma*); and in the fourth part, "the laudable ethical attitudes" (*al-akhlāq al-mamdūḥa*). Each one of the four parts contains ten religious principles (*uṣūl*).[9]

Jawāhir al-Qurʾān belongs to the late period of al-Ghazālī's writing career. A late date of authorship is confirmed through an assessment of its language and contents and through the fact that al-Ghazālī mentions in this book several of his previous works as we will see below. Furthermore, the book includes an autobiographical note in which al-Ghazālī refers to his way of life before he dedicated himself to Sufism.[10] Recent attempts to date al-Ghazālī's writings chronologically agree that *Jawāhir al-Qurʾān* was written at some point between 1102/495 and al-Ghazālī's resuming of teaching in Nīshāpūr 1106/499.[11] However, towards the end of the treatise, al-Ghazālī makes a statement which

---

9 *Jawāhir*, 66f. The abovementioned edition of *Jawāhir al-Qurʾān* prepared by Khadīja M. Kāmil includes *Kitāb al-Arbaʿīn*, pp. 193–459, as the editor considers it the third part of the *Jawāhir*. Otherwise, both treatises have been edited and published as two separate books. Earlier editions of *Kitāb al-Arbaʿīn*: *Kitāb al-Arbaʿīn fī uṣūl al-dīn*, ed. by Muḥyī ad-Dīn Ṣabrī l-Kurdī, Cairo: Al-Maṭbaʿa al-ʿArabiyya, 1344, and an edition done by Muḥammad Muḥammad Jābir, Cairo: Maktabat al-Jundī, 1964. A partial English translation: *Ghazali on the Principles of Islamic Spirituality: Selections from Forty Foundations of Religion*, annotated and explained by Aaron Spevack, Vermont: Jewish Lights Publishing, 2011.

10 *Jawāhir*, p. 96/63.

11 George Hourani, "A Revised Chronology of Ghazālī's Writings," in: *Journal of the American Oriental Society* 104 (1984): 289–302, p. 299; Alexander Treiger, *Inspired Knowledge in Islamic Thought. Al-Ghazālī's theory of mystical cognition and its Avicennian foundation*, Routledge, 2012, p. 12, assumes that "*Jawāhir* was written in or shortly after 495/1101–2." Treiger does not include *al-Maqṣad al-asnā fī sharḥ asmāʾ Allāh al-ḥusnā* (*The Loftiest Goal in Explicating the Meanings of God's Most Beautiful Names*) in the list of books al-Ghazālī refers to in *Jawāhir*: p. 105/77. ʿAbd ar-Raḥmān Badawī, *Muʾallafāt al-Ghazālī*, 2nd Edition, Kuwait: Wakālat al-maṭbūʿāt, 1977, pp. 143–148, does not suggest for *Jawāhir* any date of authorship.

The Kuwaiti scholar Fahd Sālim Khalīl ar-Rāshid has recently published the book *Iʿrāb al-Qurʾān* attributed to the Abbasid philologist az-Zajjāj (d. 923/309) as Jāmiʿ al-ʿUlūm

may help dating its completion around or shortly after September 1106/ Muharram 500, when Ismāʿilites assassinated the vizier Fakhr al-Mulk who put al-Ghazālī under pressure to resume teaching in Nīshāpūr.[12] Wondering how people could keep distracted from preparing "the ship of rescue" for themselves and others, although they are aware of the eschatological danger of this attitude, al-Ghazālī adds as an important reason why one has to be prepared that "God let the country be shadowed by a tyrannical power (*sulṭān^an^ qāhir^an^*) which wants to raid into it, kill some of the people and enthrone others."[13] This statement about life threatening political chaos with strong consequences affecting the rulers and urging people to renounce the world and concentrate on the Hereafter could contain an allusion to the murder of Fakhr al-Mulk for whom al-Ghazālī was a mentor.[14]

3 Qurʾānic Hermeneutics and Symbolism

From the beginning of the treatise on, al-Ghazālī deploys a highly metaphoric language to describe the Qurʾān. In a strong rhetorical manner, he critically addresses those who recite the Qurʾān extensively, "have its study as occupation" and grasp only "some of its apparent meanings and sentences":

> How long will you wander on the shore of the sea, closing your eyes to the wonders of the meanings of the Qurʾān? Has the time not come for you to sail to the midst of these meanings in order to see their wonders, travel to their islands and pluck their delicacies, or rather to dive into their depth, so that you become wealthy by obtaining their jewels? Don't you harm yourself by being deprived of their pearls and jewels, as you remain looking at their shores and outward appearances (*ẓawāhirihā*)?[15]

al-Bāqūlī ʿAlī bin al-Ḥussain al-Iṣbahānī's (d. 542/1147) book titled *Jawāhir al-Qurʾān*, Alger: Dār al-Jāʾiza, 2012.

12 Frank Griffel, *Al-Ghazālī's Philosophical Theology*, Oxford: Oxford University Press, p. 53. Cf. farther: Farouk Mitha, *Al-Ghazālī and the Ismailis. A Debate on Reason and Authority in Medieval Islam*, London/New York: L. B. Tauris in association with The Institute of Ismaili Studies, 2001.

13 Jawāhir, 110/85.

14 Kenneth Garden, "Coming Down from the Mountaintop: Al-Ghazālī's Autobiographical Writings in Context," in: *The Muslim World* 101 (2011): 581–596, p. 594f.

15 Jawāhir, 67f./19. Although the addressee is in the second person singular, the speech may be understood as a general statement, not directed to a particular person.

In this emphatic introduction, al-Ghazālī depicts the person who merely deals with the verbal text of the Qurʾān, without exploring its inner meanings, as a person who wanders on the shore, while intentionally closing his eyes. Instead, hidden aspects of the Qurʾān become accessible to the reader whose aim is to penetrate to the deep meanings of the Qurʾānic text. For al-Ghazālī, this is the way how Sufis read the Qurʾān; their interpretation of the Qurʾān is, in the *Jewels* as well as elsewhere,[16] preferred to the traditional way of exegesis. However, in the present context, the metaphoric description of the Qurʾān as a sea bears ideas that obviously go beyond al-Ghazālī's earlier discussion of the external rules and internal activities (*aʿmāl al-bāṭin*) required while reciting the Qurʾān, in the eighth book of the *Iḥyāʾ*.

Al-Ghazālī's language is paradoxical; on one hand, he urges the reader to approach the book and investigate its depth and various parts, while the image of the sea used to describe the Qurʾān stands for the incomprehensible depth of God's book and the extreme diversity of its contents that are inexplorable to the human mind, on the other.[17] However, the activity people are urged to undertake is a duty worthy to be pursued; it promises to be extremely rewarding, as the Qurʾān is the source of "the knowledge of the ancients and the moderns" (*ʿilm al-awwalīn wa-l-ākhirīn*). In order to indicate their high, though different, values, al-Ghazālī compares the various forms of knowledge waiting to be discovered in the Qurʾān to alchemistic materials and precious stones. His stated aim of this treatise is to guide the reader "to the manner of the journey, diving and swimming," which allows the reader to obtain forms of knowledge hidden in the Qurʾān.[18]

Al-Ghazālī uses the names of red sulfur, jewels and precious materials in order to depict the forms of knowledge preserved in the Qurʾān and rank them according to their value. He declares these names as "descriptive allegories (*istiʿārāt rasmiyya*)[19] with underlying hidden symbols and signs (*wa-taḥtahā rumūz wa-ishārāt khafiyya*)."[20] In agreement with an important principle of

16 Cf. Abū Ḥāmid al-Ghazālī, *Iḥyāʾ ʿulūm ad-dīn*, ed. ʿAbd al-Muʿṭī Amīn Qalʿajī, 2nd Ed., Beirut: Dār Ṣādir, 2004, 5 volumes, Book 8: *Kitāb Ādāb tilāwat al-Qurʾān*, last chapter, vol. 1, pp. 362–389. English: Muhammad Abul Quasem, *The Recitation and Interpretation of the Qurʾān. Al-Ghazālī's Theory* (London etc.: Routledge & Kegan Paul, 1982, rep. 1984) and in: Muhammad Abul Quasem, "Al-Ghazālī in Defense of Ṣūfistic Interpretation of the Qurʾān," in: *Islamic Culture* 53 (1979): 63–86, especially pp. 68–79.

17 Cf. Q 18:109.

18 Jawāhir, p. 68/20.

19 I decided for the text variant "*istiʿārāt rasmiyya*" (S) instead of "*istiʿārāt wa-tasmiya*" (K), which means "allegories and nomination."

20 Jawāhir, p. 87/49.

Sufi hermeneutics of the Qur'ān, al-Ghazālī states that "there is no word [of the verses containing knowledge of God and the right path leading to Him] without an underlying symbol and a sign to a hidden meaning, which are known to those who are aware of the analogy and correspondence (*al-muwāzana wa-l-munāsaba*) between the world of possession and perception (*ʿālam al-mulk wa-sh-shahāda*) and the unseen world of dominion (*ʿālam al-ghayb wa-l-malakūt*)."[21]

Considering the words of the Qur'ān as symbols and signs, which bear hidden meanings in regard to God's essence, attributes and acts as well as to the path leading to Him, corresponds to al-Ghazālī's bi-partite spiritual cosmology. According to it, every existent in the world of perception (*ʿālam ash-shahāda*) "is an icon (*mithāl*) of a spiritual matter in the world of dominion." Understood as an image of an unseen spiritual matter, an object of perception reflects the "quintessence and meaning" of this matter (*ka'annahu huwa fī rūḥihi wa-maʿnāhu*)," although it does not resemble it in regard "to its form and shape (*wa-laysa huwa huwa fī ṣūratihi ka-qālibihi*)." The physical icon in the world of perception functions as "an ascending ladder (*mirqāt*) to the spiritual meaning which is from that world."[22]

Perceived as a totality of icons, the physical world appears as a medium of ascension to the spiritual world. As such, it resembles the peel (*al-qishr*); there is no way to reach the core (*al-lubb*) but through it. Similarly, there is no way to reach the spiritual world but through the physical world. Al-Ghazālī compares the connection between the existents in the world of perception and the existents in the spiritual world to events seen in dreams and reflecting reality in the world.[23] In order to illustrate how things in both worlds share common essential qualities, al-Ghazālī refers to revealing the truth through dream interpretation.[24] For instance, a man who dreamt of himself sealing mouths of men and vaginas was told by Ibn Sīrīn that he was a person who called out to prayer before dawn in Ramadan, proclaiming the beginning of a new fasting day and thus prohibiting food and sexual intercourse.[25] Al-Ghazālī concludes that the act of "sealing mouths and vaginas shares with the call for prayer before dawn the quintessence (*rūḥ*) of the seal, which is prohibition," although both acts differ regarding the form.[26]

21 Jawāhir, p. 88/49.
22 Jawāhir, p. 88/49.
23 Jawāhir, p. 88/49.
24 Jawāhir, p. 88f./50.
25 This and similar examples are abbreviated in *Mishkāt al-anwār*, (ed. Buchman, p. 29).
26 Jawāhir, p. 89/50.

The real meanings of matters of "the world of dominion" (*ʿālam al-malakūt*) are not explicitly presented in the Qur'ān, but "through allegories" (*bi-amthila*) taken from "the world of perception" (*ʿālam ash-shahāda*).[27] Al-Ghazālī gives two reasons for the necessity of allegorization in the Qur'ān, which are not related to the nature of the text itself, but to the situation of its reader from a Sufi point of view:

1. The first reason for allegorical depicting of heavenly matters in the Qur'ān is that the state of life in this world resembles the state of sleep. "People are asleep; they wake up when they die."[28] Therefore, matters of "the Unseen" (*al-ghayb*) which are kept in the "Preserved Tablet" (*al-lawḥ al-maḥfūẓ*) are not revealed to the humans in this state but allegorically "by means of icons (*illā bi-l-mithāl*)." When people die, they become aware of "the realities and the spirits" of the allegories, "and they know that those allegories were peels and shells for those spirits".[29]
2. Secondly, allegories are important because the readers of the Qur'ān, when they concentrate "on the sensuous" (*al-ḥiss*), think that "there is no other meaning of it but the imagined one (*al-mutakhayyal*)," thus neglecting the spiritual. On the contrary, allegorization allows people to perceive and comprehend heavenly matters in this life according to their ability of perception. In order to get to this point, one has to cut off the relationship to the material world and reach a high level of asceticism "through spiritual self-training and struggle" (*bi-r-riyāḍa wa-l-mujāhada*).[30] In this regard, the prophet Muhammad serves al-Ghazālī as a role model. The "mysteries" (*asrār*) of the heavenly world remain "veiled from the hearts which are defiled by the love of the [lower] world (*ad-dunyā*);" for those people "the shells of the Qur'ān do not open to show its jewels at all."[31]

27 Al-Ghazālī acknowledges that these allegories caused people to be confused and misguided, as they ignorantly believed that God resembles humans (*jahālat at-tashbīh wa-ḍalālat at-tamthīl*): Jawāhir, 91/53.

28 Jawāhir, 91/53. Al-Ghazālī repeats this statement as a *ḥadīth* in some of his writings, see for instance: *Al-Munqidh min aḍ-ḍalāl*, ed. Farid Jabre, Beirut: Al-Lajna al-Lubnāniyya li-tarjamat ar-rawāʾiʿ, 1969, p. 13; al-Ghazālī, *Deliverance from Error*, Translated and Annotated by Richard J. McCarthy, Louisville: Fons Vitae, 1999, p. 57. However, the statement cannot be identified in *ḥadīth*-collections.

29 Jawāhir, 91/53.

30 Jawāhir, 92/55f.

31 Jawāhir, 93/57.

Corresponding with his bi-partite cosmology, al-Ghazālī presents the view that every material being bears a spirit (*rūḥ*) which is its essence and its virtue, meaning the essential quality which makes up the sense and the purpose of its existence. Adequate understanding of any object of knowledge requires, therefore, knowledge of its essence, which brings to the knower different epistemological and spiritual benefits:

> Everything has a definition and an essential property (*ḥadd wa-ḥaqīqa*) that is its spirit [quintessence] (*rūḥuhu*); if you have found the spirits [quintessences] [of things], you have become a spiritual [human being] (*rūḥāniyy^{an}*).[32]

This hermeneutical principle has also to be applied to the interpretation of Qurʾānic verses, which attribute to God bodily organs or corporeal qualities. Each one of such expressions has "a spiritual, not a corporeal meaning."[33] As an example of allegoric statements and how they should be interpreted, al-Ghazālī mentions the prophetic saying: "The heart of the believer lies between two fingers of the Compassionate."[34] As it is inconceivable for al-Ghazālī that God could have physical organs, he shifts the verbal meaning of the finger into the purpose of its existence, i.e. that what makes its quintessence. He interprets "the quintessence of the finger (*rūḥ al-iṣbaʿ*)" as "the ability to quickly and repeatedly turn [something] over and over (*surʿat at-taqlīb*)." In silent reference to another prophetic statement,[35] he interprets God's two fingers as "the touch of the angel and the touch of Satan (*lammat al-malak wa-lammat ash-shayṭān*)"; exposed to both of them, the heart of the believer is misled by the later and rightly guided by the former. As they act under God's control, the angel and Satan resemble allegorically two of His fingers; they share with fingers "the quintessence of fingership (*rūḥ al-iṣbaʿiyya*)".[36]

In a further example, al-Ghazālī interprets "the pen" (*al-qalam*) in Q 96:4–5 as the divine power by which knowledge is transmitted into the hearts of

32 Ibid.

33 Jawāhir, 90/51.

34 Ibid.: "*Qalb al-muʾmin bayna iṣbaʿayni min aṣābiʿ ar-raḥmān.*" See for this *ḥadīth* and its various wordings: *Ṣaḥīḥ Muslim*, 16:209; *Musnad Aḥmad*, 11:130; *Sunan at-Tirmidhī*, 4: 390–391.

35 *Jawāhir*, 89, n. (b). Cf. *Sunan at-Tirmidhī*, 5:204.

36 Jawāhir, 89/50.

human beings.[37] In this and other cases, al-Ghazālī interprets Qurʾānic statements through linking them to objects of theology. Thus, he adds to expressions spiritual meanings which reflect their essence. Here the question arises: How does the reader of the Qurʾān discover the real meaning of its contents? Al-Ghazālī states that the Qurʾān itself "casts" (*yulqī*) to the reader, who is not dominated by "blind imitation" (*taqlīd*) and has undertaken the adventure of diving into the depth of the text, that what this person is able to understand (*kull mā yaḥtamiluhu fahmuka*). The Qurʾān reveals its true and hidden meanings to the spiritual reader according to the reader's ability to understand. This happens in a mysterious way; as if in a dream, the reader would read "in spirit" (*bi-rūḥik*) the "Preserved Tablet" (*al-lawḥ al-maḥfūẓ*); only spiritually qualified readers are able to bear the knowledge obtained in this way. Obtaining true knowledge from the Qurʾān affects the reader, farther changing him into a spiritual human being who can perceive even the mysteries of paradise.[38]

Saying that the Qurʾān casts the meanings into the mind of the interpreter does not mean that the interpreter shall remain passive, receiving these meanings without an own endeavor to understand. The combination of receiving casted meanings and spending efforts to obtain them is indicated by al-Ghazālī through comparing the "interpretation of the Qurʾān" (*taʾwīl*) to the "interpretation of dreams" (*taʿbīr*); in both cases, the interpreter, who is sensitive to the spirit of things, deals with "signs" (*ishārāt*) in order to actively expose the real meanings behind them.[39]

3.1 *Classification of the Contents of the Qurʾān*

Al-Ghazālī declares that it is "the mystery of the Qurʾān, its purest pith and ultimate aim" to call the people to God, "the Most Powerful, the Highest, the Lord of the Hereafter and this world, and the Creator of heaven and earth, what between them and what beneath the soil."[40] Based on these attributes,

37 Jawāhir, 90/51. See Ibn Taymiyya's critique against this interpretation in Yahya Michot's contribution in the present volume.

38 Jawāhir, 90/51f.

39 Jawāhir, 90f./52. See on the connection al-Ghazālī makes between *taʾwīl* and dream interpretation: Martin Whittinham, *Al-Ghazālī and the Qurʾān*, pp. 47f., where it is correctly noted that al-Ghazālī's interpretation seems to be taken form *Rasāʾil Ikhwān aṣ-Ṣafāʾ* (*The Epistels of the Brethren of Purity*). Further indications to al-Ghazālī's reliance on the *Ikhwān*: ibid., 69.
It should be added that *taʾwīl* is for al-Ghazālī a movement of interpretation from the literal sense of an expression to its essential meaning. Cf. Whittingham, *Al-Ghazālī and the Qurʾān*, pp. 32–35.

40 Jawāhir, 68f./21.

he divides the Suras and verses of the Qurʾān into six categories (*anwāʿ*) which are divided into two groups. The first group includes "the precedents, the important principles," the other group includes "the subsequent, specific, succeeding" categories which complete the principles.[41] Each one of the categories is connected to a form of religious knowledge, which is described as a precious material substance, as shall be presented in the following.

The first category of Qurʾānic Suras and verses is dedicated to "making [God] known (*taʿrīf*)". This category deals with "explaining the knowledge of God" (*sharḥ maʿrifat Allāh*).[42] The knowledge of God is "the highest, the noblest (*al-aʿlā, al-ashraf*)" form of knowledge because all other forms of knowledge "are sought for its sake, and it is not sought for anything else."[43] This kind of knowledge includes "the knowledge of the essence of the True (*maʿrifat dhāt al-ḥaqq*), the knowledge of His attributes (*maʿrifat aṣ-ṣifāt*) and the knowledge of His acts (*maʿrifat al-afʿāl*)." The knowledge of God is symbolically called "red sulfur" (*al-kibrīt al-aḥmar*).[44] The reason al-Ghazālī gives for this symbolic

41 Jawāhir, 69/21.

42 Jawāhir, 70/23.

43 Jawāhir, 84/43. Abū Zayd, *Mafhūm an-naṣṣ*, p. 251, states that, by declaring the knowledge of God the highest purpose which all kinds of knowledge should serve, al-Ghazālī shifts the purpose of revelation from sending down God's commandments which aim at the well-being of the community to presenting the "speaker" to whom the individual tries to ascend.

44 Jawāhir, 70/23. According to medieval Arabic sources, *al-kibrīt al-aḥmar* is a very rare substance. It appears in idioms and proverbs as a point of comparison for things which can rarely be found, as it is stated for instance in Abū l-Faḍl Aḥmad al-Maydānī, *Majmūʿ al-amthāl*, edited and annotated by Jān ʿAbdallah Tūmā, 4 Volumes, Beirut: Dār Ṣādir, 1422/2002, Vol. 2, p. 450: "*aʿazz min al-kibrīt al-aḥmar*," or in Ibn Ṭufail, *Ḥayy bin Yaqẓān*, ed. Alber Naṣrī Nādir, Beirut: Dār al-mashriq, 1986, p. 20 (used by Ibn Ṭufail to emphasize that books written by the people of demonstration on Ibn Sīnā's "oriental philosophy" did not exist in Andalusia in his time). Occupied with magic powers, it is also called "the stone of the wise": Manfred Ullmann, *Wörterbuch der klassischen arabischen Sprache* I, Wiesbaden: Harrassowitz, 1970: 28a–b ("*man ẓafira bihi ẓafira bi-murādihi*," "who obtains it, obtains whatever he wishes"). In alchemistic circles it is a code name for the elixir used to change cheap into precious metals: Manfred Ullmann, *Die Natur- und Geheimwissenschaften im Islam*, Leiden: Brill, 1970, p. 258. The description of *al-kibrīt al-aḥmar* in medieval medical writings bears legendary features. According to ps.-Aristotle, it appears "in the 'West' at the coast of the Oceanus." It ignites and shines at night. Ibn Samajūn (d. 1002/392) states in his great compendium of the sayings of earlier and later physicians and philosophers about remedies (*al-Jāmiʿ li-aqwāl al-qudamāʾ wa-l-muḥdathīn min al-aṭibbāʾ wa-l-mutafalsifīn fī l-adwiya al-mufrada*) that this substance is a kind of a precious stone (*jawhar*) which is excavated by ants in a particular valley which King Solomon had

designation lies in the value and effect ascribed to red sulfur which means "the alchemy by which substances are turned from their base qualities into precious qualities, so that by it stone (*al-ḥajar*) becomes changed into corundum (*yāqūt*[an]) und copper (*an-nuḥās*) into pure gold (*dhahab*[an] *ibrīz*[an])". Al-Ghazālī justifies this specific designation by drawing the following analogy: In the same way that people who benefit from these precious materials "obtain access to the pleasures of the world, which are actually turbid and disturbed and will pass away in the near future," the knowledge of God "turns the essence of the heart from the vices of the beast and the error of ignorance into the purity of the angelic nature (*al-malakiyya*) and its spirituality, so that the heart ascends from the lowest to the highest, and obtains by it the pleasure of being near to the Lord of the worlds and beholding His noble face always and eternally."[45] Stating the possibility of beholding God's face in the afterlife al-Ghazālī goes beyond the orthodox position in Sunni theology which rejects that God could ever be seen with human eyes.

Al-Ghazālī ranks the forms of knowledge included in the knowledge of God and assigns to each one of them a specific kind of corundum (*yāqūt*). Since "ruby" (*al-yāqūt al-aḥmar*) is "the most magnificent and rarest" jewel obtained through alchemy, it stands symbolically for the knowledge of the divine essence, which "is the narrowest in scope, most difficult to acquire, most puzzling to thinking, and furthest from receiving discussion. For this reason, the Qurʾān contains only allusions and signs (*talwīḥāt wa-ishārāt*) of it; most references amount to absolute sanctification [...] and absolute glorification".[46]

visited. With the exception of the statement that the ants excavate it, this story is identical with the account in al-Khalīl's *Kitāb al-ʿAin* (Al-Khalīl bin Aḥmad al-Farāhīdī, *Kitāb al-ʿAyn*, ed. Mahdī al-Makhzūmī and Ibrāhīm as-Sāmarrāʾī, 8 volumes, Beirut n.d., Vol. 5, p. 430). This is the earliest Arabic lexicon, authored in the second half of the eighth century. Also, the great encyclopedic scholar Abū r-Rayḥān al-Bīrūnī (d. 1048) mentions in his book on gems (*al-Jamāhir fī maʿrifat al-jawāhir*) *al-kibrīt al-aḥmar* as a name for the "gold elixir" (*iksīr adh-dhahab*); he ascribes it, however, to the red ruby (*yāqūt aḥmar*): Fabian Käs, *Die Mineralien in der arabischen Pharmakognosie*, Part 2, Wiesbaden: Harrassowitz, 2010, p. 921.

45 Jawāhir, 93f./59.

46 Jawāhir, 70/23, 94/59. As an example for "absolute sanctification" of God in the Qurʾān, al-Ghazālī mentions Q 42:11, "Like Him there is naught," and Sura 112, "Say: 'He is God, One, God, the Everlasting Refuge, who has not begotten, and has not been begotten, and equal to Him is not any one' "; for absolute glorification, he mentions Q 6:100f.: "Glory be to Him! High be He exalted above what they describe! The Creator of the heavens and the earth" (Arberry's Translation).

A lower rank in the hierarchically constructed knowledge of God is the knowledge of the divine attributes (*aṣ-ṣifāt*); "the scope related to them is wider, and the space of speech about them [in the Qur'ān] is broader." Verses mentioning God's knowledge, power, life, speech, wisdom, and other attributes are numerous. The jewel that symbolizes this form of knowledge is "the bluish-grey corundum" (*al-yāqūt al-akhab*).[47]

The knowledge of the "divine acts" (*al-afʿāl*) is symbolically described as the "yellow corundum" (*al-yāqūt al-aṣfar*).[48] God's acts are too numerous to be counted; they are to be compared to "a sea which shores are wide and its ends cannot be investigated." As God is the real existent who caused all beings to exist, nothing else exists but God and His deeds; "all that exists besides Him is actually His deed." However, the Qur'ān includes of God's deeds only those which are "manifest in the visible world," like the parts of the physical world, "which appear to the senses. The noblest of His deeds, the most wonderful of them, and those which point most clearly to the glory of their maker are, however, those which are not visible to the senses, but belong to the world of dominion (*ʿālam al-malakūt*)." Al-Ghazālī counts among them the various groups of angles and devils.[49]

The second category of Qur'ānic Suras and verses is dedicated to "presenting (*taʿrīf*) the way of advancing towards God."[50] Al-Ghazālī explains this approach as "being devoted to Him" (*at-tabattul ilayhi*), which means a twofold attitude of (1) "dedicating oneself to Him" (*al-iqbāl ʿalayhi*) by "the adherence to the remembrance [of God]" (*bi-mulāzamat adh-dhikr*) and (2) turning away from everything else" which distracts from Him by "opposing passion, cleansing oneself from the troubles of the world and purifying the heart from them."[51] Knowledge of pursuing the path to God (*as-sulūk*) and of the state of attainment (*al-wuṣūl*) to Him "is a deep sea among the seas of the Qur'ān." The verses which deal with this subject are "the shining pearls" (*ad-durr al-azhar*). Green emerald (*az-zumurrud al-akhḍar*) stands for the passages which depict people's state on reaching the end of the journey and being rewarded or punished by God. Al-Ghazālī describes Paradise as a "comprehensive expression" (*al-ʿibāra al-jāmiʿa*) for the different kinds of "repose and delight" for those who attain God. Similarly, Hell is a "comprehensive expression for the humiliation and punishment" which those face who neglect pursuing this path.

47 Jawāhir, 70/23f.
48 Jawāhir, 70/23.
49 Jawāhir, 71/24.
50 Jawāhir, 72/25.
51 Jawāhir, 72/26.

This category of verses, which al-Ghazālī estimates to be as much as a third of the Qur'ān, includes also the "preceding conditions" of each one of both states. These conditions are expressed with terms such as resurrection, reckoning, balance etc.[52]

A forth category of Qur'ānic verses is about the "states of those who pursued the path [of God]" (*as-sālikīn*), such as the prophets, and "those who deviated from" it (*an-nākibīn*), such as the opponents of the prophets, the idolaters and the devils. The benefit of this category of verses lies in raising fear among the people and warning them to be more cautious in their life. "It includes secrets, symbols and signs (*asrār wa-rumūz wa-ishārāt*) which require extensive contemplation (*tafakkur*)." Among the numerous verses of this category is "grey umber and fresh blooming aloe-wood" (*al-ʿanbar al-ashhab wa-l-ʿūd ar-raṭib al-akhḍar*).[53]

The fifth category of Qur'ānic verses is about defending faith by arguing against the infidels and disclosing their lies in regards to blasphemy, insulting the prophet and denying the Day of Judgment. In these verses is the "greatest antidote" (*at-tiryāq al-akbar*).[54] In analogy to the greatest antidote that cures man from "deadly poisons," which cause physical death in this perishable world, the "demonstrative arguments" (*al-muḥājjāt al-burhāniyya*) contained in the Qur'ān cures the heart from "the poisons of heresies, passions and errors," which cause spiritual death by preventing the poisoned from journeying to the "world of holiness" (*ʿālam al-quds*).[55]

The sixth category of Qur'ānic verses concerns cultivating the stages of the path leading to God (*ʿimārat manāzil aṭ-ṭarīq*), the manner of taking provision and getting prepared through having weapons to repel thieves and bandits on the way. Since the body serves as a "vehicle" (*markab*) for the soul on its journey to God,[56] this category includes all legal verses which deal with the material needs of life necessary to preserve the body and the offspring and avert all matters which would corrupt and destroy them. Part of this category are the legally permitted or prohibited things (*al-ḥalāl wa-l-ḥarām*) extending from food and marriage affairs to fighting the unbelievers and the unjust people. These are "the restrictive ordinances of legal judgments" (*ḥudūd al-aḥkām*); al-Ghazālī calls them "strongest musk" (*al-misk al-adhfar*).[57]

52 Jawāhir, 74/28.

53 Jawāhir, 74f./29.

54 Jawāhir, 75/29f.

55 Jawāhir, 94/59f.

56 Jawāhir, 75/30.

57 Jawāhir, 76f./30f.

The reason for this designation is that, in analogy to the strongest musk "which man carries and from which rises up a fragrant smell that makes it so much known and apparent" that it cannot be hidden, "the science of jurisprudence, the knowledge of the judgments of the revealed law" (*ʿilm al-fiqh wa-maʿrifat aḥkām ash-sharīʿa*) "renders the name [of the possessor] fragrant, brings fame to him, and elevates his rank."[58]

In sum, al-Ghazālī divides the suras and verses of the Qurʾān into ten categories dedicated to the following topics: the divine essence, the divine attributes, the divine deeds, the afterlife (*al-maʿād*), the straight path (*aṣ-ṣirāṭ al-mustaqīm*), the states of the prophets, the states of the saints (*awliyāʾ*), the states of God's enemies, contending with the unbelievers (*muḥājjat al-kuffār*) and the restrictive ordinances of legal judgments (*ḥudūd al-aḥkām*). While the first two of these categories are exclusively dedicated to topics purely divine, the final seven of them are concerned with the humans. The third category in this account serves as a kind of transition between the two divisions, as it deals with God's deeds in the universe. This category is also important in regards to al-Ghazālī's connection of the Qurʾān and secular sciences. Based on his conviction that there is nothing useless in the world,[59] al-Ghazālī adds a final category of Qurʾānic verses, which he symbolically describes as "the aloe-wood" (*al-ʿūd*). Just the way this substance as such seems not to be useful, and only when it is burnt disseminates a smell, are "the hypocrites and God's enemies" useless, and only when they are severely punished "the smoke of fear" (*dukhān al-khawf*) arises from the Qurʾānic description of their punishment and penetrates the hearts inciting the people to seek the highest paradise and the dwelling near God, and to "turn away from error, heedlessness and following the passion."[60]

One of al-Ghazālī's purposes in *Jawāhir al-Qurʾān* certainly is to present the Sufi interpretation of the Qurʾān as the only adequate way to deal with the revealed text. For this reason, he presents "the jewels and the pearls" of the Scripture as a valuable result of Sufi interpretation. The "jewels and pearls" to be earned through an introspective study of the Qurʾān are forms of knowledge related to God's essence, attributes and deeds in the universe as well as to the well-being of the Muslim community and the spiritual Sufi path. These forms of knowledge can be extracted out of the Qurʾānic text through a specific

58 Jawāhir, 94/60.

59 See on this topic: Eric Ormsby, *Theodicy in Islamic Thought*, Princeton: Princeton University Press, 1984.

60 Jawāhir, 94f./60f.

hermeneutical approach which penetrates through the text to reach the inner meanings included in it. The hermeneutical approach presented in the *Jewels* is the alternative al-Ghazālī suggests not only to traditional exegesis, but also to esoteric Bāṭinism and rational Muʿtazilism. While the Bāṭiniyya marginalized the verbal text of the Qurʾān in favor of extracting the hidden meanings of the text by means of esoteric instruction, Muʿtazilite thinkers pleaded for a rational interpretation of the Qurʾānic text, as such.[61] According to al-Ghazālī, the verbal text does not lose its value in favor of the inner meanings, as the Bāṭinites taught.[62] Opposing both positions, he holds the verbal text of the Qurʾān for important and worthy to be taken seriously in the interpretation, as it serves as the only possible way to reach the inner level of the text.[63] However, it is not through rational, but spiritual interpretation which goes beyond rational restrictions, that the hidden meanings of the text can be discovered.[64]

The other group al-Ghazālī had to deal with in his career were the philosophers. The terrain of their intellectual activity consists primarily of rational sciences. Al-Ghazālī's response to them is the subject of the following part of this article.

---

61 For a Muʿtazilite reading of the Qurʾān, see for instance: Daniel Gimaret, *Une Lecture Muʿtazilite du Coran. Le Tafsīr d'Abū ʿAlī al-Gjubbāʾī (m. 303/915) partiellement reconstitute à partir de ses citateurs*, Louvain-Paris: Peters, 1994. Cf. Jawāhir, 78/34f. Al-Ghazālī criticizes here the Muʿtazila who, according to his view, "held the Qurʾān to be merely letters and sounds, and on this conviction based the theory that it is created, since letters and sounds are created." He approves their punishment and ascribes to them the disaster of being limited to the "farthest peel" (*al-qishr al-aqṣā*).

62 Al-Ghazālī attacks the Bāṭiniyya severely in several writings. See for instance: *Faḍāʾiḥ al-bāṭiniyya wa-faḍāʾil al-Mustaẓhiriyya*, ed. by ʿAbd ar-Raḥmān Badawī, Cairo: Ad-Dār al-Qawmiyya, 1383/1964, written in 487/1094. Partial translation in Richard J. McCarthy, *Freedom and Fulfillment.* An Annotated Translation of Al-Ghazālī's *al-Munqidh min al-Ḍalāl* and Other Relevant Works of al-Ghazālī, Boston: Twayne Publishers, 1980; Reprint in: Al-Ghazālī, *Deliverance from Error*, n. 24 above.

63 Similarly, al-Ghazālī states in *Kitāb Ādāb tilāwat al-Qurʾān*, Book 8 of *Iḥyāʾ ʿulūm ad-dīn*, vol. 1, p. 386. English: Muhammad Abul Quasem, *The Recitation and Interpretation of the Qurʾān*, p. 94, that it is impossible to reach the inner sense of the text (*al-bāṭin*) without mastering the verbal text itself (*iḥkām aẓ-ẓāhir*).

64 Abū Zayd, *Mafhūm an-naṣṣ*, p. 248, points out critically that al-Ghazālī develops the traditional dualism of the exterior (*aẓ-ẓāhir*) and the interior (*al-bāṭin*) of the text to the point that dualism does not only apply to the level of the meanings and the semantics of the text, but, furthermore, extends to the very structure of the text. In this sense, the interior of the text consists of the totality of mysteries, jewels and truth, while the exterior does not mean more than shells and peal.

4 The Qur'ān as Stimulus to Knowledge

The main aim of al-Ghazālī's spiritual hermeneutics of the Qur'ān in the *Jewels* is to demonstrate a method which enables the reader to penetrate beneath the outward of the text in order to extract its pure meanings. A major benefit of this endeavor is "to know how all sciences (*ʿulūm*) branch off" from the ten categories of Qur'ānic verses and how these sciences are ranked in regard to nearness to and remoteness from "the intended purpose" (*al-maqṣūd*), which is the knowledge of God.[65]

In the *Jewels*, al-Ghazālī develops a unique classification of religious sciences, which is the most comprehensive one among the seven classifications of the sciences he undertakes in several books of his.[66] Here he divides the sciences into two types: The "sciences of the shell" (*ʿulūm aṣ-ṣadaf*) and the "sciences of the pith" (*ʿulūm al-lubāb*).

4.1 *The Sciences of the Shell*

In the same way jewels and pearls are kept within shells that are the first thing to perceive, "the Arabic language" serves as the "shell and the garment (*kiswa*) of the jewels of the Qur'ān." Five sciences which branch from each other, according to the way how meaningful word groups develop,[67] deal with the words

65 Jawāhir, 78/34.

66 Alexander Treiger, "Al-Ghazali's Classifications of the Sciences," offers a comprehensive survey of these classifications. Based on that, he undertakes a characterization of al-Ghazālī's works related to these sciences, using the classification in the *Jawāhir* as a point of reference. Martin Whittingham, *Al-Ghazālī and the Qur'ān*, pp. 44–47, presents the classification of religious sciences in the *Jawāhir*. Hava Lazarus-Yafeh, *Studies in al-Ghazzālī*, Jerusalem: The Magnus Press 1975, p. 357ff., presents the division of sciences made by in the *Iḥyā'*. See for other divisions ibid., p. 395 n. 17. Franz Rosenthal in his remarkable monograph *Knowledge Triumphant. The concept of knowledge in medieval Islam*. With an Introduction by Dimitri Gutas. Leiden: Brill, 2007, does not take the treatment of sciences in *Jawāhir al-Qur'ān* into consideration. It is also neglected in Michael Marmura, "Ghazali's Attitude to the Secular Sciences and Logic," in: George F. Hourani (ed.), *Essays on Islamic Philosophy and Science*, Albany: State University of New York Press, 1975, pp. 100–111.

67 In *Jawāhir*, p. 78/34, al-Ghazālī offers a logical explanation for the sequential order of the abovementioned disciplines: "This is because the first of the parts of meanings with which speech is composed is the sound; then by being articulated the sound becomes letters; then the assemblage of letters makes a word; the specification of some of the assembled letters makes [the combination] Arabic language; then the way how letters are articulated attributes to it the quality of syntax; then the specification of one of the different syntaxes makes one of the seven standard readings; then when there is a proper

of the Qurʾān: philology (*ʿilm al-lugha*) branches off the words; from it syntax (*ʿilm an-naḥw*) emerges, followed by "the science of readings" (*ʿilm al-qirāʾāt*), out of which "phonetics" (*ʿilm makhārij al-ḥurūf*) develops. The fifth science in this category is the "science of outward exegesis" (*at-tafsīr aẓ-ẓāhir*). The "sciences of the shells and the peel (*ʿulūm aṣ-ṣadaf wa-l-qishr*) are not of the same rank." Al-Ghazālī uses the analogy to the structure of the shell and the jewel to rank sciences. The shell has two sides: one is inward-facing the jewel and therefore is closely similar to it because of nearness and "continuity of contact." The other one is the exterior side, "closely resembling all other stones." Similarly, the shell of the Qurʾān has an outer surface which is "the sound" (*aṣ-ṣawt*); therefore, "the science of letters" (*ʿilm al-ḥurūf*), i.e. phonetics, is far away from the inward side of the shell and, thus, from the "jewel itself."[68] Proceeding from the outward to the inward side of the shell, "the philology of the Qurʾān" is closer than phonetics to the jewel; syntax is the closest to it among the sciences included in this category. Apparently, al-Ghazālī evaluates these sciences in a rational way: the value of a particular science is not based on whether this science is strictly attributed to the Qurʾān, but rather on its objective value due to its usefulness for understanding the meaning of texts, including the text of the Qurʾān. Thus, although "the science of readings" is more specifically connected to the Qurʾān than philology and syntax, it belongs to the "superfluous [sciences] which can be spared, contrary to philology and syntax which are indispensable."[69] Similarly, despite the fact that all those who utilize the abovementioned sciences in dealing with the Qurʾān actually "turn around" its "shell and the peel," they are of different ranks; "the philologist and the grammarian are of higher rank than the one who knows only the science of readings."[70]

The highest among the "sciences of the shells" is, as has been mentioned, "the science of outward exegesis," as it is pursued for the sake of explaining the Qurʾānic text. Among the layers of the shell it is, symbolically, the closest to the pearl and resembles the pearl to a large extent, so that the majority of the people "think that it is the pearl itself and there is nothing more valuable behind it."[71] In al-Ghazālī's view, this is certainly not true.

Arabic word to which syntax is applied, it has become the indicator of a meaning; then it demands outward exegesis."

68 Jawāhir, 78/34f.

69 Jawāhir, 79/36.

70 Jawāhir, 79/36.

71 Jawāhir, 80/36. Al-Ghazālī compares the "science of outward exegesis (*at-tafsīr aẓ-ẓāhir*)" to "the science of *ḥadīth*" declaring this also as a "science of the shell": Ibid., 80/37.

4.2 *The Sciences of the Pith*

The second type of sciences related to the Qurʾān consists of "the sciences of the pith." These are, again, of two different levels. The lower level (*aṭ-ṭabaqa as-suflā*) includes three sciences:

1. The knowledge of the stories narrated in the Qurʾān (*qaṣaṣ al-qurʾān*). The need for this science is limited.[72]
2. The science of *kalām*-theology (*ʿilm al-kalām*). It consists in "contending with the unbelievers and disputing with them." Its purpose is to "repel errors and heresies and remove doubts" related to religious teachings, in order "to guard the layman's religious beliefs (*ḥirāsat ʿaqīdat al-ʿawāmm*) against the confusion caused by the heretics. This science does not concentrate on revealing the truth." Al-Ghazālī states that he "explained" *kalām*-theology on two levels: On the lower level, he wrote *ar-Risāla al-qudsiyya* (*The Epistle from Jerusalem*),[73] of a higher level is *al-Iqtiṣād fī l-iʿtiqād* (*Economy in Belief*).[74] Furthermore, he relates to *kalām*-theology his famous *Tahāfut al-falāsifa* (*The Incoherence of the Philosophers*)[75] as well as his writings against the Bāṭinites.[76] He states that this science has "an instrument" (*āla*) by which the methods of debate (*al-mujādala*) and dispute (*al-muḥājja*) "by means of true demonstration" (*bi-l-burhān al-ḥaqīqī*) can be distinguished. In fact, al-Ghazālī does not name this instrument, but it can hardly be doubted that he refers to the Aristotelian

72 Jawāhir, 81/38.

73 Al-Ghazālī wrote this epistle in Jerusalem. An edition of the Arabic text with introduction, English translation and comments in: Abdel Latif Tibawi, "Al-Ghazālī's Sojourn in Damascus and Jerusalem," in: *Islamic Quarterly* 9 (1965): 65–122. Al-Ghazālī incorporated the treatise in the second book of his *Iḥyāʾ*.

74 *Al-Iqtiṣād fī l-iʿtiqād*, ed. by Ibrahim Agah Çubukçu and Hüsseyin Atay, Ankara: Nur Matbaasi, 1962. Partial English translation: *Al-Ghazali on Divine Predicates and their Properties*, by A. Abu Zayd, Lahore: Sh. Muhammad Ashraf, 1970.

75 *The Incoherence of the Philosophers / Tahāfut al-Falāsifa*. A parallel English-Arabic text, edited and translated by Michael E. Marmura, Provo: Brigham Young University Press, 1997.

76 He mentions following writings: (1) *Faḍāʾiḥ al-Bāṭiniyya wa-faḍāʾil al-mustaẓhiriyya* (*Infamies of the Bāṭinites and Virtues of the Supporters of al-Mustaẓhir*), ed. by ʿAbd ar-Raḥmān Badawī, Cairo: Ad-Dār al-Qawmiyya, 1383/1964. This polemical book was written in 1094 at the request of the caliph al-Mustaẓhir (r. 487/1094–512/1118). German translation: *Streitschrift gegen die Batinijja-Sekte*, translated with comments by Ignaz Goldziher. Reprint: Brill: Leiden 1956; (2) *Ḥujjat al-ḥaqq wa-qawāṣim al-bāṭiniyya* (*The Proof of the Truth and Backbreakers of the Baṭinites*) published with an introduction by Ahmed Ateş in: *İlâhiyat Fakültesi Dergisi* (1954): pp. 23–54, Arabic text: pp. 33–43; (3) *Mufaṣṣal al-khilāf fī uṣūl ad-dīn* (*Explanation of Disagreement in the Principles of Religion*) which I was not able to identify.

logic. In form of a silent confirmation that the Aristotelian logic is this instrument, he adds the titles of his two books *Miḥakk an-naẓar fī l-manṭiq* (*The Touchstone of Reasoning in Logic*) and *Miʿyār al-ʿilm* (*Criterion of Knowledge in the Art of Logic*) at this point.[77]

3. The third science of the lower level of the sciences dealing with "the pith" of the Qur'ān is the science of *fiqh*. Al-Ghazālī explains the ample need for the various areas of this science, as it is concerned "first with the well-being in this world (*ṣalāḥ ad-dunyā*) and then with the well-being in the hereafter (*ṣalāḥ al-ākhira*)."[78] He states that this is the reason why the jurists are granted fame and reverence and are preferred to "preachers, [religious] story-tellers and *kalām*-theologians." The great influence and renown earned by the jurists led, however, to excessive expanding of the multiple branches of this science. Al-Ghazālī expresses his regret that he "wasted a good part of [his] life writing books on its disputed problems [...] and composing works on creeds and arranging them." In this regard, he mentions his books in jurisprudence *al-Basīṭ, al-Wasīṭ, al-Wajīz* and *Khulāṣat al-mukhtaṣar*.[79]

Based on the need for each one of these three sciences in the community, al-Ghazālī ranks those who are in charge of them. He ascribes to the preachers and religious story-tellers the lowest rank in this category. He considers the ranks of the *faqīh* and the *mutakallim* to be close to each other; the need of the community for the former is more extensive, for the latter more intensive.[80]

The "higher level" (*aṭ-ṭabaqa al-ʿulyā*) of the sciences of the pith consists of the knowledge which establishes "the precedents and the roots (*as-sawābiq*

---

77 Jawāhir, 81/38f. *Kitāb Miḥakk an-naẓar fī l-mantiq*, ed. by Muḥammad Badr ad-Dīn an-Naʿsānī l-Ḥalabī and Muṣṭafā l-Qabbānī d-Dimashqī, Cairo: al-Maṭbaʿa al-Adabiyya, n.d. *Miʿyār al-ʿIlm fī fann al-mantiq*, ed. by Muḥyī d-Dīn Ṣabrī l-Kurdī, Cairo: Al-Maṭbaʿa al-ʿArabiyya, 1927. Cf. on this: J. Janssens, "Al-Ghazālī: The Introduction of Peripatetic Syllogistic in Islamic Law (and Kalām)," in: *MIDEO* 28 (2010): 219–233.

78 Jawāhir, 81/38f.

79 *Al-Basīṭ* is unpublished; it is a summary of al-Juwainī's *Nihāyat al-Maṭlab*; *Al-Wasīṭ fī l-madhhab*, published with an-Nawawī's commentary (*At-Tanqīṭ fī sharḥ al-Wasīṭ*) and three other commentaries, ed. by Aḥmad Maḥmūd Ibrāhīm and Muḥammad Muḥammad Tāmir, Cairo: Dār as-Salām, 1418/1997; *Al-Wajīz fī fiqh al-Imām ash-Shāfiʿī*, 2 volumes, ed. by ʿAlī Muʿawwaḍ and ʿĀdil ʿAbd al-Mawjūd, Beirut: Dār al-Arqam bin Abī l-Arqam, 1418/1997. *Al-Khulāṣa al-musammā* [sic] *Khulāṣat al-mukhtaṣar wa-naqāwat al-muʿtaṣar, ta'līf ḥujjat al-Islām wa-barakat al-anām al-imām Abī Ḥāmid Muḥammad b. Muḥammad b. Muḥammad al-Ghazālī*, ed. Amjad Rashīd Muḥammad ʿAlī, Jeddah: Dār al-Minhāj, 1428/2007.

80 Jawāhir, 82/40f.

wa-l-uṣūl) of the important sciences." The noblest form of knowledge is that of God and the Last Day, since it deals with the ultimate "destination (*al-maqṣad*). Below it is the knowledge of the straight path and the manner of traversing it. This is to know how to purify the soul, to remove [from it] the obstacles of the destructive qualities and beautify it with the saving qualities."[81] Al-Ghazālī presents his *Iḥyāʾ ʿulūm ad-dīn* as an example of this knowledge focusing on the refinement of the human soul and occupying, thus, a higher position than *fiqh* and *kalām*.[82] The knowledge of God is to be sought progressively through ascending gradually from "contemplating God's deeds" (*tafakkarū*) to further "observing [His] attributes" (*mulāḥaẓat aṣ-ṣifāt*), and finally to "observing [His] essence" (*mulāḥaẓat adh-dhāt*). Most people do not reach this highest grade of knowledge.[83] In respect to nobleness, the knowledge about the afterlife ranks lower. It is strictly about the awareness of the human being of his "relation to God" and, based on that, of his fate in the hereafter. In regard to his authorship on the abovementioned forms of knowledge, al-Ghazālī asserts that despite his short life, being busy with many tasks and calamities and having only few helpers and companions, he wrote some books which he did not disclose, because "most people's understanding would be wearied by it, and the weak, who are the most traditional in knowledge, would be harmed by it." This kind of knowledge is appropriate to be disclosed to one who "avoids the knowledge of the outward" (*ʿilm aẓ-ẓāhir*) and follows the Sufi path in searching for God. Al-Ghazālī states that it is "unlawful for those into whose hands that book falls, to disclose it except to one who possesses all these qualities."[84]

These statements were echoed by later philosophers in Andalusia. Ibn Ṭufail reports in the introduction to his philosophical-mystical story *Ḥayy bin Yaqẓān* that al-Ghazālī in "*Kitāb al-Jawhar*" mentions that he authored books "including explicitly the truth" (*kutub*[an] *maḍnūn*[an] *bi-hā ʿalā ahlihā*) for those who are qualified; these books did not, in fact, reach Andalusia, but were confused with

81 Jawāhir, 83/42.

82 Jawāhir, 83f./42f.

83 Jawāhir, 84/43. On al-Ghazālī's concept of "*tafakkur*" see: Mizue Kato, "The Meaning of Tafakkur in al-Ghazali's Thought," in: *Bulletin of the Society for Near Eastern Studies in Japan* 49 (2006): 150–164, and Benjamin Abrahamov's contribution in the present volume.

84 Jawāhir, 84f./43f. Al-Ghazālī indicates here presumably to his *al-Maḍnūn bi-hi ʿalā ghayr ahlihi*, in M. M. Abū l-ʿAlāʾ (ed.), *al-Quṣūr al-ʿawālī min rasāʾil al-imām al-Ghazālī*, 4 vols. (Cairo: Maktabat al-Jundī, 1390 [1970]), vol. 3, p. 124–169. Much awaited is publishing the extensive study: M. Afifi al-Akiti, The *Maḍnūn* of al-Ghazālī: A Critical Edition of the Unpublished *Major Maḍnūn* with Discussion of His Restricted, Philosophical Corpus, D.Phil. diss., 3 vols., University of Oxford 2008.

others.[85] Ibn Rushd who accused al-Ghazālī of self-contradiction in dealing with the philosophers found evidence for his accusation in al-Ghazālī's above-mentioned statements: Abū Ḥāmid, in his *Tahāfut al-falāsifa*, charged the philosophers with apostasy in regards to three propositions and declared them heretics in regards to 17 others,[86] employing "arguments which created doubts and accusations which caused confusion. He lead, thus, many people astray from both philosophy and religion. Consequently, he said in his book known as *Jawāhir al-Qur'ān* that that what he stated in the *Tahāfut* are [merely] dialectical statements and that the truth is but included in *al-Maḍnūn bi-hi 'alā ghayri ahlihi*."[87]

Having discussed "the religious sciences that must necessarily exist in the world, so that traversing the path of God and journeying to Him may become easy," al-Ghazālī turns to the secular sciences. He mentions "medicine, astrology, astronomy, physiology and anatomy, magic and the knowledge to prepare talismans, and others," without describing or ranking them. He gives three reasons why he does not discuss the secular sciences in the same way as he did with the religious sciences: (1) "the well-being of this world and the Hereafter does not depend on knowing them," (2) the secular sciences are too numerous to be enumerated and described, and (3) some sciences are already too well-known that it would be superfluous to describe them.[88]

Consequently, based on both his conviction that the human ability to obtain knowledge is limited and that all sciences branch off the infinite Qur'ān, al-Ghazālī develops an open conception of science, according to which sciences cannot be counted or limited. In support of this open conception of science, he presents the following arguments which he became aware of "by means of clear insight free from doubt" (*bi-l-baṣīra al-wāḍiḥa allatī lā yutamārā fīhā*): (1) Human beings are incapable of obtaining comprehensive knowledge about sciences, as there are, in the present, "in possibility and potentiality

85 Abū Bakr ibn Ṭufail, *Ḥayy bin Yaqẓān*, ed. by Alber Naṣrī Nādir, Beirut: Dār al-Mashriq, 1986, pp. 23f.

86 Against al-Ghazālī's critique of philosophy in the *Tahāfut* Ibn Rushd wrote his famous *Tahāfut at-tahāfut* (*The Incoherence of the Incoherence*), ed. Maurice Bouyges, 3rd Ed., Beirut: Dār al-Mashriq, 1992. Al-Ghazālī declared in his *Tahāfut* that philosophers who deny physical resurrection, believe that God knows only the universals and that the world is eternal are to be declared apostates. A summary of his arguments is in *Al-Munqidh*, pp. 23f.

87 Ibn Rushd, *Al-Kashf 'an manāhij al-adilla fī 'aqā'id al-milla*, ed. by Muṣṭafā Ḥanafī with Introduction and Comments by Muḥammad 'Ābid al-Jābirī, Beirut: Markaz Dirāsāt al-Waḥda al-'Arabiyya, 1998, pp. 150f.

88 Jawāhir, 85/45.

(*fī l-imkān wa-l-quwwa*) kinds of sciences (*aṣnāf*^an^ *min al-ʿulūm*), which still exist, although it is extremely difficult for man to grasp them." (2) Similarly, there are sciences "which once came into existence, but have now been effaced;" no one has knowledge about them. (3) Finally, there are "sciences, which man's power can by no means comprehend and acquire;" only some of the angels drawn near to God can do that. Al-Ghazālī adds that though the ability of angels to acquire knowledge is greater than the ability of humans, it is nonetheless limited; only God's knowledge has no limits and is always existent and present.[89]

In a deductive rational way, al-Ghazālī connects all secular sciences to the Qur'ān. He develops this connection using the following syllogism:

- A major part of the Qur'ān is about God's innumerable deeds in the universe, which are the created beings;
- God's deeds are the objects of all – past, present and future – human sciences which actually emerge to deal with them;
- Ergo: The origins of sciences (*awāʾiluhā*) are embedded in the Qur'ān.[90]

That they originate out of the Qur'ān is one side of the intrinsic connection al-Ghazālī establishes between secular sciences and the revealed book.[91] He goes a step farther to make sciences indispensable for understanding the Qur'ān: without them, the meaning of Qur'ānic statements cannot be understood fully. In order to illustrate this view, al-Ghazālī gives examples: Only a person who has comprehensive medical knowledge can fully understand the meaning of Abraham saying in the Qur'ān that God cures him when he falls ill.[92] Verses which mention the sun and the moon and their movements can adequately be understood by one who knows astronomy.[93] The Qur'ānic statement: "O Man! What deceived thee as to thy generous Lord who created thee and shaped thee and wrought thee in symmetry and composed thee after what

89 Jawāhir, 85/45f.

90 Jawāhir, 86/46.

91 Al-Ghazālī points out the above explained connection between the Qur'ān and the sciences without further explanation in *Kitāb Ādāb tilāwat al-Qur'ān*, Book 8 of *Iḥyāʾ ʿulūm ad-dīn*, vol. 1, p. 384. English: Muhammad Abul Quasem, *The Recitation and Interpretation of the Qur'ān*, p. 88.

92 Al-Ghazālī refers to Q 26:80. He obviously acknowledges to medicine an active role by curing illnesses, what has important implications for his views on causality. See Hans Daiber's contribution in the present volume with extensive bibliographical information on the topic.

93 Al-Ghazālī refers to Q 55:5; 10:5; 75:7–10; 22:61; 35:13; 57:6; 36:38.

form He would?"[94] cannot be perfectly understood but by one "who knows the anatomy of man's limbs and internal organs, their number, their kinds, the wisdom underlying them, and their benefits [...] which is an ancient science." These examples demonstrate that the Qur'ān includes "general accounts (*majāmiʿ*) of knowledge possessed by the ancients and the moderns."[95] The dimensions and the details of these accounts, however, can only be discovered through scientific research.

Al-Ghazālī does not only take into consideration the rational sciences, but expands his conception to include the "obscure sciences (*ʿulūm ghāmiḍa*) which most people neglect to seek, and probably would not understand if they are told about by someone who is knowledgeable in them."[96] This position differs clearly from the evaluation of sciences he undertakes in *Kitāb al-ʿIlm* (*The Book of Knowledge*), the first book of the *Iḥyāʾ*. There, he distinguishes between "praiseworthy" (*maḥmūda*) and "blameworthy" (*madhmūma*) sciences; astrology and magic sciences belong to the latter category.[97] This obvious contradiction can possibly be explained by the difference in the nature of both works. While the *Revival* is written for a wider readership, the *Jewels* seem to address a narrow circle of Sufi readers or those who want to be prepared to the Sufi way of life.[98]

Another dimension of the connection between the Qur'ān and sciences is that their innumerability serves as an evidence for the ideal limitlessness of the Qur'ān.[99] In this sense, the more sciences become known to us, the more we become aware of the infinite nature of this scripture. This intrinsic relation of the Qur'ān and sciences serves as a stimulus for Muslims to pursue the study of sciences without any restriction, as this endeavor can be considered as an act of admiration towards the Qur'ān and its revealer. In this sense, al-Ghazālī defends acquiring scientific knowledge by stating that sciences, as they make the knowledge of God's deeds available, help improve man's endeavor to know

94 Q 82:6–8 (Arberry).

95 Jawāhir, 86f./46f.

96 Jawāhir, 87/48. As an example al-Ghazālī refers to God's shaping of Adam and breathing His spirit in him as mentioned in Q 15:29 and 38:72.

97 Abū Ḥāmid al-Ghazālī, *Iḥyāʾ ʿulūm ad-dīn*, ed. by ʿAbd al-Muʿṭī Amīn Qalʿajī, 5 volumes, Beirut 2004, *Kitāb al-ʿIlm*, Vol. 1, pp. 19–124, here pp. 49–65; English: Nabih Amin Faris, *Book of Knowledge. Being a Translation with Notes of the Kitāb al-ʿIlm of al-Ghazzālī's Iḥyāʾ ʿulūm al-Dīn*, 4th Ed., Lahore: Muhammad, 1974, pp. 67–99.

98 For further comparison the classification of the sciences in both sources see Treiger, "Al-Ghazālī's Classifications," p. 6–10.

99 Jawāhir, 86/46. Al-Ghazālī paraphrases here Q 18:109: "If the sea were ink for the Words of my Lord, the sea would be spent before the Words of my Lord are spent."

God. Therefore, one should keep searching for rational knowledge, as provided by secular sciences and, at the same time, "reflect on the Qur'ān and seek its wonderful meanings in order to encounter the general accounts (*majāmiʿ*) of the sciences of the ancients and the moderns," which the Qur'ān includes. Detailed knowledge is not included in the Qur'ān. Details are to be sought outside the scripture which motivates the believer to go beyond its contents and seek extensive knowledge.

In al-Ghazālī's conception, there is no conflict between the Qur'ān and sciences. On the contrary, they exist in mutual interdependence: Sciences emerge out of the human need to understand God's deeds which the Qur'ān documents in a general way. Sciences help, simultaneously, exploring the deep meanings of Qur'ānic statements. In order to illustrate this connection, al-Ghazālī shows within his hermeneutical treatment of the first Sura *al-Fātiḥa* how scientific knowledge helps the believer to deeply understand the magnitude of God's mercy (*raḥma*), as it is demonstrated in His creation. Stating that God has created each creature "in the most perfect and best kind, and has given it everything it needs," al-Ghazālī describes impressively how the mosquito, the fly, the spider and the bee, "the smallest" among animals, live.[100] As an example, I present his description of the life of the bee:

> Look at the bee and the innumerable wonders of its gathering honey and [producing] wax. We want to make you aware of the geometry of its hive. It builds its hive on the figure of the hexagon so that space may not be narrow for its companions because they become crowded in one place in a great number. If it should build its hives circular, there would remain, outside the circles, empty unused spaces since circles are not contiguous to one another. Likewise are other figures. Squares, however, are contiguous to one another. But the shape of the bee is inclined to roundness and so inside the hive there would remain unused corners as, in the circular shape outside the hive, there would remain empty unused spaces. Thus, none of the [geometrical] figures other than the hexagon approaches the circular figure in contiguity, and this is known by geometrical proof.[101]

100 Jawāhir, 99/67.

101 Jawāhir, 100/68f. A similar description of insects and the hives in connection with the form of the bees as signs of God's love and mercy are presented in the 36. book of the *Iḥyā': Kitāb al-Maḥabba wa-sh-shawq wa-l-uns wa-r-riḍā*, in: *Iḥyā' ʿulūm ad-dīn* (ed. Qalʿajī), vol. 5, p. 33f. English: Al-Ghazālī, *Love, Longing, Intimacy and Contentment. Kitāb al-Maḥabba wa'l-shawq wa'l-uns wa'l-riḍā*. Book XXXVI of *The Revival of The Religious Sciences, Iḥyā' ʿulūm al-dīn*, with an Introduction and Notes by Eric Ormsby, Cambridge: The Islamic

Combining empirical observation with geometrical knowledge al-Ghazālī explains why, due to the shape of the bee, the hexagon is the best possible form of the hives. The bee which does not possess man's rational faculty is "guided" by the merciful God. Rational knowledge leads man, however, to discover the wonders of the bee and obtain deeper appreciation of God's "wonders [...], kindness and mercy." Furthermore, knowledge is progressive; a sample of a lower rank stimulates man to seek knowledge of a higher quality (*al-adnā yunabbih ʿalā l-aʿlā*).[102] If the Qur'ān is a sea of knowledge without shores, there is no better way to dive into it in order to extract its jewels and pearls but by means of rational sciences.[103] Nevertheless, rational knowledge itself is not the end; it is the means to reach a higher level of meta-rational, spiritual knowledge. All in all, in correspondence with the limited ability of human beings to obtain knowledge, the amount of knowledge exposed to them is "definitely small in relation" to the knowledge which "has not been exposed" and which exclusively God and His angels possess.[104]

Al-Ghazālī states that the knowledge of God's uncountable deeds which demonstrate His glory is "infinite" (*lā nihāya lahā*); it is a "paradise with no boundaries." The "paradise of different forms of knowledge" (*jannat al-maʿārif*), according to al-Ghazālī, is better than the paradise which "consists of bodies" and is limited due to the limited nature of bodies.[105] This statement is a clear refutation of the literal understanding of sensual descriptions of paradise in the Qur'ān, in which the pleasures of "eating and sexual intercourse" (*al-akl wa-n-nikāḥ*) are emphasized.[106] In this sense, al-Ghazālī silently excludes from his selection verses dealing with the afterlife. For him, this issue is subject to "absolute faith" in rewarding those who know God and obey Him and punishing those who deny God and disobey Him; details are not inevitably required.[107]

Texts Society, 2011, pp. 76f. On al-Ghazālī's fondness for plants and animals see Margaret Smith, *Al-Ghazālī the Mystic*, London: Luzac & Co., 1944, pp. 48–54.

102 Jawāhir, 100/69.

103 Contrary to this interpretation, Abū Zayd, *Mafhūm an-naṣṣ*, p. 255, remarks critically that by turning the text to an infinite "sea of sciences and mysteries" from which the human mind can merely by chance grasp tiny superficial pieces of knowledge al-Ghazālī diminishes the human ability to discover the natural laws and "isolates" the text of the Qur'ān from the realms of human knowledge.

104 Jawāhir, 100/69. Al-Ghazālī indicates that the Book of Gratitude (*Kitāb ash-Shukr*) and the Book of Love (*Kitāb al-Maḥabba*) of *Iḥyāʾ ʿulūm ad-dīn*, contain "allusions" (*talwīḥāt*) to the above mentioned ideas.

105 Jawāhir, 108/83.

106 Cf. for instance Q. 55: 46–76; 56: 12–38.

107 *Jawāhir*, 191/224.

In contrary to the sensual qualities of paradise in the Qur'ān, al-Ghazālī dedicates the eighteenth chapter of the *Jewels* to describe the conditions of those who possess the desire (*shahwa*) to know God, His attributes and especially His deeds (*al-ʿārifūn*). Their paradise is the true paradise and their pleasure exceeds incommensurably the sensual pleasures promised in the Qur'ān.[108] They "look at those dedicating themselves to the base desires in the same way as prudent men (*al-ʿuqalāʾ*) look at boys dedicating themselves to the pleasure of play" and "laugh" at them.[109] With this comparison, al-Ghazālī renders rationality a part of the Sufi experience he presents as the best approach to the Qur'ān. Regarding his view that bliss in the afterlife is a result of possessing knowledge in this world, al-Ghazālī is on the same line with the Muslim philosophers preceding him.[110]

Another important aspect is al-Ghazālī's conviction that revealed knowledge is not given to everybody. With the exception of the prophet Muhammad, knowledge of the true meanings of the Qur'ānic verses is available only to those who are "capable" of understanding them.[111] In order to get to this level, one has to stop the exclusive dependency on traditional interpretations supported by statements of the companions of the prophet Muhammad[112] and to start self-training in "spiritual struggle and piety" (*al-mujāhada wa-t-taqwā*), which results in guidance granted by God.[113] God's granted guidance requires that man's desire is true and that he endeavors to seek knowledge with help of "those who have insight" (*ahl al-baṣīra*). The goal is to achieve the ability of perceiving all beings, even the inanimate, as living entities and understand their language. Al-Ghazālī connects this highly speculative idea to the Qur'ān which states that all beings without exception glorify God. Only when this stage of perception is reached, the hidden secrets of the Qur'ān can be understood.[114]

---

108 Al-Ghazālī utilizes Qur'ānic terminology to describe the paradise of those who possess such mystical knowledge (*al-ʿārifūn*): Q 3:133; 69:23; 56:32f.

109 Jawāhir, 109f./85.

110 For the philosophical view that happiness in the afterlife is a continuity of the happiness in this world caused by theoretical knowledge see, for instance: Abū Naṣr al-Fārābī, *On the Perfect State* (*Mabādiʾ ārāʾ ahl al-madīna al-fāḍila*). Revised Text with Introduction, Translation, and Commentary by Richard Walzer. Oxford University Press, 1985, Part v, Ch. 16, § 4, p. 266f.; Martin A. Bertman, "Alfarabi and the Concept of Happiness in Medieval Islamic Philosophy," in: *The Islamic Quarterly* 14 (1970): 122–125.

111 Jawāhir, 90/52.

112 Jawāhir, 90/52.

113 Jawāhir, 92/56f. To confirm that God rewards with guidance those who strive, al-Ghazālī quotes Q 29:69.

114 Jawāhir, 93/57. Al-Ghazālī quotes Q 17:44 and 41:11. Cf. for instance Q 24:41; 59:24.

Al-Ghazālī appears to make the Qurʾān a stimulus to pursue all kinds of scientific knowledge. He develops his argumentation as follows: The more you know, the more capable you will be to recognize the miracles of God and the signs of His mercy. Hereby it is to benefit from the accumulated knowledge of mankind over generations, regardless of whether this knowledge comes from Muslims or non-Muslims. Knowledge, as such, serves the faith. However, al-Ghazālī's conception of knowledge is not limited only to rational knowledge. It also encompasses forms of knowledge, which are considered irrational – a loose tolerant attitude which, due to a Sufi worldview, accepts equally rational and irrational forms of knowledge. Through sharpened senses of the mind, as a result of successful mystical training, the close connection between the visible and the hidden world can be perceived and the inner meaning behind the outer shell of every existent can be captured. Every being, even the inanimate, articulates itself meaningfully. It is just that one has to possess enough sensitivity to understand the language of being. This ability is given, however, only to the few, i.e. to the master Sufis.

Al-Ghazālī's theory in the *Jawāhir*, that all sciences branch out of the Qurʾān, has been understood in a way that it became fundamental for the development of the "scientific interpretation" (*at-tafsīr al-ʿilmī*) of the Qurʾān, which later became an aspect of its miraculous nature (*iʿjāz al-Qurʾān*). Inspired by this treatise, several books have been written throughout the following generations in order to uncover scientific truths and discoveries which are included in the Qurʾān in mysterious ways.[115] Particularly, contemporary Muslim authors try extensively to affirm a deep relationship between their scripture, on one hand, and natural sciences and technological progress, on the other. This happens in various ways and with different intentions. For some, the Qurʾān does not contradict the discoveries of modern sciences.[116] Others collect scientific data to

---

115 The Egyptian scholar Amīn al-Khūlī (1895–1966), *Manāhij tajdīd fī n-naḥū wa-l-balāgha wa-t-tafsīr wa-l-adab. Al-Aʿmāl al-kāmila*, Vol. 10, Cairo: Al-Hayʾa al-Miṣriyya al-ʿĀmma li-l-Kitāb 1995, p. 217f., summarizes this interpretation of al-Ghazālī's connecting the sciences to the Qurʾān. He counts the books which written after al-Ghazālī's *Jawāhir* to demonstrate the miraculous scientific nature of the Qurʾān. See on this topic J. J. G. Jansen, *The Interpretation of the Qurʾān in Modern Egypt*, Leiden: Brill, 1974, pp. 38ff.; J. Jomier & P. Caspar, "L'exégèse scientifique du Coran d'après le Cheikh Amîn al-Khûlî," *MIDEO* 4 (1957): 269–280.

116 Representative of this position is the French physician Maurice Bucaille in his book *La Bible, le Coran et la science: les Écritures Saintes examinées à la lumière des connaissances modernes*, Paris: Seghers 1976.

present an evidence for the miraculous nature (*iʿjāz*) of the Qurʾān.[117] Another extreme view is that of those who present the Qurʾān as a source of scientific knowledge and all kinds of sciences.[118] Accordingly, scientific facts are predicted in the Qurʾān and the achievements of modern science serve as proofs for its divine nature. The Qurʾān functions, therefore, as the final authority in science, attesting not just to the validity of a scientific discovery but also to its invalidity. It contains the criteria according to which scientific truth should be determined; reading it renders acquiring scientific knowledge unnecessary.[119]

As it has been stated, al-Ghazālī's connection of sciences and the Qurʾān differs from the above mentioned positions. In his view, the Qurʾān does not include scientific, but theological statements referring to God's creating activity; the Qurʾān is, thus, a document of God's deeds in the universe. As sciences are developed by humans to investigate what God actually created, they are related to the Qurʾān. Therefore, intensive knowledge leads to an increasingly comprehensive perception of God's might and mercy. Al-Ghazālī's conception of science does not tie sciences to the Qurʾān; it lets them, indirectly, emerge out of it, allowing them to enjoy a certain degree of autonomy against the scripture, as they have to flourish in order to help the readers of the scripture understand it.

5 Rationalized Spirituality in Response to Philosophy

Jawāhir al-Qurʾān bears clear philosophical features which show its author responding, by means of philosophy, to former Muslim philosophers, particularly Ibn Sīnā. One of these features is brought to light through explaining the purpose of employing symbols in the Qurʾān: This is, according to al-Ghazālī, an "example" (*unmūdhaj*) to show adequate people how "spiritual meanings related to the world of dominion" (*al-maʿānī r-rūḥiyya al-malakūtiyya*) are expressed in the Qurʾān by means of "descriptive common expressions"

117 For instance: W. Abū s-Suʿūd, *Iʿjāzāt ḥadītha ʿilmiyya wa-raqamiyya fī l-Qurʾān*, Beirut 1991, and Ṭāriq Suwaydān, *Iʿjāz al-Qurʾān al-karīm. Min al-iʿjāz al-ʿadadī fī l-Qurʾān*, n.p. n.d.

118 Prominent representatives of this view are: Zaghlūl an-Najjār, *Sources of scientific knowledge. The geographical concepts of mountains in the Qurʾān*, Herndon, VA 1991; Keith Moore, *The developing human. Clinically oriented embryology. With Islamic additions: Correlation studies with Qurʾān and ḥadīth*, Jeddah 1983; ʿAbd al-Majīd az-Zindānī, *al-Muʿjiza al-ʿilmiyya fī l-Qurʾān wa-s-sunna*, Cairo n.d. and other publications.

119 See for an overview on this topic: Ahmad Dallal, "Science and the Qurʾān," in Jane Dammen McAuliffe (Ed.), *Encyclopaedia of the Qurʾān*, 6 Vols., Vol. 4, Leiden: Brill 2004, pp. 540–558.

(*bi-l-alfāẓ al-ma'lūfa ar-rasmiyya*) so that the people can understand its deep meanings. As al-Ghazālī adheres firmly to the belief that the Qur'ān consists of God's revealed words, ascribing the utilization of symbols to the Qur'ān means, in al-Ghazālī's conception, that God utilizes these symbols intentionally in order to train spiritually qualified people to decipher the real meanings in His book and uncover His messages which are given through signs existing in all beings.[120] On the contrary, those who are unqualified should better not look at these signs, but rather be occupied with things which al-Ghazālī obviously considers trivial, such as the poems of al-Mutanabbī,[121] strange matters in Sībawayh's grammar,[122] Ibn al-Ḥaddād's regulations of rare matters of divorce[123] or tricks of disputations in *kalām*-theology."[124] This list shows al-Ghazālī's depreciation of some genres of Arabic literature and his disdain of the obsession with strange cases of grammar, *fiqh* and *kalām*, since, to his mind, spending time on this kind of issues is not helpful in pursuing the path of God. Remarkably, works of logic and philosophy are not listed as useless. Reason could be that al-Ghazālī considers those who are qualified to study logic and philosophy as able to scrutinize the nature of things and, therefore, to be qualified to reflect upon God's signs in the universe. In other words: it seems that al-Ghazālī holds those who are intellectually unable to pursue philosophical studies for unable to recognize God's attributes.[125]

Al-Ghazālī states, furthermore, that this method pursued in the Qur'ān in order to train its readers to intellectually decipher signs shall be imitated by the teachers in dealing with their students. During the course of his interpretation of some suras which are, according to prophetic statements, attested with

---

120 Cf. Jawāhir, 95, 101/62, 70.

121 Abū ṭ-Ṭayyib al-Mutanabbī (303/915–354/965) is one of the greatest Arab poets. He is especially known for his panegyric and egomaniacal poems – a reason for the Sufi al-Ghazālī to ironically reject him.

122 Sībawayh (ca. 148/760–ca. 180/793) is a celebrated grammarian and philologist who through his *Kitāb* greatly influenced the development of Arabic grammar.

123 Muḥammad Ibn al-Ḥaddād (264/878–344/-956) was a *shāfiʿī* jurist in Egypt.

124 Jawāhir, 101/69.

125 Similarly argues Averroes in his famous *Faṣl al-maqāl* in justification of the study of philosophy: Ibn Rushd (Averroes), *Kitāb Faṣl al-maqāl with its Appendix (Ḍamīma) and an Extract from Kitāb al-Kashf ʿan manāhij al-adilla*, Arabic text edited by George F. Hourani, Leiden: Brill, 1959, p. 1; English: Averroes, *On the Harmony of Religion and Philosophy*. A translation with introduction and notes, of Ibn Rushd's *Kitāb Faṣl al-maqāl*, with its appendix (*Ḍamīma*) and an extract from *Kitāb al-Kashf ʿan manāhij al-adilla*, by George F. Hourani, Leiden: Brill, 1961, p. 1.

special features,[126] al-Ghazālī refrains from explaining the reason why the 36. sura *Yā' Sīn* is called in a *ḥadīth* "the heart of the Qur'ān".[127] Instead, he encourages the reader to discover, by his own effort, the reason for this designation "in analogy" (*'alā qiyās*) to similar interpretations included in the *Jewels*. In a clearly pedagogical manner, he declares that "awareness out of one's own efforts (*at-tanabbuh*) increases the intellectual activity more than becoming aware due to others' efforts (*at-tanbīh*)" and that such an awareness, once happened, leads man to become "accustomed to thinking (*idmān al-fikr*), due to coveting investigation and knowledge of secrets." In doing that, the true meaning of the "striking verses of the Qur'ān" (*qawāri' al-Qur'ān*) will be opened to the trained reader. These verses are, according to al-Ghazālī, his selection in the present treatise.[128]

Transmitting ideas via signs and hints was a method ascribed to philosophers since antiquity and was known to the Arabs. For instance, al-Fārābī states that Plato intentionally used "symbols and riddles" (*ar-rumūz wa-l-alghāz*), so that only those who deserve and are intellectually eligible could acquire the knowledge and wisdom contained in his books.[129] Although Aristotle's writings are characterized through clarity, well order and transparency of ideas, he also authored his books, according to al-Fārābī, in a way that allowed only the experts to fully understand their meaning.[130] Aristotle, whom the Arabs considered as the chief philosopher throughout ages, used to express his ideas in an ambiguous way for three reasons: in order to find out if the student

126 In addition to sura 36, *Yā' Sīn*, al-Ghazālī discusses in this context sura 1, *Al-Fātiḥa*, (Ch. 12, 13, 17), the Verse of the Throne, *Āyat al-kursī*, Q. 2:255 (Ch. 14), and sura 112, *Al-Ikhlāṣ* (Ch. 15). M. Whittingham, *Al-Ghazālī and the Qur'ān*, 72–80, presents al-Ghazālī's interpretation of these passages.

Ibn Taymiyya, *Majmū' Fatāwā*, ed. 'Abd ar-Raḥmān bin Muḥammad bin Qāsim, 35 Vols., Vol. 17, Medina 1425/2004, p. 49f., 113–122, discusses al-Ghazālī's classification of some Qur'ānic verses as more excellent than others in *Jawāhir*, beginning of Chapter 11, particularly his interpretation of sura 112. Ibn Taymiyya, who seems to accept some of al-Ghazālī's interpretations, refers to the accusation generally made against al-Ghazālī that he made "philosophical ideas" (*ma'ānī l-falsafa*) "the interior of the Qur'ān" (*bāṭin al-Qur'ān*): ibid., 120.

127 *Musnad Aḥmad*, Awwal musnad al-Baṣriyyīn, 19789; *Sunan at-Tirmidhī*, Kitāb Faḍā'il al-Qur'ān, 2887; *Sunan ad-Dārimī*, Kitāb Faḍā'il al-Qur'ān, 3416 (http://hadith.al-islam.com/Loader.aspx?pageid=261).

128 Jawāhir, 107/81.

129 Abū Naṣr al-Fārābī, *Kitāb al-Jam' bayna ra'yay al-ḥakīmayn*, ed. Alber Naṣrī Nādir, 3rd Ed., Beirut: Dār al-Mashriq, 1968, p. 84.

130 Ibid., 85.

was qualified by nature to study, to withhold philosophy from those who are unqualified, and to train the students to endeavor intellectually.[131] Using symbolic and ambiguous language in philosophical writings was, therefore, mainly motivated by both keeping philosophy away from those who are not qualified to deal with it and training the intellectual abilities of the students. Al-Ghazālī seems to have adopted this educational method in training young Sufis how to deal with the Qur'ān.

However, the most significant philosophical feature in *Jawāhir al-Qur'ān* is, in my view, al-Ghazālī's classification of the sciences connecting them to the Qur'ān. For almost all classifications in Arabic before al-Ghazālī were undertaken by philosophers.[132] This method resembles al-Fārābī's and Ibn Sīnā's previous dealing with sciences from a philosophical point of view. The former describes in his *Iḥṣā' al-ʿulūm* (*The Enumeration of Sciences*) the "famous sciences" (*al-ʿulūm al-mashhūra*) and their parts presenting the objectives and qualities of each one of them. He divides the sciences into five areas: philology, logic, mathematics including music, physics, metaphysics and social sciences including *fiqh* and *kalām*. Ibn Sīnā, for his part, divides in the epistle *Fī aqsām al-ʿulūm al-ʿaqliyya* (*On the Divisions of the Rational Sciences*) "philosophy" (*al-ḥikma*) into "an abstract theoretical and a practical part." Logic with

131 Abū Naṣr al-Fārābī, *Mā yanbaghī an yuqaddam qabla taʿallum falsafat Arisṭū*, in id., *Mabādi' al-falsafa al-qadīma*, Cairo 1328 [1910], p. 14.

132 Al-Kindī, "Risālat al-Kindī fī kamiyyat kutub Arisṭū," in: *Rasā'il al-Kindī l-falsafiyya*, ed. Muḥammad ʿAbd al-Hādī Abū Rida, Kairo: Dār al-Fikr al-ʿArabī, n.d., pp. 362–374; al-Fārābī, *Iḥṣā' al-ʿulūm*, ed. by ʿUthmān Amīn, Cairo: Maktabat al-Anğlū al-Miṣrīya, 1968; Ikhwān aṣ-Ṣafā', *Rasā'il, Risāla* 1.7, Chapters: *Faṣl fī ajnās al-ʿulūm* & *Faṣl fī l-ʿulūm al-ilāhiyya*. 4 Vols., Vol. 1, Beirut: Dār Ṣādir n.d., pp. 266–275; Ibn Sīnā, *Fī aqsām al-ʿulūm al-ʿaqliyya*, in: *Tisʿ rasā'il*, Constantinople: 1298 [1880], pp. 71–80. Studies dealing with the classification of sciences by the *falāsifa*: Osman Bakar, *Classification of Knowledge in Islam: A Study in Islamic Philosophies of Science*, Islamic Texts Society, Cambridge 1998; Hans Daiber, "Qosṭā ibn Lūqā (9. Jh.) über die Einteilung der Wissenschaften," in: *Zeitschrift für die Geschichte der arabisch-islamischen Wissenschaften*, 6 (1990): 93–129; Louis Gardet and M. M. Anawati, *Introduction à la théologie musulmane: essai de théologie comparée*, J. Vrin, Paris 1948, pp. 94–124; Dimitri Gutas, *Avicenna and the Aristotelian Tradition: Introduction to Reading Avicenna's Philosophical Works*, Leiden and New York 1988, pp. 149ff.; Christel Hein, *Definition und Einteilung der Philosophie: Von der spätantiken Einleitungsliteratur zur arabischen Enzyklopädie*, Frankfurt am Main 1985; Michael Marmura, "Avicenna and the Division of Sciences in the *Isagogè* of His *Shifā'*," in: *Journal for the History of Arabic Science*, 4 (1980): 239–251 [repr. in Michael Marmura, *Probing in Islamic Philosophy: Studies in the Philosophies of Ibn Sina, al-Ghazali and Other Major Muslim Thinkers*, Binghamton 2005, pp. 1–15]; Miklós Maróth, "Das System der Wissenschaften bei Ibn Sīnā," in: Burchard Brentjes (Ed.), *Avicenna – Ibn Sina (980–1036)*, Halle 1980, vol. 2, pp. 27–32.

its nine parts is attached to them, as the instrument (*āla*) which leads man to acquire sound judgments.[133] The purpose (*ghāya*) of theoretical philosophy, according to Ibn Sīnā, is the "truth" (*al-ḥaqq*), the purpose of practical philosophy is "goodness" (*al-khayr*). Based on the extent of their relation to "matter and motion" (*al-mādda wa-l-ḥaraka*), the three parts of theoretical philosophy are ranked: "the lowest science" is physics, mathematics is the intermediate one, and metaphysics is the highest.[134] The major part of the treatise consists of brief statements on the essential qualities of each one of the various disciplines branching off these sciences.[135] The practical sciences are also divided, in an Aristotelian manner, into three parts according to the state of the individual. The first part is ethics dealing with the moral conduct of the individual; the second part, economics, deals with the management of the household; and the third part, politics, deals with leadership and guidance of human communities. Ibn Sīnā does not rank the three practical sciences; he seems to consider them as strongly interdependent.[136] However, he assigns to each one of them reference works of Greek philosophy.[137] In his other treatise *ʿUyūn al-ḥikma* (*Springs of Wisdom*), he states that the "origin (*mabdaʾ*)" of the three practical disciplines of philosophy is "obtained from the Divine Sharīʿa (*mustafād min jihat ash-sharīʿa al-ilāhiyya*); the perfection of their rules (*kamālāt ḥudūdihā*) can be made manifest (*tastabīn*) by means of the Divine Sharīʿa, as well."[138] Thus, there are good reasons to assume that al-Ghazālī was influenced by these works to classify Qurʾānic verses and connect several sciences to the Qurʾān according to a certain hierarchical order. Particularly, the statement he makes from a theological point of view that the origins (*awāʾilihā*) of secular sciences lie in the Qurʾān reveals an Avicennian impact, as Ibn Sīnā's abovementioned statement shows. Furthermore, by assigning books of his own to each one of the religious sciences, he appears to be following Ibn Sīnā's example in assigning classical books of philosophy to most of the rational sciences.[139]

133 *Fī aqsām*, 79f.

134 *Fī aqsām*, 72f.

135 *Fī aqsām*, 74–79.

136 *Fī aqsām*, 73f.

137 See: Georges Tamer, *Islamische Philosophie und die Krise der Moderne. Das Verhältnis von Leo Strauss zu Alfarabi, Avicenna und Averroes*, Leiden: Brill, 2001, pp. 63f.

138 Ibn Sīnā, *ʿUyūn al-ḥikma*, ed. by ʿAbd ar-Raḥmān Badawī, 2nd Ed., Kuwait, Beirut 1980, p. 16. In *Rasāʾil Ikhwān aṣ-ṣafāʾ* (*The Letters of the Brethren of Purity*), Beirut: Dār Ṣādir, n.d., mathematical, natural and psychological sciences as well as the matters of religion are extensively discussed in 52 treatises.

139 Cf. the discussion of al-Ghazālī's attitude towards the philosophers, particularly Ibn Sīnā, provided in Treiger, *Inspired Knowledge in Islamic Thought*, pp. 81–101. I don't share

The philosophical features of al-Ghazālī's hermeneutical treatment of the Qur'ān and deriving all kinds of sciences out of it, however, are not essential, but functional in his conception. They serve the purpose of establishing a rationally balanced Sufi understanding of the Qur'ān and its relation to sciences. In general, al-Ghazālī adopts philosophical concepts and adapts them in order to establish something different from that what the philosophers had offered. Philosophy provides him with stones he needs to erect his own building which also includes Qur'ānic and mystical elements. *Jawāhir al-Qur'ān* can, thus, be considered as al-Ghazālī's response to the rationalistic approach of the philosophers in dealing with forms of knowledge. Occupied with rational tools, al-Ghazālī presents the Qur'ān as a corpus anti-philosophy, as a source of knowledge, as a cosmos parallel to the created world. Holding the Qur'ān in his hand, he develops results contrary to the ideas of the philosophers. While the philosophers hold philosophy for a universal field of knowledge, al-Ghazālī presents the Qur'ān in the *Jewels* as an infinite, inexhaustible sea which shows numerous forms of knowledge, though hides what is preserved for those who are qualified to discover it. In his view, the text of the Qur'ān as such is a treasure of signs and allusions and an attraction for those who desire to obtain knowledge. In order to earn the wealth preserved there, they have to be intellectually and spiritually trained and occupied with adequate scientific tools. While the philosophers predominantly adhere to rational sciences, al-Ghazālī propagates an open conception of science, which includes, in addition to the rational, the religious and even the "obscure" esoteric sciences. While the philosophers are interested in enumerating and classifying sciences, al-Ghazālī holds sciences, as such, for innumerable. Presumably in a critical hint against al-Fārābī's and Ibn Sīnā's classification of philosophical sciences, al-Ghazālī asserts that sciences actually defy human counting, since humans are incapable of estimating the existence of sciences over the course of the history of human civilization. Furthermore, rational sciences constitute only a part of the totality of sciences. In this sense, al-Ghazālī goes beyond the limits of rationality drawn by the philosophers. Some segments of his project show clear philosophical color, indeed; nevertheless, they are not the final ones which ultimately determine the nature of the project and its purpose. Opposing the philosophical way of discussing sciences may explain the lack of philosophical terminology in this book.[140]

Treigers radical interpretation of al-Ghazālī as "a kind of a 'Trojan horse,' which brought Avicenna's philosophy into the heart of Islamic thought." Ibid., p. 104. Al-Ghazālī's reception of Ibn Sīnā's philosophy is too complex to be considered as mere smuggling.

140 Hava Lazarus-Yafeh, *Studies in al-Ghazzālī*, Jerusalem: The Magnus Press, 1975, p. 249.

Like the philosophers, al-Ghazālī determines that eternal bliss is the result of searching for and obtaining knowledge in life. However, he differs from the philosophers in regards to the quality of knowledge which leads to that state. He ascribes eternal bliss to those who possess knowledge of God and His deeds in the visible world – a judgment which seems to be a reply to the philosophers' view that eternal happiness is given through rational knowledge.[141] The knowledge he presents in *Jawāhir al-Qur'ān* is not exhausted in, but based on the rational study of beings in order to achieve a better knowledge of their creator who is seen as acting in and through every part of the creation. The knowledge al-Ghazālī advocates transcends rationality, without eliminating it. Al-Ghazālī uses the chariot of theoretical and practical rationality to ascend to a level of spiritual knowledge according to which God appears to be the sole existent and sole agent in the universe.[142]

6 Conclusions

Al-Ghazālī's approach in the *Jewels* is characterized through a complex synthesis of an Ash'arite-Sufi understanding of the Qur'ān, mixed with philosophical elements.[143] With the Ash'arites identifying the Qur'ānic text as the speech of God and, thus, as an attribute of His divine essence, it was no more the verbal text of the Qur'ān which deserves to be focused on, as the Mu'tazilites had advocated, but rather, the meanings of the divine speech. The Sufis, for their part, defined the purpose of human existence on earth as the achievement of individual eternal salvation in the hereafter through ascetic dedication to God. They emphasized a spiritual reading of the Qur'ān. In this context, al-Ghazālī, a committed Sufi with clear rational features, has to perform an intellectual tightrope act of Qur'ānic hermeneutics. While stressing an esoteric sense of Qur'ānic statements, he, against the Bāṭinites, does not neglect the value of the verbal text of the Qur'ān; he states that only through it, it is possible to penetrate to the deep meanings preserved within. While stressing the spiritual

141 See: Al-Fārābī, *Kitāb Taḥṣīl as-sa'āda*, ed. Ja'far Āl Yāsīn, Beirut: Dār al-Andalus 1401/1981. Partial translation by Muhsin Mahdi in R. Lerner and M. Mahdi (Eds.), *Medieval Political Philosophy: A Sourcebook*, New York: Glencoe, 1963, pp. 59–83.

142 Cf. Annemarie Schimmel, "Reason and Mystical Experience in Sufism," in: Farhad Daftari (Ed.), *Intellectual Traditions in Islam*, London/New York: L. B. Tauris in association with The Institute of Ismaili Studies, 2000, pp. 130–145.

143 Cf. Richard M. Frank, *Al-Ghazālī and the Ash'arite School*, Durham and London: Duke University Press, 1994.

knowledge of the text as the purpose of interpreting the Qurʾān, focusing on contents which lead to eternal bliss, he develops, in response to the philosophers, an open conception of science, which includes all forms of religious and non-religious knowledge, and connects them intrinsically to the Qurʾān.[144]

According to al-Ghazālī's bi-partite cosmology, the world is divided into two parts, a material and a spiritual one. Both parts truly exist; the existence of the visible world is, however, temporary, while the unseen world is eternal. The world of perception is a world of images and symbols. In al-Ghazālī's semiotics of being, every existent in the visible world serves as a sign for an existent in the invisible heavenly world. The world of perception is, therefore, a collection of signs indicating to realities which exist beyond sensual perception. These realities appear only to the inner sight of persons in possession of adequate spiritual training. Similarly, the text of the Qurʾān includes all forms and kinds of knowledge, to which Qurʾānic words and expressions indicate. In accordance with the bi-partite structure of each the world and the Qurʾān, al-Ghazālī presents a bi-partite system of religious sciences divided into a higher and a lower level. Sciences in each one of these two groups are, again, hierarchically ranked. In order to let the reader understand how the religious sciences, together with their respective subjects, are ranked in relation to each other, al-Ghazālī ascribes, symbolically, to each one of them a precious object available in the world of sense perception. The jewels, pearls and other materials, as such, are valuable; their values differ from each other. They serve as symbols for forms of religious knowledge. An existing entity itself, each one of these symbols has a certain value which makes it adequate to symbolize an abstract object of religious knowledge.[145]

---

144 Cf. Nicholas Heer, "Abū Ḥāmid al-Ghazālī's Esoteric Exegesis of the Koran," in: Leonard Lewisohn (Ed.), *The Heritage of Sufism*, 3 Vols., Vol. 1. *Classical Persian Sufism from its Origin to Rumi (700–1300)*, Oxford: Oneworld, 1999, pp. 235–257. *Jawāhir al-Qurʾān* is not treated.

145 Abū Zayd, *Mafhūm an-naṣṣ*, p. 278, considers that al-Ghazālī's transforming the words of the Qurʾān into symbols causes the interpretation of the Qurʾān (*taʾwīl*) to become a process of transformation (*taḥwīl*), such as that practiced by alchemists. Understanding the Qurʾān becomes, thus, a specialty of a minority of those who claim possessing a conjunction with the true world of spiritual ideas – the world which can be truly entered after death. (Ibid., p. 272f.) Abū Zayd adds that the relation between the symbol and the symbolized matter, in al-Ghazālī's conception, is "a relation of altering and transforming" (*al-qalb wa-t-taḥwīl*) based on knowing the common semantic meaning shared by both the symbol and the symbolized matter. The jewels and pearls mentioned in the *Jawāhir* are used as "images" indicating directly to the "truths of the Qurʾān," where their real meanings turn to be of mere metaphoric nature. (Ibid., p. 278f.) His harshest point of

Al-Ghazālī ranks the forms of knowledge using the names of well-known alchemistic and precious materials as symbols to demonstrate their different value. Utilizing alchemistic terminology to describe subjects of knowledge fits into the ultimate understanding of alchemy, predominant in pre-modern times, as a way to conceive of the secrets and the essence of things. Accordingly, searching for gold in metals resembles, basically, the search for God – a view obviously shared by al-Ghazālī.[146] In his conception, the used symbols do not substitute the forms of knowledge; they serve as concrete perceptible indicators to them. Based on al-Ghazālī's view of all existents, visible and invisible, as being connected to each other in chains of analogy, this approach appears plausible, as unusual as it actually is. Each existent in the world of perception points to a reality in the unseen world, which could be understood as an invitation for qualified readers, i.e. the Sufis, to both perceive the connections between both worlds and, furthermore, interpret the text of the Qurʾān appropriately.

According to al-Ghazālī, due to the cognitive limitations of human nature, there is no other way to obtain knowledge of the spiritual realities but through knowing the essence of the apparent images and symbols.[147] It is "impossible" for a living person to reach the spiritual world but through spiritual interpretation of the images and symbols in the material world.[148] By means of imagination (*al-khayāl*), the interpreter passes from the perceived "image" (*al-mithāl*) to the spiritual "reality" (*al-ḥaqīqa*) which the image bears,[149] from the fading "world of senses" (*ʿālam al-ḥiss*) into the eternal "world of dominion" (*ʿālam al-malakūt*). This method applies to the investigation of the world as well as to the interpretation of the Qurʾān. The spiritually trained observer of the world

critique against al-Ghazālī is that al-Ghazālī's usage of names of jewels, pearls and rubies as indications for different parts of the Qurʾān is an attempt to provide Muslims with a kind of compensation for not being capable of adequately understanding the Qurʾān. This approach paved the way in Islamic culture for treating the written text of the Qurʾān as "'something' precious" which can hardly be understood, but, rather, made an ornament or a talisman (Ibid., p. 297).

146 Cf. on Sufis and alchemistic practices Regula Forster, "Auf der Suche nach Gold und Gott. Alchemisten und Fromme im arabischen Mittelalter," in: Almut-Barbara Renger (Ed.), *Meister und Schüler in Geschichte und Gegenwart. Von Religionen der Antike bis zur modernen Esoterik*, Göttingen: V&R Unipress 2012, 213–230, especially pp. 219–224. Books of alchemy were ascribed to al-Ghazālī, although their authenticity has been doubted: Ullmann, *Die Natur- und Geheimwissenschaften im Islam*, 227.

147 Jawāhir, p. 92.

148 Jawāhir, p. 88.

149 Jawāhir, p. 91.

passes by means of imagination from the visible image to the reality beyond it; similarly, the spiritually trained interpreter of the Qur'ān passes from the external shell of the Qur'ānic text to the interior truth which is its pith.[150] Obviously, al-Ghazālī ascribes to imagination a mediator role between sensual perception and knowledge of truth. In doing that, he follows Aristotle who argues in *De Anima* that no one can learn or understand anything without sense perception and that thinking is not possible without images (*phantasmata*).[151] Imagination (*phantasia*) delivers to the intellectual faculty the objects of sense perception.[152] Aristotle's teaching was utilized by al-Fārābī to describe how the First Chief (*ar-ra'īs al-awwal*) of the Virtuous City (*al-madīna al-fāḍila*), as a prophet, receives knowledge from the Active Intellect (*al-ʿaql al-faʿʿāl*) and transmits the received knowledge to the people in an understandable way.[153]

Al-Ghazālī deduces non-religious sciences out of the Qur'ān: As the Qur'ān is a theological document of God's uncountable deeds in both the visible and the invisible world, and sciences exist in order to deal with these deeds, the origins of sciences are embedded in the Qur'ān. However, the relationship between the Qur'ān and non-religious sciences does not end here: scientific knowledge helps understand the deep meanings of Qur'ānic statements. The more we know, the better we grasp God's intentions revealed in the Qur'ān. Al-Ghazālī presents the Qur'ān, thus, as a stimulus to obtain knowledge and master sciences. The Qur'ān does not replace rational sciences, but rather confirms their necessary existence. Rational sciences do not deliver knowledge indispensable for salvation. However, they provide the person seeking salvation with necessary findings which help him improve his epistemological and spiritual state, as well. In the same way as al-Ghazālī sees the combination of "theoretical knowledge" (*al-ʿilm*) and "practice" (*al-ʿamal*)[154] necessary to pursue the mystical path, he seems to intrinsically connect scientific knowledge to

---

150 Abū Zayd, *Mafhūm an-naṣṣ*, p. 271, states critically that from a hermeneutical point of view the statements of the Qur'ān resemble, in al-Ghazālī's conception, the perishable world as well as the dreams; they are not the truth, but contain esoteric true meanings which can be reached through interpretation. The words of the Qur'ān become, thus, "symbols for hidden truths which exist in the ideal world, the world of spirits and meanings".

151 Aristotle, *De Anima*, with translation, introduction and notes by R. D. Hicks, Cambridge: Cambridge University Press, 1907, 432a7ff.

152 Ibid., III, 3.

153 Abū Naṣr al-Fārābī, *On the Perfect State*, Part V, Ch. 15, § 10, p. 244f. Cf. Hans Daiber, "Prophetie und Ethik bei Fārābī (gest. 339/950)," in: Christian Wenin (ed.), *L'homme et son Univers au moyen Âge*, Louvain la Neuve 1986: 729–753.

154 Jawāhir, III/87.

spiritual development as complementary components of the human endeavor to obtain cognitive knowledge about God.

Al-Ghazālī's open conception of science allows the establishment of deep connection between science and revelation out of the text of the Qur'ān. Based on a tolerant-inclusive attitude, he combines faith and knowledge in mystical harmony. In that, al-Ghazālī is not a rationalist; he is a mystic who does not discard rationality, but integrates it in his conception of knowledge. Rationality is highly estimated in this conception; however, it does not occupy the highest rank. This is preserved, in al-Ghazālī's mind, for spiritual knowledge obtained by "tasting" (*dhawq*) the truth of beings.[155] In his view, the world is a nexus of different analogic layers, the lower ones of them lead to the higher; the visible world of senses (*ʿālam ash-shahāda*) consists of "symbols and signs" (*rumūz wa-ishārāt*), representing higher realities in the invisible world (*ʿālam al-ghayb*), which cannot be intellectually captured by reason. For al-Ghazālī, the intellect is not the highest authority of knowledge; it is inferior to the spirit (*ar-rūḥ*) which cognizes the world by means of the eye of the heart (*al-baṣīra*) through mystical contemplation. Knowledge acquired in this manner serves the anagoge of the spirit, working its way up the order from lower to higher objects of knowledge. The lower objects serve, thus, as pointers to higher ones. The intellect is not excluded from this process of cognition; it delivers to the spirit the knowledge that it can achieve.

Al-Ghazālī's occupation with the idea of individual salvation in the Hereafter and how this can be reached through theoretical knowledge and practical behavior in this world leads him to suggest an esoteric reading of the Qur'ān, which focuses on eschatologically relevant meanings which are to be uncovered through contemplating over the text. However, an esoteric reading of the Qur'ān opens the door for arbitrary interpretations of a text which is of universal validity and normative power in Muslim societies. Al-Ghazālī seems to be aware of the fact that the hermeneutical approach he suggests in *Jawāhir al-Qur'ān* is appropriate only for a small group of people who are intellectually, morally and spiritually on a level that would require from them not to be distracted from striving to pursue a Sufi way of life. He was accustomed to say different things to different people according to their different skills.

155 Cf. Eric Ormsby, "The Taste of Truth: The Structure of Experience in Al-Ghazālī's Al-Munqidh min al-Ḍalāl," in: Wael B. Hallaq and Donald P. Little (Eds.), *Islamic Studies Presented to Charles J. Adams*, Leiden: Brill, 1991, 133–152.

CHAPTER 5

Al-Ghazālī at His Most Rationalist

The Universal Rule for Allegorically Interpreting Revelation (al-Qānūn al-Kullī fī t-Taʾwīl)

Frank Griffel

Around the year 715/1315, the Mamlūk theologian Ibn Taymiyya (d. 728/1328) wrote a monumental refutation of rationalist theology in Islam, *Rejecting the Notion That Revelation and Reason Would Contradict Each Other* (*Darʾ taʿāruḍ al-ʿaql wa-n-naql*).[1] In that book, which in its modern edition stretches over more than 4,000 pages in 11 volumes, he addresses the teachings of a number of thinkers beginning with the early theologians of the 2nd/8th century and the Muʿtazilites. He focuses primarily, however, on *falāsifa* such as Ibn Sīnā (Avicenna, d. 428/1037), Ibn Rushd (Averroes, d. 595/1198) and thinkers whom Ibn Taymiyya regarded as their followers among the theologians of Islam, like al-Ghazālī (d. 505/1111), Ibn Tūmart (d. 524/1130), or Fakhr ad-Dīn ar-Rāzī (d. 606/1210). Quite unusual for this kind of literature, Ibn Taymiyya begins his *Darʾ taʿāruḍ* right after the *basmala* and a brief *khuṭba* with a relatively long quote that he introduces as coming from "someone" ("*qāla l- qāʾil*"). In that quote the "someone" explains the principle he applies regarding passages where the outward sense of revelation (*ẓawāhir naqliyya*) differs from what has been decisively established through reason (*qawāṭiʿ ʿaqliyya*). In these cases, so the quoted position, the two conflicting sources of knowledge cannot both be true; subsequently one must be dismissed and the other be given priority. "Giving priority to revelation (*as-samʿ*)," the quote continues, "is impossible because reason is the foundation of revelation. Dismissing the foundation of a thing is dismissing the thing itself and giving priority to revelation would be dismissing revelation and reason altogether. This is why prioritizing reason is necessary."[2] Subsequently, revelation needs to be interpreted allegorically (*yutaʾawwalu*) wherever its outward sense clashes with reason.[3]

1 In regards to dating, see the editor's introduction to Ibn Taymiyya, *Darʾ taʿāruḍ al-ʿaql wa-n-naql aw-muwāfaqat ṣaḥīḥ al-manqūl li-ṣarīḥ al-maʿqūl*, ed. M. Rashād Sālim, 11 vols., Beirut: Dār al-Kunūz al-Adabiyya, n.d. [1980]), 1: 7–10. All quotations from this text rendered in English are my own translation.

2 Ibn Taymiyya, *Darʾ taʿāruḍ al-ʿaql wa-n-naql*, 1: 4.

3 Arab. *taʾwīl* means to understand a word or textual passage in a way that differs from the apparent or outward meaning (*ẓāhir*). I translate it as "allegorical interpretation," because

 | DOI 10.1163/9789004290952_006

The view that "reason is the foundation of revelation" (*al-ʿaql aṣl an-naql*) is the main premise of the position quoted – and opposed – by Ibn Taymiyya at the beginning of his *Darʾ taʿāruḍ*. Ending the quote Ibn Taymiyya adds:

> [Fakhr ad-Dīn] ar-Rāzī and his followers made this position into a universal rule (*qānūn kullī*) in regard to that which can be concluded from the Books of God and the words of His prophets and that which cannot be concluded from them. That is why [ar-Rāzī and his followers] refuse to accept conclusions based on information that comes from the prophets and the messengers about God's attributes and similar things that the prophets inform [us] of. These people believe that reason (*al-ʿaql*) contradicts [this information].[4]

In his work *Establishing [an Understanding] of Divine Transcendence* (*Taʾsīs at-taqdīs*), Fakhr ad-Dīn ar-Rāzī has a two-page-passage where he describes his attitude towards verses in revelation where the outward wording of the text (*ẓawāhir*) is in conflict with reason. There, he described this attitude as "the universal rule that should be applied for all ambiguous verses [in revelation]" (*al-qānūn al-kullī al-marjūʿ ilayhi fī jamīʿ al-mutashābihāt*). Ibn Taymiyya's quote – which he ascribes to "someone" – does indeed include many elements of ar-Rāzī's teachings in this passage,[5] yet it also includes phrases and formulas that Fakhr ad-Dīn would not have used, chief among them the claim that "reason contradicts [information that comes from the prophets]" (*al-ʿaql yuʿāriḍu* [*mā jāʾat bihi l-anbiyāʾ*]) and that "reason is the foundation of revelation" (*al-ʿaql aṣl an-naql*). Why Fakhr ad-Dīn would not have said these two phrases will become clear at the end of this chapter.

Ibn Taymiyya's claims, therefore, must be taken with a grain of salt and read in the context of his polemic. In essence, he clarifies that the very position that provoked him to write his grand refutation is the one that "reason is the foundation of revelation" (*al-ʿaql aṣl an-naql*). Those scholars who are guilty

---

the English word "interpretation" does not include the aspect of rejecting the apparent or outward meaning.

4 Ibn Taymiyya, *Darʾ taʿāruḍ al-ʿaql wa-n-naql*, 1: 4–5.

5 See Fakhr ad-Dīn ar-Rāzī in his *Taʾsīs at-taqdīs*, edited under the title *Asās at-taqdīs*, ed. Muḥyī d-Dīn Ṣabrī l-Kurdī et al., Cairo: Maṭbaʿat Kurdistān al-ʿIlmiyya, 1328 [1910–11], 210. On this passage from Fakhr ad-Dīn ar-Rāzī and Ibn Taymiyya's response in the *Darʾ taʿāruḍ* see Nicolas Heer, "The Priority of Reason in the Interpretation of Scripture: Ibn Taymīya and the Mutakallimūn," in: *The Literary Heritage of Classical Islam: Arabic and Islamic Studies in Honor of James A. Bellamy*, ed. M. Mir, Princeton: Darwin Press, 1993, 181–95.

of subscribing to that position make it into a "universal rule." Ibn Taymiyya's understanding of the connection between this position and the universal rule goes back to a small work by al-Ghazālī. Analyzing that small work will reveal what Ibn Taymiyya's accusation truly means, as well as disclose what he has in mind when he says his opponents take the position that reason is a foundation (*aṣl*) of revelation.

1 The "Universal Rule" (*qānūn kullī*) in a Letter of al-Ghazālī

Following the passage given above, Ibn Taymiyya informs his readers that the "universal rule" (*qānūn kullī*) is not Fakhr ad-Dīn ar-Rāzī's invention:

> About this rule (*qānūn*) that they apply, [we say that] another group has preceded them and one of them was Abū Ḥāmid [al-Ghazālī]. He posited a rule (*qānūn*) in response to questions put before him about certain revealed texts that posed problems for the one who asked him. These questions are similar to the ones that the Qāḍī Abū Bakr ibn al-ʿArabī asked al-Ghazālī. The Qāḍī Abū Bakr ibn al-ʿArabī rejected many of the answers he got [from al-Ghazālī] and said: "Our teacher Abū Ḥāmid [al-Ghazālī] entered into the bellies of the *falāsifa*; and when he wanted to get out of there, he couldn't." The Qāḍī Abū Bakr ibn al-ʿArabī reported from al-Ghazālī himself that he had said: "My merchandise in *ḥadīth* studies is meager." Abū Bakr ibn al-ʿArabī himself applied a different rule and based himself on the method of Abū l-Maʿālī [al-Juwaynī] and others before him, such as the Qādī Abū Bakr al-Bāqillānī.[6]

Ibn Taymiyya was enormously well read in the history of Islamic theology and he summarizes here in a nutshell what modern researchers over the past fifty years have also suspected: the short text by al-Ghazālī that circulates under the title *The Universal Rule of Allegorically Interpreting Revelation* (*al-Qānūn al-kullī fī t-taʾwīl*) was initially a written response to questions put to him by his student Abū Bakr ibn al-ʿArabī (d. 543/1148).[7]

In 1968, the Lebanese scholar Iḥsān ʿAbbās presented the content of a manuscript in Rabāṭ that preserved certain questions which Abū Bakr ibn al-ʿArabī had put to al-Ghazālī, including the latter's response. ʿAbbās' description of

---

6 Ibn Taymiyya, *Darʾ taʿāruḍ al-ʿaql wa-n-naql*, 1: 5–6.

7 On Abū Bakr ibn al-ʿArabī see Griffel, *Al-Ghazālī's Philosophical Theology*, New York: Oxford University Press, 2009, 62–71.

the text of the letter suggests that the short epistle *al-Qānūn al-kullī fī t-taʾwīl* has derived from it.[8] Ibn Taymiyya states cautiously that al-Ghazālī's written response to Abū Bakr ibn al-ʿArabī concerning the principles of how to interpret revelation allegorically "is similar" to the text where al-Ghazālī puts down his rule about the interpretation of revelation. In my recent book on al-Ghazālī I was less cautious in the conclusions I draw from the evidence that we have: the text of *responsa* to Abū Bakr ibn al-ʿArabī's questions *is* the very same text that circulates as al-Ghazālī's *al-Qānūn al-kullī fī t-taʾwīl*;[9] or, to put it the other way round, the short text circulating as al-Ghazālī's *al-Qānūn al-kullī fī t-taʾwīl* stems from written answers he gave to questions by his student Abū Bakr ibn al-ʿArabī. Ibn Taymiyya provides additional evidence to confirm this conclusion: "the Qāḍī Abū Bakr ibn al-ʿArabī reported from al-Ghazālī himself that he had said: 'My merchandise in *ḥadīth* studies is meager.' "[10] We find that sentence, verbatim, close to the end of al-Ghazālī's *al-Qānūn al-kullī fī t-taʾwīl*, which makes it quite certain that this work was originally the letter to Abū Bakr ibn al-ʿArabī that Ibn Taymiyya refers to. Indeed, after the bulk of the research on this chapter had been completed, an edition of al-Ghazālī's response to Ibn ʿArabī's question was published. It is based on a single manuscript, initially from the Zāwiyat an-Nāṣiriyya in Tamegroute in southern Morocco and now at Morocco's National Library in Rabat. The edition confirms that al-Ghazālī's *al-Qānūn al-kullī fī t-taʾwīl* is an excerpt from his response to Ibn al-ʿArabī. It is compiled mostly from the discussion to the ninth question in a letter that is much longer than *al-Qānūn* and that includes answers to 17 different question.[11]

8 Iḥsān Abbās did not draw that latter conclusion. For a description of the text in the unidentified manuscript from Rabat's Bibliotheque génèrale (al-Khizānā al-ʿāmma) of which there was apparently once a film (MS: 297–3) at the library of the American University of Beirut, Iḥsān Abbās' workplace; see his article, "Riḥlat Ibn al-ʿArabī ilā l-Mashriq kamā ṣawwarahā Qānūn at-taʾwīl," *al-Abḥāth* (Beirut) 21 (1968): 59–91, esp. 68–70.

9 Griffel, *Al-Ghazālī's Philosophical Theology*, 71.

10 Arab. *anā muzjā l-biḍāʿa fī l-ḥadīth*; Ibn Taymiyya, *Darʾ taʿāruḍ al-ʿaql wa-l-naql*, 1: 6.

11 Al-Ghazālī, *Ajwibat al-Ghazālī ʿan asʾilat Ibn al-ʿArabī*, ed. Muḥammad ʿAbdū (Beiruṭ: Dār al-Kutub al-ʿIlmiyya, 1433/2012), 74–94. The edition is based on MS Rabat, National Library, Q555, foll. 1b–14b. This is most probably the MS that Iḥsān ʿAbbās has worked with. I am grateful to Pierre-Alain Defossé in Rabat for pointing me to this edition. It made me realize that there is at least one other manuscript of this text, namely MS Paris, Bibliothèque Nationale, no. 5639 (Fonds Archinard), which I had misidentified in an earlier study (*Al-Ghazālī's Philosophical Theology*, 308, n. 61) as a manuscript of a different text of al-Ghazālī.

The text of *al-Qānūn al-kullī fī t-taʾwīl* is preserved in three manuscripts in libraries at Cairo and Istanbul.[12] There are no known copies of this work in European libraries or in Iran. It is known since at least the late 19th century and mentioned in Carl Brockelmann's list of works by al-Ghazālī.[13] An edited version of the text, based on a single manuscript from the Cairo National Library,[14] was published in Cairo, in 1940, under the misleading title *The Rule of*

---

12 MS Cairo, Dār al-Kutub al-Miṣriyya, *majāmiʿ* 180, foll. 89b–96b and two MSS at the Süleymaniye Yazma Eser Kütüphanesi in Istanbul: MS Ayasofya 2194, foll. 92a–100b and MS Carullah 1075, foll. 1a–8a. The Cairo MS was copied in Muḥarram 1133 / November 1720. It is briefly described in the catalogue of MSS at the Khedivial Library at the Darb al-Gamāmīz in Cairo. See *Fihrist al-kutub al-ʿarabiyya al-maḥfūẓa bi-l-Kutubkhāna al-Khidīwiyya*, 7 vols., Cairo: al-Maṭbaʿa al-ʿUthmāniyya, 1301–1309 [1883–1891], 7: 231–32. A more thorough description is in ʿAbd ar-Raḥmān Badawī, *Muʾallafāt al-Ghazālī*, 2nd ed., Kuwait: Wikālat al-Maṭbūʿāt, 1977, 168–171. The two MSS at the Süleymaniye Kütüphanesi are also late copies of the 11th/17th or 12th/18th centuries. MS Ayasofya 2194 is incomplete at the end, having lost its last folio. Badawī, *Muʾallafāt al-Ghazālī*, 168, mentions a third MS in Istanbul, Bayezid Umumi Kütüphanesi, Veliyeddin Efendi 1075. According to *Defter-i kütüpkhaneh-yi Veliyeddin*, Istanbul: Dersaadet Maḥmut Bey Maṭbaası, 1303 [1885–86], 60, however, MS Veliyeddin Efendi 1075 is a copy of a super-commentary on Kemalpaşazadeh's commentary on al-Abharī's *Hidāyat al-ḥikma*. Badawī most probably confused the Veliyeddin Efendi and the Carullah collections in Istanbul, a likely confusion given that the full name of the latter is "Carullah Veliyeddin."

13 Carl Brockelmann, *Geschichte der arabischen Litteratur*, 2nd. ed., 2 vols. (Leiden: Brill, 1943–49), 1: 422, no. 21, refers to the Cairo MS. Brockelmann mentions that the text has been edited by A. J. Casas y Manrique in Uppsala (Sweden) 1937. This, however, is an error. M. J. Casas y Manrique, *Ǧāmiʿ al-Ḥaqāʾiq bi-taǧrīd al-ʿalāʾiq: Origen y texto*, Uppsala: Almquist & Wiksell, 1937, is a study of MS 402 at the University Library in Uppsala, which contains a text ascribed to al-Ghazālī. The MS is described in C. J. Tornberg's catalogue, *Codices arabici, persici et turcici Bibliothecae Regia Universitatis Upsaliensis*, Lund: Impensis Reg., 1949, 262–63, and the text is, according to Casas y Manrique's study, not by al-Ghazālī.

14 Al-Ghazālī, *Qānūn at-taʾwīl*, ed. Muḥammad Zāhid al-Kawtharī, Cairo: Maktab Nashr ath-Thaqāfa al-Islāmiyya, 1359/1940. The text in this edition has been reprinted several times, most importantly in three small reprints all published with the title *Qānūn at-taʾwīl*. Two reprints bear al-Kawtharī's name as the editor on the title page, the first published in Cairo (Maktabat al-Azhariyya li-t-Turāth, 2006), the second distributed as a supplement (*hadiyya*) to *Majallat al-Azhar* (Cairo) 58.4 (Rabīʿ II 1406 / Dec. 1985–Jan. 1986). There is also a reprint of this text edited by Maḥmūd Bījū and published in Damascus under his own imprint in 1413/1993. The text was also reprinted within several collective volumes of epistles by al-Ghazālī, for instance in *Majmūʿat rasāʾil al-Imām al-Ghazālī*, ed. Aḥmad Shams ad-Dīn et al., 7 vols., Beirut: Dār al-Kutub al-ʿIlmiyya, 1409–14/1988–1994, 7: 121–32. Muḥammad Zāhid al-Kawtharī (1296–1371/1878–1952), the editor of the book, was an influential Ḥanafī jurist from Turkey who settled in Cairo in the 1920s and who

Allegorical Interpretation (*Qānūn at-taʾwīl*).[15] Neither the edition nor any of the manuscripts of this text suggest that the text goes back to questions that were put to al-Ghazālī by Abū Bakr ibn al-ʿArabī.

The text of this short epistle consists of a series of questions – some quite weird questions, as we will see – and of al-Ghazālī's responses to them. He begins his answers by promising a "universal rule" (*qānūn kullī*), which consists, as we will also see, of general remarks on the conflict between reason and revelation as well as three "recommendations" (singl. *waṣiyya*) that should be followed when engaging in allegorical interpretation (*taʾwīl*) of revelation. On the following pages, I shall present this work and contextualize it within the corpus of al-Ghazālīs œuvre. In its edition and in the manuscripts, the *Universal Rule of Interpretation* (*al-Qānūn al-kullī fī t-taʾwīl*) is only about a dozen pages long. The book is, however, quite important for our understanding of al-Ghazālī's thinking on prophecy and related issues. Furthermore, it probably had some impact on Fakhr ad-Dīn ar-Rāzī and certainly on Ibn Taymiyya, for whom the phrase "universal rule" (*qānūn kullī*) becomes a theological program ascribed to his opponents.

The text of *al-Qānūn al-kullī fī t-taʾwīl* has not been studied closely thus far; only a few excerpts of it have been translated into English and Turkish, and it has been mentioned in passing a handful of times in the Western secondary literature on al-Ghazālī.[16] What al-Ghazālī means by "the universal rule" of allegorical interpretation, however, has not been clarified; neither has his

---

edited important classical Arabic texts. He was a staunch Ashʿarite and a vocal critic of Ibn Taymiyya. See the collection of introductions to his editions, Muḥammad Zāhid al-Kawtharī, *Muqaddimāt al-Imām al-Kawtharī*, Cairo: Dār ath-Thurayyā, 1418/1997. That volume also contains two biographical articles on al-Kawtharī but it unfortunately lacks the one-page introduction al-Kawtharī wrote to his edition *Qānūn at-taʾwīl*.

15 Note that al-Ghazālī uses the phrase *qānūn at-taʾwīl* twice in one of his other works; see his *Fayṣal at-tafriqa bayna l-Islām wa-z-zandaqa*, ed. Sulaymān Dunyā, Cairo: ʿĪsā l-Bābī l-Ḥalabī, 1381/1961, 184, 187, 195.

16 Nicholas Heer, "Al-Ghazali's The Canons of Ta'wil," in: *Windows in the House of Islam: Muslim Sources on the Spirituality and Religious Life*, ed. John Renard, Berkeley: University of California Press, 1998, 48–54, provides an English translation of the middle part of the work as well as a brief paraphrase of its content. Already in 1930, Mehmet Şerafettin Yaltkaya (1879–1947) gave a paraphrase of the text in his Turkish article "Gazali'nin Te'vil Hakkında Basılmamış Bir Eseri," *Darülfünun İlahiyat Fakültesi Macmuası* (Ankara) 4 (1930): 46–58. The article is based on MS Istanbul, Carullah 1075. *Al-Qānūn al-kullī* is briefly mentioned in Maurice Bouyges, *Essai de chronologie des œuvres de al-Ghazali (Algazel)*, ed. Michel Allard, Beirut: Imprimerie Catholique, 1959, 58–59 (no. 44), 115 (no. 162), in Badawī, *Muʾallafāt al-Ghazālī*, 168–171 (no. 44), and in Martin Whittingham, *Al-Ghazālī and the Qurʾān: One Book, Many Meanings*, London and New York: Routledge, 2007, 2.

intriguing explanation of the word "Satan" (*shayṭān*) in revelation ever been presented to a Western readership.

2 Authorship and Dating

The existence of *al-Qānūn al-kullī fī t-taʾwīl* is well-documented, even from a relatively early point. A text with the title *al-Qānūn al-kullī* was ascribed to al-Ghazālī by one of his earliest bibliographers, Tāj ad-Dīn as-Subkī (d. 771/1370).[17] As-Subkī's contemporary al-Wāsiṭī (d. 776/1374), who in his biography of al-Ghazālī has an even more extensive list of works than the former, mentions a work with the title *Qānūn at-tāʾwīl*.[18] In his biographical article (*tarjama*) on al-Ghazālī, al-Wāsiṭī also quotes him as having said: "My merchandise in *ḥadīth* is meager"[19] – this is the memorable quote coming from the end of *al-Qānūn al-kullī fī t-taʾwīl*, suggesting that by the 8th/14th century the letter to Abū Bakr ibn al-ʿArabī circulated as an independent work of al-Ghazālī.[20] Based most probably on as-Subkī's testimony or on his own knowledge of a copy, the bibliographer al-Murtaḍā az-Zabīdī (d. 1205/1791) also includes a text with the title *al-Qānūn al-kullī* in his list of al-Ghazālī's works.[21] Recently, Martin Whittingham questioned al-Ghazālī's authorship of this small work. He was, as far as I know, the first to do so – though Whittingham concedes that some sections of the work may well be authentic, "the work when taken as a whole exhibits features highly uncharacteristic of al-Ghazālī, notably a disorderly structure and a self-effacing comment acknowledging limitations

---

17 As-Subkī, *Ṭabaqāt ash-shāfiʿiyya al-kubrā*, ed. Maḥmūd M. aṭ-Ṭanāḥī and ʿAbd al-Fattāḥ M. al-Ḥilū, 10 vols. (Cairo: ʿĪsā l-Bābī l-Ḥalabī, 1964–76), 6: 227.

18 Al-Wāsiṭī's work (*Aṭ-Ṭabaqāt al-ʿaliyya fī manāqib ash-shāfiʿiyya*) is yet unedited. The *tarjama* on al-Ghazālī, however, is edited in ʿAbd al-Amīr al-Aʿsam, *Al-Faylasūf al-Ghazālī: Iʿādat taqwīm li-munḥanā taṭawwurihi ar-rūḥī*, 3rd ed., Beirut: Dār al-Andalus, 1981, 167–94. *Kitāb Qānūn at-taʾwīl* is mentioned twice in that list on pp. 183 and 185. Al-Wāsiṭī's list of works by al-Ghazālī is also printed in Badawī, *Muʾallafāt al-Ghazālī*, 471–74.

19 Arab. *anā muzjā l-biḍāʿa fī l-ḥadīth*; al-Aʿsam, *Al-Faylasūf al-Ghazālī*, 179.

20 The quote, however, may also have been repeated in one of Abū Bakr ibn al-ʿArabī's numerous works; many of them are still unedited. ʿAmmār Ṭālibī, an expert on Abū Bakr ibn al-ʿArabī, noted that al-Ghazālī admitted his limited expertise in *ḥadīth*-studies to Abū Bakr and that the latter preserved the quote, see Ṭālibī's *Ārāʾ Abī Bakr ibn al-ʿArabī l-kalāmiyya*. 2 vols., Algiers: al-Sharika al-Waṭaniyya li-n-Nashr wa-t-Tawzīʿ, n.d. [1974], 1: 56.

21 Murtaḍā az-Zabīdī, *Itḥāf as-sāda al-muttaqīn bi-sharḥ Iḥyāʾ ʿulūm ad-dīn*, 10 vols. (Cairo: al-Maṭbaʿa al-Maymaniyya, 1311 [1894]), 1: 42.

in the author's knowledge of the science of hadith."[22] These reasons, however, are not convincing: classical Muslim biographers of al-Ghazālī regarded the self-effacing comment on his lack of expertise in *ḥadīth*-studies as authentic and I see no reason to doubt their judgment; and while it is true that the initial structure of the work is indeed disorderly, confusing, and un-Ghazalian, this passage at the beginning represents the questions put to al-Ghazālī – it is not authored by him, but merely records another's inquiry. Once the great scholar raises his voice, the work exhibits the usual well-structured style of composition so typical of al-Ghazālī.

Establishing the connection to Abū Bakr ibn al-ʿArabī allows us to date this text and locate it within al-Ghazālī's oeuvre.[23] Abū Bakr ibn al-ʿArabī was a student of al-Ghazālī in Baghdad during the relatively short period of a couple of months in the summer of 490/1097. This took place after al-Ghazālī had quit his teaching position at the Niẓāmiyya, after he had been to Damascus and Jerusalem, and after he had performed the *ḥājj*. That summer, al-Ghazālī stayed in Baghdad at the "Ribāṭ of Abū Saʿd right across from the Niẓāmiyya madrasa."[24] He departed there in the fall, making his way to his hometown Ṭābarān in the district of Ṭūs in Khorāsān, in today's northeast Iran. Abū Bakr ibn al-ʿArabī left us a vivid description of his brief period of studies with al-Ghazālī, giving the impression that their relationship was quite intimate. In his autobiographical report of his travels in the Muslim east, Abū Bakr Ibn al-ʿArabī writes:

> I developed strong ties with him [viz., al-Ghazālī] and I became inseparable from his carpet. I seized his isolation and his agility, and every time

22 Whittingham, *Al-Ghazālī and the Qur'ān*, 2.

23 An earlier dating was undertaken by Bouyges, *Essai de chronologie des œuvres de al-Ghazali*, 58–59. Based on a comparison with the subject matter of *Fayṣal at-tafriqa*, Bouyges, dated the text to al-Ghazālī's "period of retreat," that is, from 488–499/1095–1105. Bouyges, however, was unaware of the connection to Abū Bakr ibn al-ʿArabī, and was also wrong in his dating of the *Fayṣal*. That book was written partly as an apology to the accusation of harboring unbelief, an accusation that came up during the controversy over al-Ghazālī's teaching activity at the Niẓāmiyya madrasa in Nishapur after 499/1106. On the connection of the *Fayṣal* to the Nishapurian controversy see Richard M. Frank, *Al-Ghazālī and the Ashʿarite School*, Durham: Duke University Press, 1994, 76–77. On the controversy itself see, Kenneth Garden, "Al-Māzarī al-Dhakī: al-Ghazālī's Maghribi Adversary in Nishapur," *Journal of Islamic Studies* 21 (2010): 89–107.

24 Griffel, *Al-Ghazālī's Philosophical Theology*, 64, 65, quoting Abū Bakr ibn al-ʿArabī, *Qānūn at-taʾwīl*, ed. Muḥammad Sulaymānī, Beirut: Dār al-Gharb al-Islāmī, 1990, 111.

> he attended to me, I exhausted him with my expectations. He allowed me [to share] his place and I was with him in the morning, the afternoon, at lunchtime, and at dinner, whether he was in casual clothes or in his formal attire. During these times, I could ask him without restraint, like a scholar at a place where the shackles of enquiry are entrusted [to him]. I found him to be welcoming towards me regarding instruction and I found him true to his word.[25]

It is highly likely that al-Ghazālī's response to Abū Bakr's questions was generated in this short period in Baghdad during the summer of 490/1097. Later, when Abū Bakr was himself an accomplished scholar, he quotes other responses he obtained from al-Ghazālī, and we must assume that they all come from this period. It is not, of course, impossible that after their personal meeting in Baghdad the two remained in contact through letters. But during the years al-Ghazālī stayed in Ṭābarān, Abū Bakr ibn al-ʿArabī was a traveling itinerant, passing from Baghdad to Damascus to Jerusalem, ultimately lingering in Alexandria in Fāṭimid Egypt. It took Abū Bakr five years after his meeting with al-Ghazālī before he returned to his home in Seville in 495/1102.

There is other evidence within the text of the letter that supports the assumption that it was written in 490/1097, that is, during the time that al-Ghazālī worked on his ethical magnum opus, the *Revival of the Religious Sciences* (*Iḥyāʾ ʿulūm ad-dīn*).[26] Despite the fact that the subject matter of this letter touches on many themes that al-Ghazālī deals with in his later works – most importantly his *Decisive Criterion for Distinguishing Islam from Clandestine Unbelief* (*Fayṣal at-tafriqa bayna al-Islām wa-z-zandaqa*) and his *Restraining the Ordinary People from the Science of Kalām* (*Iljām al-ʿawāmm ʿan ʿilm al-kalām*) – none of these works are mentioned. Of his earlier works al-Ghazālī mentions only *Explaining the Marvels of the Heart* (*Sharḥ ʿajāʾib al-qalb*), the 21st book of *Iḥyāʾ ʿulūm ad-dīn*, dealing with matters of the soul, which is referred to twice in our text.[27] This suggests that, though parts of the *Iḥyāʾ* were already available,

---

25 Abū Bakr ibn al-ʿArabī, *Qānūn at-taʾwīl*, 112–13; see also Griffel, *Al-Ghazālī's Philosophical Theology*, 65–66.

26 For the dating of al-Ghazālī's *Iḥyāʾ ʿulūm ad-dīn* to the first years after he left the Baghdad Niẓāmiyya, 488/1095, see Bouyges, *Essai de chronologie des œuvres de al-Ghazali*, 41–44, and George F. Hourani, "A Revised Chronology of Ghazālī's Writings," *JAOS* 104 (1984): 289–302, esp. 296–97.

27 Al-Ghazālī, *al-Qānūn al-kullī fī t-taʾwīl*, ed. al-Kawtharī, pp. 14, 15 / MS Ayasofya 2194, fol. 100a / MS Carullah 1075, foll. 7b, 8a. In the following footnotes I will refer to the page

neither the *Fayṣal at-tafriqa* nor the *Iljām al-ʿawāmm* existed when the letter was written. These two books are now dated close to end of al-Ghazālī's life.[28]

It is difficult to say whether the title of this epistle goes back to al-Ghazālī himself. There are indications that al-Ghazālī kept copies of his letters and that some of them were published after his death out of the body of papers he left behind.[29] The lack of reference to Abū Bakr ibn al-ʿArabī in the manuscript tradition of *al-Qānūn al-kullī fī t-taʾwīl* suggests that this tradition is not based on the recipient's copy of the letter. The Rabat MS described by Iḥsān ʿAbbas seems to represent a manuscript tradition that does, however, go back to Abū Bakr ibn al-ʿArabī's copy. It mentions the recipient, but not the title *al-Qānūn al-kullī fī t-taʾwīl*.[30] Thus, it is quite possible that we are dealing with two different manuscript traditions of the text, one based on the recipient's copy of the letter, represented by the Rabat MS, and another based on the sender's copy of the letter and represented by the three manuscripts that are the basis of this study. If that is the case, then the title *al-Qānūn al-kullī fī t-taʾwīl* may well go back to al-Ghazālī or someone who published this epistle based on his bequest.

We should at least point out that Abū Bakr himself wrote a substantial monograph with the title *The Rule of Interpretation* (*Qānūn at-taʾwīl*) that deals with al-Ghazālī's teachings on *taʾwīl*, which interestingly enough he does not fully adopt. Ibn Taymiyya was aware of this when he says that Abū Bakr applied a different rule of interpretation based on al-Juwaynī and al-Bāqillānī.

---

and folio-numbers of these three textual witnesses in this order divided by slashes. The reader should keep in mind that MS Ayasofya 2194 lacks the end of the text, which means that the second reference to *ʿAjāʾib al-qalb* is missing from the text in that MS.

28 For the dating of *Fayṣal at-tafriqa* into the period after 500/1106 see fn. 23. *Iljām al-ʿawāmm* is regarded as the last of al-Ghazālī's work, finished only shortly before his death in 505/1111. See Griffel, *Al-Ghazālī's Phlosophical Theology*, 266. This dating is now somewhat challenged by a quote in Ibn Taymiyya's *Bughyat al-murtād* from al-Ghazālī's *Mishkāt al-anwār*. In that quote the text of *Mishkāt al-anwār* refers to *Iljām al-ʿawāmm* as a work that has been completed before *Mishkāt al-anwār*. See Yahya Michot's contribution to this volume. Compared to most available MSS of *Mishkāt al-anwār* as well as all its editions, this is a *lectio difficilior* and should raise our attention. Even if the status of *Iljām al-ʿawāmm* as al-Ghazālī's last work needs to be revised, however, it would still fall within the late period of al-Ghazālī's life given that it is not mentioned in any other of his works.

29 See for instance the collection of his Persian letters *Makātīb-i fārisī-yi Ghazzālī be-nām-i Fażāʾil al-anām min rasāʾil Ḥujjat al-Islām*, ed. ʿAbbās Iqbāl Āshtiyānī (Tehran: Kitābfurūsh-i Ibn Sīnā, 1333 [1954]), which was published by a relative after his death and must be based on copies of al-Ghazālī's letters which he had preserved in his library.

30 See fn. 9 as well as the recent edition of the Rabat manuscript mentioned in footnote 11.

3 Content of the Epistle

Al-Qānūn al-kullī fī t-tāʾwīl can be divided into three parts. The first part of the text – two pages out of roughly twelve in the edited version – are the questions of the questioner, most probably Abū Bakr ibn al-ʿArabī. They begin by quoting a certain *ḥadīth*. The Prophet is reported of having said: "Satan runs in the blood vessels of one of you" (*inna sh-shayṭāna yajrī min aḥadikum majrā d-dam*). The questioner sees a number of problems related with this *ḥadīth*. After the *basmala* and the author's name, the epistle begins by saying that it deals with "explaining the meaning" (*bayān maʿnā*) of the *ḥadīth* that we just quoted. It continues with the questions that were put to al-Ghazālī:

> Is Satan a mixture like water in water or is he fully contained throughout [the blood vessels]? Does the direct contact that Satan has with the hearts come about through some process of imagining (*takhāyul*) from outside and the hearts carry this [imagination] to the outward senses where it becomes manifest? And does the devilish infiltration (or: temptation, *waswās*) come from the outward senses? Or does Satan's substance affect the substance of the hearts directly? And is there something in common between that what prophecy describes here and between something similar when jinns are presented to humans in the guise of animals or different guises of this kind, such as the presentation of angels – peace be upon them – to the prophets in the guise of humans, or other examples like these? May this be clarified for him to whom it may happen that he has visual presentations of this kind, which then may acquire some material firmness as it has happened with angels.
>
> Is there a way to reconcile what revelation here says about the jinns and the satans with the teachings of the *falāsifa*? Are these examples and expressions of the four humors that are within the body in order to govern it, or not?[31]

If this translation seems clumsy, it is because the original Arabic text is even clumsier. The questioner is not an experienced writer, throwing out ideas and suggestions without developing any of them. Even if this list were derived from a personal conversation where the questions had been clarified, this part of the letter is poorly structured and often quite difficult to understand. There are all kinds of inquiries about subjects mentioned in the Qurʾān and in the *ḥadīth* corpus. Can the talk of epileptic people (*maṣrūʿūn*) be connected to prophecy,

---

31 Al-Ghazālī, *al-Qānūn al-kullī fī t-taʾwīl*, 4 / 92b / 1b.

the questioner asks; what about the *ḥadīth* saying that Satan takes a fast flight when he hears the call to prayer?[32] What about the information, also coming from the *ḥadīth* corpus, that the satans nourish themselves from manure and bones? How can that be, given that there is elsewhere information that they have no bodily needs?[33] What about the *barzakh*? Is it closer to Paradise or to Hell?[34] And why does the *ḥadīth* say that Paradise is as wide as heaven and earth, when it must be contained somewhere within the bounds of those two?[35] Also, what is the "pool of the messenger of God" (*ḥawḍ rasūl Allāh*) that is also mentioned in several *ḥadīth*s?[36] Some of these questions – like the inquiry about the type of excrement left by satans – clearly touch on delicate subjects. For all this, the questioner demands an answer from al-Ghazālī.

It is clear that the questioner shares a number of premises with al-Ghazālī that are not explicitly mentioned in the questions. First, revelation is understood as referring to both the text of the Qurʾān as well as that of the *ḥadīth* corpus. This is also true for the word "prophecy" (*nubuwwa*). Al-Ghazālī held the same position and never in his writings on *taʾwīl* does he distinguish between

32 See Muslim ibn al-Ḥajjāj, *aṣ-Ṣaḥīḥ*, Kitāb aṣ-Ṣalāt, bāb 8.

33 On "*shayṭān*" in the *ḥadīth* corpus see See Arent J. Wensinck et al. (eds.), *Concordance et indices de la tradition musulmane*, 8 vols., Leiden: Brill, 1936–88, 3: 125–31 and Arent J. Wensinck, *A Handbook of Early Muhammadan Tradition, Alphabetically Arranged*, Leiden: Brill, 1927, 210–12. I couldn't locate the sources for this information in the canonical *ḥadīth* corpus. Note that Abū Bakr ibn al-ʿArabī is considered a very thorough *ḥadīth* scholar who wrote a long commentary on at-Tirmidhī's collection: *ʿĀriḍat al-aḥwadhī bi-sharḥ Ṣaḥīh at-Tirmidhī*, ed. Jamāl Marʿashlī, 14 parts in 8 vols., Beirut: Dār al-Kutub al-ʿIlmiyya, 1997.

34 The *barzakh* ("barrier" or "separation") is mentioned three times in the Qurʾān (23:100; 25:53; 55:20). The questioner seems to understand *barzakh* as referring to a space in between Paradise and Hell, similar to the *limbus*, or Limbo, in Christian Latin theology. That understanding is later confirmed in al-Ghazālī's answer, when he says the *barzakh* may be the station between Paradise and Hell for those who have done neither good nor bad, like the insane or those who have not been reached by the message of Islam (*al-Qānūn al-kullī*, 6 / – / 8a). On *barzakh* see Christian Lange, art "Barzakh," in *Encyclopaedia of Islam. THREE*, available online at http:www.brillonline.nl,; Mona M. Zaki, "Barzakh," in *Encyclopaedia of the Qurʾān*, ed. Jane D. McAuliffe, 6 vols., Leiden: Brill, 2001–06, 1: 204–7, and B. Carra De Vaux, "Barzakh," in *Encyclopedia of Islam. New Edition*, ed. H. A. R. Gibb et al. 12 vols., Leiden and London: Luzac and Brill, 1954–2009, 1:1071–72.

35 Later, in his *Fayṣal at-tafriqa*, 179, al-Ghazālī will address this problem and offer a solution. He does not respond to this question in this letter.

36 See, for instance, al-Bukhārī, *aṣ-Ṣaḥīḥ*, Kitāb ar-Riqāq, bāb 52–53, or Muslim ibn al-Ḥajjāj, *aṣ-Ṣaḥīḥ*, Kitāb al-Faḍāʾil, bāb 9. On the Day of Resurrection, Muhammad is said to meet his community at this pool. See A. J. Wensinck, art. "Ḥawḍ," in *Encyclopedia of Islam. New Edition*, 3: 286.

verses in the Qurʾān and *ḥadīth*: both are regarded as revelation, and both need to be reconciled with reason.[37] Second, the questioner knows something about Avicennan cosmology and prophetology, inasmuch as he regards it helpful to understand phenomena like angels, jinns, and satans. He knows that for the *falāsifa*, the word "angel" is simply a reference to celestial intellects and/or souls, and he entertains the thought that jinns and satans may be objects of a similar kind, that is, celestial immaterial intellects that have certain influences on human minds. For his part, al-Ghazālī held the prophetology of Ibn Sīnā (Avicenna, d. 428/1037) to be a valid explanation of the phenomenon of divine revelation;[38] he expresses this opinion most outspokenly in another letter addressed to Abū Bakr ibn al-ʿArabī which the latter would later quote in one of his works.[39]

Al-Ghazālī's response to these questions falls into two parts: in the first part, he criticizes the questioner for the nature of his questions, gives some general remarks about the apparent conflict between reason and revelation, and lists three general "recommendations" about how to approach the texts of revelation. This part stretches over little more than six pages, which is about half of the text.[40] It is in this section that al-Ghazālī promises his "universal rule" (*qānūn kullī*), a rule claimed to be applicable in all cases where the outward sense of revelation (*ẓāhir*) clashes with what is known by reason (*ʿaql*). The second part of his answer of less than four pages, i.e. almost a third of the text, is a detailed discussion of a very limited number of the problems brought up by the questioner. Far from engaging with all that is presented, al-Ghazālī picks out a few questions and states his positions, though at least one of the questions that are left unanswered here will be picked up in a later work of al-Ghazālī.[41] His pattern of response is to fall back on the prophetology of Ibn

---

37 Griffel, *Al-Ghazālī's Philosophical Theology*, 106.

38 See M. Afifi al-Akiti, "The Three Properties of Prophethood in Certain Works of Avicenna and al-Ġazālī," in: *Interpreting Avicenna. Science and Philosophy in Medieval Islam. Proceedings of the Second Conference of the Avicenna Study Group*, ed. Jon McGinnis, Leiden: Brill, 2004, 189–212 and Frank Griffel, "Al-Ġazālī's Concept of Prophecy: The Introduction of Avicennan Psychology into Ašʿarite Theology," *Arabic Sciences and Philosophy* 14 (2004): 101–44.

39 Griffel, *Al-Ghazālī's Philosophical Theology*, 67–69.

40 Al-Ghazālī, *al-Qānūn al-kullī fī t-taʾwīl*, 6–12 / 94a–98b / 2a–6a. This part has been translated into English in Heer, "Al-Ghazali. The Canons of Ta'wil."

41 See fn. 35. Al-Ghazālī himself brings up another example of a *ḥadīth* that is later discussed in *Fayṣal at-ṭafriqa*, 179. In *al-Qānūn al-kullī*, 11 / 98a / 5b (Engl. transl. 53) al-Ghazālī mentions the *ḥadīth* saying that on the Day of Resurrection death will appear as a white spotted ram (*kabsh amlaḥ*) and will be sacrificed (see e.g. al-Bukhārī, *aṣ-Ṣaḥīḥ*, Kitāb Tafsīr

Sīnā and to give rational and scientific explanations – according to the understanding of rationality and science of his time – of the textual problems that he chooses to explain. Before we go into the part that deals in general terms with the rules of how to approach the apparent conflict between reason and revelation, I first analyze this last part and present al-Ghazālī's explanation of the *ḥadīth* about Satan running in one's blood vessels.

4 An Avicennan Explanation of the Meaning of "Satan" (*ash-shayṭān*) in Revelation

The *ḥadīth* that is quoted at the beginning of this epistle is considered reliable (*ṣaḥīḥ*); Ibn Māja, Abū Dawūd, and al-Bukhārī all have versions of it. Al-Bukhārī reports from various sources that once two of the "helpers" (*anṣār*) among the people in Medina looked with an obvious sexual desire at the young and beautiful Ṣafiyya bint Ḥuyayy (d. *c.* 50/670), one of the Prophet's wives. The Prophet chided them and said: "Satan runs in the blood vessels of humans and I fear that something of it has reached into the souls of you two."[42] For the questioner, this *ḥadiṭh* poses a problem: how can it be explained that a creature like Satan, who is usually understood as a disobedient angel or a fallen jinn, runs in human blood vessels?[43] In his answer, al-Ghazālī says that a full explanation would take too much space and merely hints at the correct position. "The meaning is not," he says, "that Satan's body mixes with the body of the human in a mixture like water with water." Rather, the effects of Satan are diffused throughout the body of the human and circulate within the body just like the atoms of blood circulate throughout his body. The idea that is hinted at here – but not spelled out – is that of a *jism laṭīf*, a "subtle body." In early *kalām* literature, angels, jinns, and satans are bodies made of such smoke-like,

---

sūrat Maryam, bāb 1). Death, says al-Ghazālī, cannot change into a ram because the former is an accident (*ʿaraḍ*) while the latter is a body (*jism*), indicating that the *ḥadīth* must be interpreted allegorically. That example is also discussed in book 31 of al-Ghazālī's *Iḥyāʾ ʿulūm ad-dīn*; see Richard Gramlich, *Muḥammad al-Ġazzālīs Lehre von den Stufen der Gottesliebe. Die Bücher 31–36 seines Hauptwerkes eingeleitet, übersetzt und kommentiert*, Wiesbaden: F. Steiner, 1984, 64–65.

42 "*inna sh-shayṭān yajrī min al-insān majrā d-dam wa-innī khashītu an yulqiya fī anfusikumā shayʾan*"; al-Bukhārī, *aṣ-Ṣaḥīh*, Kitāb al-Iʿtikāf, bāb 11. Cf. also Ibn Māja, *as-Sunan*, Kitāb aṣ-Ṣiyām, bāb 65. For other similar versions see Wensinck, *Concordance*, 1: 342.

43 For the more traditional understanding of Satan (Arab. *ash-shayṭan* and *Iblīs*) in *tafsīr* literature see Andrew Rippin, art. "Devil," in *Encyclopaedia of the Qurʾān*, 1: 524–28 and T. Fahd and A. Rippin., art, "Shayṭān," in *Encyclopaedia of Islam. New Edition*, 9: 406–9.

subtle material that is invisible to us.[44] Al-Ghazālī, however, uses the concept differently. No longer Satan himself, but his effects (*athar ash-shayṭān*) are the "subtle body" and the effects of Satan are phenomena of the soul. Al-Ghazālī explains how Satan affects humans: Humans find within themselves certain devilish temptations or devilish whisperings (*wasāwis*, singl. *waswās*).[45] These are often impressions presented to the outer senses. They are in character similar to the inspiration (*ilhām*) that some extraordinary humans – here he means the Sufi saints – receive. Al-Ghazālī explains the infiltrations of Satan in the following way:

> The devilish whispers (*wasāwis*) from Satan are similar to the inspiration (*ilhām*) from the angel. We find different thoughts (*khawāṭir*) unexpectedly in our hearts, some of them call us to follow our passion, others call to follow its opposite. These thoughts (…) fall into different groups according to causes [that they have.] […] Since they are different thoughts, their causes are different. Revelation (*sharʿ*) calls the cause from which inspiration is obtained "an angel" (*malak*) and that from which the devilish whisper is obtained "a Satan" (*shayṭān*). "Inspiration" is an expression that refers to a thought which is sent to do good, and "devilish whisper" is an expression of [a thought] that is sent to do evil, and [the words] "the angel" and "the devil" are expressions of their two causes.[46]

The comparison to *ilhām* (inspiration) puts us onto some familiar territory. From other writings of al-Ghazālī we know that *ilhām* is a lower form of prophecy that is given to *awliyāʾ*, "friends of God" or Sufi saints, which produces visions and foreknowledge of the future. Recent research has shown that in his understanding of prophecy al-Ghazālī depends thoroughly on Ibn Sīnā. He fully applies the three prophetical properties of Ibn Sīnā: that is, imaginative prophecy through a strong faculty of imagination (*takhayyul*), intellectual prophecy through strong *ḥads*, and the performance of miracles through an exceptionally

44 Josef van Ess, *Theologie und Gesellschaft im 2. und 3. Jahrhundert Hidschra. Eine Geschichte des religiösen Denkens im frühen Islam*. 6 vols., Berlin: Walter de Gruyter, 1991–97, 3: 264, 369–73, 4: 534.

45 There is a popular notion in the *ḥadīth* corpus that each person has his or her own satan, who is resting on the shoulder as a constant tempter; see Muslim ibn al-Ḥajjāj, *aṣ-Ṣaḥīḥ*, Kitāb Ṣifāt al-munāfiqīn, bāb 16 and Andrew Rippin in his art. "Shayṭān," 408b.

46 Al-Ghazālī, *al-Qānūn al-kullī fī t-taʾwīl*, 13 / 99a / 6b.

powerful practical faculty of the soul (*quwwa nafsiyya ʿamaliyya*).[47] One of the reasons why Ibn Sīnā's philosophical explanation of prophecy was so attractive to al-Ghazālī was its applicability to the superior insights of Sufi saints and to the "wondrous deeds" (*karāmāt*) they perform. The Sufi saints have these three properties – imaginative and intellectual revelation plus a certain practical capacity – to a degree that allows them to have *ilhām* (inspiration) and perform certain wondrous deeds. In fact, like Ibn Sīnā, al-Ghazālī argues that all humans have some share in these properties, some more, some less. Most people just have a very small share and prophets are exceptionally blessed with them. The *awliyāʾ* are somewhere in between and their inspiration is an expression of their superior connection to the celestial realm.[48]

There is an interesting element in Ibn Sīnā's teaching about prophetical miracles that is very important for al-Ghazālī. Ibn Sīnā asserts that the same practical faculty of the soul that allows prophets to perform miracles also allows sorcerers to perform sorcery (*siḥr*). Both, the prophet and the sorcerer, affect objects outside of themselves through strong powers they have within their souls. Prophets do this intending to benefit humanity – namely, to be accepted as prophets and to validate their message – while sorcerers (singl. *sāḥir*) use this faculty with evil intentions, mostly to enrich themselves.[49] Al-Ghazālī adopted this explanation of *siḥr* from Ibn Sīnā.[50] For al-Ghazālī the fact that both the prophetical miracle and sorcery are effects of the same human faculty leads to the conclusion that these are most often indistinguishable. This, in turn, makes him abandon the prophetical miracle as a marker for prophecy, a fact that will also become important in this text.

47 On those three properties (singl. *khāṣṣa*) see Dag N. Hasse, *Avicenna's De Anima in the West. The Formation of a Peripatetic Philosophy of the Soul 1160–1300* (London/Turin: The Warburg Institute / Nino Aragno Editore, 2000), 154–65 and Herbert A. Davidson, *Alfarabi, Avicenna, and Averroes, on Intellect. Their Cosmologies, Theories of the Active Intellect, and Theories of Human Intellect*, New York: Oxford University Press, 1992, 116–23.

48 Frank Griffel, "Muslim Philosophers' Rationalist Explanation of Muḥammad's Prophecy," in *The Cambridge Companion to Muhammad*, ed. by Jonathan E. Brockopp, New York: Cambridge University Press, 2010. 158–179, esp. 174–77. The analysis there is based on al-Ghazālī, *al-Munqidh min aḍ-ḍalāl / Erreur et deliverance*, ed. Farid Jabre. 3rd ed., Beirut: Commission libanaise pour la traduction des chefs-d'œuvre, 1969, 41–43.

49 Ibn Sīnā, *al-Ishārāt wa-t-tanbīhāt*, ed. Jacob Forget, Leiden: Brill, 1892, 220–221. Al-Ghazālī copied this passage in his report of philosophical teachings, MS London, British Library, Or. 3126, fol. 284a.

50 Griffel, *Al-Ghazālī's Philosophical* Theology, 197–198 and al-Akiti, "Three Properties of Prophethood," 19.

In accord with Ibn Sīnā's explanation of sorcery and prophetical miracles, al-Ghazālī teaches that devilish infiltrations and the Sufis' inspiration have one and the same cause. In the case of the saints' inspiration, the human is motivated to do good; in the case of the "devilish infiltrations," he or she is motivated to do moral evil. Both are distinct effects of the same cause. Al-Ghazālī clarifies:

> This is like a fire by which the sides of a house are lit bright and its ceiling is turned black. We know that brightness is the opposite of blackening and we know that the cause of brightness is the opposite of the cause of blackening. The cause of brightness is the light of the fire and the cause of blackening is its smoke. Through this [comparison] we know that the cause of the devilish whisper is different from the cause of the inspiration. This is indeed so. It remains to inquire whether that cause is an accident or not rather a substance that does not inhere in something else. It is evident that it is not an accident but a substance. Then it remains to inquire whether it is living or not living. From indications in revelation and also from certain rational aspects it becomes evident that it is living.[51]

This is all al-Ghazālī says on this subject in this epistle. According to revelation, saintly inspirations and devilish infiltrations have different causes: the first come from angels, the latter from satans. Yet these two very different phenomena, so al-Ghazālī, may have a common cause on a higher level. The cause of brightness on the inner walls of a house is the light of the fire, and the cause for the darkening of its ceiling is the smoke of the fire. As such, radiance and darkness, although opposites of one another, are, in turn, caused by the same fire. Analogously, al-Ghazālī asserts that the cause of devilish whispers is Satan and the cause of saintly inspiration is an angel; on a higher level, however, their cause is identical in essence. The cause of saintly inspirations was well known to Ibn Sīnā and subsequently to al-Ghazālī: these are the celestial souls, which, already possessing knowledge of future events, transmit parts of that knowledge to the humans to which they are connected.[52] Here, al-Ghazālī extends Ibn Sīnā's teachings on the matter to devilish infiltrations

51 Al-Ghazālī, *al-Qānūn al-kullī fī t-ta'wīl*, 13 / 99a–b / 6b.

52 Ibn Sīnā's *al-Ishārāt wa-t-tanbīhāt*, 210–11 and Davidson, *Alfarabi, Avicenna, and Averroes, on Intellect*, 121–22.

(*wasāwis*), something Ibn Sīnā, as far as I can see, never did.[53] Al-Ghazālī combines two Avicennan ideas, the first about the cause of revelation and saintly inspiration and the second about the fact that prophetical miracles and sorcery are both caused by the same faculty in humans. For al-Ghazālī, "Satan" and "the angels" are names for mere intermediaries – as the comparison with the fire in a room suggests – between the devilish infiltrations and the inspiration and their higher cause, the celestial soul. Or, and that seems even more likely, the words "Satan" or "angels" are two different names for the true cause of saintly inspirations and devilish infiltrations. This real cause is a celestial soul. The celestial souls are considered living substances that directly influence human behavior.

In this epistle al-Ghazālī contrasts his own explanation with a number of alternatives, the most interesting of which is the one he ascribes to "the *falāsifa*." In other writings such as the *Incoherence of the Philosophers* (*Tahāfut al-falāsifa*) or his autobiography *The Deliverer from Error* (*al-Munqidh min aḍ-ḍalāl*), the name "*falāsifa*" is usually used as a cipher that stands in for Ibn Sīnā and his followers. Not so in this text. The *falāsifa*, says al-Ghazālī, would reject his interpretation and would rather say the *ḥadīth* is a reference to the four humors that run in every human body. According to the *falāsifa*, so al-Ghazālī, there can be no direct interference of Satan – which here means a celestial soul – with human bodies. The *falāsifa* do not deny that celestial souls affect human bodies; rather, they assert that they do so through other intermediate causes, among them the four humors. Al-Ghazālī, in contrast, seems to put forward a theory where the celestial souls have direct influence on human souls and their faculties. Ibn Sīnā held the very same position, namely that the influence of celestial souls on humans can be direct. It can also be indirect, of course, through intermediaries such as the four humors and others. The *falāsifa* whose teaching al-Ghazālī reports in this epistle, however, seem like a constructed group, un-Avicennan and, if anything, closer to the teachings of the Greek physician Galen (d. *c.* 217 CE). They don't seem like a real group but rather a construct of al-Ghazālī, created in order to contrast his own teachings against them and thus pre-empt the likely accusation that his own teachings are derived from the *falāsifa*, i.e. from Ibn Sīnā and his followers.

Other explanations in this short epistle are also influenced by Ibn Sīnā's philosophical explanation of prophecy. In an epileptic fit (*ṣarʿ*), so al-Ghazālī, we may say that the epileptic is possessed by a jinn; the word "jinn," however, really refers to "the cause (*sabab*) for the occurrence of ideas, representa-

---

53 Ibn Sīnā never seems to have been concerned or confronted with an explanation of what *ash-shayṭān* refers to in revelation.

tions, and imaginations in his heart."[54] That cause is again a celestial soul. The celestial soul that is the cause of revelation, so al-Ghazālī, is sometimes called "a tablet," sometimes "an Imām," and sometimes "a book." Al-Ghazālī here refers to Qur'ānic passages that mention the "preserved tabled" (*al-lawḥ al-maḥfūẓ*, 85:22), a "clear Imām" (*imām mubīn*, 15:79), or "a clear book" (*kitāb mubīn*, 6:59, 10:61, and elsewhere), and he understands these phrases implicitly as referring to the celestial souls that are the causes of divine revelation. The connection between the epileptic and the celestial soul is clarified in the following passage:

> The heart is like a mirror, and the tablet (*al-lawḥ*) is like a mirror, yet between them is a veil. If the veil is withdrawn you see in the heart the pictures that are on the tablet. The veil is whatever keeps you occupied[55] and the heart is in this world occupied. Most of its occupation is to think about what sense perception produces for it. Most of its occupation is thinking (*al-tafakkur*) about what sense perception conveys to it. Thus, it is always occupied when it has sense perception. When sense perception is inactive during sleep or during an epileptic fit and when there is no other occupation inside itself, such as some corrupted mixture [of the humors], then maybe the heart sees some of the pictures that are written on the tablet.[56]

This passage bears numerous references to Avicennan teachings about prophecy. The imaginative faculty (*al-quwwa al-mutakhayyila*), for instance, can in ordinary people only connect to the celestial souls when the senses are not at work. There is also an implicit reference to a famous passage in al-Ghazālī's *Iḥyā' 'ulūm ad-dīn* about a contest between Greek and Chinese painters: in this passage, a king asks two groups of artists, one Chinese and one Byzantine-Greek (*rūmī*), each to paint one half of a chamber in order for him to judge whose work is superior. Each group working separately, they are separated by a veil and cannot see their competitors' efforts. When the veil that separates the chamber is lifted, the Greek painters reveal a vivid portrait of God's creation emblazoned using brilliant and shining colors. In contrast, the Chinese painters had simply polished their side so thoroughly that it perfectly mirrored the painting of the Greeks. The king is highly impressed by both groups. The Greek painters, so al-Ghazālī, represent the way of "the philosophers and the scholars"

54 Al-Ghazālī, *al-Qānūn al-kullī fī t-ta'wīl*, 15 / 100b / 7b–8a.

55 According to the edition. The two MSS have: "The veil is the occupation."

56 Al-Ghazālī, *al-Qānūn al-kullī fī t-ta'wīl*, 15 / 100b / 7b–8a.

(*al-ḥukamāʾ wa-l-ʿulāmāʾ*) who comprehend God by acquiring the sciences and obtained their "picture" (*naqsh*) within their souls, while the "friends of God" (*al-awliyāʾ*) – meaning the Sufis – perceive God through the manifestation of His splendor upon their polished hearts.[57] This parable appears in book 21 of the *Iḥyāʾ*. This book, *Explaining the Marvels of the Heart* (*Sharḥ ʿajāʾib al-qalb*) is the only work of al-Ghazālī mentioned in this letter, and it is certainly not wrong to use this letter in interpreting the parable. Like in the case of Sufi saints, the veil that is between the soul of the epileptic and the celestial tablet is withdrawn, which makes the epileptic have insights into the "unknown" (*al-ghayb*). He has privileged access to the celestial souls' knowledge.

5 Five Attitudes to the Relationship between Reason and Revelation

At the beginning of his answer to the inquirer's questions, al-Ghazālī promises a "universal rule" (*qānūn kullī*) about how to deal with cases of conflict between the outward sense (*ẓāhir*) of revelation and the results of a reasonable inquiry. Al-Ghazālī begins his response by stating how much he "dislikes plunging into these questions and giving answers. But since these requests may come again, I will mention a universal rule (*qānūn kullī*) that one can benefit from on this occasion."[58]

If we take al-Ghazālī by his word, then the "universal rule" is what comes right after this sentence and what is introduced by "... and I say ..." The text continues:

> At first glance and after a superficial examination [it appears] that there is a clash (*taṣādum*) between what reason dictates (*al-maʿqūl*) and what has been transmitted [in revelation] (*al-manqūl*). Those who have plunged into this question divide into [1] those who exaggerate in focusing on what has been transmitted (*al-manqūl*); [2] those who exaggerate in focusing on what reason dictates (*al-maʿqūl*); and [3] those in the middle, who wish to bring [reason and revelation] together and reconcile [them]. Those in the middle [again] divide into [3.1] those who make the dictates of reason (*al-maʿqūl*) fundamental and what is transmitted

57 Al-Ghazālī, *Iḥyāʾ ʿulūm ad-dīn*, 5 vols., Cairo: Muʾassasat al-Ḥalabī wa-Shurakāʾihi, 1387/1967–68, 3: 28–29. The story also appears in al-Ghazālī's *Mīzān al-ʿamal*, ed. Muḥyī d-dīn Ṣabrī l-Kurdī, Cairo: al-Maṭbaʿa al-ʿArabiyya, 1342 [1923], 37–8.

58 Al-Ghazālī, *al-Qānūn al-kullī fī t-taʾwīl*, 6 / 94a / 2b. See also Heer, "The Canons of Taʾwil," 48.

(*al-manqūl*) secondary and who do not pay much attention to research into the latter; [3.2] those who make what is transmitted fundamental and what is dictated by reason secondary and who do not pay much attention to research into the latter; and [3.3] those who make each of the two fundamental and who desire [or: strive][59] to combine the two and bring them together (*at-taʾlīf wa-t-talfīq baynahumā*). There are, therefore, five groups."[60]

On the following three pages al-Ghazālī describes these five groups without, however, identifying them by name.[61] Each of the groups represents a certain attitude towards reason and revelation that range between the extremes of a strict literalism on the one hand and a radical rationalism on the other. Regarding someone who adheres excessively to rationalism, there is agreement among Muslim scholars, al-Ghazālī adds, that such a rationalist – who dismisses any conflicting scriptural passage by describing it as an imagination (*taṣwīr*) of the prophet invented solely to benefit (*maṣlaḥa*) the masses (*ʿawāmm*) – is an unbeliever "who should have his head cut off."[62] The description of these two extreme groups is very much parallel to passages in al-Ghazālī's later *Fayṣal at-tafriqa*, where these two attitudes are identified with Aḥmad ibn Hanbal's followers and with the *falāsifa*.[63] Regarding the latter, al-Ghazālī repeats his earlier legal condemnation at the end of his *Tahāfut al-falāsifa*.[64] In between these two extremes are a more moderate group of rationalists, "who reject what they find difficult to interpret," and a more moderate group of literalists "who realize the clash between the dictates of reason and the outward meaning only in some fringe issues of the rational sciences." The fifth and last attitude, which, with regard to its combination of literalism and rationalism, lies right in the middle of these five groups, is that of al-Ghazālī himself. This group, which has found truth (*al-firqa al-muḥiqqa*), denies that there is opposition or contradiction (*taʿāruḍ*) between reason (*al-ʿaql*) and revelation (*ash-sharʿ*). Instead

59 The latter (*yasʿā*) in al-Kawtharī's edition. The two MSS from Istanbul have *yashūqu*, "desire."

60 Al-Ghazālī, *al-Qānūn al-kullī fī t-taʾwīl*, 6 / 94a–94b / 2b. My translation has adopted many suggestions in Nicholas Heer, "The Canons of Ta'wil," 48.

61 Al-Ghazālī, *al-Qānūn al-kullī fī t-taʾwīl*, 6–10 / 94a–97a / 2b–4b. This passage is available in an English translation in Heer, "The Canons of Ta'wil," 48–52.

62 Al-Ghazālī, *al-Qānūn al-kullī fī t-taʾwīl*, 7 / 95a / 3a. Heer, "The Canons of Ta'wil," 49.

63 Al-Ghazālī, *Fayṣal at-tafriqa*, 184, 192.

64 Al-Ghazālī, *The Incoherence of the Philosophers / Tahāfut al-falāsifa. A Parallel English-Arabic Text*, ed. and transl. Michael E. Marmura, 2nd. ed. (Provo [Utah]: Brigham Young Univ. Press, 2000), 226.

of taking extremes, they employ both reason and revelation as two important foundations (singl. *aṣl*) of their inquiry.[65]

Within his explanation of these five attitudes towards the conflict between reason and revelation, al-Ghazālī indicates that the question of which passages in revelation need to be interpreted allegorically depends on a proper distinction of what is (1) possible according to reason, (2) impossible according to reason, and what (3) reason cannot decide to be either possible or impossible.[66] Again that is a subject he later dealt with in his *Fayṣal at-tafriqa*, where he explains what is here just indicated.[67] Within this context of what is impossible according to reason, al-Ghazālī hints at some examples of doctrinal disputes between these five groups, regarding, for instance, the meaning of such words as "the above" (*al-fawq*) or "sitting upright" (*al-istiwāʾ*) when applied to God.

Al-Ghazālī's explanation of the attitude of the fifth group, that is to say, the one that has a correct position, leads him into three "recommendations" (*waṣāyā*, singl. *waṣiyya*). Two of these three "recommendations" will later be turned into independent books of al-Ghazālī. The first recommendation is simply an admission of ignorance and an expression of the *bi-lā-kayf* attitude of Ashʿarite *kalām*: one should not aspire to a complete understanding of revelation, inasmuch as some passages in revelation are simply incomprehensible and not meant to be interpreted by reason. This position is confirmed by the Qurʾānic declaration that "of knowledge, you have been given but little."[68]

The second recommendation expresses al-Ghazālī's rationalism most clearly: never deny the testimony of reason. Or, as al-Ghazālī puts it: "A [valid] rational demonstration is never wrong."[69] If reason is properly applied in a demonstrative argument – a *burhān* – then it cannot assert any falsehood. Reason is the witness for revelation through which the latter's truth is known. Revelation tells us about details that reason might not be able to prove, but reason is the character witness of the truth of revelation, without which the truth of revelation would not be accepted: "How can the truthfulness of a witness

65 Al-Ghazālī, *al-Qānūn al-kullī fī t-taʾwīl*, 9 / 97b / 4a. Heer, "The Canons of Ta'wil," 51

66 Al-Ghazālī, *al-Qānūn al-kullī fī t-taʾwīl*, 8 / 95b–96b / 3b–4a. Heer, "The Canons of Ta'wil," 50–51.

67 Al-Ghazālī, *Fayṣal at-tafriqa*, 187. I try to explain al-Ghazālī's ideas on this subject in my *Al-Ghazālī's Philosophical Theology*, 110–16.

68 Q 17:85.

69 Arab. "*lā yakdhibu burhānu l-ʿaqli aṣlan*"; al-Ghazālī, *al-Qānūn al-kullī fī t-taʾwīl*, 10 / 97a / 5a. Heer, "The Canons of Ta'wil," 52.

be known through the testimony of a character witness who is wrong?"[70] The character witness must be right in order to convince the court of the truthfulness of the chief witness in a trial. The chief witness (*ash-shāhid*) in this comparison is revelation, which informs us about things hidden from any other source of knowledge. The character witness (*muzakkī*) that testifies for the chief witness' truthfulness (*ṣidq*) is reason. The whole edifice of revealed religion, al-Ghazālī argues in this letter, rests on reason, and if reason were unreliable the reliability of revelation could not be established.

This recommendation will later be turned into his book *Fayṣal at-tafriqa*, where al-Ghazālī also deals with the rule that the conclusions of apodictic arguments or demonstrations (singl. *burhān*) must be accepted.[71] Nowhere, however, is he as blunt and as direct as in this letter. In his *Fayṣal at-tafriqa* he will stress the Ashʿarite principle that revelation must be interpreted allegorically whenever its outward sense clashes with the dictates of reason. There, he will also establish demonstrative reasoning in the Aristotlian sense of indubitable premises with correct syllogisms as the yardstick of reason. Yet, even in the *Fayṣal*, he does not declare that a demonstrative argument can never be wrong, although that is clearly implied.

Finally, the third recommendation is not to engage in allegorical interpretation (*taʾwīl*) when one is unsure about the intention (*murād*) of the revealed text. In cases where there are various opposing possibilities for what the text may mean, one should simply refrain from specifying any one of them. This recommendation will later also be turned into a book: in *Restraining the Ordinary People from the Science of Kalām* (*Iljām al-ʿawāmm ʿan ʿilm al-kalām*) al-Ghazālī gives very clear guidance to his scholar-colleagues as to what can and should be divulged about one's insight into the meaning of revelation and what should not. The principle that only well-established and very un-ambiguous interpretations should ever come over the lips of a scholar stands high upon that list.[72]

---

70 Arab. *"fa-kayfa yuʿrafu ṣidqu sh-shāhidi bi-tazkiyati l-muzakkī l-kādhib?" al-*Ghazālī, *al-Qānūn al-kullī fī t-taʾwīl*, 49 / 97b / 5a.

71 Al-Ghazālī, *Fayṣal at-tafriqa*, 188. See also Griffel, *Al-Ghazālī's Philosophical Theology*, 120–21.

72 In *Iljām al-ʿawāmm ʿan ʿilm al-kalām*, ed. Muḥammad M. al-Baghdādī (Beirut: Dār al-Kitāb al-ʿArabī 1406/1985), 53–86, al-Ghazālī formulates seven "duties" (singl. *waẓīfa*) contingent on all aiming at an understanding of passages in revelation where the *ẓāhir* is different from what reason mandates. Several of those duties reiterate the command to refrain from *taʾwīl* wherever one has doubt about what revelation refers to. See Griffel, *Al-Ghazālī's Philosophical Theology*, 266–68.

6 Verifying Revelation through Reason

In the middle part of the epistle, al-Ghazālī explains and also analyses five different attitudes that scholars have developed in regards to that relationship. Most interesting is, of course, the description of his own attitude, which comes up in two places, first, when he explains the fifth group of scholars and, second, when he puts forward his three recommendations. We have already pointed out that the second recommendation – that no demonstrative argument can be wrong – appears here in its most explicit form in al-Ghazālī's oeuvre. Yet, though not as explicitly stated, this teaching is at least implicitly expressed in other works, most importantly his *Fayṣal at-tafriqa*. In the description of the fifth group, however, al-Ghazālī does include a teaching that is truly novel, to the extent that it would be considered *bidʿa* ("heretical innovation") by some – or even many – of his peers within the Ashʿarite school.

The fifth group stands in the middle of the five attitudes and it "brings together the study of what reason dictates and what has been transmitted" from revelation.[73] Members of this group accept both the *maʿqūl* and the *manqūl* as foundations to their views and deny a conflict between these two. The underlying reason why these two do not conflict with one another is the fact that reason verifies revelation:

> Whoever says that reason (*ʿaql*) is not true also says that revelation is not true because it is only through reason that the truth of revelation (*ṣidq ash-sharʿ*) is known. Were it not for the truth of that reason (*ṣidq dhālika l-ʿaql*)[74] we would not know the difference between the true prophet and the false one (*al-mutanabbī*), nor between the person who speaks truth and the one who tells an untruth (*aṣ-ṣādiq wa-l-kādhib*).[75]

Al-Ghazālī justifies his rationalist attitude and the fact that he gives reason an equally central role as revelation because, he says, *only* reason can distinguish the true prophet from an imposter by judging whether his message is compatible with what reason dictates. Traditionally, Ashʿarite theologians verified the claims of a true prophet and distinguished him from an impostor

73 Arab. "*hiya al-firqa al-mutawassiṭa al-jāmiʿa bayna al-baḥth ʿan al-maʿqūl wa-l-manqūl*"; al-Ghazālī, *al-Qānūn al-kullī fī t-taʾwīl*, 9 / 96b / 4a. Heer, "The Canons of Ta'wil," 51.

74 According to MS Ayasofya 2194. The edition and the other MS have: "Were it not for the evidence of reason (*ṣidq dalīl al-ʿaql*) [...]."

75 Al-Ghazālī, *al-Qānūn al-kullī fī t-taʾwīl*, 9 / 96b / 4a–b. See also the slightly different Engl. trans. in Heer, "The Canons of Ta'wil," 51.

only through the acceptance of miracles performed in history and testified through an uninterrupted chain of tradition (*tawātur*). In early Ashʿarism up to al-Ghazālī only miracles could confirm prophecy and thus verify revelation. Any human attempt to distinguish prophet from impostor by judging his message, his moral rules, or his conduct assumes knowledge of what is true, false, right, or wrong prior to the revelation and it must therefore be dismissed. For early Ashʿarites up to the generation of al-Ghazālī, revealed religion rested on a prophetic miracle combined with a challenge to the Prophet's opponents which they cannot meet.[76]

We know that al-Ghazālī did differ from this position and did not hold that all prophecy must be established by miracles.[77] Though al-Ghazālī did not deny the existence of prophetic miracles, he describes them as a poor method for establishing something as important as revealed religion. As we have already learned, miracles can be easily confused with sorcery; as such, they are an unreliable criterion for the truth of revelation. In his *Ihyāʾ ʿulūm ad-dīn*, al-Ghazālī supports this assertion by recounting the story of the Golden Calf: "Everyone who became a believer by seeing a snake inadvertently became an unbeliever when he saw a calf,"[78] that is to say, all those Israelites who were convinced of Moses' prophethood by his miracles were also persuaded, by means of sorcery, to accept the false prophet who made them built the Golden Calf.[79] Thus, for al-Ghazālī, true prophecy cannot be established by miracles; too often people are mistaken, confusing genuine miracles with magic.

In his autobiography *al-Munqidh min aḍ-ḍalāl*, al-Ghazālī suggests a different criterion which he likens to Sufi practice. To begin, al-Ghazālī acknowledges that every human is endowed with a means to judge the claims of a prophet. That means is independent from the truth of revelation and is independent from any miracles that may have been performed. Here, in the *Munqidh*, this means not rational knowledge but "experience" (*tajriba*): reenacting revelation's ritual prescriptions, (for instance, during prayer or fasting in Ramadan) or reciting the revelatory text (i.e., the Qur'ān), provides a repeated and openly perceived positive effect on the soul. The kind of knowledge that al-Ghazālī describes in the *Munqidh* is theoretical knowledge about the effects of a prophet's work. The experience of that theoretical knowledge is, however described in practical terms:

76 Griffel, "Al-Ġazālī's Concept of Prophecy," 101–104.

77 Griffel, *Al-Ghazālī's Prophetical Theology*, 194–201.

78 Ibid., 197, see al-Ghazālī, *Iḥyāʾ*, 4: 315.

79 Q 20:83–98.

> If you have understood the meaning of prophecy and spent much time reflecting (*aktharta an-naẓar*) on the Qur'ān and the *akhbār*, you will acquire the necessary knowledge that Muhammad – God's blessings and peace be upon him – was on the highest level of prophecy. This is supported by the personal experience (*tajriba*) of what he says about the ritual duties and the effects they have on the purification of souls (lit. hearts, *qulūb*).[80]

We know that a revelation is true when studying it leads to the soul's experience of healing or improvement. It is the repeated experience of the prophet's healing work on one's soul, so to speak, that creates certainty about his prophecy. Here, in the *Munqidh*, rationality (*ʿaql*) is not named as a criterion for judging the truth of revelation, although the use of reflection (*naẓar*) in the quotation above may be a veiled hint at rationality. In the *Munqidh*, however, the stress is on experience (*tajriba*), and that is mostly the experience of religious practice. Al-Ghazālī calls this kind of experience *dhawq*, "tasting," and he connects it to what Sufis do and how they experience religion.

The position that we can distinguish a true prophet from an imposter by judging his message according to reason is a more radical rationalism than what al-Ghazālī suggests in his *al-Munqidh min aḍ-ḍalāl*. Why is it different? Did al-Ghazālī change his attitude between the year 490/1097 when he most likely wrote this epistle and 500/1106, when he wrote his autobiography? While this is not impossible, there is evidence that al-Ghazālī never changed his stance on this issue; indeed, there is evidence that his position in *al-Qānūn al-kullī fī t-taʾwīl* was his true position. The kind of verification he put forward in *al-Munqidh min aḍ-ḍalāl* may be a different representation of that position, one that aims at diminishing the role of reason and stressing the role of experience (*tajriba*). Apparently, al-Ghazālī presented his very rationalist position on the verification of prophecy in two ways: in the first, inscribed in a private letter to a personal student, he admitted to what can only, in the context of Ashʿarite theology, be regarded as a rationalist innovation; in the second, inscribed in an autobiography addressed to a wider audience, he expressed his view in terms that moderated its rationalist tone.

Evidence for this interpretation can be found in *The Correct Balance* (*al-Qisṭās al-mustaqīm*), unanimously accepted to be a late work written just before the *Munqidh* in the period shortly before al-Ghazālī's teaching activity at the Niẓāmiyya madrasa in Nishapur (c. 499/1106). Al-Ghazālī writes:

80 Al-Ghazālī, *al-Munqidh min aḍ-ḍalāl*, 43.

> Likewise, I gained belief in the truthfulness of Muhammad (*āmantu ana bi-ṣidqi Muḥammad*) – peace be upon him – and the truthfulness of Moses – peace be upon him – not by reason of the splitting of the moon and the changing of a stick into a serpent, for that way is open to much ambiguity and one should not rely on it. [...] Rather, I learned the balances [viz. syllogistic arguments] from the Qurʾān, and then I weighted by it all the [suggested] knowledge about God (*al-maʿārif al-ilāhiyya*), and about the states in the afterlife, about the punishment of the wicked and the reward of the obedient, just like I mention in [my] book *Jawāhir al-Qurʾān*, and I found all of this in agreement with what is in the Qurʾān and in the *akhbār*. Thus, I obtained certain knowledge (*tayaqqantu*) that Muhammad – peace be upon him – is truthful and that the Qurʾān is true (*ḥaqq*).[81]

Here, al-Ghazālī uses a terminology that he coined himself and that he explains elsewhere in *al-Qisṭās al-mustaqīm*. In that language, he explains that he scrutinized the available knowledge about God by means of, as he says, "the balances" (*al-mawāzīn*), a word that refers to the syllogistic method of logic. Using a rigid rational analysis, he was able to determine which teachings about God and the afterlife are true. Once the truth about those two subjects has been determined in such a rationalist way, al-Ghazālī compares it to divine revelation and found that it is in agreement (*muwāfaqa*) with what he found to be true through reason. This gave him certain knowledge that the Qurʾān is true divine revelation. This position is the same as the one in his letter to Abū Bakr ibn al-ʿArabī, where al-Ghazālī says that "it is only through reason (*ʿaql*) that the truth of revelation is known."

7 Conclusions

Al-Qānūn al-kullī fī t-taʾwīl is, despite its brevity, an important textual witness for our understanding of al-Ghazālī's attitude towards divine revelation. The text is closely related to his *Fayṣal at-tafriqa* yet it represents an earlier engagement with the strategy of allegorically interpreting revelation wherever its outward meaning (*ẓāhir*) conflicts with what is known from reason.[82] Here, al-Ghazālī takes a position that is much more rationalist than in the *Fayṣal*

81 Al-Ghazālī, *al-Qisṭās al-mustaqīm*, ed. Victor Chelhot, Beirut: Imprimerie Catholique, 1959, 81.

82 See fnn. 35, 41, 63.

and many of his other writings: "Would reason be wrong then perhaps it would also be wrong when it establishes [the truth] of revelation since it is through reason that we know [the truth] of revelation."[83] Revelation is verified by comparing its message with what is decisively known from reason. Passing the test of reason, the prophets' message should then be accepted as divine revelation. Such a view had never before been put forward by a theologian of the Ashʿarite school. That this truly was al-Ghazālī's position on this subject can be corroborated from comments in his other works, where this view is not explained but merely hinted at. The passage I have quoted from *al-Qisṭās al-mustaqīm* is one of the most conclusive. More detailed is a brief comment about reason and revelation in the introduction of his *Choice Essentials of the Science of the Principles* [*of Law*] (*al-Mustaṣfā fī ʿilm al-uṣūl*), a work also from his late period. There, al-Ghazālī says:

> Reason points towards the fact that the Prophet tells the truth; it then dismisses itself and commits itself to accept whatever is conveyed by the sayings of the prophets regarding [the subjects] of God and the Last Day, provided reason has no independent way of perceiving this and also doesn't judge it impossible.[84]

Another indication to this position is in al-Ghazālī's autobiography *al-Munqidh min aḍ-ḍalāl*. There, he says that if one has understood the meaning of prophecy and "spent much time reflecting on the Qurʾān and the *akhbār*" one will acquire necessary knowledge about Muhammad's prophecy.[85] "Reflecting" (*an-naẓar*) may well mean comparing the Qurʾān and the *ḥadīth* with what is known from reason. If so, it would hint to a teaching that al-Ghazālī never fully explained in any work other than this letter to one of his students. This latter remark in particular has confused many of his readers and triggered a number of comments in the field of Ghazālī studies.[86]

---

83 *"law khadhaba al-ʿaqlu fa-laʿallahu khadhaba fī ithbāti ash-sharʿi idh bihi ʿarafnā sh-sharʿ"*; al-Ghazālī, *al-Qānūn al-kullī fī t-taʾwīl*, 10 / 97a–98b / 5a. See also the Engl. transl. in Heer, "Al-Ghazali. The Canons of Ta'wil," 52.

84 Arab. *"al-ʿaql yadullu ʿalā ṣidq an-nabī"*; al-Ghazālī, *al-Mustaṣfā min ʿilm al-uṣūl*, ed. Ḥamza ibn Zuhayr Ḥāfiẓ, 4 vols. (Medina [Saudi Arabia]: al-Jāmiʿa al-Islāmiyya – Kulliyyat ash-Sharīʿa, 1413 [1992–93]), 1: 14.

85 See fn. 80 above.

86 See Duncan B. MacDonald, "The Life of al-Ghazzālī, with especial references to his religious experience and opinions," *Journal of the American Oriental Society*, 20 (1899): 71–132, esp. 96; Arend Th. van Leeuwen, *Ghazālī als Apologeet van de Islam* (Leiden: E. Ijdo, 1947) 95–98, 181; Vincenco M. Poggi, *Un classico della spiritualià musulmana* (Rome: Libreria

Here, in his letter to Abū Bakr ibn al-ʿArabī, al-Ghazālī explains the argument that underlies that comment. In a first step he claims that the results of a demonstrative argument (*burhān al-ʿaql*) cannot be but correct and true.[87] Secondly, what is established through demonstrative arguments functions as a character witness (*muzakkī*) for the truth of revelation.[88] Once reason has established that a certain revelation is truthful and trustworthy, that revelation is accepted in its entirety as a source of information on subjects where reason has nothing to say, such as God's attributes or the afterlife, for instance. The outline of this argument was already known from the later rationalist Ashʿarite Fakhr ad-Dīn ar-Rāzī. In his *Exalted Pursuits* (*al-Maṭālib al-ʿāliya*), his major work on theology, he says that the most advanced way to verify revelation is to compare it with what is known from reason. In a first step we establish through reasonable inquiry what is true (*ḥaqq*) in theoretical knowledge and what is right (*ṣawāb*) in practical knowledge. In a second step we study the claims of a certain prophet, "and if we find that his message includes a strong incitement for people to change from falsehood to truth, then we know that he is a true prophet and that one has to follow him.[89] Thus far it had been assumed that Fakhr ad-Dīn ar-Rāzī was the first Ashʿarite to use this method to verify revelation.[90] Now, we can say that al-Ghazālī preceded him in this.

This way of thinking about revelation is different both from earlier Ashʿarites and from the *falāsifa*. Earlier Ashʿarites would not have accepted that the divine message is verified by something as fallible and uncertain as human theoretical knowledge. Al-Ghazālī counters that with his acceptance of demonstration (*burhān*) as an infallible way to establish truth; here, he agrees

dell'Università Gregoriana, 1967): 242–245; George F. Hourani, "Ghazālī on the Ethics of Action," in: *Journal of the American Oriental Society*, 96 (1976): 69–88, esp. 87–88; Richard M. McCarthy in the notes to his English translation of al-Ghazālī, *Deliverance from Error* (Louisville [Kenn.]: Fons Vitae, 2000), 120; and Frank, *Al-Ghazālī and the Ashʿarite School*, 67–68.

87 See fn. 69 above.

88 See fn. 70 above.

89 This passage seems to be distorted in the standard edition of Fakhr ad-Dīn ar-Rāzī, *al-Maṭālib al-ʿāliya min al-ʿilm al-ilāhī*, ed Aḥmad Ḥijāzi as-Saqqā, 9 parts in 5 vols., Beirut: Dār al-Kitāb al-ʿArabī, 1987, 8: 103. A *lectio difficilior* is offered in an earlier part-edition of this work, published under the title *an-Nubuwwāt wa-mā yataʿallaq bihā*, ed. Aḥmad Ḥijāzi as-Saqqā, Cairo: Maktabat al-Kulliyya al-Azhariyya, 1985, 163. See also Fakhr ad-Dīn ar-Rāzī's short compendium *Maʿālim uṣūl ad-dīn*, ed. Ṭāhā ʿAbd ar-Raʾūf Saʿd, Cairo: al-Maktaba al-Azhariyya li-t-Turāth, 2004, 98–101. On these teachings of Fakhr ad-Dīn see Sabine Schmidtke, *The Theology of al-ʿAllāma al-Ḥillī*, Berlin: Klaus Schwarz, 1991, 151–2.

90 Griffel, "Al-Ghazālī's Concept of Prophecy," 104–13, 141.

with the *falāsifa*. Against the *falāsifa*, al-Ghazālī asserts that once reason has legitimated the truth of revelation, it is revelation that must be preferred in fields beyond the ken of the demonstrative method. That the prophetic message becomes a source of knowledge exceeding the demonstrative method is a notion the *falāsifa* would never have accepted. For *falāsifa* such as Ibn Sīnā or Ibn Rushd, who stood in the tradition of al-Fārābī, revelation is merely a different way of expressing the very same truth established by demonstrations. Revelation could never exceed reason and it cannot be accepted as a source of knowledge that is superior to apodeixis (*burhān*).

What, then, is the vaunted "universal rule" (*al-qānūn al-kullī*) regarding the practice of allegorically interpreting revelation? If we follow the words of al-Ghazālī's epistle, this rule is the insight that there is no clash (*taṣādum*) between reason and revelation, even though one may have such an impression ("at first glance and after a superficial examination").[91] It is best to accept both reason and revelation as foundations (singl. *aṣl*) of one's knowledge and to deny any opposition (*taʿāruḍ*) between the two. This is the most moderate of the five approaches to the question, bringing together (*jamaʿa*) reason and revelation. All these, however, are only theoretical statements. In terms of practical guidance about how to pursue one's allegorical interpretation (*taʾwīl*) of difficult passages in revelation, the universal rule consists of three recommendations (singl. *waṣiyya*): (1) show patience and do not aspire to achieve a complete understanding of divine revelation; (2) do not assume that the conclusion of a truly demonstrative argument could be wrong; and (3) do not engage in allegorically interpreting revelation wherever there are different possibilities of what the text may mean.

It should be noted that later in his *Fayṣal at-tafriqa* al-Ghazālī will again use the word "rule" in connection to allegorical interpretation. The "rule of allegorical interpretation" (*qānūn at-taʾwīl*) in that work is much more specific and consists in the principle that one can only engage in allegorical interpretation (*taʾwīl*) of a revealed text once a demonstrative argument (*burhān*) has proven that the outward meaning (*ẓāhir*) of a passage in revelation is impossible.[92] In that work, apodeixis (*burhān*) becomes the yardstick for engaging in allegorical interpretation. Here, in this brief epistle, apodeixis is the yardstick for

---

91 Arab. *"fī awwal an-naẓar wa-ẓāhir al-fikr"*, al-Ghazālī, *al-Qānūn al-kullī fī t-taʾwīl*, 6 / 94a / 2b. Heer, "The Canons of Ta'wil," 48.

92 al-Ghazālī, *Fayṣal at-tafriqa*, 184, 187. On the "rule of allegorical interpretation" (*Qānūn at-taʾwīl*) in the *Fayṣal* see Griffel, *al-Ghazālī's Phiosophical Theology*, 111–122 and idem, *Apostasie und Toleranz im Islam: Die Entwicklung zu al-Ġazālīs Urteil gegen die Philosophie und die Reaktionen der Philosophen*, Leiden: Brill 2000, 304–19, 333–5, 432–33, and 466–67.

verifying revelation. If one compares these two works, the short epistle circulating under the title *al-Qānūn al-kullī fī t-taʾwīl* from 490/1097 represents an earlier and less methodologically firm stage of thinking about *taʾwīl*. The rationalist background of both works, however, is the same and it is expressed clearer and more explicit here than in the *Fayṣal at-tafriqa*.

At last, we must return to the beginning of this chapter and ask whether Ibn Taymiyya is correct in claiming that "ar-Rāzī and his followers" considered the position that reason is the foundation (*aṣl*) of revelation to be a "universal rule." Ibn Taymiyya is both right and wrong about this: he is wrong when he implies that Fakhr ad-Dīn and al-Ghazālī call reason the foundation (*aṣl*) of revelation. Al-Ghazālī says that the best position about the conflict between reason and revelation is to make both reason *and* revelation "an important foundation."[93] Only the most radical group on the side of the rationalists, whom al-Ghazālī identifies with the *falāsifa*, adopts reason as the sole foundation of their inquiry. Ibn Taymiyya is also wrong when he implies that al-Ghazālī and Fakhr ad-Dīn ar-Rāzī believed that "reason contradicts [information that comes from the prophets]" (*al-ʿaql yuʿāriḍu [mā jāʾat bihi al-anbiyāʾ]*). Rather, in this epistle al-Ghazālī is keen to deny that there is opposition or contradiction (*taʿāruḍ*) between reason (*al-ʿaql*) and revelation (*ash-sharʿ*). Such opposition is only an impression; in reality (*ḥaqq^an^*) no such opposition exists.[94] Ibn Taymiyya is, therefore, probably wrong when he suggests that Fakhr ad-Dīn had said or implied that reason is the foundation of revelation, being privileged therefore to oppose it.

Still, there is a level where Ibn Taymiyya's accusations seem correct. All depends on what one means by "foundation" (*aṣl*) and there, the two parties have a different understanding. In this letter, al-Ghazālī uses *aṣl* to mean "principle source of information." He is right to say that the moderates – including, of course, him and his followers – use both reason and revelation as sources once the veracity of the latter has been established. Ibn Taymiyya's main accusation against his rationalist opponents in Muslim theology is that they see reason as the foundation of revelation. "Foundation" here means "principle means of verification." Ibn Taymiyya's opponents say that a rejection of reason would include a rejection of revelation: "Dismissing the foundation of a thing is dismissing the thing itself."[95] Al-Ghazālī and Fakhr ad-Dīn ar-Rāzī both believed that revelation is verified through reason and at least al-Ghazālī

93 *"al-firqatu [...] al-jāʿilatu kulla wāḥid^in^ minhumā aṣl^an^ muhimm^an^*; al-Ghazālī, *al-Qānūn al-kullī fī t-taʾwīl*, 9 / 97b / 4a. Heer, "Al-Ghazali. The Canons of Ta'wil," 51.

94 See fn. 65.

95 See fn. 2.

expressed explicitly that a rejection of reason would also lead to a rejection of revelation. Reason is the "character witness" of revelation, as al-Ghazālī puts it, and if reason could be wrong on anything, how could we assume that it is right when it testifies to the truth of revelation? "One who calls reason wrong also calls revelation wrong," al-Ghazālī says in this epistle, "because it is through reason that the truth of revelation is known."[96] This is the position that Ibn Taymiyya opposed and it seems clear that this is what he means with "reason being a foundation of revelation" (*al-ʿaql aṣl an-naql*). If the truth of revelation can only be known through reason, then reason is its foundation. This is how Ibn Taymiyya understood al-Ghazālī's letter to Abū Bakr ibn al-ʿArabī and this is why for him the "universal rule" is identical with the principle that "reason is the foundation of revelation."[97] He was right, however, only as long as one understands "foundation" (*aṣl*) to refer to the position that revelation is verified through reason. About Ibn Taymiyya's *Darʾ taʿāruḍ* we can now conclude: What triggered its writing was – according to its introductory passage – the view held by opponents of his such al-Ghazālī and Fakhr ad-Dīn ar-Rāzī that revelation is verified through reason and that the truth of revelation stand or falls with the truth of reason.

96 "*man kadhdhaba al-ʿaqla fa-qad kadhdhaba ash-sharʿa idh bi-l-ʿaqli ʿurifa ṣidqu ash-sharʿ*"; al-Ghazālī, *al-Qānūn al-kullī fī t-taʾwīl*, 9 / 96b / 4a–b. Heer, "Al-Ghazali. The Canons of Ta'wil," 51. See also fn. 75 and 83.

97 Ibn Taymiyya, *Darʿ taʿāruḍ*, 1: 4: "ar-Rāzī and his followers make this position to a universal rule".

CHAPTER 6

The Comedy of Reason

Strategies of Humour in al-Ghazālī

Eric Ormsby

For philosophers – let alone theologians – humour is no laughing matter. Indeed, as a contemporary scholar reminds us, laughter "is a serious subject."[1] True, there is Democritus of Abdera, known as "the laughing philosopher," about whom that ancient gossip Aelian (c.170–235 AD) wrote, "Democritus laughed at everyone and said they were all mad which led his fellow citizens to call him '*gelasīnus*.' "[2] But the laughter of Democritus leaves a bitter aftertaste: it springs from mockery. Of course, philosophers from Aristotle to Bergson have shown a conspicuous interest in laughter, that puzzling yet quintessentially human trait. In a solemn discussion of why we laugh when we are tickled, Aristotle says that one reason is that "human beings are the only animals that laugh"; in this sense, man is not "the rational" but "the laughing animal" (*zoīon gelastikon*).[3] Aristotle's interest, like that of most philosophers – Western as well as Islamic – is analytical and theoretical. What provokes laughter? What is its mechanism? Why do we laugh at some things and not others? Philosophers analyze humour but rarely incorporate it into their arguments or recognize it as a useful stratagem. According to Henri Bergson in *Le Rire*, his classic treatise of 1924, "laughter addresses itself to pure intelligence."[4] Bergson was doubtless unaware that his view had been anticipated in part by the Muslim philosopher Abū Sulaymān al-Manṭiqī as-Sijistānī several centuries earlier. As reported by Abū Ḥayyān at-Tawḥīdī, the philosopher held that laughter occurs when our articulate reason (*nuṭq*) collides with our innate "animality" (*ḥayawāniyya*).[5] A joke fills us with amazement (*taʿajjub*) and our reason struggles to understand

---

1 Geert Jan van Gelder, in his Introduction to Franz Rosenthal, *Humor in Early Islam*, Leiden, 2011, p. xiv.

2 Aelian, *Historical Miscellany* [*Varia Historia*], book 4, chapter 20, ed./tr. N. G. Wilson, Cambridge, MA: Harvard, 1997, p. 205.

3 *De partibus animalium*, 673a8 and 28.

4 Bergson, *Le Rire: Essai sur la signification du comique*, in *Oeuvres*, Paris, 1959, p. 389.

5 At-Tawḥīdī, *Muqābasāt*, Baghdad: Matbaʿat al-Irshād, 1970, p. 294; see also Rosenthal, *Humor in Early Islam*, p. 137.

 | DOI 10.1163/9789004290952_007

the source of this amazement while our animality directs our response to the joke either inwardly or outwardly, producing amusement or anger, as the case may be. This is one aspect of the "comedy of reason" in my title; humour stimulates reflection. But from another perspective, there seems to be something irrational, maybe even non-rational, about laughter; it not only "castigates morals," it castigates reason too. Certainly, philosophers as well as theologians avail themselves of irony, mockery and caricature of opposing views: think of the well-honed tactic of *reductio ad absurdum*. But such devices, like the laughter of Democritus, have harsh echoes; it is not that they aren't sometimes funny but that they are lacking in two of the profoundest aspects of true humour: gaiety and geniality. With the possible exceptions of Nietzsche and Kierkegaard, philosophers tend to be resolutely humourless. A book entitled *The Humour of Heidegger* would be a very slim volume indeed.

Here I want to argue that al-Ghazālī avails himself of the devices of humour in many of his works and that he does so strategically. I want to argue this in the teeth of the evidence, so to speak. For no one would embark upon a reading of the *Iḥyāʾ ʿulūm ad-dīn* or the *Tahāfut al-falāsifa* or others amongst his works with any expectation of rollicking high humour. Nevertheless, I find that al-Ghazālī does use humour quite consciously in several of his works. Sometimes this is humour of a conventional sort but at others, his humour is broader, subtler, infused with a rare geniality. To recognize this is to understand something fundamental about his work, and particularly about the *Iḥyāʾ ʿulūm ad-dīn*.

Over the past several years, while working on a translation of Book 36 of the *Iḥyāʾ*, the *Kitāb al-Maḥabba*, I was often struck by the variousness of al-Ghazālī's style; he moves from the sarcastic and even the smutty to the sublime; he can be harsh and hectoring at one moment, rapt and lyrical at the next. He displays a wide range of tones in his prose and he modulates those tones to surprising effect. In working closely with the Arabic text, my first concern was to get it right; that is, to understand what al-Ghazālī was actually saying and to convey that understanding in accurate English. But of course, accuracy is not simply a matter of fidelity to the meanings of the text nor is it mere lexical accuracy alone. There is an accuracy of style and tone that is essential to translation too. Too often, I think, we read al-Ghazālī for *what* he says but pay too little attention to *how* he says it. But can we really understand what he is saying if we are deaf to the tones in which he expresses himself? In this respect, I believe, al-Ghazālī stands squarely in the tradition of classical *adab* literature. His use of tales and anecdotes, his quips and rejoinders, his mischievous rhymes at the expense of opponents, his recourse to snippets of verse, the very playfulness of much of his discourse, links him to such predecessors as al-Jāḥiẓ, at-Tawḥīdī,

Miskawayh and ar-Rāghib al-Iṣfahānī as closely as the actual content of his thought links him to earlier philosophers, theologians and Sufi masters.[6] In working with my nose close to the text, as it were, I became increasingly aware of al-Ghazālī's frequent recourse to the stratagems and devices of the *udabāʾ*; and yet, I wasn't always sure that what struck me as humorous in certain passages was intended as such. Was I reading something into the text, or was I reading it in a way alien to the author's intentions?

These questions lead me to two obvious objections which I need to address before proceeding. First, humour is notorious for its elusiveness, its intrinsic slipperiness. While we can agree that man is the only animal that laughs – I leave aside the hyena, the kookaburra and the jackass as mere simulators of human laughter – we don't all agree on what makes us laugh. What one person finds hilarious another finds insipid, and the same is true of cultures. Georges Tamer has put this well in the Introduction to his fascinating collection *Humor in der arabischen Kultur* when he notes that the forms of humour

> vary in different ages and cultures, so that what seems to be a universal quality of humankind reveals itself in fact to be essentially determined by the specific individual and social contexts in which it occurs. To deal in a scholarly way with humour reveals itself, indeed, to be a humourless business.[7]

This is a genuine difficulty. The barriers of time and place appear insuperable. What provoked laughter in al-Ghazālī's Baghdad is likely to fall flat in 21st century Columbus, Ohio: nothing falls flatter than an ancient joke mummified by eons of incomprehension. On the other hand, certain jokes enjoy a lively immortality wherever they are told; like proverbs or folktales, they travel the world without benefit of passport. In his witty introduction to Franz Rosenthal's recently re-issued classic *Humor in Early Islam*, Geert Jan van Gelder remarks that "jokes and anecdotes have a habit of jumping like fleas, easily attaching themselves from one person to another."[8] One such flea has had an exceptionally

---

6 See Wilferd Madelung, "Ar-Rāġib al-Iṣfahānī und die Ethik al-Ġazālīs," in *Islamkundliche Abhandlungen: Fritz Meier zum sechzigsten Geburtstag*, ed. R. Gramlich, Wiesbaden: Franz Steiner Verlag, 1974, pp. 152–163, though this pioneering study deals with ethical rather than literary influence. To my knowledge no one has yet made a study of al-Ghazālī's prose style, let alone his literary and rhetorical flourishes.

7 Georges Tamer (ed.), *Humor in der arabischen Kultur/Humor in Arabic Culture*, Berlin: Walter de Gruyter, 2009, p. ix.

8 Franz Rosenthal, *Humor in Early Islam*, Leiden: Brill, 2011, p. xii.

long life and has sprung in myriad directions. In his *Notes and Essays on the 'West-Eastern Divan,'* that marvellous collection of lyric poems based on Arabic and Persian motifs written in his old age, Goethe re-tells a humorous anecdote about Nasreddin Hoja, whom he calls (with reference to Timur Lenk), "the dread world-destroyer's jocular companion in both tent and battlefield:"

> Timur was an ugly fellow; he was blind in one eye and lame in one foot. One day when Hoja was with him, Timur scratched his head – it was time for a haircut – and commanded that the barber be summoned. After he'd shaved his head the barber put a mirror in Timur's hand, as usual. Timur looked at himself in the mirror and found his appearance exceedingly ugly. He started to weep over this, Hoja began to weep too, and the two of them went on weeping for a few hours. At this one of Timur's companions comforted him and entertained him with strange tales so that he might forget everything. Timur stopped crying but Hoja did not; in fact, he began crying even more strongly. At last Timur said to Hoja: "Listen! I looked in the mirror and I saw how ugly I was. I was saddened by this because not only am I emperor but I also have great property and many slaves, and yet, I am so very ugly; that's why I cried. But why do you keep on crying without cease?" The Hoja replied, "If you looked in the mirror just once and at the sight of your own face you couldn't stand looking at yourself, what should we do who have to look at your face by day and by night? If we don't weep, who should?"[9]

The story was already centuries old when Goethe read and repeated it; the laughter it provokes still overleaps the centuries.

There is another possible objection to what I am proposing. Namely, how does al-Ghazālī himself view humour and more specifically, joking? Doesn't he tend to condemn it? In several passages, al-Ghazālī does condemn laughter and joking. In one such, he asks, "Why is joking called *muzāḥ*?" And he replies, with a play on the verb *azāḥa* – which means both "to jest" and "to drive away" – "Because it pulls the man who laughs away from the Truth."[10] In the same context he notes that "nobody laughs on his death-bed,"[11] for "laughter is a sign of

---

9 J. W. von Goethe, *West-östlicher Divan*, ed. Karl Richter, Munich: Hanser, 1998, pp. 209–210. [*Sämtliche Werke nach Epochen seines Schaffens*, vol. 11.1.2]

10 *Iḥyā'* (Beirut, 1996), 3: 137, -2: *li'annahu azāḥa ṣāḥibahu 'an al-ḥaqq* (which could also be read, of course, as "away from God").

11 Ibid.

heedlessness (*ghafla*) of the Hereafter."[12] Despite these strictures, which occur in his treatment of "the vices of the tongue" in the *Iḥyāʾ*, his final position is more nuanced than this might suggest; he fully recognizes that, as al-Jāḥiẓ had stated over two centuries before, in the opening pages of his *Book of Misers*, "laughter lies at the root of human nature" (*wa-huwa* [*aḍ-ḍaḥk*] *shayʾun fī aṣl aṭ-ṭibāʿ*).[13] Moreover, laughter, like weeping, comes ultimately from God; as proof, al-Jāḥiẓ cites the Qurān: "It is He who makes [one] laugh and weep and it is He who causes death and brings life."[14] Al-Jāḥiẓ draws out the implications of the striking chiasmus of this verse by noting that God "put laughter opposite life and weeping opposite death."[15]

With regard to joking or banter (*muṭāyaba*), al-Ghazālī writes, "When gaiety (*inbisāṭ*) and goodness of heart are present, joking and bantering are not forbidden. But know that what *is* forbidden is excessiveness (*ifrāṭ*) or persistence (*mudāwama*) [i.e., in jocularity]. Persistence involves a preoccupation with playfulness and jest and though playfulness is licit, persistence in it is reprehensible. Excess, on the other hand, produces too much laughter. Too much laughter kills the heart and incites resentment under certain circumstances."[16] (Interestingly enough, Bergson held a similar view, remarking that "in the end, to produce its complete effect, the comical requires something like a momentary anaesthesia of the heart.")[17]

Al-Ghazālī's reflections on joking and laughter stem from an ethical and juridical perspective. How, for example, he asks, does laughter relate to the Sunna of the Prophet? Now we know on the authority of certain traditions that the Prophet not only laughed but joked and indeed, played practical jokes. One of the best-known of these occurred when he informed an elderly woman that old women would not be allowed into paradise; she was upset by this, naturally enough, but then the Prophet quoted Qur'ān 56:35 which states that all the women in paradise will be virgins (and hence young) again.[18] Moreover, according to one report, the Prophet "used to laugh until his back teeth were

---

12 Ibid.

13 Al-Jāhiẓ, *Kitāb al-Bukhalāʾ* (Beirut, 1991), 1:28; tr. C. Pellat, *The Life and Works of Jāḥiẓ*, Berkeley: University of California Press, 1969, p. 238.

14 *Wa-annahu huwa aḍḥaka wa-abkā wa-annahu huwa amāta wa-aḥyā*; Q: 53:44.

15 *Kitāb al-Bukhalāʾ*, 1: 28.

16 *Iḥyāʾ*, 3:137 (*wa-kathrat aḍ-ḍaḥk tumīt al-qalb*).

17 Bergson, *Le Rire*, p. 389.

18 Rosenthal, *Humor in Early Islam*, pp. 5–6.

visible."[19] In several hadiths we are told that "the Emissary of God smiled and laughed" (*fa-tabassama rasūl Allāh ḍāḥik^an*).[20] Al-Ghazālī gives the following telling tradition: "The Emissary of God saw Ṣuhayb eating dates when one of his eyes was infected. He asked, 'Do you eat dates when you have an eye infection?' He said, 'O Emissary of God, I eat only on the other side,' meaning on the sound side of his face, and the Emissary of God laughed."[21] One of his Companions remarked that "he had never seen anyone who smiled as much as the Prophet did."[22] To the question as to why laughter may be reprehensible, since we know that the Prophet and his Companions laughed and joked, al-Ghazālī replies:

> If you can do what the Prophet and his Companions did – namely, to joke but to speak only the truth, not to wound the heart nor to be excessive in joking, and to limit it to infrequent occasions, then nothing prevents you from doing so. But it is a great mistake for a man to set about joking as a way of life or to go on and on with it and overdo it, and then excuse himself by clinging to the behaviour of the Prophet.[23]

The notion that joking should "speak only the truth" is important; it lies at the heart of al-Ghazālī's own use of humour.[24] In his discussion of the faults of the tongue, al-Ghazālī lists the criteria for "permissible jocularity" (*muzāḥ mashrūʿ*). First, the joke must be far from falsehood; when the Prophet said to Anas, "O you with the two ears!" (*yā dhā l-udhunayni!*), it was both gently amusing and incontrovertibly true. Second, a joke should neither be exaggerated nor

19 *Iḥyāʾ*, 2:398–99; 3:137. See Ulrich Marzolph, *Arabia ridens*, Frankfurt, 1992, vol. 1, p. 29; cf. also R. Sellheim, "Das Lächeln des Propheten" in *Festschrift A. Jensen*, Munich, 1964, pp. 621–30.

20 Cited in Ludwig Ammann, *Vorbild und Vernunft: Die Regelung von Lachen und Scherzen im mittelalterlichen Islam*, Hildesheim: George Olms, 1993, p. 40, on the authority of both Abū Dāwūd and A.b. Ḥanbal.

21 *Iḥyāʾ*, 2:22; tr. D. Johnson-Davies. *On the Manners relating to Eating*, Cambridge: Islamic Texts Society, 2000, p. 49.

22 Ammann, *Vorbild und Vernunft*, p. 42. See *Iḥyāʾ*, 2:398.

23 *Iḥyāʾ*, 3:138; cf. also Zabīdī, *Itḥāf*, 7:948.

24 Al-Ghazālī may have taken this precept in its particular formulation from Miskawayh, a known influence; see the latter's *Tahdhīb al-akhlāq*, ed. C. Zurayq, Beirut: American University of Beirut Press, 1966, p. 195 and especially, p. 198 where we read that "the Emissary of God joked but he spoke only the truth." In the same passage, Miskawayh lists joking (together with mockery, *istihzāʾ*) as one of the provocations to anger and sees it as an occasional *casus belli*.

long-drawn-out, a stricture already enunciated by al-Jāḥiẓ.[25] Third, a joke must not cause bad feeling or enmity; elsewhere, in his *Mīzān al-ʿamal*, al-Ghazālī lists unkind jokes as one of the main causes of anger.[26] Fourth, a joke must neither intimidate nor frighten. Fifth, all bawdiness must be avoided. Finally, sixth, a joke should be expressed in fine words; or, as al-Ghazālī, puts it, in friendly words and well-meaning expressions.[27]

Here matters of decorum are intertwined with ethical concerns. If most writers on the subject condemn excess, and especially that boisterous horse-laughter known as *qahqaha* in Arabic,[28] al-Ghazālī stands out for his insistence on truthfulness in jest. This criterion guides his practice. Let me now offer a few examples.

Irony

Al-Ghazālī often avails himself of irony for humorous effect, especially at the expense of doctors and most especially, of the *ʿulamāʾ*;[29] religious scholars are recurrent objects of scorn in the *Iḥyāʾ* and in other works. In the *Bidāyat al-hidāya*, for example, he invokes a *ḥadīth* in which the Prophet says that he is more apprehensive about the *ʿulamāʾ as-sūʾ*, "the scholars of wickedness," than he is about Dajjāl himself.[30] Al-Ghazālī seldom misses an opportunity to expose such scholars to gibes, sideswipes, and caustic dismissals.[31] In the

25 Al-Jāḥiẓ, *Kitāb al-Bukhalāʾ*, 1:28.

26 *Mīzān al-ʿamal*, ed. S. Dunyā, Cairo, Dār al-Maʿārif al-Miṣriyya, 1964, p. 322; tr. ʿAbd-Elṣamad ʿAbd-Elḥamīd Elschazlī, *Das Kriterium des Handelns*, Darmstadt: Wissenschaftliche Buchgesellschaft, 2006, p. 179.

27 For an excellent analysis, see Birgit Krawietz, "Verstehen Sie Spaß? Ernsthafte Anmerkungen zur schariat-rechtlichen Dimensionen des Scherzens," in Tamer (ed.), *Humor in der arabischen Kultur/Humor in Arabic Culture*, pp. 29–47, esp. p. 38. See *Iḥyāʾ*, 2:325 and 3:138.

28 On this, see Ammann, *Vorbild und Vernunft*, p. 131.

29 James Montgomery suggests that "irony" may be best rendered in Arabic by *muzāḥ*, the word I have translated here as "joking." See his "Al-Jāḥiẓ on Jest and Earnest" in Tamer (ed.), p. 233.

30 *Bidāyat al-hidāya* [printed on the margins of *Minhāj al-ʿĀbidīn*, Cairo, 1337], p. 5, *line*-2.

31 For an especially stinging example, see his comments on the *fuqahāʾ* in his *Fayṣal al-tafriqa* where he accuses them of unbridled appetite, fawning, money-grubbing, sucking up to the rich and powerful and an obsession with devising legal subterfuges; he concludes by noting that "all they possess of the religious sciences is knowledge of such things as the rules of ritual purity and whether or not water distilled from saffron can be

following example, he puts a wry twist on the fault known as *ghafla*, "heedlessness" or perhaps better, "slovenly complacency," which he elsewhere denounces roundly. In explaining why it is impermissible to share mystical knowledge with ordinary people – most of whom he says are "like the baffled man about whom the saying was coined, 'When he is mounted on his donkey, he keeps looking for his donkey' "[32] – he states:

> If people were to share in [mystical knowledge], the world would go to ruin. Wisdom requires that heedlessness exist for the world to thrive. If all people were to eat only permitted food for 40 days, the world would fall apart because of their austerity; markets, not to mention livelihoods, would be ruined. Even more, if religious scholars were to eat nothing but permitted foods, they would become occupied only with themselves; their tongues and their feet would grind to a halt and cease from much that they do.[33]

On one level, of course, this is sheer common sense; in regard to the religious scholars, however, the irony seems to me unmistakable. The very continuance of the world depends on their heedlessness.

Al-Ghazālī often uses the example of sexual impotence to ironic effect. Those who cannot experience the truth through "taste" (*dhawq*) are like the impotent man who cannot appreciate the pleasures of sexual intercourse and so denies them. Al-Ghazālī draws homely comparisons to make this point and again, the effect is gently humorous.

> To assert to young boys that the pleasures of sexual intercourse are superior to those of playing with a polo stick is impossible, just as it is to assert to the impotent that sexual pleasure is superior to the pleasure of sniffing violets; the impotent man has lost the ability by which he could perceive this pleasure. But he who is unimpaired by impotence and who possesses an intact sense of smell perceives the difference between the

used for ritual purification;" in Sherman A. Jackson (tr.), *On the Boundaries of Theological Tolerance in Islam*, Oxford: Oxford University Press, 2002, pp. 87–88.

32 *Iḥyāʾ*, 4:340; tr. E. Ormsby, *Love, Longing, Intimacy and Contentment: Kitāb al-Maḥabba wa'l-shawq wa'l-uns wa'l-riḍā. Book XXXVI of The Revival of the Religious Sciences: Iḥyāʾ ʿulūm al-dīn*, Cambridge: Islamic Texts Society, 2011, p. 87.

33 *Iḥyāʾ*, 4:355; tr. Ormsby, *Love, Longing, Intimacy and Contentment*, p. 126.

> two pleasures. On this there is nothing to say but: He who has tasted knows (*man dhāqa ʿarafa*).[34]

The introduction of the polo stick and the sniffing of violets imparts a sly humour to what is otherwise a serious point. In the late work *Ayyuhā l-walad*, he is much blunter:

> An impotent man wrote to a friend of his to tell him what the pleasure of sex was like. So [the friend] wrote back to him, "O so-and-so, I thought you were just impotent! Now I know that you are impotent *and* stupid.

The friend's rejoinder is funny but, in keeping with al-Ghazālī's criterion of truthfulness in jest, it has a serious point. As he goes on to explain, "This pleasure has to do with direct experience – if you attain it you know it – otherwise the description of it is not furnished through talking and writing![35]

Sufi Humour

Like his Sufi predecessors such as Abū Ṭālib al-Makkī or al-Qushayrī, from whom he took so much, al-Ghazālī likes to use tales and anecdotes to reinforce his arguments; quite often these are blithely facetious. This is one facet of his various stratagems of persuasion; after all, a funny story, like a good joke, sticks in the mind. Many of these anecdotes exemplify a peculiar Sufi humour, hard to define but quite unmistakable; they are at once droll and paradoxical, and they stimulate reflection. Henry Corbin has suggested that such Sufi humour represents an attempt to establish a certain distance from the self.[36] It is part of a discipline of detachment.

Out of many possible examples, consider the following apologue by Farīd ad-Dīn ʿAṭṭār in Edward Fitzgerald's whimsical translation:

> A fellow all his life lived hoarding gold,
> And dying, hoarded left it. And behold,
> One night his son saw peering through the house

34 *Iḥyāʾ*, 4:327; ibid., p. 49.

35 al-Ghazālī, *Ayyuhā l-walad*, tr. Tobias Mayer, Cambridge: Islamic Texts Society, 2005, p. 24.

36 H. Corbin, "Mystique et humour chez Sohravardī" in *Collected Papers on Islamic Philosophy and Mysticism*, ed. M. Mohaghegh and H. Landolt, Tehran; Montreal: The Institute of Islamic Studies, McGill University, 1971, pp. 16–38, esp. pp. 26–27.

A man, with yet the semblance of a mouse,
Watching a crevice in the wall – and cried –
"My Father?" "Yes," the Musulman replied,
"Thy Father!" "But why watching thus?" "For fear
Lest any smell my treasure buried here."
"But wherefore, Sir, so metamousified?"
"Because, my Son, such is the true outside
Of the inner soul by which I lived and died."[37]

Fitzgerald has caught the essential humour of the fable by his witty coinage "metamousified," which, needless to say, exists not in the words of the original but in its inner spirit. In keeping with al-Ghazālī's stricture on truthfulness in jest, it uses humour to deliver a serious truth.

As a further illustration, closer to home, consider the following little tales about Abū Saʿīd b. Abī l-Khayr (d. 1049/440), a Khorasanian saint of the previous generation whom al-Ghazālī often quotes. Once a man said to Abū Saʿīd, "I saw your disciple So-and-So on the road last night and he was blind drunk!" The saint replied, "Praise be to God! At least he was on the road." Again, in later life he became quite fat, a fact which exposed him to criticism from grimmer – and thinner – colleagues. One of them said to him, "Your throat is so thick that it hardly fits through your collar!" Abū Saʿīd replied, "To me it seems even more remarkable that my neck, thanks to all that God has bestowed on me, fits at all in the frame of the seven heavens!"[38] This reply contains the characteristic elements of "Sufi humour": it is at once exuberant and self-mocking; yet, while it expresses genuine gratitude to God, it is slyly self-aggrandizing. It uses humour to make a complex and paradoxical point. (As Fritz Meier has shown, for this saint – known for his expansive cheerfulness[39] – jubilance and corpulence were intimately conjoined.)

Al-Ghazālī shares much of this geniality with his Khorasanian countryman. But his humour can also be harsh. It is significant, I think, that he turns

37 Edward Fitgerald, *Selected Works*, ed. Joanna Richardson, London: Rupert Hart-Davis, 1962, pp. 287–288. For the original Persian, see *Manṭiq al-ṭayr*, ed. Ṣādiq Gawharīn, Tehran, 1978, pp. 57–58, and for a more literal translation, *The Speech of the Birds: Concerning Migration to the Real*, tr. Peter Avery, Cambridge: The Islamic Texts Society, 1998, pp. 94–95. For a brilliant modern verse translation, see Dick Davis and Afkham Darbandi (trs.), *The Conference of the Birds*, Penguin, 1984, p. 49.

38 Fritz Meier, *Abū Saʿīd-i Abū l-Ḫayr (357–440/967–1049): Wirklichkeit und Legende*, Leiden; Tehran: Brill, 1976, p. 271.

39 Ibid., p. 136 (He is *shādhvārī*). For further discussion, see also pp. 270–275.

to anecdote when he wishes to be most scathing. Thus, on the subject of Baghdad, he quotes the Sufi master Ibn al-Mubārak (d. 181/797–8). When asked "what is your opinion of Baghdad?" that saint exclaimed, "There I saw only raging policemen and anxious businessmen and baffled reciters of the Qur'ān." Again, when Fuḍayl ibn ʿIyāḍ (d. 187/803/4) asked a visiting Sufi where he lived and the man replied, "Baghdad," Fuḍayl "averted his face and said, "When we ask him where he dwells, he answers, 'In the nest of darkness.' " Even stronger is the statement al-Ghazālī cites by Bishr ibn al-Ḥārith (d. 226 or 7/840 or 841) who declared, "Someone who worships God in Baghdad is like one who worships him in the toilet."[40]

It is possible that such denunciations of Baghdad, which al-Ghazālī obviously relishes, may represent an oblique, retrospective justification for his own abrupt departure from that city after his 'conversion' to the Sufi way. But there are other anecdotes which he seems to include purely for their entertainment value, though even these have a serious underlying point. For example:

> Of Junayd it is related that he said, "Our master Sarī [as-Saqaṭi] was sick and we could neither find a remedy for his illness, nor could we discover its cause. We were told of a clever doctor and so we took a vial of Sarī's urine to him. The doctor looked at it again and again for a long time and then he said, "I see that this is the urine of a man in love." Junayd went on, "I was stunned. I fell into a faint and the vial dropped from my hand. I went back to Sarī and told him what had happened. He smiled and said (of the doctor), 'What a sharp-eyed son-of-a-bitch!' " [*qātalahu Allāhu mā abṣarahu!*] I said, "O Master, does love show even in the urine?" He replied, 'Yes.' "[41]

Here is one more – one of many, I should say – which al-Ghazālī relates in Book XI of the *Iḥyā'* in a discussion of table manners, again, I think, simply to amuse (though it too makes a serious point):

> Abū Wā'il said, 'I went with a friend of mine to visit Salmān [al-Fārisī] and he presented us with barley bread and coarsely ground salt. My friend said, 'If there were some wild thyme in this salt, it would be tastier.'

40 For these anecdotes, see *Iḥyā'*, 4:374; tr. Ormsby, *Love, Longing, Intimacy and Contentment*, pp. 175–176.

41 *Iḥyā'*, 4:356; ibid., p. 129. For the use of urine in diagnosis, see Peter E. Pormann and Emilie Savage-Smith, *Medieval Islamic Medicine*, Edinburgh: Edinburgh University Press, 2007, p. 55, and, for a fraudulent such diagnosis, p. 92.

> Salmān went out and pawned his ablution bowl and brought some wild thyme. When we had eaten my friend said, 'Praise be to God who has made us content with what we've been provided.' Salmān said, 'Had you been content with what had been provided, my ablution bowl would not be in the pawnshop.'[42]

Such charming tales, little more than jokes in many cases, are nevertheless important because they illustrate a fundamental characteristic not only of Sufi humour but of al-Ghazālī's own form of Sufism. They are characterized by that same gaiety – that *inbisāṭ* – which typifies the practice of such earlier masters as Abū Saʿīd b. Abī l-Khayr. And I would argue that they constitute an essential aspect of the *Iḥyāʾ*. They are an intrinsic part of its pervasive and thoroughgoing humanity.

This light-heartedness finds its warrant in the fact that, as al-Ghazālī tells us, God Himself is given to laughter. Al-Qushayrī, one of his masters, had declared that "God's laughter is the manifestation of His beneficence."[43] Thanks to Georges Tamer, we know that, improbably enough, there is humour in the Qurʾān.[44] In the *Kitāb al-Maḥabba*, al-Ghazālī takes this further in one of the tales he inserts about Burkh al-Aswad, the black slave who is part of that company of 'holy fools' out of whose mouths wisdom comes in the form of jokes and gibes and boisterous wrangles with God.[45]

During a drought, Moses asks Burkh to beseech God for rain. Burkh rebukes God for withholding the rains and says, "What's this that You are doing? Is this what You call mildness? Whatever are You thinking? Are you short on springs of water? Have the winds refused to obey You? Are Your supplies exhausted?... You created compassion and commanded kindness. Will You show us that now You are hindered?" Burkh went on in this vein until the rains came pouring down and "drenched the Israelites" and in less than a day the grass sprang up to their knees. Moses was irritated with Burkh but God revealed to him, "Burkh makes me laugh three times a day."[46]

---

42 *Iḥyāʾ*, 2:13; D. Johnson-Davies, *On the Manners relating to Eating*, p. 25.

43 Qushayrī, *Risāla*, 404; cited in Ammann, *Vorbild und Vernunft*, p. 47.

44 G. Tamer, "The Qurʾān and Humor," in Tamer (ed.), *Humor in der arabischen Kultur/Humor in Arabic Culture*, pp. 3–28; cf. also Mustansir Mir, "Humor in the Qurʾān," *The Muslim World*, 81:3–4 (October 1991), pp. 179–193.

45 See H. Ritter, *The Ocean of the Soul*, Leiden: Brill, 2003, pp. 165–187, for a thorough, and hilarious, account; on Burkh in particular, see pp. 538 and 584.

46 *Iḥyaʾ*, 4:359; tr. Ormsby, *Love, Longing, Intimacy and Contentment*, p. 139. The anecdote is also given in Ritter, *The Ocean of the Soul*, p. 584 (citing al-Makkī, *Qūt al-qulūb*, 2:65–66, where al-Ghazālī no doubt found it).

Causality and Caricature

As a final example of al-Ghazālī's use of humour, this time at the expense of the contortions of reason itself, I want to offer a few comments on the notorious 17th chapter of the *Tahāfut al-falāsifa* in which he rejects – or appears to reject – natural causation. As is well known, he opens this chapter with a blatant denial of cause and effect, adducing a series of examples which seem to fly in the face of common sense. Cotton burns when touched by a flame, death follows decapitation, eating and drinking satisfy hunger and quench thirst, and so on. Such phenomena merely coincide, he claims, they are not causally linked. Fire burns cotton, and cotton is consumed, not because of some intrinsic quality in either substance but because such is God's "habit" or "custom" (*ʿāda*).

This seems straightforward but in fact, it is not. For as he writes in the 35th Book of the *Iḥyāʾ* (written not long after the *Tahāfut*):

> If you were to wait for God Most High to create satiety in you without bread, or to create in bread a motion towards you, or to enjoin an angel to chew it for you and see that it reaches your stomach – that would simply display your ignorance of the practice of God Most High.[47]

Here too, in the notion of an angel chewing your bread for you, we see the characteristic Ghazalian sense of irony in play.

In pursuing his argument, ostensibly in defence of the Ashʿarite denial of secondary causality, al-Ghazālī introduces a curious counter-argument which is as surprising as it is comical. It represents a caricature of his own presumed Ashʿarite position. Moreover, it is an extravagant elaboration – virtually, a lampooning – of the very concept of "intellectual admissibility" (*tajwīz ʿaqlī*) – the notion that whatever can be imagined can exist – which he had espoused earlier in such Ashʿarite doctrinal works as *al-Iqtiṣād fī l-iʿtiqād*.[48] To deny cause

---

47 *Iḥyāʾ*, 4:282; tr. Richard Gramlich, *Muḥammad al-Ġazzālīs Lehre von den Stufen zur Gottesliebe*, Wiesbaden: Franz Steiner Verlag, 1984, pp. 565–566; tr. D. Burrell, *Faith in Divine Unity and Trust in Divine Providence*, Louisville: Fons Vitae, 2001, p. 74.

48 For a famous critique of this notion, see Maimonides, *The Guide of the Perplexed*, tr. S. Pines, Chicago: University of Chicago Press, 1963, vol. 1, pp. 206–209 [113a–114b]: "They [i.e., the Mutakallimūn] are of the opinion that everything that may be imagined is an admissible notion for the intellect ... They also say with regard to all things that are existent and perceptible that supposing anything among them should be bigger than it is or smaller or different from what it is in shape or place – should a human individual, for instance, have the size of a big mountain having many summits overtopping the air, or should there exist an elephant having the size of a flea, or a flea having the size of an

and effect is to inundate existence with bizarre and patternless events on the grounds that if they are conceivable, they are also possible. It is also, as Ibn Rushd argued in his rebuttal of al-Ghazālī, an invalidation of the intellect itself: "He who denies causes must deny the intellect [...] Denial of cause implies the denial of knowledge, and denial of knowledge implies that nothing in this world can really be known."[49] This, however, is just the sort of wildly "unknowable" world that al-Ghazālī had already presented in his *Tahāfut al-falāsifa*:

> If someone leaves a book in the house, let him allow as possible its change on his returning home into a beardless slave boy – intelligent, busy with his tasks – or into an animal; or if he leaves a boy in the house, let him allow the possibility of his changing into a dog; or if he leaves ashes, the possibility of its change into musk; and let him allow the possibility of stone changing into gold and gold into stone. If asked about any of this, he ought to say: 'I don't know what's in the house at the moment. All I know is that I left a book in the house but maybe now it's a horse which has fouled my library with its piss and dung, and I've left a jar of water in the house too, but it may have turned into an apple tree by now. God is capable of everything; it isn't necessary for a horse to be created from sperm or a tree from a seed. In fact, it isn't necessary for either of them to be created from anything. Maybe God has created things that didn't exist before.' Moreover, if such a person looks at somebody he has just seen and is asked whether such a person is a creature that was born, let him hesitate and say that it's not impossible that some fruit in the marketplace has turned into a human. For God has power over every possible thing, and this thing is possible.[50]

This is funny, and deliberately so; it has a Marx Brothers zaniness. It is a witty caricature of the Ashʿarite position, put in the mouth of a critic of that school. In one sense, of course, it is simply the sort of *reductio ad absurdum* of the Ashʿarite position which a proponent of causality might make, though boisterously exaggerated for effect; but in another sense, it is a mockery of such

elephant – all such differences would be admissible from the point of view of the intellect" (p. 206).

49 Ibn Rushd, *Tahāfut al-Tahāfut*, tr. S. Van den Bergh, London: Gibb Memorial Trust, 1954, vol. 1, p. 319.

50 *Tahāfut al-falāsifa*, ed./tr. M. Marmura as *The Incoherence of the Philosophers*, Provo: Brigham Young University Press, 1997, pp. 173–74 (modified). For a longer discussion of this passage, see my *Ghazālī*, Oxford: One World, 2008, pp. 76–86.

critics, since we all know that the world does not proceed in this topsy-turvy fashion. For all practical purposes, God's 'custom' is as dependable as cause and effect. But it seems to me too that in a sly way, al-Ghazālī's pre-emptive parody of his own supposed position is also meant to demonstrate that neither position can be proved by reason alone. Though al-Ghazālī was no proponent of "the equipollence of proofs" (*takāfuʾ al-adilla*),[51] his argument here appears to lead to such a suspended conclusion. Reason cannot establish to a certainty that what appears to be secondary cause and effect is not simply the working of God's "habit," but neither can reason prove that the world operates in accord with divine habit. Rather, something beyond reason, some meta-reason, is required to discern the true nature of creation. The passage parodies the presumptions of human reason taken to the extreme and humour is the vehicle of that parody. Al-Ghazālī uses the surprise of humour, the shock of a joke, both to satirize reason and to startle it awake.

Conclusion

Al-Ghazālī's use of humour in its various guises is but one facet of the profound humanity of his work, and of the *Iḥyāʾ* in particular. The *Iḥyāʾ* begins with the *Book of Knowledge* and progresses through all aspects of human life from daily ritual obligations, through ethics and manners, destroying vices and saving virtues, to the deathbed itself; it is no exaggeration to say of it that "all human life is here." For al-Ghazālī no detail of human life is too slight or too negligible to be drawn into a forceful analogy. He was a keen observer of the human scene. Whether he speaks of chess – of which he remarks wryly that those who love the game "never shut up about it" – or of polo or of the dealings of the marketplace or of the delights of sexual pleasure – a pleasure, he tells us, which prefigures those of paradise – he is alert to the humdrum complexities of human life. His tenderness in speaking of children, whose interests and games he often mentions, is one of the most moving aspects of this humanity. Out of many examples, let me mention just one. In speaking of the "signs of love," he uses this example:

> When a boy has set his heart on something, he will not let go of it; if it is taken from him, he weeps and screams until it is given back to him. When

51 On this theological position, ultimately a legacy of the Stoic 'ισοσθένεια των λόγων, see J. van Ess, *Die Erkenntnislehre des ʿAḍudaddīn al-Īcī*, Wiesbaden: Franz Steiner Verlag, 1966, pp. 221–229.

> he goes to sleep he takes it with him inside his clothes. When he wakes, he returns to it and holds it tight. Whenever he has to part with it, he cries; whenever he finds it again, he laughs. Whoever fights him over it he hates; whoever gives it to him he loves.[52]

No one who has lived with a small child and his favourite toy can doubt that this passage is based on personal observation. It is a tender, a genial, observation, employed for a higher purpose but nonetheless, profoundly human. Such instances of affectionate regard, of humour in its broadest and most amiable aspect, are strewn throughout the *Iḥyāʾ*. They represent one of the many and varied tones which al-Ghazālī employs and which make his prose so often memorable.

His sense of humour exemplifies that gaiety, that geniality, that *inbisāṭ*, so fundamental to certain Sufis; and, of course, such purposeful humour will become more conspicuous in later times, especially in the verse-tales of ʿAṭṭār and Rūmī where humour frequently plays a central role. But the humour which al-Ghazālī deploys has deeper roots as well as a profounder purpose. For laughter – truthful laughter, as it were – presages the ultimate joy of paradise. His older contemporary Nāṣir-i Khusraw, another Khorasanian, explained the link between laughter and joy in his final work, the *Jāmiʿ al-ḥikmatayn*, where he states – echoing the remark of Aristotle with which we began – that:

> Of all the animals only man, who possesses a rational soul, partakes of laughter. The philosopher-sages have posited one definition of man as 'living-laughing' and laughing is a manifestation of happiness. This particular human trait of laughter stands as proof that ultimate bliss is proper to the intellect.[53]

I suspect that despite their massive differences, doctrinal as well as political, al-Ghazālī would have agreed with this statement by the Ismāʿīlī poet and philosopher. What Nāṣir states explicitly al-Ghazālī advances implicitly. For al-Ghazālī the human intellect is a faculty attuned to a very specific pleasure; as he says, "By its very nature the intellect demands knowledge; knowledge is its pleasure." It is "through intellect that man apprehends knowledge of God;

52 *Iḥyāʾ*, 4:352; tr. Ormsby, *Love, Longing, Intimacy and Contentment*, p. 118.

53 *Jāmiʿ al-ḥikmatayn*, ed. H. Corbin and M. Mo'in (Tehran; Paris, 1953), p. 116 (paragraph 113); tr. E. Ormsby, *Between Reason and Revelation: Twin Wisdoms Reconciled*, London: I. B. Tauris, 2012, pp. 112–113.

hence, it is the most resplendent of traits."[54] The capacity for laughter is, like intellect itself – with which it is so unexpectedly allied – an ineradicable component of the human being. It is no accident that laughter simultaneously baffles reason and nourishes it. Laughter is a manifestation of joyousness; it too is a foretaste, as well as a promise, of paradise. For in the end, "joy is the very substance of the intellect."[55]

---

54 *Iḥyāʾ*, 4:326; tr. Ormsby, *Love, Longing, Intimacy and Contentment*, p. 43.

55 *Jāmiʿ al-ḥikmatayn*, p. 116 (paragraph 113); tr. Ormsby, *Between Reason and Revelation*, p. 112.

CHAPTER 7

Al-Ghazālī on the Emotions

Taneli Kukkonen

The centrality of moral psychology to al-Ghazālī's overall project cannot be disputed. Al-Ghazālī produces a lengthy account of the virtues and their acquisition already in the early *Scale of Action* (*Mīzān al-ʿamal*) while in the *Revival of the Religious Sciences* (*Iḥyāʾ ʿulūm ad-dīn*), mapped out in full if not yet released in 490/1097, the need for spiritual purification and self-mortification acquires a fresh urgency and in effect becomes the leading theme for the public side of al-Ghazālī's authorship. In the works deriving from the *Revival* (the *Book of the Forty* and the *Chemistry of Happiness*)[1] the materials from that book's second half are revisited and amplified, and al-Ghazālī's later books and treatises circle back to the same themes. Though its significance should not be exaggerated, of some interest is al-Ghazālī's appeal to Muhammad's saying that the struggle against our own base inclinations is the greater *jihād*.[2]

For all this, the psychological underpinnings of al-Ghazālī's ethics have only received scant attention. Mohamed Sherif's 1975 monograph, *Ghazali's Theory of Virtue*, provides the reader with many of the basic building blocks, but Sherif's approach is more compilatory than analytic.[3] The same goes for the other treatments I know of that describe al-Ghazālī's understanding of the spiritual path and its underlying anthropology: these, too, veer towards the descriptive.[4] Several studies, meanwhile, have established al-Ghazālī's indebtedness to the

* I thank the Swedish Collegium for Advanced Study for the opportunity to conduct the research necessary for this article, the European Research Council (project acronym SSALT, ID201767) for the funding that enabled its completion, and the Universities of Jyväskylä and Otago for their patience while this was going on.

1 These are the *Kitāb al-Arbaʿīn* and the *Kīmiyā-yi saʿāda*, respectively.

2 See *Mīzān al-ʿamal*, ed. Sulaymān Dunyā, Cairo: Dār al-maʿārif bi-Miṣr, 1964, x, 239; *Iḥyāʾ ʿulūm ad-dīn*, Cairo: Lajnat Nashr al-thaqāfa al-islāmiyya, 1937–1938, XXII, *bayān* 8, 1462.19–1463.1. The chapter headings for the *Iḥyāʾ* follow M. Afifi al-Akiti's suggested system in "Index to Divisions of al-Ghazālī's Often-Cited Published Works," *The Muslim World* 102.1 (2012): 70–200.

3 M. A. Sherif, *Ghazali's Theory of Virtue*, Albany: State University of New York Press, 1975.

4 See, e.g., Nicholas L. Heer, "Moral Deliberation in al-Ghazālī's *Iḥyāʾ ʿulūm al-dīn*," in *Islamic Philosophy and Mysticism*, ed. Parviz Morewedge, Delmar: Caravan Books, 1981, 163–176;

 | DOI 10.1163/9789004290952_008

writings of, for example, al-Ḥārith al-Muḥāsibī (d. 243/857), Abū Ṭālib al-Makkī (d. 386/996), Miskawayh (d. 421/1030) and through him Bryson and Galen, Abū ʿAlī Ibn Sīnā (d. 428/1037), and al-Qushayrī (d. 465/1072): but these studies, too, have been short on analysis, being concerned more with showing that al-Ghazālī uses the works of others than examining what he does with them.[5]

Yet, it seems implausible that al-Ghazālī, who – lest we forget – was an inveterate tinkerer, would not also have adjusted and retooled the many materials he incorporated into his account of moral psychology. At the very least he will have made note both of the affinities and of the discrepancies between, as well as within, the various theologians', philosophers', and Sufis' accounts of human agency and moral deliberation. He will, no doubt, also have registered the various overlapping and contending schemata of virtues that came associated with them, and he will have felt the need to make some modicum of sense of this. The afterword to the *Scale of Action*, completed in 1095/488, already says as much. Al-Ghazālī has a rhetorical reader question the way that some of what he has to say accords with the *madhhab* of the Sufis, some with that of the Ashʿarites, some with what other *kalāmī* authors have to say. In other words, the text all but challenges al-Ghazālī to show the consistency in his own presentation.[6]

Al-Ghazālī's actual answer to this pointed question is notoriously elusive. All he says in the *Scale of Action* is that one may modify one's style of address according to whether one is speaking publicly, in a private school setting, or

---

Mohammad Abul Quasem, *The Ethics of al-Ghazālī: a Composite Ethics in Islam*, Delmar: Caravan Books, 1978.

5 In addition to the studies already cited see, e.g., Margaret Smith, "The Forerunner of al-Ghazālī," *Journal of the Royal Asiatic Society* (1936): 65–78; Wilferd Madelung, "Ar-Rāġib al-Iṣfahānī und die Ethik al-Ġazālīs," in *Islamkundliche Abhandlungen. Fritz Meier zum sechzigsten Geburtstag*, ed. Richard Gramlich, Wiesbaden: Franz Steiner Verlag, 1974, 152–163; Jules Janssens, "al-Ghazālī's *Mīzān al-ʿAmal*: An Ethical Summa Based on Ibn Sīnā and al-Rāghib al-Iṣfahānī," in *Islamic Thought in the Middle Ages: Studies in Text, Transmission and Translation, in Honour of Hans Daiber*, eds. Anna Akasoy & Wim Raven, Leiden: Brill, 2008, 123–137; and Yasien Mohamed, "The Ethics of Education: Al-Iṣfahānī's *Al-Dharīʿa* as a Source of Inspiration for al-Ghazālī's *Mizān al-ʿAmal*," *The Muslim World* 101.4 (2011): 633–657. Richard Gramlich's four-part translation of *Qūt al-qulūb*, published under the title *Die Nahrung der Herzen*, Wiesbaden: Franz Steiner Verlag, 4 vols. 1991–1995, deserves special mention for how exhaustively it documents al-Ghazālī's use of al-Makkī.

6 See *Mizān* XXXII, 405.

in the recesses of one's own heart.[7] A charitable way to interpret this claim (as opposed to one that would, say, charge al-Ghazālī with rank dissimulation or incoherence) would be to say that al-Ghazālī in the latter part of his career was eager to use any available means in calling upon his fellow Muslims to reform their faith, and that this very much included his writings in moral psychology: no harmonization was necessary, because the point was the action and not the theory. And all this may indeed be perfectly true. Such an explanation would account for why al-Ghazālī's later writings are short on polemic and instead make a show of demonstrating how all the relevant authorities come together in harmony (a harmony that has been preordained by al-Ghazālī, of course).[8] But all this is still not to say that there would be no theoretical backdrop at all to al-Ghazālī's seemingly disjointed accounts of the various virtues and vices, or to his exhortations for people to change their ways. Indeed, al-Ghazālī's commitment both to a correspondence theory of truth and to the dependable operation of God's *sunna* in the world dictate that a unitary account must undergird the different presentations given to our moral striving in various contexts, even if the exact formulation should prove elusive.

Rather than attempting a yet greater catchment of the materials from which al-Ghazālī was working – undoubtedly much remains to be done on that front – the following essay takes the modest goal of flagging up some features in al-Ghazālī's account of moral psychology that are of systematic interest.[9] I focus mainly on two issues: the desiderative dynamics of the soul and its parts, and the role that appetite and spirit play in explaining the workings of our lower or animal soul. Our picture of al-Ghazālī's views needs to be reconstructed from bits and pieces, because he nowhere provides a full and comprehensive treatment of the passions and their psychological basis. Indeed, there is much that al-Ghazālī takes for granted, and many important features to which only passing reference is made (and even then in unlikely settings). Further research is needed in order to assess the level of al-Ghazālī's originality when it comes to the issues; what I think can reasonably be said at this stage is that al-Ghazālī's account is in some ways greater than the sum of its parts.

---

7 In the *Revival* a similar tripartition of sciences (*ʿulūm*) is attributed to Sahl at-Tustarī: *Iḥyāʾ* II, *faṣl* 2, *masʾala* 2, 173.4–5.

8 For an attractive portrayal of this viewpoint see Eric Ormsby, *Al-Ghazali*, Oxford: Oneworld, 2008.

9 Accordingly, references, e.g., to Aristotle and to Galen, should not be taken to suggest that al-Ghazālī would necessarily have personally read either author; it is only that the former raise certain theoretical issues to which the latter can be seen to respond.

1 The Pleasure Principle

A starting point is offered by the famous statement of God's messenger according to which God gave each person a *fiṭra*, an innate or original human nature, which most commentators considered to be simple and unspoiled.[10] The best-known among al-Ghazālī's many references to *fiṭra* are located in contexts where the subject of discussion is the array of human cognitive functions; accordingly, what has drawn most commentators' attention is the question of the acquisition of right and wrong religious belief.[11] These are indeed concerns highlighted in the second half of the hadith, which draws attention to the fact that it is one's parents who turn one into a Jew, a Christian, or a Magi (i.e. Zoroastrian). This side of the hadith's interpretation has ably been handled by Richard M. Frank, Frank Griffel, and others, and there is no reason to return to it here.[12]

We might expect an emphasis on the soundness of our *fiṭra* to spill over into the realm of our evaluative judgements as well. This is indeed what we find in al-Ghazālī: wherever there is a variant on the Prophetic tradition in al-Ghazālī's later hortatory writings, and whenever he simply refers to *fiṭra* without explicitly referring to the *ḥadīth*, it is invariably with the aim of reassuring the reader that human nature as it was originally created is perfectly made and fitted for the happiness that God has intended for it. In no uncertain terms al-Ghazālī states that our heart's desire is, by the heart's very nature, to rush to meet the Lord and to delight in His presence. Accordingly, to set one's

10 For the concept of *fiṭra*, which is notoriously hard to translate with a single word, see Duncan B. Macdonald, sv. 'Fiṭra' in *EI*²; Camilla Adang, "Islam as the Inborn Religion of Mankind: The Concept of *Fiṭrah* in the Works of Ibn Ḥazm", *Al-Qanṭara* 21 (2000): 391–410.

11 Most famous is the reference to *fiṭra* in the introduction to the *Deliverer from Error: Al-Munqidh min aḍ-ḍalāl*, ed. J. Ṣalībā & K. ʿAyyād, Beirut: Commission libanaise pour la traduction des chefs-d'œuvre, 2nd ed. 1969, 10.21–11.6; see also, e.g., *Iḥyāʾ* XXI, *bayān* 6, 1369.9ff.

12 See Richard M. Frank, "Al-Ghazālī on Taqlīd. Scholars, theologians, and philosophers," *Zeitschrift für Geschichte der arabisch-islamischen Wissenschaften* 7 (1991–1992): 207–252; Frank Griffel, "Al-Ghazālī's Use of 'Original Human Disposition' (*Fiṭra*) and its Background in the Teachings of al-Fārābī and Avicenna," *The Muslim World* 102.1 (2011): 1–32; also Taneli Kukkonen, "Al-Ghazālī's Skepticism Revisited," in *Rethinking the History of Skepticism*, ed. Henrik Lagerlund, Leiden: E. J. Brill, 2010, 29–59; Taneli Kukkonen, "Receptive to Reality: Al-Ghazālī on the Structure of the Soul," *The Muslim World* 102.3–4 (2012): 541–561.

sights on anything other than God is always a deviation from the heart's true purpose and from our original nature.[13]

Operative here is what I call 'the pleasure principle,' that is, the generic notion that the exercise of our capacities is not only pleasurable in itself, but rightfully so. The pleasure that accompanies any act of cognition is due to a natural conformity between the perceptible object and the perceiving subject, a conformity that had long been recognized by both the Platonic and the Aristotelian traditions.[14] In Peripatetic terms this is to say that each modality of perception finds its natural satisfaction and fulfilment in realizing its affinity with its object – in taking on the form without the matter, as the process is famously described in Aristotle's account of sense-perception.[15] This process carries with it an affective component, which is why the cognizing subject will experience pleasure in accordance with how powerful the perception is. What remains to be said is that the pleasures of knowledge far surpass those of sensation and other embodied forms of cognition, either because of the exalted nature of reason's objects or by virtue of the inherent dignity of the reasoning power itself. This, too, is found already in Aristotle. Yet it is in later Greek Platonism that the theme really assumes central stage and where it is explicitly linked with a soteriology that connects the human being's final destiny with the soul's ontological grounding in the divine realm.[16]

Al-Ghazālī, whose philosophical readings on the subject are found principally in Ibn Sīnā and in the *Letters of the Brethren of Purity* (*Rasā'il Ikhwān aṣ-Ṣafā'*), confirms all of the elements of this picture several times over in

---

13 See, e.g., *Iḥyā'* XXII, *bayān* 4, 1451.14–22; *Iḥyā'* XXXII, *shaṭr* 2, *rukn* 1, *bayān* 2, *aṣl* 2, 2215.15–18; *Iḥyā'* XXXVI, *bayān* 5, 2611.3–6; *Mīzān* III, 195–196; ibid., XXII, 308–310; *Al-Maqṣad al-asnā fī sharḥ ma'ānī asmā' Allāh al-ḥusnā*, ed. F. Shehadi, Beirut: Imprimerie Catholique, 2nd ed. 1982, 44.

14 Plato (?), *Seventh Letter*, 344a; Aristotle, citing Empedocles, *De an.* 1.2, 404b10–15.

15 *De an.* 2.12.

16 To connect the dots in Aristotle see *Met.* 1.1.980a21–b28; *De an.* 2.12–3.3; *De an.* 3.8; for the superiority of theoretical reasoning *Met.* 1.2.982b25–983a11 and more obliquely *Met.* 12.9; *NE* 10.7–8. It is worth noting how among al-Ghazālī's proximate or remote sources, Galen presents a somewhat different analysis: consonant with an instrumental view of the operation of the motive faculties (appetite and spirit perform needed functions within our mortal life, but that is all), Galen contends that any experience of pleasure that attaches to the use of our faculties does so only incidentally, as an added motivational factor to ensure that these are exercised sufficiently often. See the Arabic compendium (*mukhtaṣar*) of *Peri ēthōn* edited by P. Kraus, "Kitāb al-Akhlāq li-Jalīnūs," *Bulletin of the Faculty of Arts of the University of Egypt* 5.1 (1937): 1–51, at 34 (hereafter "Galen, *Akhlāq*").

the *Revival*, most prominently in the *Book of Love, Longing, Intimacy, and Contentment*. The perceiving subject naturally inclines towards those perceptible objects that conform to the perceiver's own nature (*yuwāfiq ṭabʿ al-mudrik*), since the latter bring the perceiver pleasure. Indeed, the very word "love is an expression for a given nature's inclination towards something that is pleasurable" (*al-ḥubb ʿibāra ʿan mayl aṭ-ṭabʿ ilā sh-shayʾ al-muladhdh*),[17] which again is equivalent to the soul's inclination towards that which somehow conforms to it.[18] Put another way, every pleasant thing is loved (*kull ladhīdh maḥbūb*), and this precisely because of the pleasure it brings.[19] Because pleasures follow upon perceptions and because each of our natural faculties has been created for the sake of our necessary interfacing with the world as it is, none of the soul's faculties, whether of the cognitive or the motive variety, are devoid of pleasure or pain.[20] And because we are endowed with the power of intellection, our love can extend even to the divine realm and to divine things, which by their own nature transcend the sensual and the bodily.[21] The exalted nature of such objects means that choosing any lesser form of good amounts to a betrayal of our heart's true calling.[22]

This, however, leaves us with a bit of a puzzle, since plainly people *do* desire things other than God and His dominion. In a world governed by a benevolent and almighty divinity, what could ever have resulted in such a perversion of our natural disposition towards the perfection specific to us as human beings? The full answer to this question cannot be provided within the confines of a single essay (I sketch out one possible explanation elsewhere);[23] here, it is enough to point out how al-Ghazālī regards it as axiomatic that God cannot be perceived directly in this life, and that even indirect glimpses of divine reality can only be won either (a) by virtue of an exceptional prophetic endowment; or else (b) through great spiritual perseverance. For this reason alone, most people will never achieve an acquaintance with the pleasures that accompany the contemplation of the divine: because "a human being only loves that with

17 See *Iḥyāʾ* XXXVI, *bayān* 2, 2584.9–14.

18 Ibid., *bayān* 10, 2636.13, 2637.10.

19 Ibid., *bayān* 2, 2588.3.

20 Ibid., *bayān* 4, 2602.21–2603.4.

21 Ibid., *bayān* 2, 2585.10–14.

22 See also *Mīzān* III, 195–196; *Mīzān* XXII, 308 straightforwardly characterizes an attachment to worldly pleasures as a sickness.

23 See T. Kukkonen, "Al-Ghazālī on Error," in *Islam and Rationality: The Impact of al-Ghazālī*, Vol. II, ed. Frank Griffel, Leiden: Brill, forthcoming.

which he is acquainted";[24] or, to take the opposing side, because since "what is not perceived through personal tasting (*dhawq*) cannot be greatly desired,"[25] it is not unlikely that people should go astray in their yearnings. Those whose perceptions do not surpass the sensory and the imaginary domains will not only be unable to feel the kind of love towards God that would draw them closer to Him; they may even be inclined to deny the existence of this kind of desire, as well as the existence of its object.[26] In sum, for al-Ghazālī whosoever is found lacking in the love of God has never really made acquaintance with Him, and such a person's "understanding is limited to his appetites and to his sensations."[27]

What one should notice is that al-Ghazālī is explicit in assigning different pleasures to different natures, even if these converge upon the existence of one and the same living being. Our different faculties respond to different features of the outside world and accordingly find their satisfaction in different facets of our existence. Thus the eyesight's pleasure lies in seeing attractive forms, the ear's in hearing measured melodies, the sense of touch's in the soft and the smooth, etc.[28] This accords with al-Ghazālī's overall ontological pluralism, but it also provides him with the tools to account for the way that appetite and spirit – as per Plato, the motive aspects of human existence associated with natural and animal life – can act at odds in regards to our God-given power of reasoning, as well as with one another.[29] To act on a certain impulse is to identify with the part or power of the soul that produced it, and although only one of these acts of identification is the correct one (that which recognizes the rational part as representing our true self), all of them are possible.[30]

To sum up, al-Ghazālī posits that our innate nature (*fiṭra*) is inherently unstable, being equally amenable to suggestions low and high due to its teth-

24 "*Lā yuḥibbu l-insān illā mā yaʿrifuhu*": *Iḥyāʾ* XXXVI, *bayān* 2, 2584.7–8; similarly, e.g., *Iḥyāʾ* XXXIII, *shaṭr* 2, *bayān* 4, 2348.7; ibid., *shaṭr* 2, *bayān* 7, *q.* 3, *sabab* 2, 2376.15.

25 *Iḥyāʾ* XXIII, *qawl fī shahwat al-farj*, 1525.10.

26 Cf. *Iḥyāʾ* XXXVI, *bayān* 2, 2585.5–14.

27 Ibid., *bayān* 3, 2593.4–6.

28 Ibid., *bayān* 2, 2584.19–22.

29 For the Platonic and Aristotelian background in general see Hendrik Lorenz, *The Brute Within: Appetitive Desire in Plato and Aristotle*, Oxford: Oxford University Press, 2006.

30 See here the Prolegomena to al-Ghazālī's *Alchemy of Happiness*, where al-Ghazālī bears on his reader to acknowledge that if eating, sleeping, and sexual intercourse are where one's pleasure is found, then a beast is what one is, etc. Galen (*Akhlāq*, 38–39) expresses this differently; each of the soul's parts has its own 'appetite' and the relative strengths of these appetites account for the different directions in which a personality will develop.

ering in this world and the next.[31] The formulation made famous by al-Ghazālī, though found already in the Arabic compendium of Galen's treatise *On morals*, is that we can rise to the level of angels or sink to the level of beasts.[32] The former, which is our true calling, happens with the flourishing of our rational and contemplative side, while the latter fate will befall us if we give in to our animal instincts.[33] But what might account for the fact that some people incline one way while the rest go in the direction of the other?

2 Nature and Nurture

Al-Ghazālī in fact allows for considerable variation when it comes to the strength of people's natural dispositions (*gharīza*) at birth. This is most obviously true for cognitive ability: a select few are born with an intellect that is blazing in its insight from the first moment of its appearance, while some are correspondingly dim-witted, and the great majority of people fall somewhere in between.[34] But al-Ghazālī is similarly willing to countenance a broad level of variation when it comes to our moral makeup. Some people enjoy innate perfection (*kamāl fiṭrī*), meaning that they are created faithful, generous, and brave; while in others the opposing qualities – namely, infidelity, stinginess, and cowardice – are already entrenched from the beginning.[35] This teaching, too, goes back to Galen, who argued against the Stoics in favour of an inherent variation in humanity's moral qualities.[36]

---

31 See, e.g., *Mīzān* XV, 258–259; *Iḥyā'* XXI, *bayān* 11, 1392.16–17; cf. also *Iḥyā'* XXII, *bayān* 2, 1441.12, where the example is that of our ability to give equally as well as to withhold.

32 For Galen see *Akhlāq*, 40: the reference to angels, or *malā'ika*, can scarcely have derived from Galen's original Greek, having its origin instead in the redactive/translation process. The metaphor is so prevalent in al-Ghazālī that any listing of its instances will end up woefully incomplete: for just those sources cited in this study see, e.g., *Iḥyā'* VI, *faṣl* 2, 431.15–22 and *Iḥyā'* XXI, *bayān* 4, 1360.8–17; *Mīzān* V, 209–210 and XIX, 286–287; and *Maqṣad*, 44–46.

33 In fact, those who do not reach out to the higher world are worse than beasts, since the latter at least have not dishonoured their higher calling: *Mishkāt*, 11.6–9; *Iḥyā'* XXXI, *rukn* 2, *bayān* 2, *rutba* 2, 2124.1–10; *Iḥyā'* XXXII, *shaṭr* 1, *bayān* 5, 2189.15–19.

34 *Iḥyā'* I, *bāb* 7, 150.8–151.20; *Iḥyā'* XXI, *bayān* 9, 1383.1–19; *Mīzān* VI, 219.

35 *Mīzān* VI, 219, XIV, 257, and XV, 258–259; compare, also, *Iḥyā'* XXII, *bayān* 4, 1449.5–10 and *Iḥyā'* II, *faṣl* 2, 163.8–10, which seem to encompass both cognitive and moral *fiṭra*.

36 See *Akhlāq*, 29–30; Richard Walzer, *Greek into Arabic*, Cambridge, Mass.: Harvard University Press, 1962, 158–161.

What this means for the prophetic program of moral improvement is that different people will find its implementation hard or easy, each according to their abilities. This may not seem entirely fair to us, but al-Ghazālī would hardly flinch, seeing as he is willing to accept without hesitation the yet more pointed conclusion that all of our supposed moral striving is attributable to God in the first place via His angels, just as the road to perdition on the part of the sinner is attributable to God through the mediation of the devil (see below). What matters to al-Ghazālī in the present context is merely that moral improvement be possible in the first place. This must surely be the case: God has instructed us to reform our character, and he would not command us to do what is impossible.[37] Children are especially susceptible to becoming good and evil.[38] In a rather lovely phrase, al-Ghazālī likens the child's heart to a precious, uncut jewel devoid of any shape or form.[39]

Al-Ghazālī is furthermore keen to underline how a person's psychological makeup is shaped by her or his entire life's experience. Above all this is a matter of habituation. Whatever we have been taught to appreciate and have had the chance to sample on multiple occasions is what we ultimately come to enjoy the most. The more graphic examples adduced by al-Ghazālī have to do with the disgusting habits criminals and miscreants may learn to regard as pleasurable: the gambler will love the roll of the dice even when it brings ruin; the criminal will boast of his steadfastness on the cross or under the whip; the effeminate man will take pleasure in plucking out his hair and delight in the company of similar people, and so forth.[40] But people may also develop a genuine passion for relatively innocuous or frivolous pastimes such as bird-watching, lute-playing, backgammon, and chess;[41] also – and this is of particular importance to al-Ghazālī – there is no reason why prayer and a life of devotion should not become second nature to a person as well, given practice.

There is a communal aspect to these activities and evaluative judgements that bears noting. We are, as a rule, introduced to specific activities and taught to appreciate them by others, and certainly we always find reassurance in the reinforcement provided by like-minded people. More generally, what all these strange passions confirm is that good as well as bad character traits are

---

37 *Iḥyāʾ* XXII, *bayān* 3, 1444.14–1448.21; *Mīzān* XXII, 247; cf., however, *Iḥyāʾ* II, *faṣl* 3, *rukn* 3, *aṣl* 5, 195.14–18, where al-Ghazālī claims in good Ashʿarite fashion that God can impose impossible obligations on His servants.

38 *Iḥyāʾ* XXII, *bayān* 10, 1477.23–1478.3.

39 Ibid., 1474.2–7.

40 Ibid., *bayān* 4, 1450.17–1451.14.

41 *Iḥyāʾ* XXIII, *qawl fī shahwat al-farj*, 1527.11–14.

resilient, yes – they are sticky, one might say – but they are neither innate nor impervious to change. All character-based proclivities are essentially subrational responses to our environment: they are conditioned reactions to things and experiences that we either embrace or shun. Al-Ghazālī's definition of character (*khulq*), derived from Galen by way of Miskawayh, is accordingly that it denotes "a fixed psychological state (*hay'a*), one from which actions flow with ease and without any need for cogitation or consideration" (*ghayr ḥāja ilā fikr wa-rawiyya*).[42]

This leads, naturally enough, to a fundamental distrust of the passions. If "everything that is beloved is also worshipped, and the servant is bound by that which he serves,"[43] then allowing ourselves to desire something other than God is tantamount to remaining beholden to some aspect of this world. This itself is tantamount to a corresponding inability to set God above everything else. This part of al-Ghazālī's ethics, at least, stands firmly in the Sufi tradition, as demonstrated by his ample use of Islamic spiritual literature to illustrate the point. But al-Ghazālī's analysis of how the functionality of the passions figures into this is of some interest:

> Falling outside the pale of monotheism are those who follow their passion (*hawā*), for anyone who follows his passion makes this into that which he worships. God said, "Have you seen the one who divinized his passion" (45:23) and the Messenger of God likewise said, "Of the earthly things worshipped as god, the thing most hated by God is passion". In point of fact, upon consideration one comes to understand that the idol-worshipper does not worship the idol, instead, he worships his passion, since his soul inclines (*mā'ila*) towards the religion of his fathers and he follows this inclination, and the soul's inclination towards familiar things is one of the meanings that the expression 'passion' denotes.[44]

The notion that the pagan worships his passion helps to explain an otherwise inexplicable phenomenon. What does the idolater get out of worshipping an otherwise inert and unresponsive statue? There are, after all, as al-Ghazālī

---

42 *Iḥyā'* XXII, *bayān* 2, 1440.21–22. As documented by several scholars, Miskawayh has exactly the terminology al-Ghazālī does: see *Tahdhīb al-akhlāq*, ed. Constantine K. Zurayk, Beirut: American University of Beirut, 1967, 31. Galen's phrasing in the Arabic compendium, by comparison, is "without forethought or choice" (*bi-lā rawiyya wa-lā ikhtiyār*): Galen, *Akhlāq*, 25.

43 *Iḥyā'* XXXVI, *bayān* 6, 2617.7–8.

44 *Iḥyā'* I, *bāb* 3, *bayān* 2, *lafẓ* 4, 57.1–5; cf. *Mīzān* XI, 240.

says elsewhere, no realities attached to the names that the idol-worshippers use for their gods, in fact, there is nothing at all there for anybody to worship. These are signifiers without the signified, so to say, which would make of their adoration the ultimate exercise in futility.[45] Nevertheless, al-Ghazālī's model allows for an explanation of sorts. Those who worship false gods have grown accustomed to channelling their desires in a particular direction through the example of others, and in the fullness of time they have learned to take pleasure in the act of offering itself – that is, in the passionate attachment to a particular set of practices and, one presumes, to the pleasures attached to their social dimensions. Again the social aspect of habituation is subtly underlined, with the implication that it is up to the community and the individual teacher to foster healthy habits and inclinations in those who are as of yet susceptible to instruction. This had better be accomplished early, lest bad habits set in and the task of improvement becomes impossible or nearly so.[46]

3 The Appetite and the Spirit

Up to this point, our account has proceeded on a rather generic level: *qalb*, or the heart, as the principle that naturally desires to meet its Lord, and *hawā*, or passion, as its opposite. Thus far al-Ghazālī could well claim that he is merely following in the footsteps of many Sufi masters. When it comes to the more detailed technical analysis of the soul's motions and its innate and acquired characteristics, however, it soon becomes evident (as has been documented by many scholars) that al-Ghazālī draws on the toolkit of the *falāsifa*. This is signalled straight away by his equation of the Sufis' lower self with the combined forces of appetite (*shahwa*) and spirit (*ghaḍab*), the two being the seat of all the blameworthy attributes (*aṣ-ṣifāt al-madhmūma*).[47] Rather than Ibn Sīnā, al-Ghazālī's primary source appears to have been Miskawayh, mediated through ar-Rāghib al-Iṣfahānī. It is in Miskawayh's version that al-Ghazālī relates the late ancient synthesis of Platonic, Aristotelian, and Stoic virtue theory: the four cardinal virtues, with a number of subordinate virtues listed under each, with each one analysed as the mean between two extremes. While

45 *Maqṣad*, 32–33; see Taneli Kukkonen, "Al-Ghazālī on the Signification of Names," *Vivarium* 48.1–2 (2010): 55–74, at 71–72.

46 The fourfold division of souls according to how susceptible they are to moral improvement is another favourite theme of al-Ghazālī's: see, e.g., *Iḥyā'* XXII, *bayān* 3, 1446.3–21 and *Mīzān* XII, 249–250.

47 *Iḥyā'* XXI, *bayān* 1, *lafẓ* 3, 1351.6–9.

an exposition of the virtues and their relation to the specifically religious virtues (called by al-Ghazālī the praiseworthy or salvific character traits) could easily fill the rest of this article, or indeed an entire volume, the groundwork in this respect has been done by scholars such as Sherif, Quasem, Mohamed, and others.[48] I therefore turn my attention instead to how al-Ghazālī conceives of the parts of the soul and their characteristic activities as the psychological basis both for virtue and for vice.

Crucial here is how appetite and spirit are positioned relative to one another and how they develop as parts of the human psyche.[49] To take first things first, the deep-rooted nature of our primal appetites stems simply from the fact that their seat – the concupiscible faculty – has been instilled in us at birth.[50] This makes the appetitive part the hardest of all to subjugate, and altogether impossible to eradicate within the confines of our embodied existence. It is, moreover, by virtue of the reason that the appetitive faculty is perfected before the intellect that it becomes so easy for the appetites to hold sway over the soul.[51] This dominion may extend to the eventual rationalization of our irrational desires. Any sane person, after all, however warped his or her perceptions may be, will always desire to attain some apparent good:[52] and since one of Satan's tricks is to dress up evil in the guise of a good,[53] it is eminently easy for us to fall into the trap of seeking out excuses for our appetites. We may come to rationalize our desire for a particular person, for instance, making believe that only he or she can ever satisfy the emptiness in our hearts. This both (1) makes a mockery of the true love which we should feel exclusively for God and at the same time (2) represents a perversion of the natural order, where the appetites should obey the intellect and not the other way around – none of which, of course, matters one whit to the person in the thrall of lust.[54]

---

48 See the references in nn. 3–5.

49 The relative rankings of *thymos* and *epithumia* vary in late antique thought: see Kevin Corrigan, "The Organization of the Soul: Some Overlooked Aspects of Interpretation from Plato to Late Antiquity," in *Reading Ancient Texts. Volume II: Aristotle and Neoplatonism: Essays in Honour of Denis O'Brien*, eds. Suzanne Stern-Gillet & Kevin Corrigan, Leiden: E. J. Brill, 2007, 99–113.

50 *Iḥyāʾ* XXII, *bayān* 3, 1445.21–1446.2; *Mīzān* XII, 248–249.

51 *Iḥyāʾ* XXXI, *rukn* 1, *bayān* 4, 2090.5–2091.1.

52 Conversely, an inability to decide on a goal is one of the distinguishing hallmarks of insanity: see *Mīzān* XVII, 275–276.

53 *Iḥyāʾ* XXI, *bayān* 11, 1396.12–13.

54 *Iḥyāʾ* XXIII, *qawl fī shahwat al-farj*, 1527.5–10; cf. *Mīzān* XI, 246; *Iḥyāʾ* XXI, *bayān* 5, 1363.18–1364.5.

Al-Ghazālī sometimes calls the appetites by the name of beastly attributes (*aṣ-ṣifāt al-bahīmiyya*). These are foregrounded at birth, while the predatory (*sabʿiyya*) attributes assume precedence later: this change coincides with the first dawning of our ability to discriminate (*tamyīz*).[55] Indeed, one indication of the connection between the spirited part of the soul and the power of reasoning is that they develop together – for instance, shame can only occur with the dawning of the intellect.[56] Al-Ghazālī also contends that giving preponderance to the demands of the spirit over those of mere appetite already bespeaks a certain refinement of the soul.[57]

In al-Ghazālī's many metaphors regarding the three parts of the soul and their interaction, reference is made repeatedly to the role of the spirit in bringing appetence to heel. In one simile the spirit becomes the hunter's dog, while the appetite is the beast on which he rides; in another, the appetite is merely a pig.[58] This confirms that al-Ghazālī, similar to ar-Rāghib al-Iṣfahānī, regards the spirit as inherently more amenable to the suggestions of the intellect than appetite could be.[59] Then again, anger is also the ghoul of reason (*ghūl al-ʿaql*), meaning that it can twist the intellect to its own purposes in even more fiendish ways than the appetite can.[60] Thus, for instance, the love of status (*jāh*) is the most entrenched of the soul's attachments to this world, making it all too easy for Satan to manipulate honour-seeking individuals into erroneously equating their worldly prominence with their everlasting good.[61]

The power of habituation lies in the psychophysical connection between the various faculties of the animal soul, the organs with which they are associated, and the actions that issue from them. Al-Ghazālī talks up this connection as a mystery and a divine secret,[62] but it must be said that in al-Ghazālī's own view there is nothing especially mysterious about the process, given how he

---

55 *Iḥyāʾ* XXXI, *rukn* 2, *bayān* 1, 2101.19–2102.4.

56 *Mīzān* XX, 288; *Iḥyāʾ* XXII, *bayān* 10, 1474.16.

57 This is the case even if the enjoyment of the presence of the Lord naturally supersedes both, or should do so: see *Iḥyāʾ* XXXVI, *bayān* 4, 2605.8–18; ibid., 2609.11–23.

58 See *Iḥyāʾ* XXI, *bayān* 3, 13:57.4–10; ibid., *bayān* 5, 1362.17ff.

59 On this see Yasien Mohamed, "The Metaphor of the Dog in Arabic Literature," *Tydskrif vir Letterkunde* 45.1 (2008): 75–86. The similes appear to derive from Middle Platonic sources, as the Arabic summary of Galen's *Peri ēthōn*, al-Kindī's *Treatise on the soul*, and Miskawayh's *Reformation of Morals* all present variants of the same tradition: for al-Kindī in particular see *Qawl fī n-nafs*, in *Rasāʾil al-Kindī*, ed. M. Abū Rīda, Cairo: Dār al-fikr al-ʿarabī, 2 vols. 1950–1953, 1: 273–274.

60 *Iḥyāʾ* XXI, *bayān* 12, 1400.12; *Mishkāt*, 42.10.

61 *Iḥyāʾ* XXXII, *shaṭr* 1, *bayān* 7, 2205.15–22.

62 *Mīzān* XIII, 251–252; *Iḥyāʾ* II, *faṣl* 4, *masʾala* 2, *iṭlāq* 1, 212.3–4; *Iḥyāʾ* XXII, *bayān* 4, 1451.23–1452.3.

himself describes anger, for example, as the excitation of the blood around the heart much in the same way Aristotle had.[63] Moreover, al-Ghazālī himself explicitly points to how the imprints left by the objects of appetite are retained by the inner senses and thus leave their mark also on the heart, which again provides a fully naturalistic explanation of the manner in which both animal and human souls become accustomed to responding in a certain way to repeated stimuli.[64] This implies an intimate relation between a raw sensation (whether sense-perception or the evaluative sort, as in the appetites and the spirit being stimulated) and the representation of it as something pleasant or unpleasant. And all of this matches Avicenna's presentation of animal and human psychology.[65] Many of the specific examples al-Ghazālī uses in his discussion of habituation, meanwhile, go back to al-Kindī's treatise *On the Means of Dispelling Sorrows*.[66]

An important part of al-Ghazālī's understanding of character-building is his affirmation with Aristotle that this cannot be done through reasoning and argument alone, but must instead be instilled through practice. Echoes of the *Nicomachean Ethics* can be heard, e.g., in the way al-Ghazālī describes the moral education of youngsters. The young can be brought to pray, but this will be by way of simple praise and punishment and through showing a good example, rather than through any serious understanding of everlasting life. Good character traits are thus inculcated and their desirability established long before their theoretical basis can be grasped, since the discerning faculty (*tamyīz*), which is the highest one possessed by children, does not yet reach beyond that which is immediately at hand.[67]

4 Moderation and Apathy

Al-Ghazālī maintains that both appetite and spirit have been created for a reason: they have a positive function in our daily lives insofar as they ensure that

63 *Iḥyāʾ* XXV, *qawl* 1, *bayān* 2, 1647.15ff.

64 *Iḥyāʾ* XXI, *bayān* 11, 1390.19–1391.4.

65 For Avicenna see Simo Knuuttila, *Emotions in Ancient and Medieval Philosophy*, Oxford: Oxford University Press, 2004, 218–226.

66 Helmut Ritter & Richard Walzer, "Uno scritto morale inedito di al-Kindî," *Memorie Della Reale, Accademia Nazionale Dei Lincei, Classe Di Scienze Morali, Storiche e Filologiche* (6th series) 8 (1938): 5–63, at 33–34.

67 *Iḥyāʾ* XXXII, *shaṭr* 1, *bayān* 2, 2185.1–12; cf. *Iḥyāʾ* XXXIII, *shaṭr* 2, *bayān* 6, 2358.21–2359.20; for Aristotle on this very important point see Myles F. Burnyeat, "Aristotle on Learning to be Good," in *Essays on Aristotle's Ethics*, ed. Amélie Oksenberg Rorty, Berkeley: University of California Press, 1980, 69–92.

we have adequate nutrition, that we procreate, and that we act in defence of our essential interests, etc.[68] This already means that the extirpation of our passions can never be the goal: rather, as the Messenger of God had indicated, "the best of affairs is the middle course."[69] In addition, one may consider how impossible it would be to root out the passions altogether. Even attempting such a feat is liable to result only in despondency and melancholy.[70]

In the *Revival* al-Ghazāli furthermore lets his readers in on a secret. The reason teachers urge their charges to cut off all worldly ties and eliminate the passions is that this is the best way to ensure even a modicum of success. With greed, lust, anger, and pride being such primal forces, it would be foolish to signal to the average aspirant that a moderation of these passions would be enough. Such an easy-going attitude would only lead to moral laxity, and so the responsible spiritual guide will rather recommend great rigour and austerity. Nonetheless, it is the virtuous mean that is the real aim of the instructor.[71]

All this has led commentators to maintain that al-Ghazālī sticks to an Aristotelian program of *metriopatheia*, or the moderation of the passions, as opposed to the Platonic or Stoic ideal of *apatheia*, i.e. the belief that one should rid oneself of the passions entirely.[72] However, there is a twist peculiar to al-Ghazālī's presentation of the metriopatheic ideal that I have not encountered anywhere else. Consider the following argument for staying the middle course between excess and defect:

> An eagerness to spend money directs the heart [and its attentions] towards spending, just as an eagerness to withhold it turns the heart towards withholding: the perfection of the heart lies in being healed of both urges. Since such a thing is not [attainable] in this life, what ought to be sought is what most closely resembles a lack of such characteristics and what is most remote from both extremes, i.e. the mean. Lukewarm water is neither hot nor cold but in between the two and, as it were, free of the characteristics of both: generosity lies similarly between

68 See *Iḥyā*ʾ XXI, *bayān* 2, 1353.18–1354.10; *Iḥyā*ʾ XXII, *bayān* 3, 1446.24–1447.10; *Iḥyā*ʾ XXIII, *qawl fī shahwat al-farj*, 1525.7–11; *Iḥyā*ʾ XXV, *qawl* 1, *bayān* 2, 1646.20–1647.19; *Iḥyā*ʾ XXXVI, *bayān* 4, 2602.22–2603.4.

69 *Iḥyā*ʾ XXII, *bayān* 3, 1448.6–7; *Iḥyā*ʾ XXIII, *bayān* 4, 1518.21 and 1520.2–3; *Iḥyā*ʾ XXV, *qawl* 1, *bayān* 2, 1650.10–11; ibid., *bayān* 3, 1652.17–1653.4.

70 See *Mīzān* X, 237–238 and cf. *Iḥyā*ʾ XXII, *bayān* 3, 1446.22ff.

71 Ibid., 1448.16–21; also *Iḥyā*ʾ XXIII, *bayān* 4, 1518.22–1519.9.

72 See, e.g., T. Kukkonen, "The Self as Enemy, the Self as Divine: A Crossroads in the Development of Islamic Anthropology," in *The Ancient Philosophy of Self*, eds. Juha Sihvola & Pauliina Remes, Dordrecht: Springer, 2008, 205–224.

> extravagance and stinginess, courage between cowardice and recklessness, moderation between voraciousness and indifference, and so it goes with the rest of the character traits. It is thus the extreme in matters that is reprehensible.[73]

Certainly many of the surface elements here support the notion that Aristotelian moderation is the goal. Notice, however, the precise way al-Ghazālī arrives at this conclusion: the mean is recommended because it is what comes closest to pure apathy. The latter, not the former, is what would be truly desirable, other things being equal: it is only because in this world we cannot rid ourselves altogether of all the urges related to our embodied life that an approximation of apathy (rather than the real thing) becomes necessary.

The example of lukewarm water derives already from the *Scale of Action*. In that context, al-Ghazālī further specifies that the aim of all this is that one's bodily preoccupations no longer distract one from the pursuit of one's true happiness.[74] Coming back to the *Revival*, al-Ghazālī lauds the lightness and, as it were, the transparency of the virtuous soul.[75] The effect, once more, is that of underscoring how the virtuous person simply will not give consideration to corporeal pleasures and pains, since the sought-after stance is one of consummate indifference.

In fact, the only way al-Ghazālī ever defends the urges of the animal soul is in terms of their utility. For instance, al-Ghazālī maintains that the Qur'ān only condones the emotion of aggression in the context of confronting unbelievers, because this way there is no fear of a cessation in the struggle that is a divinely imposed obligation.[76] Alternatively, one can point to the utility of anger in the kind of vigorous self-defence in which all animals must sometime engage. Our appetite for food and sex can likewise be seen as valuable when it comes to certain aspects of our worldly existence, viz., our need to replenish ourselves and to procreate: in addition, they serve to give the corporeally inclined a hint, however inadequate, of the spiritual bliss that the believer is promised in the afterlife.[77]

But even if this is far from being a wholly world-denouncing stance, it is also a far cry from the Aristotelian picture where – when it comes to the passions –

73 *Iḥyā'* XXII, *bayān* 3, 1448.10–16.

74 *Mīzān* XV, 262.

75 *Iḥyā'* XXIII, *bayān* 4, 1520.4–5.

76 *Iḥyā'* XXII, *bayān* 3, 1447.7–8.

77 *Iḥyā'* XXIII, *qawl fī shahwat al-farj*, 1525.7–8; *Mīzān* XVI, 271; cf. *Iḥyā'* XXXII, *shaṭr* 2, *rukn* 2, *bayān* 2, *ṭaraf* 2, 2262.1–2263.8.

the mean is the ideal because a certain emotional responsiveness simply is the correct and most appropriate way for us to act and feel. The Aristotelian well-rounded person, we will remember, is one who is suitably impassioned in matters large and small, at the right time, in the right measure. For al-Ghazālī, by contrast, the ideal is the sage whose sole desire is for God, while any detraction from this constitutes a failing of a greater or a lesser magnitude. The virtues are developed as the mean between two extremes *because* this is what brings us closest to the angels who feel nothing at all towards the world.[78] To return to the example given above, the appropriately generous person neither hoards wealth nor is concerned with how to spend it: the generous soul is indifferent to money, or as indifferent to it as this world will allow.

Whence could this argument derive? It certainly seems like something that an Aristotelianizing Platonist – or a Platonizing Aristotelian – from late antiquity would say, and there would be any number of channels through which such an argument could have reached al-Ghazālī. However, I have yet to identify a single source, whether proximate or remote, that would offer this exact defence of *metriopatheia* as the next best thing to apathy.[79] Whatever its provenance, I would submit that al-Ghazālī puts forward his argument because it provides a tighter fit for his preferred hierarchy of desires than does the fundamentally pluralist Aristotelian model. For al-Ghazālī, it is axiomatic that whosoever loves anything else at all besides God has not yet perceived where true human happiness lies.[80] This is because one cannot love two things at once: as long as one loves something else, one does not truly love God. Al-Ghazālī likens the heart to a jar which cannot accommodate vinegar until it has been emptied of water.[81] He also cites a proof-text from the Qurʾān according to which God has not created two hearts in man's body.[82] As such, all this asserts unequivocally that all continuing attachments to worldly affairs are only distractions and shortcomings.[83]

A further corollary, one that may seem surprising until one stops to think about it, is that self-denial is never its own end. We are dealing here with something other than the familiar complaint, common since at least al-Muḥāsibī, that asceticism can easily be twisted into a tool for bolstering one's worldly

78 *Iḥyāʾ* XXIII, *bayān* 4, 1519.10–16.

79 I thank Simo Knuuttila and David Konstan for discussing with me possible Greek and Christian antecedents. I may well be missing some perfectly obvious source.

80 *Iḥyāʾ* XXXII, *shaṭr* 2, *rukn* 1, *bayān* 2, *aṣl* 2, 2215.15–18; ibid., *rukn* 2, *bayān* 1, 2245.15–17.

81 *Iḥyāʾ* XXXVI, *bayān* 6, 2617.1–2; cf. *Iḥyāʾ* XXI, *bayān* 4, 1359.19–20.

82 Q 33:4.

83 See *Iḥyāʾ* XXIII, 3: 93.36–38.

reputation, though this notion too finds a place in al-Ghazālī. Nor is al-Ghazālī content merely to point out that anyone who continues to obsess over this or that aspect of their animal nature is shown by the very gesture to be continually preoccupied with it.[84] Al-Ghazālī's proper point is that the final aim is for the positive acts prescribed by God to become delightful and desired for their own sake. Once virtuous habits – the salvific religious qualities – become entrenched, they come to be loved for their own sake and are found to be pleasant, while the opposite is the case with evil and ugly actions.[85] This in turn will lead to a point where one's love of God and the desire to meet him overshadow all else.[86] Al-Ghazālī reproduces in clear terms the aesthetic colouration of Aristotelian virtue ethics – actions divide into the beautiful and the ugly, in the eyes of God as well as in the eyes of the properly habituated human being – with the added corollary that one's love of God is the most intense erotic relationship one can ever have. Al-Ghazālī goes to great lengths in his efforts to detoxify the erotic connotations of the spiritual aspirant's love for God and desire to seek His company, but he never backs down from the central premise that this is an admirable goal to have and an even more exalted one to attain.[87]

This will accordingly make of perseverance only a relative and not an absolute good. It is vastly superior to slackness in religious matters, to be sure, but it remains inferior to that willing commitment to God's purpose which comes easy to the well-adjusted believer. The latter state is what the true lover of God will aim at, and indeed what the true lover of God will find comes naturally to her or him.[88] To the sincere believer all worldly things will cease to matter either way: just as the heart cannot contain two loves at once, so also it cannot be at once given to both love and hate. This spells the end to all hate in the heart of the true lover of God.[89] A related point can be teased out of a passage where al-Ghazālī scolds those who would be eunuchs for the sake of God, or who starve themselves to a wraith-like state, for losing the right balance in religious matters. Contrary to appearances, al-Ghazālī in stating this

---

84 In another place, al-Ghazālī astutely observes that one who hates oneself is equally as self-absorbed as one who loves himself; see *Iḥyāʾ* XXXIV, *shaṭr* 1, *bayān* 1, 2401.20–2402.4; cf. *Iḥyāʾ* XXI, *bayān* 6, 1368.1–8, where obsessing over the minutiae of religious works or one's own failings is similarly described as an impediment.

85 *Iḥyāʾ* XXII, *bayān* 4, 1449.17–19.

86 Ibid., 1450.11–15.

87 See Eric Ormsby's "Introduction" to his English translation of al-Ghazālī's book of *Love, Longing, Intimacy and Contentment*, Cambridge: Islamic Texts Society, 2011, xi–xxxix.

88 *Iḥyāʾ* XXI, *bayān* 6, 1369.9–19; *Iḥyāʾ* XXXII, *shaṭr* 1, *bayān* 5, 2189.21–2190.14; *Iḥyāʾ* XXXVI, *bayān* 15, 2663.5ff.; *Mīzān* XIV, 255.

89 *Iḥyāʾ* XXXIV, *shaṭr* 1, *bayān* 1, 2402.4–6.

opinion wishes neither to denigrate the worth of abstinence nor to deny the need among the many for spiritual striving. What he wants to say, rather, is that the truly spiritually perfect will be able to recognize intellectually the intended benefit in both sustenance and sexual congress without getting carried away by either in the least. The virtuous heart will thus be able to approach all worldly goods with a deep but detached sense of gratitude, while for the unrefined hearts and minds the very same things constitute a real and present danger.[90]

5 Propassions and the Formation of the Will

One development in ancient theories of the emotions is the originally Stoic distinction between passions proper and the so-called propassions (the Greek *propatheiai*) or first motions of the soul.[91] The origins of this theoretical distinction lay in the need to explain what appear to be unmistakable psychophysical reactions to one's perceptions (pointedly including ones identical to physical reactions associated with arousal, fear, and the like) while at the same time holding fast to the Stoic tenet that all of a person's emotions should remain under the sage's rational control and that one can withhold assent from even the most violent bodily urgings. The solution that the Stoics hit upon – ruthlessly caricatured, albeit in an admiring fashion, in Aulus Gellius' *Attic Nights*,[92] from which the following example is taken – was that the sage in a raging storm may be beset by a case of the jitters, turn pale, or otherwise manifest every sign of being afraid. Yet one cannot say that the sage has felt fear, just as long as her or his power of reason has not rushed to the false judgement that there would be anything truly worrisome about the situation (it is assumed here that the sage should adopt a wholly impersonal point of view with regard to all things, and that according to such a viewpoint personal peril really is an indifferent matter). The Stoic theory of propassions later became transformed through its Christian appropriation, where the emphasis came to rest on passing thoughts (*logismoi*), those unsavoury suggestions of the soul that arise unbidden and without warning. Most Christian thinkers came to regard such incipient notions as uncontrollable and as an ineradicable part of our mortal existence. The moral responsibility of the spiritual aspirant, consequently, was

90 *Iḥyāʾ* XXXII, *shaṭr* 2, *rukn* 2, *bayān* 1, *qisma* 6, 2248.16–18.

91 For the development of the Stoic theory of *propatheiai* see K. Abel, "Das Propatheia-Theorem: ein Beitrag zur stoischen Affektenlehre," *Hermes* 111 (1983): 78–97; Knuuttila, *Emotions*, 62–67 and for the medieval Latin continuation, ibid., 178–195.

92 *Noctes Atticae* 19.1.

to quiet such thoughts as they occurred and quash any desire to obey their suggestions.[93]

The ancient discussions are echoed in al-Ghazālī's deliberations regarding the issue of whether a person should be reprimanded for the involuntary suggestions (*khāṭir*, pl. *khawāṭir*) in which his senses and base appetites necessarily involve him. After making a basic distinction that allows for divinely inspired suggestions as well, al-Ghazālī makes a point familiar from the writings of the desert fathers: even if one is to shut out the distractions and temptations produced by one's outer senses, one's imagination will still bring up images and suggestions sufficient to lead astray any aspiring ascetic. Because of the ineradicability of the basic forces of appetite and spirit, one's spiritual struggle will consequently continue until the advent of death.[94] Nevertheless, because this is so, the first involuntary notions that arise in one's soul entirely unannounced cannot yet provide cause for blame or punishment: such inner speech (*ḥadīth an-nafs*) simply is what it is, the crucial thing being what we make of it. Al-Ghazālī further specifies that the first incipient desire cannot be censured either, since it, too, is an inclination of our nature (*mayl aṭ-ṭabʿ*). Similar to the Stoicizing Christian teachers, al-Ghazālī contends that only those who assent to their incipient thoughts or give in to their desires are to be censured, since these are matters that are up to human beings themselves.[95]

One has to wonder about the coherence in drawing the line here, seeing as how al-Ghazālī is otherwise perfectly willing to ascribe both animal and human actions to fully determined or 'necessitating' antecedent causes.[96] In the present context, it is enough to note how according to al-Ghazālī "occurrent notions are the starting point to action since an occurrent notion (*khāṭir*) sets in motion desire (*raghba*), desire moves resolve (*ʿazm*), resolve moves intent (*niyya*), and intent moves the limbs."[97] Though the language is, as in much of the *Revival*, resolutely non-technical, I believe al-Ghazālī's thought is most easily explicable if we situate it against a broadly Peripatetic backdrop. A useful starting point is the standard formulation of the Aristotelian practical

93 See Richard Sorabji, *Emotion and Peace of Mind*, Oxford: Oxford University Press, 2000, 343–371; Knuuttila, *Emotions*, 122–176; on the influential theory of Evagrius in particular, whose works were known also in Arabic circles, Kevin Corrigan, *Evagrius and Gregory: Mind, Soul and Body in the 4th Century*, Farnham: Ashgate, 2009, 73–101.

94 *Iḥyāʾ* XXI, *bayān* 11, 1397.19–1398.9.

95 Ibid., *bayān* 13, 1416.11–1421.8.

96 *Iḥyāʾ* XXXII, *shaṭr* 2, *rukn* 1, *bayān* 2, 2213.15–2214.3; on this point in the context of al-Ghazālī's general cosmology see Frank Griffel, *Al-Ghazālī's Philosophical Theology*, Oxford: Oxford University Press, 2009, 216–221.

97 *Iḥyāʾ* XXI, *bayān* 11, 1391.9–10.

syllogism: given one universal premise ("the good lies in seeking pleasure") and one particular one ("here is something pleasurable"), the cognitive process naturally and necessarily results in action being taken (indulging in pleasures). Compare this with how al-Ghazālī in the *Book of Repentance*, which opens the final quarter of the *Revival*, illustrates the contentious principle that the God's "servant is compelled in the choice that is ascribed to him."[98] His example is that of our desire for, then consumption of, food:

> God created the right hand and the delectable food and the stomach's appetite for that food; He also created the heart's knowledge that the food will set the appetite to rest. Furthermore He created the mutually opposing occurrent notions regarding this particular food – whether it contains something harmful in conjunction with satisfying one's appetite, and whether or not there is something objectionable in its consumption that would preclude its consumption. Then He created the knowledge that no such objection exists: then, with the convergence of all these causes, the instigating will resolves to consume the food. Following upon the vacillation of opposing notions and the fixation of the appetite upon the food, the resolve of the intellect is called choice (*ikhtiyār*). There is no question about its emergence once its causes have become complete, and with the advent of the will's resolve – through God's creation of all this – the hand moves without fail in the direction of the food: after the will and the power have become complete, action follows necessarily.[99]

This is not the place to consider the so-called secret of destiny (*sirr al-qadar*), that is, the determinist problematic to which al-Ghazālī alludes.[100] Rather, what catches the eye is that precisely along the lines of the practical syllogism, the endpoint in any chain of deliberation is action itself (rather than, say, some belief concerning action). When al-Ghazālī, in what follows, says that "every piece of knowledge whose purpose it is to instigate action has not discharged

98 *Iḥyāʾ* XXXI, *rukn* 1, *bayān* 2, 2084.12.

99 Ibid., 2084.13–19.

100 It appears to me that al-Ghazālī is quite happy to concede that all acts of deliberation and subsequent resolution have sufficient antecedent causes, and that consequently everything that goes into a particular human decision can ultimately be traced to the eternal decree of God (*al-qaḍāʾ al-azalī*): for a comparison see, e.g., *Iḥyāʾ* XXXIII, *shaṭr* 2, *bayān* 3, 2346.11–18. For a discussion that makes use of further materials see Th.-A. Druart, "Al-Ghazālī's Conception of the Agent in the *Tahāfut* and the *Iqtiṣād*: Are People Really Agents," in *Arabic Theology, Arabic Philosophy: From the Many to the One*, ed. James E. Montgomery, Leuven: Peeters Press, 2006, 425–440.

its duty if it does not actually instigate it,"[101] he means that the practical aspect of our reasoning faculty is geared towards action, not theories about action. In the *Scale of Action* al-Ghazālī goes so far as to say that on the scale of overall human excellence, practical knowledge is inferior to action itself.[102] All of this, of course, properly reflects the Aristotelian parameters according to which practical knowledge has to do with life as it is led. We do not study virtue in order to know things about it, but in order to become good ourselves.[103]

In uncertainty, al-Ghazālī contends, God comes to the assistance of reason, while Satan and his host fly to the aid of vice.[104] Both the angelic and the demonic impulses that influence our decisions ultimately issue from God: despite the appearance in some passages of the *Revival* of an autonomous force operating contrary to God's purpose, and notwithstanding the accusations that were levelled against him by uncomprehending early readers of the *Revival* as well as the *Niche of Lights*, there is no question here of an overall cosmological dualism. The ontological standing given to Satan in the cosmic scheme is in any case not a matter for investigation within the science of actions, a genre to which the *Revival* professedly belongs.[105] Suffice it to say that Satan's weapons are passion and the appetites, however he may have come by them, and that the reality of these impulses and their effectiveness in turning people's hearts away from God testify to their origin in a secondary cause (*sabab*) of a distinctive nature.

6 Postscript: Executive Justice?

In traditional Platonic fashion, al-Ghazālī lists the four cardinal virtues as wisdom, courage, temperance, and justice. He furthermore states that their perfection is intertwined: at heart, all virtue is of a unitary character.[106] As the

101 *Iḥyāʾ* XXXI, *rukn* 1, *bayān* 3, 2087.12–13.

102 Theoretical knowledge and contemplation outrank them both: *Mīzān*, 229–230.

103 Aristotle, *Nicomachean Ethics* 2.1. In the *Book of Love, Longing, Intimacy, and Contentment* al-Ghazālī puts it that knowledge comes both first and last: we want to know how to act, but in the final end we act in order to know, since contemplation is our ultimate aim (*Iḥyāʾ* XXXVI, *bayān* 6, *sabab* 2, 2618.17–17). The *Book of Fear and Hope* postulates that the true goal of both knowledge and action is the intimate understanding of God (*Iḥyāʾ* XXXIII, *shaṭr* 2, *bayān* 5, 2358.17).

104 See *Mīzān* XI, 244; Q 2:257 is cited as a proof-text.

105 *Iḥyāʾ* XXI, *bayān* 11, 1395.17–19.

106 *Mīzān* IX, 233–234 and XVI, 264–273.

foundations (*uṣūl*) of good character, the cardinal virtues are also tagged to the three parts of the soul, as follows:

> In one's inner aspect (*al-bāṭin*) there are four things, all of which must be good for the perfection of good character: when the four are in repose, balanced and proportionate, then one attains to good character. These [four] are the faculty (*quwwa*) of knowledge, the irascible faculty, the appetitive faculty, and the faculty of justice [mediating] between the three faculties in question.[107]

What attracts one's attention is that in the schematic outline given above, al-Ghazālī tacitly acknowledges the orphan status of the virtue of justice. Justice does not latch on to any one of the recognized parts of the soul; instead, it lies somehow in between. This of course reflects the Platonic conception according to which justice simply *is* the appropriate harmony obtaining between the three parts of the soul (or the state, or the cosmos). Accordingly, al-Ghazālī still describes justice in the *Scale of Action* solely in terms of a harmoniously ordered relation within, as well as between, the three parts of the soul and their characteristic virtues. When all three souls are maximally improved and when appetite and spirit are made subject to reason then justice, as the sum of all of the virtues, is achieved.[108] Yet al-Ghazālī also hints at a more scintillating, although much more problematic, conception of justice, as evidenced by the fact that he chooses to call justice a faculty or power in the afore-cited passage. To get at this, we must first look at its natural ally in the regulation of the passions, namely reason.

One genuinely curious feature of al-Ghazālī's account of the virtues is his contention that there is an excess as well as a defect to the deployment of reason. In contrast to the mainstream of *falsafa* and the Greek rationalist tradition, al-Ghazālī holds that it is possible for one to be too clever for one's own good: to be more specific, an excess of ratiocination will lead to "swindling, wiliness, trickery, and cunning."[109] As a general rule, if the use of reason is put to

---

107 *Iḥyāʾ* XXII, *bayān* 2, 1441.18–21.

108 See *Mīzān* IX, 233–234; *Mīzān* XIX, 286; notably, al-Ghazālī evokes here the concept of religious law (*sharīʿa*) and its perfection.

109 "*Jurbuza wa-makr wa-khidāʿ wa-dahāʾ*": *Iḥyāʾ* XXII, *bayān* 2, 1443.6. The four expressions are near-synonyms, with the first term deriving from Persian and having the connotation of confidence tricks and the like: see Tim Winter's note to his translation, *On Disciplining the Soul*, Cambridge: Islamic Texts Society, 1995, 20.

corrupt ends, then this will result in malice and duplicity (*khubth wa-jurbuza*).[110] The explanation mirrors that given by Miskawayh in his *Reformation of Morals*, where it is also said that wily and duplicitous behaviour issue from a faulty intellect when the power of reason is wrongfully subjected to the mercies of the passions.[111]

Common to Miskawayh and al-Ghazālī seems to be the systematizing urge to have some vice stand on either side of each designated virtue for the sake of symmetry and systematicity. Miskawayh is more thoroughgoing with his project, as he even has justice flanked (rather unconvincingly) by two opposing vices. Al-Ghazālī by contrast sticks to the more common conception according to which justice only has one opposite, tyranny (*jūr*).[112] A more important difference with Miskawayh shows itself in the contrasting ways that Miskawayh and al-Ghazālī deal with the question of what forms the excess of reasoning can take. Miskawayh's explanation is rather awkward: in essence, he suggests that some people are too *quick* to reason, with their mind leaping from thing to thing at such a pace that they do not properly pause to reflect on the objects of their knowledge and grasp their essence. In effect, Miskawayh charges his over-thinkers with a form of mental impatience.[113] This path is not available to al-Ghazālī, who in general follows Avicenna's theory when it comes to explaining concept-formation and intellection.[114] In the Avicennian picture, quick-wittedness (*dhakāʾ*) and intuition (*ḥads*) are unqualified intellectual virtues – indeed, both are distinctive hallmarks not only of philosophical titans but also of prophets. The ability to jump to conclusions and from there to further grounding principles is what intellection is all about, since to grasp some one thing in its quiddity is to grasp its causes and its place in the network of necessary relations between all things.[115] Thus, quick-wittedness could never be a

110 See *Mīzān* XVII, 275; *Iḥyāʾ* XXII, *bayān* 2, 1442.20.

111 See Miskawayh, *Tahdhīb*, 26.

112 Cf. ibid., 28 with *Mīzān* XVI, 273 and *Iḥyāʾ* XXII, *bayān* 2, 1442.18–19.

113 *Tahdhīb*, 26–27.

114 See Alexander Treiger, *Inspired Knowledge in Islamic Thought. Al-Ghazālī's theory of mystical cognition and its Avicennian foundation*, London: Routledge, 2012.

115 For remarks on Ibn Sīnā's notion of perfect contemplation see, e.g., Dimitri Gutas, "Intellect Without Limits," in *Intellect et imagination dans la philosophie médiévale*, eds. M. C. Pacheco & J. F. Meirinhos, Turnhout: Brepols, 2006, 3 vols., 1: 351–372. Space does not permit any proper reflection on the subject, but it seems to me that a picture such as Miskawayh's is only possible in the context of something like a popularizing version of al-Kindī's noetics, where the intelligibles are acquired directly and as a whole. Here, it may indeed make sense to think that a kind of dwelling upon each intelligible separately may be of some positive value; in the Avicennian picture, in contrast – where the very

negative indicator to al-Ghazālī. Accordingly, already al-Ghazālī's early *Scale of Action* specifies that it is practical reason that is susceptible to excess as well as defect and practical reason that may as a consequence also become corrupted.[116] The theoretical intellect, which in al-Ghazālī's exposition in the *Scale of Action* gets designated as the only true form of reason,[117] does not suffer from this fault. When it comes to an understanding of the realities of things (*ḥaqāʾiq al-ashyāʾ*), the heart, which is just another name for intellect in al-Ghazālī's estimation, can never get its fill; to the contrary, it is rightfully insatiable unto infinity since its objects, viz., the intelligibles, are likewise without end.[118]

Whatever the background or justification, al-Ghazālī holds that the reasoning faculty can itself prove unruly despite the fact that reason is supposed to rule over appetite and spirit. This leads one to suspect that something else is needed to provide reason with guidance. And it is here that justice, it seems to me, comes to occupy a curious new role within al-Ghazālī's moral psychology, at least if we are to go by the (admittedly very sketchy) evidence offered by the *Revival*. In a tantalizing formulation, al-Ghazālī notes that it is the 'faculty' or 'power' of justice (*quwwat al-ʿadl*) that is responsible for placing the appetite and the spirit under the rule of reason.[119] Whence derives this newly minted executive power of justice? I am quite unsure, and in fact find it perfectly possible that al-Ghazālī himself would prove shaky if pressed on the point. Nevertheless, we may take notice of how elsewhere in the *Revival* al-Ghazālī proclaims that all the noble and beautiful character traits are reducible to knowledge and power (*ʿilm wa-qudra*).[120] The parallel to the primary characteristics of the Godhead is quite explicit and apparent, and gives rise to the notion that al-Ghazālī might want to reinforce a more general division of labour within every intentional agent between a discerning power and an executive power.

A further analogy from the side of angelology may prove helpful at this point. In explaining the salvific virtue of patience, al-Ghazālī underlines how

---

notion of intelligibility has to do with perceiving a network of necessary causal relations – the alacrity with which connections are made can only be a good thing.

116 *Mīzān* XVI, 266.

117 Ibid., 264–265.

118 Al-Ghazālī's contention that there is no limit to what the intellect can know sets him apart from the mainstream of *falsafa*, though it is much more in line with what some Ashʿarite *mutakallimūn* had proposed: for formulations of this doctrine see, e.g., *Maqṣad*, 57–58; *Iḥyāʾ* XXI, *bayān* 4, 1358.22–23; ibid., *bayān* 6, 1370.8–10; *Iḥyāʾ* XXXVI, *bayān* 3, 2597.3–13; ibid., *bayān* 9, 2630.6–8.

119 *Iḥyāʾ* XXII, *bayān* 2, 1442.6.

120 *Iḥyāʾ* XXXVI, *bayān* 2, 2590.4–5.

patience is a fixed state (*ḥāl*) arising out of an understanding of the harm that will result from following the passions.[121] This means that a cognitive component is necessary when it comes to the higher-order virtues such as continence: it is, however, never enough in and of itself. If argument could make men good, Aristotle had observed, philosophers would have perfected society long ago, but that has not happened.[122] Thus, as al-Ghazālī puts it, the light of guidance (*nūr al-hidāya*), which in itself is an angelic force, must be supplemented by another angel, one that fortifies. The former is described as knowledge (*ʿilm*), the latter as power (*qudra*[123]). Based on certain theological precepts, it seems, al-Ghazālī by the time of writing the *Revival* had arrived at the notion that all intentional action relies, for its explication, on the postulation of two powers: one that proposes a notion, and one that effects it. As in heaven, so also on earth. This is a curious notion indeed, and one rather wishes one knew what to do with it. Unless I am seeing things, there may be a subtle parallel drawn here between the fortifying and guiding angels and the efficient and final modes of causality in the Avicennian cosmos. But it is all very vague, and rather unsatisfying.

What al-Ghazālī ends up saying is that the guiding angel, when all is said done, ranks higher than the fortifying angel,[124] which is to say that all power must in the end bow to knowledge. In Aristotelian as well as Avicennian terms, final causality trumps efficient causality in the sense that it is for the sake of the end that actions are undertaken. It is in fact hard to see that al-Ghazālī would ever make much of his innovation of a separate executive faculty, if ever he meant to. In the realm of created being, the notion of any autonomous power of implementation runs ashore on the grounds of the 'secret of destiny' (see above); in the sphere of the divine mystery, the purported absolute freedom of the divine power turns out to be a much more problematic concept than would first appear.[125] It may be that al-Ghazālī's suggestion that the human character traits be reduced to knowledge and power represents a serious case of conceptual overreach, a systematizing urge taken a step too far. Overall, it seems as though it is more in the expansive treatment of the subrational faculties

121 *Iḥyāʾ* XXXII, *shaṭr* 1, *bayān* 2, 2181.8–10.

122 *NE* 10.9.

123 *Iḥyāʾ* XXXII, *shaṭr* 1, *bayān* 2, 2180.9–2181.2.

124 Ibid., 2181.16–17.

125 See Richard M. Frank, *Creation and the Cosmic System: Al-Ghazālī and Avicenna*, Heidelberg: Carl Winter-Universitätsverlag, 1992; Taneli Kukkonen, "Possible Worlds in the *Tahāfut al-Falāsifa*: Al-Ghazālī on Creation and Contingency," *Journal of the History of Philosophy* 38.4 (2000): 479–502.

that the philosophical interest is to be found in al-Ghazālī's moral psychology. Here, a comprehensive treatment of the workings of the practical intellect would be a first-order *desideratum*. For now, it is to be hoped that the present exposition of the lower parts of the soul can serve to point the way to further studies.

CHAPTER 8

Sex, Marriage and the Family in Al-Ghazālī's Thought

Some Preliminary Notes

Avner Giladi

Introduction

An official publication issued in 1990 by the Egyptian Ministry of Information, under the title "Facts and data on family planning"[1] raises, among others, the question: "What are the most important motives for practicing birth control?" In a short text charged with religious terminology, of all Muslim scholars it is al-Ghazālī who is referred to as a supporter of birth control.[2] Al-Ghazālī's rational attitude toward this question, to which I will return later, in addition to his authority and intellectual ability to cope with relevant theological and ethical issues – such as that of *tawakkul* ("trust in God"), as he does so forcefully in the fourth part of *Iḥyāʾ ʿulūm ad-dīn* ("The Revival of the Religious Sciences")[3] – makes his writings a source of legitimization, almost nine hundred years after his death, for a family planning project.

The impact of al-Ghazālī's thought on posterity is beyond the scope of this paper. I assume, however, that for many Muslims of later generations al-Ghazālī's way of discussing practical matters has other advantages, in addition to its salient rational character. His "shrewd eye for the humble realities of real life,"[4] the sensitivity to human psychology that he brings to his treatment of legal issues, his profound understanding of the complexity of the human soul, and, on top of all this, his pedagogical skills – that is, his logical, clear and

* I wish to thank Ms Liz Yodim for her help in editing the text of this paper.

1 Wizārat al-Iʿlām, al-Hayʾa al-ʿĀmma li-l-Istiʿlāmāt, Markaz al-Iʿlām wa-t-Taʿlīm wa-l-Iittiṣāl, *Ḥaqāʾiq wa-maʿlūmāt ʿan tanẓīm al-usra*, [Cairo], 1990. I am grateful to Prof. Uri M. Kupferschmidt for bringing this publication to my attention.

2 Ibid., pp. 16–17. See also pp. 12, 14.

3 L. Lewisohn, "Tawakkul," *EI*[2], x, pp. 376–378; Eric Ormsby, *Ghazali: The Revival of Islam*, Oxford: Oneworld, 2008, pp. 130–132.

4 Ormsby, *Ghazali*, p. 112.

 | DOI 10.1163/9789004290952_009

sophisticated methods of guidance – to a great extent render his message universal, reaching readers across borders of time, certainly, but also of culture.[5]

Trying to explain the lack of a comprehensive history of Islamic ethics, Montgomery Watt, in his foreword to Muhammad Abul Quasem's *The Ethics of al-Ghazālī*, points out that Islamic moral values are so similar to those of Judaism and Christianity that "they hardly deserved separate attention";[6] there is, however, one exception: family ethics. Basim Musallam, in *Sex and Society in Islam*, and more recently Geert van Gelder, in *Close Relationships: Incest and Inbreeding in Classical Arabic Literature*, to mention just two examples, have convincingly shown how sexual morality is related to other aspects of family ethics and law in the Persian and the three monotheistic cultures, and how it can be used as a criterion according to which each one of them is distinguished and characterized.[7]

"Marriage rules help to define a religion and a culture," observes Van Gelder. For instance, "the alleged practices of the Zoroastrians are a recurrent motif in Arabic literature, used to distinguish between 'us' and 'them'; and heretical sects are not rarely credited with a sexual free-for-all or holding women as communal sex objects, with all the implications of possible incest."[8]

Al-Ghazālī's views on the family – on gender relations and the status of women, on marriage, sex, birth control, divorce, child rearing and education – have not been dealt with comprehensively and systematically, at least not within Islamic studies in the West, as far as I am aware. Some attention has been given to the place al-Ghazālī's notions of femininity and sexuality occupy in his Sufi world view, in a wider context of the status of women and attitudes

---

5 Ormsby, *Ghazali*, p. 36; Avner Giladi, "Islamic Educational Theories in the Middle East: Some Methodological Notes with Special Reference to Al-Ghazālī," *Bulletin of the British Society for Middle Eastern Studies*, 14 (1988), pp. 3–10, especially pp. 6–8. An example of al-Ghazālī's long-term and cross-cultural influence, i.e., his impact upon Jewish thought, particularly from the 12th through the 15th century AD (5th through 9th century AH), is given in Steven Harvey's contribution to this volume.
On the comparison Aḥmad ibn Taymiyya made between al-Ghazālī and Maimonides, the greatest and most influential Jewish thinker in the Middle Ages and beyond, see Hava Lazarus Yafeh, *Studies in al-Ghazzali*, Jerusalem: The Magnes Press, 1975, p. 523.

6 Muhammad Abul Quasem, *The Ethics of Al-Ghazālī: A Composite Ethics in Islam*, Selangor, Malaysia: Published by the author, 1975, p. 9.

7 Basim F. Musallam, *Sex and Society in Islam: Birth control before the nineteenth century*, Cambridge: Cambridge University Press, 1983, pp. 10–11. See also, G.-H. Bousquet, *L'Ethique sexuelle de l'Islam*, Paris: Desclée de Brouwer, 1990, especially chapter 2.

8 Geert Jan Van Gelder, *Close Relationships: Incest and Inbreeding in Classical Arabic Literature*, London and New York: I. B. Tauris, 2005, p. 5. See also pp. 181–183.

toward sexuality in Islamic-mystical cosmology and morality, as well as to his concepts of childhood.[9]

Without ignoring the role of al-Ghazālī as the most prominent theorist of Orthodox Sufism, the sources of his notions on the family in the writings of earlier Muslim philosophers, such as Ibn Miskawayh,[10] and Sufis, particularly Abū Ṭālib al-Makkī,[11] and the possible impact of his writings on later mystics, I approach this theme from a different angle, that of Family History, the field of research that focuses on family structures and functions in different socio-historical circumstances as well as on the changes in gender and generational relations within families, on both the theoretical and the practical level.[12] In the case of al-Ghazālī this approach is justified if we take into account his authority as a spiritual leader and as a "renewer of religion" (*mujaddid ad-dīn* or *muḥyī d-dīn*)[13] in wide circles of Muslims in his time and beyond; we must also take into account the audience he had in mind while compiling not only his *sharʿī* collections but also the first two parts of *Iḥyāʾ ʿulūm ad-dīn*, an audience which included, beside Ṣūfī novices, other, "regular" believers as well, although, admittedly men only.[14]

---

9 See, for instance, Abul Quasem, pp. 110–112; Kaoru Aoyagi, "Transition of Views on Sexuality in Sufism: Al-Makkī, al-Ghazālī, and Ibn ʿArabī," AJAMES (*The Journal of Japan Association of Middle East Studies*) 22 (2006), pp. 1–20, especially pp. 4–11; T. J. Winter's Introduction to *Al-Ghazālī on Disciplining the Soul: Kitāb Riyāḍat al-nafs and on Breaking the Two Desires: Kitāb Kasr al-shahwatayni*, Cambridge: The Islamic Texts Society, pp. xv–xcii; Avner Giladi, *Children of Islam: Concepts of Childhood in Medieval Muslim Society*, Houndmills and London: Macmillan and St Antony's College, Oxford, 1992, pp. 45–60, 64–65.

10 Giladi, *Children of Islam*, pp. 49–50.

11 Abū Ṭālib Muḥammad b. ʿAlī al-Ḥārithī al-Makkī, *Qūt al-qulūb fī muʿāmalat al-maḥbūb wa-waṣf ṭarīq al-murīd ilā maqām at-tawḥīd*, Cairo: Muṣṭafā al-Bābī al-Ḥalabī, 1961, II, pp. 489–529. The relationship of al-Makkī's work to al-Ghazālī's writings is well documented in Richard Gramlich's *Die Nahrung der Herzen. Abū Ṭālib al-Makkīs Qūt al-qulūb*, eingeleitet, übersetzt und kommentiert, 3 Vols., Stuttgart: Franz Steiner Verlag 1992–1995.

12 Tierry Bianquis, *La famille arabe médiévale*, Bruxelles: Éditions Complexe, 2005; H. Benkheira, A. Giladi, C. Mayeur-Jaouen et J. Sublet, *La famille en Islam d'après les sources arabes*, Paris: Les Indes Savantes, 2013, Introduction.

13 On al-Ghazālī's self image as the person sent, according to a divine promise, at the beginning of the 6th Hijri century to renew Islam, see Abū Ḥāmid Muḥammad al-Ghazālī, *al-Munqidh min aḍ-ḍalāl wa-l-mūṣil ilā dhī l-ʿizza wa-l-jalāl*, edited by Jamīl Ṣalībā and Kāmil ʿIyād, Beirut: Dār al-Andalus, 1967, p. 122: *Wa-qad waʿada Allāh subḥānahu bi-iḥyāʾ dīnihi ʿalā raʾs kull miʾa wa-yassara Allāh taʿālā [lī] al-ḥaraka ilā Naysābūr li-l-qiyām bi-hādhā l-muhimm.*

14 Marshall G. Hodgson, *The Venture of Islam: Conscience and History in a World Civilization*, Chicago and London: The University of Chicago Press, 1974, II, p. 190: "Some advice he

The questions to be asked are therefore: what is the perception of "the family" this great thinker and educator has in mind? What are the guidelines he formulates for his students/novices and other readers concerning their family life? How does he combine his expertise as a jurist (*faqīh*) with Ṣūfī lore in his discussion of the subject? And, finally, how is the reality of family structure and function in his time, including his own experience as husband and father (to daughters only?),[15] reflected in his writings? In my short paper, I offer some partial, tentative answers to these questions which, due to the richness, complexity and originality of al-Ghazālī's thought, and due to the scope of his writing, deserve further research.

Sex, Marriage and the Family in *Iḥyāʾ ʿulūm ad-dīn*

Here we come to a set of preliminary questions concerning the place allocated to sex, marriage and the family within al-Ghazālī's *magnum opus, Iḥyāʾ ʿulūm ad-dīn*, compiled apparently between 1095 and 1096 AD (488 and 489 AH),[16] where most of the material on this subject is concentrated: how are these themes interwoven into the general plan of the whole collection? And, what is the relation between their location and their content?

The *Iḥyāʾ* as a whole, intended to deal with *ʿilm al-muʿāmala* ("The science of behavior and relationship"),[17] is designed in such a deliberate way that each text within it has its premeditated place (see appendix below).[18] *ʿIlm al-muʿāmala*, being a preparatory stage for those young scholars of the Law

---

[al-Ghazālī] gave presupposed a *man* (not a woman) whose trade allowed him a fair amount of leisure during his day [...] Only a person whose time could be largely devoted to religion could afford to make use of the Sharʿi life to the full as Ghazālī interpreted it" (emphasis added). See Ormsby, *Ghazali*, pp. 111–112, where the author complains about the tendency of social historians to ignore the *Iḥyāʾ*, which, in his view, is a rich source for this kind of history. As an example, Ormsby presents one of the many parables al-Ghazālī uses in this collection, a parable that reflects his paternal sensitivity and psychological insight. For more examples, see below.

15 *Wa-lam yuʿqib illā al-banāt*, according to ʿAbd al-Ghāfir b. Ismāʿīl al-Fārisī (d. 529 AH), as cited in al-Subkī's *Ṭabāqāt ash-Shāfiʿiyya al-kubrā*. See, ʿAbd al-Karīm al-ʿUthmān, *Sīrat al-Ghazālī wa-aqwāl al-mutaqaddimīn fīhi*, Damascus: Dār al-Fikr, n.d., p. 46.

16 For a general survey of the structure, contents and character of the *Iḥyāʾ*, see, for instance, Lazarus-Yafeh, pp. 363–373; Ormsby, *Ghazali*, pp. 111–138.

17 Lazarus-Yafeh, pp. 359–360.

18 On the "architecture of the Iḥyāʾ," see Ormsby, *Ghazali*, pp. 113–115.

who are spiritually qualified for acquiring *ʿilm al-mukāshafa* ("The science of revelation and vision"),[19] comprises studies of various aspects of the Muslim's outward behavior (*aʿmāl al-jawāriḥ*, lit. "actions of the limbs"), as well as those of his inner moral-psychological traits (*aʿmāl al-qulūb*, lit. "actions of the hearts").[20] Accordingly, the collection is divided into two symmetrical parts, each of which is opened with a pair of introductory books and is split itself into two parts that consist of ten books each. Hence, we get forty books altogether, a figure charged with religious significance in Islam and particularly in the Ṣūfī tradition.[21] Add to this the "vertical" dimension of the collection's plan: most of the books in the first half deal with themes regularly treated in legal compilations, although here they are enriched by the typical Ṣūfī element of introspection – *daqāʾiq al-ādāb al-bāṭina* or *ash-shurūṭ al-bāṭina*; that is, moral-psychological "secrets" (*asrār*), a term which appears in the titles of Books II–VII of the First Quarter: "The secrets of ritual purity," "The secrets of prayer," "The secrets of almsgiving," etc. In this way, al-Ghazālī hopes to attract advanced students of Law, who are accustomed to the four-part structure of Islamic legal compilations, and to convince them to adopt Ṣūfī attitudes towards religious commandments. Those students who successfully follow his instructions in the first twenty books, ten on *ʿibādāt* ("Matters of worship and service") and ten on *ʿādāt* ("Manners and customs"), are invited to pass on to an elevated stage, namely, to embark on a process of disciplining the soul according to the methods suggested in the ten books of the third quarter devoted to *muhlikāt* ("Things leading to destruction"). Now, he who has purified his soul is allowed to "climb up" and reach a higher stage, that of *munjiyāt* ("Things leading to salvation"), dealt with in the fourth quarter of the *Iḥyāʾ*. This final part discusses the different stations and states of the Ṣūfī wayfarer.[22]

As a jurist, loyal to a system of law that is comprehensive and total, al-Ghazālī discusses, in the second quarter of the *Iḥyāʾ* (*Rubʿ al-ʿādāt*), questions such as "gain and earning a livelihood," "lawful and unlawful things," "association with friends and companions" [23] and "travel";[24] he also does not shrink from dealing

---

19 Lazarus-Yafeh, *Studies in al-Ghazzali*, pp. 360–363.

20 For al-Ghazālī's exposition of his deliberations in structuring the *Iḥyāʾ*, see the general introduction to the collection: Abū Ḥāmid Muḥammad al-Ghazālī, *Iḥyāʾ ʿulūm ad-dīn*, Cairo: Muʾassasat al-Ḥalabī, 1967 I, pp. 9–13, especially pp. 10–13.

21 Annemarie Schimmel, *Mystical Dimensions of Islam*, Chapel Hill: The University of North Carolina Press, 1978 (Third printing), p. 94; Ormsby, op. cit.

22 Schimmel, ibid., p. 95.

23 Ormsby, *Ghazali*, p. 117.

24 Ibid.

with the most intimate aspects of human life, namely, marriage and procreation, both encouraged by the Sharīʿa. For some Ṣūfīs, on the other hand, the option of seclusion and celibacy, although perhaps not frequently espoused by others, seemed legitimate.[25] As a result, the question of marriage and family life in the context of Ṣūfī training found its way also into the third quarter of the compilation (*Rubʿ al-muhlikāt*). Interestingly enough, in both cases, the theme of family ethics and sexuality is raised in connection with that of eating manners. In *Rubʿ al-ʿādāt*, "The book on etiquette of marriage" (*Kitāb Ādāb an-nikāḥ*)[26] follows "The book on table manners" (*Kitāb Ādāb al-akl*), the first in this quarter. In *Rubʿ al-muhlikāt*, "The book on breaking the hold of the two desires" (*Kitāb Kasr ash-shahwatayni*; viz., the desires of the stomach and that for sex), comes third, just after two introductory books. The importance of these themes, reflected in the prominent place allocated in the *Iḥyāʾ* to the books on *ādāb al-akl*, *ādāb an-nikāḥ* and *kasr ash-shahwatayni*, is explained by al-Ghazālī's observation (based on the Greek philosophical-ethical tradition, particularly that of Plato and Aristotle) that eating and sex are the most powerful, yet the most morally dangerous, desires (*shahawāt*).

The faculty of desire and that of anger (*ghaḍab*) are subdivisions of the motive faculty (*muḥarrika*) in the animal soul (*an-nafs al-ḥayawāniyya*) – in itself an essential component of the human soul. The desire of the stomach assures one's individual survival while the sexual impulse is responsible for the preservation of the species as a whole; thus "both servants help the body survive" (*khādimāni li-baqāʾ al-badan*).[27] In order to achieve the moral ideal of "equilibrium" (*ʿadl*, lit. "justice"), *shahwa* as well as *ghaḍab* should be subordinate to reason (*ʿaql*) and to religious law (*sharʿ*).[28]

The existential dependence of human beings on bestial cravings from the very moment of their birth makes these passions extremely difficult to curb and balance:

---

25 Arin Shawkat Salamah-Qudsi, "A Lightning Trigger or a Stumbling Block: Mother Images and Roles in Classical Sufism," *Oriens* 39 (2011), pp. 199–226, especially p. 204.

26 In the Qurʾān, the term *nikāḥ* is interchangeably used to designate sexual intercourse and marital union. See Khaleel Mohammed, "Sex, Sexuality and the family" in Andrew Rippin (ed.), *The Blackwell Companion to the Qurʾān*, Oxford: Blackwell, 2006, pp. 298–307, especially 299.

27 *Iḥyāʾ* III (*Kitāb Riyaḍat an-nafs*), p. 73: *Fa-law inqaṭaʿat shahwat aṭ-ṭaʿām la-halaka al-insān wa-law inqaṭaʿat shahwat al-wiqāʿ la-nqaṭaʿa an-nasl*; *Iḥyāʾ* III (*Kitāb Sharḥ ʿajāʾib al-qalb*), p. 7; Abū Ḥāmid Muḥammad al-Ghazālī, *Mīzān al-ʿamal*, Cairo: Maktabat al-Jundī, 1973, pp. 107–116. See also id., *Faḍāʾiḥ al-bāṭiniyya*, ed. ʿAbd ar-Raḥmān Badawī, Kuwait: Dār al-Kutub ath-Thaqāfiyya, n.d., p. 200.

28 *Iḥyāʾ*, III (*Kitāb Riyāḍat an-nafs*), p. 69. Cf. Sherif pp. 24–31.

> [T]he capacities for desire, anger and pride are all present in the human creature; however, the most difficult to deal with and the least susceptible to change is that of desire (*wa-lākinna aṣʿabahā amr*[an] *wa-aʿṣāhā ʿalā t-taghyīr – quwwat ash-shahwa*), which is the oldest capacity in man. For it is the first thing to be created in a child (*idh aṣ-ṣabiyy fī mabdaʾ al-fiṭra tukhlaq lahu ash-shahwa*).[29]

In *Kitāb Kasr ash-shahwatayni*, al-Ghazālī confirms yet again that

> [t]he greatest of the mortal vices which a man may harbour is the desire of the stomach (*shahwat al-baṭn*) [...] After the belly, which is the very well-spring of desires and the source of diseases and disorders, comes the desire for sex and voracious appetite for women (*shahwat al-farj wa-shiddat ash-shabaq ilā l-mankūḥāt*).[30]

Inculcating eating manners in Muslims from a very early age is therefore crucial since – as al-Ghazālī repeats in a chapter he dedicated, in *Kitāb Riyāḍat an-nafs*, to the moral education of children – "[t]he first trait to take control of [the child] will be greed for food" (*wa-awwal mā yaghlib ʿalayhi min aṣ-ṣifāt sharah aṭ-ṭaʿām*) and "he is to be disciplined [first] in this regard" (*fa-yanbaghī an yuʾaddaba fīhi*).[31]

The connection between, on the one hand, the location of each of the books on family and sexual ethics within the *Iḥyāʾ* and their contents and general character, on the other, is clear. *Kitāb Ādāb an-nikāḥ* is directed at a large and diversified body of readers: potential mystics, but also those who prove unable to succeed in completing the long Ṣūfī training and who therefore read the *Iḥyāʾ*, or rather the first half of it, in search of guidance on how to achieve a meaningful and decent Islamic life.

---

29 *Iḥyāʾ* III (*Kitāb Riyāḍat an-nafs*), p. 72. English translation by Winter, p. 26. Cf. Abul Quasem, pp. 108–112.

30 *Iḥyāʾ* III (*Kitāb Kasr ash-shahwatayni*), p. 102; English translation by Winter, p. 106. On page 132, however, al-Ghazālī presents the sexual drive as most powerful and most difficult to control: *Iʿlam anna hādhihi ash-shahwa (shahwat al-farj) hiya aghlab ash-shahawāt ʿalā l-insān wa-aʿṣāhā ʿinda al-hayajān ʿalā l-ʿaql.*

31 *Iḥyāʾ* III (*Kitāb Riyāḍat an-nafs*), p. 93. English translation by Winter, p. 76. Cf. Giladi, *Children of Islam*, pp. 57–58. See also Norbert Elias, *The Civilizing Process*, Oxford UK and Cambridge USA: Blackwell, 1994, especially pp. 42–56. On the connection between food and sex – *al-aṭyabāni* – in Arabic literature, see Geert Jan van Gelder, *Of Dishes and Discourse: Classical Arabic Literary Representations of Food*, Richmond: Curzon, 2000, pp. 109–118.

In his efforts to harmonize two religious approaches towards marriage – the supportive, *sharʿī*, attitude and the reserved one (expressed by several Zuhhād and Ṣūfīs) – al-Ghazālī offers in *Kitāb Ādāb an-nikāḥ* an extremely interesting discussion, rich not only in sophisticated legal, theological and ethical arguments but also, as I said, in psychological insights. Particularly interesting in this context is his "theory of relativity," the nucleus of which we find in al-Makkī's *Qūt al-qulūb*,[32] that proposes different formulas for (or total withdrawal from) family life that should be adapted to the personal circumstances, capabilities and religious aspirations of each believer. "The discourse on sexual desire" in *Kitāb Kasr ash-shahwatayni* is not only shorter than in *Kitāb Ādāb an-nikāḥ*, but also, due to its aim and therefore location in the third quarter of the *Iḥyāʾ*, is focused more on the practical questions of sexuality and family involved in the training of Ṣūfī novices. The fact that al-Ghazālī raises the problem of homosexuality here and not in *Kitāb Ādāb an-nikāḥ*, common as it probably was within groups of male novices who apply the recommendation not to get married,[33] is another indication of his purpose in writing this book.

To close this part of my paper, I should add that references to the family and its components are scattered throughout the *Iḥyāʾ*, frequently in the form of isolated sayings, examples and aphorisms. For instance, the reaction of an ailing child and his parents when a repulsive medicine is prescribed illustrates different attitudes toward life here, in this world, involving temporary harm, vis à vis the eternal existence in the hereafter where the ephemeral suffering on earth may emerge as useful (*aḍ-ḍārr fī l-ḥāl nāfiʿ fī l-maʾāl*).[34] The child, who is naturally unaware of the long-term merit of a medicine, refuses to consume it. Likewise, a caring, loving, yet shortsighted mother rejects a blood-letting treatment for her child while his father, who is conscious of its long-term benefits, supports it.[35] Hidden in the distinction between the emotional response of the mother and the rational approach of the father is a justification of the hierarchy in the patrilineal-patriarchal family where the father, the supreme authority, serves as guardian (*walī*) of his children, although the

32 Al-Makkī II, pp. 528–529.

33 For a warning directed at male novices against close relationships with young men (*ṣuḥbat al-aḥdāth; mujālasat al-aḥdāth wa-mukhālaṭatihim*), see, for instance, Abū al-Qāsim ʿAbd al-Karīm al-Qushayrī, *ar-Risāla al-Qushayriyya*, eds. ʿAbd al-Ḥalīm Maḥmūd and Maḥmūd b. ash-Sharīf, Cairo: Dār al-Maʿārif, 1994 II, p. 580. Such an advice, included in a chapter which al-Qushayrī dedicates to "counsel for novices" (*Bāb al-waṣiyya li-l-murīdīn*) seems to reflect a real dilemma.

34 Iḥyāʾ IV (*Kitāb aṣ-Ṣabr wa-sh-shukr*), p. 124.

35 Ibid.

mother temporarily holds the right to custody of her (husband's) young children (*ḥaḍāna*).[36]

A close observation of the stages of children's physical and mental development as well as parental psychology is mirrored in a description of the wonders of God's creation and His mercy in *Kitāb at-Tafakkur* ("The book of meditation"), where al-Ghazālī draws attention to, among other things, parental emotions as a divine device to protect the helpless infant (*thumma ḥannana qulūb al-wālidayni ʿalayhi li-l-qiyām bi-tadbīrihi fī l-waqt alladhī kāna ʿājiz*[an] *ʿan tadbīr nafsihi*).[37]

Such examples may reveal a little about al-Ghazālī himself as a father "who has observed his children; who has understood, and sympathized with, their small passions and sorrows."[38]

In what follows I will briefly discuss al-Ghazālī's views on marriage and the family, on sexuality – with emphasis on birth control – and on women and gender relations.

Marriage

By raising the question 'to be (married) or not to be,' al-Ghazālī draws attention to a practical issue with which novices had to cope. These beginners might have had in mind early examples of ascetics – *zuhhād* – and Ṣūfī role models such as Ibrāhīm b. Adham[39] and Abū Sulaymān ad-Dārānī,[40] who, in an effort to dedicate themselves exclusively to God, led a celibate life contrary not only to the mainstream Islamic tradition but also to the custom among many

36 Avner Giladi, "Ṣaghīr," *EI*², VIII, pp. 821–827, especially p. 824; id., "Guardianship," in Jane Dammen McAuliffe, (ed.), *Encyclopaedia of the Qurʾān* [EQ], Leiden and Boston: Brill, II (2002), pp. 373–375; Y. Linant de Bellefonds, "Ḥaḍāna", *EI*², III, pp. 16–19; Susan A. Spectorsky, *Women in Classical Islamic Law: A Survey of the Sources*, Leiden and Boston: Brill, 2010, pp. 188–189

37 Iḥyāʾ IV (*Kitāb at-Tafakkur*), p. 545. Cf. Giladi, *Children of Islam*, pp. 45–49. On analogies al-Ghazālī draws from sexual life, see, for instance, his *al-Maqṣad al-asnā – sharḥ asmāʾ Allāh al-ḥusnā*, Cairo: Maktabat al-Jundī, n.d., p. 38 (to exemplify the advantage of *gnosis* – *maʿrifa* – as a means to attain religious truths: a child and an impotent adult cannot grasp the pleasure of sexual intercourse unless, when the former becomes mature and the latter healthy, they experience it directly). See also Orsmby, p. 80.

38 Ormsby, *Ghazali*, p. 112.

39 d. 776 or 790 AD/159 or 173 AH.

40 d. 830 AD/215 AH.

great Ṣūfīs, including al-Ghazālī himself.[41] They might also have been familiar with earlier mystical texts on the subject, for instance, the chapter on "What is preferable – to get married or to abandon marriage altogether" (*Dhikr at-tazwīj wa-tarkihi – ayyuhumā afḍal*) in Abū Ṭālib al-Makkī's *Qūt al-qulūb* from the 10th century AD (3rd century AH).[42]

The Qurʾān and Islamic tradition, including the biographies of the Prophet Muhammad, praise marriage and parenthood and approve of sexual intercourse for procreation as well as for sexual fulfillment (see below).[43] The Prophet is said to have explicitly rejected monasticism – *rahbāniyya* – a position many Ṣūfīs accepted.[44] Al-Ghazālī, as al-Makkī earlier, does not ignore these traditional trends; on the contrary, he openly introduces them in detail.

In *Kitāb Kasr ash-shahwatayni*, however, due to the specific discussion of Ṣūfī training, the formula suggested by al-Ghazālī is rather simple and unequivocal: despite the positive purposes of marriage, namely, first, "that by knowing [... the sexual] delight he is able to draw an analogy which suggests to him what the delight of the Afterlife must be like" (*an yudrika ladhdhatahu* [*ladhdhat al-wiqāʿ*] *fa-yaqīsa bihi ladhdhāt al-ākhira*),[45] and, second, procreation, allowing "the human race to continue and the world to abide" (*baqāʾ an-nasl wa-dawām al-wujūd*),[46] nevertheless "sexual desire also contains evils which may destroy both religion and the world (*wa-lākin fīhā* [*fī shahwat al-wiqāʿ*] *min al-āfāt mā yuhlik ad-dīn wa-d-dunyā*) if it is not controlled and subjugated and restored to a state of equilibrium (*iʿtidāl*)."[47] It is the examination of these advantages and disadvantages of marriage that results in al-Ghazālī's clear conclusion: "[i]t is a condition that the aspirant (*murīd*) remain celibate at the outset (*fī l-ibtidāʾ*), until such a time as his *gnosis* (*maʿrifa*) becomes well-established. This,

41 Winter, p. XLIII; Schimmel, pp. 36–37, 427–428. See also, Avner Giladi, "Herlihy's Theses Revisited: Some Notes on Investment in Children in Medieval Muslim Societies," *Journal of Family History* 36 (2011), pp. 235–247, especially pp. 240–241.

42 Al-Makkī II, pp. 489–529. Cf. Schimmel, p. 428.

43 Harald Motzki, "Marriage and Divorce," *EQ* III (2003), pp. 276–281; A. J. Wensinck, *A Handbook of Early Muhammadan Tradition*, Leiden: Brill, 1960, pp. 143–146 (s.v. "Marriage"); Musallam, *Sex and Society*, pp. 10–11; Abdelwahab Bouhdiba, *Sexuality in Islam*, London: Routledge and Kegan Paul, 1985, pp. 7–13; Avner Giladi, "Birth Control," *EI*[3] IV (2009), pp. 108–113, especially p. 109.

44 Sara Sviri, "Wa-rahbāniyyatan ibtadaʿūhā: an Analysis of Traditions Concerning the Origins and Evaluation of Christian Monasticism," *Jerusalem Studies in Arabic and Islam* 13 (1990), pp. 195–208.

45 *Iḥyāʾ* III (*Kitāb Kasr ash-shahwatayni*), p. 126. English translation by Winter, p. 165.

46 Ibid.

47 Ibid. cf. *Mīzān al-ʿamal*, pp. 109–111.

however, is the case only if he is not overcome by desire. If he is so overcome he should break it [i.e., break its hold] with constant hunger and fasting. Should his desire still not be subjugated, and he find himself unable to restrain his eyes, for instance, even if able to preserve his chastity, then for him marriage is the better state, for it will quieten his desire."[48]

As I have said, *Kitāb Ādāb an-nikāḥ*, written with a larger (male) readership in mind, deals with the subject in a more comprehensive and profound way, combining legal, theological, and moral-psychological deliberations; yet, the text offers the reader less unequivocal solutions. Although here, too, al-Ghazālī takes into account potential moral flaws, *Kitāb Ādāb an-nikāḥ* as a whole reflects a positive attitude toward marriage, expressed from the very first lines of the book's introduction. Indeed, in the first chapter he deals at length with the "Advantages and disadvantages of marriage" (*Fī t-targhīb fī n-nikāḥ wa-t-targhīb ʿanhu*);[49] if the latter scale had outweighed that of the former, after all he would not have proceeded to a guide for legally and morally valid marriage in Chapter 2, "Conditions of a woman and stipulations of the marriage contract" (*Fīmā yurāʿī ḥālat al-ʿaqd min aḥwāl al-marʾa wa-shurūṭ al-ʿaqd*).[50] He also closes the book with the fascinating chapter on the "Etiquette of cohabitation, what should take place during the marriage, and the obligations of husband and wife" (*Fī ādāb al-muʿāshara wa-mā yajrī fī dawām an-nikāḥ wa-n-naẓar fīmā ʿalā z-zawj wa-fīmā ʿalā z-zawja*).[51]

In Chapter One of *Kitāb Ādāb an-nikāḥ*, al-Ghazālī lists five advantages of marriage, namely: (a) "begetting children" (*al-walad*), justified – through a teleological argumentation – by God's way of creating human beings of two genders; (b) "fortifying ones-self against the Devil [...] and satisfying sexual desire" (*at-taḥaṣṣun min ash-shayṭān* [...] *wa-dafʿ ghwāʾil ash-shahwa*); (c) "companionship" (*tarwīḥ an-nafs wa-īnāsuhā*); (d) "ordering the household" (*tafrīgh al-qalb ʿan tadbīr al-manzil*); and, finally, under Ṣūfī inspiration, (e) "disciplining the self and training it to be mindful [...] and respectful of the rights of the wives (*mujāhadat an-nafs wa-riyāḍatuhā bi-r-riʿāya wa-l-wilāya wa-l-qiyām bi-ḥuqūq al-ahl*), tolerating their manners, enduring harm from them [i.e., at their hands], striving to reform them [...] striving toward

48 *Iḥyāʾ* III (*Kitāb Kasr ash-shahwatayni*), p. 128. English translation by Winter, p. 172.

49 Lit. "to make marriage desirous and, on the contrary, to awaken an aversion to it," *Iḥyāʾ* II (*Kitāb Ādāb an-nikāḥ*), pp. 27–46. English translation: Madelain Farah, *Marriage and Sexuality in Islam: A translation of al-Ghazālī's Book on the Etiquette of Marriage from the Iḥyāʾ*, Salt Lake City: University of Utah Press, 1984, pp. 47–77.

50 *Iḥyāʾ* II (*Kitāb Ādāb an-nikāḥ*), pp. 46–54. English translation by Farah, pp. 79–91.

51 *Iḥyāʾ* II (*Kitāb Ādāb an-nikāḥ*), ibid., pp. 54–77. English translation by Farah, pp. 93–126.

making lawful gains for their sake," etc. (*wa-ṣ-ṣabr ʿalā akhlāqihinna wa-ḥtimāl al-adhā minhunna wa-s-saʿy fī iṣlāḥihinna wa-irshādihinna ilā ṭarīq ad-dīn wa-l-ijtihād fī kasb al-ḥalāl li-ajlihinna*).[52] He then presents only three disadvantages: (a) "inability to seek lawful gain" (*al-ʿajz ʿan ṭalab al-ḥalāl*); (b) "failure to uphold wives' rights" (*al-quṣūr ʿan al-qiyām bi-ḥaqqihinna*); and (c) "distractions from God" (*an yakūna al-ahl wa-l-walad shāghil^an^ lahu ʿan Allāh taʿālā*).[53] In concluding this chapter, al-Ghazālī instructs the reader how to use these two lists for introspection, how to weigh the merits versus the flaws from one's own personal point of view, and then decide for oneself whether to marry: "To judge that a person is absolutely better off [by] being married or single falls short of taking into consideration all these matters (*fa-l-ḥukm ʿalā shakhṣ wāḥid bi-anna al-afḍal lahu an-nikāḥ aw al-ʿuzūba muṭlaq^an^, quṣūr ʿan al-iḥāṭa bi-majāmiʿ hādhihi al-umūr*). Rather, such advantages and disadvantages can be considered a precept and a criterion against which the novice should measure himself (*bal tuttakhadh hādhihi al-fawāʾid wa-l-āfāt muʿtabar^an^ wa-miḥakk^an^ wa-yaʿriḍu al-murīd ʿalayhi nafsahu*)."[54] This is an outstanding example of one of the most salient characteristics of al-Ghazālī's perception of human behavior, his "theory of relativity," as mentioned above. Indeed, in the light of the model of the Prophet Muhammad, who, unlike Jesus, "armed himself with strength and combined the virtue of worship and that of marriage,"[55] the Ṣūfī novice for whom "the disadvantages [of marriage] are nonexistent in his case and the benefits are all present"[56] should marry, but for others the case may be different and the solutions accordingly various.

Sex and Birth Control

In al-Ghazālī's discussion of birth control in the third chapter of *Kitāb Ādāb al-nikāḥ*, we find "the most thorough statement of the Islamic permission to

52 *Iḥyāʾ* II (*Kitāb Ādāb an-nikāḥ*), pp. 31–42. English translation by Farah, pp. 53–71. An example of a Biblical prophet, Jonah, who endured harm at the hand of a wicked wife after having asked God to "hasten upon him in this life whatever punishment He has prepared for him in the hereafter," is brought by al-Ghazālī in *Iḥyāʾ* II (*Kitāb Ādāb an-nikāḥ*), p. 42 (English translation by Farah, pp. 69–70). Jonah is described as *ṣābir* (steadfast) in her company.

53 *Iḥyāʾ*, II (*Kitāb Ādāb an-nikāḥ*), pp. 42–45. English translation by Farah, pp. 71–74.

54 *Iḥyāʾ*, II (*Kitāb Ādāb an-nikāḥ*), p. 44. English translation by Farah, p. 74.

55 *Iḥyāʾ*, ibid., p. 46. English translation by Farah, p. 77.

56 *Iḥyāʾ*, ibid., p. 44. English translation by Farah p. 74.

use contraception," as Basim Musallam puts it.[57] It reflects a rational approach to a sensitive intimate-personal and familial issue related to wider theological and moral questions, revealing an open and flexible attitude toward human sexuality. À propos the quotation from the Egyptian pamphlet at the opening of these notes, we should keep in mind the difference between the social background of the discussion of birth control in the 11th–12th century AD (6th–7th century AH), on the one hand, and that of our time, on the other. In a period when high rates of birth were counterbalanced by similarly high rates of infant and child mortality, the question of birth control was dealt with in terms of individual and familial interests, rather than as a socio-political problem of coping with overpopulation as is the case, for instance, in contemporary Egypt.

While justifying the religious duty to marry and procreate in the first chapter of *Kitāb Ādāb an-nikāḥ*, al-Ghazālī assesses, in the third chapter, the practice of coitus interruptus (*ʿazl*) in certain circumstances and for several purposes, and defines such an act as legally neutral (*mubāḥ*) or at the most *makrūh* (reprehensible) but only in its limited meaning of "abandoning a virtue" (*tark al-faḍīla*).[58] Indeed, *ʿazl* contradicts the appropriate Islamic way of life (*ādāb*). Nevertheless, neither the very act nor some of the motivations behind it are unlawful (see below). Al-Gahzālī decisively defends his position vis-à-vis the opposite legal opinion and, basing himself on *ḥadīth* sources and on biological concepts, rebuts the argument of a similarity existing between *ʿazl* and abortion (*ijhāḍ*) or even infanticide (*waʾd*). Accepting the Hippocratic and Galenic theory that "both male and female contribute equally to the formation of the embryo, that both have 'semen,'"[59] he compares the sexual act to the "offer" (*ījāb*) "and acceptance" (*qabūl*) in Islamic contractual law.[60] He who withdraws his offer prior to his partner's acceptance cannot be blamed for breaching an agreement.

Al-Ghazālī sanctions birth control, motivated by economic considerations, when sexual relations take place either between a Muslim man and his own concubine, "to prevent [... her] from bearing a child so that she will not qualify for manumission upon [... his] death" (*ḥifẓ al-mulk ʿan al-halāk bi-istiḥqāq*

57 Musallam, *Sex and Society*, p. 17.

58 *Iḥyāʾ* II (*Kitāb Ādāb al-nikāḥ*), p. 65. English translation by Farah, p. 109.

59 Musallam, *Sex and Society*, pp. 39–53; id., "The Human Embryo in Arabic Scientific and Religious Thought" in G. R. Dunstan, (ed.), *The Human Embryo: Aristotle and the Arabic and European Traditions*, Exeter: University of Exeter Press, 1990, pp. 32–46, especially 32–38.

60 *Iḥyāʾ* II (*Kitāb Ādāb an-nikāḥ*), p. 66. English translation by Farah, p. 110. Cf. Musallam, *Sex and Society*, p. 18.

al-ʿatāq),[61] or between a Muslim man and his free wife. This is in order "to avoid hardships associated with large families (*al-khawf min kathrat al ḥaraj bi-sabab kathrat al-awlād*) and protect oneself from the temptation to pursue illegitimate ways of augmenting one's income" (*dukhūl madākhil as-sūʾ*).[62] Other Muslim scholars supported birth control out of concern for the unborn – for instance, the fear of the enslavement of children – or out of an inability to provide for their education and proper upbringing.[63]

In addition, al-Ghazālī allows the practice of *ʿazl* in order to preserve one's wife's beauty and shapeliness, to secure continuing enjoyment (on the part of men), and to protect her against the life-threatening dangers of childbirth (*istibqāʾ jamāl al-marʾa wa-simanihā li-dawām at-tamattuʿ wa-istibqāʾ ḥayātihā khawf*[an] *min khaṭar aṭ-ṭalq*).[64] On the other hand, when the initiative to avoid pregnancies for similar reasons of "fear of labor pains, child birth and nursing" comes from a wife (*an tamtaniʿa al-marʾa li-taʿazzuzihā* [...] *wa-t-taḥarruz min aṭ-ṭalq wa-n-nifās wa-r-riḍāʿ*),[65] al-Ghazālī rejects it.[66] The difference is explicable: most Muslim jurists, including al-Ghazālī, lived in an urban environment, where the cost of living was higher than in the countryside. They approached the subject of birth control from a perspective of their own patriarchal responsibility for family well-being.[67] Guarding their right to make decisions pertaining to their family size (although, according to Islamic law, a free woman, who is entitled to bear children and enjoy intimate relations, should be consulted before *ʿazl* is applied), they refer exclusively to the motivation and the technique men mostly use, namely, coitus interruptus. At the same time, they ignore those forms of contraception used by women, leaving the latter to physicians and pharmacologists.[68]

Be that as it may, the method al-Ghazālī applies to justify birth control and the legitimacy he confers on "satisfying sexual desire" – that is, as one of the purposes of marriage, which he supports by equating the pleasures of sex with those of Paradise – make him an outspoken representative of a well-established trend in Islamic culture. In the 9th/3th century, al-Jāḥiẓ (d. 869 CE/255 AH)

61 *Iḥyāʾ*, ibid. English translation by Farah, p. 111.

62 Ibid.

63 Musallam, *Sex and Society*, pp. 25–26.

64 *Iḥyāʾ*, II (*Kitāb Ādāb an-nikāḥ*), p. 66. English translation by Farah, p. 110.

65 Ibid.

66 Ibid., where al-Ghazālī condemns also "fear of having female children" (*al-khawf min al-awlād al-ināth*) as the pretext for *ʿazl*, typically suggested by men.

67 Musallam, *Sex and Society*, pp. 28–38.

68 Giladi, "Birth Control," pp. 110–111.

already observed that human beings are the only creatures on earth who, while having sexual relations, occasionally use contraceptive measures: "When he is adverse to having a child, he practices coitus interruptus (*idhā kariha al-walad, ʿazala*)".[69]

The position of Muslim jurists vindicates intercourse for the sole purpose of sexual fulfillment: "the idea of a total, absolute Eros that is its own end," in the words of Abdelwahab Bouhdiba,[70] is understandable if we take into account Islamic sexual morality and the nature of the institution of marriage: Muslim men may have up to four wives at a time, may engage in sexual intercourse with their concubines and may divorce and replace their wives relatively easily.[71] Nevertheless, in the spirit of his moral ideal of *iʿtidāl*, al-Ghazālī preaches moderation and denounces excess in sex and amorous passion (*ʿishq*), the latter constituting "utter ignorance of the intended purpose of sexual congress." Passionate lovers, he says, "will only be satisfied with one person in particular, which thing heaps abasement upon abasement and enslavement upon enslavement."[72] However, in spite of al-Ghazālī's seemingly anti-romantic, practical approach towards marriage – mirrored, for instance in his instructions for men on how to select their wives[73] – his discussion does not altogether lack a sentimental dimension. This is revealed in his description of the Prophet Muhammad's profound love of his young wife ʿĀ'isha, "the first love which occurred in [the time] of Islam" (*awwal ḥubb waqaʿa fī l-islām*),[74] and his recommendations to men to express emotions and to be considerate in the course of sexual encounters (see below).

Al-Ghazālī's Attitude toward Women

Following the early conquests, the expansion of Islam in the Middle East and beyond established contacts between the Arab-Muslim conquerors and the local elites in the big cities. With the socio-cultural adaptation involved in the processes of settlement and urbanization, the position of Muslim women,

69 ʿAmr b. Baḥr al-Jāḥiẓ, *Kitāb al-Ḥayawān*, ed. ʿAbd as-Salām Muḥammad Hārūn, Cairo, 1938, I, p. 110.

70 Bouhdiba, p. 158.

71 Musallam, *Sex and Society*, p. 11.

72 *Iḥyā'* III (*Kitāb Kasr ash-shahwatayni*), p. 127. English translation by Winter, pp. 168–169.

73 *Iḥyā'* II (*Kitāb Ādāb an-nikāḥ*), p. 48.

74 Ibid., p. 56.

particularly in the cities, considerably deteriorated.[75] The Qur'ān reveals the concept of divine wish to create a world based on bivalence and dual relations, a "harmonious unity of the sexes,"[76] but at the same time introduces the outlines of a patrilineal-patriarchal structure of the family, established, however, on new Islamic values. Qur'ānic commentators, collectors of *ḥadīth*, and jurists in the classical period of Islam (7th–11th centuries AD/1th–5th AH), while interpreting the seemingly contrasting messages of the Qur'ān, stressed men's superiority at the expense of the more egalitarian aspects of the holy text. They emphasized restrictive norms with the distinct purpose of legitimizing the new status of women in Islam.[77]

Against this backdrop, Sufism offers a more complex, ambivalent attitude toward women. "The Sufis were well aware of the positive aspects of womanhood," says Schimmel, and "were more favourable to the development of feminine activities than were other branches of Islam [...] The very fact that the first true saint of Islam was a woman – the great lover Rābi'a al-'Adawiyya – certainly helped to shape the image of the ideal pious woman."[78] Muḥyī d-Dīn Muḥammad b. 'Alī Ibn al-'Arabī (d. 1240/638), one of the greatest Ṣūfīs of Islam, represents this exceptional approach. He did not hesitate to study with women and to instruct his daughter, to whom he was strongly attached, in theology. On the mystical theoretical level, he developed the notions of the feminine dimension of the divine and the complementarity of the sexes.[79]

No trace of this more balanced Ṣūfī attitude toward women is to be found either in *Kitāb Ādāb an-nikāḥ* or in *Kitāb Kasr ash-shahwatayni*, both compiled,

75 Leila Ahmed, "Early Islam and the Position of Women: The Problem of Interpretation," in Nikki Keddie and Beth Baron, eds., *Women in Middle Eastern History: Shifting Boundaries in Sex and Gender*, New Haven and London: Yale University Press, 1991, pp. 58–73, especially 58–59; id. *Women and Gender in Islam*, New Haven and London: Yale University Press, 1992, Chapters 2, 3.

76 Bouhdiba, p. 213.

77 Barbara Freyer Stowasser, "The Status of Women in Early Islam," in Freda Hussain (ed.), *Muslim Women*, New York: St Martin's Press, 1984, p. 38. See also, Asma Barlas, "Women's Reading of the Qur'ān," in Jane Dammen McAuliffe, (ed.), *The Cambridge Companion to the Qur'ān*, Cambridge: Cambridge University Press, 2006, pp. 255–258.

78 Schimmel, pp. 426, 429; Ahmed, in Keddie and Baron, p. 66. A short survey of Ṣūfī attitudes toward women is to be found in the Introduction to Sara Sviri, *The Sufis: An Anthology*, Tel Aviv: Tel Aviv University Press and MAPA, 2008, pp. 51–53 (in Hebrew) with references to Rkia Cornell, *Early Sūfi Women*, Louisville, Kentucky, 1999, pp. 15–70 and R. J. W. Austin, "The Sophianic Feminine in the Work of Ibn 'Arabi and Rūmi," in L. Lewisohn, (ed.), *The Heritage of Sufism*, Oxford: Oneworld, 1999–2003, II, pp. 233–245.

79 Ahmed, in Keddie and Baron, pp. 69–70; id., *Women and Gender*, pp. 99–100; Aoyagi, pp. 12–15.

as I have mentioned, for males only. On the contrary, al-Ghazālī is revealed in these books as a fanatic misogynist, particularly in the way he selects *ḥadīth* reports, even "weak" ones,[80] that carry a normative message of the total submission of women to men, some of which – notably those that hold infertile women in contempt – were of an accentuated instrumental, contemptuous and humiliating character. For instance, "A straw mat in the corner of the house is preferable to a barren woman" (*al-ḥaṣīr fī nāḥiyat al-bayt khayr min imraʾa lā talidu*)[81] and "a black child-bearer is better than a beauty that cannot give birth" (*sawdāʾ walūd khayr min ḥasnāʾ lā talidu*).[82] It should be emphasized that this is contrary to the spirit of the Qurʾān, inasmuch as the holy book of Islam, while admitting the religious significance of having many offspring, presents infertility not necessarily as retribution but as another revelation of both God's will and His wisdom in creation.[83]

No wonder, then, that al-Ghazālī compares a woman's status in marriage to that of a slave, *li-annahā raqīqa bi-n-nikāḥ, lā mukhliṣ lahā*[84] and, quoting a *ḥadīth* report, requires that a wife "pleases her husband when he looks at her, obeys him when he commands her and guards his memory and his possessions when he is absent."[85] In another quoted report, the Prophet is described as saying: "Were I to command someone to prostrate himself before another, I would command the wife to prostrate herself before her husband on account of the magnitude of her obligation to him."[86]

---

80 Adrien Leites, "Ghazzālī's Alteration of *ḥadīths*: Processes and Meaning," *Oriens* 40 (2012), pp. 133–148.

81 *Iḥyāʾ* II (*Kitāb Ādāb an-nikāḥ*), p. 33. English translation by Farah, p. 57 – not to be found in the collections of canonical traditions.

82 *Iḥyāʾ* II (*Kitāb Ādāb an-nikāḥ*), pp. 33–34. English translation, ibid.; again, not to be found in the collections of canonical traditions. Cf. Abū Naṣr b. al-Faḍl Ṭabarsī (the Imāmī scholar of the 12th century AD), *Makārim al-akhlāq*, Cairo: Maktabat al-Qāhira, n.d., p. 158: *Al-marʾa as-sawdāʾ idhā kānat walūd*[an] *aḥabb ilayya min al-ḥasnāʾ al-ʿāqir*. Here the saying is attributed to "one of the ʿulamāʾ."

83 Q 42: 49–50: "To God belongs the Kingdom of the heavens and earth; He creates what He will (*yakhluqu mā yshāʾu*); He gives to whom He will females (*yahabu li-man yashāʾu ināth*[an]), and He gives to whom he will males (*wa-yahabu li-man yashāʾu adh-dhukūr*) or He couples them, both males and females (*aw yuzzawijuhum dhukrān*[an] *wa-ināth*[an]), and He makes whom He will barren (*wa-yajʿalu man yashāʾu ʿaqīm*[an]). Surely He is All-knowing, All-powerful." *The Koran Interpreted*, translated by Arthur J. Arberry, Oxford: Oxford University Press, Reissued, 2008, p. 504.

84 *Iḥyāʾ*, II (*Kitāb Ādāb an-nikāḥ*), p. 53. English translation by Farah, p. 91.

85 *Iḥyāʾ*, II (*Kitāb Ādāb an-nikāḥ*), p. 51; English translation by Farah, p. 88 (and note 37, on the origin of this ḥadīth report).

86 *Iḥyāʾ* II (*Kitāb Ādāb an-nikāḥ*), p. 73. English translation by Farah, p. 121. See Abū Bakr ʿAbdallāh Ibn Abī -d-Dunyā, *Kitāb al-ʿIyāl*, ed. ʿAbd al-Raḥmān Khalaf, al-Manṣūra, 1997,

Al-Ghazālī is also an ardent supporter of keeping women secluded within private spaces with very restricted access to the public sphere: although "[t]he Prophet permitted women to go to the mosques," says al-Ghazālī, "the appropriate thing now [...] is to prevent them [even from doing so] except for the old [ones]" (*wa-ṣ-ṣawāb al-ān al-manʿ illā li-l-ʿajāʾiz*).[87]

In the light of this basic approach, al-Ghazālī's few considerate expressions are to be read either as a softer – yet still arrogant and patronizing – version of his negative view (for instance, men should treat their wives with mercy and patience due to the latter's "mental deficiency," "*li-quṣūr ʿaqlihinna*," he says),[88] or as motivated mostly by egoistic male interests. Thus, he calls men to take into account the woman's needs in the context of sexual intercourse; simultaneous orgasms were considered by medieval physicians – Muslims, Christians and Jews alike – as necessary for conception: "Let him proceed with gentle words and kisses" (*wa-li-yuqaddim at-talaṭṭuf bi-l-kalām wa-t-taqbīl*), or "once the husband has attained his fulfilment, let him tarry until his wife also attains hers" (*fa-l-yatamahhal ʿalā ahlihi ḥattā taqḍiya hiya ayḍan nahmatahā*).[89] But when, in *Kitāb al-Murāqaba wa-l-muḥāsaba* ("The book of observation and introspection"), the eighth book of the fourth part of the *Iḥyāʾ*, he dedicates a section to "saintly women who undertook great hardship [in the path of religion]," al-Ghazālī, again, cannot hide his contempt for the "fair sex": "He who is unable to follow *even* the example of women, deserves to be despised," he says.[90]

To Conclude

In his discussion of marriage, sex and the family, al-Ghazālī proves that not only the big questions about the mystic's Path, such as those raised in the fourth part of the *Iḥyāʾ*, but also the very practical aspects of the Muslim daily

pp. 309–312, within a chapter on "Man's rights over his wife" (pp. 304–317). This specific ḥadīth report is repeatedly quoted here, with various chains of transmitters, alongside others, emphasizing the wife's obligation to obey her husband and satisfy him.

87 *Iḥyāʾ* II (*Kitāb Ādāb an-nikāḥ*), p. 60. English translation by Farah, p. 100.

88 *Iḥyāʾ* II (*Kitāb Ādāb an-nikāḥ*), p. 54. English translation by Farah, p. 94.

89 *Iḥyāʾ* II (*Kitāb Ādāb an-nikāḥ*), pp. 63–64. English translation by Farah, pp. 106–107. Cf. Ron Barkai, "Greek Medical Traditions and Their Impact on Conceptions of Women in the Gynecological Writing in the Middle Ages" in Yael Azmon, *A View into the Lives of Women in Jewish Societies*, Jerusalem: The Zalman Shazar Center for Jewish History, 1995, pp. 115–142, especially pp. 133–135 (in Hebrew).

90 *Iḥyāʾ* IV, p. 514, emphasis added.

life deserve profound religious, and indeed intellectual consideration. The discussion of the legitimacy of contraception from a Muslim point of view is an illuminating example of such an examination. It is also one of the most impressive representations of the Islamic approach to human sexuality, which unfortunately escaped Michel Foucault when he compared, in the second part of *The History of Sexuality*, the sexual ethics of Christianity to that of the ancient world.[91]

Both in *Kitāb Ādāb an-nikāḥ* and *Kitāb Kasr ash-shahwatayni*, al-Ghazālī tries to reconcile the well-rooted Islamic tradition in favour of marriage, family life, and procreation as well as an open, positive approach toward human sexuality – all expressed so clearly in the Prophet Muhammad's way of life – with the ascetic tendency to renunciation and abstinence as represented by several prominent Zuhhād and Ṣūfīs. The results of al-Ghazālī's attempt are best reflected in *Kitāb Ādāb an-nikāḥ*, written for a readership that, though exclusively male, was more varied than that of *Kitāb Kasr ash-shahwatayni*. Equipped with methodological means of analysis, an observational ability and profound psychological understanding, al-Ghazālī develops a "theory of relativity" to be applied by each individual (again, male) Muslim according to his personal situation.

Enriched by the Ṣūfī inclination to introspection, the discussion on *Ādāb an-nikāḥ*, with the attention that the author gives to the complexities of the human soul and to individual differences, is a model of a humanistic approach existing within a theo-centric worldview. If not for his disregard of the feminine half of humanity, we could title al-Ghazālī "a humanist," with all the reservations involved in using a term created in a different place and time.

It is exactly al-Ghazālī's efforts to harmonize different attitudes towards family life that highlight the preference Islam as a religion and culture gives to human sexuality, marriage and procreation, all – unlike the Christian dominant approach – free of guilty feelings. His discussion of these themes presents in the best possible way the traditional Islamic point of view with its various nuances and options for application. I assume that these characteristics of al-Ghazālī's deliberations, in addition to his spiritual authority in general, made *Kitāb Ādāb an-nikāḥ* a guide for family ethics for a large audience of educated Muslims. From this perspective, this and other relevant texts are essential for the study of Family History in Islamic contexts.

My notes should be taken as just a starting point for further meticulous research of al-Ghazālī's complex views on the family and their relation to

91 Michel Foucault, *The History of Sexuality, Vol. 2: the Use of Pleasure*, New York: Vintage Books, 1990.

other domains of his thought. Except for *Qūt al-qulūb* by al-Makkī, which no doubt supplied al-Ghazālī with much of the 'raw material' for the texts with which I have dealt here, other legal and Ṣūfī sources that might have inspired him should be located and compared with his relevant writings. In addition, the themes of sexuality and family are discussed in other books authored by al-Ghazālī, in addition to *Iḥyāʾ* and *Mīzān*. A systematic comparison can shed light on changes in his views over the course of time. And finally, an endeavour to gather more details on al-Ghazālī's own family life, hinted at in his writings or explicitly described in his biographies, may explain some of his opinions in this domain.

Appendix: The Structure of *Iḥyāʾ ʿUlūm ad-Dīn*

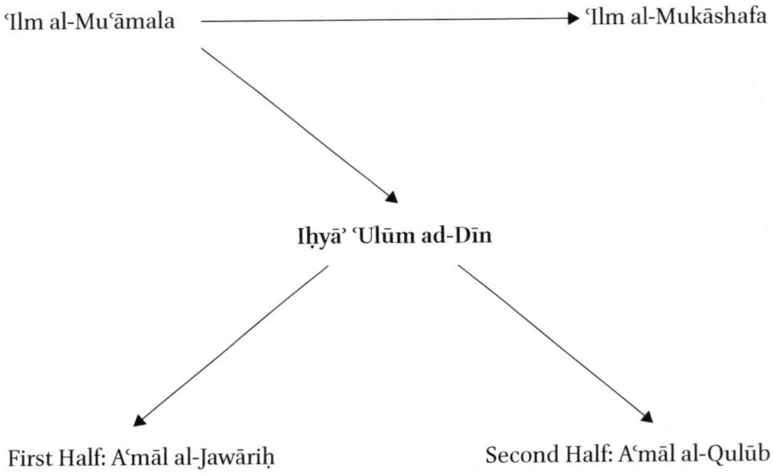

First Quarter – ʿIbādāt		**Third Quarter – Muhlikāt**	
Book I:	*al-ʿIlm*	Book I:	*Sharḥ ʿajāʾib al-qalb*
Book II:	*Qawāʿid al-ʿaqāʾid*	Book II:	*Riyāḍat an-nafs*
Book III:	*Asrār aṭ-ṭahāra*	Book III:	***Kasr al-Shahwatayni***
Book IV:	*Asrār aṣ-ṣalāt*	Book IV:	*Āfāt al-lisān*
Book V:	*Asrār az-zakāt*	Book V:	*Dhamm al-ghaḍab wa-l-ḥiqd wa-l-ḥasad*
Book VI:	*Asrār aṣ-ṣawm*	Book VI:	*Dhamm ad-dunyā*
Book VII:	*Asrār al-ḥajj*	Book VII:	*Dhamm al-bukhl*
Book VIII:	*Ādāb tilāwat al-Qurʾān*	Book VIII:	*Dhamm al-jāh wa-r-riyāʾ*
Book IX:	*Al-Adhkār wa-d-daʿwāt*	Book IX:	*Dhamm al-kibar wa-l-ʿujb*
Book X:	*Tartīb al-awrād wa-tafṣīl iḥyāʾ al-layl*	Book X:	*Dhamm al-ghurūr*
	↓		↓

Second Quarter – ʿĀdāt		**Fourth Quarter – Munjyāt**	
Book I:	*Ādāb al-akl*	Book I:	*at-Tawba*
Book II:	***Ādāb an-nikāḥ***	Book II:	*aṣ-Ṣabr wa-sh-shukr*
Book III:	*Ādāb al-kasb wa-l-maʿāsh*	Book III:	*al-Khawf wa-r-rajāʾ*
Book IV:	*al-Ḥalāl wa-l-ḥarām*	Book IV:	*al-Faqr wa-z-zuhd*
Book V:	*Ādāb al-ulfa wa-l-ukhuwwa*	Book V:	*at-Tawḥīd wa-t-tawakkul*
Book VI:	*Ādāb al-ʿuzla*	Book VI:	*al-Maḥabba wa-sh-shawq*
Book VII:	*Ādāb as-safar*	Book VII:	*an-Niyya wa-l-ikhlāṣ wa-ṣ-ṣidq*
Book VIII:	*Ādāb as-samāʿ wa-l-wajd*	Book VIII:	*al-Murāqaba wa-l-muḥāsaba*
Book IX:	*al-Amr bi-l-maʿrūf*	Book IX:	*at-Tafakkur*
Book X:	*Ādāb al-maʿīsha wa-akhlāq an-nubuwwa*	Book X:	*Dhikr al-mawt wa-mā baʿdahu*

CHAPTER 9

The Duties of the Teacher

Al-Iṣfahānī's Dharīʿa *as a Source of Inspiration for al-Ghazālī's* Mīzān al-ʿAmal

Yasien Mohamed

1 Introduction

Early literary contributions to *adab* as an educational concept prepared the background for the educational thought of ar-Rāghib al-Iṣfahānī (d. 452/1060),[1] whose *Kitāb adh-Dharīʿa ilā makārim ash-sharīʿa* (*The Book of Means to the Noble Virtues of the Revealed Law*) was a source of inspiration for al-Ghazālī (d. 504/1111) as he composed *Mīzān al-ʿamal*.[2] *Mīzān al-ʿamal*, or *The Scale of Action*, is an ethical treatise written either during al-Ghazālī's tenure in Baghdad or shortly after his departure from the city.

1 Ar-Rāghib al-Iṣfahānī, Abū l-Qāsim al-Ḥusayn b. Muḥammad b. al-Mufaḍḍal is well known for his Qurʾānic lexicon, *Kitāb Mufradāt alfāẓ al-Qurʾān*, but less known for his *Kitāb adh-Dharīʿa ilā makārim ash-sharīʿa*, ed. Abū l-Yazīd al-ʿAjamī, Cairo 1987, which is a work of Islamic philosophical ethics. All reference is to this Cairo edition, but there are some textual variations in an edition printed in Tehran; see ar-Rāghib al-Iṣfahānī, *Kitāb al-Dharīʿa ilā makārim ash-sharīʿa*, ed. Sayyid Ali Mir Lawhi Falawurjani, Iṣfahān: University of Iṣfahān, 1997. For information on his life and ethical thought see Yasien Mohamed, "Al-Rāghib al-Iṣfahānī's Classical Concept of the Intellect," *Muslim Educational Quarterly*, 1995, 13 (1) pp. 52–61; "The Ethical Philosophy of al-Rāghib al-Iṣfahānī," *Journal of Islamic Studies*. 1996, 6 (1) pp. 51–75; "The Unifying Thread Intuitive Cognition of the Intellect in al-Fārābī, al-Isfahānī and al-Ghazālī," MAAS *Journal of Islamic Science*, 1996, 12 (2) pp. 27–47; " 'Knowledge and Purification of the Soul,' An Annotated Translation with Introduction of al-Iṣfahānī's Kitāb al-Dharīʿa ilā Makārim al-Sharīʿah" (pp. 58–76; 89–92), *Journal of Islamic Studies*, 1998, 9 (1) pp. 1–34. The most extensive contribution on al-Iṣfahānī to date is my *The Path to Virtue: The Ethical Philosophy of al-Rāghib al-Iṣfahānī*, Kuala Lumpur: International Institute of Islamic Thought and Civilization, 2006.

2 Al-Ghazālī, *Mīzān al-ʿamal*, ed. Sulayman Dunyā, Cairo: Dār al-Maʿārif, 1964. All reference is to this edition, but for variations we may refer to other Arabic editions. See al-Ghazālī, *Mīzān al-ʿamal*, ed. Aḥmad Shamsuddīn, Beirut: Dār al-Kutub al-ʿIlmiyyah, 1989; al-Ghazālī, *Mīzān al-ʿamal*, ed. ʿAlī Bū Milḥim, Beirut: Dār wa-Maktabat al-Hilāl, 1995; al-Ghazālī, *Mīzān al-ʿamal*, ed. Maḥmūd Bijū, Damascus: Dār at-Taqwā, 2008. For a German translation see *Das Kriterium des Handelns* (*Ghazzali's* Mīzān al-ʿAmal), translation with notes by Abd-Elṣamad Abd-Elḥamīd, Darmstadt: WBG, 2006.

 | DOI 10.1163/9789004290952_010

This article will focus on the etiquette (*adab*) of education with respect to the duties of the teacher. I will compare the view of al-Iṣfahānī with al-Ghazālī to determine the extent to which al-Iṣfahānī's *Dharīʿa* was a source of inspiration for al-Ghazālī's *Mīzān*. We attempt to show how al-Ghazālī appropriated and refashioned a particular section of *Dharīʿa* as a source text. This will contribute to a better understanding of the sources that shaped al-Ghazālī's ethics in general and his educational thought in particular.

To begin, a writer's thought and style are shaped by a variety of influences. The theory of intertextuality helps us understand that no author is completely original. His text is a product of previous texts, whether they creep into it consciously or unconsciously, and whether he acknowledges the previous texts or not. According to Barthes,[3] a text is a multidimensional space in which a variety of writings, none of them original, blend and clash. The author's power and originality lies in the way he blends these writings and not on the dependence of one particular work.

All literature is intertextual: "All literary texts are woven out of other literary texts, not in the conventional sense that they bear the traces of 'influence' but in the more radical sense that every word, phrase or segment is a reworking of other writings which precede or surround the individual work."[4] Although our focus is on al-Iṣfahānī's *Dharīʿa*, we must assume that other writings also serve as sources upon which al-Ghazālī drew for his content and style. No scholar, no matter how great, is completely original, and al-Ghazālī is no exception. In spite of his criticism of the philosophers, there is evidence to suggest that he was inspired by their writings, albeit in the form of Arabic translations, or mediated through the works of Ibn Sīnā or ar-Rāghib al-Iṣfahānī. Thus, al-Ghazālī's *Mīzān* must necessarily be a product of a variety of sources; this article, however, aims to demonstrate the impact of one specific source only. Our intention is not to undermine the originality of al-Ghazālī, but we must not treat his treatise as a closed-off entity. Though our approach may appear contradictory in that we invoke the power of intertextuality, on the one hand, and acknowledge the revisionary skill of the author on the other, this is our way of bridging the gap between traditional assumptions about authorial power and control and the poststructuralist claim that authors neither create their own texts nor control them, but are themselves products of pre-existent cultural discourses. Thus, the poststructuralist Barthes affirms: "We know that a text consists not of a line of words [...] but of a multi-dimensional space in which are married

---

3 Roland Barthes, *Image-Music-Text*, London: Fontana, 1977; cf. Terry Eagleton, *Literary Theory: An Introduction*, Oxford: Blackwell, 1983.

4 Ibid., p. 138.

and contested several writings, none of which is original: the text is a fabric of quotations resulting from a thousand sources of culture."[5] Indeed, powerful philosophical ideas are prevalent in the air and permeate the thinking of the author, and often unconsciously. However, we can also make a case for the author, as we do for al-Ghazālī, who makes deliberate and intentional choices for his source text, and refashions them for his own purpose.

I will examine the structure of *Mīzān*, but more importantly, I will concentrate on the 'structuration'[6] of the text, or the way the structure of the text came into being; that is to say, I want to bring to the reader's attention the literary context in which *Mīzān* was produced. I have chosen the *Dharīʿa* for comparison because of its literary resemblance to *Mīzān*. Consideration of length will only allow a comparison of the educational section in these two texts.

Al-Ghazālī's ideas on moral education are not new to us, but are derived mainly from *Iḥyāʾ ʿulūm ad-dīn* (*The Revival of the Religious Sciences*), especially *Kitāb al-ʿIlm* (*The Book of Knowledge*) and *Kitāb Riyāḍat an-nafs* (*Disciplining the Soul*).[7] Studies on his *Mīzān al-ʿamal* are scanty, however, and to date no detailed examination of the educational section of *Mīzān* has been published, even though it is nearly identical to the education section of the Book of Knowledge in the *Iḥyāʾ*. Hence, comparing *Dharīʿa* to the *Mīzān* is like comparing it to the *Iḥyāʾ*. We have chosen *Mīzān* for comparison with *Dharīʿa* because of the strong similarity between these two texts, but also because such a comparison has certainly never been undertaken in great detail until now.

To understand the literary sources that inspired *Mīzān*, we need to examine the literature on moral education and *adab* that preceded it, especially Miskawayh's (d. 421/1030) *Tahdhīb al-akhlāq* (*The Refinement of Character*) and al-Iṣfahānī's *Kitāb al-Dharīʿa*. Many scholars have just assumed that the main source of philosophical ethics for al-Ghazālī was *Tahdhīb*,[8] but new research –

5 Roland Barthes, "The Death of the Author" in Hazard Adams (ed.), *Critical Theory since Plato*, Florida, Harcourt Brace Javanovich: 1971, p. 1132.

6 This term is used in Roland Barthes, "The Structuralist Activity" in ibid., pp. 1128–1130; cf. Terry Eagleton, *Literary Theory*, University of Minnesota Press, who used the term with reference to Barthes (p. 139).

7 See for example, al-Ghazālī, *On Disciplining the Soul and on Breaking the Two Desires, Books 22 and 23 of the Revival of the Religious Sciences*, translated with an introduction and notes by T. J. Winter, Cambridge: Islamic Texts Society, 1995.

8 See for example, the work of Lenn E. Goodman, "Morals and Society in Islamic Philosophy," in Brian Carr (ed.), *Companion Encyclopedia of Asian Philosophy*, London: Routledge, 1997, pp. 1000–1023. Goodman assumed that Islamic philosophical ethics came to an end with Miskawayh, and there is no mention of al-Iṣfahānī.

especially the research of Madelung,[9] Daiber[10] and Sherif[11] – has thrown light on *Dharīʿa* as the primary source of influence on al-Ghazālī's *Mīzān*. Giladi states that we should review the educational literature before al-Ghazālī to determine the extent to which he has been influenced by it, and the extent to which he has improved on it.[12] In pursuing this goal, Giladi provides a useful list of bibliographical information regarding works that were written in the medieval period, but makes no mention of al-Iṣfahānī.[13]

Al-Ghazālī was mainly interested in the moral education of children and adults and the training of Sufi mystics; a more explicitly Sufi slant on moral education is contained in *Ayyuhā l-walad*.[14] Al-Ghazālī's writing on children's education as reflected in *Iḥyāʾ* was probably inspired by Miskawayh, who wrote a substantial chapter on it in his *Tahdhīb al-akhlāq*. As for *Mīzān*, the main source of inspiration is primarily *Dharīʿa*, except for chapter one, which is an attempt to steer ethics in the direction of Sufism.

In *Mīzān* we have an ethics, but with a difference. Al-Ghazālī established an extensive theoretical basis for adopting an ethics informed by Sufi practices.[15] Most jurists and theologians concur that faith must be expressed in good deeds, but differ on the status of these good acts and how these impact the definition of a believer. Al-Ghazālī favoured the Sufi method of self-realization,

9 Wilferd Madelung, "Ar-Rāġib al-Iṣfahānī und die Ethik al-Ġazālīs," in Richard Gramlich, ed., *Islamwissenschaftliche Abhandlungen Fritz Meier zum sechzigsten Geburtstag*, Wiesbaden, Franz Steiner Verlag, 1974, pp. 152–63.

10 Hans Daiber, "Griechische Ethik in islamischem Gewande: Das Beispiel von Rāġib al-Iṣfahānī," in Burkhard Mojsisch and Olaf Pluta, eds., *Historia Philosophiae Medii Aevi: Studien zur Geschichte der Philosophie des Mittelalters*, 2 vols., Amsterdam, 1991–92, I, pp. 181–92.

11 Mohamed Ahmed Sherif, *Ghazali's Theory of Virtue*, Albany: State University of New York Press, 1975. In appendix 1 (pp. 170–176) Sherif discusses the authenticity of the *Mīzān*, refuting the argument of M. Watt, who holds that the philosophical ethics of the *Mīzān*, since written after the *Iḥyāʾ*, cannot be the work of al-Ghazālī as it gives primacy to the role of reason. Sherif alludes to the close textual resemblance between the *Dharīʿa* and the *Mīzān*, and mentions modern scholars such as L. Massignon, M. Bouyges, G. F. Hourani and ʿAbd ar-Raḥmān Badawī, who accept it as an authentic work of al-Ghazālī.

12 Avner Giladi, "Islamic Educational Theories in the Middle Ages: some Methodological Notes with Special reference to al-Ghazali," *British Society for Middle Eastern Studies*. Bulletin, 1988; 14:1, pp. 3–10.

13 Ibid., pp. 3–10.

14 Al-Ghazālī, *Letter to a Disciple: Ayyuhā 'l-Walad*, trans. Tobias Mayer, Cambridge: Islamic Texts Society, 2005.

15 Ebrahim Moosa, *al-Ghazali and the Poetics of Imagination*, Chapel and London: The University of North Carolina Press, 2005, p. 205.

but also acknowledged other approaches among the jurists, theologians and philosophers.[16] For Aristotle, habituation of moral action is essential for character development.[17] Miskawayh and al-Iṣfahānī integrated the principle of habituation into their philosophical ethics and al-Ghazālī, borrowing the principle from al-Iṣfahānī, placed it within a Sufi context. This is not the only Greek element that filtered through to al-Ghazālī via al-Iṣfahānī; the former also integrated a portion of Platonic psychology, with its tripartite division of the soul into the rational, concupiscent and irascible faculties – as in Aristotle, balance between these faculties led to the virtues of wisdom, courage, temperance and justice.[18] Thus, it is clear al-Ghazālī was open to philosophy, as has been confirmed by two recent articles by Garden[19] and Janssens.[20] Garden views al-Ghazālī's *Munqidh* as an apologetic attempt to demonstrate his rejection of philosophy; this is a response to charges against his *Iḥyāʾ*, which critics alleged to be inspired by philosophy itself. Janssens discusses the Aristotelian division between the theoretical and practical sciences, which al-Ghazālī adopts for his epistemology. The duties of the teacher fall under the practical sciences, which are designed for religious and moral practice in Islam.

Unmistakably, the Qurʾān is a common source for both al-Iṣfahānī and al-Ghazālī. The former inspired the latter to use the Qurʾān to support philosophical ethics. This is obvious by the manner in which Qurʾānic verses are arranged for a particular ethical context. Al-Ghazālī embraced philosophical ethics and integrated it into a Qurʾānic and Sufi context. Yet, influence does not imply a lack of originality; al-Ghazālī's originality lies in providing a philosophical basis for his Sufi ethics or, as it were, a Sufi orientation for his philosophical ethics. The first chapter of *Mīzān* provides an intellectual justification for combining knowledge (*ʿilm*) and practice (*ʿamal*). Practice is not merely the practice of Platonic virtues, but also religious and mystical virtues such as *tawba* (repentance) and *tawakkul* (trust). These philosophical and mystical virtues lead to the purification of the self, which is the key to the intuitive knowledge of God.

16 Ibid., p. 253.

17 Cf. Aristotle, "Eudemian Ethics," in *Complete Works of Aristotle: The Revised Oxford Translation*, trans. Ed. J. Barnes, vol. 2, Princeton: Princeton University Press, 1984, esp. p. 1932.

18 See Mohamed, *The Path to Virtue*, chapter 5.

19 See Kenneth Garden, "Coming Down from the Mountaintop: al-Ghazali's Autobiographical Writings in Context," in *The Muslim World*, ed. M. Afifi al-Akiti, 101 (4), 2011, pp. 581–596.

20 See Jules Janssens, "Al-Ghazali between philosophy (*falsafah*) and Sufism (*taṣawwuf*): His Complex Attitude in the Marvels of the Heart (*ʿAjaʾib al-Qalb*) of the Ihya Ulum al-Din," in *The Muslim World*, ed. M. Afifi al-Akiti, 101 (4), 2011, pp. 614–632.

Al-Iṣfahānī's *Dharīʿa* reflects an interesting blend of Greek and Islamic influences, and unlike Miskawayh's *Tahdhīb al-akhlāq*, he quotes extensively from the Qurʾān and hadith. According to Najjār, al-Ghazālī and al-Iṣfahānī have often been compared; the former used to admire the latter's *Dharīʿa*, and used to take it along with him on his travels.[21] In any case, al-Ghazālī employs it extensively, often quoting passages verbatim; he nevertheless does not acknowledge his sources in several of his works, including *Mīzān al-ʿamal* and *Iḥyāʾ*. According to Madelung, as much as half of *Mīzān* is derived from *Dharīʿa*, and much of it also found its way into *Iḥyāʾ*, where portions of the *Dharīʿa* are incorporated into al-Ghazālī's mystical ethics.[22]

Al-Ghazālī does not acknowledge the works of al-Iṣfahānī, but this does not signify a vendetta against al-Iṣfahānī in particular; rather, it was the oral and written tradition of the time to draw upon the ideas, statements and compositions of previous authors without acknowledgement. Al-Ghazālī rarely cites his sources. In his autobiography, he mentions specifically the names of Abū Ṭālib al-Makkī (d. 386/996) and al-Muḥāsibī (d. 243/857) as sources of inspiration for his Sufi ideas; al-Iṣfahānī is not acknowledged at all – in fact, there is no mention of al-Iṣfahānī in any of al-Ghazālī's works. Though al-Ghazālī was critical of Greek thought, it cannot be that he neglected mentioning al-Iṣfahānī simply because his ethics were inspired by Greek ethics. Indeed, al-Ghazālī was himself influenced by Greek philosophy, and he states in the *Munqidh* that there is no reason to reject philosophy if its wisdom does not contradict the Qurʾān and Sunna. Despite this, however, al-Ghazālī refutes allegations that he was inspired by the ancient philosophers; he responds, in a section on ethics, that he arrived at much of his ideas either through independent investigation or from researching Sufi sources. For al-Ghazālī, the wisdom of the philosophers ultimately came from the mystics or the Prophets.[23] Of course, al-Ghazālī deliberately ignores Ibn Sīnā – whom he famously charges with blasphemy – even though some philosophical and psychological concepts filtered through to al-Ghazālī by Avicennian channels.[24]

---

21 Al-Iṣfahānī, *Tafṣīl an-nashʾatayni wa-taḥsīl as-saʿādatayni*, ed. A. Najjār, Beirut, 1988, pp. 20–21.

22 Wilferd Madelung, "Ar-Rāġib al-Iṣfahānī und die Ethik al-Ġazālīs," p. 153.

23 Al-Ghazālī, *al-Munqidh min aḍ-ḍalāl: Majmūʿ rasāʾil al-imām al-Ghazālī*, ed., Aḥmad Shamsuddīn, Beirut: Dār al-Kutub al-ʿIlmiyyah, 1988, p. 44; W. Montgomery Watt, *Deliverance from Error and the Beginning of Guidance*, Kuala Lumpur: Islamic Book Trust, 2005, pp. 27–28.

24 Jules Janssens, "al-Ghazzali and his use of Avicennian texts [XI]," in *Problems in Arabic Philosophy*, ed. M. Maroth, Pilisesala, The Avicenna Institute of Middle Eastern Studies,

Despite his critique of philosophy and his scepticism that reason could produce certitude, al-Ghazālī wrote three philosophical works that prepared the ground for his subsequent systematic writings on theology: *Miʿyār al-ʿilm* (*The Criterion of Knowledge*), *Miḥakk an-naẓar* (*The Touchstone of Thought*) and *Mīzān al-ʿamal* (*The Scale of Action*). *Miʿyār* and *Miḥakk* are works of logic, and *Mīzān* is a work of philosophical ethics. Al-Ghazālī mentions *Miʿyār* in several different places in *Mīzān* as his own book. This not only provides the internal evidence for the authorship of *Mīzān*, but also for its chronology as a work that followed *Miʿyār*.[25]

Recent research by Janssens, al-Akiti and myself compared these two works and came to a similar conclusion about the close resemblance between them.[26] Janssens provides a brief overview of similar passages in these two texts, including the duties of the teacher, in order to identify *Dharīʿa* as a source for *Mīzān*. I compare these two texts in detail with reference to the duties of the student, and conclude that all ten duties in *Mīzān* can be traced to *Dharīʿa*. A similar comparison is attempted in this article but with reference to the duties of the teacher. Thus, for a full picture of the intertextual relation of these two works the reader should also refer to my article dealing with the duties of the student.

Al-Ghazālī integrates philosophical, religious and Sufi elements in his *Mīzān al-ʿamal*, which, according to Madelung, was written before al-Ghazālī's period of retreat into Sufism (488/1095–499/1106);[27] according to al-Akiti, *Mizān* is

---

2003, pp. 37–49; cf. Janssens, *Ibn Sina and his influence on the Arabic and Latin World*, Ashgate: Variorum, 2006.

25 See for example, *Mīzān*, p. 179, where al-Ghazālī states: *ʿalā shurūṭ allatī dhakarnāhu fī Miʿyār al ʿilm* ("according to the rules [of logic] that we have mentioned in [the work entitled] *Miʿyār al-ʿilm*").

26 Previous research on al-Iṣfahānī's educational impact on al-Ghazālī appeared in my *The Path to Virtue: The Ethical Philosophy of al-Rāghib al-Iṣfahānī*, chapter 10; see also my "The Ethics of Education: al-Isfahanı's *al-Dharīʿa* as a Source of Inspiration for al-Ghazali's *Mīzān al-ʿAmal*" in *The Muslim World*, ed. M. Afifi al-Akiti, 101 (4), 2011, pp. 633–657, for a comparison of the two texts with reference to the duties of the student. For a slight comparison, see also Jules Janssens, "Al-Ghazali's *Mizan al-Amal*: An Ethical Summa based on Ibn Sina and al-Raghib al-Isfahani," in *Islamic Thought in the Middle Ages: studies in text, transmission and translation, in honour of Hans Daiber*, edited by Anna Akasoy and Wim Raven, Leiden: Brill, 2008, pp. 123–138. See also M. Afifi Alakiti, *The Madnun of al-Ghazali: A Critical Edition of the Unpublished Major Madnun with Discussion of his Restricted Philosophical Corpus*, 3 vols., dissertation, University of Oxford, 2008, vol. 1, pp. 92–93, nn. 235 and 238, for sections dealing with the connection between the *Dharīʿa* and the *Mīzān*.

27 Madelung, "ar-Raghib al-Iṣfahānī und die Ethik al-Gazālis," p. 152.

a philosophical work written before *Tahāfut*, but after *Maʿārij*. In any case, it is clear that *Mīzān* is an earlier book, and represents al-Ghazālī's attempt to clarify his own thoughts about the relationship between philosophical ethics and Sufism. *Mizān* provided the rational justification for his Sufi oriented ethics in *Iḥyāʾ* and *Ayyuhā l-walad*. We turn now to an in-depth comparison of the education section of *Dharīʿa* and *Mīzān*.

2 Duties of the Teacher in al-Iṣfahānī

The first duty of the teacher is "to be sympathetic to students and treat them as his children." The teacher should not be a tyrant, but like a loving father, revered inasmuch as he imparts knowledge to the student that is useful both in this world and the Hereafter.

> The duty of the teacher is to treat his students as his children. He is more important to them than their own parents as Alexander responded when he was asked: 'is your teacher more honoured to you than your father'? He replied: 'Indeed my teacher, for he is the cause of my eternal life but my father is the cause of my transient life'. The Prophet (ṣ) also stated: "I am to you like a father." So the teacher of virtue should follow the Prophet's example as he is the successor of the Prophet in guiding people. Like the Prophet, the teacher should be kind to his student as God states: *He* [Muhammad] *is deeply concerned for you and full of kindness and a mercy towards the believers* [emphasis added].[28]

As children love their father and siblings, so should students love their teacher and their colleagues. The teacher's relationship with students – even the ones who misbehave – should be based on love and sympathy.

The second duty of the teacher is to gently, not bluntly, dissuade the student from misbehaviour. Implicit dissuasion is more effective than explicit dissuasion for five reasons. One of the reasons is that explicit dissuasion incites rebellion:

> The Prophet said: 'If people were prohibited from making porridge from the camel's dung, they would have done it, stating, "We would not have

28 *Dharīʿa*, p. 244; Q. 9:128. The translation of this verse and all subsequent verses are by Majid Fakhry in *The Qur'an: A Modern English Version*, London: Garnet Publishing House, 1997.

> been forbidden to do it if there had not been some good in it."' An apt example of this is when Adam and Eve were commanded not to eat the forbidden fruit from the tree.[29]

The autocratic method of teaching makes the student stubborn and doggedly determined to violate prohibitions. A gentle and subtle approach is recommended.

The third duty of the teacher is to follow the example of the Prophet who did not expect payment for knowledge that God had granted him.

> The teacher should know that selling knowledge for worldly gain violates divine wisdom. God has intended wealth [as a means of] providing food and clothes for the body. And the body is intended to serve the soul, and the soul intended to serve knowledge. Knowledge is the master to be served and should not serve anything else; but wealth should be the servant, not master of anything. Thus, he who uses knowledge to serve wealth has made knowledge a servant, when it should be the master to be served.[30]

The fourth duty[31] of the teacher/sage (*ḥakīm*) and scholar (*ʿālim*) is to protect the ignorant student from pursuing the inner realities of knowledge, and to limit his knowledge in accordance with his understanding. The teacher should impart that which is within the grasp of the student, in order to prevent him from being confused and averse to the subject. In substantiation, al-Iṣfahānī quotes two sayings from the Prophet and one attributed to Jesus:

> The Prophet said: 'Speak to people according to the knowledge they possess, and refrain from [talking about] that which they have no knowledge, or is it that you would have God and His Prophet to be belied?' The Prophet also said: 'When you talk to people about a matter they do not understand, they will go away.' Jesus, the son of Mary, said: 'Impart not wisdom to those who cannot absorb it; this is itself a violation of wisdom. Impart it to those who can understand, otherwise (withholding) it will be an injustice to them. Be like the intelligent physician who only dispenses medicine when it will be beneficial.'[32]

---

29 *Dharīʿa*, p. 245.

30 Ibid., p. 246.

31 Ibid., pp. 247–250.

32 Ibid., pp. 247–248.

The teacher should therefore give instruction in knowledge that the student will be responsive to, and he should speak to him according to his level of understanding.[33]

Al-Iṣfahānī then explains the criteria to be considered when instructing students with advanced knowledge and wisdom. Substantiating his case with Qur'ānic verses and a hadith, he espouses the view that on the Day of Judgment the teacher will be punished for withholding knowledge from the deserving and will be likewise punished for disclosing knowledge to the non-deserving. The non-deserving are like orphans that are not mentally matured and so cannot be entrusted with wealth. Such orphans are likely to abuse it and in the process destroy themselves and others.

> Just as it is incumbent on the sages,[34] if they find the feeble-minded attain the age of maturity, they should remove all obstacles in their way, and hand over to them responsibility for their own wealth as God states: *Test orphans until they reach marriageable age; then, if you find they have sound judgment, hand over their property to them* [emphasis added];[35] similarly, sages who find the mature seekers of guidance receptive to knowledge should impart knowledge to them in accordance with their merit. Knowledge is an acquirement that leads to the eternal life, but wealth is an acquisition by which we are assisted in this worldly life. The [teacher] who imparts knowledge to the non-deserving should be punished, but if he withholds knowledge from the deserving who is receptive to it, he should also be punished.[36]

Al-Iṣfahānī distinguishes between the layman and the elite. The layman should not slacken in his commitment to the revealed law; otherwise, doubt will enter his soul.[37] A restless person seeking knowledge of reality, however, should be encouraged to specialise in certain areas of knowledge,[38] and to attain to the

---

33 Ibid., p. 249.

34 Ibid., p. 249, the Cairo edition has the word *ḥukkām*, but the Iṣfahān edition reads *ḥukamā'* (sages).

35 Cf. Q. 4:6.

36 *Dharīʿa*, p. 249.

37 Rosenthal, *Knowledge Triumphant*, pp. 306–308. Rosenthal states that al-Iṣfahānī assigned value to doubt, inasmuch as it might lead to obtaining certainty; al-Iṣfahānī was also conscious of the role of doubt in creating sectarianism and disunity in the Muslim community. Doubt was therefore not something he would recommend for the general public, but only for mature students and advanced scholars.

38 *Dharīʿa*, pp. 249–250.

level of the intellectual elite. On the other hand, the wicked and mentally weak should be prevented from such specialization. The ordinary layman, for his part, should rather keep to his craft or trade; the teacher should not expect him to specialize in a particular branch of knowledge. If the ordinary person does specialize he may neglect his craft, which is important for the development of the land (*ʿimāra*).

Whoever is preoccupied with the development of the earth, whether in a trade or profession, must confine himself only to the amount of knowledge that befits his social standing and requirements for the general worship of God. The only other knowledge permitted such a layman is the knowledge that fills his soul with the desire for paradise and the fear of hell-fire, as mentioned in the Qurʾān. Doubt and confusion should not be instilled in such a person.[39]

Furthermore:

> If a person in early advanced communities comes forward to the educated to specialise in philosophy and true knowledge to surpass the level of the masses and to attain the level of the elite, he will be tested first. If he does not have a [philosophical] temperament, or is ill-prepared for such knowledge, he should be discouraged and prevented from pursuing it. But if he is good-natured and receptive to learning, then he must enter the House of Wisdom provided that he is committed to it. He should then not be allowed to leave [the House] until he has acquired all the knowledge demanded of him or unless he dies.[40]

Gradation in knowledge and method is central to al-Iṣfahānī's educational philosophy. The teacher should gently correct the student and earnestly discourage him from knowledge beyond his grasp. The student or layman who is not ready for higher knowledge should keep to his own study or profession; this prevents confusion and laxity in commitment to the revealed law and craft.

The Fifth Duty

The fifth duty is for the teacher to set a moral example and to practice what he preaches. Al-Iṣfahānī uses the term 'the preacher' (*al-wāʿiẓ*) here instead. The preacher, also an educator, is the intermediary between the sage and the common folk; the sage, after all, cannot communicate directly with the masses. This is not his fault, but the shortcoming of the common folk who cannot understand him. To facilitate the transfer of knowledge from the sage to the

39 Ibid., pp. 249–250.

40 Ibid., p. 250.

common man, the preacher acquires wisdom from the sage and passes that wisdom to the masses according to their understanding; by this mechanism, the wisdom of the sages filters through to the common folk.

The preacher can only affect the common folk by his moral example. This is consistent with the first duty of the student in al-Iṣfahānī, which is to purify the soul of vices. The preacher's moral example is crucial to effecting moral transformation; students are inclined to follow the preacher's visible actions, not his audible words. As such, a good preacher should be like the sun that supplies the moon with light rays, yet contains itself more than what it radiates; this is like fire, which melts iron, yet itself has a greater glow than the iron. The Qur'ān describes the antithesis of such a person:

> [You will find] among the people a person whose discourse about life in this world displeases you, and who calls God to vouch for what is in his heart, although he is your worst enemy. And when he departs, he roams the land sowing corruption therein and destroying crops and livestock; but God does not like corruption.[41]

As mentioned, the preacher benefits people more through his outer actions than his inner knowledge, inasmuch as his inner knowledge cannot be seen, but his external actions can be; al-Iṣfahānī compares the preacher's relationship to the masses with the doctor's role with his patients. If the doctor tells people to avoid poisonous food, but eats it himself, his behaviour would appear preposterous. Similarly, the preacher who acts immorally[42] likewise appears preposterous. Another analogy is the relation between the printer and the printed, or the shadow and the possessor of the shadow.

> It is said that the preacher compared to the preached is like the printer compared to the printed. Just as it is impossible to imprint into clay that which is not sketched in the engraver, it is impossible for the soul of the preached to obtain virtue when it is absent in the soul of the preacher. Thus, if the preacher's speech is devoid of action, the preached will only learn from his speech but not his action. Also, the relationship of the preached and the preacher is like the relation between the shadow and the possessor of the shadow. As it is impossible for the shadow to be crooked when its possessor is [standing] straight up, so it is impossible

41 Ibid., p. 254; cf. Q. 2:204–205.

42 Ibid.

> for the preached to be upright while the preacher is crooked in character.[43]

Thus, the teacher should be a moral example for the student, who learns by imitation. If the teacher is corrupt, the child will learn to be corrupt; if the teacher is morally upright, the child will learn to be morally upright. Good character is a matter of habit. If the teacher practices good habits, the child will try to follow his good example.

3 Duties of the Teacher Compared with al-Ghazālī

Al-Iṣfahānī identifies five main duties of the teacher; in al-Ghazālī there are eight duties of the teacher. These duties will be compared, pointing out similarities and differences with respect to content and style. To avoid repetition we will only compare the passages in *Mīzān* with similar passages in *Dharīʿa*. As will be seen, al-Ghazālī relies heavily on al-Iṣfahānī's structure and argument, adding or excising very little.

The first duty, as noted above, is to treat students with love and affection, just as one would treat one's own children. The passage containing this first duty[44] in al-Ghazālī is shorter than al-Iṣfahānī's, but the idea is the same and the style is similar. They both quote the same hadith about the Prophet being a father to his companions, and the same statement from Alexander describing the greater respect accorded to the teacher compared to the parent.[45] They both quote two of the same Qur'ānic verses. The passages are not identical, but they have a similar style and use of citations. The difference is that verses 9:128 and 19:5–6 are absent in the *Mīzān*; furthermore, the sentence which reads "all scholars are travelling towards God, the Almighty, and they are treading the path that requires the fostering of love" is absent in the *Dharīʿa*.

The second duty, corresponding to the fourth duty[46] in al-Ghazālī, is to dissuade the student from evil ways, implicitly rather than explicitly; explicit dissuasion will not prevent the evil action of the sinner, but will instead make him more determined in his vile action. Al-Ghazālī is brief, leaving out

43 Ibid., p. 255.

44 *Mīzān*, p. 363f.

45 Al-Ghazālī mentions the same idea in the *Munqidh*; however, no *ḥadīth* or quotation from Alexander is cited there. See al-Ghazālī, *al-Munqidh*, p. 81; Watt, *Deliverance from Error*, p. 81.

46 *Mīzān*, p. 364f; cf. al-Ghazālī, *Letter to a Disciple*, p. 42, p. 54.

al-Iṣfahānī's five reasons for gentle dissuasion, though he quotes the same hadith about making porridge from the camel's dung and the story of Adam and Eve who ate the forbidden fruit. He omits the poetic verse mentioned in *Dharīʿa*.

The third duty, which corresponds with the second duty[47] in *Mīzān*, is to imitate the Prophet, who was instructed by God not to accept any form of remuneration for services and to maintain an attitude of detachment from the world. We know that this attitude of detachment became the turning point in al-Ghazālī's life; leaving Baghdad to follow the path of asceticism, he aimed to overcome pride, develop sincerity by doing things to please God, not for fame and wealth. Al-Ghazālī states in his autobiography:

> It had already become clear to me that I had no hope of the bliss of the world to come save through a God-fearing life and the withdrawal of myself from vain desire. [...] It was also clear that this was only to be achieved by turning away from wealth and position and fleeing from all time-consuming entanglements. [...] After that I examined my motive in my work of teaching, and realized that it was not a pure desire for the things of God, but that the impulse moving me was the desire for an influential position and public recognition. I saw for certain that I was on a brink of a crumbling bank of sand and in imminent danger of hell-fire unless I set about to mend my ways.[48]

Both al-Iṣfahānī and al-Ghazālī quote the same Qurʾānic verse: "Say: No reward for this do I ask of you."[49] Both presumably intend this verse to stress the importance of sincerity in transmitting knowledge; knowledge should be pursued or taught not for the sake of wealth or position, but for the sake of God. Both agree that wealth is inferior to knowledge: wealth should serve the body and knowledge should serve the soul; neither should one be mastered by the acquisition or exercise of affluence. Al-Iṣfahānī develops the point logically, showing the relations of the lower external virtues to the soul: wealth serves food and clothes, which in turn serves the body, which in turn serves knowledge, which in turn serves the soul. Al-Ghazālī makes the same point, using the same Arabic words, but does not mention that wealth serves food and clothes.

47 *Mīzān*, p. 366f.

48 Al-Ghazālī, *al-Munqidh min aḍ-ḍalāl*, in *Majmuʿah rasāʾil al-Imām al-Ghazālī*, Beirut: Dār al-Kutub al-ʿIlmiyyah, 1986, p. 59; cf. Montgomery Watt, *al-Ghazali: Deliverance from Error*, pp. 48–49.

49 Q. 6:90.

This is a minor difference. Al-Iṣfahānī states: "Knowledge is served, not a servant, and wealth is a servant, not served" (*fa-l-ʿilm makhdūm ghayr khādim wa-l-māl khādim ghayr makhdūm*). This sentence is repeated almost verbatim in *Mīzān*, except that *ghayr* is replaced with *laysa*.

The fourth duty of al-Iṣfahānī corresponds to the sixth duty[50] in al-Ghazālī. The teacher's duty is to instruct in accordance with what is in the grasp of the student. This prevents the student from becoming confused and from loathing the subject. To substantiate the trueness of this duty al-Iṣfahānī quotes four hadith, a saying from Jesus, a saying from ʿAlī, and five Qurʾānic verses. Al-Ghazālī quotes the same four hadith, the same saying from Jesus, and three of the same Qurʾānic verses. These many quotations tend to affect the coherence of the style for the modern reader. However, for the Arabic reader, they press home the central message that the teacher should not withhold knowledge from those students who are ready for it, nor impart knowledge to those who are not ready for it.

The second part of the fourth duty in al-Iṣfahānī corresponds with the seventh duty[51] in al-Ghazālī. The teacher's duty is to teach the basics to the slow student. If he teaches the advanced sciences he will confuse the student, who will as a result neglect his worship and his craft, never attaining the level of the elite. The craft is important for the development of the earth (*ʿimārat al-arḍ*), which benefits society greatly. Al-Ghazālī shares the same idea as al-Iṣfahānī with slight differences in style. Some sentences are almost identical, and others are reformulated. Unlike al-Iṣfahānī, al-Ghazālī mentions the need for honesty and trustworthiness in the craft. For both, the craft is not an end in itself, but a means to benefit the society. The society's welfare in turn is instrumental to the welfare of the hereafter. This is consistent with the idea that wealth should serve the body and the body should serve the soul. Thus, all activity, be it a craft or the pursuit of science, must lead to the purification of the soul, and ultimately to happiness in the hereafter.

For al-Iṣfahānī a student who is wicked or does not have the intellectual ability should be prevented from specializing in a particular branch of knowledge and entering the House of Wisdom; but if he is good-natured and intellectually capable, he should be encouraged to enter the House of Wisdom, and should remain there till his death or until he has acquired all the knowledge expected of him.[52] Al-Ghazālī concurs with al-Iṣfahānī that a wicked student, or one with a bad character, should be prevented from any study of a higher

---

50 *Mīzān*, pp. 365–367; cf. al-Ghazālī, *Letter to a Disciple*, p. 46.

51 *Mīzān*, pp. 369–370.

52 *Dharīʿa*, pp. 249–250.

order. He does not mention, like al-Iṣfahānī, that he should remain in the institution until his death. To describe the academic institution, al-Iṣfahānī uses *Dār al-Ḥikmah* (House of Wisdom) and al-Ghazālī uses *Dār al-ʿIlm* (House of Knowledge).

The fifth duty of al-Iṣfahānī deals with the preacher, who acts as an intermediary between himself and the common folk, and who ought to set the moral example as people are more inclined to imitate the outward actions of the teacher. This corresponds with the eighth duty[53] of the teacher in al-Ghazālī, who does not mention the word 'preacher' as the intermediary, but the 'teacher.'

> The teacher's action should not contradict his words, for that will drive people from seeking his guidance and from the right path. While knowledge is comprehended through the mind, action is comprehended through the eyes. The people who see with their eyes (*asḥāb al-baṣāʾir*) are far greater in number compared to those who see through their minds. He should focus more on refining his actions than on improving and disseminating knowledge.[54]

They both give the example of the doctor who warns people not to take something poisonous, but then consumes it himself. Al-Iṣfahānī specifically uses poisonous food as an example; for his part, al-Ghazālī names anything that is poisonous. Unlike al-Iṣfahānī, al-Ghazālī mentions that people might even be enticed to taste the poisonous substance that the doctor has prohibited. Their motivation, al-Ghazālī suggests, is that the doctor may be regarded as selfishly withholding from the patient what he himself enjoys. They both share the analogy of the printer and the printed; but al-Iṣfahānī develops the analogy in a more complete and logical manner:

> Just as it is not possible to imprint into clay that which is not sketched in the engraver, it is not possible for the soul of the preached to obtain virtue when it is absent in the preacher.[55]

In al-Ghazālī, "the relation between the guide and the guided is like the relationship between the stamp and the clay."[56]

---

53 *Mīzān*, pp. 370–372; cf. al-Ghazālī, *Letter to a Disciple*, p. 50, for the use of the word "preacher."

54 Ibid., p. 371.

55 *Dharīʿa*, p. 254.

56 *Mizān*, p. 371.

Al-Iṣfahānī also gives the example of the shadow and the possessor of the shadow; al-Ghazālī gives the relatively analogous relationship between the shadow and the cane: that is, if a cane is curved, the shadow of the cane cannot be straight. They both cite the same hadith about bad innovation. Al-Iṣfahānī quotes five Qur'ānic verses. Al-Ghazālī quotes one verse from *sūrat al-Baqarah* commanding mankind to practice what is preached; for the same divine command, al-Iṣfahānī quotes from *sūrat aṣ-Ṣaff*.

Here again, the duty of the teacher to practice what he preaches is strongly emphasised by al-Ghazālī; this has clearly preoccupied his mind before his departure from Baghdad, and this may partly explain his sense of guilt and depression during his spiritual crisis. As a case in point, al-Ghazālī attacks Ibn Sīnā's attitude towards *khamr*, or wine. In his autobiography al-Ghazālī is critical of those people who are polite to Islam, but do "not refrain from drinking wine and various immoral practices." Seeking to justify their habits, they assure themselves that they are "sufficiently wise to guard against" the enmity which is wine's direct product. Al-Ghazālī refers to Ibn Sīnā who, although praising the revealed law, acknowledges that he drinks wine, albeit for medicinal purposes, not for pleasure.[57] Al-Ghazālī argues that it is precisely Ibn Sīnā's well-regarded philosophical mind that will cause others to imitate him. The other extreme is that people reject the rational sciences, partly due to the laxity of morals. Thus, al-Ghazālī was not only concerned with the problem of lapsed morals, but also the problem of the neglect of the rational sciences.

From the foregoing we note that these five duties in al-Isfahānī correspond to the duties in al-Ghazālī. From al-Iṣfahānī's fourth duty, he derives the sixth and seventh duties; thus, the five duties in al-Iṣfahānī are equal to the six duties in al-Ghazālī. Al-Ghazālī added two more duties (the third and fifth), which gives us a total of eight duties of the teacher. We shall now turn to an exposition of these two additional duties.

Al-Ghazālī's third duty[58] is that the teacher should not withhold from the student any advice or allow him to attempt the work of any grade unless he is qualified for it. Furthermore, he should be reminded that the purpose of knowledge is not for worldly pleasure and power, but for the sake of God and the happiness of the hereafter. However, should he intend to pursue knowledge for the sake of power and prestige, he should not be stopped.

> If [the teacher] notices a person who seeks knowledge only for position or boasting with scholars, he should not be prevented from study. His

57 Al-Ghazālī, *al-Munqidh*, p. 74; Montgomery Watt, *Deliverance from Error*, p. 69.

58 *Mīzān*, p. 365f.

> preoccupation with learning with such an [ignoble] intention is better than evading learning, for the knowledge he acquires could make him aware of the hereafter and its realities.[59]

Al-Ghazālī states that such people may do things for the sake of boasting, but eventually realize the insincerity of their intention. His autobiography tells us that al-Ghazālī studied for the sake of fame, but came to realize his insincere intention, and so resolved to shun worldliness and to purify his soul of all vices.[60] Not surprisingly, therefore, al-Ghazālī has a tolerant approach to such boastful students. He knows from his own experience that he was boastful himself at one stage, but this did not prevent him from coming to a realization of his vice and resolving to improve. It is his knowledge of right and wrong that saved him; or rather it is ultimately through God's grace that he was saved, for it is God that endowed him with this knowledge. Echoing his own life experiences, al-Ghazālī declares that the arrogant student should continue to pursue knowledge in the hope that it would sensitise him to his proud ego. Al-Ghazālī himself chose knowledge over ignorance, which enabled him to be more critical of his own vices.

Al-Ghazālī's fifth duty[61] is an original contribution, and cannot be traced to a source in al-Iṣfahānī. Al-Ghazālī warns that a teacher should never disparage other sciences in front of students, lest they become discouraged in pursuing those sciences; for example, teachers of jurisprudence should not disparage

---

59 Ibid., p. 365. This duty should not be confused with the seventh duty of the teacher, which is to prevent a student of bad character from further study. Possessing the wrong motives for study, however, does not imply a corrupt character; a person who studies for the sake of fame can always correct himself later in life, knowledge apparently conferring, in its attainment, a benefic effect.

60 The idea of tolerating the boastful student being able to change is another piece of evidence suggesting that the *Mīzān* was written just after al-Ghazālī's departure from Baghdad; after all, it was through his own experience of boastfulness that enabled al-Ghazālī to realise the way of the Sufis and to make the change for the better. There is a statement in the *Iḥyā'*, however, which confirms to him that this realization comes from experience and personal observation: see the third duty of the teacher in the *Iḥyā'*, "There is no better proof for this than personal experience and observation"; cf. Nabih Amin Faris, *al-Ghazzali the book of Knowledge*, Lahore: Sh. Muhammad Ashraf, 1979, p. 148. This statement is absent in the third duty of the *Mīzān*, which implies that al-Ghazālī must have added it to the *Mīzān* when reformulating the duty in the *Iḥyā'*. This is further evidence that the *Mīzān* could not have been written after the *Iḥyā'* as assumed by M. Watt; the statement in the third duty of the *Iḥyā'* was as a result of the eleven years of spiritual experience and search.

61 *Mīzān*, p. 365.

the rational sciences. Interestingly, there is no mention of the rational sciences (*al-ʿulūm al-ʿaqliyya*) in the education section of *Iḥyāʾ*. In its place, al-Ghazālī states that the teachers of jurisprudence should not belittle the teachers of the science of hadith. Perhaps this suggests that during the time of writing *Mīzān*, al-Ghazālī was still in his philosophical phase, and so looked more favourably towards the philosophical sciences than in the later period after his conversion to Sufism.[62] In his *Munqidh*, al-Ghazālī expresses his concern for those who are impressed with the philosophers' mathematical precision, but then end up blindly following their corrupt ways and beliefs.[63] Here again, he must have had Ibn Sīnā in mind as an example of such a philosopher. People who are captivated by such philosophers should be restrained from pursuing the sciences. This point accords with the sixth duty of the teacher in *Mīzān*; the caution in *Mīzān*, however, seems to be directed mainly at dialectical theology or *kalām*, which can confuse the masses. The idea of respecting all the sciences, however, is consistent with the tenth duty of the student in al-Ghazālī.[64]

The teacher should rather make the student aware of the value of the knowledge that is above his level so that he can be preoccupied with it once he has completed the branch of knowledge that he is currently studying. If he is studying two subjects concurrently,[65] he should rather finish the study of the one, and then complete the other, taking care of the importance of gradation in learning.[66]

As can be observed from the preceding comparisons, al-Ghazālī adopts the five duties of al-Iṣfahānī. He divides the fifth duty into two separate duties, and adds two of his own duties that cannot be found in the *Dharīʿa*. In our comparison of the five duties of al-Iṣfahānī with the eight duties in al-Ghazālī, we noted that the ideas are basically the same, with some minor differences. The quotations from the Qurʾān, hadith, and poetic verses are mostly identical, used for the same topic, and presented in the same sequence. For some duties, al-Ghazālī cites fewer Qurʾānic verses than al-Iṣfahānī; in one duty al-Ghazālī quotes a different Qurʾānic verse to express the same meaning and message. He appears to have used *Dharīʿa* as a rough draft to select, delete and reconstruct a new systematic and coherent discussion on the duties of the teacher.

---

62 This further supports the assertion that the *Mīzān* was written when al-Ghazālī was still in his philosophical and theological phase in Baghdad, or shortly after his departure from the capital.

63 Al-Ghazālī, *al-Munqidh*, p. 38; Watt, *Deliverance from Error*, pp. 21–22.

64 See Mohamed, "The Ethics of Education", pp. 633–657.

65 The idea of concurrent subjects is not mentioned in the *Iḥyāʾ*.

66 *Mīzān*, p. 366.

Al-Ghazālī does not extract the duties from *Dharīʿa* slavishly, but adapts them to his own context. He paraphrases some passages from it and adopts some passages or sentences with minor changes such as using a different analogy or a different term. The *Dharīʿa* is not just a static source that al-Ghazālī simply picks from and rearranges, but he refashions the material into alternative fields of interpretation. Al-Ghazālī responds to the source text; he does not merely agree with it, but recasts it for his own purpose, namely, to suit the theme of *Mīzān*, which is partly a preparation for his Sufi ethics. Needless to say, this was not his only source of inspiration; he was also inspired by Ibn Sīnā, insofar as a reactive attack can be considered inspiration. Al-Ghazālī was also inspired by the early Sufi masters such as al-Muḥāsibī, and tried to provide a philosophical basis for the Sufi emphasis on the purification of the self.

In terms of content, both al-Ghazālī and al-Iṣfahānī deal with ethics as a practical science to be lived. This is the key to true education, which must lead to the intuitive knowledge of God. This higher knowledge is achieved when the soul is purified of vices and adorned with virtue. It is only then that it becomes receptive to the true knowledge of God. Since the focus of ethics is practical, the teacher should not only teach, but also embody the moral virtues through his personal example. Knowledge and practice must go together, and the teacher must embody exemplary conduct so that good qualities can pass to his students. For both al-Iṣfahānī and al-Ghazālī, education should be a means of controlling the lower self by the higher faculty of reason through a process of moral training. The establishment of good moral habits will lead the student to acquire virtues until his self can express them naturally, without any conscious effort. This philosophical basis of ethics is not new in al-Iṣfahānī and al-Ghazālī; it has its precedents in the Aristotelian ethical legacy. What is new, rather, is that these two figures directed this purification to the intuitive knowledge of God. This higher knowledge of God is also the ultimate goal of the Sufis; in light of this, al-Ghazālī provided a way to arrive at this knowledge through the practical program of Sufi meditation and obedience to the teacher or spiritual master.[67]

Conclusion

Mīzān al-ʿamal provided al-Ghazālī with a philosophical basis for a Sufi-oriented ethics, which he later developed in detail in the *Iḥyāʾ*. We cannot also ignore the influence of Miskawayh, but the philosophical thrust of his ethics

---

67 Al-Ghazālī, *Letter to a Disciple*, p. 34.

filtered through to al-Iṣfahānī, whose *Dharīʿa* became a mediating source of philosophical ethics for al-Ghazālī.

Thus, al-Ghazālī uses *Dharīʿa* as a primary source for his educational duties and even for most of his quotations from the Qurʾān and hadith, which he cites mostly in the same context and the same order as al-Iṣfahānī. Al-Ghazālī is not a plagiarist, however, but utilizes *Dharīʿa* as a framework, refashioning it and originally rewriting it into a systematic exposition of the duties of the teacher. Al-Ghazālī later incorporated all of these duties of the teacher into *Iḥyāʾ* with little modification. Al-Ghazālī's *Mīzān* is richer and more systematic, and this may be attributed to his talent in exploiting his primary sources, including the *Dharīʿa* to the fullest. Though the *Dharīʿa* cannot be reduced to a simple source from which we can measure contours of textual difference, it provides a highly relevant, pre-written text that al-Ghazālī variously adapts to provide alternative textual possibilities. Al-Ghazālī does not only rewrite parts of *Dharīʿa*, but also re-presents the Qurʾānic ethics of al-Iṣfahānī to suit a new readership that is both philosophical and Sufi-minded.

Al-Ghazālī's ethics is directed, both in terms of his method and aim, at the knowledge of God (*maʿrifa*). The Sufi slant to his educational ethics is most concisely formulated in his *Letter to a Disciple*, which echoes some duties of the teacher in *Mīzān*, although the former is specifically meant for his own disciples in Ṭūs. This is one of the last works written in the Sufi lodge in Ṭūs, where he acted as a Sufi master, or *murshid*, and provided practical guidance to his disciples.[68]

It is hoped that this chapter will contribute to a better understanding of the sources that shaped al-Ghazālī's ethical thought and writing as contained in *Mīzān*, a book which provided the intellectual clarification and justification for connecting ethics as a practical science to Sufism. Al-Ghazālī used it as a touchstone for a detailed practical programme of ethical action in *Iḥyāʾ*. The *Iḥyāʾ*, in turn, had an impact on later Jewish[69] and Christian thinkers.

---

68 Ibid., p. 16, p. 24.

69 See for example, al-Ghazālī's duties of the teacher and the student in the Book of Knowledge in the *Iḥyāʾ*, and the clear parallels with the duties of teachers and students in Maimonide's *Book of Knowledge*; cf. Steven Harvey, "al-Ghazali and Maimonides and their Books of Knowledge" in Jay M. Harris, ed. Cambridge: Harvard University Press, 2005. Thanks to the author for supplying me with this article; see also the contributions by Harvey, Ivry, and Takahashi in this present volume.

CHAPTER 10

Revisiting al-Ghazālī's Crisis through His *Scale for Action* (*Mizān al-ʿAmal*)

Kenneth Garden

Accounts of al-Ghazālī's life and thought have traditionally divided both into two distinct phases: an early phase spent as a traditional religious scholar, and a later phase spent as a Sufi. This division is based on al-Ghazālī's own account of his life in his *Deliverer from Error* (*Al-Munqidh min aḍ-ḍalāl*). According to this book, the transition came in 488/1095, when the forty year old Muslim intellectual concluded a life-long quest for a criterion for certain knowledge by embracing Sufism, having previously investigated and rejected *kalām*, philosophy, and Ismaʿīlī Shiism. Actually embarking upon Sufi practice, though, came only at the end of a long internal struggle against his attachment to his worldly position as head of the Niẓāmiyya madrasa in Nishapur. Only a spiritual breakdown that left him unable to speak or digest food forced him to renounce his position and pursue the Sufi path; it was through this path that he aimed to attain both the certain knowledge of his original quest and also salvation. Thereafter, his spiritual practice and writings would be dedicated to Sufism.

The account in the *Deliverer* was the starting point of all major al-Ghazālī biographies for over a century, but acceptance of it has eroded over the past two decades. There can be little doubt now that the rejection of philosophy and embrace of Sufism that al-Ghazālī describes in the *Deliverer* was a deliberate misrepresentation of his own thought. His writings after 488/1095 betray a profound debt to the philosophy he claims to have rejected, especially to the thought of Ibn Sīnā.[1] This is true even in his great masterpiece *The Revival of*

* I would like to thank Georges Tamer for graciously hosting the conference that occasioned this article and the exchange of ideas that improved it.

1 Al-Ghazālī's debt to Ibn Sīnā had been noticed by earlier scholars, such as Mohamed Sherif, *Ghazali's Theory of Virtue*, Albany: SUNY Press, 1975. But the breakthrough studies on this subject were written by Richard Frank, especially *Creation and the Cosmic System: al-Ghazâlî & Avicenna*, Abhandlungen der Heidelberger Akademie der Wissenschaften Heidelberg: Carl Winter Universitätsverlag, 1992, and *Al-Ghazālī and the Ashʿarite School*, Curham: Duke University Press, 1994. Further important work has been done by Jules Janssens, "Al-Ghazzâlî's *Tahâfut*: Is it Really a Rejection of Ibn Sînâ's Philosophy?," *Journal of Islamic Studies* 12, no. 1 (2001), pp. 1–17; Frank Griffel, *Al-Ghazālī's Philosophical Theology*,

 | DOI 10.1163/9789004290952_011

the Religious Sciences (*Iḥyāʾ ʿulūm ad-dīn*), long portrayed as an encyclopedic exposition of his new-found Sufism. Furthermore, *The Deliverer from Error*, in which he presents his account, has been shown to be an artful construct that aims to establish its author's authority and to deflect charges of being a philosopher and Ismaʿīlī.[2]

Still, we know that 488/1095 did represent a turning point in his life. He *did* renounce his position at the Niẓāmiyya madrasa in Baghdad. We know that, even if philosophy continued to play an important role in his thought and writing, he *did* present himself as a Sufi for the remainder of his post-Baghdad life. How far, then, must we go in questioning the account in the *Deliverer*, and what more can we learn about al-Ghazālī's famous departure from Baghdad that would be more in keeping with what we know about the development of his thought?

This article will turn to a different source to re-examine the significance of al-Ghazālī's crisis and renunciation of his position and public teaching. If the *Revival of the Religious Sciences*, a work of ethics, was the major expression of al-Ghazālī's post-Baghdad thought, then we can expect his ethical writing on the eve of his departure to reflect his deliberations leading up to this turning point. Such a work exists in the form of *Mīzān al-ʿamal, The Scale of Action*, a short book al-Ghazālī wrote in 488/1095.[3] The *Scale* shows al-Ghazālī in a very

---

Oxford: Oxford University Press, 2009; M. Afifi al-Akiti, "The Good, The Bad, and the Ugly of Falsafa: al-Ghazālī's *Maḍnūn, Tahāfut, and Maqāṣid*, with Particular Attention to their Falsafī Treatments of God's Knowledge of Temporal Events," in *Avicenna and His Legacy: A Golden Age of Science and Philosophy*, ed. Y. Tzvi Langermann, Turnhout, Belgium: Brepolis, 2009, pp. 51–100; and Alexander Treiger, *Inspired Knowledge in Islamic Thought: Al-Ghazali's Theory of Mystical Cognition and its Avicennian Foundation*, London and New York: Routledge, 2011.

2 See Franz Rosenthal, "Die Arabische Autobiographie," *Analecta Orientalia* 14, no. Studia Arabica I (1937), pp. 1–40; Josef van Ess, "Quelques remarques sur le *Munqidh min aḍ-ḍalâl*," in *Ghazâlî: La raison et le miracle, Table ronde* UNESCO, *9–10 décembre 1985*, ed. A.-M. Turki, Paris: Éditions Maisonneuve et Larose, 1987, pp. 57–68; Stephen Menn, "The Discourse on the Method and the Tradition of Intellectual Autobiography," in *Hellenistic and Early Modern Philosophy*, ed. Jon Miller and Brad Inwood, Cambridge: Cambridge University Press, 2003; Kenneth Garden, "Coming Down from the Mountaintop: Al-Ghazālī's Autobiographical Writings in Context," *Muslim World* 101, no. 4 (2011), pp. 581–596; *The First Islamic Reviver: Abū Ḥāmid al-Ghazālī and his Revival of the Religious Sciences*, Oxford: Oxford University Press, 2013, pp. 153–155.

3 Hourani dates the *Scale* to 488/1095, by situating it before his departure from Baghdad, but after two other works to which it is related. He points out that the *Scale* refers six times to *The Standard of Knowledge* (*Miʿyār al-ʿilm*), a work on logic. He presents the *Standard*, in turn, as an appendix to the *The Incoherence* (or, as Treiger has recently argued, *Precipitance*) *of the Philosophers* (*Tahāfut al-falāsifa*), which refers to the *Standard* as a work already written. In

different frame of mind than the one depicted in the *Deliverer*, and dealing with a very different set of issues than the quest for certain knowledge and salvation. The author of the *Scale* appears supremely self-confident, not wracked by spiritual turmoil. He is concerned not with epistemological certainty, but with methods of attaining felicity (*saʿāda*) in the afterlife, a state above the salvation (*najāt*) of the majority, and the fact that so few are moved

---

the introduction to the *Standard*, al-Ghazālī states that he wrote the book for two reasons, one of which was to clarify terms used in *The Precipitance*, which strengthens the inference that the two works are of a piece. In the conclusion of the *Standard*, al-Ghazālī announces his intention to write the *Scale* on the topic of practice (*ʿamal*), though as a stand-alone work for those with no desire to read the *Standard*. The *Precipitance* is thought to have been written in 487/1094, which makes a very good case for dating the *Scale* to 488/1095. See George Hourani, "A Revised Chronology of Ghazâlî's Writings," *Journal of the American Oriental Society* 104, no. 2 (1984), pp. 289–302, esp. 292–295; Abū Ḥāmid al-Ghazālī, *Miʿyar al-ʿilm*, Beirut: Dār al-Kutub al-ʿilmiyya, 1990, 27, 334. Montgomery Watt has claimed that much of the *Scale of Action* consists of forged interpolations, a claim rebutted at length by Mohamed Sherif. Montgomery Watt, "The Authenticity of Works Attributed to al-Ghazâlî," *Journal of the Royal Asiatic Society* (1952): pp. 24–45; *vide* esp. 38–40 & 45. Sherif, *Ghazali's Theory of Virtue*, 170–76. Some have suggested that the *Scale* was written significantly *after* 488/1095 and represents a later stage of al-Ghazālī's thought, a claim made most recently in the introduction to a German translation of that work: Abū Ḥāmid Al-Ghazālī, *Das Kriterium des Handelns*: Aus dem Arabischen übersetzt, mit einer Einleitung, mit Anmerkungen und Indices herasugegeben von ʿAbd-Elṣamad ʿAbd-Elḥamīd Elschazlī, Darmstadt: Wissenschaftliche Buchgesellschaft, 2006. That the *Criterion* was written in 488/1095 at the latest is strongly suggested by the fact that material found in that book was further refined in book 21 of the *Revival of the Religious Sciences, The Marvels of the Heart* (*Kitāb Sharḥ ʿajāʾib al-qalb*), and was therefore written before al-Ghazālī's departure from Baghdad, as he is known to have begun reading publically from the *Revival* in Damascus shortly after his departure.

Frank Griffel has suggested an intriguing third possibility to me, which is that the *Scale* could have been written significantly *before* 488/1095 and only published in that year, in which case it would represent an earlier phase of al-Ghazālī's thinking. Evidence for this is that, as we shall see, the *Scale* plainly states that al-Ghazālī had not begun practicing Sufism at the time of writing, while al-Ghazālī's student for a short time during his brief stop-over in Baghdad on his way back to Khorasan in 490/1097, Abū Bakr Ibn al-ʿArabī, reports that al-Ghazālī had begun practicing Sufism *five years earlier*, that is, in 485/1092. I cannot disprove this possibility. Still, I think it is unlikely. Parallels between the *Scale* and the *Revival* that I will discuss below, suggest a rather shorter period of development between the two works. Furthermore, the urgency with which al-Ghazālī discusses the imperative of bringing his fellow Muslims to purse felicity in the hereafter through knowledge and practice fits well with the assumption that he devoted himself to this mission a short time later by leaving his position in Baghdad and writing and promoting the *Revival of the Religious Sciences*, which aims at precisely this.

to pursue it. These methods include Sufism, but also philosophy, and it can be confidently inferred from the text that the author of the *Scale* sees himself as a philosopher, not a Sufi. The *Scale* suggests that al-Ghazālī's subsequent decision to abandon his position in Baghdad and take up Sufi practice and self-presentation was not a first step on his quest for felicity. Rather, al-Ghazālī undertook this for two different reasons. One was to perfect through the Sufi method his already considerable attainments in the quest for felicity achieved through the philosophical method. The other was to make himself a more compelling example and guide for those with the talent for Sufism (though not philosophy) who nevertheless remained indifferent to the imperative to seek felicity in the hereafter.

The Scale of Action

The Scale for Action, compared to the *Revival*, is a very short book, a small fraction of the size of the later work. It contains 32 short chapters of a few pages each that aim as much to persuade the reader to seek felicity as to provide guidance in doing so. Its opening chapters are devoted to convincing the reader that the reward of felicity for all of eternity outweighs any price one could pay in a short lifetime. The *Scale* presents a psychological model that explains the workings of the soul and body, the ways in which human beings are diverted from attaining the felicity that is the purpose of their creation, and the means of pursuing felicity through knowledge and ethical practice. It presents two methods for this pursuit – namely philosophy and Sufism – and then dedicates its second half to detailing the path.

It has been shown that al-Ghazālī adapted much of the content of the *Scale* from earlier works, especially ar-Rāghib al-Iṣfahānī's *adh-Dharīʿa ilā makārim ash-sharīʿa*, but also various works of Ibn Sīnā.[4] However, the opening chapters,

4 Several studies have shown the *Scale* to be an adaptation of the ethical thought of Ibn Sīnā and ar-Rāghib al-Iṣfahānī. See the extensive critical introduction to ar-Rāghib al-Iṣfahānī, *The Path to Virtue: The Ethical Philosophy of Al-Rāghib al-Iṣfahānī*, An Annotated Translation, with Critical Introduction, of *Kitāb al-Dharīʿah ilā Makārim al-Sharīʿah*, trans. Yasien Mohamed, Kuala Lumpur: International Institute of Islamic Thought and Civilization, 2006. See also Yasien Mohamed, "The Ethics of Education: Al-Iṣfahānī's *al-Dharīʿa* as a Source of Inspiration for al-Ghazālī's *Mīzān al-ʿAmal*," *The Muslim World* 101, no. 4 (2011), pp. 633–657; and Jules Janssens, "Al-Ghazālī's *Mīzān al-ʿAmal*: an Ethical Summa Based on Ibn Sīnā and al-Rāghib al-Iṣfahānī," in *Islamic Thought in the Middle Ages: Studies in Text, Transmission and Translation in Honour of Hans Daiber*, ed. Anna Akasoy and Wim Raven, Leiden: Brill, 2008, pp. 123–137 esp. 137, n. 29.

which urge the pursuit of felicity, and chapters 7 and 8, which discuss the relative merits of philosophy and Sufism as methods for attaining felicity, seem to be al-Ghazālī's entirely original composition. This suggests that these two issues – urging pursuit of felicity and determining the best method for attaining it – were al-Ghazālī's major objectives in composing this work.

The Ghazālī that emerges from the *Scale* is a philosopher critical of existing philosophical schools. He is intrigued by Sufism and has inquired into selectively adopting some of its practices, but the Sufi guide he consulted has forbidden him from proceeding. The *Scale* presents both philosophy and Sufism as paths to the highest felicity in the afterlife (*as-saʿāda al-ukhrawiyya*), philosophy being the surer of the two, though suitable for only a small elite qualified to pursue it. Sufism is the path best suited to most of those who pursue felicity, and those for whom Sufism is more appropriate should not be exposed to philosophy. But al-Ghazālī holds out the possibility of a more perfect felicity, through subsequent Sufi practice, for those philosophers who have reached the limit of what their method can attain. This is not the position al-Ghazālī presents himself as holding vis-à-vis philosophy and Sufism in the *Deliverer*. Neither are these the concerns he presents himself there as weighing on the eve of his departure.

Felicity in the Hereafter is Attained through Knowledge and Practice

The very first point al-Ghazālī makes in the *Scale* is that the highest imperative in human life is attaining felicity (*saʿāda*) in the hereafter. Felicity is not the same as simple salvation (*najāt*), which most Muslims can hope to attain, but is a state of pleasure that surpasses the pleasure of the saved in the hereafter. It is pursued through knowledge and practice (*ʿilm wa- ʿamal*), and its substance is likewise to be understood in terms of these, particularly knowledge.

> [...] success and salvation are not attained except through knowledge and practice together... knowledge is nobler than practice, for it is as though practice serves the attainment of knowledge and is guided by knowledge until it arrives in its mark.[5]

5 Abū Ḥāmid al-Ghazālī, *Mīzān al-ʿamal*, ed. Muḥammad Bījū, Damascus: Dār at-Taqwā, 2008, 26. Though al-Ghazālī uses the term "salvation" (*an-najāt*) here rather than "felicity," this sentence comes in response to the following question: "You have clarified to me that following the way of felicity is the resolution of rational men, and that indifference in this is the

Al-Ghazālī goes so far as to claim of knowledge that "the unique characteristic for the sake of which human beings were created is reason (*al-ʿaql*) and grasping the true essences of things."[6]

Practice consists of training the self to act ethically by cultivating habitual virtues such as wisdom and courage and eliminating habitual vices such as foolishness, cowardice, or rashness. Ethical training is necessary because the default disposition among human beings is to follow the dictates of their passions: anger and the appetites for food and sex. The passions, al-Ghazālī writes, have their uses. In order for the human soul to gather knowledge of the true essences of things, it has to exist in the world, and worldly existence requires a body. The body, in turn, requires anger for the sake of defending itself, and the appetites for the sake of sustaining itself and reproducing the species. Al-Ghazālī compares feeding the body to feeding a horse that one rides into battle.[7] But satisfying the passions for most people becomes an end in itself rather than a means to an end. This leads to engrossment in the affairs of the world and heedlessness of the goal of attaining felicity in the afterlife. Thus, taming the passions – practice – becomes a prerequisite for focusing on attaining knowledge.

Once the passions are tamed, the intellect (*ʿaql*) is freed to pursue knowledge, though not just any knowledge. What is ultimately desired is knowledge of God. Al-Ghazālī calls the pursuit of this knowledge the "theoretical science" (*al-ʿilm an-naẓarī*), whose domain he defines as:

> Knowledge of God, his attributes, angels, books, prophets, and the kingdoms of the heavens and the earth, the marvels of the human and animal souls insofar as they are related to the omnipotence of God, not with respect to their essence. The highest goal is the knowledge of God and God's angels. It is necessary to know them because they are intermediaries between God and the Prophet. And likewise knowledge of prophecy and the Prophet, because the Prophet is an intermediary between human beings and angels just as the angel is an intermediary between God and the Prophet. This chain continues to the least of the theoretical sciences. The utmost of them is the knowledge of God, but the discussion of this

heedlessness of the ignorant, but how can someone who does not know the path follow it? How can I know that knowledge and practice are the path such that I can dedicate myself to it?" This being the case, it is clear that the reference to "salvation" in the response refers more specifically to felicity.

6 Ibid., 36.

7 Ibid., 54.

> branches out in all directions because each refers to the others as the details are many.[8]

Any phenomenon in existence is of interest, not for itself, but because it is a creation of God; just as we may come to know an author more closely by examining his writings, al-Ghazālī asserts, so too can we come to know the Creator by studying His creation.[9]

Unlike practice, knowledge of the divine is not a means to the end of felicity – it is felicity itself.[10] "The felicity and perfection of the soul," consists in its "being inscribed with the truths of divine matters and uniting with them to the point that it is as though [the soul] were they [i.e., the divine truths]."[11] The result of this is a drawing near (*taqarrub*) to God. Al-Ghazālī is quick to specify that this proximity is not in space, but in quality (*maʿnā*) and to denounce the ecstatic claims of Sufis like al-Ḥallāj and Abū Yazīd al-Bisṭāmī to have attained union with God, which he insists is impossible.[12] The soul was created for this perfection and thirsts for it. But there are infinite gradations of this perfection and thus of felicity, which will only truly be grasped after death, the separation of the soul from the body and the cessation of the appetites, sensory data, and imaginings. Death, then, is the drawing back of the curtain on Reality.[13]

The Two Schools that Pursue Felicity through Knowledge and Practice are Philosophy and Sufism

Al-Ghazālī refers explicitly in the *Scale* to only two methods for pursuing felicity through knowledge and practice: Sufism and philosophy. Al-Ghazālī gives an account of the difference between these two methods in two different

---

8 Ibid., 49.

9 Ibid., 39.

10 "The felicity, pleasure, and repose of every entity lies the in attaining its unique perfection ... the unique perfection of a human being lies in grasping the reality of the intelligibles (*al-ʿaqlīyāt*) as they truly are without imaginings or sensory data that animals also share," ibid., 27. Al-Ghazālī makes this point more explicitly in the *Revival*; see, Abū Ḥāmid al-Ghazālī, *Iḥyāʾ ʿulūm ad-dīn*, 5 vols., Beirut, 1997, vol. 4, pp. 116–17. For a discussion of salvation and felicity in al-Ghazālī's thought and its relation to the Science of Unveiling, see, Alexander Treiger, "The Science of Divine Disclosure: Al-Ġazālī's Higher Theology and its Philosophical Underpinnings," PhD diss., Yale University, 2008, 62–68.

11 Al-Ghazālī, *Mīzān*, 42.

12 Ibid., 34.

13 Ibid., 27.

passages in the *Scale*.[14] The second of these is longer and more detailed and comes in chapter 7, entitled "The Separation of the Path of the Sufis from the Path of Others with Respect to Knowledge" (*Bayān mufāraqat ṭarīq aṣ-ṣūfiyya fī jānib al-ʿilm ṭarīq ghayrihim*). It is the more important of the two because it not only expounds the difference between Sufis and philosophers but presents al-Ghazālī's experience of and critique of Sufism as well as his tentative proposal of a third way that combines aspects of both paths.

Al-Ghazālī defines the difference between the Sufis and philosophers as follows:

> Know that with respect to practice they are in agreement; its aim is the elimination of bad traits (*aṣ-ṣifāt ar-radiyya*) and the purification of the soul of bad morals. But with respect to knowledge, they disagree, and the paths of the Sufis and the paths of the theoreticians (*nuẓẓār*) [read: "philosophers" – I will account for the difference in terminology below] of the people of knowledge part ways in this matter. The Sufis do not encourage acquiring and studying the sciences or studying the compositions of writers on inquiring into the truths of matters. Rather, they say that the path begins with eliminating sinful traits, cutting all ties, and devoting all of one's attention to God Most High.[15]

This is not to say that the Sufis are not interested in attaining knowledge of the truths of matters. The difference lies in the way in which they acquire such knowledge. After immersing themselves in single-minded attention to God,

> Nothing remains for [the Sufi practitioner] but to wait for what appears from an opening (*futūḥ*) the likes of which appeared to the saints. This is a portion of what appeared to the prophets. It may be a matter like a fleeting flash of lightening that does not persist. Then it may return, though it may be delayed. If it returns it may persist or it may be dazzling. If it persists, its persistence may lengthen or may not. Its likeness may follow in close succession and may not be limited to a single discipline (*fann*).[16]

The Sufi approach to knowledge, then, is to trust that it will come through divine inspiration after perfection in ethical practice.

14 Ibid., 26 and 43–45.

15 Ibid., 43.

16 Ibid., 44.

More striking than the description of Sufi acquisition of knowledge is al-Ghazālī's account of where he received his information. His source is a Sufi *shaykh* whom he approached about practicing Sufism under his guidance only to be rejected. He writes,

> At the time when my desire to pursue this path was sincere I consulted with an authority and spiritual guide of the Sufis (*matbūʿ muqaddam min aṣ-ṣūfiyya*) about [the practice of] continually reciting the Qur'ān, and he forbade me.[17]

The reason al-Ghazālī was rejected is not given and neither does he tell us when in his life it occurred.[18] But the fact that he prefaces this man's account of the Sufi method with a story of having been rejected by him as a disciple plainly implies that he had not subsequently practiced Sufism such that he could have given his own first-hand account. While there is evidence in other sources that al-Ghazālī's acquaintance with Sufism was long-standing[19] and that he had begun practicing Sufism shortly after his arrival in Baghdad,[20] this

17 Ibid., 43. *Muqaddam* has the sense of supervisor or guardian, which I take to mean the man was a *shaykh* who guided novices in their practice. This makes sense given that al-Ghazālī consulted him about practicing Sufism, presumably under his guidance. In more contemporary use, a *muqaddam* is a person deputized by a shaykh to train disciples on his behalf. The term may have had this connotation in al-Ghazālī's day as well. See Mark Sedgwick, *Against the Modern World: Traditionalism and the Secret Intellectual History of the Twentieth Century*, Oxford: Oxford University Press, 2009, p. 87.

18 It is very tempting to try to draw inferences from the few details present here. In the following chapter of the *Scale*, as we shall see shortly, al-Ghazālī tentatively describes a third way of pursuing felicity, namely the pursuit first of philosophy and then of Sufism once the insights of philosophy have been exhausted. We might speculate that he inquired into Sufism in conjunction with his speculation about such a third way. We might also speculate that he was rejected because he asked about trying a single Sufi practice, namely continually reciting the Qur'ān, while the *shaykh* demanded total dedication. The evidence, though, is too slender to make such inferences.

19 Esp. his youthful acquaintance with al-Fāramadhī – see Treiger, *Inspired Knowledge in Islamic Thought*, p. 1 and n. 3.

20 Abū Bakr Ibn al-ʿArabī, al-Ghazālī's student for a short time in Baghdad in 490/1097, reports that al-Ghazālī had begun practicing Sufism already in 486/1093; Frank Griffel accepts Abū Bakr's account. I am skeptical. As we shall see, already in the *Scale* al-Ghazālī is evasive about his discussion of philosophy, preferring to present the *Scale* as a work devoted to Sufism. Furthermore, the *Scale* describes philosophy and Sufism as identical with respect to practice but differing with respect to the pursuit of knowledge. Thus Al-Ghazāli may have felt that he could, in good faith, present his earlier philosophically

is a clear statement from al-Ghazālī himself that he had not pursued the Sufi path at the time of his writing the *Scale* in 488/1095. More importantly, the fact that al-Ghazālī was not a practitioner of Sufism, one of only two paths to the felicity whose pursuit al-Ghazālī so fervently advocates in the *Scale*, must lead us to infer that he was a practitioner of the other path: philosophy.

This impression is strengthened by the account later in the same chapter of the philosophical method. While the account of Sufism is presented with reference only to itself, the account of philosophy is presented as a critique of Sufism from a philosophical perspective. The philosophers ("theoreticians"), al-Ghazālī writes, do not deny the Sufi method of focusing on practice, but they hold that it is extremely unlikely to succeed in attaining the knowledge that is its goal. Cutting ties to the world to the degree the Sufi path requires is nearly impossible, and if it is achieved is more likely to lead to confusion, delusion, bodily illness and melancholy. Without previous training in "the true demonstrative sciences" (*al-ʿulūm al-ḥaqīqiyya al-burhāniyya*), the theoreticians charge, the Sufi will take delusional imaginings to be the truth. How many a Sufi, they ask, has been captivated by an imagined insight for ten years that he could have seen through in an instant had he been schooled in the sciences first? A more reliable way to seek knowledge is to pursue knowledge and practice in tandem, taming the passions but also pursuing rational inquiry into the divine matters.

While this critique is placed in the mouth of the philosophers rather than in al-Ghazālī's own voice, it is a critique he certainly shares. He allows it to stand without contradiction, and provides no corresponding critique of the philosophers from a Sufi standpoint. More importantly, he presents his own preference explicitly in the following chapter, entitled, "The Primary of the two Paths" (*Bayān al-ūlā min at-ṭarīqayn*).

---

guided ethical practice as Sufi, and he may have preferred to do so in his discussions with Abū Bakr, seeing him as better suited to Sufism than philosophy. Abū Bakr presents himself as having an ascetic bent during his travels in the East. As I will show in the final section of this essay, there is further evidence for al-Ghazālī's later adoption of Sufism in that the secondhand description of Sufism found in the *Scale* is reproduced in book 21 of the post-Baghdad *Revival of the Religious Sciences*. That al-Ghazālī had no more personal experience of the Sufi path at the time of writing this passage of the *Revival* suggests that his Sufi practice remained limited even in his first months after leaving Baghdad. See Abū Bakr Ibn al-ʿArabī, *al-ʿAwāṣim min al-qawāṣim*, ed. ʿAmmār Ṭālibī, Cairo: Maktabat Dār at-turāth, 1997, 24; Griffel, *Al-Ghazālī's Philosophical Theology*, 42; and ʿAmmār Ṭālibi, *Ārāʾ Abī Bakr ibn al-ʿArabī l-kalāmiyya*, Algiers: Ash-Sharika al-Waṭaniyya li-n-nashr wa-t-tawzīʿ, 1974, vol. 1, pp. 58–59 (Ṭālibī quotes Abu Bakr's unpublished *Sirāj al-murīdīn*).

In that chapter he writes that, in his opinion, there is no way of saying absolutely which is the superior method for attaining felicity, for this depends on the personality and circumstances of each would-be practitioner. To follow philosophy and its simultaneous pursuit of knowledge and practice, one must be young enough to be trainable, smart enough to grasp philosophical sciences, and fortunate enough to have a qualified instructor. If any of these conditions are not met, it is preferable to pursue ethical practice alone, that is, Sufism. Al-Ghazālī specifies that only a few of the few who resolve to pursue felicity will meet these criteria, making philosophy the path of the elite and Sufism the path of the many.[21] While on the surface this relative approach does not give absolute precedence to one school over another, there is a clear hierarchy: Al-Ghazālī does not even entertain the possibility that a person qualified for the study and practice of philosophy might choose to pursue Sufism instead. Combining this discussion with the critique of Sufism presented in the previous chapter of the *Scale* makes al-Ghazālī's preference for philosophy – and the rationale for this preference – clear.

This is further demonstrated by his own practice as evidenced by his writings at the time. The *Scale for Action* is a book of ethics, that is, practice, which is part of both the philosophical and the Sufi path. But al-Ghazālī wrote it as a companion piece to a previous work, *The Standard of Knowledge* (*Miʿyār al-ʿilm*),[22] a book on logic. He announces his intention in the *Standard* to write the *Scale* and refers several times in the *Scale* to the *Standard*.[23] The two works together are a guide to the simultaneous pursuit of knowledge and practice, the hallmark of the philosophical path.

Furthermore, the discussion of ethics in the *Scale* is drawn from philosophy rather than Sufism. His ethical psychology is ultimately Platonic, describing the soul as possessing three faculties (*quwā*): the rational (*qūwat at-tafakkur*), the irascible (*qūwat al-ghaḍab*, i.e., anger), and the concupiscent (*qūwat*

21 Al-Ghazālī, *Mīzān*, 46–47. Al-Ghazālī makes it clear later in the *Scale* that most people will not pursue felicity and that this is a mercy from God: if all people abandoned their professions civilization would go to ruin; ibid., 132–133. The vast majority of people, then, will not pursue felicity at all. A minority will pursue it through Sufism; the elite of this minority will pursue philosophy, and, as we shall see below, al-Ghazālī suggests that the elite of these elite will pursue first philosophy and then Sufism. It is important to bear this in mind: in his urgent summons to pursue felicity, al-Ghazālī is addressing the small fragment of his pre-modern society that was literate and inclined to the study of religious sciences.

22 Al-Ghazālī, *Miʿyār al-ʿilm*. For the relation of the *Standard* to the *Precipitance* and to the *Scale*, see n. 4 above.

23 The *Scale* refers several times to the *Standard*; see ibid., 15, 44, 50, 57.

ash-shahwa, i.e., the appetites).[24] He defines virtue in an Aristotelian way as a mean between a vice of excess and a vice of deficit.[25] His list of the cardinal virtues that flow from the correct balancing of the three faculties further follows Aristotle.[26] The Sufi method he describes on the authority of the spiritual guide he once consulted – namely cutting ties to the world and meditating on God alone – is not reproduced in the *Scale*, and the Sufi-derived virtues of the fourth quarter of the *Revival* do not appear in the *Scale*. There are examples of ethical self-discipline that refer to Sufi training under the direction of a *shaykh*,[27] and, more importantly, al-Ghazālī does claim in two later chapters of the *Scale* that it is a work of Sufism.[28] But the content of the work contradicts these claims: the very guide to pursuing felicity through knowledge and practice in which al-Ghazālī's discussion of the two paths is contained is written according to the philosophical method.

A Third Way

Al-Ghazālī's discussion of Sufism and philosophy does not end with this, but goes on to point towards a third possible method that synthesizes the two. Given al-Ghazālī's plain statement that he has not practiced Sufism and the tone with which he discusses this synthesis, it is clear that such a hybrid remains a hypothetical prospect for him. He describes this third possibility as follows:

> [Another possibility] is a young man of innate intelligence who has spent his youth in the pursuit of knowledge, who is drawn to this [i.e., philoso-

24 Ibid., 50.

25 Ibid., 73–78. See especially p. 74 where he introduces the concept and p. 75 where he weaves the conception of virtue as a mean between a vice of excess and a vice of deficit into the Islamic tradition by equating the mean with *aṣ-ṣirāṭ al-mustaqīm* (cf. Q 1:6).

26 Ibid., 50–51. For further discussion of balancing the faculties to attain the cardinal virtues as well as parables that clarify this concept, see pp. 53–55. For the main discussion of the virtues, see Chapter 16, *bayān ummahāt al-faḍāʾil*, pp. 73–78.

27 See for example ibid., 70. Here he gives advice to Sufi *shaykhs* on how to guide their disciples in their training. After a preceding discussion on how a doctor should treat a sickness by countering, for example, an excess of heat with a substance that induces coldness, he explains how a *shaykh* who treats the souls of his disciples should treat an excess of pride by prescribing actions the disciple would find humiliating. The reference is to the Sufi *shaykh*, but the ethical framework of understanding virtue as a mean between two possible extremes is philosophical.

28 Ibid., 131, 133 (chapter 27) and 163 (chapter 32).

> phy] after training in the other sciences, but training within the framework of the science he is drawn to (*tanabbah lahu baʿd al-irtiyāḍ bi-anwāʿ min al-ʿulūm wa-lākin bi-hadhā an-nawʿ min al-ʿilm alladhī tanabbah lahu*)[29] – such a person as this is prepared for both paths together. His first task is to advance along the path of study to the point that he attains from the demonstrative sciences (*al-ʿulūm al-burhāniyya*) that which it is within human capacity to grasp through effort and study. Following those who have preceded him is sufficient provision for this. Once he has attained this to the extent possible, such that there remains no science of these kinds of sciences that he has not attained, there is no harm after this in choosing seclusion from humankind, turning away from the world and devoting himself to God. If he waits, perhaps there will be opened to him through that path that which is obscure to the climbers of this path [i.e. philosophy].[30]

The combination of Sufism and philosophy is sequential, then, and reserved for the elite of the elite. Of those drawn to pursue felicity, only a few will be qualified for the study and practice of philosophy. Only a few of these few will exhaust the possibilities of the philosophical method and be free to explore Sufi practice as a possible route to more profound knowledge and thus greater felicity.

A better sense of the kind of additional insight that may be attained by a philosopher who pursues Sufi practice after the completion of the philosophical curriculum is given in a parable al-Ghazālī provides in a previous chapter of the *Mizān* which is also found in the *Revival*. A king invites Byzantine and Chinese artists to decorate opposite walls of a single hall so that he can judge between their artistry. A curtain is hung down the middle of the room so that neither group of artists can see the other. The Byzantines request exotic pigments for painting and the Chinese request supplies for polishing alone, which evokes surprise. After some time, the Byzantines announce that they are finished and the Chinese announce that they are finished as well. The curtain

29 In this section of chapter 8, between the description of the "few of the few" who are qualified for the study of philosophy and the passage presented here, there is a brief aside in which al-Ghazālī criticizes scholars who are dependent on the authority and conclusions of other scholars (*muqallid*) as opposed to being masters of their field, qualified for independent investigation and conclusions. This description of the approach to the study of the sciences of the young man qualified for both philosophy and Sufism seems to be contrasted to the *muqallid* – he should study the sciences philosophically, that is finding demonstrative proofs for the various principles he assents to.

30 Al-Ghazālī, *Mīzān*, 47.

is raised, revealing a splendid painting on the Byzantine wall and its still more dazzling reflection on the other wall, which has been polished by the Chinese to a mirror-like finish.[31]

As Alexander Treiger has noted, the content of the truth revealed by the two methods (philosophy and Sufism respectively) is the same, though the Sufi method reveals it with greater brilliance and clarity.[32] Combining the two would create a method that joins the surety of rational investigation to the superior quality of mystical insight.

Al-Ghazālī certainly saw himself as a candidate for this hybrid path – he describes himself as a youth of innate intelligence with a thirst for independent authority in the sciences in the *Deliverer* and hints at a similar self-regard in the *Scale*.[33] But this third way remained a theoretical possibility for him at this point. It was not a path he had himself taken, and he retained his doubts about its possibility. There is a strong note of hesitancy in his description of this third path quoted above: "there is no harm" in following it; "perhaps" it will lead to deeper insight still.

Are the "Theoreticians" and the Philosophers One and the Same?

This discussion of al-Ghazālī's comparison of Sufism and philosophy has so far avoided a significant distinction in his terminology in the *Scale*. The only explicit uses of the term "philosophers" (*falāsifa*) come in the second and third chapters of the book, while all subsequent discussions of those I have referred to as "philosophers" – including the important comparison of philosophy and Sufism in Chapter Seven and discussion of the superior of the two methods in Chapter Eight – refer not to "philosophers" as such but to "theoreticians" (*nuẓẓār*). Is the term "theoreticians" just another way of referring to "philosophers?" The answer is "yes," but with a meaningful distinction.[34]

The explicit uses of the term "philosophers," four in all, come in chapters two and three of the *Scale*, in which al-Ghazālī attempts to convince the reader of the reality of felicity and to urge him to pursue it. Al-Ghazālī refers here to a wide variety of groups – two different schools of philosophers; common

31 Ibid., 45.

32 Treiger, *Inspired Knowledge in Islamic Thought*, 68.

33 al-Ghazālī, *Mīzān*, 29. This passage will be discussed below.

34 Alexander Treiger also analyzes this passage and likewise concludes that "theoreticians" is a reference to philosophers. See Treiger, *Inspired Knowledge in Islamic Thought*, 66–68, especially n. 16.

believers, Jewish, Christian, and Muslim; as well as Sufis – and he does this in order to make the point that there exists a consensus among very disparate schools of thought that felicity in the hereafter exists, even if they conceive of it in different ways.

Clearly, al-Ghazālī does not agree with each group's conception of felicity or with their broader creed or doctrines; after all, he includes Jews and Christians in his list. He shows explicit reservations, too, about some of philosophers he does mention. His first reference is to a school of philosophers that hold that the pleasures of the afterlife will in fact be rational, though some may experience these rational pleasures as bodily ones. He refers to this group as "Islamic metaphysicians among the philosophers" (*al-ilāhiyyīn al-islāmiyyīn min al-falāsifa*).[35] The second reference is to philosophers who hold that the rational pleasures of the afterlife will bear no resemblance to bodily pleasures, a position he also attributes to the Sufis. He refers to this group as the "metaphysicians among the philosophers" (*al-ilāhiyyūn min al-falāsifa*), neglecting to refer to them as "Islamic."[36] A final mention of the consensus between Sufis and philosophers generally on the reality of felicity refers to "The Sufis and the philosophers who believe both in God and the Last Day" (*al-falāsifa alladhīna āmanū bi-l-lāh wa-l-yawm al-ākhir ʿalā l-jumla*) to distinguish them from other philosophers who do not.[37]

After these few highly qualified references to philosophers, the word never again appears in the *Scale*. The Sufis, paired twice in this early discussion with the philosophers, are subsequently contrasted to the "theoreticians," as we have seen. The theoreticians in turn, though plainly a group that also believes in the reality of felicity in the afterlife, are not mentioned in chapter two among the groups that share this consensus. In his subsequent discussions of the theoreticians, al-Ghazālī never qualifies their status as Muslims as he did for some of the philosophers. What are we to make of this distinction?

The source of the word "theoretician" (*nuẓẓār*) in the *Scale* would seem to be the "theoretical science" (*al-ʿilm an-naẓarī*) mentioned above, the science of attaining knowledge of God, which is opposed to the "practical science" (*al-ʿilm al-ʿamalī*), which contains ethics, along with politics and economics.[38] This very taxonomy of theoretical and practical sciences is philosophical, as Avner

35 Al-Ghazālī, *Mīzān*, 19.

36 Ibid., 20.

37 Ibid., 26.

38 Ibid., 49–50.

Giladi has shown,[39] as is the broader framework of the *Scale of Action* and its companion work the *Standard of Knowledge*, as discussed above. This alone presents a good case for the identity of the theoreticians and philosophers.

Another, simpler piece of evidence is that the term "theoretician" does not occur in the earlier discussion of those groups that hold that felicity is gained through knowledge and practice, and the term "philosopher" does not appear in the latter discussion of the different methods for attaining felicity. If the theoreticians are a distinct third group that shares the position of the Sufis and philosophers concerning felicity and its pursuit, why not mention them in the first discussion? And if the philosophers are a distinct third group with a method for attaining felicity in the hereafter, why not present them and their method alongside the Sufis and theoreticians in the second discussion? This, too, strongly implies that al-Ghazālī is dealing throughout with only two groups and their respective methods for attaining felicity through knowledge and practice: the Sufis and the philosophers/theoreticians.

Further evidence comes from an early use of the term "theoretician" in the *Scale*. In the discussion of the consensus on the reality of otherworldly felicity al-Ghazālī in Chapter Two describes one group that does not share this consensus. Of them he writes,

> They are the masses of fools who are not known by their names and are not counted among the group of the theoreticians (*zumrat an-nuẓẓār*). They claim that death is utter non-existence, that there is no punishment for obedience or disobedience, and that a human being returns after death to non-existence as he was before his existence. It is not allowable to call them a sect, because a sect refers to a group and this school of thought is not a group and cannot be attributed to a known theoretician (*nāẓir maʿrūf*). Rather such a one is to be considered a useless fool whose appetites have overwhelmed him and who has been mastered by Satan ... He deceives some sinners by ascribing this creed to one known for the intricacies of the sciences like Aristotle or Plato or to a sect like the philosophers.[40]

First, those described here sound very much like a group of philosophers al-Ghazālī refers to in the *Deliverer from Error*, whom he calls there the Naturalists (*aṭ-ṭabīʿīyūn*), who say that upon death a human being "is

39 Avner Giladi, "On the Origins of Two Key Terms in al-Ġazālī's *Iḥyāʾ ʿulūm al-dīn*," *Arabica* XXXVI, no. 1 (1989), pp. 81–93; 86.

40 Al-Ghazālī, *Mīzān*, 20–21.

annihilated, and if he is annihilated, it is not reasonable to posit the return of the annihilated."[41] He dismisses this group as heretics (*zanādiqa*) and contrasts them to another philosophical school, the metaphysicians (*al-ilāhiyyūn*), much as he does in this passage of the *Scale*. The fact that he refrains in the *Scale* from referring to this group as philosophers and takes pains to contrast them to philosophers can only be explained by his wanting to preserve the reputation of philosophy as such, his earlier reservations regarding specific schools of philosophy notwithstanding.

More important, though, is his use of the term "theoretician" in this passage. This group cannot be considered to be among the theoreticians and are not associated with the teachings of a known theoretician. Presumably, then, the metaphysicians he mentions earlier in this chapter of the *Scale*, as well as Plato and Aristotle and the philosophers he refers to at the end of this passage, can be considered theoreticians, which shows an overlap between the two terms. By extension, we could take "theoretician" in this passage to refer to the Sufis as well, but this possibility is excluded by the explicit contrast of Sufis and theorists later in the book. "Theoreticians" are those who seek knowledge of the true affairs of things through the theoretical science (*al-ʿilm an-naẓarī*), which is to say philosophers, including some philosophers some of whose tenets al-Ghazālī rejects.

To understand the distinction between the two terms we must consider the context of their use. In chapters Two and Three, al-Ghazālī seeks to convince his reader to believe in, and therefore to pursue, felicity in the hereafter; he attempts this by pointing to a consensus on its reality among existing groups in the world. This being the case, he must refer to existing philosophical thinkers and schools of thought, some of whose tenets he did not accept. The metaphysicians he refers to by name in the *Deliverer* are Socrates, Plato, Aristotle, al-Fārābī, and Ibn Sīnā, and he divides their teaching into acceptable, innovative, and constituting unbelief.[42] We can assume he had something similar in mind when he qualified them as "Islamic metaphysicians" in the *Scale*. Discussions of theoreticians, by contrast, do not refer to distinct individuals or schools, but to the practice of philosophy as al-Ghazālī himself conceives of it, and as such there was no need to apologize for, qualify, or critique it. By this taxonomy, the Islamic metaphysicians among the philosophers are also theoreticians, seeking theoretical knowledge of God, but not all theoreticians adhere to those blameworthy tenets that distinguish the Islamic metaphysicians. This

41 Abū Ḥāmid al-Ghazālī, "*Al-Munqidh min aḍ-ḍalāl*," in *Majmūʿat rasāʾil al-imām al-Ghazālī*, ed. Aḥmad Shams ad-Dīn, Beirut: Dār al-Kutub al-ʿIlmiyya, 1997, vol. 7, 35–36.

42 Ibid., 36–37.

being the case, it is legitimate to discuss the later chapters of the *Scale* on Sufis and theoreticians in terms of a distinction between Sufis and philosophers.

The Turning Point of 488/1095

In the *Deliverer*, al-Ghazālī paints a picture of himself on the eve of his departure from Baghdad as an inward-looking man, motivated by a quest for certain knowledge, who had examined and rejected a number of methods of attaining it, including philosophy. Though convinced that Sufism was the method he sought, and though he had grown anxious about his own salvation, he was unable to bring himself to leave his prestigious position in Baghdad to practice Sufism. His anxiety, by the will of God, grew to the point that he lost the ability to speak and therefore to teach, and lost his ability to digest food. Only through this crisis did he find the resolve to leave Baghdad, travel to Damascus, and finally become a Sufi.

This portrait of al-Ghazālī during his last days at the Niẓāmiyya Madrasa in Baghdad, uncertain and inward-looking, concerned with his personal fate in the afterlife, an enemy of philosophy and fully convinced by Sufism, finds no echo in his intellectual commitments and musings on the brink of his departure from that city. If al-Ghazālī was also motivated by a desperate lack of a criterion for certain knowledge and an attendant uncertainty, he betrays none of this in the *Scale of Action*, written in the very year of his departure. On the contrary, he expresses the utmost self-certainty. Not only does he present himself as possessing a means to sure knowledge, but he is prepared to share this knowledge with his reader. Writing of the method of pursuing felicity through knowledge and practice, al-Ghazālī declares that there are two types of people in this matter, those who follow the authority of others as a sick man follows the directions of his doctor, and those who rise to the authority of the doctor themselves. He offers to guide the reader in attaining this latter rank, writing,

> The potential for calamity (*khaṭb*) in this is great, the subject is extensive, and the qualifications for this matter do not appear in the ages except in a single rare individual (*illā li-wāḥid fard shādhdh*). But we will inform you of it and raise you from the lowlands of following the authority of others (*taqlīd*) and guide you to the smoothness of the path.[43]

43 Al-Ghazālī, *Mīzān*, 29.

There can be little doubt that al-Ghazālī saw himself as just this "rare individual," a forerunner of his claim in the *Deliverer* to be the divinely appointed renewer of the fifth Islamic century.[44] Sufism played no role in securing this conviction of his own insight; he informs us in the *Scale* that his attempt to practice Sufism under the guidance of a shaykh was rebuffed and that his knowledge of Sufi practice is second hand. Al-Ghazālī's self-certainty and conviction that he had secured a high degree of the felicity that is the aim of human existence came from philosophy, from pursuing ethical self-perfection and theoretical investigation of existence and its Creator in conjunction.

We know from independent sources that al-Ghazālī did take up Sufi practice and presented himself as a Sufi after he left Baghdad. The *Scale* suggests two reasons for this that have nothing to do with a sudden shattering of his convictions. For one, as we have seen, al-Ghazālī tentatively suggests a third way to felicity that combines philosophy with Sufism. For the most talented philosophers – and plainly al-Ghazālī saw himself as belonging to this elite of the elite – the subsequent practice of Sufism may add the luminous clarity of mystical insight to the rational conclusions of philosophy. Alexander Treiger has argued that the tentative proposal of the *Scale* becomes a fixed feature of al-Ghazālī's later thought.[45] The lure of the greatest possible felicity may well have drawn al-Ghazālī to the path that the *shaykh* he cites in the *Scale* had forbidden him to follow without giving up all of his worldly attainments. The wavering between resolve and procrastination he describes in the *Deliverer* may well have been his experience of the decision to leave Baghdad and all it represented for the sake of perfecting the knowledge of God he had attained by means of philosophical investigation through subsequent Sufi practice.

This proposal is a variation on the interior, spiritual view of al-Ghazālī's life, described in the *Deliverer* and embraced by generations of scholars. But there is another, quite different reason for embracing Sufism. At the time he wrote the *Scale*, al-Ghazālī was not worried about his own attainment of felicity. Rather, one of the key motives in writing the book, as the first two chapters show, is the desire to lead his fellow Muslims to felicity. Saving his fellow Muslims and guiding those who may be so guided to some degree of felicity was not merely a matter, as he knew, of articulating doctrines that were correct, but of articulating them in a compelling manner. In this, the messenger mattered as much as the message. In another passage of the *Scale* he writes,

44 Al-Ghazālī, *Al-Munqidh min aḍ-ḍalāl*, 75–76.

45 Treiger, "The Science of Divine Disclosure: Al-Ġazālī's Higher Theology and its Philosophical Underpinnings," 307.

> Know that the reason for [the failure of most people to pursue felicity] is heedlessness in contemplating (*at-tafakkur fī*) these matters that we have mentioned – for this heedlessness is constantly upon them, filling every hour of their day, and they cannot realize this as long as their appetites are dominant, as they are. *Truly, the one who would make them aware of this is a preacher of faultless conduct* (*wāʿiẓ zakī s-sīra*), *and the land is empty of them* (emphasis added).[46]

Al-Ghazālī saw it as his mission to rouse his fellow men from their heedlessness – not merely to convey the right ideas and to convey them convincingly, but to become himself the most effective messenger for them. We find this sentiment again in Chapter Twenty-seven of the *Scale*, entitled "Exposition of the duties of the student and teacher in the Sciences that Lead to Felicity" (*Bayān waẓāʾif al-mutaʿallim wa-l-muʿallim fī l-ʿulūm al-musʿida*). This is the longest chapter of the *Scale* by far, highlighting al-Ghazālī's concern with pedagogy. The eighth of eight duties of the teacher is that "the teacher of the Practical Science (*al-ʿilm al-ʿamalī*) – I mean the legal sciences (*ash-sharʿiyyāt*) – practice what he teaches."[47] Again, an effective guide must guide by example.

In addition to testing his hypothesis that more luminous insight was to be found through the practice of Sufism after the completion of the philosophical curriculum, al-Ghazālī took up Sufi practices – and identity – to present himself as an inspiring model for those he hoped to attract to the pursuit of felicity. We see this pedagogical concern also in the fact that al-Ghazālī did not retreat into the obscurity of spiritual retreat after leaving Baghdad, concerned only with cultivating his own felicity; he immediately began writing and reading from the *Revival of the Religious Sciences*, which aimed to refocus the religious sciences on the quest for felicity though a method that al-Ghazālī in that work refers to as the Science of the Hereafter (*ʿilm al-ākhira*).

Being a Sufi was also effective because al-Ghazālī had not one message to deliver, but two, at least: the philosophical method for the elite who were qualified to follow it, and the Sufi method for the majority who were not. By presenting himself as a Sufi, he could reach this majority and convince them through his personal example. But al-Ghazālī did not neglect those few who were qualified for philosophy (and perhaps Sufism beyond philosophy). After all, they were the most promising students and the most likely to attain felicity.

46 Al-Ghazālī, *Mīzān*, 25.

47 Ibid., 139. Under the duties of the teacher in this chapter, we also find the injunction not to teach students material that is too advanced for their understanding, which echoes the discussion of the three meanings of "school" discussed above. Ibid., 138–39.

Though he had taken up Sufi practice, he continued to write works specifically for this group, a body of writings he referred to as his "restricted" (*maḍnūn*) corpus.[48] Even in his more popular works, he does not write from a Sufi perspective alone. His *Revival of the Religious Sciences*, from which he began reading publically already in Damascus, shortly after his departure from Baghdad, advocates and details not Sufism, but what al-Ghazālī calls the Science of the Hereafter, a method for pursuing felicity in the hereafter that comprises both Sufism and philosophy. But in the *Revival*, al-Ghazālī announces that he will treat practice alone and not knowledge of God. By so limiting his discussion, al-Ghazālī restricts his treatment of the path to felicity to ethics alone, the shared terrain of Sufism and philosophy, avoiding discussion of the method of obtaining the knowledge that is the substance of felicity that divides the two disciplines. This allows al-Ghazālī to write a book that is accessible to the majority of those who pursue felicity in the hereafter while not denying the validity of the philosophical approach.

It is worth noting that the description of the Sufi path that al-Ghazālī gives in the *Scale* on the authority of the Sufi Shaykh who forbade al-Ghazālī to practice is given nearly verbatim in Book Twenty-one of the *Revival*, though without attributing it to the Sufi authority or telling the story of having been refused his guidance. The critique of Sufism from the perspective of the "theoreticians" is also found in that book. This could indicate that Book Twenty-one, "the Marvels of the Heart" (*Kitāb Sharḥ 'ajā'ib al-qalb*) represents the earliest section of the *Revival*. It may also indicate that at the time of writing it, al-Ghazālī still had had no deeper personal experience of Sufi practice than he had when he wrote the *Scale of Action*.

Conclusion

We have seen that al-Ghazālī's intellectual convictions and spiritual mission on the eve of his spectacular departure from Baghdad were very different than he later portrayed them in the *Deliverer*. He had not rejected philosophy, was not trying to find the fortitude to embrace Sufism, and was not anxious about his own salvation. Rather, he had critically embraced philosophy and saw himself as having made profound progress in its practice. He hoped to sharpen his insight and raise his degree of felicity through the practice of Sufism, but more than that, he hoped, as a Sufi, to be able to rouse men from their heedlessness and to lead them to the method of the pursuit of felicity for which the majority

48 A term coined by Afifi al-Akiti in "The Good, the Bad and the Ugly of *Falsafa*."

was suited. We cannot know what exactly transpired in al-Ghazālī's heart or mind as he broke with a life he had led for more than a decade and had trained for over many years before that. It was, no doubt, a dramatic event that led him in directions he could not have imagined as he wrote the *Scale* on the brink of taking that step. But the *Revival of the Religious Sciences*, the fruit of this embarkation and the blueprint for the agenda to which he dedicated the remainder of his life, shows that his understanding of the paths to felicity and the means of calling men to follow them remained largely unchanged.

CHAPTER 11

Al-Ghazālī on Knowledge (*ʿilm*) and Certainty (*yaqīn*) in *al-Munqidh min aḍ-Ḍalāl* and in *al-Qisṭās al-Mustaqīm*

Luis Xavier López-Farjeat

In his well-known autobiographical treatise entitled *Deliverance from Error* (*al-Munqidh min aḍ-ḍalāl*),[1] al-Ghazālī relays the most important account of his personal encounter with skepticism and the intellectual itinerary that he traveled in order to attain the certainty of truth. While trying to find the correct method for the attainment of truth, al-Ghazālī deals with some epistemological difficulties that have bearing on contemporary discussions on the sources of knowledge and its connection with certainty, and, specifically, on the epistemic controversies related to skepticism, foundationalism, and fallibilism.

In the opening section of the *Munqidh*, al-Ghazālī states a problem[2] that is found in some epistemological discussions, namely, the connection between

1 I use the Arabic version *al-Munqidh min aḍ-ḍalāl*, ed. Jamīl Ṣalībā and Kāmil ʿAyyād, Beirut: Dar al-Andalus, 1981; and the English version *Deliverance from Error: An Annotated Translation of Al-Ghazali's al-Munqidh min al-Dalal including Five Key Texts*, trans. R. J. McCarthy, Boston: Twayne Publishers, 1980, 61–143. I quote McCarthy's translation (slightly modified when necessary) indicating the paragraph and the page, and the Arabic version of Ṣalībā and ʿAyyād indicating the page. There is a trivial discussion on al-Ghazālī's sincerity around these 'confessions'. In the introduction to his translation McCarthy (McCarthy 1980, 23–26) presents the different standpoints in this respect. Beyond this discussion I have no doubt of the historical value of the treatise. In my view it is a puzzling text that (a) presents critical arguments against the Bāṭinites; (b) makes important contributions in order to understand al-Ghazālī's sympathy with Sufism; and (c) suggests significant clues for understanding the relations between philosophy and theology in al-Ghazālī's thought.

2 "(…) I began by saying to myself: 'First I must seek for the knowledge of the true meaning of things, therefore, I must inquire into what the true meaning of knowledge is.' Then it became clear to me that sure and certain knowledge is that in which the thing known is made so manifest that no doubt clings to it, nor is it accompanied by the possibility of error and deception, nor can the mind even suppose such a possibility. Furthermore, safety from error must accompany the certainty to such a degree that, if someone proposed to show it to be false – for example, a man who would turn a stone into gold and a stick into a snake – his feat would not induce any doubt or denial. For if I know that ten is more than three, and then someone were to say: 'No, on the contrary, three is more than ten, as is proved by my turning

 | DOI 10.1163/9789004290952_012

knowledge and certainty. In this direction, a well-known contemporary epistemological principle with Cartesian roots is 'we should believe nothing that we do not know for certain.' Or, as al-Ghazālī suggests: 'we *know some proposition X* when we are sure that it is not possible to find an error in it.' Thus, if someone tries to show that a proposition such as "ten is more than three" is false and he or she proves it by means of something miraculous, that should not make us change our mind – some propositions are irrefutable. The *Munqidh*, however, shows al-Ghazālī's crisis when he finds that there is no certainty in knowledge. This distrust of knowledge drove al-Ghazālī to skepticism. After God cured him, however, he began to inquire into the different methods employed by the seekers of the truth. The *Munqidh* reveals a particular epistemic itinerary: from knowledge to skepticism and from skepticism to reasoned faith.

Here, I argue that al-Ghazālī is a foundationalist who adopts skepticism as a starting point in his epistemology, with the intention of showing that the only way to avoid skepticism is to argue that the first principles or primary truths on which knowledge is grounded are intuitively apprehended. This solution is directly connected to the knowledge of God. It is God who ultimately grounds all knowledge. But how can we know God? Al-Ghazālī's question on the nature of knowledge is, then, simultaneously the question of the correct way of knowing God. In order to find an answer to the question on the knowledge of God, I moved to al-Ghazālī's logical-religious treatise called, *The Correct Balance* (*al-Qisṭās al-mustaqīm*).[3] In this short work, al-Ghazālī connects philosophical logic with revelation and conceives intellectual knowledge as the best way to know God. I argue, however, that this does not make al-Ghazālī a radical rationalist; rather, he is reforming traditional Islamic theology and is adopting logical argumentation in order to provide an original (though problematic) understanding of the relationship between reason and revelation. Indeed, al-Ghazālī thinks that they are not contradictory, but entirely compatible. The

this stick into a snake – and if he were to do just that and I were to see him do it, I would not doubt my knowledge because of his feat. The only effect it would have on me would be to make me wonder how he could do such thing. But there would be no doubt at all about what I knew!'

I realized, then, that whatever I did not know in this way and was not certain of with this kind of certainty was unreliable and unsure knowledge, and that every knowledge unaccompanied by safety from error is not sure and certain knowledge" (al-Ghazālī, *al-Munqidh* 7, 55, trans. McCarthy, slightly modified; Arabic 63–64).

3 I use the Arabic version *al-Qisṭās al-mustaqīm*, ed. M. Bījū, Damascus: Al-Maṭbaʿa al-ʿIlmiyya, 1993, and the English version included in al-Ghazālī, *al-Munqidh* trans. McCarthy, 287–332. I quote McCarthy's translation indicating the paragraph and the page, and the Arabic version of Bijū indicating the page.

use of philosophical logic within theology radically changes the traditional conception of revelation as something miraculous and attained by means other than human reason.

1

Al-Ghazālī's *al-Munqidh min aḍ-ḍalāl* starts with the question regarding the true meaning of knowledge (*'ilm*): "certain knowledge is that in which the thing known is made so manifest that no doubt (*rayb*) clings to it, nor is it accompanied by the possibility of error and deception, nor can the mind even suppose such a possibility."[4] This definition is close to the Aristotelian notion of *apodeixis*.[5] According to Aristotle, this kind of reasoning is reserved, in the strict sense, to mathematics and metaphysics.[6] And, certainly, al-Ghazālī uses a mathematical example that makes it clear that there are some propositions that prove the infallibility of reason: "ten is more than three" is an irrefutable proposition. It is a necessary assertion that guarantees the certainty of knowledge. For Aristotle, necessary propositions are not reserved to mathematics. The first principles, and those principles in which each science and discipline are grounded, are also proofs of the infallibility of reason. In addition, Aristotle affirms that reason is infallible in the case of empirical realities. According to some contemporary scholars, Aristotle grounds knowledge in a group of self-evident, irrefutable principles and, in this sense, he is avoiding skepticism.[7] Yet we should ask – as al-Ghazālī himself asked – what would happen if these principles broke down.

Al-Ghazālī claims that the only cognitions of which we can have certainty are sense-data (*al-ḥissiyyāt*) and self-evident truths (or 'necessary things': *aḍ-ḍarūriyyāt*). He decides, however, to test whether or not we can truly have

---

4 Al-Ghazālī, *al-Munqidh* 7, 55, trans. McCarthy; Arabic 64.

5 See Aristotle, *The Complete Works of Aristotle*, ed. Jonathan Barnes, Princeton: Princeton University Press, 1984, *Posterior Analytics* 1, 2, 71b18–24.

6 Aristotle, *The Complete Works of Aristotle*, ed. Barnes, *Posterior Analytics* 1.1–2, 71a1–72b4; *Metaphysics* books 3 and 4. See also *Mathematik und Metaphysik bei Aristoteles*, ed. Andreas Graeser, Bern & Sttutgart: Haupt Verlag, 1987.

7 Enrico Berti, *L'unità del sapere in Aristotele*, Padua: CEDAM, 1965, 156; Terence Irwin, *Aristotle's first principles*, Oxford: Oxford University Press, 1988, 196–198; Jonathan Barnes, commentary on *Aristotle Posterior Analytics*, Oxford: Clarendon Press, 1993, 261–267; Orna Harari, *Knowledge and demonstration. Aristotle's Posterior Analytics*, Dordrecht/Boston/London: Kluwer Academic Publishers, 2004, 39–62.

certainty. The results of this testing are very similar to those of Descartes:[8] empirical observation is an imperfect source of knowledge because it induces doubt. Reason is able to show the falsehood of sense-data, and it is reasonable to believe that reason is trustworthy. Still, if reason acts as a judge of the sense-data, perhaps there is a judge that is beyond reason and that could declare the falsehood of judgments. The sort of philosophical problem that follows the possibility of a judge of reason is well known: how is it possible to distinguish whether one is dreaming or whether one is awake? Al-Ghazālī confesses that given that he could not find a satisfactory answer to this problem he turned skeptic in fact but not in doctrine.[9]

The distinction between dreaming and waking states is a well-known problem in the history of philosophy. From Descartes' evil demon[10] to Putnam's brain-in-a-vat experiment,[11] the possibility of dreaming while we are allegedly

8 In this respect two articles offer interesting parallels: the first one is from Sami M. Najm, "The Place and Function of Doubt in the Philosophies of Descartes and Al-Ghazālī." *Philosophy East and West* 16, 3/4(1966): 133–41; the second one is from Tamara Albertini, "Crisis and Certainty of Knowledge in al-Ghazālī (1058–1111) and Descartes (1596–1650)." *Philosophy East and West* 55 (2005): 1–14. Although Descartes's proposal in the *Meditations* is very similar to al-Ghazālī's, there is no evidence that Descartes was aware of the *Munqidh*. Mustafa Abu-Sway, in *Al-Ghazzālyy. A Study in Islamic Epistemology* (Kuala Lumpur: Dewan Bahasa dan Pustaka, 1996), 142, mentions the alleged existence of a translated copy of the *Munqidh* in Descartes' library in Paris, with his comments in the margin, but Abu-Sway himself affirms that there is no account of the nature of these comments. Ignacio L. Götz, "The Quest for Certainty: al-Ghazālī and Descartes," *Journal of Philosophical Research* 92 (2003): 13–16, says that there are different opinions on this alleged influence. He mentions that while Catherine Wilson states that Descartes definitely read al-Ghazālī's work, V. V. Naumkin affirms that there is not much information in support of such a claim. Since according to Götz there is no evidence of a Latin translation of the *Munqidh* before Descartes' time, he offers some other alternative following scholars such as Sharif and Zakzouk: (a) perhaps he knew about al-Ghazālī in the works of Aquinas and Ramon Llull; (b) it was translated orally for Descartes by some scholar of Arabic – after all, Descartes had contact with some Orientalists like Jacobus Golius (1596–1667), who taught Arabic and mathematics at the University of Leiden; (c) it is known that a student of Golius, Levinius Warner, had a manuscript copy of the *Munqidh* which is now at the Rijks Universiteit of Leiden. It seems that the more convincing alternative is that perhaps Descartes exchanged ideas with Golius and his circle not only about mathematics but also about Islamic matters.

9 Al-Ghazālī, *al-Munqidh* 15, 57, trans. McCarthy; Arabic 67–68.

10 René Descartes, *Meditations on First Philosophy* in *Meditations and Other Metaphysical Writings*, ed. D. Clarke, Harmondsworth, Middlesex: Penguin, 1998, 22.

11 Hilary Putnam, *Reason, Truth and History*, Cambridge: Cambridge University Press, 1982, 1–21.

awake has been discussed and is an open door for skepticism. Al-Ghazālī could not find a satisfactory argument to distinguish waking life from dreaming. He was genuinely perplexed by the fact that it is possible to believe the reality of certain dreamed things and circumstances while we are asleep. His argument is as follows: if it is true that we believe what is happening in our dreams (while we are asleep) and we find that those imaginings and beliefs are unsubstantial when we wake up, what guarantees that there is not another state that has the same relation as waking has to dreaming? Al-Ghazālī is asking for a certain and infallible source of knowledge as well as for a method that could justify it; after two months without finding a consistent source and justification for knowledge, of course, he became a skeptic.[12] Later on, however, he fortunately was healed by God: his soul regained its health and balance and once again he accepted the self-evident data of reason. The restoration of al-Ghazālī's soul did not come from a 'rational proof' or from argumentation. It came from a light that, according to him, "is the key to most knowledge."[13]

It is not easy to understand the metaphor of "light."[14] From an epistemological standpoint, it would be difficult to explain it in the way that al-Ghazālī describes it, namely, as a "light which God casts into the heart".[15] I shall not discuss the way in which this "illumination" affects our heart (following the Aristotelian tradition, al-Ghazālī shared with other thinkers the belief that intelligence (*noūs*) is located in the heart and not in the brain). I shall point out, however, that the action of an external agent, namely God, is a resource that guarantees that knowledge is well grounded. But God is not replacing

12 In my view, this is a very particular kind of skepticism. Certainly, it is neither the skepticism of Sextus Empiricus nor that of the Islamic thinker Ibn ar-Rāwandī; rather, it seems to be a sort of methodological skepticism. Some of al-Ghazālī's biographers think, however, that this skepticism was a sincere crisis that deeply affected even his emotional stability. For an interesting and valuable approach to al-Ghazālī's skepticism see Leor Halevi, "The Theologian's Doubts: Natural Philosophy and the Skeptical Games of Ghazālī," *Journal of the History of Ideas* 63, 1 (2002): 19–39, and Taneli Kukkonen, "al-Ghazālī's Skepticism Revisited," in *Rethinking the History of Skepticism. The Missing Medieval Background*, ed. G. Henrik Lagerlund, Leiden: Brill, 2010, 29–60.

13 Al-Ghazālī, *al-Munqidh* 15, 57, trans. McCarthy; Arabic 68.

14 Al-Ghazālī's treatise *The Niche of Lights* (*Mishkāt al-Anwār*), trans. David Buchman, Provo: Brigham Young University Press, 1998, for example, is a mystical treatise where he deeply explores this metaphor. Franz Rosenthal's *Knowledge Triumphant. The Concept of Knowledge in Medieval Islam*, Leiden: Brill, 2007, pp. 155–193, is truly helpful for understanding the sense of this metaphor among Sufis. For more on this topic, see Girdner's contribution to this volume.

15 Al-Ghazālī, *al-Munqidh* 16, 58, trans. McCarthy; Arabic 68.

reason; we must be careful when understanding al-Ghazālī's metaphor of light because it does not have exactly the same sense as in Sufism – that is, it is not a sort of ecstasy or mystic encounter in which human understanding is invalidated. For al-Ghazālī, this light is an illumination from God that makes human knowledge possible. He argues, therefore, that our first epistemological attitude does not arise from knowledge *per se*. Previous to knowledge, we acquired a group of first principles or primary truths that enable the foundation of knowledge. Those principles come from God. Thus, al-Ghazālī's conception of knowledge is distinctly foundationalist. This means that knowledge begins with an illumination or, in other words, with an 'intuition' that leads us to some principles or propositions that can be known with certainty. In order to confirm the consistency of those first principles that are supported by God and at the same time support knowledge, al-Ghazālī tests other sources of knowledge, as I show in the next section.

2

After defending the sort of foundationalism explained above, al-Ghazālī evaluates the epistemological categories of whom he calls "the seekers of the truth" (*aṣnāf aṭ-ṭālibīn*). The analysis starts with the dialectic method of the *mutakallimūn*. Al-Ghazālī's description of the *kalām* underlines its apologetic use for the preservation of the traditional Islamic creed and the refutation of the confusions and innovations introduced by heretics. The science of *kalām* is characterized precisely by its dialectic or polemic method. This means that it deals with probable premises. Although al-Ghazālī was a theologian and wrote long treatises against innovative conceptions of religious dogma, in the *Munqidh* he concedes that there is something defective in the theologians' methodology.[16] When theologians argued against their adversaries, says al-Ghazālī, "they relied on premises which they took over from their adversaries, being compelled to admit them by uncritical acceptance deriving from the Qur'ān and the Traditions."[17] This is where the methodological defects are found: theological polemics are devoted to showing the inconsistencies and the illogical conclusions of those who have been considered innovators

---

16 Al-Ghazālī's critiques concerning theology are intriguing. Although he is usually considered a theologian, he could also be taken for a "religious thinker" discussing theological matters. Al-Ghazālī was familiar with the methodology of the *mutakallimūn* and certainly he could be considered an Asha'irite.

17 Al-Ghazālī, *al-Munqidh* 23, 59, trans. McCarthy; Arabic 72.

and, in their discussions, the theologians assume that the religious tradition that comes from the community, the Book, and the Tradition should not be analyzed. In contrast, al-Ghazālī suggests that those sources of religion should also be critically analyzed because, otherwise, theologians would not be able to dispute with those who admit only truths of reason. This is why, sooner or later, theology resorts to philosophy; it is also why Islamic theologians began to study the true nature of things. Nevertheless, given that this was not the aim of theology, those theologians sympathetic to philosophy failed to clarify those matters in disagreement.[18]

Al-Ghazālī recognized the power of philosophy and its capacity to find errors in other sciences. Philosophy is grounded on logic, the science of perfect reasoning. Thus, this science – and specifically the art of demonstration – leads to certainty. Although certainty is guaranteed by demonstration, al-Ghazālī was not satisfied with it. He was suspicious of the coherence of philosophical arguments. Concretely, he distrusted them because some philosophers attained false conclusions despite apparently having argued correctly. In the autobiographical *Munqidh*, he does not absolutely repudiate philosophical argumentation; rather, he condemns the unbelief and godlessness of most of the philosophers and expresses his disapproval of the infidelity and heresy involved in some of their conclusions.

According to al-Ghazālī, logic and mathematics are paradigmatic philosophical disciplines with infallible and accurate methodologies. He does not criticize the logical and mathematical methods *per se*. Both are rational disciplines and there is no objection against them.[19] Something quite different

18 Al-Ghazālī, *al-Munqidh* 24, 60, trans. McCarthy; Arabic 72–73.

19 Though logic and mathematics are safe disciplines because they do not deal with religious matters, al-Ghazālī mentions some inconveniences related to them. Mathematics is a paradigmatic discipline since it is accurate and entirely true. The evils related to mathematics are not due to its intrinsic methodology; rather, the first evil of mathematics comes from the people who marvel at its accuracy and surmise that every philosophical argument reaches the same exactness – clearly, not every philosophical discipline works with the same clarity and precision as mathematics does. Thus, people do not distinguish between mathematical and other kinds of philosophical assertions, holding instead that philosophy is always accurate; it is easy to become an unbeliever this way. A second evil related to mathematics emerges when some ignorant Muslims reject mathematical accuracy, believing it to be dangerous for religion. Something similar happens with logic: philosophers trust in apodictic demonstrations because they lead to certitude, so in many cases they distrust those disciplines that cannot satisfy the argumentative conditions of demonstration. Another common critique against philosophers is that they frequently think that they have proved something when actually they have erred in their

happens with the rest of the philosophical disciplines, however: al-Ghazālī devotes some paragraphs to show the inconsistencies of physics, metaphysics, politics, and ethics.

Errors in physics and metaphysics are related. Al-Ghazālī mentions that he has already faced these, and especially the metaphysical errors, in the *The Incoherence of the Philosophers* (*Tahāfut al-falāsifa*), a treatise in which he refutes philosophical heresies or innovations. He is concerned specifically with three issues, common among philosophers, which are offensive to every Muslim: (a) denial of the resurrection of the body; (b) the claim that God knows universals but not particulars; and (c) affirmation of the eternity of the world. These questions contradict the religious dogmas of the resurrection of the body, of divine omniscience, and of creation respectively. Despite these errors, however, there is nothing to be condemned in the theologians who subscribe to some philosophical views, such as "the denial of the divine attributes, and their assertion that God knows by His essence, and not by a knowledge superadded to His essence."[20]

With regard to politics, al-Ghazālī affirms that philosophers have taken the general maxims of revelation and have not added anything different; and regarding ethics, he asserts that philosophers have simply adopted what has been said by the Sufis. The product of this philosophical mixture of prophetic utterances, the sayings of the Sufis, and the presentation of the qualities and habits of the soul was a confusing ethical teaching. At this point, al-Ghazālī concludes that the source of knowledge can be found neither among the common opinions discussed by theologians, nor amongst the apodictic arguments presented by the philosophers, nor within the resultant eclectic combination of religion and philosophy the philosophers had demonstrated.

After dealing with philosophy, al-Ghazālī turns his attention to those who follow the teachings of the infallible Imām. Given that al-Ghazālī explains that they follow the authority (*taʿlimiyya*) of the Imām, in his translation McCarthy refers to them as the Taʿlīmites or authoritarians. The Arabic text refers to the *Bāṭiniyya*.[21] Al-Ghazālī mentions that while he was reading the writings of this sect, the Caliph asked him to write a book revealing the true meaning of their esoteric doctrine; he wrote, therefore, the short treatise entitled *The Infamies of the Bāṭinites and the Virtues of the Mustaẓhirites* (*Faḍāʾiḥ al-Bāṭiniyya wa-faḍāʾil al-Mustaẓhiriyya*). *Bāṭiniyya* is a pejorative term that means, precisely, 'esoteric';

---

arguments and are incapable of realizing it. See al-Ghazālī, *al-Munqidh* 36–44, 63–65, trans. McCarthy; Arabic 79–82.

20 Al-Ghazālī, *al-Munqidh* 48–67, trans. McCarthy; Arabic 84.

21 Al-Ghazālī, *al-Munqidh*, Arabic 69.

it is the one that al-Ghazālī uses several times within his treatises to designate his Isma'ili adversaries. Therefore, there are reasons to suspect that the followers of the Imām are the Isma'ilis, and al-Ghazālī basically disapproves of their servility to authority (*ta'limiyya*). The notion of authority is quite relevant for them but al-Ghazālī is skeptical about their notion of an infallible Imām. This skepticism also presents an epistemological problem. For the followers of the infallible Imām, the source of knowledge is authority; in this sense, it is not necessary to search for the truth in the philosophical disciplines or in independent judgments.

Al-Ghazālī explains that some Muslims give priority to personal judgment or reasoned opinion (*ra'y*) over blind adhesion to the criterion of authority; here emerges a complex epistemological problem: which of these sources is safer? The followers of the infallible Imām think that it is safer to discard reason (*an-naẓar*) and replace it with authoritative instruction (*ta'līm*). Al-Ghazālī, however, disagrees with both alternatives. Independent reasoning is not trustworthy if it is reduced to the opinion or personal criterion of a jurist. As we shall see, though, if reasoning is assisted by logic, then it is definitely valid and trustworthy. In this last sense, independent reasoning should not be identified as reasoned opinion but as formal argumentation.

To trust in authority is problematic. We have to inquire into its legitimacy. This matter is not easy since there are many founders of theological and juridical schools and there are differences between them. If every Muslim has to follow an authority, this should remove the differences between the schools. In other words, if 'Alī was the first Imām, why did he not eradicate the differences? The fact is that there are many differences among the Muslim sects and if someone decides to follow a specific authority, they previously have to judge whether or not that leader is legitimate.[22] Al-Ghazālī says, for instance, that if someone follows Abū Ḥanīfa or ash-Shāfi'ī, or another religious authority, it is necessary to exercise independent reasoning in order to judge which is the best qualified authority; as such, it is not possible to discard personal judgment. Thus, when the followers of the Imām argue for the infallibility of authority, present the role of the Imām as the only alternative for eradicating the discrepancies, and invite their people to discard judgment, they simply emphasize differences rather than dissolve them.

22 Certainly, it is common to find that people actually follow a specific authority because they were educated in that tradition. Al-Ghazālī rejects this possibility because it would lead us to believe that there is no true religion and that each person becomes Jew, Christian, Muslim, or follows a sect instead of another because the force of tradition instead of the truth itself.

Al-Ghazālī adds one last element to his critique of the followers of the infallible Imām. What he criticizes is not just the strong role of authority in their theory, but also the ambiguity of the arguments they employ when discussing theological matters, especially the legitimacy of their Imām. It is for this reason that, as mentioned before, al-Ghazālī called them Bāṭinites or 'esoteric.'

If the followers of the infallible Imām are the Ismaʿīlis as I think they are, it is fair to stress that al-Ghazālī is not completely impartial in his critique of them; one could even say that some of his accounts are crude and simplistic, and some scholars have already pointed out distortions in al-Ghazālī's descriptions.[23] I do not intend to dwell on a detailed analysis of these distortions. What I want to stress is al-Ghazālī's intention when he argues against the Ismaʿīli conception of authority; he is defending reason against what he considers an irrational attitude that – paradoxically – is supported by rationality. The Ismaʿīlis invite their followers to abandon the use of reason because it is fallible. The Ismaʿīlis argue the following: reason is fallible; a proof of this fallibility is that judgments may be right or wrong, however rational they appear. Given this risk, therefore, it is better to discard reason entirely and replace fallible opinions with an external infallible authority, i.e., *taʿlīm*. Al-Ghazālī refutes authoritarianism, but his argument works also as a refutation of epistemological fallibilism. He reiterates, however, that choosing to believe in an authority is a rational decision. As such, even the authority of instruction (*taʿlīm*) and the knowledge gleaned from it refer ultimately to rationality. Here, we find an epistemological problem that is relevant even today: how should laypersons evaluate the testimony of experts or of authority? It seems that a solution to this problem would have to appeal to logical competencies, and this is what al-Ghazālī argues.

Having rejected the Ismaʿīli notion of authority as a valid source of knowledge, al-Ghazālī offers a careful analysis of Sufi mysticism. For him, the way of the Sufis is definitely the most attractive alternative. He agrees with some Sufi concerns (for instance, the emphasis on practice instead of theory, or their promotion of asceticism), yet he rejects ecstasy as the only means of knowing the

23 Eric Ormsby observes that al-Ghazālī's views on the Ismaʿilis are incomplete because they are based principally only on the doctrines propounded by Ḥasan-i Ṣabbāḥ, the leader of the Nizārī Ismāʿīlīs in Syria. According to Ormsby, al-Ghazālī's attacks are too diffuse and it seems that sometimes he misreads their texts deliberately (Eric Ormsby, *Ghazali: The Revival of Islam*, Oxford: Oneworld Publications, 2008, 99–104. For the polemical reception of al-Ghazālī's writings on the Ismaʿilis, the work of Farouk Mitha, *Al-Ghazālī and the Ismāʿīlīs*, London: I.B. Tauris, 2001 (esp. pp. 19–27; 86–102) is quite helpful.

truth, warning against the excesses of this kind of spirituality, which include, for instance, the primacy of ecstasy over worship.

Sufis have spiritual interests that move them away from theologians, philosophers, and the followers of the infallible Imām. The concept of knowledge (*ʿilm*) is radically different for Sufis because they are not interested in offering a theoretical account of knowledge; their main concern is mysticism.[24] Mystical experience is intangible, something that surpasses words and rational understanding. The Sufi conception of knowledge as light is quite different from the philosophical conception of knowledge as thought, and al-Ghazālī is conscious of this distinction.

3

Now, if within the *Munqidh kalām*-theology, philosophy, and authoritative instruction (*taʿlīm*) have been discarded as sources of knowledge, what would count as a valid source? As I mentioned in the first section, the source of knowledge is God for al-Ghazālī, since God ultimately provides the basis of all knowledge. But how can we know God? Do we know Him by intuition? God presents Himself in revelation; yet, do we understand revelation as a mystical experience, or as an intellectual one? As I mentioned at the beginning, it is possible to propose an answer going beyond the *Munqidh* and finding its connections with another treatise entitled *The Correct Balance* (*al-Qisṭās al-mustaqīm*). There, al-Ghazālī connects philosophical logic with revelation and maintains that the intellectual or philosophical way of understanding revelation is the best way to know God. This means that al-Ghazālī moderates some of his critiques of philosophy and, as he does in other writings, he must therefore harmonize philosophy – and specifically logic – with revelation. In this sense, I think that al-Ghazālī, proposing a radical identification of logic and revelation, reforms traditional Islamic theology. In my view, al-Ghazālī has already argued as a reformer when criticizing the methodology of his peers in the *Munqidh*; this does not mean, however, that he is abandoning his vocation – rather, he has a methodological alternative in mind. The key for finding this sort of reformed methodology is the treatise *The Correct Balance*. In the *Munqidh*,

24 I do not intend to offer an in depth study of the nature of mystical knowledge. Although I think it is an interesting issue, it is beyond the scope of the epistemological problems with which we are dealing. For more on this issue, see Franz Rosenthal, *Knowledge Triumphant: The concept of knowledge in medieval Islam*, Leiden: Brill, 2007, 58–69; 176–193.

there are significant allusions to this work: (a) al-Ghazālī refers to it in order to find a way to avoid false beliefs;[25] (b) he mentions that in that treatise he has also studied a way to end disagreement among men;[26] (c) he affirms that in the *Qisṭās* he has explained "the scale for weighing knowledge and showing that he who fully understands it has no need of an infallible Imām";[27] and, (d) later on, he resorts to the same treatise to identify the treatment for those who claim to be perplexed because of the teachings of the authoritarians.[28]

I find these references to be particularly important because they validate the source of knowledge explained by al-Ghazālī in the *Qisṭās*. In terms of contents, the *Qisṭās* is largely devoted to an explanation of Aristotelian syllogism. Thus, we find there a philosophical theology of sorts and, in this sense, both a reformed version of *kalām* and an illuminating explanation of how theology resorts to different kinds of syllogisms. The *Qisṭās* offers a particular explanation of the "correct balance" between reason and revelation; as such, it contains a sort of apology for logical reasoning. Thus, the *Qisṭās* should be read as a key text for finding a precise answer to the question of what should be used as a source for understanding revelation and comprehending the knowledge of God. It is the place where we should find the correct way of carrying out theological investigation (without committing the errors that al-Ghazālī has attributed to theologians in the *Munqidh*) and the correct way of using philosophical argumentation (carefully examining the syllogistic structure of every argument in order to avoid false conclusions).

Al-Ghazālī wrote several works on logic; he was, after all, truly interested in an in-depth understanding of the different kinds of syllogisms and argumentative strategies. The *Qisṭās* is his only treatise devoted explicitly to the use of syllogisms in the Qur'ān.[29] In my view, al-Ghazālī is reforming traditional theology for two basic reasons: (a) he is convinced that "philosophical logic," that is, the demonstrative method (not the dialectic of the ordinary dogmatic theologians), can be perfectly incorporated into revelation and, therefore, that

25 Al-Ghazālī, *al-Munqidh* 68, 73–4, trans. McCarthy; Arabic 95.

26 Al-Ghazālī, *al-Munqidh* 70, 74, trans. McCarthy; Arabic 96.

27 Al-Ghazālī, *al-Munqidh* 76, 76, trans. McCarthy; Arabic 98.

28 Al-Ghazālī, *al-Munqidh* 140, 93, trans. McCarthy; Arabic 124.

29 The use of syllogism for interpreting the Qur'ān is the starting-point of the remarkable work of Rosalind W. Gwyne, *Logic, Rhetoric, and Legal Reasoning in the Qur'ān*, London: Routledge Curzon, 2004. In her work, she includes over thirty varieties of explicit and implicit arguments in the Qur'ān. In my opinion, the most interesting chapters are the sixth and seventh, both devoted to the presence of rhetorical arguments in the Book. For a related topic see J. van Ess, "The Logical Structure of Islamic Theology," in *Logic in Classical Islamic Culture*, ed. G. von Grunebaum, Wiesbaden: Harrasowitz, 1970, 21–50.

there is no contradiction between revelation and reason; (b) he is radically changing theological methodology, since he thinks that theologians should verify revealed assertions (in this sense, he definitely thinks that logic is the most perfect scientific method; perhaps that is why he does not criticize logical and mathematical methodologies *per se* in the *Munqidh*). The methodological perfection of logic and mathematics allows us to admit both of these disciplines as paradigmatic. Thus, they should be the correct disciplines for understanding revelation, that is, for knowing God. Certainly, al-Ghazālī is more interested in the philosophical argumentative arts than in arithmetical, geometrical, and astronomical matters. For his aims, the nature of the syllogism, the methods of proofs, the rules of demonstration, and the combination of premises provide a more adequate methodology.

Nevertheless, al-Ghazālī's intentions in the *Qisṭās* go beyond the mere comprehension of syllogisms. One of the basic subjects discussed in the *Qisṭās* is the perfection of knowledge, that is, the supreme way to know God. As Abrahamov[30] has pointed out, this is one of the most discussed matters among scholars working on al-Ghazālī. Some have argued that al-Ghazālī states that the best way to know God is the mystical experience as taught by the Sufis. Watt, for instance, has argued that he combines both ways, the mystical and the intellectual, simultaneously or at different times.[31] In my view, Abrahamov is right when he maintains that al-Ghazālī emphasizes the intellectual way. But this alternative offers some more difficulties: in this case it is relevant to understand the complex overlapping of philosophy and theology, and the relation between logic and revelation. Otherwise, it is easy to misunderstand al-Ghazālī's conception of theology and to understand his views as if he were a radical rationalist thinker. Although al-Ghazālī showed some disagreement with philosophy, he considered logic to be a valid method of verification. Thus, he selected it as the most appropriate way for attaining certitude. Al-Ghazālī trusted in logic as a valid way of interpreting the Qur'ān and, in this sense, of knowing revelation.

Trusting logic implies that it provides helpful tools for interpreting the Qur'ān and, obviously, that human reason is necessary for knowing God. With this in mind, it is clearer why al-Ghazālī criticized the Isma'īlis' intention of discarding reason in the *Munqidh*, and also why the mystical practices of the

---

30 Binyamin Abrahamov, "Al-Ghazālī's Supreme Way to Know God," *Studia Islamica* 77 (1993): 141–168.

31 Ibid., 141.

Sufis did not entirely satisfy him.[32] Al-Ghazālī believed in the superiority of philosophical reasoning if the conclusions reached were the correct ones. He wanted to show to the followers of the esoteric sect, who rejected logic, that when used correctly logic does not contradict revelation. On the contrary, revelation incorporates logic and it helps prevent arbitrary interpretations of the Qur'ān. Another issue would be whether the aim of the *Qisṭās* was to convince the former sect about the methodological advantages of logic and, further, to show them how the Qur'ān itself has a syllogistic basis (this would mean that logic is a discipline that is present in revelation). It seems that al-Ghazālī's main purpose was to refute the Ismaʿīlis (that is, the esoteric Bāṭinites) and certainly this is what he does. In my view, both purposes are important. It is very significant, however, that his arguments are not restricted to disproving the invalidation of reason. He presents a meticulous analysis of several Qur'ānic assertions using Aristotelian and Stoic syllogistic.

In his classic work, *Muslim Intellectual*, Watt[33] asks why it was necessary for al-Ghazālī to argue in that way, namely, by trying to find a Qur'ānic justification for the different types of syllogism (the first, second, and third Aristotelian figures explained in the *Prior Analytics*, and the conjunctive and disjunctive syllogisms from the Stoics). According to Watt, the *Qisṭās* is a puzzling treatise consisting of forced interpretations of Qur'ānic passages. Two of al-Ghazālī's other works are devoted to the explanation of logic: these, *The Standard of Knowledge* (*Miʿyār al-ʿilm*) and *The Touchstone of Thinking* (*Miḥakk an-naẓar*), are very technical because they were written for a philosophical audience. In contrast, the *Qisṭās* is not exactly a specialized treatise. It is possible that the audience for which this treatise was written could not understand logical technicalities. Thus, Watt[34] concludes that al-Ghazālī "spend[s] time on trivialities of this kind" precisely because he was trying to explain logic to those people who were ignorant of it. In my opinion, the *Qisṭās* is not exclusively a treatise designed to teach basic logic. At the beginning of this essay, I referred to the *Qisṭās* as a logical-religious treatise because I think that it is devoted to

32 It is true that especially at the end of his life, al-Ghazālī followed, in many aspects, the practices of the Sufis. In *The Revival of Religious Sciences* (*Iḥyāʾ ʿulūm ad-dīn*), for instance, there are many passages that confirm his decision to follow that path. Although he admits the limited capacity of reason, this does not necessarily means that he rejected its usefulness in verifying our knowledge and especially in avoiding errors.

33 W. Montgomery Watt, *Muslim Intellectual: a Study of al-Ghazālī*, Edinburgh: University Press, 1963, 69–70.

34 Ibid., 70.

integrating logic into revelation.[35] Al-Ghazālī shows that there is no contradiction between reason and religion, and that, in fact, religious assertions have a syllogistic structure. Thus, he believed that it was possible to posit the existence of a positive relationship between logic and revelation.

4

The *Qisṭās* presents an allegorical conversation between al-Ghazālī and a Bāṭinite. The latter asks al-Ghazālī whether true knowledge is perceived by the "independent" balance of reasoning (*raʾy*) or by the balance of analogy (*qiyās*).[36] Obviously, the Bāṭinite explains that both means are risky because they are contradictory; being ambiguous, they have been a cause of disagreement among believers. As such, following an infallible authority is safer than trusting the means of reason. Al-Ghazālī summarily rejects the need to obey some infallible authority as the right method for attaining the truth; yet, he also rejects the two means mentioned by the Bāṭinite, namely, *raʾy* and *qiyās*. He argues, then, that he weighs knowledge with the "correct balance," an obvious allusion to a verse in the Qurʾān: "weigh with a just balance."[37]

This balance consists of five scales emerging from the Book that God sent down and whereby He taught the Prophets to weigh knowledge. According to al-Ghazālī, familiarity with these five scales is a prerequisite for attaining true knowledge. Yet, I must reiterate, these five scales can be identified with the five kinds of syllogisms presented by Aristotle and the Stoics. Al-Ghazālī, however, does not explain them as part of a philosophical discipline, but as the technique of weighing or balancing established by God in the Qurʾān. He states: "[K]now that the balances of the Qurʾān are basically three: the balance of equivalence, and the balance of concomitance, and the balance of opposition. But the balance of equivalence is divided into three – the greater, the middle, and the lesser. So the total is five."[38]

Al-Ghazālī explains the greater balance of equivalence (*mīzān at-taʿādul*) in chapter two. Chapters three and four are devoted to the middle balance

---

35 On al-Ghazālī's purposes of the *Qisṭās* see Angelika Kleinknecht, "Al-Qisṭās al-Mustaqīm: Eine Ableitung der Logik aus dem Koran," in *Islamic Philosophy and the Classical Tradition*, ed. S. M. Stern, A. Hourani, and V. Brown, Oxford: Cassirer, 1972, 159–87; and Martin Whittingham, *Al-Ghazālī and the Qurʾān*, London: Routledge, 2007, 81–101.

36 Al-Ghazālī, *al-Qisṭās* 1, 245, trans. McCarthy; Arabic 11–12.

37 Q. 17:35.

38 Al-Ghazālī, *al-Qisṭās* 12, 248, trans. McCarthy; Arabic 18.

of measurement (*al-mīzān al-awsaṭ*) and the lesser balance of measurement (*al-mīzān al-aṣghar*), respectively. Chapters five and six concern the balance of concomitance (*mīzān at-talāzum*) and the balance of opposition (*mīzān at-taʿānud*), respectively. The other five chapters deal with different matters related to the five balances: chapter seven concerns false syllogisms; chapter eight argues that Muhammad is the only authoritative teacher and that he established the revealed truth by means of syllogisms; chapter nine deals with the different debates among believers; chapter ten explains why *raʾy* and *qiyās* are not the correct means of inquiry.

I shall now focus on chapter eight in order to show that al-Ghazālī provides an original alternative for harmonizing reason and revelation which, as mentioned previously, transforms the traditional conception of revelation as something miraculous and unattainable by reason. Al-Ghazālī opts for intellectual knowledge as the best way of knowing God. This means, as I shall show, that reasoning – that is, logic – provides a subjective certainty to the believer concerning revelation, which itself is true *quoad se*.

The greater balance of equivalence is the categorical syllogism, which, as McCarthy's translation recalls, is explained in Aristotle's *Prior Analytics*.[39] Al-Ghazālī explains that this is the syllogism that Abraham used with Nimrod:

> Know that the Greater Balance is that which the Friend [Abraham] used with Nimrod. So from him we have learned it, but by means of the Qurʾān. Nimrod claimed divinity. And "God" by agreement, is a designation of "the one who can do everything [is omnipotent]." So Abraham said: "God is my God, because He it is who makes to live and causes to die: He can do it and you cannot do it!" Nimrod replied: "I make to live and cause to die," meaning that he makes the semen live by coitus and causes to die by killing. Then Abraham knew that it would be difficult for him to understand his error. So he turned to what would be clearer for Nimrod and said: "God brings the sun from the east: do you bring it from the west" – and he who misbelieved was astonished. And God Most High praised Abraham saying: "And that was Our proof which We brought to Abraham against his people".[40]

---

39 Aristotle, *The Complete Works of Aristotle* (*Prior Analytics*), ed. Jonathan Barnes, 1.4, 25b, 26–26b.

40 Al-Ghazālī, *al-Qisṭās* 17, 250, trans. McCarthy; Arabic 21.

According to al-Ghazālī, Abraham's response could be converted into two syllogisms:

> Whoever can make the sun rise is God [one principle]
> But my God can make the sun rise [a second principle]
> [Therefore] my God is God – and not you, Nimrod.[41]

And:

> My Lord is the one who makes the sun rise.
> And the one who makes the sun rise is a god.
> So it follows from it that my Lord is a god.[42]

The first syllogism, as McCarthy[43] points out, is a DARII; but the second violates a basic rule given by Aristotle for the first figure syllogisms, namely, that the minor premise must be affirmative and the major premise must be universal. It seems, however, that al-Ghazālī is trying to build a BARBARA.

The middle balance (the second figure in *Prior Analytics*)[44] is explained in chapter three. In this case the rule is that one premise must be negative, the major must be universal, and the conclusion must be negative. Al-Ghazālī builds a CESARE:

> The moon is a thing which sets.
> But God is not a thing which sets.
> Therefore the moon is not a God.[45]

He also presents a FESTINO:

> Sons [of God] are not chastised [by God].
> But you are chastised [by God].
> Therefore, you are not sons [of God].[46]

---

41 Al-Ghazālī, *al-Qisṭās* 18, 250, trans. McCarthy; Arabic 21–22.

42 Al-Ghazālī, *al-Qisṭās* 22, 251, trans. McCarthy; Arabic 23.

43 See McCarthy's annotation to al-Ghazālī, *al-Qisṭās* 18, 250.

44 Aristotle, *The Complete Works of Aristotle* (*Prior Analytics*), ed. Jonathan Barnes, 1.5, 26b34–28a.

45 Al-Ghazālī, *al-Qisṭās* 36, 254, trans. McCarthy; Arabic 28.

46 Al-Ghazālī, *al-Qisṭās* 36, 254, trans. McCarthy; Arabic 30.

And a defective CAMESTRES:[47]

> Every friend desires to meet his friend
> But the Jew does not desire to meet God.
> Therefore, [it follows necessarily from this that] he is not the friend of God.[48]

The lesser balance (the third figure in *Prior Analytics*)[49] is explained in chapter four. According to Aristotle, in this case the minor premise must be affirmative and the conclusion must be particular. Al-Ghazālī builds a DARAPTI:

> Moses is a man.
> Moses is one upon whom the Scripture was sent down.
> Some man has had sent down upon him the Book [Scripture][50]

The other two syllogisms, the balance of concomitance and the balance of opposition, are the *modus tollens* and *modus ponens*, respectively. In the first case, al-Ghazālī uses the typical conjunctive conditional, "if P, then Q; but not Q; therefore not P":

> If the world has two gods, heaven and earth would have gone to ruin.
> But it is a known fact that they have not gone to ruin.
> So there follows from these two a necessary condition, viz. the denial of the two gods.[51]

A second example in the same direction is:

> If there had been with the Lord of the Throne other gods, they assuredly would have sought a way to the Lord of the Throne.
> But it is a known fact that they did not seek that.

---

47 As McCarthy (255–256, n. 43) points out, perhaps it would be more correct to state this syllogism as follows: Every friend of God desires to meet his friend God. But the Jew does not long to meet God. Therefore the Jew is not a friend of God.

48 Al-Ghazālī, *al-Qisṭās* 43, 255, trans. McCarthy; Arabic 30.

49 Aristotle, *The Complete Works of Aristotle* (*Prior Analytics*), ed. Jonathan Barnes, 1.6, 28a10–29a.

50 Al-Ghazālī, *al-Qisṭās* 48, 257, trans. McCarthy; Arabic 32.

51 Al-Ghazālī, *al-Qisṭās* 54, 258, trans. McCarthy; Arabic 36.

> So there follows necessarily the denial of gods other than the Lord of the Throne.[52]

For the *modus ponens* al-Ghazālī resorts to the typical disjunctive conditional, "P or Q; but not P; therefore Q":

> We or you are in manifest error.
> But it is known that We are not in error.
> So there follows from their coupling a necessary conclusion, viz. that you are in error.[53]

This explanation of syllogisms is so basic that we may think that the aim of the *Qisṭās* is, as I mentioned before, to explain logic to beginners; indeed, the presentation of syllogisms is the same as that which we find in every standard manual of logic. Given the rejection of independent reasoning and analogy, however, it can also be read as a subtle criticism of the way in which some theologians and jurists argued. Independent reasoning (*raʾy*) is used in jurisprudence when there is a situation with no definite resolution either in the Qurʾān or in the hadith. If this happens, it is the personal criterion of the jurist which states the best resolution. Thus, the conclusion in those difficult cases comes from the experience, intellectual capacity, and moral disposition of the jurist, and not from an argument. From a logical standpoint, this could be a weak source of knowledge. Analogical reasoning (*qiyās*) could be also a weak and defective source of knowledge if it is understood mainly as inductive reasoning or as a paradigm.[54] For example, a jurist could reason as follows: 'Zayd became a governor and he began to act with arrogance; and so did Omar and Ahmad; thus, if Arfan became governor, he will be arrogant.' This is an ordinary case of a paradigm which proceeds by comparing similar particular cases and transferring them to another particular case. The weakness of both independent reasoning and analogy lies in that these argument types engender probability, and not certainty.

52 Al-Ghazālī, *al-Qisṭās* 54, 258, trans. McCarthy; Arabic 36–37.

53 Al-Ghazālī, *al-Qisṭās* 60, 260, trans. McCarthy; Arabic 39.

54 For the use of *qiyās* in the Islamic legal theory see Nabil Shehaby, " 'Illa and Qiyās in Early Islamic Legal Theory," *Journal of the American Oriental Society* 102, 1 (1982): 27–46. For the use of logic and formal arguments in the legal practice see Wael B. Hallaq, "Logic, Formal Arguments and Formalization of Arguments in Sunnī Jurisprudence," *Arabica* 37 (1990): 315–58.

Al-Ghazālī introduces these syllogistic forms because he wants to go beyond the probability of independent reasoning and analogy and also to avoid invalid arguments and false conclusions. Thus, he shows that logic is crucial because it strengthens arguments as well as detects defective, vague, and fallacious elements. Paradoxically, in chapter eight al-Ghazālī's interlocutor still distrusts logic: even though this discipline is useful for discerning between correct and incorrect arguments and between those who have the right doctrine and those who have erred, a safer alternative is to rely on authority and avoid such subtle discussions.[55] Al-Ghazālī believes that his interlocutor is a servile conformist that shows the same attitude shown by people who have learned their creeds from parents or teachers, not from weighing their beliefs:

> Your knowledge of the true Imām is not "necessary". For it is either servile conformism to parents, or it is weighed by one of these balances the syllogisms that he has explained along the *Qisṭās*. For every cognition that it is not primary necessarily comes to be in its possessor through the existence of these balances in his soul, even though he is not conscious of it. For you know the correctness of the balance of assessment [*at-taqdīr*: valuation] because of the order [systematic arrangement] in your mind of the two principles, the empirical and the sensible. It is also so for other persons without their being conscious of it. One who knows that this animal, for example, does not bear offspring because it is a mule, knows [this] by the arrangement of two principles, even though he is not conscious of the source of his knowledge. Similarly every cognition in the world which comes to be in a man is like that. So if you have accepted the belief of infallibility in the true Imām, or even in Muhammad – Peace be upon him! – from parents and comrades by servile conformism, you are no different from the Jews [Chelhot's[56] edition adds: and the Christians] and the Magicians [Zoroastrians]: for so they have done. But if you have accepted [it] from weighing with one of these balances, you may have erred in one of the fine points, and so you ought not to trust therein.[57]

After these words, the Bāṭinite is perplexed. He thinks that al-Ghazālī has blocked both sources of knowledge, both authority and weighing. Al-Ghazālī

55 Al-Ghazālī, *al-Qisṭās* 91, 268, trans. McCarthy; Arabic 55.

56 Al-Ghazālī, *al-Qisṭās al-Mustaqīm*, ed. V. Chelhot (Vol. IV, 1959). Bījū's edition does not mention the Christians.

57 Al-Ghazālī, *al-Qisṭās* 92, 268, trans. McCarthy; Arabic 55–56.

argues, however, that if an assertion causes difficulties, it should be submitted to the balance. Though it is true that our cognitions may err, the balance is the best way to detect errors and to remove doubts from our minds. In other words, careful logical analysis of every argument is the most trustworthy source of knowledge; it is also the best route to attain certainty. The "correct balance" guarantees knowledge, including the knowledge of God. This is in contrast with the traditional Muslim theologians, who verify the truth by appealing to the miracles of the Prophet and to tradition (*tawātur*). Both are criticized by al-Ghazālī: trusting a master who has been taught by his master, who in turn has been authorized by another master, is a technique that may be subject to errors, especially when the uninterrupted chain of authorizers is long;[58] also, to trust in someone who changes a stick into a snake may be a trick of deception and could result in ambiguities.[59]

5

In conclusion, al-Ghazālī has reformed traditional theology. He denies that revealed truth is grounded on miracles or tradition; instead, he states that there are logical arguments that certify it. This does not mean that reason is above revelation as, according to al-Ghazālī, some Islamic philosophers thought; rather, it means that both divine revelation and demonstrative proof (*burhān*), which is furnished by human reason, lead to the same conclusions. Al-Ghazālī's conception is quite coherent: in the *Munqidh* he has argued that there are some principles of knowledge – primary truths or evident data of reason – that come from God. Logical reasoning is part of these acquired principles that support knowledge. We know them by intuition, that is, immediately, and, just as it happens in foundationalist epistemologies, they guarantee knowledge. In other words, we have an immediate notion of truth that is a prerequisite for giving assent to revelation. According to the *Qisṭās*, if someone assents to revelation because of tradition or miracles, they have some kind of belief, but not a perfect belief. Certain belief is attained only when no contradiction is found, which occurs after comparing the immediate notion of truth with revelation. Indeed, there can be no contradiction because both the first principles of knowledge and revelation proceed from the same source, namely, God.

58 Al-Ghazālī, *al-Qisṭās* 98, 270, trans. McCarthy; Arabic 58.

59 See al-Ghazālī, *al-Qisṭās* 98–100, 270, trans. McCarthy; Arabic 58–60.

Logic and revelation are, then, independent for al-Ghazālī. In fact, logical reasoning is temporarily prior to revelation. But logic is not above revelation, nor does revelation replace logical reasoning. Logic leads to truth. Revelation is true *quoad se*. In this sense, they are connected: if syllogisms are used properly, they will lead to the same conclusions as revelation. This does not mean, of course, that the truth of revelation comes from logic. Logic is a method for verifying revelation, which, as was said, is itself true *quoad se*; this verification is needed because revelation seems not to be evident *quoad nos*. Al-Ghazālī admits that the Qur'ān contains hidden or invisible (spiritual) meanings[60] that demand interpretation. The syllogism is the path to unraveling these hidden meanings. It is crucial to adopt the best method for understanding the Qur'ān; otherwise it is easy to get caught up in ambiguities, giving rise to doubt, and logic is helpful for avoiding this ambiguity. Yet, there is another implicit problem: if the divine message comes from God, there should be no doubt about its truth; in fact, however, there is doubt. This is an interesting epistemological difficulty – it could be that someone is not certain of some matter of which there is no doubt; revelation could be true *quoad se*, but if it is incoherent to the subject, it proves to be a useless message, at least for that subject. Considering this, it is necessary for revelation to be accepted as something coherent *quoad nos*. Here is where reason comes in play. Al-Ghazālī believed in the superiority of logical reasoning as the best means for attaining certainty about prophecy (*yaqīn bi-n-nubuwwa*), that is, for accepting it as something true *quoad nos*.

The divine message has an inner dimension (*kalām nafsī*), but it also has an external expression (*ʿibāra*). Since the external expression has led to some differences in interpretation, it is necessary to find a method of verification in order to guarantee the truth of revelation and to eliminate ambiguities and interpretive differences among Muslims. Revelation, as it has been explained, can be verified neither by the authority of the Imām nor by miracles; instead, the proper method of verification is the syllogism. In fact, the rules of the syllogism regulate the way in which Qur'ānic expressions are used. This is precisely what al-Ghazālī has shown in the *Qisṭās*: the syllogism is the best method to detect formal errors and is the correct route for attaining the truth. In this sense, al-Ghazālī reasons in the same manner as the philosophers do, with an important difference: logic must not alter the content or inner dimension of the divine message. Philosophers have altered revelation, arguing that it contradicts demonstrative reasoning. Furthermore, they have tried to subordinate revelation to logic, whereas, according to al-Ghazālī, logic is incorporated into revelation. God being both the source of revelation and the ultimate source of

60 Al-Ghazālī, *al-Qisṭās* 72–73, 263, trans. McCarthy; Arabic 45–46.

knowledge, it is not possible to find a contradiction between reason and the divine message.

With the acceptance of logic as the most perfect route for attaining the truth, al-Ghazālī has completed the particular itinerary that I pointed out in the opening lines of this essay: he has moved from knowledge to skepticism and from skepticism to reasoned faith. Al-Ghazālī suggests that every assertion and every belief can be expressed syllogistically because that is the way in which human thought works. Given al-Ghazālī's sympathy for Sufism, the centrality of logic in the *Munqidh* and the *Qisṭās* should be disconcerting. Nevertheless, as I have noted, al-Ghazālī is not exactly rejecting Sufism, but observing that even in this case, the verification of knowledge is a necessary prerequisite. Al-Ghazālī apparently holds to a philosophical theology where both revelation and rationality coexist harmoniously. It is true that al-Ghazālī criticized philosophy, but he also adopted many views coming from his adversaries, al-Fārābī and Ibn Sīnā (Avicenna). He follows these two, especially Avicenna,[61] in regards to many metaphysical and logical issues; even prompting Averroes, one of the most famous critics of al-Ghazālī, to state that "he adhered to no single doctrine in his books, but was an Ashʿarite with the Ashʿarites, a Sufi with the Sufis, and a philosopher with the philosophers."[62] Thus, how can we interpret al-Ghazālī's intellectual ambivalences? What are the implications of the seeming contradictions in his understanding of knowledge and in his conception of theology?

In exploring these questions, I do not conclude that al-Ghazālī maintains a relative position, as Averroes suggests; rather, al-Ghazālī gave priority to logic as the appropriate method of verification. Since the science of the syllogism embodies the law that rules our thinking, it therefore provides the criteria that must be followed in order to discern whether or not knowledge is valid. Since revelation is not self-evident, it is necessary to follow the principles of reasoning that, according to al-Ghazālī, are presented by the Qurʾān itself. If the Book provides the "scales" or principles of reasoning, this means that revelation itself states the necessity of appealing to logical reasoning for verifying Qurʾānic verses. In this sense, the Qurʾān itself provides the method that shall be followed for understanding the divine message. According to al-Ghazālī,

61 It is not my intention to address these in detail, but cf. Binyamin Abrahamov, "Al-Ghazālī's Supreme Way to Know God", 165–67 and Frank Griffel, "Al-Ġazālī's Concept of Prophecy: The Introduction of Avicennan Psychology into Ašʿarite Theology," *Arabic Sciences and Philosophy* 14 (2004): 113–44.

62 Averroes, *On the Harmony of Religion and Philosophy*, trans. George F. Hourani, London: Luzac & Co., 1961, 144.

the Book has been composed with beautiful verses that can be converted into formal arguments with premises and conclusions. If these syllogisms are valid, we can conclude that: (a) the Qur'ān can be read systematically; (b) logic is helpful for avoiding ambiguities and equivocal interpretations of the divine message (for instance, those of the extremists); and (c) logic is useful for verifying that both reason and revelation lead to the same conclusions.

In this, al-Ghazālī has suggested a particular hermeneutic where revelation validates reason and reason verifies revelation. If logic is the best method of verification and the appropriate path to achieve the certainty of knowledge, this must lead us to conclude that al-Ghazālī is a rationalist for whom logical reasoning and revelation are equivalent. There would be no difference between assenting to a mathematical proposition and assenting to revelation. Indeed, al-Ghazālī is quite sure that there are differences between the certainty involved in mathematics and the certainty involved in the assent given to revelation. In my view, in the two treatises that I have analyzed, al-Ghazālī concludes that the assent to revelation, that is, faith, depends on knowledge: it is not possible to believe without knowing.

Knowledge – logical reasoning – is a necessary prerequisite for attaining the truth of the divine message. Religion, however, could not be reduced to the assent of some theoretical assertions; Islam is something much more complex than a sophisticated set of arguments. That is why al-Ghazālī's last writings – for instance his masterpiece, *The Revival of Religious Sciences* – were devoted to the worship and ritual obligations that Muslims must follow, to applied ethics, to the rejection of those acts that destroy the human soul, and to the exercise of the virtues that lead to salvation. At the end of his life al-Ghazālī worked intensely on the connection between knowledge and action; this being so, al-Ghazālī's conception of religion must be understood from both theoretical and practical perspectives. In the *Munqidh* and in the *Qisṭās* al-Ghazālī has shown that logical reasoning is the appropriate method for verifying the divine message. The practice of the revealed commandments, however, is reserved to other treatises.[63]

63 I wish to thank the Center of Theological Inquiry at Princeton for supporting my research on epistemology of religion in Medieval philosophy, of which this paper is part.

CHAPTER 12

Ghazālī's Hermeneutics and Their Reception in Jewish Tradition

Mishkāt al-Anwār (*The Niche of Lights*) and Maimonides' *Shemonah Peraqim* (*Eight Chapters*)

Scott Michael Girdner

1 Introduction

In this chapter, I will compare the conceptual relationship between the final chapter, or veils section, of al-Ghazālī's *Mishkāt al-Anwār* (*The Niche of Lights*) and the seventh chapter of Maimonides' *Shemonah Peraqim* (*Eight Chapters*),[1] as well as the thought of Maimonides and al-Ghazālī generally. I hope to move beyond a simple contrast of Maimonides' rationalist approach to tradition and al-Ghazālī's traditionalist critique of rational disciplines, such as philosophy and theology, by highlighting their similar conception of an encounter with the limits of reasoning. Specifically, I consider the use of philosophical psychology and ethics by both authors in their interpretations of traditional sayings concerning the veils of God. I outline their shared interpretation of the unveiling of God's face in terms of the philosophical concept of the Necessary Existent. Finally, I describe the hermeneutics and attribute doctrines that the authors employ to interpret God's face. I consider these issues in terms of a

* I thank Diana Lobel for reading and commenting on a draft of this chapter and the participants at the conference for valuable comments and discussion. I examine additional aspects of the reception of *Mishkāt al-Anwār* and al-Ghazālī's hermeneutics in Jewish tradition, including the medieval Hebrew translations of the work, elsewhere.

1 All citations of these works are from the following editions: al-Ghazālī, *Mishkāt al-Anwār*: a dual language edition published as Ghazālī, *The Niche of Lights*, trans. David Buchman, Provo, Utah: Brigham Young University Press, 1998; hereafter: *Mishkāt al-Anwār*. Maimonides, "Eight Chapters," in *Ethical Writings of Maimonides*, ed. Raymond L. Weiss with Charles Butterworth, New York: Dover Publications, Inc., 1975, 59–104; hereafter: *Shemonah Peraqim* – cf. *Shemonah Peraqim* (*Haqadamah le-masekhet Avot*). Arabic text with Hebrew translation by Yitzhaq Sheilat. in id., *Haqdamot ha-Rambam la-Mishnah*, Jerusalem, 1994. Full bibliographic information is given in the first citation of texts, followed by abbreviated citations. In translated texts, subsequent abbreviations of English and Arabic citations to the same title are represented by: En./Ar.

 | DOI 10.1163/9789004290952_013

broader question: how do Maimonides and al-Ghazālī resolve their apparently paradoxical conception of God as simultaneously knowable and unknowable? I will not argue here that the veils section of al-Ghazālī's *Mishkāt al-Anwār* was a direct influence on the seventh chapter of Maimonides' *Shemonah Peraqim* (*Eight Chapters*), though I do not preclude that possibility.[2]

2 Overview and Background of *Mishkāt al-Anwār* and *Shemonah Peraqim*

Mishkāt al-Anwār is a late work that, according to al-Ghazālī, is intended to provide an interpretation of the famous "Light Verse" (Q 24:35) of the Qur'ān as well as a *ḥadīth*, referred to in this discussion as the 'veils *ḥadīth*,' which al-Ghazālī interprets in the veils section of the work. The philosophical and mystical nature of al-Ghazālī's exposition of this traditional source material in *Mishkāt al-Anwār* is unmistakable, and the philosophical aspect gave rise to controversies regarding al-Ghazālī's relationship to philosophy. For instance, the renowned philosopher Ibn Rushd famously suggested that al-Ghazālī's position on philosophy was inconsistent, with particular reference to the veils section of *Mishkāt al-Anwār*.[3] More recently, prominent scholars of the Islamic intellectual tradition have supported aspects of Ibn Rushd's reading in a manner that suggests a need to revise traditional conceptions of al-Ghazālī.[4]

2 Ibn Rushd's citation of *Mishkāt al-Anwār* in his *al-Kashf ʿan manāhij al-adilla* and Ibn Ṭufayl's citation of the work in the introduction to his *Ḥayy ibn Yaqẓān* demonstrate its presence in al-Andalus and the Maghreb in the lifetime of Maimonides. Ibn Rushd, *Al-Kashf ʿan manāhij al-adilla*, ed. Muḥammad ʿĀbid al-Jābarī, Beirut: Markaz Dirāsāt al-Waḥda al-ʿArabiyya, 1998, 151. cf. William Henry Temple Gairdner, "Al-Ghazālī's Mishkāt Al-Anwār and the Ghazālī-Problem," *Der Islam* 5, no. 2 (1914): 133; hereafter: Gairdner, "Al-Ghazālī's Mishkāt Al-Anwār and the Ghazālī-Problem." Ibn Ṭufayl, *Ḥayy ibn Yaqẓān*, in *Two Andalusian Philosophers: the story of Hayy ibn Yaqzan & The Definitive Statement*, trans. by Jim Colville, New York: Kegan Paul International, 1999, 9; cf. id. *Risālat Ḥayy ibn Yaqẓān* in Maḥmūd ʿAbd al-Ḥalīm. *Falsafat Ibn Ṭufayl wa-risālatuhu Ḥayy ibn Yaqẓān*, Cairo: Maktabat al-Anjlū al-Miṣrīyat, n.d., 63–4: available at: http://www.wdl.org/en/item/7443/ (1/10/2012).

3 Ibid.; Ibn Rushd cites the veils section of *Mishkāt al-Anwār* as proof of al-Ghazālī's commitment to the worldview of the philosophers, but Ibn Ṭufayl apparently disagrees.

4 See, e.g.: W. Montgomery Watt. "A Forgery in al-Ghazālī's *Mishkāt*?" *Journal of the Royal Asiatic Society of Great Britain and Ireland* (1949): 18–19; hereafter: Watt. "A Forgery"; Binyamin Abrahamov, "Al-Ghazālī's Supreme Way to Know God," *Studia Islamica*, 77 (1993): 141–68; hereafter: Abrahamov, "Al-Ghazālī's Supreme Way"; Herbert Davidson, *Alfarabi, Avicenna, and Averroes*, New York: Oxford University Press, 1992, 127–44; hereafter: Davidson, *Alfarabi, Avicenna, and Averroes*. cf. Farid Jabre, *La Notion De Certitude Selon Ghazali Dans Ses Origines Psychologiques Et Historiques*. Beyrouth: Université Libanaise, 1958, esp. 180–206, 315–326. On

This chapter cannot fully detail the complex place of philosophy in *Mishkāt al-Anwār*, but I have argued elsewhere that al-Ghazālī employs philosophical content to accomplish his own distinctive purpose in a manner that is largely consistent with his interest in mysticism, his earlier critique of philosophy, and his traditional association with the rational traditionalism of the Ashʿarī school of theology.[5]

Shemonah Peraqim is the title given to Maimonides' introduction to his commentary on *The Chapters of the Fathers* (*Pirqei Avot*) in the *Mishnah*, the rabbinic law code from the third century of the Common Era, which is part of the authoritative collection of rabbinic commentary, the *Talmud*. Maimonides composed the *Eight Chapters* in Arabic, drawing on Jewish tradition as well as Greek and Arabic philosophical tradition. In particular, Maimonides tried to harmonize philosophical psychology and ethics with traditional Jewish practices, texts, and conceptions of piety in *Shemonah Peraqim*. Maimonides says in his introduction that he does not wish to take credit for the work of others; nonetheless, he explicitly refuses to cite his philosophical sources, both in order to avoid prolixity and lest his audience should reject a true statement based on the reputation of his source.[6] As Herbert Davidson has shown, the "modern philosophers" to whom Maimonides refers, and avoids naming, overwhelmingly seem to be a single source: namely, the Muslim philosopher al-Fārābī.[7] It is noteworthy that Davidson finds Maimonides departing from his heavy reliance on al-Fārābī in chapters five and seven, because the images and interests of chapter seven are so similar to the veils section of *Mishkāt al-Anwār*.[8]

---

the general issue of revising traditional conceptions of al-Ghazālī see especially: Richard M. Frank, *Al-Ghazālī and the Ashʿarite School*, Durham: Duke University Press, 1994; id., *Creation and the Cosmic System: Al-Ghazālī and Avicenna*, Abhandlungen Der Heidelberger Akademie Der Wissenschaften, Philosophisch-Historische Klasse, Heidelberg, Germany: Winter, 1992; hereafter: Frank, *Creation and Cosmic System*.

5 My dissertation argued that attention to how al-Ghazālī develops his interpretations of Qur'ānic passages is particularly revealing of his intentions in his use of philosophical content in *Mishkāt al-Anwār* and does not require a major revision of traditional conceptions of his life and work: Scott Girdner, "Reasoning with Revelation: the significance of the Qur'ānic contextualization of philosophy in al-Ghazālī's *Mishkāt al-Anwār* (*The Niche of Lights*)," (Ph.D. diss., Boston University, 2010), hereafter: Girdner, *Reasoning with Revelation*.

6 *Shemonah Peraqim*, 60–1.

7 Herbert Davidson, "Maimonides' *Shemonah Peraqim* and Alfarabi's *Fuṣūl Al-Madanī*," in *Proceedings of the American Academy for Jewish Research*, 31 (1963): 33–50; hereafter: Davidson, "Maimonides' *Shemonah Peraqim* and Alfarabi's *Fuṣūl Al-Madanī*." According to Davidson, "over half of the strictly philosophic sections in *Shemonah Peraqim* are built around direct quotations from that book (al-Farābī's *Fuṣūl Al-Madanī*)." ibid., 41.

8 Davidson, "Maimonides' *Shemonah Peraqim* and Alfarabi's *Fuṣūl Al-Madanī*," 37–40.

3 Philosophical Psychology and Ethics

In *Mishkāt al-Anwār* and *Shemonah Peraqim*, al-Ghazālī and Maimonides employ a philosophical psychology that ultimately derives from Aristotle. As noted, Maimonides is frank about his reliance on his consciously unspecified philosophical sources; on the other hand, al-Ghazālī clearly relies on philosophical sources as well, though he does not state this explicitly.[9] Both authors use this philosophical psychology to describe the human soul and its various parts, such as its appetites and faculties, as well as the way these interact to account for ethical character and the acquisition of knowledge. For both al-Ghazālī and Maimonides, humans have an animal soul that includes certain appetites; an ethical person must regulate these appetites in accordance with the distinguishing characteristic of the human soul, namely, the rational intellect and its faculties. There is a reciprocal relationship between intellect and appetite here: even as an ethical person employs the intellect to regulate appetites, the appetites must be regulated for the intellect to function properly. Only if this relationship is modulated successfully can humans realize their proper end as the rational animal, which is the theoretical or intellectual contemplation of God.

The veils *ḥadith* states: "God has seventy veils of light and darkness; were he to lift them, the august glories of His face would burn up everyone whose eyesight perceived Him."[10] Al-Ghazālī employs this *ḥadith* to describe both

9 On philosophical sources and content in *Mishkāt al-Anwār*, see: Binyamin Abrahamov. "Al-Ghazālī's Supreme Way"; id., "Ibn Sīnā's Influence on Al-Ghazālī's Non-Philosophical Works," *Abr-Nahrain* 29 (1991), 1–17. Davidson, *Alfarabi, Avicenna, and Averroes*, 132f. Frank, *Creation and the Cosmic System, passim.* Girdner, *Reasoning with Revelation.* Frank Griffel, *The Philosophical Theology of al-Ghazali: A Study of His Life and His Cosmology*, New York: Oxford University Press, 2009, 245–64; hereafter: Griffel, *The Philosophical Theology of al-Ghazali.* Hermann Landolt, "Ghazālī and 'Religionswissenschaft': Some Notes on the *Mishkat Al-Anwar*," *Asiatische Studien* 45, no. 1 (1991): 19–72; hereafter: Landolt, "Ghazālī and 'Religionswissenschaft'." Alexander Treiger, "Monism and Monotheism in al-Ghazālī's *Mishkāt al-Anwār*," in *Journal of Qur'ānic Studies*, 9 (2007): 1–27; hereafter: Treiger, "Monism and Monotheism; id. "The Science of Divine Disclosure: Ghazālī's Higher Theology and its Philosophical Underpinnings." (PhD diss., Yale University, 2008); id. *Inspired Knowledge in Islamic Thought: Al-Ghazali's Theory of Mystical Cognition and Its Avicennian Foundation*, New York: Routledge, 2011. A. J. Wensinck. "Ghazālī's *Mishkāt al-Anwār* (Niche of Lights)," in *Semetische Studien uit de Natatenschaap van Professor Dr. A. J. Wensinck*, Leiden: A.W. Sijthoff's Uitgeversmaatchappij, 75 (1933): 183–209. Martin Whittingham, *Al-Ghazālī and the Qur'ān: One Book, Many Meanings*, New York: Routledge, 2007.

10 *Mishkāt al-Anwār*. 1, 44. Note that Ghazālī gives the *ḥadīth* in a slight paraphrase relative to the standard canonical versions; cf. Buchman's note, ibid., and A. J. Wensinck, *Concordance et indices de la tradition musulmane*, New York: E. J. Brill, 1992, 1:424.

the contemplation of God as the goal of human life and the proper ordering of the various parts of the human soul toward this end. He designates three broad classes of veils – those of darkness, darkness mixed with light, and pure light – and explains that the veils, pertaining to humans, represent obstacles to true perception of God. The veils of pure darkness are moral vices; they represent drives such as the irascible and concupiscent appetites. The mixed veils correspond to intellectual vices; these are associated with the improper operation or incorrect understanding of the imaginative, reflective, or rational faculties – that is, the higher faculties of the soul. The final broad class of seekers comprises those with veils of pure light. These properly order and orient the appetites and higher faculties of their souls toward knowledge of God.[11]

In earlier chapters of the *Shemonah Peraqim*, Maimonides summarizes the appetites and faculties of the soul and presents contemplation of God as the end of human life.[12] The seventh chapter illustrates this goal through Maimonides' interpretation of an authoritative tradition that "some of the prophets saw God from behind many veils, while others saw Him from behind a few veils," and that Moses had only one veil.[13] These traditional reports largely function the way the veils *ḥadith* does in *Mishkāt al-Anwār*, that is, they allow Maimonides to explain how philosophical psychology and ethics account for varying types of knowledge of God:

> ... some vices are rational, such as ignorance, stupidity, and slow understanding; and some are moral, such as lust, arrogance, irascibility, [etc.] ... all these vices are veils separating man from God, may He be exalted.[14]

---

11 This summary draws on al-Ghazālī's description of the vices in the context of the philosophical psychology and ethics in his exposition of Q 24:40, which he gives just before his interpretation of the veils *ḥadīth*. His interpretation of this verse links the psychological interpretation he gives to the Light Verse (Q 24:35) and the veils *ḥādīth*, the exposition of which is his stated purpose for writing *Mishkāt al-Anwār*. His interpretations of all of these show an integrated development of his interest in philosophical ethics and psychology; *Mishkāt al-Anwār*, 36–43; cf. Girdner, *Reasoning with Revelation*, 393–437.

12 Maimonides summarizes the philosophical psychology and ethics in chapters one through four, and presents contemplation of God as the end of human life in chapter five: "Man needs to subordinate all his soul's powers to thought [...] and to set his sight on a single goal: the perception of God (may He be glorified and magnified), I mean, knowledge of Him, in so far as that lies within man's power." *Shemonah Peraqim*, 75, 77–8. cf. ibid., 15.

13 Maimonides interprets a Rabbinic statement that Moses "looked through a transparent glass" (*B.T.*, Revamot, 49b) as meaning that Moses had only one diaphanous veil; *Shemonah Peraqim*, 80–1, 102n2.

14 *Shemonah Peraqim*, 81.

As in *Mishkāt al-Anwār*, the veils that obscure true perception of God are moral vices, which pertain to the appetites, and rational vices, which pertain to the proper ordering of the higher faculties of the soul toward the knowledge of God that is its end.[15] Al-Ghazālī and Maimonides set knowledge of God as the end of human life, but they simultaneously assert that God is unknowable.[16] Philosophical psychology partially resolves this apparent paradox: psychological concepts allow al-Ghazālī and Maimonides to draw distinctions between the diverse ways an object of knowledge, such as God, may be perceived by the various faculties. These concepts also allow them to distinguish the extent to which it may be known, given the effects of vices on human perception.

4 The Face of God: Philosophical Conceptions of Divinity as the Necessary Existent

After describing the veils in terms of vices, Maimonides considers the single veil of Moses with reference to the theophany in Exodus 33:18–23: Moses requests to see God, but is only permitted a vision of God's back and not his face. Maimonides says that the human intellect, attached to a material body, is the single veil between Moses and "the perception of the true reality of God's existence."[17] Maimonides presents the veil in terms of the faculties of the soul, namely the intellect; but note especially that the object of perception is "the true reality of God's *existence*." Maimonides explains this intellectual

15 Maimonides and al-Ghazālī deploy their conception of the veils as vices differently in at least one major respect: they situate prophecy differently within the context of human susceptibility to vice. Though prophets for Maimonides represent the extreme limit of human capability to know God, they are still susceptible to vice and remain veiled to a greater or lesser extent: for example, Solomon was veiled by the moral vice of lust which affected his sexual appetite; David could be cruel; Elijah was irascible, and so forth; *Shemonah Peraqim*, 81–82. Al-Ghazālī seems to present prophecy more in accordance with the general Islamic theological position that a Prophet is preserved from sin (*maʿṣūm*) and that distinctions should not be made between the prophets (cf. Q 2:136, 285). Al-Ghazālī distinguishes Prophets from other classes of people in the veils section, while Maimonides distinguishes Moses from other Prophets; *Mishkāt al-Anwār*, 52. cf. ibid. 13.

16 On the unknowability of God, see, for example, *Mishkāt al-Anwār*, 17, 23–4, 28; *Shemonah Peraqim*, 83, 94–95. Moses Maimonides, *The Guide of the Perplexed*, trans. Shlomo Pines, Chicago: University of Chicago Press, 1963, 1:59, 139; hereafter: *The Guide*. See discussion of this passage below.

17 *Shemonah Peraqim*, 83.

perception of God's existence with an apparent allusion to the philosophical concept of the Necessary Existent, most associated with the philosopher Ibn Sīnā. This concept draws on an observation of phenomenal existence as contingent, or having the possibility of not existing, and argues that there must be a necessary existent who makes actual the potential existence of contingent beings. Maimonides explains that the true perception of the reality of God's existence means:

> [...] to attain in one's soul with regard to the verity of His existence what none of the other beings share with that existence, so that one finds His existence firmly established in his soul and distinct from the existence of the other beings found in his soul.[18]

It appears that the true perception of God's existence, symbolized by the unveiling of God's face, is an understanding of God as belonging to a unique class of existence as the Necessary Existent. This is further supported by Maimonides' discussion of the theophany of Moses and the meaning of seeing God's face in *The Guide of the Perplexed* (I:54):[19] there, in the course of a long exposition of the theophany, Maimonides elaborates how God can be described as gracious in giving existence, and states: "For He, may He be Exalted, brings into existence and governs beings that have no claim upon Him with respect to being brought into existence and being governed."[20] Thus, creatures, depending on God for their existence, have a necessary relationship with him; contrarily, God does not have a necessary relationship with any other being. The only necessity that pertains to God is the necessity of his own existence as manifest in his relationship to contingent creatures.

---

18 Ibid.

19 *The Guide*, 124–5. Maimonides also discusses the theophany in I:21 of *The Guide*, 48–9. For Maimonides' conception of necessary existence, cf. *The Guide*, introduction to book II, 238, II:1, 248; also book one (*Sefer Ha-Madda*ʿ) of his *Mishneh Torah*, see id., in *A Maimonides Reader*, ed. Isadore Twersky, Springfield, New Jersey: Behrman House, 1972, 43–4; hereafter *Mishneh Torah*. Also cf. *Shemonah Peraqim*, 83; see below, note 22.

20 *The Guide*, 125. Describing God's necessary existence in *Mishneh Torah*, Maimonides says: "The basic principle of all basic principles and the pillar of all sciences is to realize that there is a First Being who brought every existing thing into being [...] for all beings are in need of Him; but He, blessed be He, is not in need of them nor of anyone of them. Hence, His real essence is unlike that of any of them." ibid., 43–4. The parallels between Maimonides' language here and *Mishkāt al-Anwār* are striking; cf. *Mishkāt al-Anwār*, 16, 23.

Al-Ghazālī, in a similar discussion in *Mishkāt al-Anwār*, also makes apparent allusions to the philosophical concept of the Necessary Existent in the context of providing his interpretations of a scriptural reference to the face of God and the meaning of the unveiling of God's face in the veils *ḥadith*.[21] According to al-Ghazālī, consideration of existence is multifaceted. Such consideration is not simply concerned with the actuality of existence for any particular being, but also the quality of its existence as either possible or necessary. An object may be considered as existing in some respects and not existing in others:

> [...] each thing has two faces: a face towards itself, and a face toward its Lord. Viewed in terms of the face of itself, it is nonexistent; but viewed in terms of the face of God, it exists. Hence, nothing exists but God and his face: "Everything is perishing except His face."[22]

God, as the Necessary Existent, is unconditioned by any possibility for non-existence; meanwhile all other existents are "perishing" in some respect, because they are conditioned by the possibility of non-existence. In the broader context of this quote, al-Ghazālī clearly employs the ontological categories of Ibn Sīnā and his conception of the Necessary Existent in his understanding of God's face. Any doubt about this may be removed when one considers that Ibn Sīnā himself employed this same verse in his explanation of these concepts.[23]

---

21 In *Mishkāt al-Anwār*, al-Ghazālī refers to the face of God in multiple instances – recall that the veils *ḥadīth* is concerned with the unveiling of God's face – and consistently interprets the face in terms of the philosophical conception of God as the Necessary Existent, as well as the ontological categories such as possible and necessary existence which form the basis of Ibn Sīnā's concept of the Necessary Existent: *Mishkāt al-Anwār*, 16–17, 20, 51–2.

22 *Mishkāt al-Anwār*, 17; Q 28:88.

23 See, for example, Ibn Sīnā, *ash-Shifāʾ, al-Ilāhīyāt*, a dual language edition published as M. E. Marmura, *The Metaphysics of the Healing*, Provo, Utah: Brigham Young University Press, 2005, 284; hereafter: *ash-Shifāʾ*. cf. Ibn Sīnā's commentary on book *Lambda* of Aristotle's *Metaphysics* in ʿA. Badawī, *Arisṭū ʿinda al-ʿArab*, Kuwait: Wakālat al-Maṭbūʿāt, 1978, 25–6. Compare esp. the parallels between *ash-Shifāʾ* and al-Ghazālī's discussion in id. *Al-Maqṣad al-asnā fī sharḥ maʿānī asmāʾ Allāh al-ḥusnā*. ed. Fadlou Shehadi, Beirut: Dar al-Machreq, 1982, 47.; cf. al-Ghazālī, *Al-Maqṣad al-asnā fī sharḥ maʿanī asmāʾ Allāh al-ḥusnā*, translated as *Al-Ghazali on the Ninety-nine Beautiful Names of God* by D. Burrell and N. Daher, Islamic Texts Society, 1992, 35; hereafter: *Al-Maqṣad*. En./Ar. For discussion of these parallels, see: Alexander Treiger, "Monism and Monotheism," 9, 16, 22n.43; Richard M. Frank, *Creation and the Cosmic System* 16, 62n.118; Girdner, *Reasoning with Revelation*, 344–55. Also recommended: Ghazālī, *Kitāb Ādāb tilāwat al-Qurʾān* in: *Iḥyāʾ ʿulūm ad-dīn*. Wa-bi-hāmishihi al-Mughnī ʿan ḥaml al-asfār fī takhrīj mā fī al-iḥyāʾ min akhbār li-Zayn ad-Dīn Abī al-Faḍl ʿAbd ar-Raḥīm b. al-Ḥusayn al-ʿIrāqī. Wa-bi-dhaylihi

Thus, as with Maimonides, al-Ghazālī associates the unveiling of God's face with His necessary existence.

Both al-Ghazālī and Maimonides describe the moment of unveiling of God's face in terms of the philosophical concept of the Necessary Existent. What does this common interest tell us of the apparent paradox regarding knowledge of God? How can the true perception of God's face, which is the unobtainable perception of His essence, be understood as the philosophical concept of the Necessary Existent? This concept is intelligible and can be understood by the human intellect; both authors expound it in a variety of works.[24] The concept itself provides a partial resolution: if one accepts the premises and the argument, one can know that there is a Necessary Existent; but – to speak anthropomorphically – one cannot know "who" that being is. To speak more philosophically, we can know *that* God exists (*innīya*); but we cannot know his essence or quiddity (*māhīya*)[25] through the formal processes

Taʿrīf al-aḥyāʾ bi-faḍāʾil al-Iḥyāʾ li-ʿAbd al-Qādir b. Shaykh b. ʿAbd Allāh al-ʿAydarūs. Wa-l-imlāʾ ʿan ishkālāt al-Iḥyāʾ, al-Qāhirah: Dār as-Salām, 2003, 324; translated as *The Recitation and Interpretation of the Qurʾān: al-Ghazālī's theory* by Muhammad Abul Quasem, Kuala Lumpur: University of Malaysia Press, 1979, 66–7; hereafter: *Iḥyāʾ, K. at-Tilāwa* En./Ar.

24 For example, see citations for Maimonides' discussions in notes 21 and 22 above. For al-Ghazālī see, e.g.: *Al-Maqṣad*, En. 35, 51/Ar. 47, 64. For discussion of al-Ghazālī's use of the concept of God's necessary existence in a variety of works, with particular reference to his scheme of four stages of *tawḥīd* and his concept of mystical experience, see: Girdner, *Reasoning with Revelation*, 627–633, 640–50.

25 Maimonides follows Ibn Sīnā and al-Farābī in using the term "*innīya*" ("indeed-ness") which derives from the emphatic particle *inna*. In *The Guide* (1:58), Maimonides says: "we are only able to apprehend the fact that He is and cannot apprehend His quiddity." ibid. 135; cf. *Shemonah Peraqim*, 95 and notes 28–9 below. In *Mishkāt al-Anwār*, al-Ghazālī first evokes the categories of existence which support the argument for the Necessary Existent and asserts that God's essence is unknowable, inasmuch as he is too great for any relation or comparison (ibid., 16–17). After an excursus on mystical experience, the significance of which will be discussed below, al-Ghazālī makes a pun with a similar term *hūwīya* (concerned with existence as distinct from quiddity) and ultimately alludes to Ibn Sīnā's conception of his argument for the Necessary Existent as *burhān aṣ-ṣiddīqīn* (the proof of the righteous), while employing the same Qurʾānic allusions and interpretations that Ibn Sīnā uses to distinguish his proof from other proofs; ibid. 20–1; cf. Ibn Sīnā, *al-Ishārāt wa-t-tanbihāt*, ed. J. Forget, Leiden 1892, vol. 3: 482–3; hereafter: *al-Ishārāt*. On *burhān aṣ-ṣiddiqīn*, see note 28. For discussion of the term *innīya*, see: R. M. Frank, "The Origin of the Arabic Philosophical Term *anniyya*," *Cahiers de Byrsa*, 6 (1956): 181–201 (also in id., *Philosophy, Theology and Mysticism in Medieval Islam. Texts and Studies on the Development and History of Kalam*, I, ed. by D. Gutas, Variorum CS Series, 833, Ashgate 2005). For Maimonides' use of the term see Diana Lobel, "'Silence Is Praise to You':

of definition and logical demonstration.[26] In this sense, God remains both knowable and unknowable. Here, it is worth emphasizing that the argument for the Necessary Existent is not a purely *a priori* ontological argument that begins with a definition of God's essence and identifies this with necessary

---

Maimonides on Negative Theology, Looseness of Expression, and Religious Experience," *American Catholic Philosophical Quarterly* 76:1 (spring 2002): 26 and n. 4, 45–6 and n. 82; hereafter: Lobel. "Silence Is Praise." For discussion and references to scholarship on the term, see Diana Lobel, *A Sufi-Jewish Dialogue: philosophy and mysticism in Baḥya Ibn Paqūda's* Duties of the Heart, Philadelphia: University of Pennsylvania Press, 2007, 281n. 25; hereafter: Lobel, *A Sufi-Jewish Dialogue*; and Marmura's note in *ash-Shifā'*. 383n.1, where he identifies an article by d'Alverny as providing a good survey of the scholarship: M.-Th. D'Alverny, "Anniyya-Anitas," in *Mélanges offerts a Étienne Gilson*, Toronto: Pontifical Institute, 1959. For more recent discussions, see: Peter Adamson, "Before Essence and Existence: al-Kindi's conception of being," *Journal of the History of Philosophy*, 40:3 (2002), 297–312; and Cristina D'Ancona. "Platonic and Neoplatonic terminology for being in Arabic Translation" in *Studia Graeco-Arabica*, The Journal of the Project: *Greek into Arabic Philosophical Concepts and Linguistic Bridges*, available at: http://www.greekintoarabic.eu/uploads/media/SGA_I_2011.pdf (1/17/2012).

26 In *Shemonah Peraqim*, Maimonides says: "It has also become clear in metaphysics that by our intellects we are unable to attain perfect comprehension of His existence, may He be exalted. This is due to the perfection of His existence and the deficiency of our intellects. His existence has no causes by which He could be known." ibid., 94–5; cf. *Mishkāt al-Anwār*, 17, 23, 51. Maimonides and al-Ghazālī follow Ibn Sīnā in this regard: concluding his discussion of the Necessary Existent, Ibn Sīnā says: "It has become clear, then, that the First has no genus, no quiddity (*māhīya*) [... and] that He has no definition and [there is] no demonstration (*burhān*) for him, rather he is the demonstration of all things; indeed there are for him only the clear and evidential proofs (*ad-dalā'il al-wāḍiḥa*)" (*ash-Shifā'*, 282–3). Thus, Ibn Sīnā acknowledges that his argument for the Necessary Existent does not meet the formal criteria of full syllogistic demonstration. Marmura asserts that the argument for the Necessary Existent is a *burhān inna*, which demonstrates *that* something necessarily exists; but it is not a *burhān lima*, which demonstrates *why* something necessarily exists. One cannot construct a demonstrative syllogism (*burhān lima*) which would explain "why," because one cannot define God as a term in the manner needed for such a syllogism (ibid., 282–3, 383n.1, 415n.11). Herbert Davdison explains: "a truly demonstrative syllogism must be framed with propositions that are 'prior to' and the 'causes of,' the conclusion. It is more precisely, a syllogism in which the middle term is the *cause* of the presence of the major term in the minor term. Since there is nothing prior to, and the cause of, the presence of actual existence in the necessarily existent by virtue of itself, a demonstrative syllogism leading to the existence of an entity of the description is impossible": Herbert A. Davidson, *Proofs for Eternity, Creation, and the Existence of God in Medieval Islamic and Jewish Philosophy*, New York: Oxford University Press, 1987, 298–99; hereafter: Davidson, *Proofs*. In contrast the proof (*dalīl* or *burhān inna*) offered by Ibn Sīnā for the Necessary Existent is "a syllogism wherein the middle term is the *effect* rather

existence. Rather, it is an *a posteriori* cosmological argument, moving from an observation of contingent existence to the need for a Necessary Existent and leaving the essence of such a being unknowable.[27] To convey this idea of God's unknowable essence and distinguish it from the act of creation, Maimonides and al-Ghazālī draw on the hermeneutics and attribute discourse of *kalām*, or theology.

5 The Face of God: Theological Hermeneutics and Conceptions of the Divine Attributes

One way to resolve the paradox of God as simultaneously knowable and unknowable is to distinguish between the acts and essence of God. This distinction allows one to claim that God is knowable, inasmuch as he can be understood as the agent of acts which are intelligible; he remains unknowable,

than the *cause* of the presence of the major term in the minor term; it is a chain of reasoning that moves not from the prior to the posterior, but from the posterior to the prior, from the presence of the effect to the existence of the cause. Stated in another way, a strictly demonstrative syllogism established both 'that' a certain proposition is true and 'why' it is true, where as a 'proof' establishes only that it is true." (ibid., 299); cf. Michael Marmura. "Avicenna's Proof from Contingency for God's Existence in the *Metaphysics* of the *Shifā'*," *Mediaeval Studies*, 42 (1980), 337–52.

27 The *a posteriori* nature of the argument and its reasoning from effect to cause makes it a cosmological argument. *A priori* ontological arguments, such as Anselm's argument, begin with a concept or definition and deductively show its logical consistency. Ibn Sīnā's argument for the Necessary Existent brings in one datum from observation of the actual universe: "there is no doubt that something exists" (or, there is no doubt that there is existence: *lā shakka anna hunā wujūd[an]*), Ibn Sīnā, *an-Najāt*, ed. Muḥyiddīn Ṣabrī l-Kurdī, Tehran: Murtazavi, 1346, SH, 235; hereafter: *an-Najāt*; cf. Davidson, *Proofs*, 303. Because of this, when Ibn Sīnā famously asserts the superiority of his "metaphysical" proof of God over kinematic proofs such as Aristotle's unmoved mover, he cannot mean that it is superior because it is an ontological argument, employing *a priori* demonstration (even though it derives from a consideration of existence itself); see *al-Ishārāt*, 3: 482; cf. the distinction between *burhān inna* and *burhān lima* in the preceding note. Davidson argues that Ibn Sīnā considers it superior because: (1) it establishes the cause of existence, not simply the cause of motion; (2) it establishes the cause of all existents, both corporeal and incorporeal, and not simply the corporeal or movable existents (Davidson, *Proofs*, 288). Perhaps it would be best to speak of the argument as having both cosmological and ontological elements; for a detailed analysis of the issue and scholarly debate concerning it, see: Toby Mayer, "Ibn Sīnā's '*Burhān al-Ṣiddiqīn*'," in *Journal of Islamic Studies*, 12:1 (2001), 18–39; cf. *The Guide*, 1:71, 182–3; cf. *Mishkāt al-Anwār*, 23, cf. 17, 52.

however, in terms of a full comprehension of his essence. The tradition of *kalām*, or theology, provided both Ghazālī and Maimonides with resources for drawing such distinctions.[28]

In the seventh chapter, Maimonides does not elaborate the theological concepts he uses to interpret God's face and back in the theophany in Exodus 33:18–23. His discussion of the theophany in 1:21 of *The Guide of the Perplexed*, however, makes the theological distinction between attributes of act and essence its primary concern:

> God, may he be exalted, hid from him (Moses) the apprehension called that of the face and made him pass over to something different; I mean the knowledge of the acts ascribed to Him, may he be exalted, which, as we shall explain are deemed to be multiple attributes.[29]

While the divine face (or essence) remains veiled for Moses, God granted him knowledge of his 'back' or divine acts and attributes. A similar discussion of the theophany of Moses in 1:54 asserts that God is known with respect to his

28 The position of both al-Ghazālī and Maimonides regarding *kalām* is complex, controversial to some extent, and cannot be detailed here; nevertheless, they were both clearly critical of *kalām*. In particular, they both shared a criticism of the dialectical and rhetorical modes of argumentation deployed in the tradition, seeing it as inferior in terms of logical demonstration and very limited in its utility. Nonetheless, both al-Ghazālī and Maimonides do engage *kalām* critically and their thought is, at the least, influenced by the tradition in this regard. Of course al-Ghazālī actually wrote *kalām* works, but he considered these as belonging to a particular mode of discourse that did not fully represent his own thought. A tendency in some scholarship to present al-Ghazālī primarily as a *mutakallim* (rather than a jurist, philosopher, or mystic) obscures how close Maimonides was to al-Ghazālī in his criticisms of *kalām*. Maimonides engages and alludes to *kalām* positions in a variety of places in *Shemonah Peraqim*; for example, in chapter one, he is critical of the theologians (ibid., 63); but see esp. chapter eight, where he criticizes the theologians on the issue of divine volition (ibid., 87) and generally engages *kalām* conceptions of freewill and divine predetermination. Though Maimonides took pains to distinguish his positions from those of the *mutakallimūn*, his arguments show considerable sympathy with Muʿtazilī tradition in its conception of the divine attributes and human free will (see esp. ibid., 84–5, 94). For Maimonides' famous summary of the history of *kalām* see *The Guide*, 1:71, 175–84. Al-Ghazālī also engages with, and alludes to, a variety of *kalām* doctrines and schools in *Mishkāt al-Anwār*: see, for example, 49–50. For extensive citations on al-Ghazālī's criticism of *kalām*, see references in note 41.

29 *The Guide*, 1:21, 48–9.

attributes of action.[30] The following five chapters explain Maimonides' conception of the limits of attributing any qualities to God and the need to logically negate all qualities attributed to the divine essence. In 1:59, Maimonides states his objective: "one should know the impossibility of everything which is impossible with reference to Him."[31] Ultimately, Maimonides sees the highest degree of knowledge of God that humans may attain as dependent on formal logical demonstration. Nonetheless, logic does not positively demonstrate anything about the unknowable essence of God; it only allows for a better understanding of the logical impossibility of attributing any quality to God. Maimonides elaborates this in a seemingly mystical tone:

> [...] apprehending [God] consists in the inability to attain the ultimate term in apprehending Him.[32] Thus all the philosophers say: we are dazzled by His beauty, and He is hidden from us because of the intensity with which He becomes manifest, just as the sun is hidden to eyes that are too weak to apprehend it.[33]

30 Seeing the back, according to Maimonides, corresponds to the request of Moses that God show him his ways (Exodus 33:13), and the display of God's goodness (Ex. 33:19): "all my goodness – alludes to the display to him of all existing things of which it is said: And God saw everything that he had made, and, behold, it was very good. By their display, I mean that he (Moses) will apprehend their nature and the way they are mutually connected so that he will know how He governs them in general and in detail [...] that is, he has grasped the existence of all My world with a true and firmly established understanding. For the opinions that are not correct are not firmly established. *Accordingly the apprehension of these actions is an apprehension of His attributes, may He be exalted, with respect to which He is known*" (emphasis added: *The Guide*, 1: 54, 124).

31 Ibid., 1:39, 139.

32 Ibid. Maimonides employs a slightly paraphrased Sufi expression here: *idrākuh huwa al-ʿajz ʿan nihāyat idrākih*. In a variety of works al-Ghazālī employs the *ḥadīth*: *al-ʿajzu ʿan darki al-idrāki idrāk* (the failure to attain perception is perception, or apprehension is the inability to apprehend). Al-Ghazālī appears to use this *ḥadīth*, attributed to Abū Bakr, in a systematic way. I hope to develop a separate study of his use of it and his sources. cf. e.g. *al-Maqṣad*, En. 42/Ar. 54; cf. also *Iḥyāʾ ʿulūm ad-dīn., K. at-Tawḥīd*, 1605; and al-Ghazālī, *Kitāb al-Arbaʿīn fī uṣūl ad-dīn*. ed. ʿAbd al-Qādir Makrī, Jiddah: Dār al-Minhāj li-n-Nashr wa-t-Tawzīʿ, 2006, 92; hereafter: *al-Arbaʿīn*. Finally, cf. id. *Maqāṣid al-falāsifa*, ed. Sulaymān Dunyā, Miṣr: Dār al-Maʿārif, 1961, 252; see also: Lobel, *A Sufi-Jewish Dialogue*, 39, 255n.27.

33 Ibid. Compare the similar prayer in 1:59: "Glory then to Him who is such that when the intellects contemplate His essence, their apprehension turns into incapacity; and when they contemplate the proceeding of His actions from His will, their knowledge turns into ignorance; and when the tongues aspire to magnify Him by means of attributive

In *Shemonah Peraqim*, he says:

> The inadequacy of our intellects to perceive Him is like the inadequacy of the light of [our] vision to perceive the light of the sun. That is not due to the weakness of the light of the sun, but to the latter being stronger than the light [of vision] which wants to perceive it.[34]

Maimonides insists that truth is known by means of reason through logical demonstration; but he equally asserts that this mode of perceiving truth will be exhausted and overwhelmed in its encounter with the divine. Al-Ghazālī describes this condition of being overwhelmed by an encounter with the divine in strikingly similar terms in *Mishkāt al-Anwār*:

> [...] it is not unreasonable that God's light be hidden, that its hiddenness derive from the intensity of its disclosure, and that heedlessness of it stems from the radiance of its brightness. So glory be to Him who is hidden from creatures through the intensity of His manifestation and veiled from them because of the radiance of his light![35]

Both authors share a conviction that God exhausts all human efforts to perceive him. In these quotes they draw on a Sufi and Neoplatonic image of God as hidden by his overabundant manifestation in order to highlight that the failure of perception is in the human faculties that are dazzled and blinded by the intensity of God.[36] Whatever their means of arrival at this point, Maimonides and al-Ghazālī seem to be in strong agreement about the end and purpose of human life, which is contemplation of a God who eludes and dazzles. Yet, the distinct manner of their arrival at this point of harmony is significant. Maimonides feels that scripture and the truth regarding the divine attributes that it describes are essentially rational. Scripture speaks in symbolic terms because few people are truly rational; therefore rational truths

---

qualifications, all eloquence turns into weariness and incapacity!" ibid., 137; cf. Lobel, *A Sufi-Jewish Dialogue*, 39.

34 *Shemonah Peraqim*, 95. He continues: "This subject has been frequently discussed, and all the discourses are correct and clear."

35 *Mishkāt al-Anwār*, 23–24; see note 35 above and 38 below.

36 Ibn Sīnā uses very similar Sufi-Neoplatonic language as well, e.g. at the end of his *Ḥayy b. Yaqẓān*: Ibn Sīnā, *Rasāʾil ash-Shaykh ar-Raʾīs Abū ʿAlī l-Ḥusayn b. ʿAbdallāh b. Sīnā fī asrār al-ḥikmah al-mashriqīyah* (*Traites Mystiques d'Abou ʿAlī Hosain b. ʿAbdallāh b. Sīnā ou d'Avicenna*), ed. with French translation by A. F. Mehren, Leiden: E.J. Brill, 1899, 21 (of the Arabic text of *Ḥayy b. Yaqẓān*).

must be presented in some other manner. He follows his major influence in the *Shemonah Peraqim*, al-Fārābī, closely in this regard. This appraisal does not demean scripture for Maimonides: a truth that is not known rationally is not really known for him. Nonetheless, he does believe there are unknowable truths. Al-Ghazālī believes in unknowable truths as well, but he allows for a greater scope of human interaction with these truths. He articulates this according to both traditionalist and mystical hermeneutics, in terms of the unknowable modality of the divine attributes that are revealed in scripture.

Al-Ghazālī's psychological interpretation of the veils *ḥadīth* establishes the contemplation of God as the goal of human life. He divides the classes of the veiled seekers in terms of how aspects of the soul such as the appetites, physical senses, imagination, or reason may act as a veil obscuring true perception of God. In addition to these interests, Al-Ghazālī also takes an apparently theological interest in the proper conception of the divine attributes a prominent concern of the veils section.[37] For instance, idolaters may recognize that beauty and might are attributes of God, yet worship these in sensible form: they are "veiled" by the faculty of the senses in their perception of God's attributes.[38] Similarly, al-Ghazālī describes the last class among the mixed veiled seekers as "those who are veiled by the divine lights along with dark, corrupt, rational comparisons."[39] He presents this final class of mixed veiled

37 Again, Maimonides shows similar interest in some of his discussions, e.g. *The Guide* I:59, where he creates his own hierarchy of those who attempt to know God through different conceptions, and methods of knowing, the divine attributes; ibid., 138. Note the close proximity of this hierarchy to the passages parallel to *Mishkāt al-Anwār*, above at notes 34 & 35.

38 *Mishkāt al-Anwār*, 47.

39 Ibid., 49. Here, we see al-Ghazālī's general criticism of *kalām*: the method of reasoning is flawed, for instance in his autobiography: id., *al-Munqidh min aḍ-ḍalāl*, in *Majmūʿ rasāʾil al-Imām al-Ghazālī*, Bayrūt: Dār al-Kutub al-ʿIlmiyyah, 1994, 32–3. cf. id., *al-Munqidh min aḍ-ḍalāl*, translated in *Freedom and Fulfillment: an annotated translation of Al-Ghazālī's al-Munqidh min al-Ḍalāl and other relevant works of al-Ghazālī*, trans. R. J. McCarthy, Boston: Twayne Publishers, 1980, 59–60; hereafter: *al-Munqidh*, En./Ar., with the other works in the text cited by their Arabic title, followed by: in R. J. McCarthy, in *Freedom and Fulfillment*. cf. id. *al-Qisṭās al-mustaqīm*. ed. Victor Chelhot, Beirut: al-Maṭbaʿa al-Kāthūlīkiyya, 1959, 90; cf. id. *al-Qisṭās al-mustaqīm*, in R. J. McCarthy, in *Freedom and fulfillment*, 276; hereafter: *al-Qisṭās al-Mustaqīm*, En./Ar.; where al-Ghazālī associates theology with veils over the heart as he does in *Mishkāt al-Anwār* and, in the broader context of that work, such theology is clearly corrupt logic. Also compare id. *Kitāb Sharḥ ʿajāʾib al-qalb* in *Iḥyāʾ ʿUlūm al-Dīn*, 869–70; cf. id. *Kitāb Sharḥ ʿajāʾib al-qalb* in *Knowledge of God in Classical Sufism* (partial translation), ed./trans. John Renard, New York: Paulist Press, 2004, 302–3; hereafter: *Iḥyāʾ, K. Sharḥ ʿAjāʾib al-Qalb*, En./Ar. Note, here, that ignorance of

seekers with allusions to doctrines concerning divine attributes such as speech and will, saying "these are well known doctrines, and there is no need to go into details."[40] Al-Ghazālī's vagueness gave rise to speculation and some of the secondary scholarship curiously sees a transition from traditionalist theology toward Muʿtazilī theology at this point in the veils section.[41]

In fact, the Muʿtazilī position dominates the whole of the final sub-section discussing the mixed veiled seekers and any transition is from Muʿtazilī thought toward a more traditionalist position.[42] Al-Ghazālī's allusions to the

---

the proper use of logic is an obstacle to knowledge; thus, theology seems to veil the heart in a manner similar to the 'corrupt dark rational comparisons' in *Mishkāt al-Anwār*; cf. id. *Iḥyā', K. at-Tilāwa*, En., 70/Ar., 325, where theological partisanship is a veil that conceals understanding of the Qur'ān. Likewise, see id. *Iḥyā', K. at-tawḥīd*, 1598, where the theologians are located in the penultimate stage of *tawḥīd*; cf. id., *Fayṣal at-tafriqah bayn al-Islām wa-z-zandaqa*, ed. Muḥammad Bījū, Damascus, 1993, 71–9. Similarly, id. *Fayṣal at-tafriqah bayn al-Islām wa-z-zandaqah*. trans., R. J. McCarthy, in *Freedom and fulfillment*, 143–5; hereafter: *Fayṣal*, En./Ar., where al-Ghazālī says *kalām* is *ḥarām* except in two cases); cf. id. *Kitāb al-ʿIlm* in *Iḥyā' ʿulūm ad-dīn*, 33; also cf. id. *Kitāb al-ʿIlm* translated as *The Book of Knowledge* by Nabih Amin Faris, Lahore: Sh. Muhammad Ashraf, 1962, 47–8; hereafter: *Iḥyā', K. ʿIlm*, En./Ar. Of similar note is id. *Maʿārij al-quds fī madārij maʿrifat an-nafs*, ed. Muḥammad Bījū, Dimashq: Dār al-Albāb, 1998, 82–3; cf. id. *Maʿarij al-quds fī madārij maʿrifat an-nafs* translated as *On the Soul* by Yahya Abu Risha, Irbid, Jordan: Dar Al-Hilal for Translation & Pub., 2001, 151; hereafter: *Maʿārij al-Quds*, En./Ar. Next, cf. *al-Iqtiṣād fī al-iʿtiqād*. eds. Husayn Atay and Ibrāhīm Cubkcu, Ankara, Nur Matbaasi, 1962, 9–15; and *al-Iqtiṣād fī al-iʿtiqād* partially translated as "Al-Ghazālī on Divine Essence: a translation from the *Iqtiṣād fī al-Iʿtiqād*" by Dennis Morgan Davis (PhD. diss., The University of Utah), 2005, 92–101; hereafter *al-Iqtiṣād*, En./Ar. Finally, cf. *al-Arbaʿīn*, 80, 275; *al-Maqṣad*, En. 31/Ar. 43.

40 *Mishkāt al-Anwār*, 50.

41 Hermann Landolt, "Ghazālī and 'Religionswissenschaft'," 36. William Henry Temple Gairdner. "Al-Ghazālī's Mishkāt Al-Anwār," 15. Watt, "A Forgery," 6–7. More recently, Frank Griffel correctly identified the doctrines as Muʿtazilī; *The Philosophical Theology of al-Ghazali*, 246–8.

42 For a detailed argument on this, see: Girdner. *Reasoning with Revelation*, 408–30. For the allusions to doctrines at issue, see: *Mishkāt al-Anwār*, 50. Succinctly, the three doctrines to which al-Ghazālī alludes at this point are linked to the broader issue of his criticism of *tashbīh*, which he identifies with the Muʿtazila (see below, note 46). Al-Ghazālī routinely presents the first doctrine at issue, namely, that God's speech consists of sounds and letters, as Muʿtazilī. Likewise, he associates the third doctrine, which describes God's will as originated, with the Muʿtazilī position. The intervening doctrine is closer, but not equivalent, to the Ashʿarī position; it is still concerned with originated mental speech and is inappropriately likened to creatures. Meanwhile, the first class of those veiled by

doctrines of the final subcategory of mixed veiled seekers are consistent with his presentation of Muʿtazilī positions in other works; he syntactically links all the doctrines to which he alludes, critiquing them collectively in terms of the polemical theological category of *tashbīh*, or comparing God to creatures. This is the "corrupt rational comparison" that concerns him.[43] Al-Ghazālī makes this clear by beginning his allusions with a general characterization of this class: "[...] they understand these [divine] attributes in keeping with how they stand in relation to their own attributes."[44] Al-Ghazālī continues his interest in *tashbīh* as he turns to the first class of those veiled by pure lights:

> The first [of those veiled by pure lights] is a company of people who come to know the meanings of the attributes through verification. They perceive that ascribing the names "speaking," "desiring," "powerful,"

---

veils of pure light appears to espouse a rational-traditionalist approach to attribution (see note 48 below). For parallel discussions of these issues in al-Ghazālī's works, see: *al-Qisṭās al-Mustaqīm*, En. 278/Ar. 94, where al-Ghazālī explicitly accuses the Muʿtazila of likening creatures to God. For discussion of God's speech or word as sounds and letters, cf. esp. the discussion of letters and words in the context of a consideration of *tashbīh* and *tanzīh* in *Iḥyā', K. at-tawḥīd*, Ar., 1604; cf. *al-Maqṣad*, En., 175/Ar., 163; *Iḥyā', K. at-Tilāwa*, En., 56–7/Ar., 321; *Al-Iqtiṣād*, Ar., 113–115, 125, 153–4; cf. *al-Arbaʿīn*, 48, 91; cf. Ghazālī, *Kitāb at-Tawba* in *Iḥyā' ʿulūm ad-dīn*, 1351; cf. id. *Kitāb al-Tawba* translated as *al-Ghazzali On Repentance* by M. S. Stern, New Delhi: Sterling Publishers, 1990, 67; hereafter: *Iḥyā', k. al-tawba* En./Ar. cf. id. *Jawāhir al-Qur'ān* translated as *The Jewels of the Qur'ān* by Muhammad Abul Quasem, Bangi, Selangor, Malaysia: Jabatan Usuluddin dan Falsafa, Fakulti Pengajian Islam, Universiti Kebangsaan Malaysia, 1977, 35; hereafter: *Jawāhir*. Compare also id. *Risālah al-Qudsīyah*, translated as "Al-Ghazali's Tract on Dogmatic Theology," ed. & trans. Tibawi, in *Islamic Quarterly*, IX (1965): 85; hereafter: *ar-Risālah al-Qudsīyah*.

43 *Mishkāt al-Anwār*, 49.

44 Ibid., 50. Al-Ghazālī's concern with *tashbīh* somewhat obscures the object of his criticism, if one expects the Muʿtazila to be condemned for *tanzīh*, or emptying God of his attributes. This party errs by thinking that speaking or willing can only be understood as temporally originated in accordance with the expression of these attributes in creatures. Temporally originated attributes cannot characterize the eternal divine essence; so the will and speech must be denied as attributes which eternally characterize the divine essence. They deny God's eternal attributes because of their conception of them in terms of their human analogs. Their *tanzīh* is a product of their *tashbīh*, which is the corrupt rational comparison which veils this group. This is consistent with al-Ghazālī's other presentations of the issue and the Muʿtazila: cf. esp. *al-Qisṭās al-Mustaqīm*, En. 278/Ar. 94, where al-Ghazālī explicitly accuses the Muʿtazila of *tashbīh*; for additional references to Ghazālī's treatment of these issues, cf. above note 44.

"knowing," and so forth to His attributes is not like ascribing them to human beings.[45]

This class affirms a standard list of attributes; but they recognize the limits of rational comparisons between human and divine attributes. One might say, they piously constrain their discussion of the modality of the relationship between the divine attributes and essence in a manner suggestive of the *bi-lā kayfa wa-lā tashbīh* doctrine associated with traditionalist theology in general, including the rational traditionalism of the Ashʿarīya.[46] Indeed, the interpretation al-Ghazālī gives to the proof text he cites at this point supports such a reading.[47] The precise theological identity of this group, however, does not seem to be central to al-Ghazālī's point and theological partisanship does not provide a compelling account of his major motives. It seems more likely that

45 Ibid., 50.

46 Ibid., cf. 28. It seems likely that this approach is most readily identified with al-Ghazālī's generally Ashʿarī presentation of a balance of limited speculation and a traditionalist reticence, or pious restraint, concerning the intelligibility of the modality of God's attributes in his theological writings. In several works, al-Ghazālī suggests that his sympathies lie most closely with this traditionalist hermeneutic which limits speculation on the modality of God's attributes with the *bi-lā kayfa wa-lā tashbīh* doctrine by "not asking how" the attributes describe God, "nor comparing" him to creatures. For example, al-Ghazālī is fond of the tradition from Imām Mālik which was given in response to a question concerning how God is seated upon the throne: "the fact of sitting (*istiwāʾ*) is known but its manner is not; to believe in it is an obligation, to inquire about its manner is an innovation." Al-Ghazālī's fondness for quoting this tradition communicates his traditionalist sympathies, or at least his eagerness to appear sympathetic to traditionalist doctrine. However, his location of philosophical content in sacred sources such as the Qurʾān shows his willingness to expand such traditionalism; reason plays a central role in determining what is acceptable in this regard. For more, see Girdner, *Reasoning with Revelation*. 424–8, and chapter ten generally; cf. al-Ghazālī, *Qanūn at-Taʾwīl*, ed. M. Bījū, Damascus, 1993, 24; cf. id. *Kitāb Qawāʿid al-ʿaqāʾid* in *Iḥyāʾ ʿulūm ad-dīn*, 108, 127; hereafter: *K. Qawāʿid al-ʿaqāʾid*; cf. *Fayṣal*, En., 136 /Ar., 49; *Al-Iqtiṣād*, En. 167/Ar. 52.

47 Al-Ghazālī twice alludes to Q 26:23–7, which depicts an encounter between Moses and Pharaoh. He reads this encounter as one in which Pharaoh foolishly demands to know the quiddity of God, but Moses responds only with references to God's acts. It is significant that this allusion is used by al-Ghazālī to illustrate what he means when he says that "ascribing the names 'speaking,' 'desiring,' 'powerful,' 'knowing,' and so forth to His attributes is not like ascribing them to human beings." *Mishkāt al-Anwār*, 50, cf. 28. In other words, *tashbīh* is excluded, but attribution is preserved. For an analysis of al-Ghazālī's use of this passage relative to his presentation of various theological doctrines in *Mishkāt al-Anwār*, see: Girdner, *Reasoning with Revelation*, 429–31, 453–54.

al-Ghazālī's point is a general advocacy, and ultimately a philosophical and mystical adaptation, of the traditionalist *bi-lā kayfa wa-lā tashbīh* doctrine in as much as it involves a basic acknowledgment of the limits of human reasoning, as well as the role of revelation for understanding the nature of God and his attributes. To understand this, we need to turn to briefly consider aspects of the remaining classes of those veiled by pure light.

Al-Ghazālī subdivides the remainder of those veiled by pure lights in terms of a variety of realizations concerning the cause of motion in the heavens, and he apparently alludes to various conceptions of the efficient and final cause of celestial motion. Then, he distinguishes seekers of the cause of motion from the final category of those veiled by veils of pure light. These attain a realization that, while mysterious and controversial, clearly entails a shift of interest from God as the cause of motion in the cosmos to God as the cause of all existence. It seems that al-Ghazālī is distinguishing between rational proofs for God's existence based on motion, such as Aristotelian arguments for the unmoved mover, and proofs based on a consideration of existence, such as Ibn Sīnā's arguments for the Necessary Existent. This is confirmed by the fact that al-Ghazālī identifies those who make this distinction as "those who have arrived" at an unveiling of God's face. They come to an understanding of the Qur'ānic allusion we considered above, that is, "everything is perishing except his face" (Q 28:88). Recall that al-Ghazālī explains this passage in terms of the concept of the Necessary Existent earlier in *Mishkāt al-Anwār*. Upon the unveiling of God's face in the veils section, al-Ghazālī refers the reader back to this explanation. Thus, the unveiling of God's face conveys the truth of God as the Necessary Existent and this truth is – inasmuch as it is outlined by Ibn Sīnā's philosophy – perceived by the rational faculty; but what of the holy prophetic faculty, which al-Ghazālī attaches to his outline of the philosophical psychology that provides the framework for his interpretation of the veils *ḥadīth*?

Al-Ghazālī provides his philosophical interpretation of the meaning of everything perishing but God's face in the first chapter of *Mishkāt al-Anwār*, after which he proceeds to a long exposition of the mystical state of *fanā'*, or the ecstatic mystical experience of the extinction of the self in God. Al-Ghazālī returns to his philosophical interpretation of the face of God as his necessary existence; he also returns to this mystical interest in the ecstatic state of *fanā'* in the veils section, explicitly referencing his previous interpretations. Elsewhere, I have discussed in detail how al-Ghazālī uses his interpretation of Q 28:88 in terms of the philosophical concepts of necessary and possible existence; he employs these terms to explicate the ecstatic experience of mystical union with God in the state of *fanāʾ*.[48] Here, I can simply assert my finding that al-Ghazālī employs the ontological categories of necessary and possible existence to argue for both the possibility of such mystical experiences, and to censure what he considers to be heterodox claims of actual union with God. He presents *fanāʾ* as the realization by the mystical-prophetic faculty of the mystic's relationship as a contingent being with the necessary being of God; this realization, however, might be subjectively mistaken for unity with the divine being.[49] Apropos to the broader concern in this volume with al-Ghazālī and rationality, the realization of the mystical-prophetic faculty is not of an irrational truth; it may be partially explained in terms of Ibn Sīnā's rational concept of the Necessary Existent. What distinguishes those who have arrived from anyone who rationally understands the concept of God's necessary existence is the mode of their knowing that God's necessary existence is the source of all contingent existence: those who have arrived understand the relationship between God's necessary existence and all contingent existence both rationally and mystically. In Ṣūfī terminology, al-Ghazālī says this truth becomes a taste (*dhawq*) and a state (*ḥāl*) for them and he describes it as the ecstatic experience of *fanāʾ*, or extinction of the self.

The truths of the mystical-prophetic faculty cannot contradict reason, but they can exhaust its limits. Indeed, this is the profundity of such an experience for al-Ghazālī; it provides certainty that reason cannot provide with regard to a truth that is unknowable in its essence and must remain a mystery known by revelation: God. At this point in *Mishkāt al-Anwār*, al-Ghazālī integrates the traditionalist, rationalist, and mystical hermeneutics that he advocates in his discussion of those veiled by pure light.[50] Those who have arrived rationally

48 Girdner, *Reasoning with Revelation*, 355–79, 640–50. For al-Ghazālī's use of *al-Qaṣaṣ*/28:88, see: *Mishkāt al-Anwār*, 16–18, 52; cf. *al-Maqṣad*, En. 51, 124/Ar. 64, 137; cf. *Iḥyāʾ, K. at-Tilāwa*, En. 66–7/Ar. 324; cf. *al-Arbaʿīn*, 81.

49 Ibid., esp. 365–74. cf. *Mishkāt al-Anwār*, 16–18, 52. Cf. esp. *al-Maqṣad*, En. 125–6, 149–58/Ar. 139, 162–71. For Ghazālī's conception of the highest stage of *tawḥīd* and mystical experience in terms of a realization that only God exists, see also: *al-Maqṣad*, En. 46/Ar. 58; cf. *Iḥyāʾ, K. Sharḥ ʿajāʾib al-qalb*, in RJ McCarthy. *Freedom and Fulfillment*, 323; cf. *Iḥyāʾ, K. Sharḥ ʿajāʾib al-qalb*, En. 305/Ar., 871, 875; cf. *Iḥyāʾ, k. al-tawba*, En. 77/Ar. 1357 and *Iḥyāʾ, K. at-tawḥīd*, 1598; cf. *al-Arbaʿīn*, 276.

50 The hermeneutic is traditionalist in as much as it appears to elaborate the *bi-lā kayfa* doctrine (cf. discussion above and note 48); it is rationalist in as much as it asserts that part of what the Qurʾān and *ḥadīth* convey may be interpreted as referring to philosophical truths (e.g. God as the Necessary Existent). It is mystical in its assertion that the mysterious dimension of scripture which tradition accepts 'without asking how' and which can bear rationalist exegesis, but cannot be fully explicated by such exegesis, may be

understand the philosophical distinctions, provided by the rationalist hermeneutic, between varied arguments for God and for the concept of the Necessary Existent; nevertheless, they encounter a mysterious dimension of revelation which exhausts rationalist hermeneutics. In terms of the traditionalist hermeneutic, this mystery can only be known by revelation; thus al-Ghazālī is careful to express their realization in the language of the Qur'ān: "'Everything is perishing except his face' (Q 28:88) becomes for them a taste and a state."[51] In terms of the mystical hermeneutic, those who have arrived experience an ecstatic and subjective certainty with regard to truths that tradition simply communicates as a mystery. This experience makes the pious restraint of traditionalism into a positive encounter with something more than the limits of human reason even as it affirms these limits. At the same time, much room for the exercise of reason is found within their bounds.

6 Conclusion: Apophasis, Pious Restraint, and Encountering the Mysterious

In both the veils section of *Mishkat al-Anwār* and the seventh chapter of the *Shemonah Peraqim*, al-Ghazālī and Maimonides provide an interpretation of traditional reports concerning the veils of God in terms of a philosophical psychology and ethics which present the theoretical or intellectual contemplation of God as the end of human life; yet they paradoxically deny the possibility of knowledge of God. In addition, al-Ghazālī and Maimonides both interpret the unveiling of God's face in terms of the philosophical concept of God as the Necessary Existent. This concept allows them to identify God as known by means of the necessary relationship of contingent creatures to his being; they describe the divine essence, however, as unknowable in itself, even as they say it necessarily exists. Drawing on theological conceptualizations of the relationship of the divine attributes to the divine essence and to creatures, al-Ghazālī and Maimonides present God as unknowable in his essence. Maimonides employs a rationalist hermeneutic asserting that even the attributes, known from observation or given in revelation, cannot explain the divine essence; they must be logically negated from it by means of apophasis. Al-Ghazālī, on the other hand, maintains that the attributes of God are not to be logically negated, but personally experienced as meaningful mysteries in a

encountered personally and experienced subjectively as true. Cf. Girdner, *Reasoning with Revelation*, 349–79, 408–28, 640–50.

51 *Mishkāt al-Anwār*, 52; cf. 16–17, 20, 23. cf. discussion above, esp. notes 24 & 27.

mystical expansion of traditionalist hermeneutics. Meanwhile, his interpretation of the Qur'ān and *aḥādīth* in terms of philosophical concepts shows that though scripture can bear rational exegesis, it cannot be reduced to it.

God remains essentially unknowable for both al-Ghazālī and Maimonides, but the quality of how one approaches God's unknowable essence – which is His transcendence – is distinct, especially with regard to the issues of the human need for revelation and the nature of scripture and tradition. Functionally, though, Maimonides' rationalist approach to tradition and the philosophically and mystically expansive traditionalism of al-Ghazālī are very similar: they both recommend a personal encounter with the limits of rationality and human knowledge. Maimonides primarily conceived of this encounter philosophically, but, with Biblical exegeses and allusions to a seemingly mystical bedazzlement, presented it in traditionalist and mystical terms. Al-Ghazālī adapted the pious restraint of traditionalism, with its emphasis on the primacy and mysterious nature of revelation, to create space for philosophical and mystical approaches to the truth of that revelation. *Shemonah Peraqim* and *Mishkāt al-Anwār* reveal that both authors were profoundly influenced by the philosophical conception of the ordering of the soul for the theoretical contemplation of God as the ultimate end of human life. Both authors thought of this end as elusive and not completely obtainable; yet, its pursuit was of utmost significance, drawing holistically on all human capabilities and intellectual disciplines. They both concluded their seeking not only with a negative encounter with the limits of reason, but with a positive encounter with a mystery that transcends those limits, "who is hidden from creatures through the intensity of His manifestation and veiled from them because of the radiance of his light!"[52]

52 *Mishkāt al-Anwār*, 24; cf. above notes 35–7.

CHAPTER 13

Al-Ghazālī, Averroes and Moshe Narboni

Conflict and Conflation

Alfred L. Ivry

Two of the three persons my contribution has brought together need no introduction to the readers of this volume. Al-Ghazālī is the one whose millennial anniversary is being commemorated, and Averroes (Ibn Rushd) is his celebrated adversary, the philosopher who wished to render al-Ghazālī's "Incoherence of the Philosophers" incoherent. But who is Moshe Narboni?[1]

Moshe Narboni is a fourteenth century Jewish philosopher (d. 1362) whose surname derives from the Provençal city of Narbonne, an *ʿir vaʾem beyisrael*, a site of Jewish learning and scholarship in the Middle Ages. Moses, or Moshe, however, who is known in Latin as Maestre Vidal Bellsom, or Blasom, was actually born in Perpignan, and lived there until 1344. It was there that Narboni – as we shall call him – studied a full complement of Jewish texts: the Bible and rabbinic literature, as well as Jewish philosophy, besides medicine and Islamic philosophy. It is most probable that he studied the Muslim *falāsifa* through Hebrew translations of their work, though he may have had some Arabic as well as some Latin. He did not know Scholastic philosophy, however, and it was the luminaries of Islamic and Jewish thought of the tenth to twelfth centuries who circumscribed his intellectual horizons.

Narboni moved to Spain in mid-life, and lived in various cities there amidst the disturbances caused by warfare and the Bubonic plague. He fled Cervera together with the Jewish community in 1349 due to anti-Jewish attacks, leaving behind his possessions and books. Nevertheless, he continued writing, projecting an image of an *oecumenia* of shared learning and belief among Jews and Muslims.

---

1 A Summary of Narboni's life and work may be found in my entry, "Moses ben Joshua (Ben Mar David) of Narbonne," *Encyclopaedia Judaica*, Keter Publishing, Jerusalem, 1972, XII: 422–423. For greater detail, cf. Maurice R. Hayoun, *La Philosophie et la Théologie de Moïse de Narbonne*, Tübingen: J. C. B. Mohr (Paul Siebeck), 1989; and see Gitit Holzman, *The Theory of the Intellect and Soul in the Thought of Rabbi Moshe Narboni, Based on his Commentaries on the Writings of Ibn Rushd, Ibn Tufayl, Ibn Bajja and al-Ghazali* (Hebrew, PhD. Dissertation, Hebrew University, 1996), pp. 1–24.

© KONINKLIJKE BRILL NV, LEIDEN, 2015 | DOI 10.1163/9789004290952_014

Narboni was particularly captivated by the work of Averroes and Maimonides, and inserted them into all his philosophical studies. He wrote supercommentaries on Averroes' commentaries on Aristotle's logic, physics, metaphysics, cosmology and psychology, and towards the end of his life wrote a major commentary on Maimonides' *Guide of the Perplexed*. Narboni had studied Maimonides' work since the age of 13, enabling him to reference the *Guide* frequently, well before he wrote his commentary on it.

In addition to his supercommentaries on Averroes, Narboni wrote a commentary on al-Ghazālī's *Maqāṣid al-falāsifa*, "The Intentions of the Philosophers," and on Ibn Ṭufayl's *Ḥayy ibn Yaqẓān*, in which commentary he inserted comments on Ibn Bājja's *Tadbīr al-mutawaḥḥid*, "The Regimen of the Solitary." An early commentary on a short work of Averroes, "The Treatise on the Hylic Intellect," also known as the "Treatise on the Possibility of Conjunction,"[2] shows that Narboni had fully grasped Averroes' radical teaching on that subject, as intimated in Averroes' *Talkhīṣ kitāb an-Nafs*, his Middle Commentary on (Aristotle's) *De anima*.[3]

Narboni actually incorporated much of this Middle Commentary into his own lengthy *Ma'amar bi-Shelemut ha-Nefesh*, the "Treatise on the Perfection of the Soul";[4] introducing into it as well much of Averroes' "Treatise on the Possibility of Conjunction." In his treatise, Narboni refers as well to Maimonides' *Guide* and to a number of al-Ghazālī's texts.

Two major, if smaller, treatises that Narboni wrote deserve special mention for their relevance to issues close to his own time. The first is an early composition called *Iggeret 'al Shi'ur Qomah*, the "Epistle on *Shi'ur Qomah*;" *Shi'ur Qomah* designating an anthropomorphically imagined deity of immense proportions, encompassing the cosmos and paradoxically affirming God's indescribability. As it has been shown, Narboni wrote this epistle in an attempt to reconcile the *sefirot* of the kabbalists with the celestial spheres of the philosophers.[5]

---

2 Cf. Kalman Bland, ed. and trans., *The Epistle on the Possibility of Conjunction with the Active Intellect by Ibn Rushd with the Commentary of Moses Narboni*, New York: Jewish Theological Seminary, 1982.

3 Cf. Alfred L. Ivry, ed. and trans., *Averroës Middle Commentary on Aristotle's De anima*, Provo, Utah: Brigham Young University Press 2002.

4 Moses of Narbonne, *Ma'amar bi-Shelemut ha-Nefesh*, (*Treatise on the Perfection of the Soul*) ed. Alfred Lyon Ivry (Hebrew), The Israel Academy of Sciences and Humanities, Jerusalem, 1977.

5 Cf. Alexander Altmann, ed. and trans., "Moses Narboni's Epistle on *Shi'ur Qomah*," *Jewish Medieval and Renaissance Studies*, ed. A. Altmann, Cambridge: Harvard University Press, 1967, pp. 225–288.

The second short treatise is Narboni's *Ha-Ma'amar bi-Veḥirah*, "The Treatise on Choice," i.e., free will. He wrote this as a response to a determinist tractate (*Minḥat kena'ot*) written by one Abner of Burgos.[6] In his response, Narboni defends free will on philosophical as well as theological grounds, impugning Abner's motives in opting for a doctrine that contradicted a tenet of Judaism.[7]

Al-Ghazālī's *Maqāṣid al-falāsifa* was known to the Latin West in the 12th century translation of Dominicus Gundissalinus as *Logica et Philosophia Algazelis*, and was thought, as the title declares, to represent his true beliefs. This was facilitated by the absence in Latin of al-Ghazālī's opening and closing remarks in that work, passages in which he clearly states that one first has to know the arguments of an opponent in order to refute them. Avicenna's physics and metaphysics represented to al-Ghazālī the views he presented as the "Intentions of the Philosophers," and it is aspects of Avicenna's philosophy that al-Ghazālī then attempts to repudiate in his *Tahāfut al-falāsifa*, "The Incoherence of the Philosophers." Interestingly, Judah Halevi employs a similar, if abbreviated, strategy within the pages of his 12th century apologia, the *Cuzari*, using the views of Avicenna – who nevertheless remains unnamed by Halevi – as the position of a prototypical philosopher.

Narboni, however, could not conveniently claim ignorance, having a complete copy of *Maqāṣid al-falāsifa* before him in an anonymous Hebrew translation, correctly called *Kavvanot Ha-Filosofim*. Narboni therefore knew that al-Ghazālī claimed to be presenting Avicennian philosophy in that work, prior to refuting it. Narboni knew that, but did not believe it. Rather, he chose to believe that al-Ghazālī deliberately misrepresented his disagreement with Avicenna in order to placate the powerful foes of philosophy while nevertheless transmitting his teachings.[8] Narboni thus views al-Ghazālī as practicing a form of *taqiyya*, or dissimulation, a tactic associated with the Isma'ilis, and one which Maimonides implicitly endorses in the *Guide*.

Narboni thus considered the *Maqāṣid* to be al-Ghazālī's confirmation of Avicenna's philosophy, and his *Tahāfut* a pretended refutation. This may explain Narboni's relative neglect of the latter work, which established al-Ghazālī in

6 Cf. Zvi Avneri, "Abner of Burgos," in *Encyclopaedia Judaica*, ed. Michael Berenbaum and Fred Skolnik, 2nd ed., vol. 1, Detroit: Macmillan Reference USA, 2007, pp. 264–265. The *Minhat kena'ot* is extant in Castilian translation.

7 Cf. Maurice Hayoun, ed. and trans., "L'epître du Libre Arbitre de Moïse de Narbonne," *Revue des études juives* (CXLI (1–2), 1982), pp. 139–167.

8 Narboni's words to that effect are quoted by Holzman, p. 293. English translation by Steven Harvey, "Why Did Fourteenth-Century Jews Turn to Al-Ghazali's Account of Natural Science?" *Jewish Quarterly Review* (vol. 91, 2001) pp. 366–367, n. 24.

most readers' eyes as opposed to philosophy. Narboni, however, is not blind to al-Ghazālī's positions when they run counter to those of his beloved Averroes, and criticizes al-Ghazālī for this, though he states in the introduction to his commentary that he will simply present al-Ghazālī's views without comment. It would appear that his desire to think well of al-Ghazālī conflicted with his sense of philosophical probity.

Narboni's positive attitude towards al-Ghazālī's *Maqāṣid* is reflected in the reception that text received among Jewish readers. It was translated into Hebrew two or three times, the anonymous translation Narboni used being perhaps a revision of an earlier translation. The seventy-plus surviving Hebrew manuscripts of this work testify to its popularity among Jews interested in philosophy, and this despite Averroes' disparagement of the work. Those who did use the text were impressed with its conciseness and relatively easy style of exposition. As Narboni says in the introduction to his commentary,

> we intend (to write) a short commentary in order not to deviate from the intention of the sage, for this noble man has revealed and publicized science's secrets with wonderful brevity to those who are worthy of them. This indicates that divine providence (extends over) those who worship God (and) yearn for scientific wisdom (*ḥokhma*), though they are troubled by external hindrances. [Providence] sent this illustrious person, who has seen the spiritual world, as Abū Bakr ibn aṣ-Ṣāyigh (i.e., Ibn Bājja), has testified, to assist us (in understanding) the principles of science in a short amount of time.[9]

Despite such encomia, Narboni's acceptance of al-Ghazālī's Avicennianism is limited to its compatibility with Averroean doctrine. Narboni has little quarrel with the summaries of logic and physics that al-Ghazālī presents, unlike his discomfort with aspects of Avicenna's metaphysics. Perhaps another feature of the *Maqāṣid* that attracted Narboni is al-Ghazālī's affirmation of personal immortality and its essential similarity to the traditional religious view of Judaism; here, though, Narboni may be practicing his own bit of *taqiyya*, for as an Averroist he ought not to have shared this belief.

This becomes apparent in Narboni's comments on al-Ghazālī's treatment of the various stages that the rational faculty of the soul undergoes. Narboni has no quarrel with the conventional outline of the topic that al-Ghazālī presents: a progression from pure potentiality – *al-ʿaql al-hayūlī* or *hayulānī* – to an intellect that has primary premises and conventional propositions – *al-ʿaql*

9 Holzman, p. 288 (my translation).

bi-l-malaka – then an operational, active intellect, *al-ʿaql bi-l-fiʿl*, culminating through conjunction with the *ʿaql al-faʿʿāl*, the agent intellect, and the acquisition of theoretical intelligible propositions in the aptly named "acquired intellect," *al-ʿaql al-mustafād*. Sympathetic with this epistemological scheme as he is, Narboni could not agree with the assumption that the hylic intellect is a pure disposition to think, and he may well have doubted that the conjunction the acquired intellect achieves with the Agent intellect renders the individual intellect *per se* immortal. Narboni also had to be uncomfortable with al-Ghazālī's view that the entire soul, and not just the rational faculty, endures forever, and that it experiences pleasure or pain in an afterlife.

Here, however, Narboni has to tread carefully, for such a view was considered a tenet of both Islam and Judaism. He therefore limits himself to the remark that the soul upon death is indeed pained, as al-Ghazālī says, over its inability to conjoin with the Agent Intellect, but that is because it loses at that point the senses and imaginative faculty that are essential to acquiring intelligibles.[10] Narboni does not say that without these faculties the surviving intellect, were it to survive as an independent entity, would have no sense of self.

Narboni brings Maimonides together with al-Ghazālī in his commentary on al-Ghazālī's work, indicating in a number of places that in his opinion the Jewish philosopher followed the lead of his Muslim predecessor.[11] This is particularly noteworthy, since Maimonides does not mention al-Ghazālī at all in the *Guide*, nor include him among the authors whose works he recommends to his translator. Recent scholarship has shown, however, that there are al-Ghazālīan aspects in Maimonides' work,[12] lending credibility to Narboni's claims.

A closer look at al-Ghazālī's role in Narboni's "Treatise on the Perfection of the Soul," *Maʾamar beshelemut hanefesh*, may help us appreciate the appeal al-Ghazālī held for a fourteenth century Jewish philosopher. While the "Perfection of the Soul" (hence to be called by its Hebrew name, *Shelemut hanefesh*) is Narboni's 'own' composition, it is actually a patchwork quilt of selections taken mainly from Averroes' commentaries on the *De anima*, both his Short Commentary or Epitome, (*jamʿ* in Arabic, *qiẓẓur* in Hebrew) and his Middle Commentary, the *talkhīṣ/beʾur*. Narboni knew these texts, as well as those of al-Ghazālī, in Hebrew translation, and did not have access to Averroes'

10 Cf. Holzman, p. 303.

11 Holzman, pp. 306, 317.

12 Cf. Amira Eran, "Al-Ghazali and Maimonides on the World to Come and Spiritual Pleasures," *Jewish Studies Quarterly* 8 (2001), pp. 137–166; Alfred Ivry, "The Guide and Maimonides' Philosophical Sources," *The Cambridge Companion to Maimonides*, ed. Kenneth Seeskin, Cambridge University Press, 2005, pp. 68, 69.

Long Commentary on *De anima*, it not having been translated into Hebrew at the time. He was familiar, as has been said, with the translation of a short treatise Averroes wrote on the "Possibility of Conjunction," a text no longer extant in its Arabic original. Ever the commentator, Narboni concludes *Shelemut Hanefesh* with quotations from this Conjunction treatise, and from his own earlier commentary on it.

For the most part, *Shelemut Hanefesh* presents Averroes' understanding of Aristotle's major text on the soul, utilizing the *Short Commentary* for summarizing details of the soul's external and internal faculties of perception and apprehension; the *Middle Commentary* is used for elaborating the functions of the rational faculty, and particularly to establish the nature of the hylic intellect and its relation to the Agent Intellect.

Narboni introduces al-Ghazālī in this book to supplement, and in some places to replace, Averroes' discussion of the physical senses of perception, preferring the brevity of his remarks in al-Ghazālī's *Maqāṣid al-falāsifa*, "Intentions of the Philosophers," as well as some passages al-Ghazālī offers in his *Miʿyār al-ʿIlm*, the "Standard of Science," and in his *Tahāfut al-falāsifa*, the "Incoherence of the Philosophers." Actually, Narboni may be quoting from Averroes' citations of al-Ghazālī's *Tahāfut al-falāsifa* in Averroes' *Tahāfut at-tahāfut*, "The Incoherence of the Incoherence," for in one place at least[13] Narboni proffers Averroes' response to al-Ghazālī as found in that text.

Narboni first introduces al-Ghazālī in *Shelemut Hanefesh* shortly after beginning his paraphrase of the second Book of *De anima*, where Aristotle commences to define the soul and elaborate on its faculties. Aristotle treats the soul nearly entirely in physical terms, describing its faculties, beginning with the faculty of nutrition. He does acknowledge that the intellect is "a different kind of soul"[14] that can exist separately, but it is not until much later, in Book Three, that Aristotle develops his concept of the soul's non-physical intellectual faculty. In accessing an al-Ghazālī text here, Narboni apparently wishes to assure his reader – if not himself – of a more religiously-accommodating concept of soul.

Thus, having barely begun to paraphrase Aristotle,[15] Narboni interrupts his text at *De an.* 412b 5, where Aristotle has stated that the soul is "the first actuality (*entelecheia*) of a natural body which has organs,"[16] to expand upon the

13 *Shelemut Hanefesh* 97:22.

14 *De an.* II. 2 413b 24.

15 *Shelemut Hanefesh* 40:11.

16 Following here and below D. W. Hamlyn's translation, *Aristotle's De anima, Books II and III*, Oxford: Clarendon Press, 1968.

theme. He does this by quoting the definitions of the soul al-Ghazālī brings in *Miʿyār al-ʿilm*,[17] a handbook of logical terms of which al-Ghazālī approved.

Al-Ghazālī points out that the term 'soul' is used homonymously, meaning not just one thing in relation to human beings, animals and plants, and another to angels, but also one thing when referring to the soul as the form of the body, and another thing as a separate substance. Thus the "soul" is both "the first actuality, or perfection (*entelecheia, kamāl/shelemut*), of a natural body which has organs," as Aristotle has defined it, and it is an immaterial substance that moves the body through choice (*ikhtiyār/beḥira*), having an intelligent principle. Even in this latter case, however, the soul is spoken of homonymously, for the intelligently motivating soul is potential – at first – in humans, but actual always in angels.

Narboni continues to quote from *Miʿyār al-ʿilm*, confirming al-Ghazālī's desire to establish the presence of God in all matters pertaining to the soul, both those that seem purely physical as well as those in which the intellect plays a decisive role. Thus, al-Ghazālī is seen to say that the grain of wheat that grows and is nourished when cast on earth does so by the creation of an attribute that it formerly was not disposed to have, receiving it from the *wāhib aṣ-ṣuwar/noten ha-ẓurot*, the Grantor of Forms, *wa-huwa Allāh taʿālā wa-malāʾikatuhu*, God and his angels.

In choosing to quote Al-Ghazālī here, Narboni could appear to be following his source in modifying Aristotle's doctrine of an innate potentiality in all actualized beings, replacing it with a *kalām*-like notion of a volitional endowment of attributes originally absent from an object. Yet in depicting the Giver of Forms as both "God and his angels" al-Ghazālī, as well as Narboni, may be seen as accepting the notion of a deity Who functions as the remote formal principle of sublunar bodies, even as His "angels," the souls or intelligent principles of the spheres, function as their proximate principle. In this depiction, then, Narboni, with al-Ghazālī's *imprimatur*, moves back into the philosophical fold, albeit with a greater sense of traditional religiosity.

Without mentioning it by name, Narboni returns to *Miʿyār al-ʿilm* only one more time in this book, and much later, when he finishes quoting Averroes' Middle Commentary of *De anima*, ending at Book 3, chapter 8 of Aristotle's text. There Aristotle sums up, in his words, "what has been said about the soul,"[18] finding it is "in a way" (*pos*) all existing things, capturing the external world of intelligible and perceptible objects through its faculties of intellection and perception. The soul's faculties correspond to their objects, potential to potential,

17 Ed. Sulaymān Dunyā, Cairo: Dār al-maʿārif, 1969, p. 290.

18 *De an.* 431b 20.

actual to actual, and this leads Narboni to discuss the active and passive states of being in objects, the one a cause of change, the other an effect of it.

Narboni makes his point by quoting al-Ghazālī again, after lavishly praising him: *Hineh niqaḥ beveʾur zeh divrei hameʿir lanu beʾoro venoʾmar: katav Abū Ḥāmid zeh leshono*, that is, "now we shall take in explaining this the words of one who enlightens us with his light and say that Abū Ḥāmid (al-Ghazālī) wrote exactly as follows."[19] Al-Ghazālī is then quoted from *Miʿyār al-ʿilm*[20] to bring out the difference between forces of agency and of receptivity in things. The change that an agent causes in a passive object is limited to complementary qualities, such as the color of hair changing from black to white, or water from cold to hot. The lesson that Narboni seeks to teach through al-Ghazālī, apparently, is that change is determined by the range of possibilities potentially existing in an object; this is a natural and delimited range, as Aristotle has taught. That which is actual emerges from its potential state to actuality.

This principle has an upper limit, and it may be for that reason that Narboni refers to al-Ghazālī again, but this time from the *Maqāṣid al-falāsifa*.[21] Narboni quotes from al-Ghazālī's opening remarks about potentiality and actuality, as found in the seventh section (*qism*) of the Second part (*fann*) of the book, which is devoted to metaphysics.[22]

As al-Ghazālī's remarks indicate, the symbiosis of potentiality and actuality does not obtain with the first principle, whom al-Ghazālī refers to as *al-mabdaʾ al-awwal*, and Narboni as *haboreʾ hariʾshon*, "the first creator," in whom there is no potentiality whatsoever. While Narboni's translation of Al-Ghazālī's locution specifying God the creator is certainly appropriate, it may well be more than al-Ghazālī intended in presenting standard philosophical doctrine in the *Maqāṣid al-falāsifa*. Al-Ghazālī's *philosophical* orthodoxy here is explicit a few sentences later, when he states the lower limit to the emergence of everything potential from something actual. As he says, this doctrine requires that everything generated be preceded by something material, which is impossible for prime matter, it being eternal![23]

All other material bodies follow the path of necessity, however; everything that comes to be has to come from something already actual, the chain of causes containing both remote and proximate agents. Al-Ghazālī cites human

19 *Shelemut Hanefesh*, 134:15.

20 *Miʿyār al-ʿilm*, p. 327.

21 *Shelemut Hanefesh*, 135:4.

22 *Maqāṣid al-falāsifa*, ed. Sulaymān Dunyā, Cairo: Dār al-Maʿārif, 1961, p. 200.

23 *Shelemut Hanefesh* 135:21; *Maqāṣid*, p. 201.

sperm as the proximate cause of man's existence, and gives earth (*turāb*, for which Narboni has "dust," *ʿafar*) as the remote cause.

In so saying, al-Ghazālī is clearly expressing philosophical ideas that he does not essentially share. Narboni, in choosing to reproduce them, is not entirely comfortable with them, though as an Averroist he ought to be. He therefore goes outside his source here to locate a more religiously compatible coda, actually citing the Qurʾān in a verse that paraphrases many *āyāt* in that Scripture.[24] As Narboni has it, "Therefore, it is said in the Qurʾān that God, may He be exalted, created man from clay and placed semen (in him), heating him in a pot (i.e., the womb)."[25] This is most similar to sūra 23, verses 12 and 13, which Arberry translates rather primly as "We created man of an extraction of clay, then We set him, a drop, in a receptacle secure."[26]

As its name indicates, *Shelemut Hanefesh* is dedicated largely to describing the soul as a whole and according to all its faculties. Accordingly, Narboni presents al-Ghazālī's semi-Avicennian descriptions of the soul's faculties a number of times in this book, indicating thereby his sympathy with them. In one place, Narboni quotes from Part Two of al-Ghazālī's *Tahāfut al-falāsifa*, in which al-Ghazālī explains the philosophers' take on the natural sciences.[27] Al-Ghazālī introduces the topic saying that he must first acquaint the reader with the philosophers' view of the human soul as a self-sufficient spiritual entity, in order to show that they are unable to offer demonstrative proofs to that effect. Al-Ghazālī then proceeds, in Narboni's telling, to describe the external and internal faculties of the soul, Narboni omitting al-Ghazālī's later critique of the philosophers' argument.

As quoted by Narboni, al-Ghazālī proceeds to describe the rational faculty, with its division into practical and theoretical activities. Theoretical knowledge, i.e., knowledge of the sciences, is said to be received from the angels, a term later associated with the intelligences of the heavens. This is not to disapprove of these teachings on religious grounds, however, for al-Ghazālī concludes this section of the *Tahāfut al-falāsifa* by saying, "There is nothing in what [the philosophers] have mentioned that must be denied in terms of

---

24 See Q 22:5, and 32:7.

25 *Velakhen amar bi'lquran hashem yitʿaleh baraʾ heʾadam min haṭit vesamo shikhvat zeraʿ vehirtiḥo biqederah"; Shelemut Hanefesh* 136:7.

26 The Arabic is *wa-laqad khalaqnā l-insāna min sulālat*^{in} *min ṭīn*^{in}*, thumma ja ʿalnāhu nuṭfat*^{an} *fi qarār*^{in} *makīn*^{in}; Arthur J. Arberry, *The Koran Interpreted*, New York: The Macmillan Company, 1955, II:37.

27 Cf. Shelemut Hanefesh 97.22; Al-Ghazālī, *The Incoherence of the Philosophers*, trans. Michael E. Marmura, Provo, Utah: Brigham Young University Press, 1997, p. 182.

the religious law. For these are observed matters which God has ordained to flow according to habit (*al-ʿāda*)."[28] In Narboni's Hebrew translation this is rendered, *Ve ein davar mimmah shezakharuhu meʾasher yeḥuyav kefirato batorah, ki hem ʿinyanim niglim himshikh haʾel yitʿaleh haminhag bam*.[29]

As Marmura comments, the last sentence, that the philosophers' description of the faculties of the soul are "observed matters which God has ordained to flow according to habit" (*al-ʿāda/haminhag*), indicates that al-Ghazālī could accept what appears to be a naturally and independently necessary scheme by treating it as a habitual reality only, one that is understood to depend on Divine concurrence.

Al-Ghazālī's approval of the philosophers' description of the soul's faculties, as of the philosophers' characterization of the entire physical world, is further evident a few sentences later in the *Tahāfut al-falāsifa*, when he says that, à propos of his discourse on resurrection and the afterlife, he may well show that the *sharʿ* (given as the *Torah* by Narboni) affirms (*muṣaddiq*) the philosophers' teachings.

Resurrection and the afterlife are referred to by al-Ghazālī as *al-ḥashr wa-n-nashr*, and Narboni, in quoting al-Ghazālī, transliterates rather than translates these terms. This is unusual and puzzling, indicative perhaps of the sensitivity or ambiguity of this subject to Narboni and his translator, as well as Narboni's sensitivity to the reactions of his readers. Though Jews too believed in resurrection and an afterlife, Narboni may not have been eager to have them entertain the Islamic model alluded to by al-Ghazālī.

In non-theological areas, Narboni can be indulgent in his use of al-Ghazālī's writings. Thus, though the preface by which al-Ghazālī introduces his discussion of the faculties of the soul in the *Tahāfut al-falāsifa* alerts the reader that what follows is not al-Ghazālī's own view, Narboni repeatedly presents it as such; we are meant to believe that al-Ghazālī, as well as Narboni, fully embraces the description. On one occasion, Narboni quotes from the *Tahāfut at-tahāfut's* critique of the estimative faculty, which Averroes finds redundant.[30] This does not stop Narboni from including that alleged faculty in the passages he quotes from the *Tahāfut al-falāsifa*, as well as from portions of the *Maqāṣid al-falāsifa*.[31] Obviously, Narboni followed al-Ghazālī, and Avicenna, in accepting the reality of an estimative faculty, despite his alleged partiality to Averroes' teachings.

28 *Wa-laysa shayʾ^un mimmā dhakarūhu mimmā yajibu inkāruhu fi-sh-sharʿi; fa-innahā umūr^un mushāhadat^un ajrā Allāhu al-ʿādata bihā*; cf. Marmura, p. 185.

29 *Shelemut Hanefesh*, 99:22.

30 Ibid., 100:3; *Tahāfut at-tahāfut*, p. 818.

31 *Shelemut Hanefesh*, 103:18.

Accordingly, Narboni quotes both the *Maqāṣid* and *Tahāfut* texts as al-Ghazālī presents (practically verbatim at times) Avicenna's five-fold division of the internal senses, expanding upon Aristotle's tri-fold classification of common sense, imagination and memory. For al-Ghazālī, as for Avicenna, there is the common sense, which coordinates the various external senses' impressions of an object; an imaginative faculty that first receives impressions from the common sense and then stores them as individual images with which it may then fantasize (being then called in human beings the "cogitative" faculty, *al-quwwa al-mufakkira/hakoaḥ hameḥashev*); the estimative faculty referred to before, called *quwwa wahmiyya/koaḥ meḥashev* (again) that triggers a reaction to a perceived sensation, associating the object perceived with a meaning or "intention" (*maʿnā/ʿinyan*) that is not perceivable, such as the fear engendered by a sheep when seeing a wolf; and a memorative faculty that stores this experience and other physically-based impressions of both an individual and general sort.

Throughout, al-Ghazālī's assumption is of the existence of internal faculties functioning by themselves, 'naturally,' but in accordance with God's will. Understanding and agreeing with this, Narboni concludes by saying *ve la'el hamaskim lenakhon*, a difficult sentence that I take to mean, "and (thanks be to) God, who agrees with what is correct." That is, God approves of that which is correctly described, nature functioning according to His will.

There is one recurring motif throughout al-Ghazālī's presentations, and that is his remarking, after describing what appears to be a fully natural process, that it is God, the "Giver of Forms" (*wāhib aṣ-ṣuwar/noten haẓurot*), who is responsible for the whole process. Al-Ghazālī does not mean to indicate by this an Occasionalist doctrine,[32] since all the philosophers recognize God, however understood, as the ultimate source of being. Still, the frequency of this appellation – and Narboni's use of similar statements – is striking, giving the presentation a tone that makes it appear compatible with traditional religious sensibilities.

Narboni's partiality to al-Ghazālī's writing appears quaint at times. An instance of this occurs in al-Ghazālī's remarks on the faculty of smell, as quoted from the *Maqāṣid al-falāsifa*.[33] Al-Ghazālī relates a tale he attributes to the ancient Greeks to illustrate the principle that air is a medium that is affected by odors that mix with it, and that can carry them for many "parasangs" (the air disposed to do so by the *wāhib aṣ-ṣuwar*, of course). According to the Greek

---

32 Cf. Frank Griffel's discussion of Occasionalism in his *Al-Ghazālī's Philosophical Theology*, Oxford: Oxford University Press, 2009, pp. 125–127.

33 Al-Ghazālī, *Maqāṣid al-falāsifa*, p. 350; *Shelemut Hanefesh*, 67:3.

story, a vulture – *rakhma* in Arabic, as in the Hebrew "translation" – was said to have been attracted to the corpses on a battlefield by their odor at a distance of two hundred parasangs. A parasang – *farsakh* in Arabic (from the Persian) and *parsa'* in Hebrew – is equal to approximately two and a half miles, so that the odor carried for nearly five hundred miles, allegedly.

This is too much for al-Ghazālī who finds it impossible that a smell can carry that far, and this despite the caveat that he presented earlier, that it is the *wāhib aṣ-ṣuwar*, the Giver of Forms, who disposes the air to receive odors, and thus could conceivably have created such an occurrence. Clearly though, for al-Ghazālī, God's actions are attuned to nature's habitual order (*ʿāda*), an order he has imposed on nature, and which He seldom alters. As presented by Narboni, al-Ghazālī thus affirms God's presence in nature, mediated by the forces of nature.

This is apparent also in Narboni's chapter on the rational faculty in *Shelemut Hanefesh*, in which al-Ghazālī is quoted from the *Maqāṣid al-falāsifa* discussing the process whereby the Agent Intellect – *al-ʿaql al-faʿʿāl/hasekhel hapoʿel* – enables specific imaginative forms to become abstract intelligible universals.[34] A person's intellect is seen as naturally endowed to form abstract propositions, the Agent Intellect simply facilitating its operation. Incidentally, in this description, al-Ghazālī does not follow Avicenna's description of an Agent Intellect that dominates the process more directly. Nonetheless, al-Ghazālī recognizes that the Agent Intellect is a medium – really the principal medium – through which the Giver of Forms endows a human intellect with its own form and with its ability to conceptualize other forms, i.e., to comprehend their universal nature.

Al-Ghazālī says that the external agent of intellection is the Agent Intellect, which may equally be called an angel. He concludes by saying that the *sharīʿa*, which Narboni again renders as *torah*, affirms the instrumentality of angels in imparting knowledge to ordinary people as well as to prophets. As Narboni presents it, therefore, both he and al-Ghazālī see their legal religious traditions as fully compatible with the teachings of philosophy, both the natural philosophy of the physical world, and the metaphysical realm. The ten intelligences of the heavens (and their accompanying spheres), as well as the forms on earth and their material substrates, are constituted as they are by virtue of inspiration from and obedience to God's will.[35]

In *Shelemut Hanefesh*, then, Narboni presents al-Ghazālī as favorably inclined towards the schematic descriptions of philosophy. Narboni's positive

34 Al-Ghazālī, *Maqāṣid al-falāsifa*, p. 372; *Shelemut Hanefesh*, 105:10.

35 Al-Ghazālī, *Maqāṣid al-falāsifa*, p. 362; *Shelemut Hanefesh*, 104:3.

attitude towards al-Ghazālī may therefore require some modification of Narboni's image as a staunch Averroist. Though he seems to follow Averroes' metaphysical teachings on the annihilation of the self at the moment of conjunction with the Agent Intellect, Narboni, as reflected in his Ghazālīan extracts in *Shelemut Hanefesh*, may have retained sympathy for, and perhaps a belief in, a personal survival of the soul and a personal God.[36] Conversely, his admiration of al-Ghazālī brings out that theologian's affinity not only for the logical schemata of the philosophers, which is well known, but also for their ontological structures.[37] Highlighting al-Ghazālī's *Maqāṣid al-falāsifa* as he does, Narboni teaches us by implication that al-Ghazālī was far from considering all of the intentions of the philosophers as incoherent.

36 Cf. Ivry, "Moses of Narbonne's 'Treatise on the Perfection of the Soul': A Methodological and Conceptual Analysis," *The Jewish Quarterly Review* (LVII: 4, 1967), pp. 293–97.

37 Cf. Griffel, *Al-Ghazālī's Philosophical Theology*, p. 7.

CHAPTER 14

The Changing Image of al-Ghazālī in Medieval Jewish Thought

Steven Harvey

The title of this volume, "Islam and Rationality: the Impact of al-Ghazālī," could well be the title of the present paper with one not insignificant change: "Judaism and Rationality: the Impact of al-Ghazālī." Al-Ghazālī (d. 1111/504) was known to some Jewish thinkers – mostly twelfth century Andalusians – directly through certain Arabic writings of his that had made their way to the West;[1] he was known to many more through the thirteenth- and fourteenth-century Hebrew translations of several of his writings. As this volume underscores, al-Ghazālī was a brilliant and penetrating author in many disciplines. There is no question that his impact upon medieval Jewish thought was marked – but in which areas, and in what ways? In this paper, I will build upon recent research into al-Ghazālī's influence on Jewish thought and present a picture of the changing image of Abū Ḥāmid (as he was known in Hebrew) as he was seen by Jewish thinkers from the twelfth to the fifteenth centuries. We will see which of his writings were translated, and which of them were popular and cited. Special attention will be given to the very different ways in which the medieval Jewish reader reacted to his presentation of Aristotelian philosophy and science and to his critique of it.

When students of medieval Jewish philosophy think of al-Ghazālī's impact upon Jewish thought, what invariably comes first to mind is his critique of Aristotelian philosophy; this critique likely influenced Judah ha-Levi (d. 1141/535) in the twelfth century and Ḥasdai Crescas (d. 1411/814) at the beginning of the fifteenth century. All three thinkers used their profound and intimate knowledge of Aristotelian science and philosophy to compose devastating critiques of those teachings, which they believed were subversive to true

1 Al-Ghazālī was also known to Jewish thinkers in the East, but to a lesser extent. One important such thinker was Abū l-Barakāt al-Baghdādī (d. 1164/559). See Frank Griffel, "Between al-Ghazālī and Abū l-Barakāt al-Baghdādī: The Dialectical Turn in the Philosophy of Iraq and Iran During the Sixth/Twelfth Century," in *The Age of Averroes: Arabic Philosophy in the Sixth/Twelfth Century*, ed. Peter Adamson, London: Warburg Institute, 2011, 45–75, esp. 64–74. See also, n. 25 below.

 | DOI 10.1163/9789004290952_015

religion and could lead to unbelief. In fact, while al-Ghazālī was indeed known to both Ha-Levi and Crescas, who mentions him by name, his impact on Jewish thought went far beyond these two thinkers. One may point to three significant different ways in which the medieval Jewish philosophers related to him:

1. al-Ghazālī as a religious thinker and critic of Aristotelian philosophy, especially in his book *Tahāfut al-falāsifa*;
2. al-Ghazālī as the author of an important philosophic book of logic, science, and philosophy, *Maqāṣid al-falāsifa*;
3. al-Ghazālī as a mediocre philosopher, but successful popularizer of Aristotelian philosophy, again in his *Maqāṣid al-falāsifa.*

It is interesting to observe that in the history of medieval Jewish philosophy, al-Ghazālī – the very al-Ghazālī who exploited his wide-ranging knowledge of Aristotelian philosophy to defend his religion against the heterodox implications of that philosophy – in fact by the fifteenth century may have replaced Averroes, the most faithful Islamic Aristotelian, as the most popular source among the Jews for the study of Aristotelian natural science. Indeed, *Maqāṣid al-falāsifa* survives in its various Hebrew versions, under the title *Kavvanot ha-Filosofim,* in over seventy-five manuscripts, which makes it one of the most popular Hebrew books of the medieval period. How did this come to be? And what did the medieval Jews really think of al-Ghazālī?

In general, the writings of the early Islamic *falāsifa* – by which I mean, in particular, al-Fārābī and Avicenna (Ibn Sīnā), as opposed to the *Mutakallimūn* and the Islamic Neoplatonists – had very little impact on the medieval Jewish thinkers until Abraham ibn Da'ud, writing in 1160/555. Judah ha-Levi is the first one in the West who seems to have been quite familiar with their writings, but he writes against them. As for al-Ghazālī's influence on Ha-Levi, scholars have pointed to and debated the extent of this influence for well over a century. In her book on the *Kuzari, Between Mysticism and Philosophy: Sufi Language of Religious Experience,* Diana Lobel traces the history of the scholarly discussion of this impact from David Kaufmann's exaggerated claims of influence, not only in the critique of Aristotelian philosophy, but also in the use of certain key terms that point to the limits of human reason, such as *'ayn bāṭina* (inner eye) in discussions of prophecy. For her, discussions such as those of Julius Guttmann and David Baneth in the 1920s, which noted significant differences between the two thinkers – such as attitudes toward asceticism and universalistic versus particularistic teachings – presented a "more nuanced picture" of the relationship between them. Lobel herself, through her study, has helped clarify the nature of this influence, particularly regarding attitudes toward *kalām* and philosophy and the use of certain Sufi terms.[2] It may be added that Binyamin Abrahamov, in his review of Lobel's book, has pointed to al-Ghazalī's *Iḥyā' ʿulūm ad-dīn* as a source for certain religious and philosophical notions in Ha-Levi's *Kuzari*.[3] While Lobel clarified the influence of al-Ghazālī on Ha-Levi in her book on Ha-Levi, interestingly, in her book on Baḥya ibn Paquda, the same Lobel put an end to discussion of the possible influence of al-Ghazālī on Baḥya, an eleventh-century Jewish Sufi-influenced ethicist. In that work, she briefly surveys the hundred-year old debate on this influence and indeed points to new similarities between al-Ghazālī and Baḥya, but persuasively dismisses the claims that al-Ghazālī influenced Baḥya on the grounds that Baḥya's active writing career in Spain extended between 1050/441 to 1090/483, that is, before that of al-Ghazālī, and he thus could not have read him.[4] The literary parallels between the two authors may be explained through Baneth's claim that Baḥya and al-Ghazālī shared a common source, Pseudo-Jāḥiẓ's *Kitāb ad-Dalā'il wa-l-iʿtibār*. Lobel refers to this claim and, in the course of her book, marshals further evidence to support it.[5]

While Ha-Levi indeed seems to have been influenced by al-Ghazālī's critique of the philosophers[6] as well as by his account of *kalām*, it is Abraham ibn Da'ud, writing in Toledo twenty years after the completion of the *Kuzari*, who may have been the first Jewish author to take al-Ghazālī seriously as an

---

2 Diana Lobel, *Between Mysticism and Philosophy: Sufi Language of Religious Experience in Judah Ha-Levi's* Kuzari, Albany: State University of New York Press, 2000, esp. 6–8, 171–176.

3 Binyamin Abrahamov, review of *Between Mysticism and Philosophy: Sufi Language of Religious Experience in Judah Ha-Levi's* Kuzari, by Diana Lobel, *Journal of the American Oriental Society* 123 (2003): 244–246.

4 Diana Lobel, *A Sufi-Jewish Dialogue: Philosophy and Mysticism in Baḥya Ibn Paqūda's* Duties of the Heart, Philadelphia: University of Pennsylvania Press, 2007, 1, 14, 39, 119–122, 128, 132–133, 144, 167, 171–172, 175, 209–210. According to Lobel (1–2), Baḥya's active writing career extended between 1050–1090. Al-Ghazālī's period of literary creativity is thought to have begun in earnest with his arrival in Baghdad in 1091. See Hava Lazarus-Yafeh, *Studies in Al-Ghazzali*, Jerusalem: The Magnes Press, 1975, 46–49. Although Lobel's argument is persuasive, it is a bit confusing to write that "A century after Baḥya, al-Ghazālī joins the conversation" (*Sufi-Jewish Dialogue*, 39).

5 See Lobel, *Sufi-Jewish Dialogue*, esp. chap. 6, 117–145. She refers to Baneth's claim in her *Sufi-Jewish Dialogue*, 1, 14, 119–120, 144–145.

6 See also Barry S. Kogan, "Al-Ghazali and Halevi on Philosophy and the Philosophers," in *Medieval Philosophy and the Classical Tradition: In Islam, Judaism and Christianity*, ed. John Inglis, London: Curzon Press, 2002, 54–80. Kogan speaks of each thinker's crisis in his struggle with philosophy, and that each thinker "recovered from that crisis by selectively appropriating a part of his philosophical inheritance to reestablish a basis for religious belief and action" (55).

important source for Aristotelian science and philosophy. His book, the *Exalted Faith*, sought to alter the way Jews approached these disciplines. Ibn Da'ud is commonly considered to be the first Jewish Aristotelian, and indeed he is the first Jewish thinker to put forward a system of Aristotelian philosophy. The independent studies of Amira Eran and Resianne Fontaine, the two leading scholars of Ibn Da'ud today, have shown that al-Ghazālī's *Maqāṣid al-falāsifa* was one of the major sources for Ibn Da'ud's Avicennian Aristotelianism.[7] Ibn Da'ud apparently turned to the *Maqāṣid*, not so much for its science and philosophy – which were essentially Avicennian – but for its formulation and examples. This influence of the *Maqāṣid* is perceptible not only in the first part of the *Exalted Faith*, which deals with the basic principles of Aristotelian science and philosophy, but also in the second part, which deals with the principles of religion. Thus, for example, Fontaine has suggested the possible influence of the *Maqāṣid* in the first part in Ibn Da'ud's definition of the category of 'position,' in his discussions of common sense, in his account of the incorporeality of the intellect, and in the second part in the discussions of the Necessary Existent, the classification of attributes, the nature of prophecy, and the problem of evil.[8] Eran reached similar conclusions and, if anything, is even more certain than Fontaine of the influence of the *Maqāṣid* on Ibn Da'ud. It may be added that the case for the influence of the *Maqāṣid* is further strengthened if one recalls that Ibn Da'ud was likely the Avendauth who collaborated with Dominicus Gundissalinus on the Latin translation of the book in Toledo, perhaps shortly before writing the *Exalted Faith*.[9]

---

7 See Amira Eran, *Me-Emunah Tammah le-Emunah Ramah*, Tel-Aviv: Hakibbutz Hameuchad, 1998, 27, 76, 87, 129, 176, 217, 221, 302, 304–305, 310, 311; and T. A. M. Fontaine, *In Defence of Judaism: Abraham Ibn Daud*, Assen/Maastricht, The Netherlands: Van Gorcum, 1990, 11, 19, 62, 65, 73, 82, 99–100, 122–124, 150, 192, 260.

8 See the references in the previous note.

9 On this identification, see Fontaine, *In Defence of Judaism*, 262–262, Alexander Fidora, "Abraham Ibn Daud und Dominicus Gundissalinus: Philosophie und religiöse Toleranz im Toledo des 12. Jahrhunderts," in *Juden, Christen und Muslime. Religionsdialoge im Mittelalter*, ed. Matthias Lutz-Bachmann and Alexander Fidora, Darmstadt: Wissenschaftliche Buchgesellschaft, 2004, 10–26, and Mauro Zonta, "The Jewish Mediation in the Transmission of Arabo-Islamic Science and Philosophy to the Latin Middle Ages: Historical Overview and Perspectives of Research," in *Wissen über Grenzen: Arabisches Wissen und lateinisches Mittelalter*, ed. Andreas Speer and Lydia Wegener, Walter De Gruyter, 2006, esp. 100–101. For new very suggestive evidence of the identification of Avendauth with Ibn Da'ud, see now Yossi Esudri, "R. Abraham Ibn Da'ud and His Philosophical Book, *The Exalted Faith*: Miscellanea" (Hebrew), in *Adam le-Adam: Studies Presented to Warren Zev Harvey*, ed. Ari Ackerman, Esti Eisenmann, Aviram Ravitsky, and Shmuel Wygoda (forthcoming).

Ibn Da'ud's pioneering work of Jewish Aristotelianism was in a few decades overshadowed by Maimonides' *Guide of the Perplexed*, a work certainly influenced by Ibn Da'ud's *Exalted Faith*.[10] Yet unlike Ibn Da'ud, Maimonides had little patience for Avicenna's version of Aristotelian science. To what extent did al-Ghazālī impact upon Maimonides? Indeed, as I have elsewhere observed, al-Ghazālī is the most famous Islamic thinker not mentioned by Maimonides in the well-known letter to Samuel ibn Tibbon in which he evaluates classical and contemporary writers.[11] Not only is al-Ghazālī conspicuously absent in the letter; the fact is – at least as far as I have been able to determine – that Maimonides nowhere mentions al-Ghazālī. It is hardly conceivable that he was not familiar with al-Ghazālī's various works, for al-Ghazālī was the best known and perhaps most talked-about Islamic thinker in twelfth-century al-Andalus. His writings would have been known to all the philosophically-inclined scholars of the day, let alone to a man like Maimonides who read everything he could, including, by his own admission, the books of the *Mutakallimūn*, among the most illustrious of whom was al-Ghazālī.[12]

Maimonides certainly knew al-Ghazālī's works, although exactly how many of them is difficult to say. The truth is that it is only in the past decades that scholars have begun examining anew and in earnest the influence of al-Ghazālī on medieval Jewish thinkers, and although most of the effort has gone toward uncovering his influence on Maimonides, there is still much to do. The spur for this renewed *Quellenforschung* was no doubt Shlomo Pines' classic study, one half century ago, of the philosophic sources of the *Guide of*

10 On the influence of Ibn Da'ud on Maimonides' *Guide of the Perplexed*, see Eran, *Me-Emunah Tammah le-Emunah Ramah*, esp. 20–21, 26–27, 162–163, 250–251; Fontaine, *In Defence of Judaism*, 5; and Resianne Fontaine, "Was Maimonides an Epigone?" *Studia Rosenthaliana* 40 (2007–8): 9–26.

11 See my "Did Maimonides' Letter to Samuel Ibn Tibbon Determine Which Philosophers Would Be Studied by Later Jewish Thinkers?" *Jewish Quarterly Review* 83 (1992): 51–70, esp. 60, and id., "Alghazali and Maimonides and Their Books of Knowledge," in *Be'erot Yitzhak: Studies in Memory of Isadore Twersky*, ed. Jay M. Harris, Cambridge, Mass: Harvard University Press, 2005, 99–117, esp. 99–100. Note, however, the variant reading in one of the Oxford manuscripts of the letter, recorded by I. Shailat in the apparatus to his edition of the letter in his *Iggerot ha-Rambam*, Ma'aleh Adumim – Jerusalem: Shailat Publishing, 1995, vol. 2, 553, n. 19: "And Abū Ḥamid was the exalted of the scholars of Islam." On the tendency of the scribe of this manuscript to alter the text, see ibid., 553–554, n. 27.

12 See especially Maimonides, *Guide of the Perplexed*, trans. Shlomo Pines, Chicago: The University of Chicago Press, 1963, I, 71, 178–180. It is probable that he became familiar with al-Ghazālī's writings while he was still in the Maghrib. Al-Ghazālī's various writings would presumably have been even more accessible in Egypt.

the Perplexed.[13] Pines did not give al-Ghazālī his own heading or subsection as he did the Islamic Aristotelians and others, but he did devote five pages to him of his seven-page discussion of the influence of *kalām*. Pines seemed almost exclusively focused on the possible influence of the *Tahāfut al-falāsifa* on the *Guide*, and suggested evidence for this influence. In particular, he mentioned the antithesis in Maimonides between the God of religion Who possesses a free will through which He can transcend the order of nature, and the God of Aristotle and his followers Who of necessity acts in accordance with that order; and pointed to its roots in al-Ghazālī's conception of the nature of the divine will, which is reflected, according to him, in *Guide* II, 18. Pines' conclusion was that "no absolutely certain answer can be given to it; however the probabilities are that at the time of the writing of the *Guide* Maimonides had read the celebrated work."[14] In the past two decades, scholars such as Hava Lazarus-Yafeh, Herbert Davidson, Binyamin Abrahamov, Amira Eran, Charles Manekin – and I may add my own name – have noted similarities between al-Ghazālī's teachings and those of Maimonides in the *Guide*, or – in a few cases – argued for the direct influence of al-Ghazālī upon the *Guide* with regard to particular points.[15] Among the subjects of influence noted are the idea of particularization (*takhṣīṣ*), the treatment of knowledge of God, creation of the

13 Ibid., Translator's introduction, lvii–cxxxiv.

14 Ibid., Translator's introduction, cxxvi–cxxx (quotation on cxxvii).

15 For these references and others, see Harvey, "Alghazali and Maimonides," 100–103. In addition, see Chales H. Manekin, "Divine Will in Maimonides' Later Writings," *Maimonidean Studies* 5 (2008): 207–209. Manekin focuses on certain parallels between the discussion of creation/eternity in the *Guide* II, 25 and al-Ghazālī's *Faḍā'ih al-bāṭiniyya*. He notes the similarity between the two texts regarding the rules of interpretation of Scripture when the plain meaning is demonstrated to be false. What is more striking is his suggestion that Maimonides' statement there – that belief in the eternity of the world as Aristotle conceives it "destroys the law in its principle, necessarily gives the lie to every miracle, and reduces to inanity all the hopes and threats that the Law has held out, unless – by God! – one interprets the miracles figuratively also, as was done by the Islamic internalists [*ahl al-bāṭin*]; this, however, would result in some sort of crazy imaginings [*hadhayān*]" (*Guide*, II, 25, 328) – may have been influenced by *Faḍā'ih al-bāṭiniyya*. In that work, al-Ghazālī also refers to the crazy imaginings or *hadhayān* of the *bāṭiniyya*, precisely in connection with their allegorical interpretations of the miracles of the Qur'ān. Now Maimonides, in his various writings, does not refer only to the *hadhayān* of the internalists, but as Sarah Stroumsa has showed in several studies, uses the term to describe several different people and groups of people (see, e.g., Sarah Stroumsa, *Maimonides in His World: Portrait of a Mediterranean Thinker*, Princeton: Princeton University Press, 2009, 138–152). But in this passage from the *Guide*, the term appears, as in al-Ghazālī, in connection with the interpretation of miracles of the internalists.

world, the World-to-Come and spiritual pleasures, the passionate love (*ʿishq*) of God, and al-Ghazālī's attempt to reconcile Islam and Sufism. The suggested texts of al-Ghazālī are the *Tahāfut*, the *Maqāṣid*, and the *Iḥyāʾ*. Avner Giladi has even argued that the very title of the *Guide, Dalālat al-ḥāʾirīn*, is borrowed from al-Ghazālī's *Iḥyāʾ*,[16] where the words *dalīl al-mutaḥayyirīn* ("the guide of the perplexed") occur at least twice, each time as an attribute of God. Yet, although the evidence is mounting for al-Ghazālī's influence on the *Guide*, little attempt has been made to investigate the extent of the parallels and similarities between al-Ghazālī's philosophical thought and that of Maimonides.[17] Some scholars are beginning to point at the direction such a study may take. Davidson, for example, has recently gone so far as to claim that "virtually everything of a metaphysical character attributed by Maimonides to Aristotle but actually deriving from Avicenna can be found" in the *Maqāṣid*.[18] The recent research on the influence of Avicenna on Maimonides[19] has, I believe, prepared the way for an in-depth study of al-Ghazālī's influence on the *Guide*.

If one considers al-Ghazālī's influence on the *Guide*, as it is presented in the recent scholarship referred to above, it appears that Maimonides' primary interest in al-Ghazālī was in his metaphysics or theology, far more than his natural science. In this respect, Maimonides' interest in al-Ghazālī was basically

16 Avner Gilʿadi, "A Short Note on the Possible Origin of the Title *Moreh ha-Nevukhim*" (Hebrew), *Tarbiz* 48 (1979): 346–347. According to Gilʿadi, al-Ghazālī uses the term *dalīl al-mutaḥayyirīn* (the guide of the perplexed) at least twice in the *Revival*, each time as an attribute of God. He suggests that Maimonides may have intentionally slightly modified this phrase in his title to *Dalālat al-ḥāʾirīn* (literally, *The Instruction of the Perplexed*) to avoid exact identification with the divine attribute. See further Michael Schwarz's Hebrew trans. of the *Guide of the Perplexed*, Tel-Aviv: Tel-Aviv University Press, 2002, 11, n. 19; cf. R.J. McCarthy, *Freedom and Fulfillment*, Boston: Twayne, 1980, xliv.

17 One such attempt is Hava Lazarus-Yafeh, "Was Maimonides Influenced by Alghazali?" (Hebrew), in *Tehillah le-Moshe: Biblical and Judaic Studies in Honor of Moshe Greenberg*, ed. Mordechai Cogan, Barry L. Eichler, and Jeffrey H. Tigay, Winona Lake, Indiana: Eisenbrauns, 1997, 163–169. Some general similarities between al-Ghazālī's *Deliverance from Error* and the *Guide* were discussed by Vincenzo M. Poggi in his study of the *Deliverance, Un classico della spiritualità Musulmana*, Rome: Libreria dell'Università Gregoriana, 1967, chap. 6, 103–136. See McCarthy's summary of this discussion in his *Freedom and Fulfillment*, xliii–v.

18 Herbert A. Davidson, *Moses Maimonide: the Man and His Works*, Oxford: Oxford University Press, 2005, 104.

19 On the influence of Avicenna on Maimonides, see Steven Harvey, "Avicenna's Influence on Jewish Thought: Some Reflections," in *Avicenna and his Legacy: A Golden Age of Science and Philosophy*, ed. Y. Tzvi Langermann, Turnhout, Belgium: Brepols, 2009, 327–340, esp. 333–335, and the literature cited there. In particular, see Warren Zev Harvey, "Maimonides' Avicennianism," *Maimonidean Studies* 5 (2008): 107–119.

for the same reasons as it now appears he was interested in Avicenna.[20] It must be added, however, that Maimonides was also interested in al-Ghazālī's *Iḥyā'*, that is in al-Ghazālī, the religious scholar, in ways in which he was not interested in Avicenna. In this connection, I wish to mention as illustrations Eran's article on the influence of the *Iḥyā'* and perhaps other writings of al-Ghazālī on Maimonides' discussion of spiritual rewards and pleasures in the introduction to the section called *Ḥeleq* in his *Commentary on the Mishnah*; and my own study on the influence of the *Kitāb al-ʿIlm* of the *Iḥyā'* on Maimonides' *Book of Knowledge* in his monumental code, the *Mishneh Torah*.[21] This latter study followed the lead of Boaz Cohen and Franz Rosenthal. Cohen in a 1934 article had claimed Maimonides "was able to produce such a remarkable Code because he brought to it a mind thoroughly trained in the law and theology of the Arabs."[22] For Rosenthal, most of the contents of Maimonides' *Book of Knowledge* "can be read as a summary in miniature of al-Ghazzālī's [*sic*] *Iḥyā'*."[23] This influence of al-Ghazālī on Maimonides' legal writings probably escaped the attention of the post-Maimonidean Jewish philosophers who did not read Arabic and who were not interested in al-Ghazālī as a legal scholar, some of whom were quite convinced of al-Ghazālī's influence on Maimonides' philosophical teachings. They were, as we shall see, for the most part, interested in al-Ghazālī as a philosopher and/or as a critic of philosophy. Nonetheless, for a complete picture of the impact of al-Ghazālī on Maimonides, further research on the influence of

20 See, e.g., Harvey, "Avicenna's Influence," 333–335; Harvey, "Maimonides' Avicennianism"; and Idit Dobbs-Weinstein, "Maimonides' Reticence toward Ibn Sīnā," *Avicenna and His Heritage*, ed. Jules Janssens and Daniel De Smet, Leuven: Leuven University Press, 2002, 285–6.

21 Amira Eran, "Al-Ghazali and Maimonides on the World to Come and Spiritual Pleasures," *Jewish Studies Quarterly* 8 (2001): 137–166, and Harvey, "Alghazali and Maimonides" (above, n. 11). See further, Frederek Musall, "'Bücher der Erkenntnis': Einige Überlegungen zum Einfluss Al-Ġazālīs auf Maimonides," *Transkulturelle Verflechtungen im mittelalterlichen Jahrtausend: Europa, Ostasien und Afrika*, ed. Michael Borgolte and Matthias M. Tischler, Darmstadt: Wissenschaftliche Buchgesellschaft, 2012, 241-256.

22 Boaz Cohen, "The Classification of the Law in the Mishneh Torah," *Jewish Quarterly Review* 25 (1934–5): 529. Cohen continues: "and vigorously disciplined by their philosophy and science." For Cohen, Maimonides' idea to write the *Book of Knowledge* was "suggested to him undoubtedly" by Muslim sources (530). Cohen notes in passing that "a study of the *Ihya* with special reference to Maimonides would bring to light a number of interesting parallels" (531, n. 47).

23 Franz Rosenthal, *Knowledge. Triumphant: The Concept of Knowledge in Medieval Islam*, Leiden: Brill, 1970, 95–6. Rosenthal concludes: "It is obvious that his 'Book of Knowledge,' occurring as it does at the beginning of the *Law Code*, owes its title, its being, and its place to the attitude of Muslim civilization toward 'knowledge' and the trends and developments described in this chapter."

al-Ghazālī's legal teachings upon Maimonides, such as that of Gideon Leibson over the past two decades, is needed.[24]

By the time of Maimonides' death in 1204/600, and as a direct result of the changing political landscape in the West, Hebrew was already replacing Arabic as the language of philosophy among the Jews. While some Jews continued to read al-Ghazālī in Arabic, particularly in the East,[25] it is in Hebrew translation that al-Ghazālī made his impact on later Jewish thought. Despite Maimonides' silence on al-Ghazālī, several works of al-Ghazālī were translated in the thirteenth and fourteenth centuries into Hebrew. By far, the most important of these was the *Maqāṣid al-falāsifa*, which was translated at least twice and also summarized and commented upon. As was mentioned above, it is extant today in over seventy-five Hebrew manuscripts.[26] The *Tahāfut al-falāsifa* was not

24 On the influence of Islamic law on Maimonides, see, e.g., Gideon Leibson, "Parallels Between Maimonides and Islamic Law," in *The Thought of Moses Maimonides*, ed. Ira Robinson, Lawrence. Kaplan, Julien Bauer, Lewiston, New York: Edwin Mellen Press, 1990, 209–48, and Joel Kraemer, "The Influence of Islamic Law on Maimonides: The Case of the Five Qualifications," *Te'udah* 10 (1996): 225–44.

25 A good example is Ibn Kammūna. On Ibn Kammūna's use of several texts of al-Ghazālī, see Reza Pourjavady and Sabine Schmidtke, *A Jewish Philosopher of Baghdad: 'Izz al-Dawla ibn Kammūna (d. 683/1284) and His Writings*, Leiden: Brill, 2006, 26. For another example, see Joav Avtalion, "A Comparative Study: Abraham Maimonides' *Kitāb Kifāyat al-'ābidīn* and Abū Ḥāmid Muḥammad al-Ghazālī's *Iḥyā' 'ulūm ad-dīn*" (Hebrew), Ph.D. diss., Bar-Ilan University, 2011. This interest of Maimonides' descendants in al-Ghazālī's *Iḥyā'* is evident as well in David II Maimonides, the last known member of the Maimonidean dynasty. See, e.g., Paul Fenton, "The Literary Legacy of David ben Joshua, Last of the Maimonidean *Negidim*," *The Jewish Quarterly Review* 75 (1984–1985): 1–56, on 32. For a later example of al-Ghazālī's influence, see David R. Blumenthal, *The Commentary of R. Ḥōṭer ben Shelōmō to the Thirteen Principles of Maimonides*, Leiden: Brill, 1974, 13–14. Of course, some Jews continued to read al-Ghazālī in Arabic in the West as well, e.g., Moses ben Joseph Ha-Levi in the 13th century and Joseph ben Abraham ibn Waqār in the 14th century. See, e.g., Georges Vajda, *Recherches sur la philosophie et la kabbale dans la pensée juive du Moyen Age* (Paris: Mouton & Co, 1962), 128, 132, 204–206, 268–271, 283, 295. For an early example of the influence of the *Iḥyā'* in Arabic upon a post-Maimonidean Jewish thinker in the West, see Nahem Ilan, "Fragments of al-Ghazālī's Theory Related to Speech in the Commentary on *Avot* by Rabbi Israel Israeli of Toledo" (Hebrew), in *The Intertwined Worlds of Islam: Essays in Memory of Hava Lazarus-Yafeh*, ed. Nehemia Levtzion et al. (Jerusalem, 2002), 20–58.

26 On the Hebrew translations of *Maqāsid al-falāsifa*, and the early reception history of these translations, see Steven Harvey, "Why Did Fourteenth-Century Jews Turn to Alghazali's Account of Natural Science?" *Jewish Quarterly Review* 91 (2001): 359–376. It now seems unlikely to me that the third Hebrew translation of the book, the one by the anonymous translator, is indeed a separate independent translation. The relation between that

translated until the end of the fourteenth or beginning of the fifteenth century, but was well known through the earlier translation of Averroes' *Tahāfut at-tahāfut*. These were the primary texts through which post-Maimonidean Jewish philosophers knew al-Ghazālī, and they will be the focus of the discussion that follows on al-Ghazālī's impact on medieval Jewish thought. Mention, however, must be made of four other works:[27] (1) Abraham ibn Ḥasdai translated al-Ghazālī's early ethical treatise, *Mīzān al-ʿamal*, into Hebrew in the thirteenth century. This translation, *Mozne Ṣedeq*, was edited and published in 1839, and was prefaced with an introduction by Ibn Ḥasdai filled with praise for al-Ghazālī.[28] Early twentieth century scholarship has argued for the influence of the *Mīzān al-ʿamal* in Arabic on Abraham ibn Ezra and Ibn Da'ud. I have shown its influence also on Joseph ibn ʿAqnin, a younger contemporary of Maimonides, in his *Ṭibb an-nufūs as-salīma*.[29] (2) Jacob ben Makhir translated al-Ghazālī's logical treatise, *Miʿyār al-ʿilm*, in the thirteenth-century, and this text too had some influence on Jewish readers.[30] (3) As for the Hebrew translations of *Mishkāt al-anwār*, one may consult Scott Girdner's paper in the present volume. In this paper, Girdner also suggests the possible influence of the final sections of *Mishkāt* on the seventh chapter of Maimonides' *Eight Chapters*. The *Mishkāt* is an Islamic religious text. Why were medieval Jews so interested in it?[31] It was, after all, translated twice! In addition to Girdner, these

translation and the one by Judah ben Solomon Nathan needs to be explored further. On the many commentaries on this work, see Moritz Steinschneider, *Die hebräischen Übersetzungen des Mittelalters und die Juden als Dolmetscher*, Berlin: Kommissionsverlag des Bibliographischen Bureaus, 1893, 311–326.

27 On a partial Hebrew translation of the *Iḥyāʾ ʿulūm ad-dīn*, see Fenton, "Literary Legacy," 32, n. 39.

28 See *Mīzān al-ʿamal: Compendium doctrinae ethicae, auctore Al-Gazali Tusensi* . . . , Hebrew trans. ed. Jacob Goldenthal, Leipzig: Gebhardt & Reisland, 1839, 3–4.

29 See, e.g., *Jewish Encyclopedia*, s.v. "Ghazali, Abu Ḥamid Mohammed ibn Mohammed al-." On the influence on Ibn ʿAqnin, see Harvey, "Alghazali and Maimonides," 115–117, esp. n. 74.

30 Ben Makhir apparently thought he was translating a work by Averroes. On the influence of this work on Moses Narboni, see Alfred Ivry's contribution, "Al-Ghazālī, Averroes and Moshe Narboni: Conflict and Conflation," in the present volume. On the Hebrew translation and on the wider influence of the *Miʿyār al-ʿilm* on Jewish authors, see Mauro Zonta, "Fonti antiche e medievali della logica ebraica nella Provenza del Trecento," *Medioevo: Rivista di storia della filosofia medievale* 23 (1997): 515–594, esp. 566–567.

31 It may be observed here that while *Mishkāt al-anwār* is indeed an Islamic religious text, it is not without philosophic and general religious interest. On the philosophical aspects of the veil section, see Frank Griffel, "Al-Ghazālī's Cosmology in the Veil Section of His *Mishkāt al-Anwār*," in Langermann, *Avicenna and his Legacy* (above, n. 19), 27–49. There

questions are addressed by Erez Tsabari, who prepared editions of part three of the two Hebrew translations of *Mishkāt*, and is particularly interested in their influence on Jewish thought.[32] (4) Finally, mention must be made of the Hebrew version of the *Ajwiba* attributed to al-Ghazālī, which is extant in eleven manuscripts![33] Why was this text so popular among medieval Jews? Tzvi Langermann has been intrigued by the Hebrew *Ajwiba* for many years and has recently published an important study of it.[34] Langermann addresses the question why the treatise, translated by Isaac ben Nathan of Cordoba, was apparently so popular in Hebrew, despite the fact that the translation was done in what he characterizes as "an extremely difficult style, [where] some passages of the Hebrew version of the *Ajwiba* are simply impenetrable."[35] Langermann's "chief thesis" is that the work "is a coherent text that conveys a clear line of thought, taking an unambiguous stance on some key issues of concern to al-Ghazālī, to Muslims, and to monotheists in general," which is the reason it was so popular among Jews despite the difficult translation.[36] He also connects this interest with a statement by Moses Narboni that a certain short treatise (presumably this work) contains al-Ghazālī's secret or true position on philosophic issues that he rebutted in the *Tahāhut*.[37]

What then about the great popularity of the *Maqāṣid* in Hebrew translation? I have studied this question in two separate articles, and will simply summarize briefly my conclusions.[38] The first translation of the *Maqāṣid* was not made

---

is a lengthy citation in Arabic from the first part of *Mishkāt* in Joseph ibn Waqār's *Kitāb al-Jamī'a bayn al-falsafa wa-sh-sharī'a*; see Vajda, *Recherches*, 128. On the likely sources of the quotations of Abner of Burgos/Alfonso of Valladolid from the *Mishkāt*, see Ryan Szpiech, "In Search of Ibn Sīnā's 'Oriental Philosophy' in Medieval Castile," *Arabic Sciences and Philosophy* 20 (2010): 197–199.

32 See Erez Tsabari, "The Hebrew Translations of *Mishkāt al-anwār* by Abū Ḥāmid al-Ghazālī", (Hebrew), M.A. thesis, Bar-Ilan University, 2012.

33 The text appeared with partial German translation in Heinrich Malter, *Die Abhandlung des Abū Ḥamid al-Ġazzāli: Antworten auf Fragen, die an ihn gerichtet wurden*, Frankfurt a. M.: J. Kaufmann, 1896.

34 See Y. Tzvi Langermann, "A Judaeo-Arabic Poem Attributed to Abū Ḥamid al-Ghazali," *MEAH* 52 (2003): 183–200, esp. 189–190; and idem, "The Hebrew *Ajwiba* Ascribed to al-Ghazālī: Corpus, Conspectus, and Context," *Muslim World* 101 (2011): 680–697.

35 Langermann, "Hebrew *Ajwiba*," 686. On 682, he speaks of "the awkward, at times incomprehensible, diction of the Hebrew translator."

36 Ibid., 682.

37 Ibid., 683–684.

38 See Harvey, "Why Did Fourteenth-Century Jews Turn to Alghazali's Account of Natural Science?" and id., "Author's Introductions as a Gauge for Monitoring Philosophic Influence: The Case of Alghazali," in *Studies in Jewish and Muslim Thought Presented to*

until the very end of the thirteenth century. The fourteenth-century Jews who considered this work differed in their estimation of al-Ghazālī's real motives, whether the work reflected his own views, and the extent to which he succeeded in putting forward the actual opinions of the philosophers. Regardless of these motives, why did fourteenth-century Jews turn to al-Ghazālī's account of natural science? After all, serious students would, and for the most part presumably did, find all they needed in the commentaries of Averroes on the physical writings of Aristotle. Indeed, leading Aristotelians of the time such as Gersonides, Jedaiah ha-Penini, Ibn Kaspi, and several lesser known commentators on Aristotle, showed virtually no interest in the book. The author of the *Maqāṣid*'s most popular Hebrew translation, Judah ben Solomon Nathan, intended it as a popular way for learning science. Yet, it turns out that the most important fourteenth-century Jewish philosophers who studied the *Maqāṣid*, and even praised the work in their introductions – I have in mind specifically, Isaac Albalag, Moses Narboni, Moses ben Judah, and Abraham Avigdor – appreciated its easy-to-read style, but harshly criticized the text, and used it as a springboard for making clearer Averroes' positions and teaching true science. There is little indication that the text was used – at least not in the fourteenth century – as Judah ben Solomon intended it. However, the abundant number of Hebrew manuscripts of the text in the fifteenth and sixteenth centuries argues that it did become a very popular and well read text.[39] Why?

As explanation, I conclude with some remarks on the influence of al-Ghazālī on Ḥasdai Crescas, one of the most creative and impressive of the medieval Jewish thinkers, writing in Spain in the late fourteenth and early fifteenth centuries. Virtually every student of medieval Jewish thought realizes that there is some similarity, if not direct connection, between the thought of Crescas and that of al-Ghazālī. After all, both thinkers – each the leading scholar and teacher of his religious community of his period – used their profound knowledge of Aristotelian philosophy to defend their religion against Aristotelian heterodoxy. I have already also mentioned Judah ha-Levi in this connection; however, there is one outstanding difference between Ha-Levi and Crescas. Whereas Ha-Levi sought to attack and discredit the philosophers in any way

---

Professor Michael Schwarz, ed. Sara Klein-Braslavy, Binyamin Abrahamov and Joseph Sadan, Tel Aviv: Tel Aviv University Press, 2009, 53–66.

39 For sixteenth-century testimonies to the popularity of the *Maqāṣid* and its being "widespread among us," see Hava Tirosh-Samuelson, "The Ultimate End of Human Life in Postexpulsion Philosophic Literature," in *Crisis and Creativity in the Sephardic World 1391–1648*, ed. Benjamin R. Gampel (New York: Columbia University Press, 1997), 163–164, n. 52, and the references there.

he could, including his publicly revealing – by way of the philosopher at the outset of his *Kuzari* – the heterodox secrets of the *falāsifa*, something no *faylasūf* would ever do, Crescas was determined to play by the rules and refute the teachings of the philosophers on the basis of Aristotelian logic and proof. Ha-Levi no doubt found precedent for his betrayal of the philosophers' secrets in al-Ghazālī's proclamation of the Islamic philosophers' heterodox opinions and his concomitant charges of unbelief. Crescas, it has been claimed, found precedent for his reasoned attack against the philosophers in al-Ghazālī's *Tahāfut al-falāsifa*. This latter point – and more specifically, the direct influence of the *Tahāfut* on Crescas – was argued by Julius Wolfsohn over a century ago.[40] Harry A. Wolfson, in his monumental study of Crescas, questioned the view of all those who held that Crescas' criticism of Aristotle was inspired by al-Ghazālī's *Tahāfut*, and, in particular, raised serious doubts about Wolfsohn's conclusions about the direct influence of the *Tahāfut*. For Wolfson, even if Crescas did know the work, it was "far from being" a "predominant influence" upon him. At most, "he may have borrowed certain arguments [from it] which he has incorporated in his own work." In contrast, Wolfson claimed that Crescas "made use of Algazali's *Maḳaṣid al-Falasifah*, though this work is never mentioned by title and no direct quotation from it can be discerned."[41] In 2002 my brother Zev Harvey and I published a study on the influence of al-Ghazālī on Crescas, and affirmed Wolfson's conclusions: the *Maqāṣid al-falāsifa* had a marked and distinct influence upon Crescas; the *Tahāfut* surprisingly did not.[42]

The most striking similarity between al-Ghazālī and Crescas, apart from their common pious goal of refuting the Aristotelianism current in their day, seems to be rarely noticed by historians of Jewish philosophy. Al-Ghazālī – or, at least, the al-Ghazālī that Crescas knew – was the only Islamic student of philosophy who prefaced his critique of philosophy with a separate, clear, and even, at times, improved account of that philosophy. Likewise, Crescas was the only Jewish student of philosophy who prefaced his critique of philosophy with a separate, clear, and even, at times, improved account of that philosophy. But while their critiques were in this respect similar, there is a significant difference between

40 Julius Wolfsohn, *Der Einfluß Ġazali's auf Chisdai Crescas*, Frankfurt am Main: Kauffmann, 1905.

41 Harry A. Wolfson, *Crescas' Critique of Aristotle*, Cambridge, Mass.: Harvard University Press, 1929, 10–18.

42 See Steven Harvey and Warren Zev Harvey, "Rabbi Ḥasdai Crescas's Attitude toward al-Ghazālī" (Hebrew, with an English summary), in *The Intertwined Worlds of Islam: Essays in Memory of Hava Lazarus-Yafeh*, ed Nahem Ilan, Jerusalem: Ben-Zvi Institute, 2002, 191–210.

them. Exactly how different is difficult to say; the conventional understanding of the relation between al-Ghazālī's *Maqāṣid* and his *Tahāfut* has been challenged and rejected, increasingly in the past two decades, by leading scholars of al-Ghazālī such as Jules Janssens and Frank Griffel.[43] But even if one accepts the conventional understanding, it seems rather certain that al-Ghazālī in fact accepted most of the teachings of natural science he explicated in the *Maqāṣid* and saw no need to refute the basic principles and concepts of Aristotelian science.[44] In contrast, this is precisely what Crescas sought to do in his critique of Aristotelian physics in the *Light of the Lord*. Al-Ghazālī believed Aristotelian natural science was essentially true and, as such, posed no problem for the principles and beliefs of Islam; Crescas believed it was faulty science and at the root of heretical beliefs, thus demanding exposition and scientific repudiation.

It may be added that both thinkers made clear that they intended to concern themselves only with the arguments of the best philosophers of the day. At the time of al-Ghazālī, this meant the writings of al-Fārābī and Avicenna; at the time of Crescas, this meant the science of Aristotle and his Greek, Islamic and Jewish followers and commentators. Interestingly, al-Ghazālī is explicitly listed by Crescas as one of the important authors, thus giving legitimacy to him as a serious philosophic authority.[45] In his critique of the principles of Aristotelian physics, Crescas mentions al-Ghazālī five times by name. All of these references mention al-Ghazālī along with Avicenna and as opposed to Averroes.[46] To a great extent, by underscoring the lack of agreement among the leading philosophic authorities, Crescas weakened the philosophic position, and thus paved the way for his own teachings. In these discussions,

---

43 See, e.g., Jules Janssens, "Al-Ghazzālī's *Tahāfut*: Is It Really a Rejection of Ibn Sīnā's Philosophy?" *Journal of Islamic Studies* 12 (2001), 1–17; and Frank Griffel, "MS London, British Library, Or. 3126: An Unknown Work by al-Ghazālī on Metaphysics and Philosophical Theology," *Journal of Islamic Studies* 17 (2006), 1–42. While I find the detailed arguments of Janssens and Griffel – who differ also from each other on the relation between the two texts – compelling, I believe there is also a way to respond to the various difficulties they raise with regard to the conventional view that al-Ghazālī wrote the *Maqāṣid* shortly before the *Tahāfut* as a preparation for his refutation in it of certain teachings of the *falāsifa*. I hope to articulate this different way of viewing the *Maqāṣid* and its relation to the *Tahāfut* in a future study.

44 See, e.g., Frank Griffel, *Al-Ghazālī's Philosophical Theology*, Oxford: Oxford University Press, 2009, esp. 98–101.

45 See the passage in Wolfson, *Crescas' Critique*, 130–131.

46 Three of the passages may be found with English translation in ibid., 218–219, 222–223, and 260–261. For an account of all five passages, see Harvey and Harvey, "Crescas's Attitude toward al-Ghazālī," 201–208. A sixth mention is referenced in the previous note.

Crescas usually favored al-Ghazālī's formulations over those of Avicenna, and the *Maqāṣid* indeed was a dominant source for him in working out his arguments. This may be, to some extent, because this text was more readily at hand and more familiar to Crescas than the books of Avicenna, but it is probably also because Crescas preferred al-Ghazālī's simple and clear formulations.

There are other examples of the *Maqāṣid*'s influence on Crescas where al-Ghazālī is not cited by name.[47] In these examples too, Crescas was drawn to the work for its clear formulations and as an alternative to Averroes' presentation of Aristotle. Unlike the leading Jewish Aristotelians who preceded Crescas in the thirteenth and fourteenth centuries, the al-Ghazālī to whom he turned was neither the bold critic of the philosophers nor an unreliable popularizer of their teachings, but their competent representative and explicator. After Crescas, the *Maqāṣid* received legitimacy as an important scientific text in its own right, and Jews flocked to it, not in order to criticize it, but to learn from it.[48] Ironically, Crescas's own physics – with its new understandings of such key concepts as time, space, infinity, magnitude, void, and motion that paved the way for the scientific revolution and the overthrow of Aristotelian science[49] – would not be appreciated for centuries to come.

Al-Ghazālī was in many respects the most impressive Islamic scholar of the medieval period, and the more we discover about him, the more impressive he becomes. Not surprisingly, he exerted a significant influence on medieval Jewish thought, both through his original texts and through Hebrew translations of them. Our survey – representative, but not at all exhaustive – was intended to highlight the main areas in which al-Ghazālī impacted on Jewish thinkers and, in particular, the very different ways in which medieval Jewish readers reacted to his presentation of Aristotelian philosophy and science and to his critique of it. In so doing, we have sketched the changing image of al-Ghazālī in medieval Jewish thought.

47 See, e.g., the entry 'Algazali' in the index to Wolfson, *Crescas' Critique*, 716–717.

48 See Harvey, "Fourteenth-Century Jews" (above, n. 26), 374–376.

49 On Crescas' new conception of the universe, see Wolfson, *Crescas' Critique*, esp. 114–127. See further, Warren Zev Harvey, *Physics and Metaphysics in Ḥasdai Crescas*, Amsterdam: J. C. Gieben, 1998.

CHAPTER 15

The Influence of al-Ghazālī on the Juridical, Theological and Philosophical Works of Barhebraeus

Hidemi Takahashi

1 Introduction

It is fairly well-known that the works of al-Ghazālī were read by and exercised significant influence on not only Muslims of subsequent ages, but also Jewish scholars – who read his works in Arabic and later in Hebrew translation – and Christian scholars in the Latin West.[1] Less well-known, it seems, is the influence his writings had on the Christians living within the Near East and in particular among the Syriac-speaking Christians. Among these Syriac-speaking Christians, al-Ghazālī's writings were to serve as the source of the material, as well as the form, of a number of works by at least one major author, namely the Syrian Orthodox prelate and polymath Gregory Abū l-Faraj Bar ʿEbrāyā, commonly known in the West as Barhebraeus.

Barhebraeus was born as the son of a physician in Melitene (Malatya) in 1225/6 (622/3 AH). After a period of study in Antioch, Tripoli and, possibly, Damascus, he was ordained bishop at the age of twenty and appointed to the see of Gubos in the vicinity of Melitene. He was later translated to Aleppo, and was the bishop there when the city fell to the Mongols in 1260 (658 AH). In 1264 he was elected to the "Maphrianate of the East," the second-highest office in the Syrian Orthodox Church, with jurisdiction over those areas which had been under Persian rule in pre-Islamic times. As Maphrian Barhebraeus normally resided in Mosul and the nearby Monastery of Mar Mattai, but also made visitations to such cities as Baghdad and Marāgha, the latter of which had become a new centre of learning under the leadership of Naṣīr ad-Dīn aṭ-Ṭūsī. It was on a visit to Marāgha that he died on 30th July, 1286 (685 AH).[2]

Besides his training in Syriac and the ecclesiastical sciences, Barhebraeus clearly also had good knowledge of the Arabic language and of scientific

1 See, for example, the contributions by Girdner, Harvey and Janssens in the present volume.

2 On the life and works of Barhebraeus in general, see Hidemi Takahashi, *Barhebraeus: A Bio-Bibliography* (Piscataway: Gorgias Press, 2005).

 | DOI 10.1163/9789004290952_016

literature written in Arabic. He actually composed a number of scholarly works in Arabic, including several medical works, as well as the *Compendium of the History of the Dynasties* (*Mukhtaṣar taʾrīkh ad-duwal*), a work he is said to have begun writing at the request of Muslims and had almost completed at the time of his death. The majority of his works, however, were written in Syriac. It seems that one of the principal goals of his literary activity was a revival of learning in Syriac; he aimed to accomplish this by synthesizing the older Syriac literary heritage and the fruits of more recent scholarly activities which were available to him mostly in Arabic. One of the Muslim authors he frequently drew upon in doing so – alongside Ibn Sīnā and Barhebraeus' older contemporary Naṣīr ad-Dīn aṭ-Ṭūsī – was al-Ghazālī. It has been known for some time that a number of Barhebraeus' works are closely modelled on al-Ghazālī's, both in their overall structure and their contents. In what follows I shall provide an overview of what is known about the relationship of the works of Barhebraeus to those of al-Ghazālī, and shall then attempt towards the end of the paper to say a few words comparing the attitudes of the two authors towards philosophy and the secular sciences.

2 References to al-Ghazālī in *Candelabrum of the Sanctuary* and *Chronicon*

Before moving on to discuss those works in which Barhebraeus was influenced by al-Ghazālī, we should first mention those instances where Barhebraeus refers to the latter by name. Barhebraeus does not, as far as I am aware, mention al-Ghazālī's name in those works of his where he relied on him as his main source and inspiration. This is, in fact, very much in line with his treatment elsewhere of non-Christian sources, as well as of Christian sources close to his time, whose authors are rarely named by Barhebraeus; in contrast, he regularly cites the earlier Church Fathers.[3] There are, however, at least two instances where al-Ghazālī's name is mentioned explicitly by Barhebraeus. One of the instances occurs in his major theological work, the *Candelabrum of the Sanctuary* (*Mnārat qudshē*), namely in the fourth part of that work, which deals with the Incarnation and was probably written around 1271/2.[4] In refuting the miracles attributed to Muḥammad there, Barhebraeus mentions "Ghazālī in the Book of *Munqidh*" (GZʾLY *ba-ktābā d*-MWNQD, ܓܙܐܠܝ ܒܟܬܒܐ ܕܡܘܢܩܕ) as

3 On this point, see David G. K. Taylor "L'importance des Pères de l'Église dans l'œuvre speculative de Barhebræus," *Parole de l'Orient* 33 (2008): 63–85, esp. 77ff.

4 On the chronology of Barhebraeus' works, see Takahashi, *Barhebraeus*, 90–94.

someone who considered the sum of Muḥammad's virtuous conduct as the proof of his being a messenger and prophet (*īzgaddūtā* and *nbīyūtā*). The reference, however, is not a direct one to the *Munqidh*, since it occurs within a passage that is, rather unusually, explicitly attributed to Fakhr ad-Dīn ar-Rāzī's *Muḥaṣṣal afkār al-mutaqaddimīn wa-l-muta'akhkhirīn*.[5]

Al-Ghazālī is also mentioned by Barhebraeus in his *Chronicon*, a work which seems to have been originally composed mainly in the early to mid-1270's, and in which Barhebraeus regularly gives accounts of the scholars who lived and died during each age.

ܒܗܕܐ ܫܢܬܐ ܡܝܬ ܓܙܐܠܝ ܡܠܦܢܐ ܪܒܐ ܕܛܝܝܐ. ܘܐܬܩܒܪ ܒܛܪܣܘܣ ܕܩܝܠܝܩܝܐ. ܗܢܐ ܣܓܝ ܡܟܣܣ
ܠܛܝܝܐ ܒܡܠܦܢܘܬܗ. ܕܥܠ ܣܚܝܬܐ ܘܕܘܟܝܘܬ ܦܓܪܐ ܒܠܚܘܕ ܝܨܝܦܝܢ ܗܘܘ. ܘܫܒܩܝܢ ܕܟܝܘܬ ܠܒܐ.
ܕܡܢܗ ܢܒܥܝܢ ܚܛܗ̈ܐ ܡܬܘܡܝܢ. ܘܥܠ ܢܙܝܪܘܬܐ ܘܡܣܟܢܘܬܐ ܣܓܝ ܡܦܝܣ. ܘܐܦܩ ܬܚܘܝ̈ܬܐ ܠܐܣܩܠܬܐ ܡܢ
ܕܘܒܪ̈ܐ ܕܐܒܗ̈ܬܐ ܡܕܒܪ̈ܝܐ ܒܟܬܒܐ ܗܘ ܒܡܟܬܒܢܘܬܗ ܗܘ ܪܒܐ. ܘܡܛܠܗܕܐ ܐܬܕܟܪܢܝܗܝ.

In this year [sc. 1422 A.Gr./505 AH = 1110/1111 AD] *GZZ'LY*, the great teacher of the Muslims (*ṭayyāyē*), died and was buried in Tarsus in Cilicia. This man greatly reproached the Muslims in his teachings because they cared only about ablutions and cleanliness of the body, and neglected the purity of the heart, [the place] from which the sins spring forth. He greatly encouraged abstinence and poverty, and brought forth many examples from the conduct of the Desert Fathers in that great work of his, and for that reason we have mentioned him.[6]

---

5 *Le Candélabre du sanctuaire de Grégoire Abou'lfaradj dit Barhebraeus, Quatrième Base: de l'Incarnation*, ed. & trans. Joseph Khoury, Paris: Firmin-Didot, 1964, 118; cf. ibid. 246–249, where the original passage of the *Muḥaṣṣal* is quoted by Khoury.

6 *Gregorii Bar-Hebraei Chronicon syriacum*, ed. Paulus Iacobus Bruns & Georgius Guilielmus Kirsch, Leipzig: Boehme, 1789, 294, l. 13–18; *Gregorii Barhebrœi Chronicon syriacum*, ed. Paulus Bedjan, Paris: Maisonneuve, 1890, 276–277; cf. *Gregorii Abulpharagii sive Bar-Hebraei Chronicon syriacum*, trans. Paulus Iacobus Bruns & Georgius Guilielmus Kirsch, Leipzig: Boehme, 1789, 300–301. MSS. Oxford, Bodl. Hunt. 52 (14th c.?), 85v, b31–86r, a3; Jerusalem, St. Mark's Monastery 211 (ca. 1491/2), 127r, b15–26; Oxford, Bodl. Hunt. 1 (ca. 1498), p. 478, d2–12. There is no mention of al-Ghazālī at the corresponding place in the Arabic *Compendium of the History of the Dynasties* (*Ta'rīkh mukhtaṣar ad-duwal li-l-'allāma Ghrīghūriyūs Abī l-Faraj b. Ahrūn aṭ-ṭabīb al-malaṭī al-ma'rūf bi-Ibn al-'Ibrī*, ed. Anṭūn Ṣālḥānī, Beirut: Dār ar-Rā'id al-Lubnānī, 1983, 346; cf. Ada Rosanna Marino, "Confronto tra il *Ta'rīḫ muḫtaṣar ad-duwal* e il *Chonicon Syriacum* di Abū l-Farağ Ibn al-'Ibrī (Barebreo)," Diss., Università degli studi di Venezia Cà Foscari, 2002/3, 67). As an earlier discussion of the passage of the *Chronicon*, see Herman G. B. Teule, "Barhebraeus' Ethicon, al-Ghazâlî and Ibn Sînâ," *Islamochristiana* 18 (1992): 73–86, here 75–76.

Al-Ghazālī's name is written here (unlike in the passage of the *Candelabrum* mentioned above) with two *zayn*s in the two principal editions of the work as well as the manuscripts I have had access to.[7] The editions and manuscripts, rather disconcertingly, also place al-Ghazālī's death in Tarsus (*ṬRSWS*), rather than the historically-accurate Ṭūs (*ṬWS*). The "great work" in which al-Ghazālī discussed the "conduct of the Desert Fathers" must be the *Iḥyāʾ ʿulūm ad-dīn*, which, as we shall see, was used by Barhebraeus as the principal source of one of his works. Given what we now know of Barhebraeus' dependence on al-Ghazālī, the passage here is both inaccurate and surprisingly brief, especially when compared, for example, with the biographical accounts in the same work of Ibn Sīnā and Naṣīr ad-Dīn aṭ-Ṭūsī, two other Muslim authors whose works were used extensively as sources by Barhebraeus.[8] It may be that the brevity and inaccuracy are due to the sources used by Barhebraeus, but it may also be that Barhebraeus was not yet very familiar with al-Ghazālī's works when he wrote this passage; and it was only later, in the latter half of the 1270's, that he came to read them in greater depth.

3 Dependence of the *Book of Directions* on *Kitāb al-Wajīz*

One area in which Barhebraeus made use of al-Ghazālī as a principal source of the material for his work was that of jurisprudence. As the leader of a minority Christian community within a Muslim-majority society, Barhebraeus was required to adjudicate not only ecclesiastical matters but also civil cases internal to the community under his jurisdiction. Out of the forty chapters in his legal handbook, the *Book of Directions* (*Ktābā d-huddāyē, Nomocanon*), which may have been written in the mid- to late 1270's, the first eight deal with canon law (including matrimonial law), while the remaining thirty-two are concerned with civil law.[9] Although there are other lawbooks in Syriac

7 The name is written as a single word in the manuscripts. It is written as two separate words (*GZZ ʾLY*) in the edition by Bruns and Kirsch ("Gazaz Ali" in the Latin translation) and, no doubt following them, by Bedjan; evidently unaware of the identity of the person behind the name, Bedjan then went on to suggest an emendation of *ʾLY* to *ʿLY* (whence "Ghâzâz ʿÂlî" in the English translation by Budge).

8 See, respectively, *Gregorii Barhebræi Chronicon syriacum* [ed. Bedjan], 219–221 and 529.

9 Syriac text in *Nomocanon Gregorii Barhebræi*, ed. Paulus Bedjan, Paris-Leipzig: Harrassowitz, 1898, and *Nomocanon of Bar-Hebraeus*, ed. Yuliyos Yeshuʿ Çiçek, Glane-Losser: Bar Hebraeus Verlag, 1986. Latin translation by Joseph Aloysius Assemanus in *Scriptorum veterum nova collectio*, vol. 10, ed. A. M[aius], Rome: Collegium Urbanum, 1838, part 2, 1–268.

covering civil law,[10] this is by far the longest of such compilations composed in Syriac. Tracing their origins to communities which arose out of the schisms within the Roman Empire in late Antiquity and which soon found themselves under Muslim rule, the Syriac-speaking Christian churches, including the Syrian Orthodox Church to which Barhebraeus belonged, never had state apparatuses with which they were closely linked. A number of legal texts going back to late Antiquity have survived in Syriac, including the so-called "Syro-Roman Lawbook," but by the thirteenth century these texts would have been inadequate for covering the civil cases Barhebraeus and his colleagues in the episcopate had to deal with. It is clear that in writing the latter parts of his *Book of Directions* Barhebraeus had to have recourse to sources outside the Syriac tradition, and it was inevitably to the lawbooks of his Islamic neighbours, with whom and under whose rule the Syrian Christians lived, that Barhebraeus turned. The close similarity of both the overall structure and the contents of the civil law part of the *Book of Directions* to those of *al-Wajīz fī fiqh madhhab al-Imām ash-Shāfiʿī*, the third in length of the four handbooks of Shāfiʿī law composed by al-Ghazālī, was indicated some time ago by Nallino.[11] In a recent study, Khadra tells us that materials present in the *Book of Directions* but not in the *Wajīz* are to be found in *al-Wasīṭ fī l-madhhab*, the second longest of al-Ghazālī's four handbooks,[12] suggesting either that the civil law part of the *Book of Directions* is based on this latter work rather than the *Wajīz*, or that Barhebraeus, while using the *Wajīz* as the basis, also used the *Wasīṭ* as a supplementary source.

The first sixteen sections (*kutub*) of both the *Wasīṭ* and the *Wajīz* are concerned with Islamic religious practices. This part naturally has not been used in the *Book of Directions*, and has been replaced, as it were, by the chapters of that book on canon law. Nallino has shown that Chapters 9 and 10 of the *Book of Directions* (on wills and on inheritance) go back partly to earlier Christian

10 For an overview of the juridical literature in Syriac, see L. Van Rompay, "Juridical Literature," in *Gorgias Encyclopedic Dictionary of Syriac Heritage*, ed. Sebastian P. Brock et al., Piscataway: Gorgias Press, 2011, 238–239, with the literature cited there.

11 Carlo Alfonso Nallino, "Il diritto musulmano nel Nomocanone siriaco cristiano di Barhebraeus," *Rivista degli studi orientali* 8 (1921–23): 512–580, repr. in id., *Raccolta di scritti editi e inediti*, vol. 4, Rome: Istituto per l'Oriente, 1942, 214–300.

12 Hanna Khadra, *Le Nomocanon de Bar Hebraeus: son importance juridique entre les sources chrétiennes et les sources musulmanes* (extrait de la thèse soutenue pour obtenir le doctorat), Rome: Pontificia Universitas Lateranensis, 2005. The detailed comparison of the material in the *Book of Directions* and the *Wasīṭ* is unfortunately not in the published part of the dissertation.

laws but also contain materials borrowed from the *Wajīz*.[13] The chapters of the *Book of Directions* from Chapter 11 (on sales) to the end then correspond closely in their order to the sections of the *Wasīṭ* and the *Wajīz*, beginning with the seventeenth section of those two works (on sales, *Kitāb al-Bayʿ*).[14]

Besides in the transfer of the material relating to inheritance to before Chapter 11, there are a number of minor changes in the order, such as the transfer of the material from the very end of the *Kitāb al-Wajīz* to chapter 32 (on manumission of slaves) in the *Book of Directions*; a number of sections, such as those on warfare and booty in war, have been omitted altogether as being irrelevant for Barhebraeus' Christian subjects, deprived as they were of their own political and military institutions under Islam. Such rearrangement of the material is typical of the way in which Barhebraeus treated his sources elsewhere.[15]

Another type of change that Barhebraeus made in borrowing from al-Ghazālī's lawbooks is the adaptation of Islamic practices for Christian purposes. For a typical example of such adaptation – already noted by Nallino[16] – one might mention the application of rules concerning the pilgrimage to Mecca to the Christian pilgrimage to Jerusalem. In the sections on vows (*nudhūr*) in his handbooks, al-Ghazālī gives a number of rules related to the vow to make the *ḥajj* on foot.[17] In the corresponding chapter (chap. 38, on *nedrē*) of his

13 See Nallino, "Il diritto musulmano," 535–539. For some further comments on the influence of Islamic law on Barhebraeus' treatment of marriage and divorce in his *Book of Directions*, see Youhanna Salamah, *Séparation et divorce selon l'enseignement de Bar Hebraeus et l'implication oecuménique*, Diss., University of Ottawa, 2005, 172–177.

14 See the list of the correspondences between the *Book of Directions* and the *Wajīz* at Nallino, "Il diritto musulmano," 542–545, and between these two and the *Wasīṭ* at Khadra, *Le Nomocanon de Bar Hebraeus*, 249–257.

15 On the rearrangement of the material borrowed from Ibn Sīnā's *Kitāb ash-Shifāʾ* in Barhebraeus' *Cream of Wisdom*, see Takahashi, *Aristotelian Meteorology in Syriac: Barhebraeus, Butyrum sapientiae, Books of Mineralogy and Meteorology*, Leiden: Brill, 2004, 10–14. See further below on the rearrangement of the material borrowed from al-Ghazālī in the *Treatise of Treatises*.

16 Nallino, "Il diritto musulmano," 554.

17 *Al-Wasīṭ fī l-madhhab taṣnīf ash-shaykh al-imām ḥujjat al-Islām Muḥammad b. Muḥammad b. Muḥammad al-Ghazālī*, ed. Aḥmad Maḥmūd Ibrāhīm, Cairo: Dār as-Salām, 1417/1997, vol. 7, 275; *Al-Wajīz fī fiqh al-Imām ash-Shāfiʿī li-l-ʿallāma al-fiqhiyya al-ḥujja Abī Ḥāmid Muḥammad b. Muḥammad b. Muḥammad al-Ghazālī*, ed. ʿAlī Muʿawwaḍ & ʿĀdil ʿAbd al-Mawjūd, Beirut: Dār al-Arqam, 1418/1997, vol. 2, 234; *Al-Wajīz fī fiqh madhhab al-Imām ash-Shāfiʿī taʾlīf ḥujjat al-Islām Abī Ḥāmid Muḥammad b. Muḥammad al-Ghazālī*, ed. Aḥmad Farīd az-Zaydī, Beirut: Dār al-Kutub al-ʿIlmiyya, 2004/1425, 477; *Al-Khulāṣa al-musammā* [sic] *Khulāṣat al-mukhtaṣar wa-naqāwat al-muʿtaṣar taʾlīf ḥujjat al-Islām*

Book of Directions, Barhebraeus discusses the vow to make the pilgrimage to Jerusalem on foot, whereby he simplifies the rules given by al-Ghazālī, limiting the possible excuse for dispensation from the vow to the case of an illness; he does, however, adopt from al-Ghazālī the rule given in both the *Wasīṭ* and the *Wajīz* (but not in the *Khulāṣa*, the shortest of al-Ghazālī's four handbooks) that when one rides for a part of the journey during a first pilgrimage the vow can be fulfilled by travelling only over those stretches on foot while on a second pilgrimage.[18]

4 Use of *Iḥyāʾ ʿulūm ad-dīn* and *al-Munqidh min aḍ-ḍalāl* in *Ethicon* and *Book of the Dove*

Another area in which Barhebraeus stands under the influence of al-Ghazālī is that of moral and mystical theology. Barhebraeus' *Ethicon* (*Ktābā d-ītīqōn*), which was completed in July 1279 (678 AH), may be described as a guidebook for pious Christian living. There is no dearth of guides for monastic life in Syriac, but the *Ethicon* is unique in its kind in Syriac in that it is addressed also to the laity.[19]

The work is divided into four books (*mēmrē*), dealing with (1) the training of the body through devotional practices (i.e. prayer, fasting, pilgrimage etc., *mṭakksūt zawʿē d-durrāshā pagrānāyā*, in 9 chapters); (2) the proper conduct for the sustenance of the body (*taqnūt dubbārē d-quyyāmā pagrānāyā*, in 6 chapters; (3) the liberation of the soul from foul passions (*meṣṭall^{e}lānūt napshā men ḥashshē shkīrē*, in 12 chapters); and (4) the adornment of the soul through virtuous conduct (*meṣṭabbtānūt napshā ba-znayyā myattrē*, in 16 chapters). For those familiar with al-Ghazālī's *Iḥyāʾ ʿulūm ad-dīn*, it will be immediately obvious that these four books correspond to the four "quarters" of the *Iḥyāʾ* which deal, respectively, with matters relating to worship (*ʿibādāt*),

---

wa-barakat al-anām al-imām Abī Ḥāmid Muḥammad b. Muḥammad b. Muḥammad al-Ghazālī, ed. Amjad Rashīd Muḥammad ʿAlī, Jeddah: Dār al-Minhāj, 1428/2007, 674.

18 *Nomocanon Gregorii Barhebræi*, ed. Bedjan, 475. On the parallel adaptation of the material relating to the *ḥajj* in al-Ghazālī's *Iḥyāʾ ʿulūm ad-dīn* in Barhebraeus' *Ethicon*, see Herman G.B. Teule, "The Perception of the Jerusalem Pilgrimage in Syriac Monastic Circles," in *VI Symposium Syriacum 1992*, ed. René Lavenant, Rome: Pontificio Istituto Orientale, 1994, 311–321.

19 Edition of the whole work: *Ethicon seu Moralia Gregorii Barhebræi*, ed. Paulus Bedjan, Paris-Leipzig: Harrassowitz, 1898. Critical edition and translation of Book 1: Gregory Barhebraeus, *Ethicon. Mēmrā I*, ed./trans. Herman G.B. Teule, 2 vols., Louvain: Peeters, 1993.

customs (*ʿādāt*), things that are detrimental to the soul (*muhlikāt*) and things that lead to salvation (*munjiyāt*). The correspondence not only of the overall structure but also of a significant part of the contents of the *Ethicon* to the content of the *Iḥyāʾ* was demonstrated by Wensinck, who appended the translations of some of those parts of the *Ethicon* derived from al-Ghazālī (Book 4, chap. 15, and Book 1, chap. 5) to his translation of Barhebraeus' *Book of the Dove*.[20] More detailed studies on the relationship of the *Ethicon* to al-Ghazālī's *Iḥyāʾ* have been conducted in recent years especially by Teule, who published a critical edition of the first book of the work and has been preparing an edition of the remaining three books.[21]

Given its Christian subject matter, the *Ethicon* is clearly not a simple paraphrase or summary of the *Iḥyāʾ ʿulūm ad-dīn*. Much of its contents are derived from Christian sources, especially from earlier ascetic literature.[22] Where al-Ghazālī cites passages from the Qurʾān and the *ḥadīth*, Barhebraeus frequently replaces these passages with quotations from the Bible and the Fathers. For example, where al-Ghazālī uses quotations from the Qurʾān in talking about meditation on the wonders of the Creation,[23] Barhebraeus has a chapter "on remembrance (*ʿuhdānā*) of God and meditation (*hergā*) of the

---

20 A. J. Wensinck, *Bar Hebraeus's Book of the Dove together with Some Chapters from His Ethikon*, Leiden: Brill, 1919.

21 Cf. note 19 above. For further studies on the *Ethicon*, see the list at Takahashi, *Barhebraeus*, 203–204. To this list might now be added: Herman Teule, "A Christian-Muslim Discussion: The Importance of the Bodily and Spiritual Purity. A Chapter from the Second Memro of Barhebraeus' Ethicon on 'The Right Conduct Regarding the Sustenance of the Body,'" in *Syriac Polemics: Studies in Honour of Gerrit Jan Reinink*, ed. W. J. van Bekkum et al., Louvain: Peeters, 2007, 193–203; id., "La vie dans le monde: perspectives chrétiennes. Une étude de Memrō II de *l'Ethicon* de Grégoire Abū l-Farağ Barhebræus," *Parole de l'Orient* 33 (2008): 115–128; id., "An important Concept in Muslim and Christian Mysticism: the Remembrance of God – *dhikr Allah* – *ʿuhdōnō d-Alōhō*," in *Gotteserlebnis und Gotteslehre. Christliche und islamische Mystik im Orient*, ed. Martin Tamcke, Wiesbaden: Harrassowitz, 2010, 11–24; also Georg Günter Blum, *Die Geschichte der Begegnung christlich-orientalischer Mystik mit der Mystik des Islams*, Wiesbaden: Harrassowitz, 2009, 619–710 (Zweiter Teil, VI. Kapitel: Barʿ Ebraya: Höhepunkt und Abschluß christlich-orientalischer und islamischer Mystik); Lev Weitz, "Ghazālī, Bar Hebraeus, and 'the Good Wife'," *Journal of the American Oriental Society* 134 (2014): 203–223.

22 For a survey of the Christian sources used by Barhebraeus in his *Ethicon*, see Herman Teule, "Christian Spiritual Sources in Barhebraeus' *Ethicon* and the Book of the Dove," *Journal of Eastern Christian Studies* 60 (2008): 333–354.

23 In the section "Bayān kaifiyyat at-tafakkur fī khalq Allāh taʿālā" in *Iḥyāʾ*, Book 39, Kitāb at-Tafakkur (*Iḥyāʾ ʿulūm ad-dīn taṣnīf al-imām Abī Ḥāmid Muḥammad b. Muḥammad al-Ghazālī al-mutawaffā fī sanat 505 h.*, Beirut: Dār al-Maʿrifa, 1403/1982, IV. 435–448.

wonders of His Creation." The chapter is divided into nine sections:[24] the first two are entitled "discourse of the Fathers on the virtue of remembrance" and "on the fact that the remembrance of God is confirmed in the soul through meditation on his Creation," and the last's title is "on the fact that the mind is enlightened through sound meditation." In the remaining six sections (sections 3 to 8) we are given a hexaemeral account of the Creation, which appears to be a summary of similar accounts of the events of the Six Days as given in two other works of Barhebraeus composed around the same time as or just before the *Ethicon* (*Book of Rays* and *Ascent of the Mind*).[25] Nevertheless, a significant amount of the actual content of the *Ethicon* is derived from the *Iḥyāʾ*, especially those places where al-Ghazālī had theorised on the practices and phenomena under discussion.

Another work by Barhebraeus that is closely related to his *Ethicon* is his *Book of the Dove* (*Ktābā d-yawnā*), a shorter "spiritual guide" addressed specifically to monks, or, to be more precise, to solitaries who find themselves "without or far from a leader," as it is stated in its introduction.[26] It is divided into four chapters entitled: (1) "cultivation (*pulḥānā*) of the body practised in the monastery" (in 10 sections); (2) "cultivation of the soul perfected in the cell" (in 10 sections); (3) "on the spiritual rest of the perfect" (in 10 sections); and (4) "a tale of the author's progress in the teachings and some revelatory sentences." This work was evidently written after the *Ethicon*, and in it Barhebraeus frequently repeats in a shorter form the discussions he had conducted in the *Ethicon*, including those he originally borrowed from the *Iḥyāʾ*.

Material borrowed from the *Iḥyāʾ* in the *Ethicon* thus often resurfaces in an abbreviated form in the *Book of the Dove*. As a typical instance, we might

---

24 *Ethicon*, 4.13, ed. Bedjan (as n. 19 above), 447–466.

25 See Takahashi, "Observations on Bar ʿEbroyo's Marine Geography," *Hugoye: Journal of Syriac Studies*, 6/1 (2003): 77–130; id., "Bemerkungen zum Buch der Blitze (Ktobo d-zalge) des Barhebraeus," in *Die Suyoye und ihre Umwelt. 4. deutsches Syrologen-Symposium in Trier 2004*, ed. Martin Tamcke & Andreas Heinz, Münster: LIT, 2005, 407–422.

26 *Liber columbæ seu Directorium monachorum Gregorii Barhebræi*, ed. Paulus Bedjan, Paris-Leizpig: Harrassowitz, 1898 [= appendix to Bedjan's edition of the *Ethicon*], 521; *Abulfaragii Gregorii Bar-Hebraei mafriani Orientis Kithâbhâ dhiyaunâ seu Liber columbae*, ed. Gabriel Cardahi, Rome: Academia Lynceorum, 1898, 1; *Ktobo d-yawno meṭul duboro d-iḥidoye b-karyoto men syome d-abun ṭubtono Mor Grigoriyos mafryono qadisho d-Madnḥo d-metidaʿ Bar ʿEbroyo*, ed. Yuḥanon Dolabani, ʿUmro d-Mor Ḥananyo-Dayr al-Zaʿfarān, 1916, 1; *Ktobo d-yawno meṭul duboro d-iḥidoye b-karyoto men syome d-abun ṭubtono Mor Grigoriyos mafryono qadisho d-Madnḥo d-metidaʿ Bar ʿEbroyo. Bar Hebraeus's Book of the Dove*, ed. Yuliyos Yeshuʿ Çiçek, Glane-Losser: Dayro d-Mor Afrem Suryoyo, 1983, 1; English translation at Wensinck, *Bar Hebraeus's Book of the Dove*, 3.

mention here Barhebraeus' discussion of love. Where al-Ghazālī had begun his discussion of love in the *Iḥyāʾ* (in Book 36)[27] with a section containing quotations from the *ḥadīth* and Islamic jurists (*bayān shawāhid ash-sharʿ fī ḥubb al-ʿabd li-llāh taʿālā*), Barhebraeus began his chapter on the love of God in his *Ethicon* (Book 4, chap. 15)[28] with a section on the "sayings of the Fathers concerning love towards God" (with quotations from Antony, Basil, Evagrius, John of Dalyatha and Isaac of Nineveh). In the second section of the chapter ("on the definition of love, its divisions and its causes"), Barhebraeus first gives us a definition of love that is derived from al-Ghazālī, namely that it is "the inclination of the soul towards communion (*baytāyūtā*) with an object that can be grasped (*metdarkānā*, √drk),"[29] and goes on, as al-Ghazālī had done,[30] to enumerate five causes of love, which are: (1) perpetuation of being and the existence of the self (*ammīnūt ītūtā wa-shkīḥūt yātā*);[31] (2) accomplishment

27 *Kitāb al-Maḥabba wa-sh-shawq wa-l-uns wa-r-riḍā*, ed. Beirut 1982, IV.293–361. English translation: Eric Ormsby, *Al-Ghazali on Love, Longing, Intimacy & Contentment*, Cambridge: Islamic Texts Society, 2011.

28 Ed. Bedjan, 473–506; English translation of the chapter, with notes indicating corresponding passages of the *Iḥyāʾ*, in Wensinck, *Bar Hebraeus' Book of the Dove* (as n. 20 above), 85–117. As a discussion of the material in this chapter, see Herman Teule, "L'amour de Dieu dans l'œuvre de Bar'Ebroyo," in *Dieu Miséricorde Dieu Amour: Actes du colloque VIII Patrimoine Syriaque*, vol. 1 (Antélias: CERO, 2003), 259–275.

29 Cf. *Iḥyāʾ*, ed. Beirut 1982, IV.296.15: أنه لا يتصور محبة إلا بعد معرفة وإدراك إذ لا يحب الإنسان إلا ما يعرفه ("… that love is conceived only after knowledge and perception [*idrāk*, √drk], since man loves only what he knows"); IV.296.20: فالحب عبارة عن ميل الطبع إلى الشيء الملذ ("love is therefore the term for the inclination of nature towards a pleasing object"). For a discussion of the definition in the *Ethicon*, including a discussion of the term "*baytāyūtā*," derived from the word *baytā* ("house, family"), see Teule, "L'amour de Dieu," 264–268.

30 *Iḥyāʾ*, ed. Beirut 1982, IV.296–300.

31 *Iḥyāʾ*, ed. Beirut 1982, IV.296.23–24: فإذن المحبوب الأول للإنسان ذاته ثم اعضاءه ثم ماله وولده وعشيرته وأصدقائه. فالأعضاء محبوبة وسلامتها مطلوبة لأن كمال الوجود ودوام الوجود موقوف عليها... ("Therefore, man's first object of love is himself, then his limbs, then his possessions, his children, his family and his friends. The limbs are loved and their safety sought after, because the perfection of the existence and the perpetuation of the existence depend upon them …"); 301.8: فأما السبب الأول وهو حب الإنسان نفسه وبقاءه وكماله ودوام وجوده ("The first reason [why love should be directed towards God] is man's love for himself, his preservation, his perfection and the perpetuation of his existence").

of what benefits us (*sāʿōrūt ṭābtā*);[32] (3) outward beauty (*shuprā barrāyā*);[33] (4) inward beauty (*shuprā gawwāyā*); and (5) hidden affinity and secret similarity (*ḥyānūtā ksītā w-damyūtā gnīztā*).[34] In the *Book of the Dove*, we find a section on "the causes of love" in the third chapter.[35] The citations from the Fathers and the definition of love are omitted there, and the section begins with the list of the five causes of love, which, though phrased slightly differently, are the same as the five mentioned in the *Ethicon*: sustenance of the self (*quyyāmā da-qnōmā*), accomplishment of what benefits us, outward beauty, inward beauty, and hidden similarity (*dāmyūtā ksītā*). Barhebraeus then goes on in the rest of the section to explain how these causes relate to the love of God, summarizing what he had said on the matter in his *Ethicon* and inserting, at the same time, a number of quotations from the Bible, which he had not used in his earlier work.[36]

Beyond the *Iḥyāʾ*, the *Book of the Dove* owes a significant element of its content to another work by al-Ghazālī, namely his *al-Munqidh min aḍ-ḍalāl*. At the beginning of the fourth chapter of his *Book of the Dove*, Barhebraeus gives us an autobiographical account of his journey through life.[37] The very opening words

---

32 This corresponds to al-Ghazālī's second cause, the act of benevolence (*iḥsān*, *Iḥyāʾ*, ed. Beirut 1982, IV.298.2).

33 This is not the same as al-Ghazālī's third cause, which is the love of a thing for itself (*Iḥyāʾ*, ed. Beirut 1982, IV.298.15: السبب الثالث أن يحب الشيء لذاته لا لحظ ينال منه وراء ذاته, "The third cause is that a thing is loved for its own sake and not for the good that is conferred by it after itself"), and al-Ghazālī treats beauty, both inward and outward, as his fourth cause, but Barhebraeus does incorporate al-Ghazālī's third cause into his definition of outward beauty by saying that outward beauty "is loved for its own sake and not for the sake of something (else)."

34 Cf. *Iḥyāʾ*, ed. Beirut 1982, IV.300.18: السبب الخامس المناسبة الخفية بين المحب والمحبوب ("Fifth cause: the secret relationship between the lover and the beloved").

35 *Book of the Dove*, 3.5, ed. Bedjan, 569; ed. Cardahi, 64–65; ed. Dolabani, 56–57; ed. Çiçek, 47–48; English translation at Wensinck, *Bar Hebraeus's Book of the Dove*, 51–52; English and French translations of the section, respectively, by Sebastian Brock and Ray Jabre Mouawad also in *Textes syriaques. Dieu Miséricorde Dieu Amour. Patrimoine Syriaque Colloque VIII*, Antélias: Markaz ad-Dirāsāt wa-l-Abḥāth al-Mashriqiyya [CERO], 2002, 61–62.

36 The explanations provided here correspond to those in the third section of the chapter in the *Ethicon* (4.15.3: "on the fact that the love of God is justified in relation to all the causes"), which in turn answers to the section of the *Iḥyāʾ* on the fact that God alone is the deserving object of love ("*Bayān anna al-mustaḥiqq li-l-maḥabba huwa Allāh waḥdahu*," ed. Beirut 1982, IV.300–307).

37 Ed. Bedjan, 577–579; ed. Cardahi, 75–78; ed. Dolabani, 66–68; ed. Çiçek 55–57; Wensinck, *Bar Hebraeus's Book of the Dove*, 60–62. English translation of the passage also in

of the passage, where Barhebraeus tells us that ever since his "tender youth" (lit. "tender nails") he has been engaged in the study of various teachings, echo the beginning of the autobiographical account in the *Munqidh*,[38] and this might be interpreted as Barhebraeus acknowledging his debt to al-Ghazālī.[39] Although the passage is a short one in comparison with the *Munqidh* as a whole, this account in which Barhebraeus tells us about his engagement and subsequent disappointment with the secular sciences, his spiritual crisis, and his final salvation through mysticism, has an unmistakable similarity, both in its structure and its contents, to al-Ghazālī's account in his *Munqidh*.

5 Use of *Maqāṣid al-falāsifa* in *Treatise of Treatises*

A third area in which Barhebraeus is indebted to al-Ghazālī is that of philosophy. Among Barhebraeus' philosophical works, three cover the whole range of Aristotelian philosophy, beginning with logic and moving on to natural philosophy and metaphysics. The intermediate of the three in length, the *Treatise of Treatises* (*Tēgrat tēgrātā*), must be the earliest in date, since it is referred to in the shorter *Conversation of Wisdom* (*Swād sōpiya*), while the longest, the *Cream of Wisdom* (*Ḥēwat ḥekmtā*) was only completed in February 1286 (685 AH), just five months before the author's death. Baumstark, who quoted a pas-

Brian Colless, *The Wisdom of the Pearlers. An Anthology of Syriac Christian Mysticism*, Kalamazoo: Cistercian Publications, 2008, 172–174. For discussions of the relationship of the passage to the *Munqidh*, see Samir Khalil Samir, "Cheminement mystique d'Ibn al-ʿIbrī (1226–1286)," *Proche-Orient Chrétien* 37 (1987): 71–89; id., "Un récit autobiographique d'Ibn al-ʿIbrī," *Dirasat. Lettres & Sciences humaines*, Université Libanaise, Faculté de Pédagogie, 15 (1988): 15–51.

38 *Al-Munqidh min aḍ-ḍalāl wa-l-mūṣil ilā dhī l-ʿizza wa-l-jalāl taʾlīf ḥujjat al-Islām Abī Ḥāmid al-Ghazālī*, ed. Jamīl Ṣalībā & Kāmil ʿAyyād, Beirut: Dār al-Andalus, 1967, 26.1ff.

39 Another autobiographical account by Barhebraeus, left incomplete at his death and called the *Childhood of the Mind* (*Ṭalyūt hawnā*), is found appended to all the modern editions, as well as a number of recent (19th c.) manuscripts, of the *Book of the Dove* (see n. 26 above; the piece is usually found with collections of Barhebraeus' poems in older manuscripts). It has recently been noted that this piece is closely modelled on a Persian work by Suhrawardi, *On the State of the Childhood* (*Risāla fī ḥālat aṭ-ṭufūliyya*); see Jean Fathi, "The Mystic Story of Childhood from Suhrawardi to Bar ʿEbroyo: The Maphrian's last Syriac work and its Persian model," forthcoming in the proceedings of the Second Aleppo Syriac Colloquium: "The Life and Works of Mar Bar Ebroyo (Barhebraeus) +1286" (held at the Syrian Orthodox Archdiocese of Aleppo, 1st–4th July, 2010). Here too, the similarity of the title, as well as the opening words of the piece, to its model may be seen as the sign of an open acknowledgement of the debt by Barhebraeus.

sage from the *Treatise of Treatises* in his *Aristoteles bei den Syrern*,[40] considered the work as a whole to be a reworking of Ibn Sīnā's *ʿUyūn al-ḥikma*.[41] The passage that Baumstark quoted, a passage on the classification of the sciences from the beginning of the second part of work, does indeed look like a translation of the corresponding passage of the *ʿUyūn al-ḥikma*.[42] When we begin comparing the rest of *Treatise of Treatises* with the *ʿUyūn al-ḥikma*, however, it soon becomes clear that further correspondence between the two works is difficult to find. I have had the occasion to show elsewhere that the details of the sections of the *Treatise of Treatises* dealing with mineralogy and meteorology, as well as the overall conception of the work, have much more in common with al-Ghazālī's *Maqāṣid al-falāsifa*; indeed, a comparison of the mineralogical and meteorological material in the *Treatise of Treatises* with a number of works that are likely to have been available to Barhebraeus – including Ibn Sīnā's *ʿUyūn al-ḥikma*, as well as the same author's *Kitāb ash-Shifāʾ* and *Kitāb an-Najāt* – shows that the order in which the material is presented most closely matches the order in the *Maqāṣid al-falāsifa*, and that the wording of the material also frequently mirrors the wording in the *Maqāṣid*, although Barhebraeus has, following his usual practice, supplemented the material taken from the *Maqāṣid* with material borrowed from elsewhere (including, in this case, the Syriac version of the Pseudo-Aristotelian *De mundo*).[43]

To provide an overview of the contents of the *Treatise of Treatises* and its relationship to the *Maqāṣid al-falāsifa*, I list below the chapter headings of the work as a whole, as well as the headings of the sections within one of these chapters, together with the headings of the corresponding parts of the *Maqāṣid al-falāsifa*. For the section headings in the chapter on the divisions of Being, I have also added the corresponding headings in Ibn Sīnā's *Dānishnāma-yi ʿAlāʾī*, the principal source of al-Ghazālī's *Maqāṣid*, in order to show that the wording of the *Treatise of Treatises* more closely resembles that of the *Maqāṣid al-falāsifa* than the *Dānishnāma*, which Barhebraeus could also potentially have used given what we know about his ability to read Persian. The numbers

40 Anton Baumstark, *Aristoteles bei den Syrern*, vol. 1, Leipzig: Teubner, 1900, 164–165.

41 Baumstark, op. cit., 184, n. 1; cf. id., *Geschichte der syrischen Litteratur*, Bonn: Marcus & Weber, 1922, 317.

42 *Ibn Sina Risâleleri 1*, ed. Hilmi Ziya Ülken, Ankara: Türk Tarih Kurumu Basımevi, 1953, 13–14.

43 Takahashi, "Barhebraeus und seine islamischen Quellen. Têgrat têgrātā (Tractatus tractatuum) und Ġazālīs Maqāṣid al-falāsifa," in *Syriaca. Zur Geschichte, Theologie, Liturgie und Gegenwartslage der Syrischen Kirchen. 2. Deutsches Syrologen-Symposium (Juli 2000, Wittenberg)*, ed. Martin Tamcke, Münster: LIT, 2002, 147–175.

below following the headings in the *Treatise of Treatises* indicate the folios where each chapter/section begins in MS. Cambridge University Library, Add. 2003, the oldest manuscript of the work copied within the author's lifetime in 1276. The numbers accompanied by the letter "D" following the headings in the *Maqāṣid al-falāsifa* indicate the pages in Dunyā's 1961 edition of the work,[44] and the numbers marked "M" following the headings in the *Dānishnāma* the pages in Muʿīn's edition of the metaphysical section of that work.[45]

Treatise of Treatises *and* Maqāṣid al-falāsifa: *Chapter Headings*

Part 1. Logic	
Introduction: "Introduction before logic, and [on] what use arises from it" (ܡܥܠܢܘܬܐ ܕܩܕܡ ܠܘܓܝܩܝ ܘܡܢܐ ܗܘ ܝܘܬܪܢܐ ܕܡܢܗ̇, 3r)	[Introduction] تمهيد المنطق وبيان فائدته وأقسامه (D33)
1.1. On simple words and the five universals (ܥܠ ܡ̈ܠܐ ܦܫܝܛ̈ܬܐ. ܘܥܠ ܚܡܫ ܟ̈ܘܠܢܝܬܐ, 4r)	1.1. دلالة الألفاظ (D39); and 1.2 فى المعانى الكلية واختلاف نسبها وأقسامها (D44)
1.2. On the composition of all kinds of protases and those things that follow them (ܥܠ ܪ̈ܘܟܒܐ ܕܟܠ ܙܢ̈ܝ ܦܪ̈ܘܛܐܣܝܣ ܘܥܠ ܗ̇ܠܝܢ ܕܡܢܩܦ ܠܗܘܢ ܢܩܦܢ, 12r)	
1.3. On the second composition of affirmation (ܡܐܡܪܐ ܬܠܝܬܝܐ ܥܠ ܪܘܟܒܐ ܬܪܝܢܐ ܕܡܫܪܪܢܘܬܐ, 22v)	1.3. فى تركيب المفردات وأقسام القضايا (D53)
1.4. On apodictic syllogism in particular (ܥܠ ܣܘܠܘܓܝܣܡܘܣ ܐܦܘܕܝܩܛܝܩܐ ܕܝܚܝܕܐܝܬ)	1.4. فى تركيب القضايا لتصير قياسًا (D66)
1.5. On sophistic, or misleading, syllogisms (ܥܠ ܣ̈ܘܠܘܓܝܣܡܘܣ ܣܘܦܝܣܛܝܩܐ ܐܘܟܝܬ ܛ̈ܘܥܝܢܐ, 38v)	1.5. من الكتاب فى لواحق القياس والبرهان (D118)

44 *Muqaddimat Tahāfut al-falāsifa al-musammāt Maqāṣid al-falāsifa li-l-Imām al-Ghazālī*, ed. Sulaymān Dunyā, Cairo: Dār al-Maʿārif, 1961.

45 *Ilāhīyāt-i Dānishnāma-yi ʿAlāʾī taṣnīf-i Shaykh-i Raʾīs Abū ʿAlī Sīnā*, ed. Muḥammad Muʿīn, 2nd ed., Hamadan: Dānishgāh-i Bū ʿAlī Sīnā, Tehran: Anjuman-i Āthār wa Mafākhir-i Farhangī, 1383/2004.

Part 2. Natural philosophy (40r)	
Introduction (ܒܘܬܪܐ, on the division of the sciences)	cf. المقدمة الأولى فى تقسيم العلوم (D135); but the content of *Treatise of Treatises* here based on Ibn Sīnā's *ʿUyūn al-ḥikma*.
2.1. On theories common to all bodies (ܥܠ ܬܐܘܪ̈ܝܣ ܕܓ̈ܘܢܝܢ ܠܟܠ ܓܘܫܡ, 41r)	3.1. فى ما يعم سائر الأجسام (D304)
2.2. On simple and non-compound bodies (ܥܠ ܓ̈ܘܫܡܐ ܗܟܝܢ ܦܫܝ̈ܛܐ ܘܗܟܝܢ ܣܘܟ̈ܢܝܢ ܘܪܘܟܒܐ, 50r)	3.2. فى الأجسام البسيطة والمكان خاصة (D304); and 3.3 فى المزاج والمركبات (D335)
2.3. On the kinds of souls (ܥܠ ܙܢ̈ܝܐ ܕܢܦ̈ܫܬܐ, 57v)	3.4. فى النفس النباتى والحيوانى والانسانى (D346)
Part 3. Metaphysics (62r)	
3.1. On the division of Being (ܥܠ ܦܘܠܓܐ ܕܗܘ̇ ܕܐܝܬܘܗܝ, 128r)	2.1. فى اقسام الوجود (D140)
3.2. On the necessary being and the manner of its action (ܥܠ ܗܘܝܢ ܕܐܠܝܨ ܐܝܬܘܬܐ ܘܐܝܟܢܝܘܬܐ ܡܥܒܕܢܘܬܗ, 67r)	2.2. فى ذات واجب الوجود ولوازمه (D210); 2.3 فى صفات الأول (D223); [2.4. no heading, but وإذ قد عرفنا من ذكر صفات الأول فلا بد من ذكر أفعاله…, D253]; 2.5. فى كيفية وجود الأشياء من المبدأ الأول (D288)
3.3. Discourse on separation from matter, perception, providence, fate, and the kingdom of heaven, i.e. bliss (ܡܡܠܠܐ ܕܥܠ ܡܦܪ̈ܫܘܬܐ ܕܡܢ ܗܘܠܐ. ܘܡܪܓܫܢܘܬܐ ܘܡܦܪܢܣܢܘܬܐ ܘܚܠܩܐ ܘܡܠܟܘܬܐ ܕܫܡܝܐ ܐܘܟܝܬ ܒܘܣܡܐ, 84v)	3.5. فى ما يفيض على النفوس من العقل الفعال (D371); 3.5.2. كيفية حصول العلوم فى النفس (D372); 3.5.3. القول فى الشقاوة (D373); 3.5.4. السعادة (D374)
3.4. Discourse on prophecies, signs, visions and dreams (ܡܡܠܠܐ ܕܥܠ ܢܒ̈ܝܘܬܐ ܘܐܬ̈ܘܬܐ ܘܚܙ̈ܘܢܐ ܘܚܠ̈ܡܐ, 91v)	3.5.5. فى سبب الرؤيا الصادقة (D377); 3.5.6. أضغاث الأحلام (D377); 3.5.7. فى معرفة الغيب فى اليقظة (D378); 3.5.8. فى سبب رؤية الانسان فى يقظة صورًا لا وجود لها (D379); 3.5.9. فى أصول المعجزات والكرامات (D380); 3.5.10. فى اثبات أن النبى لا بد له أن يدخل تحت الوجود (D384)

Treatise of Treatises, Maqāṣid al-falāsifa *and* Dānishnāma: *Section Headings in Chapters on the Divisions of Being*

2.2. On the division of Being		
(1) Division of Being into substance and accident (ܦܘܠܓܐ ܕܗܘ ܕܐܝܬܘܗܝ ܠܐܘܣܝܐ ܘܠܓܕܫܐ, 67r)	2.1.1. First Division. Being is divided into substance and accident (القسمة الأولى. الوجود ينقسم الى الجوهر والعرض, D140)	[2.9. Examination of the state of the accident (پیدا کردن حال عرض, M28)]
(2) Division of Being into universal and particular (ܦܘܠܓܐ ܕܗܘ ܕܐܝܬܘܗܝ ܠܟܘܠܢܝܐ ܘܠܡܢܝܬܐ, 69v)	2.1.2. Second Division. Being is divided into universal and particular (قسمة ثانية. الوجود ينقسم الى كلى وجزئى, D174)	2.12. Consideration of the state of the reality of the universal and the particular (دانستن حال حقیقت کلی وجزئی, M39)
(3) Division of Being into finite and infinite (ܦܘܠܓܐ ܕܗܘ ܕܐܝܬܘܗܝ ܠܡܣܝܟܐ ܘܠܐ ܡܣܝܟܐ, 70v)	2.1.6. Sixth Division. Being is divided into finite and infinite (قسمة سادسة. الوجود ينقسم الى متناه وغير متناه, D193)	2.16. Examination of the state of the finitude of everything that is prior and posterior and the finitude of particular causes (پیدا کردن حال متناهی بودن هرچه ورا پیشی وسپسی است ومتناهی بودن علتهای خاص, M58)
(4) Division of Being into one and many (ܦܘܠܓܐ ܕܗܘ ܕܐܝܬܘܗܝ ܠܚܕ ܘܠܣܓܝܐܐ, 70v)	2.1.3. Third Division. Being is divided into one and many (قسمة ثالثة للوجود. الوجود ينقسم الى الواحد وكثير (D184)	2.13. Examination of the state of the one and the many and everything that is connected with them (پیدا کردن حال واحد وکثیر وهرچه بدیشان پیوسته است, M45)
(5) Division of Being into prior and posterior (ܦܘܠܓܐ ܕܗܘ ܕܐܝܬܘܗܝ ܠܩܕܡܝܐ ܘܠܐܚܪܝܐ, 72r)	2.1.4. Fourth Division. Being is divided into what is prior and what is posterior (قسمة رابعة. الوجود ينقسم الى ما هو متقدم والى ما هو متأخر, D187)	2.14. Examination of the state of the prior and the posterior (پیدا کردن حال متقدّمی ومتأخّری که پیشی وسپسی بود, M50)

(6) Division of Being into cause and result (ܦܘܠܓܐ ܕܗܘ ܐܝܬܘܗܝ ܠܥܠܬܐ ܘܥܠܘܠܬܐ, 72v)	2.1.5. Fifth Division. Being is divided into cause and result (قسمة خامسة. الوجود ينقسم الى سبب ومسبب, D189)	2.15. Examination the state of the cause and the result (پیدا کردن حال سبب ومسبّب وعلت ومعلول, M53)
(7) Division of Being into potential and actual (ܦܘܠܓܐ ܕܗܘ ܐܝܬܘܗܝ ܠܗܘܐ ܕܚܝܠܐ ܘܠܗܘܐ ܕܡܥܒܕܢܘܬܐ, 73r)	2.1.7. Seventh Division. Being is divided into what is in potential and what is in actuality (قسمة سابعة. الوجود ينقسم الى ما هو بالقوة والى ما هو بالفعل, D200)	2.17. Examination of the state of potentiality and actuality (پیدا کردن حال قوت وفعل, M61)
(8) Division of Being into necessary and possible (ܦܘܠܓܐ ܕܗܘ ܐܝܬܘܗܝ ܠܐܠܨܝܐ ܘܠܡܫܟܚܢܝܐ, 73v)	2.1.8. Eighth Division. Being is divided into necessary and possible (قسمة ثامنة. الوجود ينقسم الى واجب والى ممكن, D203)	2.18. Demonstration of the existence of the necessary and the possible (نمودن حال هستی واجب وممکن, M65)

There is one major difference in the order of the materials between *Maqāṣid al-falāsifa* and the *Treatise of Treatises* in that the section on the natural sciences, which is placed after metaphysics in the third part of *Maqāṣid*, appears in its more traditional position, before metaphysics, in the *Treatise of Treatises*. This is comparable to the way in which Barhebraeus gave his longest work on philosophy, the *Cream of Wisdom*, a more traditional Aristotelian structure than its principal model, *Kitāb ash-Shifāʾ*, by suppressing the section on the mathematical sciences and adding a section on practical philosophy, basing the latter not on a work of Ibn Sīnā but on Naṣīr ad-Dīn aṭ-Ṭūsī's Persian work on ethics, the *Akhlāq-i nāṣirī*. In the chapter on the divisions of Being, too, Barhebraeus has made one departure from the order found in *Maqāṣid* by placing the discussion of division into the finite and the infinite in the third section rather than the sixth, but otherwise the arrangement is similar to that found in *Maqāṣid* and it will be seen that the wording of the headings, too, closely resembles the wording in *Maqāṣid*.

6 Comparison of Attitudes to Philosophy

Considering Barhebraeus' use of al-Ghazālī's works in different fields of the sciences, including both those he would have classified as "internal" (ecclesiastical) and "external" (secular), one question that arises is to what extent he shared al-Ghazālī's outlook on the secular sciences and, in particular, philosophy. One of the places in which Barhebraeus discusses the secular sciences is the section on the division of the sciences in his *Ethicon*.[46] In this section, Barhebraeus tells us that teaching (*yulpānā*) is either (I) ecclesiastical (*ʿēdtānāyā*), or (II) secular (lit. 'external', *barrāyā*), and, after a discussion of the ecclesiastical sciences, goes on to give a classification of the secular sciences into what is good, bad and partly good and partly bad,[47] which may be summarised as follows:

II.1: Good
- II.1.2: Good and necessary: medicine and computation[48]
- II.1.3: Good and useful: language (*leksīs*) and grammar[49]

II.2: Bad
- II.2.1: Harmful for the soul: astrology (because it makes creatures the causes of good and bad, and so removes fear of God)[50]
- II.2.2: Harmful for the body: sorcery[51]

II.3: Partly good and partly bad, i.e. philosophy[52]
- II.3.1 and 2: Logic and mathematics (geometry, astronomy, arithmetic, music) which "sharpens, and does not corrupt, the mind" (*maḥrpā l-tarʿītā w-lā mḥattpā*)[53]
- II.3.3 and 4: Natural philosophy and metaphysics

46 *Ethicon*, 4.1, ed. Bedjan, 317–319; cf. *Ethicon. Mēmrā I*, trans. Teule, (as n. 19 above), xxv; al-Ghazālī, *Iḥyāʾ*, Bk. 1. Kitāb al-ʿIlm, Bāb 2. Fī l-ʿilm al-maḥmūd wa-l-madhmūm wa-aqsāmihā wa-aḥkāmihā (ed. Beirut, 1982, I.13–28); also *Munqidh*, Aqsām al-ʿulūm (ed. Ṣalībā-ʿAyyād 1967, 79–90).

47 The three categories correspond to al-Ghazālī's three categories of "praiseworthy," "blameworthy" and "permissible" (*maḥmūd, madhmūm, mubāḥ*; *Iḥyāʾ*, ed. Beirut, 1982, I.16).

48 Cf. *Iḥyāʾ*, ed. Beirut, 1982, I.16.12–14 (on *ṭibb* and *ḥisāb*).

49 Barhebraeus differs from al-Ghazālī in including the study of language and grammar in the secular sciences, since these disciplines (*ʿilm al-lugha wa-n-naḥw*) are counted, as is usual in the Islamic tradition, among the religious (*sharʿī*) sciences by the latter (*Iḥyāʾ*, ed. Beirut, 1982, I.17.5).

50 Cf. *Iḥyāʾ*, ed. Beirut, 1982, I.29–30 (on *aḥkām* [*an-nujūm*]), esp. 29.24–30.6.

51 Cf. *Iḥyāʾ*, ed. Beirut, 1982, I.16.20 (*ʿilm as-siḥr wa-ṭ-ṭilismāt wa-ʿilm ash-shaʿbadha wa-t-talbīsāt*); also I.29.

52 Cf. *Iḥyāʾ*, ed. Beirut, 1982, I.22.

53 Cf. n. 56 below.

Concerning natural philosophy and metaphysics, Barhebraeus tells us that four related doctrines are opposed to "ecclesiastical truth," namely those concerning (a) the eternity (in the beginning, *mtōmāyūtā* = Arabic *azal*) of the world; (b) denial of the dissolution of the heavens; (c) denial of *creatio ex nihilo*; and (d) assertion that the Creator's will is bound by His nature. He then goes on to tell us that "the rest [of the doctrines] are good and not to be condemned (*ṭābān w-lā mḥayybān*), but since the seeds of the two teachings are choked among the tares (*zīzānē*, cf. Mt. 13:25), it is not safe for the simple to go deep into them, just as it is not for those who do not know how to swim to go deep into a swelling river."

The assessment of natural philosophy and metaphysics given here is basically the same as the assessment made, for example, of natural philosophy in al-Ghazālī's *Munqidh*, namely that "its rejection is not a condition imposed by Religion, except in those particular questions we have mentioned in *Tahāfut al-falāsifa*,"[54] although the presence of the word "good" in the phrase "good and not to be condemned" gives the assessment a slightly more positive note.

A similar assessment of the various branches of the secular sciences is also given by Barhebraeus in his *Book of Directions*, in the context of the enumeration of the books which are to be read and taught in ecclesiastical schools.[55] The books mentioned there include the work on rhetoric by Antony of Tagrit, the logical works of Aristotle (including the *Poetics* and *Rhetoric*) and the books of the four mathematical sciences, which Barhebraeus describes as providing "beauty for the tongue and training for the mind."[56] Barhebraeus tells us that from the *Physics* (*Shemʿā kyānāyā*) and *Metaphysics* one should accept only as much as he himself has accepted in his two theological works, *Candelabrum of the Sanctuary* and *Book of Rays*, and only for the sake of "refutation and disputation against those who knew God but did not glorify Him as God (cf. Rom. 1:21)." He then goes on to justify the teaching of such secular sciences

---

54 *Munqidh*, ed. Ṣalībā-ʿAyyād 1967, 83.7–9: وكما ليس من شرط الدين انكار علم الطب فليس من شرطه ايضًا انكار ذلك العلم الا في مسائل معينة ذكرناها في كتاب تهافت الفلاسفة...

55 *Book of Directions*, 7.9, ed. Bedjan, 106–107. For a discussion of the passage (with references to earlier studies), see Takahashi, "Between Greek and Arabic: The Sciences in Syriac from Severus Sebokht to Barhebraeus," in *Transmission of Sciences: Greek, Syriac, Arabic and Latin*, ed. Haruo Kobayashi & Mizue Kato, Tokyo: Organization for Islamic Area Studies, Waseda University [WIAS], 2010, 16–32, here 28–30.

56 Cf. the comment that the mathematical sciences "sharpen the mind" in the *Ethicon* (n. 53 above). The words used here in the *Book of Directions* go back to Socrates of Constantinople (Scholasticus, fl. ca. 440), *Historia ecclesiatica*, III.16.27: τοῦτο μὲν εὐγλωττίας χάριν καὶ γυμνασίας τοῦ νοῦ (cf. n. 57 below).

by citing a number of passages from the New Testament where St. Paul was said to have quoted from non-Christian authors.[57] This addition is interesting in that it indicates, in the first place, that the prevailing attitude in his ecclesiastical community towards the secular sciences was such that Barhebraeus felt the need to make a justification for their study. The addition indicates at the same time that Barhebraeus took a positive interest in promoting the study of such subjects in the schools under his jurisdiction.

A further passage where Barhebraeus talks about the secular, "Greek" sciences is in the autobiographical passage in the *Book of the Dove*, which, as has been mentioned above, is modelled on *al-Munqidh min aḍ-ḍalāl*.

> I then endeavoured to apprehend the force of the wisdom of the Greeks, that is to say: logic (*mlīlūtā*), natural philosophy (*kyānāyātā*), metaphysics (*alāhāyātā*), arithmetic (*menyānē*, lit. numbers), geometry (*eskēmē*, lit. shapes) and astronomy (lit. teaching of the spheres and the movements of the luminaries). And because life is short and scholarship deep and wide, I had to read in every pursuit whatever was most essential. In the course of my studies in these teachings I resembled someone sinking in the ocean and waving his arms about in all directions in his desire to be rescued. And because in all the scholarship, internal and external, I did not find what I was seeking, I almost ended up in complete disintegration. To put it briefly: if the Lord had not sustained my failing faith at that critical time, and if he had not led me to look into the writings of the Initiated, such as Father Evagrios and others, both western and eastern, and if he had not lifted me out of the whirlpool of disintegration and destruction, I would have already despaired of the life of the soul, though not that of the body. I meditated on these works for a period of seven years, during which I despised other kinds of knowledge, though I had to study some of them superficially, not for my own sake but for the sake of others who wished to be instructed by me.[58]

The attitude taken towards the secular sciences here appears to be more negative than that found in the *Ethicon* and the *Book of Directions*. Barhebraeus tells us that he did not find what he was looking for in those sciences and that they were leading him to perdition. It will also be remembered that the term

57 All but one of these quotations are found in the defence of Greek learning by Socrates of Constantinople, *Historia ecclesiastica*, III.16.23–26 (Socrates, *Kirchengeschichte*, ed. Günther Christian Hansen, Berlin: Akademie-Verlag, 1995, 212).

58 Slightly adapted from the translation by Colless (see n. 37 above).

"wisdom of the Greeks" is one that has a negative connotation in the Christian tradition going back to St. Paul (1 Cor. 1:22), and Bahebraeus is probably being intentionally disparaging in using simple words such as "shapes" and "numbers" (as opposed to the Greek loanwords G'WMYṬRY' and 'RYTMṬYQY used in the *Ethicon*) in referring to the mathematical sciences.

Since the *Book of the Dove* is evidently a later work than the *Ethicon* and the *Book of Directions*, it may be that the difference reflects a change of attitude on Barhebraeus' part, perhaps during those years that he meditated on the works of Evagrius and others. What makes this somewhat unlikely is that one of the last works Barhebraeus wrote was his longest work on Aristotelian-Avicennian philosophy, the *Cream of Wisdom*. It may be that he wrote this work "for the sake of those who wished to be instructed" by him, but it is somehow difficult to imagine that he undertook the composition of this *magnum opus* not as a labour of love but simply for the sake of others.

It seems more likely that the difference in the attitude reflects a difference of the audience. The *Book of the Dove* was addressed to ascetics, who naturally concentrate on things other than the study of the secular sciences as, of course, they should. Works such as the *Ethicon* and the *Book of Directions*, where warnings are given against certain unacceptable tenets of philosophy, as well as the theological works mentioned in the latter – that is, the *Candelabrum of the Sanctuary* and *Book of Rays* – were written not for ascetics, but were probably intended for a more general readership consisting of the members of both the clergy and the laity; in writing them Barhebraeus was exercising his teaching authority as a Christian bishop. It is not stated for whom the philosophical works such as the *Cream of Wisdom* and *Treatise of Treatises* were intended, but two of Barhebraeus' works on the secular sciences, the astronomical *Ascent of the Mind* and the Syriac translation of Ibn Sīnā's *al-Ishārāt wa-t-tanbīhāt*, are dedicated to a specific person, the physician Simeon of Qalʿa Rūmāytā, who worked and rose to some prominence at the Mongol court, and whose nephew, the future patriarch Philoxenus Nemrod (patriarch 1283–92), was at one time a disciple of Barhebraeus.[59] This suggests that these works on the secular sciences were written for a more limited, élite audience.

Recent studies have been making it increasingly clear that the attitude of al-Ghazālī towards philosophy was more complex than appears from the traditional account of his spiritual crisis and rejection of philosophy as depicted in the *Munqidh*; these studies have revealed that he continued to be deeply

---

59 See Takahashi, "Simeon of Qalʿa Rumaita, Patriarch Philoxenus Nemrod and Bar ʿEbroyo," *Hugoye: Journal of Syriac Studies* 4/1 (2001): 45–91.

influenced by Avicennian philosophy in his later works.[60] It also appears that al-Ghazālī was more openly accepting of the views of the philosophers in those works written for a close circle of his disciples.[61] That being the case, it may be that Barhebraeus, who, as a religious leader with an interest in and appreciation of philosophy, presented different faces to different audiences, had something in common in this regard, too, with the *Ḥujjat al-Islām*.

7 Conclusion

The foregoing pages, it is hoped, give some idea of the not insignificant extent to which Barhebraeus depended on al-Ghazālī in composing his works. One factor which Barhebraeus found attractive about al-Ghazālī's writings was without doubt the clear, systematic presentation of the material he found in many of them. This would have been the case especially when he turned to the legal handbooks of al-Ghazālī as the source for his *Book of Directions*; Barhebraeus' selection of al-Ghazālī's *Maqāṣid al-falāsifa*, rather than the often more discursive works of Ibn Sīnā himself, as the principal source of his *Treatise of Treatises* may be explained in the same way. Similarly, it was no doubt the comprehensive and rational treatment of the material in the *Iḥyāʾ ʿulūm ad-dīn* that inspired and prompted Barhebraeus to use this work as the source in composing a new type of work which had no precedent in his own Syriac tradition.

Barhebraeus not only used al-Ghazālī's works to provide a structure around which to build his writings, but also borrowed and transferred the contents of large portions of them into his works. For Barhebraeus to borrow as much as he did, he must have agreed with much of al-Ghazālī had said, and found what he saw in al-Ghazālī's writings congenial and convenient for his purposes. It is significant that Barhebraeus, as a learned leader of a Christian community, could borrow so much from a leading scholar of the Islamic sciences, not only in matters pertaining to the secular sciences but also in matters that lay at the core of his religious activities. This convergence tells us much about what the two religious traditions represented by these two men share in common.

60 For an overview of the recent developments in Ghazalian studies in this respect, see Alexander Treiger, *Inspired Knowledge in Islamic Thought: Al-Ghazālī's Theory of Mystical Cognition and Its Avicennian Foundation*, London: Routledge, 2012, 1–4.

61 See, for example, Frank Griffel, "MS London, British Library Or. 3126: An Unknown Work by Al-Ghazālī on Metaphysics and Philosophical Theology," *Journal of Islamic Studies* 17/1 (2006): 1–42; also the contribution by Madelung in the present volume.

I have not been able to do much more here than to outline what we know about the use of al-Ghazālī's works as sources by Barhebraeus. What needs to be done, of course, is to examine more closely the manner in which Barhebraeus used the materials he borrowed from al-Ghazālī, adapting and altering them in certain cases to suit his own purposes. Some valuable studies have been undertaken by Teule on the changes made by Barhebraeus in applying the materials taken from the *Iḥyāʾ ʿulūm ad-dīn* to a Christian context in his *Ethicon*. It may be hoped that more work of this kind will be conducted in the future, bringing greater light to our understanding, firstly, of the works of Barhebraeus, but also, by way of reflexion, of the works of al-Ghazālī, and, in a broader context, to our understanding of the relationship between Christianity and Islam.[62]

62 It has not been possible to take account here of the relevant literature that has appeared in the years between the submission of this paper and its publication. Out of such literature, one might take note in particular of the following: On a reference to al-Ghazālī's *Maqāṣid al-falāsifa* in an Arabic work (*Kitāb Farāʾid al-qawāʾid fī uṣūl ad-dīn wa-l-ʿaqāʾid*) by ʿAbdīshōʿ bar Brīkhā, a near-contemporary of Barhebraeus who likewise composed his works in both Syriac and Arabic, see Herman Teule, "Gregory Bar ʿEbrōyō and ʿAbdishoʿ Bar Brikhā: similar but different," in *Orientalia Christiana. Festschrift für Hubert Kaufhold zum 70. Geburtstag*, ed. Peter Bruns & Heinz Otto Luthe, Wiesbaden: Harrassowitz, 2013, 543–551 (here 547). On Barhebraeus' uses of Islamic sources in his works, including those works discussed here, see now also Herman G.B. Teule, "Barhebraeus," in *Christian-Muslim Relations: A Bibliographical History*, vol. 4 (1200-1350), ed. David Thomas & Alex Mallett, Leiden: Brill, 2012, 588–609. On the *Book of Directions*, including on Barhebraeus' handling of his Islamic sources in the work, see now also Dorothea Weltecke, "Zum syrisch-orthodoxen Leben in der mittelalterlichen Stadt und zu den Hūddōyē des Bar ʿEbrōyō," in *Orientalia Christiana. Festschrift für Hubert Kaufhold zum 70. Geburtstag*, 585–613.

CHAPTER 16

R. Marti and His References to al-Ghazālī

Jules Janssens

R. Marti (or Martini) was a 13th century Dominican priest with Catalan roots. Actively involved in missionary activities, he spent some time in Tunisia prior to his death (c. 1286/685). His major work, dated to the 1270s, is the *Pugio fidei adversus Mauros et Judaeos*, an apologetic work for Christianity, "a dagger of faith against the Moors and the Jews." The book is famous for its many quotations in Hebrew; more importantly here, though, it also contains many references to Arabic-Islamic sources, including the Qur'ān, such famous Arabic thinkers as Abū Bakr ar-Rāzī, Avicenna, and Averroes. Most topically for the present discussion, al-Ghazālī figures among them as well.[1]

Although in contemporary scholarship one is well aware of this presence of al-Ghazālī in Marti's writings, as far as I know no detailed analysis of the precise extent and nature of his translations of Ghazalian texts has been made. This is all the more regrettable since we are in his case confronted with an important instance of an entirely new encounter with al-Ghazālī's thought in the Christian Latin world. In fact, Marti introduces the titles of a few of al-Ghazālī's works previously unknown in the Latin world. But that isn't all: Marti also presents new ideas absent in the *Maqāṣid al-falāsifa*, the only work with which the vast majority of the major Latin scholastics were familiar. Especially in the *Pugio*, as will become evident, Marti offers – in Latin translation – quotations and paraphrases of different Ghazalian texts, among which the *Munqidh* and, although to a lesser extent, the *Tahāfut*, figure pre-eminently. These translated fragments offer an intriguing picture of the 'critical' attitude (above all, towards philosophy) that is so typical of al-Ghazālī. However, more importantly, Marti adopts in many respects the very same attitude as al-Ghazālī's in his thought, as will become most clear in the way he structures the first part of the *Pugio*. In this respect, a striking difference comes to the fore with Thomas Aquinas. In spite of there being common passages – many of which are taken *verbatim* – in both

* I wish to thank David Twetten for having corrected the English style of the paper.

1 I have been able to access only the Leipzig 1687 edition (all references will be to this edition). See Ryan Szpiech, "Hermeneutical Muslims? Islam as Witness in Christian Anti-Judaism," http://cas.uchicago.edu/workshops/westmedcult/files/2010/11/Szpiech-Hermeneutical-Muslims.pdf, 23–24.

 DOI 10.1163/9789004290952_017

the latter's *Summa contra Gentiles* and the 'Prima pars' of the *Pugio*,[2] the basic démarche in the two works is quite different. In the *Summa contra Gentiles* the order of the four major parts is: God, creation, providence and revelation. In this order one detects the expression of a Christian (philosophico-)theological point of view. As to the *Pugio*'s 'Prima pars,' its structuring is highly influenced by al-Ghazālī's *Munqidh*, since it starts with distinguishing three major categories of philosophers. Then, it refutes the views of the 'lower' among them, i.e. the materialists and the naturalists. Thereafter it offers an indication of what is valuable in 'good' philosophy before systematically discussing three major issues: the eternity of the world, God's knowledge of the particulars and the resurrection of body and soul. Certainly, Thomas, in his *Summa*, also discusses these latter issues; he does not, however, treat them as a unity, but instead scatters them over the different parts of the work. Moreover, the *Pugio*, compared to the *Summa contra Gentiles*, adds several quotations, mainly of a 'theological' nature, derived from Arabic sources (above all, al-Ghazālī); consequently, it lacks several arguments found in the *Summa*, most of which are philosophical (viz., Aristotelian) in nature. But Marti is not merely a compiler of Arabic with a peculiar fixation on Ghazalian fragments; rather, he is a thinker who, in spite of his profound disagreement with the religious belief of his opponent, valorizes what he finds valuable and/or valid in the latter's writings.

Contrary to Marti, however, the vast majority of scholars who had access to anything of al-Ghazālī were familiar only – as we already noted – with the 12th Century Latin translation of the *Maqāṣid*, made at Toledo. This version was known in the Latin world as *Summa theoreticae philosophiae* and did not contain any preface; the preface in the Arabic editions was translated into Latin near the end of the thirteenth century. It is also only at that time that one finds the work entitled '*Intentiones philosophorum*.'[3] Marti, in his early treatise, *Explanatio simboli apostolorum*, refers to al-Ghazālī's work under the heading

2 A. Rodríguez Bachillér, *Influencia de la filosofía árabe en el* Pugio *de Raimondo Marti*. Madrid, 1969, pp. 17–18 (I owe this reference to Szpiech, 'Hermeneutical Muslims?,' p. 20, n. 38, offering further references). I will not enter here the debate which of the two works has influenced the other. Let me simply remark that the possibility of a common source has in my view also to be seriously taken into consideration, given the presence of additions and omissions on both sides and of some striking differences (e.g., only three of the five proofs for God's existence are common).

3 For more details regarding the Latin translation see my "al-Ġazālī's *Maqāṣid al-Falāsifa*, The Latin Translation of," in Henrik Lagerlund (ed), *Encyclopedia of Medieval Philosophy. Philosophy between 500 and 1500*, Springer 2011, pp. 387–90.

'*Intentiones physicarum*.'[4] This might be a scribal error for '*Intentiones philosophorum*,' as A. Cortaberria believes,[5] but this is certainly not the only possible explanation. In fact, Marti presents the work as a single book ("in libro"), and in one passage he makes direct reference to the fifth chapter of the third treatise (*maqāla*). This latter is clearly the third treatise of the Metaphysics proper, since the twenty lines quoted there all derive from it,[6] not from the end of the Physics, as Cortaberria asserted. Hence, it could be that "physicarum" is a scribal error for "metaphysicarum," especially given that the work is many times referred to as 'Algazelis Metaphysica' in Latin scholastic writings. Moreover, in some manuscripts only the Metaphysics is present, while in others the metaphysical and physical parts are given together (with or without any title), without the Logic.[7] Finally, given the absence of any title in some of the manuscripts, one may conjecture that Marti derived the title from the affirmation, present at the beginning of the treatise, that it will treat the 'intentiones huius divinae scientiae' – besides offering some 'physical' ideas necessary for an understanding of metaphysics.[8] The replacement of 'divine science' by 'metaphysics,' I add, is quite understandable since the former could be mistaken as designating the science of 'theology.' None of these points prove, of

4 See Joseph M. March, "En Ramón Martí y la seva 'Explanatio simboli apostolorum'," *Anuari de l'Insitut d'estudis catalans*, 2 (1908), 443–496 (text pp. 450–496), p. 494, 20 (afterward abbreviated *Explanatio*). It is worth noting that this edition is based on the only known XIII–XIVth Century manuscript, Tortosa, Bibliotheca de la Catedral, ms. 6. The work is generally dated 1256/57 (654/55).

5 A. Cortaberria Beitia, "Les sources arabes de l'*Explanatio simboli* du dominicain catalan Raymond Martin," *Mélanges de l'Institut Dominicain d'Études Orientales* (MIDEO), 16 (1983), 95–115, p. 110, note 18.

6 One finds the following quotations in Marti's early *Explanatio* (with only a very few minor variants):

Explanatio	Algazel's *Metaphysics* (ed. J. T. Muckle. Toronto, 1933)
494, 20–21	83, 11–12
494, 21–25	83, 24–31
494, 25–30	86, 3–11
494, 30–41	86, 17–36.

In fact, these may be grouped in pairs: in the first pair, the emphasis is on the difference between the sensual and the intelligible and on the superiority of intellectual pleasure over sensual; the second pair focuses on the fact that the intellectual pleasure of the angels is infinitely superior to all physical pleasures. Hence, there is as a common denominator within all: the superiority of intellectual pleasure over sensual pleasure.

7 For a survey of the existing manuscripts, see Ch. Lohr, "Logica Algazelis. Introduction and Critical Text," *Traditio* 21 (1965), 223–90, pp. 232–36.

8 See J. T. Muckle, *Algazel's Metaphysics. A Medieval Translation*. Toronto, 1933, p. 1, 9–12.

course, that "physicarum" is a mistake for "metaphysicarum." Nevertheless, there is also no compelling reason to accept the alternative proposal of "philosophorum." In any case, there is certainly no evidence that Marti knew the 'preface' when he composed the *Explanatio*. As a matter of fact, Marti – in line with the vast majority of the scholastics – continues to view al-Ghazālī as one of the 'philosophers' of the Saracens, and, more precisely, as one of those (clearly the superior 'philosophers', for Marti) who identified eternal happiness with knowledge of God.[9] From a doctrinal point of view, the point of this statement is to show that spiritual pleasures are higher than sensual ones. Marti finds further confirmation for the presence of this idea in al-Ghazālī by offering, as the title of the fourth *bayān* of the *Book of Love* of the *Iḥyā'*, "gloriosior et excellentior delectationum [est] cognitio Dei excelsi et contemplatio vultus eius," and by construing the title of the twenty-second chapter of *Mīzān* (rendered as '*Trutina operum*') as "quid sit beatitudo ultima."[10] Whether he had access at

---

9 Marti, *Explanatio*, p. 494, 46–7: "Ex hiis [i.e., sayings of Avicenna, al-Ghazālī and al-Fārābī] patet quod etiam apud philosophos sarracenorum beatitudo consistit in cognitione et amore Dei, non in delectatione." The Saracen philosophers referred to must include al-Ghazālī – this affirmation forms the conclusion of a section affirming that three major Arabic thinkers, i.e., Avicenna, al-Ghazālī and al-Fārābī, have in common the idea that spiritual retributions prevail over bodily ones. Note, moreover, that Marti makes no mention of any contradiction between *Maqāṣid*, on the one hand, and *Iḥyā' 'ulūm ad-dīn* and *Mīzān al-'amal*, on the other. On the contrary, what he quotes of these works 'confirmat,' if you will, the affirmation(s) of the former, and this is also the case with two works of al-Fārābī, i.e., *De auditu naturali* (*Physics*, lost in Arabic) and *De intellectu*. This strongly reinforces the impression that, for Marti, al-Ghazālī was indeed a philosopher. Hence, it looks highly probable that he included al-Ghazālī among the 'sapientes sarracenorum' (without any qualification) who did not believe in the resurrection of the body, misled as they were by the Qur'ānic description of paradise, which Marti labels as far too sensuous (*Explanatio*, p. 393, 12–5). All this makes it probable that Marti, at the time he wrote the *Explanatio*, was not aware of the existence of the *Tahāfut* or of the *Munqidh* (nor, indeed, was he seriously acquainted with any other of al-Ghazālī's religious writings). Things had changed when he wrote the *Pugio*, since he quotes fragments from both works while giving their titles (and referring to other religious works by al-Ghazālī), perhaps thanks to his travel to Tunis in 1268–69 (see A. Bonner, 'L'apologètica de Ramon Marti i Ramon Llul devant de l'Islam i del Judaism,' *Estudi generali*, Girona: Collegi Universitari, 9 [1989], 171–85, p. 174). Let me add that I do not see how Marti plays up an intellectual division within Islam that would make Avicenna and al-Fārābī (hence, not al-Ghazālī) into free-thinking rationalists who rejected the Qur'ān, as claimed by Jon Tolan, "Saracen philosophers secretly deride Islam," *Medieval Encounters*, 8/2–3 (2002), 184–208, p. 197.

10 The precise title of the chapter according to the Arabic original is: "An exposition that the noblest and loftiest pleasure (*ghāyat as-sa'ādāt wa-marātibihā*) is knowledge of God and contemplation of His blessed face and only he who is denied this pleasure can

that time to these works is not certain, given that he mentions only titles of chapters (in a paraphrastic way, in the case of *Mīzān*). As for *Iḥyā'*, it is unlikely that Marti had the complete work at his disposal since he seems to present the *Book of Penitence* (*Kitāb at-Tawba*), the thirty-first book, as an independent work rather than as a part of a whole.[11] As for *Mīzān*, as we shall see, three small (somewhat free) quotations are present in *Pugio*, but the work's title is now translated into Latin as '*Statera* (*operum*).'[12] It therefore appears likely, though not certain, that Marti was indeed in possession of a copy of this work.

It must be observed that Marti does not limit himself simply to evoking the title of the *Book of Penitence*; he literally presents two of al-Ghazālī's affirmations: (1) every society needs wise men, who, like physicians, can discern the weaknesses of men, and can remedy them, giving good advice; and (2) spiritual weaknesses are sins, and unless their existence is identified, they cannot be cured.[13] Herein one detects elements of a fragment from near the beginning of *rukn* 4, where al-Ghazālī develops three reasons why the diseases of the heart are more numerous than those of the body: (1) people suffering from spiritual diseases are usually unaware of them; (2) the invisibility of such diseases,

---

conceivably prefer any other pleasure to it". Marti clearly omits the last part and interprets 'pleasures' in terms of 'beatitude.' The title of the fourth *bayān* of the *Book of Love* of *Iḥyā' 'ulūm ad-dīn* is a good translation of the Arabic, see Al-Ghazālī, *Love, Longing, Intimacy and Contentment.* Kitāb al-Maḥabba wa'l-shawq wa'l-uns wa'l-riḍā. Book XXXVI of the *Revival of the Religious Sciences Iḥyā' 'ulūm al-dīn* – translated with Introduction and Notes by E. Ormsby. Cambridge, the Islamic Text Society, 2012, p. 42. It must be noted, however, that Marti does not refer to any specific book, but to the entire work, the title of which is given in Latin translation as '*Vivificatio scientiarum*,' hence omitting the specification *ad-dīn*, 'of religion,' in the original. If this omission does not result from a scribal error but is original with Marti, it is difficult to justify his choice. Rather, as will become immediately clear from what follows in the exposé, he probably had no direct access to the work, but just some limited information. In this respect, it is worthwhile to note that no reference whatsoever to *Iḥyā'* appears in *Pugio*.

11 Marti, *Explanatio*, p. 486, 49–50: "dicit Algazel in libro *De penitentia*." It is a well-known fact that several books of the *Iḥyā'* circulated in an independent manner. Therefore, it looks reasonable to assume that Marti either saw a copy of this kind or had indirect information about the existence of such a work. The presence of a small paraphrastical fragment (see what follows in the exposé) tips the scale in favor of the first of the two alternatives.

12 It has to be noted that 'trutina' and 'statera' are more or less synonymous, each signifying 'balance.' Hence they are both acceptable translations of *mīzān*.

13 Marti, *Explanatio*, p. 486, 50–2: "in qualibet civitate debent poni sapientes, qui sint velut physici, qui debent cognoscere infirmitates, et eas mederi, donando eis consilium. Et infirmitates spirituales sunt peccata, quae, nisi ostendantur, non possunt curari."

namely sins, makes people insensitive to them; and (3) at the present time, we lack good 'physicians' for such spiritual diseases.[14] It is obvious, then, that the *Explanatio* offers not a literal translation, but rather a free paraphrase, and even that in a highly condensed form. Nevertheless, the paraphrase is clearly inspired directly by the text, so that Marti's having direct access to the text is very plausible.[15] In sum, the *Explanatio* offers references to various works of al-Ghazālī, yet, one never gets the impression that at the time of its composition, Marti was aware of al-Ghazālī's genuine thought. Instead, in a way similar to his Latin contemporaries, he considered al-Ghazālī to be a true philosopher, as were al-Fārābī and Avicenna before him.

The *Explanatio*, compared to Marti's later work, *Pugio fidei*, shows at best a very limited knowledge of al-Ghazālī's writings hardly surpassing that of his contemporaries. With the *Pugio*, written approximately two decades later, things have changed dramatically.[16] Even a first look at the basic structure of the 'prima pars' immediately reveals a profound Ghazalian influence. In this part, Marti deals with three groups that have no religious law: (1) the 'Temporales,' who deny God's existence, among whom Marti places the Epicureans, insofar as they look after only pleasures of the flesh (in chapters 2 and 3 Marti will argue against their fundamental thesis); (2) the 'Naturales,' who deny any kind of survival of man after death (in chapter 4 Marti will argue on purely rational grounds for the immortality of the soul); and (3) the 'philosophers,' who defend the eternity of the world (criticized in chapters 6–14), deny God's knowledge of particulars (refuted in chapters 15–25), and deny the resurrection of the body (refuted in chapter 26, the last chapter of the first part). It is obvious that

---

14 Al-Ghazālī, *Iḥyāʾ ʿulūm ad-dīn*, an. ed. Maghreb, s.d., IV, 51, 7–17 (A German translation is available in R. Gramlich, *Muḥammad al-Ġazzālīs Lehre von den Stufen zur Gottesliebe*. Wiesbaden, 1984, p. 118, A 270).

15 Note that Marti almost certainly consulted the work in Arabic, since so far no known medieval Latin translation of this book (or of any other) of the *Iḥyāʾ* is known. Marti interprets al-Ghazālī's affirmations in a typical Christian framework, i.e., in that of the sacrament of confession, involving especially the need for another human person, *in casu* the priest (whom he identifies with the wise man of al-Ghazālī's text). This comes unambiguously to the fore in the introductory formula to the (paraphrastical) quotation: "Quod vero homo debeat confiteri homini dicit Algazel ...". Such a perspective is of course completely foreign to the original text, where the emphasis is more on the lack of attention of people, including on the part of so-called wise men, to spiritual diseases, and, relatedly, to the remedies that cure them.

16 March, "En Ramón Martí y la seva 'Explanatio simboli apostolorum'," p. 447 dates the composition of the *Explanatio* in the years 1256–57, while he situates the writing of the *Pugio* in 1278.

in the last case, al-Ghazālī's famous three grounds for the condemnation of the philosophers – making them guilty of unbelief – have directly influenced Marti. As for the distinction of three categories of people deprived of a religious law, it is largely inspired, as we shall see, by al-Ghazālī's distinction of three fundamental categories of philosophers in the *Munqidh*. This latter work, together with *Tahāfut*, constitutes a major source of inspiration for Marti; one also finds minor derivations from other works, i.e., from the *Mīzān*, from *Mishkāt al-anwār*, from *al-Maqṣad al-asnā* and from two otherwise unidentified works, entitled in Latin 'Probatorium' and 'Epistola ad amicum.'[17]

In the first chapter, entitled 'De diversitate errantium a via veritatis et fidei,' Marti affirms in the fourth paragraph that the 'temporales' deny that God exists.[18] He explicitly recognizes that this idea was expressed by al-Ghazālī in his 'Almonkid min Addalel,' and indeed it is said there that they, i.e., the *dahriyyūn*, the 'materialists,' are *az-zanādiqa*, atheists.[19] One might be tempted to correct 'temporales' to 'materialists,' assuming a personal rewording of Marti, as Poggi claims.[20] But no such rewording is involved. In fact, Marti has clearly understood the notion of *dahr* in the designation *dahriyyūn* as meaning 'temporal duration,' which is its common meaning. In this sense the Latin rendering of *dahriyyūn* by 'temporales' is quite understandable, although it clearly misses the technical sense in which the term is used in the present context. We, however, agree with Poggi that Marti introduces a personal element when he evokes in one and the same breath the 'Epicurei seu Carnales,' for

17 A basic survey of all these derivations can be found in A. Cortaberria, "Fuentas árabes del «Pugio fidei» de Ramón Martí: Algazel (1085–1111)," *Ciencia Tomista*, 112 (1985), 581–96. Like Cortaberria, I was unable to identify the last two works. Regarding the use of the *Munqidh*, a detailed, although not fully complete presentation has been given by Vincenzo M. Poggi, *Un classico della spiritualità musulmana. Saggio monografico sul* "Munqidh" *di al-Ġazālī*. Roma, 1967, 55–79.

18 The first chapter covers Marti, *Pugio*, f. 192–94 (In order not to multiply unnecessarily the notes, I shall not indicate the folios of the respective paragraphs, since the reader can easily identify them).

19 Al-Ghazālī, *al-Munqidh min aḍ-ḍalāl* (afterwards abbreviated *Munqidh*), traduction française avec introduction et notes par Farīd Jabre. [2]Beyrouth 1969, p. 19, 4 and 7 (Arabic – the Arabic text is that of the edition by Jamīl Ṣalība and Kāmil 'Ayyād, Damascus 1956; in what follows all references will be to the Arabic text). Attention has to be paid to the fact that Marti here presents the title of the work in transliteration, whereas on other occasions he will use the Latin translation 'Qui eripit ab errore,' as we will see shortly.

20 Poggi, *Un classico della spiritualità musulmana*, pp. 60–1.

whom the pleasures of the flesh were the highest good.[21] In the fifth paragraph the 'naturales' are presented as another group of erring people. Again, Marti explicitly refers to the *Munqidh*, but now under its Latin title 'Qui eripit ab errore.' He quotes almost *verbatim* the first half of al-Ghazālī's exposé on the *Ṭabīʿiyyūn*, the 'naturalists', i.e. philosophers devoting themselves exclusively to the study of nature, although he illustrates the marvels present in animals and plants in a more comprehensive and concrete way than in the original.[22] Marti's sixth paragraph, once more pointing to the *Munqidh* ('Algazel ubi supra'), states that the 'naturales,' having lost all fear for God ('timor Dei'), have fulfilled their basic desires as if they were beasts. This remark, which is indeed present in al-Ghazālī,[23] makes more understandable Marti's introduction of the Epicureans in the former category of the 'temporales,' insofar as they combined moral depravity with a denial of God's existence. As for the 'naturales,' they do not deny this latter, but they do deny the immortality of the soul, a doctrine the origin of which lies in Galen's notion of 'complexion' (*mizāj*). Although the fact of 'complexion' (but without any mention of Galen) is strongly emphasized in the *Munqidh* as a cause of the Naturalists' denial of the resurrection of the soul, Marti, in the seventh paragraph, obviously prefers to refer to al-Ghazālī's *Tahāfut al-falāsifa*, a title that he renders into Latin as 'Tractatus de ruina philosophorum.'[24] As to the reference, it concerns in all likelihood a brief passage inside the first discussion where al-Ghazālī explicitly mentions Galen's doctrine of complexion, noting that it follows from this doctrine that the soul would be in matter and its possibility would be related

21 Note that Marti in no way relates their evocation to al-Ghazālī, but explicitly refers to Papias (of Hierapolis), an apostolic father of the second century.

22 Al-Ghazālī, *Munqidh*, p. 19, 8–15. Marti's additional illustrations consist of such items as, for example, the wings of birds; the veins, arteries, and members in animals; or the presence of the different sense faculties in them, and so forth.

23 Ibid., 19, 19–20. Poggi has clearly overlooked this reference.

24 Most scholars now agree that this is not a correct translation, since *tahāfut* rather means 'incoherence'; see, for example, the recent translation by M. E. Marmura: Al-Ghazālī, *The Incoherence of the Philosophers*; A parallel English-Arabic text, translated, introduced, and commented by Michael E. Marmura, Provo, Utah, 1997 (hereafter abbreviated '*Incoherence*'). For a critical investigation of the *Tahāfut* as a rejection of philosophy (especially in the Avicennian line), see my "Al-Ghazzālī's *Tahāfut*: is it really a rejection of Ibn Sīnā's philosophy?," *Journal of Islamic Studies*, 13 (2002), pp. 1–19, reprinted in my *Ibn Sīnā and his Influence on the Arabic and Latin World*. Aldershot, Hampshire 2006, x. With respect to the use of 'complexion' as the English rendering of *mizāj*, though it is admittedly archaic English, it better reflects the basic meaning than does the translation '(bodily) humors'.

to matter.[25] In the eightieth paragraph, Marti evokes the third and final category of thinkers who fail to recognize the real truth, that is, the 'philosophi.'

These latter correspond to what al-Ghazālī calls the *Ilāhiyyūn*. It is obvious that for a Christian priest and theologian such as Marti, the translation 'theologi' was excluded. Based on the *Munqidh* alone, one would nevertheless have expected the translation 'philosophi primi.'[26] In his exposé, however, Marti clearly mixes elements of the *Munqidh* with others derived from the *Tahāfut*'s preface, so that the use of 'philosophi' almost appears natural. The exposé on the 'philosophi' begins with an explicit reference to the book 'Qui eripit ab errore.' Like al-Ghazālī, Marti affirms that the 'philosophers' have categorically rejected the views of the former two categories, i.e., the 'temporales' and the 'naturales.'[27] He also mentions that among the philosophers were Socrates, Plato and Aristotle, and stresses that the latter has systematically organized the sciences, logic especially.[28] To this Marti adds that even if Plato is a friend, truth is always a truer friend; though this saying is not present in the *Munqidh*, it is clear that Marti has derived it from the Preface of the *Tahāfut*, having slightly modified the wording.[29] Marti opens the ninth and last paragraph with a remark regarding the 'sequaces,' Avicenna and Alpharabius, which remark, again, is directly based on the *Munqidh*.[30] Next he offers an enumeration of the three theses in which the philosophers are heretical, i.e., their affirmation of the eternity of the world, their denial of divine knowledge of particulars, and their negation of bodily resurrection. Marti mainly uses the wordings of al-Ghazālī in the *Munqidh*, although he inverts the order.[31] At the same time, he clearly adds an element derived from *Tahāfut*, when he expresses the philosophers' theory of God's knowledge: 'Deum particularia ignorare, sed tantum universalia scire ut sunt genera et species.' Indeed, this formulation, especially its final part – viz., the specification of the knowledge of the universals in terms of their being 'genera et species,' – very strongly recalls the title of *Tahāfut*'s

25 Al-Ghazālī, *Incoherence*, p. 44, 1–2 (Arabic).

26 I base this remark on the very fact that the title of *al-Ilāhiyyāt* of *ash-Shifā'* in the medieval Latin translation is 'Liber de philosophia prima sive scientia divina.'

27 Al-Ghazālī, *Munqidh*, p. 20, 4–5. It has to be noted that he articulates this rejection in terms of a proof for God's existence, the imperishability of the soul, and of the denial that the corporeal pleasures are the highest good. This elucidation is as such absent from the *Munqidh*.

28 Ibid., p. 20, 1–3.

29 Al-Ghazālī, *Incoherence*, p. 4, 7–8 (Arabic) where the affirmation reads as follows: "Plato is a friend and truth is a friend, but truth is a truer friend" (ibid., p. 4, 14–15 [English]).

30 Al-Ghazālī, *Munqidh*, p. 20, 9–10.

31 Ibid., pp. 23, 21–24, 7.

eleventh chapter.[32] Whatever the case may be, it is beyond any reasonable doubt that the triple division of the philosophers, articulated by al-Ghazālī in his *Munqidh*, had a profound impact on Marti. It must be observed, at once, however, that Marti does not take over the more fundamental distinction that al-Ghazālī had used between four basic categories of thinkers, namely, the categories of *mutakallimūn*, bāṭinites, *falāsifa* and Sufis; Marti neglects, furthermore, al-Ghazālī's arguments in favor of these last as the best, probably seeing this as Islamic internal affairs, so to speak. Nevertheless, he certainly found most of al-Ghazālī's remarks about the philosophers highly valuable.

In the second chapter, in direct opposition to the 'temporales,' Marti offers proofs – both philosophical and religious in nature – that God exists. In the fourth paragraph, he refers explicitly to al-Ghazālī's *Mishkat al-anwār* under the Latin title 'lampas luminum.'[33] In the context of the argument of the Unmoved Mover, he mentions the *Mishkat* together with Averroes' epitome (*Algaveim*) on the *Metaphysics* in order to show that God must be identified not with the inner moving force of the ultimate sphere, but rather with its cause.[34] The actual Latin formulation is not very clear, but if I have understood it correctly, the reference seems to be to what al-Ghazālī observes regarding the second group of those veiled by pure light in the third part, where he states that the members of this group accept a mover-angel for each sphere, but perceive the Lord as the One who communicates motion to the outermost sphere.[35] Marti's final remark that a further cause would be superfluous is lacking in al-Ghazālī, however.

In the third chapter Marti opposes the Epicureans, especially their idea that the pleasure of the flesh is the highest good. At the very end of the chapter,

---

32 Al-Ghazālī, *Incoherence*, p. 128: "On showing the impotence of those among them who perceive that the First knows other(s) and knows the genera and species in a universal way."

33 Marti, *Pugio*, f. 195.

34 It has to be noted that 'Algaveim' is in all likelihood a scribal error for 'Algavemi,' the Latin transliteration of the Arabic *al-jawāmiʿ*. If this is correct, one here finds a further confirmation that the work in question is indeed an 'epitome' – there being no indication whatsoever as to the nature of the work expressed in the Arabic manuscripts; see Averroes, *On Aristotle's* "Metaphysics": an Annotated Translation edited by R. Arnzen, Scientia Graeco-Arabica, 5, Berlin-New York, 2010, pp. 1–4.

35 Al-Ghazālī, *Mishkat al-anwār*, ed. ʿAbd al-ʿAzīz as-Sayrawān. Beirut 1986, p. 186, 1–6. In the section in question al-Ghazālī probably refers to Aristotle's notion of the Unmoved Mover – see Frank Griffel, "Al-Ghazālī's Cosmology in the Veil Section of His *Mishkat al-anwār*," in Y. Tzvi Langermann (ed), *Avicenna and His Legacy* (Cultural Encounters in Late Antiquity and the Middle Ages, 8), Turnhout, 2009, 27–49, pp. 40–3.

after having mentioned both religious arguments and philosophical ones (based on Avicenna and Averroes), Marti concludes with one of al-Ghazālī's sayings from *Mīzān* ('Statera'), found in § 23: "Those who are busy with what enters their stomach, are worthy of what leaves it."[36] Although that this saying is apparently proverbial rather than of al-Ghazālī's own invention, it is evident that al-Ghazālī fully approves. One may detect therein an element that has permitted Marti to make a kind of identification between the 'temporales' and the 'carnales' without distorting al-Ghazālī's exposé in any serious way.

Though the fourth chapter on the immortality of the soul seems bereft of any reference to al-Ghazālī, Abū Ḥāmid returns in force in the fifth chapter, especially in the first half, that is, in folios 207–10. Marti notes explicitly that "hucusque verba Algazelis omnia a principio pene capituli, partim de libro 'Praecipitii vel ruina philosophorum' [i.e., the *Tahāfut*, this word being rendered by a double translation], partim de 'Epistola ad amicum' [I was no more successful than Cortaberria in identifying this text] et de libro 'Almonkid min Addalel.' "[37] Hence, no less than three writings of al-Ghazālī – namely, *Tahāfut*, the so-called 'Epistola ad amicum,' and al-Ghazālī's autobiography, *al-Munqidh min aḍ-ḍalāl* – were employed in this chapter's composition.

In this chapter, Marti begins his exposé with the remark that in the mathematical sciences and in logic there is little danger for religious belief. He therefore has reduced al-Ghazālī's presentation of both sciences in the *Munqidh* to their essential basis – that is, a basis that is free of any, or almost any objectionable idea.[38] The way Marti evokes astronomy and the phenomena of lunar and solar eclipses, however, demonstrates his combination of some elements taken from the *Munqidh* with others derived from *Tahāfut*'s second introduction.[39]

In the second paragraph, the astrologers are severely criticized, the worst of whom are the 'Demoniaci,' the so-called "Demoniacs," who are in no way philosophers, and thus cannot be properly called astronomers. As far as I can

36 Marti, *Pugio*, f. 199; the quotation refers to al-Ghazālī, *Mīzān al-'amal*, ed. A. Shams ad-Dīn. Beirut, 1989, p. 108, 14; ed. S. Dunya. Cairo, 1964, p. 308, 8–9.

37 Marti, *Pugio*, f. 210, § 9. It has to be stressed that the 'Epistola ad amicum' can in no case be identified with the famous writing *Ayyuhā l-walad*.

38 Al-Ghazālī, *Munqidh*, pp. 20, 20–23, 3.

39 Al-Ghazālī, *Munqidh*, pp. 21, 21–22, 8, respectively al-Ghazālī, *Incoherence*, pp. 5, 17–6, 12. However, Marti limits himself to noting that these sciences are demonstrative and therefore must be accepted, whereas al-Ghazālī insists that to deny these facts as established by the philosophers (scientists), can be very harmful for religion. This insistence offers a strong indication that, for him, there is no opposition possible between what is demonstratively shown by genuine reason and the data of Revelation, or, in other words, between *'aql* and *naql*.

see, this idea is not present in the *Munqidh* or in *Tahāfut*, but it could certainly have a Ghazalian origin;[40] Marti could have derived it, after all, from what he calls the 'epistola ad amicum.'

The third and fourth paragraphs explain that even if these sciences (i.e., mathematics, logic and astronomy) are true, nevertheless there are two main dangers present. The first, brought to the fore in paragraph three, consists in the conviction of one's own superiority based on one's familiarity with great authorities. Such familiarity makes people believe that they no longer need Revelation to open themselves to the divine light. It is evident that Marti substantially depends on al-Ghazālī's 'Preface' to *Tahāfut* for his discussion of this danger.[41] The other danger, which is extensively discussed in the fourth paragraph, consists in an excessive admiration for the philosophical sciences, which is the natural result of insufficient attention to their order or to the subtle nature of their wordings. Given such admiration, one too readily tends to place all the philosophical sciences on an equal level; moreover, based on such attitude, one easily forgets that an expert in one science is not necessarily an expert in another. Marti insists that many people neglect religious practice because of their firm belief in the strength of the philosophers' view; their exaltation of the gibberish of the philosophers, is due to a desire to learn the truth from fellow men, not from God. Again, the *Munqidh* inspires all of this directly.[42]

The total failure of weak-minded people occupies a central place in the fifth paragraph; as they unjustly criticize what has been demonstratively proven, they fail to do justice to philosophy.[43] Lacking divine wisdom, they fail to realize that, besides the Prophet himself, no human being's sayings should be taken as absolute truth.[44] Finally, these people sin against themselves, since,

40 Cf. al-Ghazālī's criticism of astrology in the introductory part to the third section of the first book of the *Iḥyāʾ ʿulūm ad-dīn*, where he, while following ʿUmar b. al-Khattāb, formulates three objections against astrology: (1) it leads people away from worshipping God; (2) it is guess work; and (3) it is useless. The evocation of the 'Demoniaci' in this context might be a proper addition of Marti, but this cannot be affirmed with certitude as long as the 'Epistola ad amicum' has not been identified.

41 Al-Ghazālī, *Incoherence*, pp. 1, 11–2 and 2, 8–11. Marti adds, however, the names of Euclides and Ptolemaeus to those of Socrates, Hippocrates, Plato and Aristotle.

42 Al-Ghazālī, *Munqidh*, respectively pp. 21, 1–3; 21, 8–11; 21, 3–5; and 25, 14–6.

43 This affirmation seems to have been inspired by al-Ghazālī, *Munqidh*, p. 21, 20–1, where it is indicated that there exists a great risk that people merely out of ignorance reject all of the sciences.

44 This appears to offer the logical conclusion to what earlier had been qualified as the unjust trust in great names, that is, famous men (see the previous paragraph).

in spite of having eyes, they blindly imitate the philosophers, not taking into account the latters' seriously mistaken doctrines, especially the metaphysical ones: a survey of these doctrines is present in the book 'De ruina philosophorum,' that is, *Tahāfut*, which asserts that seventeen philosophical doctrines are weak and three dangerously weak, so dangerous as to make those who hold them, in fact, infidels. This last remark is almost literally taken from the exposé on the 'metaphysical sciences,' the *Ilāhiyyāt*, in the *Munqidh*.[45] Marti adds that even for the (uncivilized) Arab shepherds, in spite of their being very close to beasts, it is clear that to measure the absent by what is present is a non-valid mode.[46] Finally, he quotes a saying of Aristotle at the beginning ('in principio') of the *Metaphysics, Alpha Ellaton* 993 b 9–11, which was indeed book one in the Arabic tradition:[47] this saying states that the relationship between our intellect and the first principles can be compared to the relationship between a bat and daylight.[48] These two last remarks appear to be lacking in the *Munqidh* and *Tahāfut*. Hence, they may have their origin in the 'Epistola ad amicum.'

In the sixth paragraph, Marti stresses that weak people are like moles that despise the eyes of the eagle. Blindly following the philosophers, they admit that the prophet can foresee the future and to do extraordinary things, but, in their aping, they explain these prophetic capacities in a natural way, ascribing them to the help of the celestial bodies. This latter observation recalls al-Ghazālī's presentation of the philosophers' view on the extraordinary powers of the

45 Al-Ghazālī, *Munqidh*, p. 23, 17–24, 7.

46 Marti, *Pugio*, f. 209, 16–8: "[those who blindly imitate the philosophers accept the mode] absentia presentibus mensurando; quem profecto mensurandi modum etiam istis pastoribus Arabum, qui omnibus hominibus sont bestiis propriores, constat esse incongruum." This affirmation is close to a similar one in al-Ghazālī, *Mīzān*, see *infra*, p. 16.

47 Already Ibn an-Nadīm, in his *Fihrist*, presents *Alpha Ellaton* as the first book (see F. E. Peters, *Aristoteles Arabus. The Oriental Translations and Commentaries on the Aristotelian* corpus. Leiden 1968, p. 49); it is also the first book commented on in Averroes' Great Commentary on the *Metaphysics*. For the Arabic translation of 993 b 9–11, see Ibn Rushd, *Tafsīr mā ba'd aṭ-Ṭabī'a*, ed. M. Bouyges. Beirut 1938, I, p. 4, 8–10.

48 The latter notion of daylight is articulated by Marti in terms of 'lumen solis,' which literally corresponds to the Arabic translation *ḍaw' ash-shams*, whereas the Greek has *phenggos to met'hemeran*. In the Greco-Latin translation this has been rendered by 'lumen diei'; see Aristoteles Latinus, *Metaphysica*. Recensio et translatio Guillelmi de Moerbeka, ed. G. Vuillemin-Diem. Leiden – New York – Köln 1995, p. 43, 13. However in the Arabic-Latin translation one finds the reading 'lumen solis', see (Averroes Latinus), *Aristotelis opera cum Averrois commentariis*. Venetiis, 1562–74, f. 28vI. Hence, it is beyond any reasonable doubt that Marti has before him an Arabic work quoting the Arabic translation of Aristotle's *Metaphysics*. Given the present context, the 'Epistola ad amicum' appears a good candidate.

prophets in the introduction to the second part, that is, on natural sciences, of *Tahāfut* (167–68).[49] In what follows, it is stressed that the prophet, on the contrary, possesses a special 'eye,' that is, a degree of intellectual capacity that is indeed beyond the normal one. This eye permits the prophet to perform miracles that disrupt the natural order as well as to know hidden things. This idea of a special eye is directly derived from the *Munqidh* (one may detect other reminiscences of the *Munqidh*, as well).[50]

While rewording a fragment taken from the section on prophecy in the *Munqidh*,[51] Marti states in the seventh paragraph that some deny that the existence of the prophets can be shown by recourse to the phenomenon of dreams which sometimes reveal what is hidden; this denial is based on the assertion that the hidden cannot be seen by the senses when awake, *a fortiori*, nor when asleep – a view which Marti completely discounts. As for al-Ghazālī, he insists that someone who is completely unfamiliar with dreams is strongly inclined to deny that hidden things can be seen while dreaming; for such a person, only the senses are the causes of perception, and perception never includes hidden things. Note, however, that Marti's reformulation remains faithful to the spirit of al-Ghazālī's affirmation.

The eighth paragraph starts with a general remark based on the *Munqidh*, namely, that the human intellect, based on so-called rational grounds, judges not only prophecy to be impossible, but also many other phenomena.[52] Marti illustrates this using two natural examples: opium and diamond. Regarding opium, Marti stresses that even a very small amount can be lethal, its excessively cooling action fatally congealing the blood in the veins; this, however, seems contrary to physics: since no combination of even the two coldest elements (i.e., water and earth) can generate such an extreme coolness, it seems impossible for a combination of two warm elements, i.e., air and fire, to produce such a chill, as is the case with opium. This first example constitutes an almost *verbatim*, albeit slightly amplified, version of al-Ghazālī's presentation of the very same example in the *Munqidh*.[53] As for diamond, designated by Marti as the stone 'qui Arabice dicitur Hajaralmech [*ḥajar al-mās*], apud aurifices Latinos esmerillus terreus,' it is stressed that it is a very hard stone,

49 Al-Ghazālī, *Incoherence*, pp. 167–68.

50 Al-Ghazālī, *Munqidh*, p. 51, 2–5 (the affirmation occurs in a section which deals with the remedying of those who have a feeble belief in the prophet). This basic passage has been supplemented with *Munqidh*, pp. 41, 17–42, 2 and 42, 13–5 (inside the part on prophecy).

51 Ibid., p. 42, 6–13.

52 Ibid., p. 51, 5–7.

53 Ibid., p. 51, 7–16.

almost impossible to break, but once placed in a recipient of iron, stone, or even wood, can be completely pulverized when hit with a leaden bar – but, Marti insists, only with a leaden bar, not with any other metal. When one tells a philosopher this, although he has never experienced it, he will deny it based on physical considerations, such as the idea that a 'lesser' cannot be when there is no 'greater,' and what something lower (e.g., a lower metal) can do, something higher (e.g., a higher metal) can also do. Thus, the philosopher measures what is present through what is absent – a logical fallacy of which even the shepherds of the camels ('pastores camelorum') are aware. Beyond any reasonable doubt, Marti bases himself in this case on an Arabic text. Again, the most probable candidate is the already mentioned 'Epistola ad amicum'; this likelihood is magnified by the conclusion of the paragraph, which asserts that not all things are as evident as they appear, as shown in the twenty questions disputed in the 'De ruina philosophorum.'

At the beginning of the ninth paragraph, Marti notes that nothing of what is correct in the sayings of the philosophers must be rejected. This affirmation is most likely based on al-Ghazālī's following rhetorical question in the *Munqidh*: if something is found in philosophy that has been proven demonstratively and that corresponds with the Qur'ān and the Sunna, why would it be rejected?[54] To illustrate this idea, Marti refers with al-Ghazālī to the example of the presence of honey in a cupping glass.[55] After indicating the titles of the three works of al-Ghazālī he has used in what preceded,[56] he remarks that it is better to refute the philosophers by the philosophers than by the saints. Herein, one may also detect a Ghazalian influence, as is well exemplified by the case of *Tahāfut*, since al-Ghazālī routinely combats the philosophers with their own arms. In what follows, Marti evokes sayings of the saints, especially of St. Augustine, whose attitude towards the philosophers he qualifies as almost identical to that of al-Ghazālī.[57] It is also worthwhile to note that among these sayings of the saints, a further reference to al-Ghazālī, more precisely to his 'liber Statera', (i.e., *Mīzān* 96, 7–9), is present.[58] This saying highlights the

54 Ibid., p. 26, 9–11.

55 Ibid., p. 26, 17–8.

56 See *supra*, p. 10. From the preceding exposé, it is clear that Marti mainly used the *Munqidh*, perhaps supplemented in an important way by the 'Epistola ad amicum'; he obviously granted the *Tahāfut* only a minor role.

57 Marti, *Pugio*, f. 211.

58 Ibid., f. 213.

necessity to combine perfect knowledge with a perfect moral attitude so as to become truly perfect and to be able to come nearer to God.[59]

In the chapters dealing with the issue of the eternity/temporality of the world, Marti leans three times on al-Ghazālī's *Tahāfut*:

1. Marti insists that because of our imagination, we always consider time (and place) as being with 'something.'[60] It is this (false) imagination that has urged the philosophers to claim that the temporal origination of the universe implies the existence of a time before a time, thereby leading them in error. Even in its highly abbreviated state, this argument is clearly based on al-Ghazālī's first discussion of the second proof in the first Question on the past eternity of the world.[61]
2. Marti, while explicitly referring to *Tahāfut*, evokes al-Ghazālī's argument from the infinity of souls in favor of the temporal duration of the world.[62] He first notes that though the philosophers invoke the necessity of reason, 'necessitas intellectus,' their adversaries can nevertheless do the same.[63] Next, he provides an almost *verbatim* Latin translation of a paragraph of *Tahāfut*, in which al-Ghazālī states that the Platonic doctrine of the existence of one single eternal soul, to which all souls return after death, is undoubtedly an even worse alternative opinion.[64] It should be noted that Marti, before offering this translation, explicitly says that he, for the sake of brevity, has omitted 'multa' of al-Ghazālī's exposé. This implies that he was in possession of a more complete text, and perhaps the totality of the work.
3. A third and last instance is present in the chapter entitled 'Quod Aristoteles non reputavit rationes, quas induxit ad probandum aeternitatem mundi, esse demonstrativas simpliciter.' Marti, once more explicitly referring to the *Tahāfut* (in fact, 12, 8–11), presents Galen's position on

59 Al-Ghazālī, *Mīzān al-ʿamal*, ed. A. Shams ad-Dīn. p. 96, 7–8; ed. S. Dunya. p. 293, 13–5.

60 Marti, *Pugio*, I, 9, f. 221.

61 Al-Ghazālī, *Incoherence*, pp. 30, 12–36, 6, especially pp. 33, 4–17 and 35, 13–36, 6 (Arabic).

62 Marti, *Pugio*, I, 12, f. 226. Concerning al-Ghazālī's argument, see the seminal study of M. E. Marmura, "Avicenna and the Problem of the Infinite Number of Souls," *Mediaeval Studies*, 22 (1960), pp. 232–39 (reprinted in his *Probing in Islamic Philosophy*, Binghamton 2005, pp. 171–79).

63 Marti summarizes and rewords part of the first objection against the first proof in al-Ghazālī first Question; al-Ghazālī, *Incoherence*, pp. 17, 16–18, 2 (Arabic).

64 Al-Ghazālī, *Incoherence*, pp. 19, 19–20, 9 (Arabic).

> this issue as non-committal, not because of his being weak-minded, but because of the complexity of the problem.[65]

Among the chapters in question, one finds in chapter 11 one further reference to al-Ghazālī's 'Liber probatorium,' concerning the improper transfer of the meaning of a term: that is, the transfer of 'creation' (factio) into the 'making of particular things.' Regarding such a transfer, according to Marti, al-Ghazālī affirms: "Facere vim in verbis ex quo sententia patet mos est brevem habentium scientiam et curtum intellectum." The same saying, although in a more understandable form (i.e., "Facere vim in verbis postquam sensus patet consuetudo est brevem habentium scientiam et curtum intellectum"), reappears in Pars tertia, Distinctio I, caput IV, f. 495, again accompanied by a reference to al-Ghazālī, but this time without mention of any precise work. So far, I looked in vain for this affirmation in al-Ghazālī's logical works, including *Miḥakk* and *Miʿyār*.

As for the chapters dealing with God's knowledge (especially of particulars), one finds, at the very beginning, a reminder that al-Ghazālī has shown that the philosophers are heretics in this matter.[66] Al-Ghazālī's name is once more present in chapter twenty-five, one of the last chapters dealing with this issue, in two different instances (f. 251 and f. 252). Each of these is located within the Latin translation Marti offers from Averroes' *Epistle Dedicatory*.[67] Note, however, that in the extant Arabic text of Averroes, the second reference to al-Ghazālī is not present. Whether Marti introduced it on his own initiative, or whether he disposed of another, more complete manuscript, needs further investigation.

Finally, in the only chapter devoted to the issue of resurrection, Marti translates a fragment of the twentieth Question of *Tahāfut* after he has offered a summary paraphrase of what precedes.[68] Again, the emphasis is on the fact that what appears at first sight impossible – for example, the resurrection of the body – should not be immediately dismissed; there are phenomena in nature, after all, that are difficult to understand, such as magnetism.[69]

---

65 Marti, *Pugio*, I, 14, f. 231. The reference is to al-Ghazālī, *Incoherence*, p. 12, 8–11 (Arabic).

66 Marti, *Pugio*, I, 15, f. 234.

67 Ibid., I, 25, ff. 251–52. Note that the translation of Averroes' *Epistle Dedicatory*, entitled in the Latin 'Epistola ad amicum,' accounts for almost the entire chapter with the exception of the last paragraph.

68 Ibid., I, 26, ff. 254. The translated fragment corresponds to al-Ghazālī, *Incoherence*, p. 226, 11–7 (Arabic).

69 *Vide supra*, p. 13.

In the remaining parts of *Pugio*, references to al-Ghazālī become extremely rare. One occurs in the eighth chapter of 'pars secunda,' where Marti – after having noted that reason shows that Jesus' miracles are the most convincing, *inter alia*, insofar as one of them consists in making the stupid man wise by the gift of the Holy Spirit – insists that the Qur'ān instigates Muslims to indulge the desires of the flesh; this drive is especially strong among the Arabs, who, of all men, are the closest to the beasts.[70] In this respect Marti refers to al-Ghazālī's *Mīzān* ('Statera factorum'), undoubtedly to the passage near the end of chapter twenty-four, where the latter affirms that among men the uncivilized Arabs and Turks are the most bestial.[71] Marti omits not only the mentioning of the Turks – in all likelihood because they were the Byzantines of his day, and hence Christians – but also the qualification 'uncivilized' (*ajlāf*), thus giving the impression that al-Ghazālī himself considered all the Arabs to be 'bestial by nature.'[72] His remark about the Qur'ānic attitude toward the pleasures of the flesh, however, could have been inspired by al-Ghazālī's qualification of the sexual appetite as recommendable (*maḥmūd*).[73] But did Marti really have access to the complete text of *Mīzān*? The three – all in all, minor – quotations present in *Pugio* indicate that at best he had access to a florilegium containing a few of its sayings. This could also explain his limited references to a few other works, such as to *Mishkāt* and to 'Liber Probatorium.' Whatever the case may be, a single reference to another Ghazalian work is also present, i.e., to *al-Maqṣad al-asnā fī sharḥ ma'ānī asmā' Allāh al-ḥusnā*, evoked by the Latin title 'Liber de Nominibus Dei.' This reference occurs in the third part, more precisely in the discussion of the name 'Shaddai' as one of the names of the Messiah.[74] Marti offers an almost literal translation of al-Ghazālī's exposé of the names *al-ghānī* and *al-mughnī*, omitting, however, the last five lines.[75] Once again one wonders whether this omission is the result of Marti's own decision, or of the fact that he lacked access to the complete text.

---

70 Marti, *Pugio*, II, 8, f. 368.

71 Al-Ghazālī, *Mīzān al-'amal*, ed. A. Shams ad-Dīn. p. 122, 14–5; ed. S. Dunya. p. 332, 20.

72 Of course, this undoubtedly reflects his missionary attitude and his profound conviction of the superiority of the Christian faith over the Muslim one; nevertheless, it is striking that he pays attention to important Muslim sources, including the Qur'ān; *vide supra*, note 1.

73 Al-Ghazālī, *Mīzān al-'amal*, ed. A. Shams ad-Dīn. pp. 111, 5–112, 6; ed. S. Dunya. pp. 314, 19–316, 11. It must be noted, however, that al-Ghazālī imposes some clear limitations on the exercise of sexual pleasures.

74 Marti, *Pugio*, III, f. 694.

75 Al-Ghazālī, *al-Maqṣad al-asnā fī sharḥ ma'ānī asmā' Allāh al-ḥusnā*, anonymous edition. Limasol 1987, p. 144, 4–12.

One must acknowledge Marti's very substantial use of the *Munqidh* and *Tahāfut* (and also of the 'Epistola ad amicum,' about which nothing seriously can be said until it is definitively identified). Still, his consultation is limited mainly to a few parts of these works: as far as the *Munqidh* is concerned, to the exposé on philosophy and, to a lesser degree, on prophecy; in regards to *Tahāfut*, to the Preface, and to parts of the first and twentieth Questions. Moreover, the instances of use usually involve more or less paraphrastical renderings. Nevertheless, the use of these works is systematic and indicates a well-planned project, a fact that accounts for Marti's preference of some passages over others. Generally speaking, Marti seems to particularly appreciate al-Ghazālī's critical attitude towards the philosophers, as well as the latter's recommendation of spiritual pleasures over the mundane ones. Even so, the evidence does not prove that he had indeed access to the full text of the *Munqidh* or of *Tahāfut*. If this is true, one wonders why he continues to qualify al-Ghazālī as 'philosophus quidam' before quoting the passage of the *Maqṣad*; given what he has said in chapter five of the first part, this remains, in any case, a puzzling statement. Had he written it before he came acquainted with the *Munqidh* and *Tahāfut*? Or, is the qualification of 'philosophus' by 'quidam' to be understood in the sense that al-Ghazālī was 'a kind of' philosopher, not in the usual sense – where philosophy opposes basic religious beliefs – but in the sense of a rationalist who fundamentally respects the data of Revelation? I am inclined to believe that 'critical philosopher' best represents Marti's opinion of al-Ghazālī, that is, that the latter offers a 'philosophical' critique against the philosophers. After all, this is a possible, and in my view, most interesting interpretation of al-Ghazālī's thought.

CHAPTER 17

Al-Ghazālī's Esotericism According to Ibn Taymiyya's *Bughyat al-Murtād*

Yahya M. Michot

Many of the simplistic images of the Damascene theologian Ibn Taymiyya (d. 728/1328) circulating nowadays are grave distortions of his ideas, both in the domain of politics and in Islamic thought, particularly in regard to Sufism and *falsafa*. Much time will probably be needed for these images to be corrected, especially among certain Islamist groups and mediocre neo-Orientalists. Several recent publications nevertheless have already paved the way towards a more accurate understanding of his ideas;[1] also, works like his magisterial *Darʾ at-taʿāruḍ*[2] have begun to receive the attention which they deserve as first-hand sources for the history of intellectual, religious and spiritual debates during the classical period of Islam.

In earlier articles, I have presented a number of Taymiyyan texts relating to, or commenting on, al-Ḥallāj, the Ikhwān aṣ-Ṣafāʾ, Avicenna, and Naṣīr ad-Dīn aṭ-Ṭūsī.[3] What about Abū Ḥāmid al-Ghazālī? The Damascene theologian's

1 See Y. Michot, *Ibn Taymiyya. Against Extremisms.* Texts translated, annotated and introduced. With a foreword by Bruce B. Lawrence (Beirut – Paris: Albouraq, Ṣafar 1433/Jan. 2012); *Muslims under Non-Muslim Rule. Ibn Taymiyya on fleeing from sin, kinds of emigration, the status of Mardin (domain of peace/war, domain composite), the conditions for challenging power.* Texts translated, annotated and presented in relation to six modern readings of the *Mardin fatwa.* Foreword by J. Piscatori (Oxford – London: Interface Publications, 2006); *Ibn Taymiyya's "New Mardin Fatwa". Is genetically modified Islam (GMI) carcinogenic?*, in *The Muslim World*, 101/2 (Hartford, April 2011), pp. 130–181; *L'autorité, l'individu et la communauté face à la* Sharīʿa *: quelques pensées d'Ibn Taymiyya*, in *Mélanges de l'Université Saint Joseph* 64 (Beirut, 2013), pp. 261–286; Y. Rapoport & S. Ahmed (eds), *Ibn Taymiyya and his Times* (Karachi: Oxford University Press, 2010); C. Bori, *Théologie politique et Islam à propos d'Ibn Taymiyya (m. 728/1328) et du sultanat mamelouk*, in *Revue de l'Histoire des Religions*, 224/1 (Paris, 2007), pp. 5–46; J. R. Hoover, *Ibn Taymiyya's Theodicy of Perpetual Optimism* (Leiden – Boston: Brill, "Islamic Philosophy, Theology and Science. Texts and Studies, 73", 2007).

2 Ibn Taymiyya, *Darʾ taʿāruḍ al-ʿaql wa-n-naql aw muwāfaqat ṣaḥīḥ al-manqūl li-ṣarīḥ al-maʿqūl*, ed. M. R. Sālim, 11 vols. (Riyadh: Dār al-Kunūz al-Adabiyya, [1399/1979]). See Y. Michot, *Vanités intellectuelles. L'impasse des rationalismes selon* le Rejet de la contradiction *d'Ibn Taymiyya*, in *Oriente Moderno*, 19 (80), n. s. (Rome, 2000), pp. 597–617.

3 See Y. Michot, *Ibn Taymiyya's Commentary on the* Creed *of al-Ḥallāj*, in A. Shihadeh (ed.), *Sufism and Theology* (Edinburgh: Edinburgh University Press, 2007), pp. 123–136; *Misled*

 | DOI 10.1163/9789004290952_018

remarkably extensive knowledge of the Ghazālian *corpus* is striking; the titles that he quotes, as surveyed by R. Y. ash-Shāmī,[4] exceed two dozen. Yet, impressive as ash-Shāmī's list appears, on its own it does not fully convey the depth of Ibn Taymiyya's engagement with the works of his predecessor. Ash-Shāmī's survey is unfortunately not exhaustive; moreover, it does not reveal that the Damascene theologian sometimes quotes lengthy excerpts from a number of al-Ghazālī's works verbatim, and comments on them in various ways. In fact, Ibn Taymiyya's information about, and grasp of, Abū Ḥāmid's corpus is far better than that of the latter's most famous challengers among the *falāsifa*, Ibn Ṭufayl and Averroes. It is accordingly the more astonishing that, in Ghazālian studies, Ibn Taymiyya has not been more often taken into consideration.[5]

In a paper presented at the International al-Ghazālī Symposium held in Isparta, Süleyman Demirel University, in May 2011, I translated and examined several pages of different Taymiyyan works relating to specific topics addressed in four prominent books of al-Ghazālī,[6] offering evaluations of the latter's thought as a whole, or discussing its sources and influence.[7] In the present paper, I take this exploration of the Damascene theologian's views on the

---

and Misleading ... Yet Central in their Influence: Ibn Taymiyya's Views on the Ikhwān al-Ṣafā', in N. El-Bizri (ed.), *The Ikhwān al-Ṣafā' and their* Rasā'il. *An Introduction* (Oxford: Oxford University Press, 2008), pp. 139–179 – Corrected version on *www.muslimphilosophy.com*; *A Mamlūk Theologian's Commentary on Avicenna's* Risāla Aḍḥawiyya: *Being a Translation of a Part of the* Dar' al-Ta'āruḍ *of Ibn Taymiyya*, with Introduction, Annotation, and Appendices, in *Journal of Islamic Studies*, Part I, 14/2 (Oxford, May 2003), pp. 149–203; Part II, 14/3 (Sept. 2003), pp. 309–363; *Vizir « hérétique » mais philosophe d'entre les plus éminents: al-Ṭūsī vu par Ibn Taymiyya*, in *Farhang*, 15–16, nos 44–45 (Tehran: Institute for Humanities and Cultural Studies, Winter-Spring 2003), pp. 195–227; *From al-Ma'mūn to Ibn Sab'īn, via Avicenna: Ibn Taymiyya's Historiography of* Falsafa, in F. Opwis & D. Reisman (eds.), *Islamic Philosophy, Science, Culture, and Religion. Studies in Honor of Dimitri Gutas* (Leiden: Brill, 2012), pp. 453–475.

4 Rizq Yūsuf ash-Shāmī, *Ibn Taymiyya: Maṣādiru-hu wa-manhaju-hu fī taḥlīli-hā*, in *Journal of the Institute of Arabic Manuscripts*, v. 38 (Cairo, 1415/1994), pp. 183–269, at pp. 244–246. See also the transliteration of this list given in Y. Michot, *An Important Reader of al-Ghazālī: Ibn Taymiyya*, in *The Muslim World* 103 (2013), pp. 131-160, here p. 132.

5 For example, there is very little use of Ibn Taymiyya in E. L. Ormsby, *Theodicy in Islamic Thought. The Dispute over al-Ghazālī's "Best of All Possible Worlds"* (Princeton: Princeton University Press, 1984), and, more recently, K. Garden, *Al-Ghazālī's Contested Revival:* Iḥyā' 'Ulūm al-Dīn *and Its Critics in Khorasan and the Maghrib*. Unpublished PhD dissertation (University of Chicago, 2005). Fortunately, however, things are improving.

6 Greek logic in the *Mustaṣfā*, philosophy and causality in the *Iḥyā'*, causality in the *Tahāfut*, intercession and prophethood in the *Maḍnūn*.

7 See Y. Michot, *Reader*. Other Taymiyyan pages on al-Ghazālī are translated in Y. Michot, *Textes spirituels d'Ibn Taymiyya (Nouvelle série). XI. Abū Ḥāmid al-Ghazālī & Fakhr al-Dīn al-Rāzī*, on *www.muslimphilosophy.com*, July 2011, pp. 1–5.

Ḥujjat al-Islam further by focusing on the first half of the former's *Bughyat al-murtād – The Goal of the Explorer.*[8] As in other publications, I will prefer to let Ibn Taymiyya speak for himself.

According to its editor, Mūsā d-Duwaysh, Ibn Taymiyya wrote the *Bughya* during his stay in Alexandria, between 1 Rabīʿ I and 2 Shawwāl 709, i.e. between August 1309 and March 1310. The work has several other titles. Ibn Taymiyya himself variously calls it *Refutation of Ibn Sabʿīn and the Unionists, Discourse against the Sabʿīnians* and *Refutation of the Unionists.*[9] Ibn Qayyim al-Jawziyya (d. 751/1350) refers to it as *The Alexandrian Questions* and Ibn ʿAbd al-Hādī (d. 744/1343) as *The Alexandrian Questions concerning the Refutation of the Heretics and the Unionists.*[10] Despite the editorial efforts of M. ad-Duwaysh, the text is still plagued with mistakes and problems leading one to wonder what sort of unpolished version it comes from: a draft by the Damascene theologian himself, or notes by one of his disciples? The Taymiyyan nature of the book is nevertheless beyond doubt and it is of the greatest interest to Ghazālian studies as a number of pages of the *Miʿyār,*[11] *Tafriqa,*[12] *Mishkāt*[13] and *Jawāhir*[14]

---

8 See Ibn Taymiyya, *Bughyat al-murtād fī r-radd ʿalā l-mutafalsifa wa-l-qarāmiṭa wa-l-bāṭiniyya ahl al-ilḥād min al-qāʾilīn bi-l-ḥulūl wa-l-ittiḥād*, ed. M. B. S. ad-Duwaysh (n.p.: Maktabat al-ʿUlūm wa-l-Ḥikam, 1408/1988; hereafter referred to, in apparatus criticus footnotes, as a boldfaced capital B, i.e., **B**), pp. 169–531.

9 See, respectively, Ibn Taymiyya, *Kitāb an-Nubuwwāt* (Beirut: Dār al-Fikr, n.d.), p. 82; *ar-Radd ʿalā Ibn Sabʿīn wa-ahl al-waḥda*; *ar-Radd alā l-manṭiqiyyīn* (*Refutation of the Logicians*), ed. ʿA. Ṣ. Sh. D. al-Kutubī (Bombay: Qayyimah Press, 1368/1949), p. 275; *al-Kalām ʿalā s-Sabʿīniyya*; *Majmūʿ al-fatāwā*, vol. 10, p. 403: *ar-Radd ʿalā l-ittiḥādiyya* (from M. ad-Duwaysh (ed.), *Bughya*, pp. 53–54).

10 *Al-Masāʾil al-Iskandarāniyya* and *Masāʾil al-Iskandariyya fī r-radd ʿalā l-malāḥida wa l-ittihādiyya*; see M. ad-Duwaysh (ed.), *Bughya*, pp. 55–56.

11 See al-Ghazālī, *Manṭiq* Tahāfut al-falāsifa, *al-musammā* Miʿyār al-ʿilm. Ed. S. Dunyā (Cairo: Dār al-Maʿārif, 1379/1960).

12 See al-Ghazālī, *Fayṣal at-tafriqa bayn al-Islām wa-z-zandaqa*, in M. M. Abū l-ʿAlāʾ, *al-Quṣūr al-ʿawālī min rasāʾil al-imām al-Ghazālī* (Cairo: Maktabat al-Jandī, 1390/1970), v. 1, pp. 123–159. See also the translation by S. A. Jackson, *On the Boundaries of Theological Tolerance in Islam: Abū Ḥāmid al-Ghazālī's* Fayṣal al-Tafriqa Bayna al-Islām wa al-Zandaqa (Karachi: Oxford University Press, "Studies in Islamic Philosophy", 2002).

13 See al-Ghazālī, *Mishkāt al-anwār*, ed. A. ʿA. ʿAfīfī (Cairo: ad-Dār al-Qawmiyya li-ṭ-Ṭibāʿa wa-n-Nashr, 1964/1383). See also the translation by W. H. T. Gairdner, *Al-Ghazzali's* Mishkat Al-Anwar (*"The Niche for Lights"*). A translation with introduction (Lahore: Sh. Muhammad Ashraf, 1952).

14 See al-Ghazālī, *Jawāhir al-Qurʾān* (Beirut: Dār al-Āfāq al-Jadīda, 1393/1973; hereafter referred to, in apparatus criticus footnotes, as a boldfaced capital J, i.e., J). See also the translation by L. Bakhtiar, *Al-Ghazzali: Jewels of the Quran* (Chicago: Kazi Publications, 2009).

are reproduced and discussed therein, in relation to the *Fuṣūṣ al-Ḥikam* of Ibn ʿArabī and the *Risālat al-Alwāḥ* of Ibn Sabʿīn.[15]

The textual imperfections of the *Bughya* should not deter scholars from paying full attention to the version of the Ghazālian writings preserved in its long quotes. The manuscripts of the *Miʿyār, Tafriqa, Mishkāt* and *Jawāhir* reproduced by Ibn Taymiyya probably predate many copies used as sources for the 20th century editions of these four books, and the *Bughya* indeed contains important variants or emendations. Four examples will suffice here.

In the *Miʿyār*, p. 292, l. 2–3, one reads: *wa-ammā ʿaql al-kull fa-yuṭlaqu ʿalā maʿnayayni, aḥaduhumā*... – "As for 'the intellect of the whole', the [expression] is used in two senses; one of which is..." In the *Bughya*'s version, p. 187, l. 14–15, the text is: *wa-ammā ʿaql al-kull fa-yuṭlaqu ʿalā maʿnayayni,* ***li-anna l-kulla yuṭlaqu ʿalā maʿnayayni,*** *aḥaduhumā*... – "As for 'the intellect of the whole', the [expression] is used in two senses **because 'the whole' is used in two senses;** one of which is..." There is obviously a *homoioteleuton* in the modern edition[16] and Ibn Taymiyya's version offers a better meaning.

In [*Fayṣal*] *at-tafriqa*, p. 135, l. 3, one reads: *qad athbata qalam^{an} ʿaqliyy^{an} lā ḥissiyy^{an} khayāliyy^{an} wa-ka-dhālika*... – which S. A. Jackson translates: "affirms the existence of a noetic pen [or hand], not a pen [or hand] perceived through the senses (*ḥiss*) or conceived of in the imagination (*khayāl*). Similar to..."[17] In the *Bughya*'s version, p. 198, l. 3, the text is: *qad athbata qalam^{an} ʿaqliyy^{an} lā ḥissiyy^{an} khayāliyy^{an}* ***lā kawniyy^{an}*** *wa-ka-dhālika*... and the translation becomes: "affirms the existence of a noetic pen [or hand], not a pen [or hand] perceived through the senses, conceived of in the imagination, **not ontological.** Similar to..." The *lectio difficilior* of Ibn Taymiyya's version is rhetorically more satisfying and enriches the meaning of the passage. Philosophically, the double parallelism drawn between *ʿaql* and *khayāl* on the one hand, *ḥiss* and *kawn* on the other, and the opposition of these two dimensions one against the other, entails a dichotomy worthy of further investigation.

---

15 A concordance of the *Bughya* and the *Miʿyār, Tafriqa, Mishkāt* and *Jawāhir* is offered in the Appendix. It covers nearly half of the text in M. ad-Duwaysh's edition (pp. 169–327, i.e. 158 pages out of 362). Between pp. 328 and 376, Ibn Taymiyya returns to the *Tafriqa* and *Mishkāt* before dealing more extensively with Ibn ʿArabī and Ibn Sabʿīn. The limits imparted to this paper made it impossible to include these supplementary quotes in our concordance and analysis.

16 Idem in the edition of M. M. Abū l-ʿAlāʾ, *Al-Ghazālī, Miʿyār al-ʿilm fī fann al-manṭiq* (Cairo: Maktabat al-Jandī, 1392/1972), p. 259.

17 S. A. Jackson, *Boundaries*, p. 100.

In the *Mishkāt*, p. 74, l. 10–11, one reads: *wa-hādhihi ḥamāqāt. Wa-ammā*... – "These are imbecilities. As for..." In the *Bughya*'s version, p. 213, l. 6–9, the text is: *wa-hādhihi ḥamāqāt.* ***Wa-qad abṭalnā jamīʿ dhālika fī kitāb "Iljām al-ʿawāmm" wa-mansha' "al-Risāla fī aḥkām az-zaygh wa-ḍ-ḍalāla."*** *Wa-ammā*... – "These are imbecilities. **We have shown the vain nature of all this in [our] book 'Restraining the Masses from Delving into the Science of *Kalām*' and in the beginning of the 'Epistle on the Legal Rulings of Deviation and Errancy.'** As for..." Here is a question for the Ghazālian specialists: does this whole sentence present in Ibn Taymiyya's version of the *Mishkāt* but absent from its modern edition affect in any way the generally accepted chronology of Abū Ḥāmid's works?

Finally, in the *Jawāhir*, p. 30, l. 17–31, l. 1, one reads: *inna kulla mā yaḥtamiluhu fahmuka, fa-inna l-Qur'āna yulqīhi ilayka*... – which L. Bakhtiar translates: "Everything that it is possible that you understand is given to you in the Qur'ān..."[18] In the *Bughya*'s version, p. 279, l. 4, the text is: *inna kulla mā* ***lā*** *yaḥtamiluhu fahmuka, fa-inna l-Qur'āna yulqīhi ilayka*... and the translation becomes: "Everything that it is **not** possible that you understand is given to you in the Qur'ān..." By the mere addition of a negation, the version of the *Jawāhir* available to Ibn Taymiyya offers an understanding of the relation between reason and revelation which is the exact opposite of the one appearing in its modern edition and L. Bakhtiar's translation.[19]

The reason why the Damascene theologian quotes long excerpts of the *Miʿyār*, *Tafriqa*, *Mishkāt* and *Jawāhir* in the *Bughya* has of course nothing to do with such textual concerns. Nor does it ensue from a desire to develop a systematic commentary on these works of the Ḥujjat al-Islam. The *Bughya* is a fatwa and, as such, its objective is fundamentally determined by the questions that its author is asked to answer. In this case, as explained in the introduction, the query relates to the authenticity of three sayings attributed to the Prophet and, hence, the lawfulness of using them in religious matters:

18 L. Bakhtiar, *Jewels*, p. 39.

19 After I had finished writing this paper, K. Garden kindly offered me a copy of the new edition of the *Jawāhir* published by Kh. M. Kāmil & ʿI. al-Sharqawī, *Jawāhir al-Qur'ān wa-duraruhu li-Ḥujjat al-Islām Abī Ḥāmid al-Ghazālī* (Cairo: Maktaba Dār al-Kutub wa-l-Wathā'iq al-Qawmiyya, 1432/2011). P. 90, this new edition has the same *mā yaḥtamiluhu* as the Beirut edition of 1393/1973 but gives Ibn Taymiyya's negative version as a variant in an *apparatus criticus* footnote.

1. INTRODUCTION[20] – The Shaykh al-Islam, the outstanding one of the outstanding scholars, Taqī d-Dīn Abū l-ʿAbbās Aḥmad b. ʿAbd al-Ḥalīm b. ʿAbd as-Salām Ibn Taymiyya of Ḥarrān, may the Exalted God have mercy upon him, was asked:
What do the masters, the scholars, the imams of the religion say about the hadith which is reported with this wording: "The first [thing] that God created was the intellect. He said to it: 'Turn forward' and it turned forward. He then said to it: 'Turn backward' and it turned backward. He said: 'By My might! I have created no creature more precious to Me than you. By you I take and by you I give. By you [comes] the reward and the punishment!'"

And about this other hadith whose wording is: "I was a treasure, unknown, and I wanted to be known. I thus created the creatures, in order that they know Me. By Me they have known Me." **[170]**

And about this third hadith whose wording is: "God was and there was nothing with him. And He is now as He was then."

Are these hadiths authentic or flawed? Or are some authentic and others flawed? And which one is authentic?[21]

Ibn Taymiyya's interest in Ghazālī in the *Bughya* comes from his conviction that the latter, like the Ikhwān aṣ-Ṣafāʾ before him, played a central role in the promotion of the hadith of the intellect and its like as arguments for blending religion and philosophy, and thus shares in the responsibility for the importance increasingly given to it amongst Muslim thinkers, despite its inauthenticity:

2. THE FIRST [THING] THAT GOD CREATED ... – It is amazing that those who want to make a synthesis between the divine Law and Greek Peripatetic philosophy took this hadith for their main reference (*ʿumda*) concerning the fundamentals of the religion, knowledge, and realization [of the truth] (*taḥqīq*). This [hadith] is invented (*mawḍūʿ*) and, yet, all those changed it and reported [it as] "The first [thing] (*awwal*^{u}) that God created was the intellect (*al-ʿaql*^{u}). He said to it: 'Turn forward.'" They took this for an argument (*ḥujja*) and considered it to correspond to what **[180]** the Peripatetic philosophers – the followers of Aristotle – say when saying: "The first of the [things] emanating from the Necessary Existent is the first intelligence."

20 These titles are added by the translator. The numbers between small boldfaced square brackets appearing in the translations refer to the pagination of the Arabic editions used.

21 Ibn Taymiyya, *Bughya*, pp. 169–170.

> This spread out in the words of many of the later [thinkers], after they saw it in the books [titled] *The Epistles of the Ikhwān aṣ-Ṣafā'*. These *Epistles* are indeed the main reference of those [people]. **[181]** They also found something similar in the words of Abū Ḥāmid [al-Ghazālī], in [various] places – although it is said that he abjured that. Thereafter, it got into the words of whoever trod on this path amongst the Jahmīs and the philosophizers – those who speak of the oneness of existence and others.
>
> This, however, is vain from many points of view. One of them is that this hadith, in this wording and with this desinential inflection (*iʿrāb*), has not been reported by any of the hadith reporters, neither with a sound chain of transmitters nor with a flawed one. Rather, the wording of the hadith which is reported – although with a flawed chain – is "When (*awwal*[a]) God created the intellect (*ʿaql*[a])…", with *awwal*[a] and *ʿaql*[a] ending with the *a* of the accusative. Now, in this there is no argument that the intellect was the first creature created.[22]

It is as part of his refutation of the philosophizers misusing this kind of "prophetic" sayings that the Damascene theologian includes long excerpts of Abū Ḥāmid's four books in the *Bughya*. After giving these quotes, he always has something to say about them: either he picks up a few short passages, reproduces them as lemmas and briefly comments on them, or he offers more elaborate reflections. He can also do both and, in fact, does not follow any straight, consistent, systematic path. It is as if he could not resist the pleasure of a criticism or an excursus. Consequently, he is repeatedly forced to remind the reader of his main objective by saying, for example *al-maqṣūd hunā…*, "The objective, here, is…" So, what is his objective? It is to question, invalidate and delegitimize the philosophical exegesis and esoteric hermeneutics of canonic, or unauthentic, scriptures promoted by al-Ghazālī and his disciples.

> 3. ILLEGITIMATE COMMENTARIES – One knows, necessarily, that the commentary (*tafsīr*) that [these philosophizers] give of the words of God Most High and of His Messenger, God pray over him and grant him peace – and, even, of the words of others – does not enter into what is meant by them – not to speak of it being what is meant by them. Rather, most of their commentaries contradict what God Most High has meant, either by that wording or by another. And when some (*ṭawāʾif*) of the people renowned for jurisprudence and Sufism utter these Islamic

22 Ibid., pp. 179–181.

expressions with [such] philosophical Qarmaṭī commentaries, they declare that they are taken from those [philosophizers], as Abū Ḥāmid [al-Ghazālī] mentions it in his book *The Standard of Knowledge* (*Miʿyār al-ʿilm*), when he speaks about the definitions and says: [185]

✳ *But we have supplied detailed definitions* ⁂[23]

✳ *The soul of the whole is a principle close to the natural bodies.* – I say: What [al-Ghazālī] says here for the [philosophers] is a topic discussed amongst them, as most of them say that the intellect itself is the principle for the bodies.

✳ *The agent intellects.* – Similarly for this saying. It is also a discussed topic, as what is named "agent intellect" among them is the last, tenth, intellect. So has [al-Ghazālī] made clear that it is ✳ *the one which makes the souls of the Adamic beings come out from potentiality to actuality*. [192]

What he has mentioned, for them, of the difference between the intellects and the souls and, [on the other hand,] the bodies, [i.e.] that those are abstracted from matter whereas the bodies are ✳ *in matter*, is based on [the idea] that the body has a matter which is a substance subsisting by itself, which is amongst the gravest vain [opinions].

✳ *Not by an abstraction* [*made*] *by something else.* – What [al-Ghazālī] has brought up[24] by saying this, concerning abstraction and their exclusion (*iḥtirāz*) of the intellected [notions], entails an homonymy about what is named "the intellect". This intellect is indeed one of the accidents whereas that one is a substance subsisting by itself. There is no doubt that what they say to establish [the existence of] that [intellect], even if it is awesome for people who have not examined it closely, [shows itself], when truly realized, of the ultimate corruption, contradiction, and confusion, as we have made clear elsewhere.

✳ *What occupies space* (*al-mutaḥayyiz*). – Similarly for what [al-Ghazālī] mentions of the *kalām* theologians about this. They indeed have controversies about it and it would deserve a detailed study for which this is not the place. [193]

---

23 The short passages in italics introduced by a star (✳) are all quotes from al-Ghazālī. The ⁂ sign indicates that Ibn Taymiyya carries on quoting verbatim an excerpt of the Ghazālian text which it would be too long to translate here or for which an English translation already exists. The exact references of all these quotations, with those of an eventual translation, are given below in the Concordance. A ∗ sign reappears in the Concordance after the reference given for the end of the long excerpts marked here by ⁂.

24 dhakara: dhakarū B

> The object of our concern (*al-maqṣūd*) here, however, is nothing else than that Abū Ḥāmid and his like confess that to make these philosophical meanings the things named by these prophetic terms participates of what these philosophizers say. When, thus, something similar to that is found in the words of one of these, it is known that he has followed their example. [I say this] lest someone who might contest that,[25] or be in doubt about it, be deluded by such [words], or [so that] the idea does not pass through his heart – because of his good opinion about whoever speaks with Islamic, prophetic, expressions – that [that speaker] does not intend by them what these philosophizers mean![26] How excellent is what the Shaykh al-Islam al-Harawī[27] said about some of the *kalām*-theologians, [though] they were in a better situation than these! "They took," he said, "the marrow of philosophy and garbed it with the bast of the Sunna."[28]

About the various points of al-Ghazālī's text which he highlights, Ibn Taymiyya obviously enjoys digging into *falsafa* or *kalām* technicalities and underlining Abū Ḥāmid's deficiencies or contradictions. However, his remarks should not distract the reader from the main argument that he makes in the first and the last paragraphs. For Ibn Taymiyya, there is a gap, a discontinuity, a contradiction even, between the true meaning of scriptural or other Islamic vocabulary and the philosophical meanings which philosophizers give them when interpreting them. These philosophical interpretations of Islamic terms are sometimes borrowed by religious scholars – that is, jurists or Sufis. A good illustration of this situation is provided by the *Miʿyār* definitions, in which al-Ghazālī explicitly acknowledges the philosophical origin of the interpretations which he gives for a number of "Islamic, prophetic, expressions."[29] Caution should therefore always be used vis-à-vis texts that one reads, even when they are written by important religious authorities: whenever their interpretations of Islamic terminology include "something similar to that," i.e. Ghazālian interpretations of the *Miʿyār* definitions type, these revered scholars are also, despite their

25 That is, that someone using such a terminology is effectively following the philosophers.

26 yaʿnīhi: baʿnīhi B

27 Abū Ismāʿīl ʿAbd Allāh b. Muḥammad al-Anṣārī l-Harawī (Herat, 396/1006–481/1089), Ḥanbalī Sufi; see S. De Beaurecueil, *EI*², art. "al-Anṣārī."

28 Ibn Taymiyya, *Bughya*, pp. 184–193.

29 Quotations given without references in my commentaries (as here) come from the texts commented on, and translated therebefore (or, sometimes, following), where they can be easily found and followed up.

fame and appearances, *de facto* followers of the philosophers and are philosophizing. Faithful to a Ḥanbalī spiritual master for whom he is known to have great respect, ʿAbd Allāh al-Anṣārī of Herat, the Damascene theologian's concern is somehow one of ideological *ḥisba*: i.e., preventing the counterfeiting of the semantic value of Islamic terminology. As he explains further through the *Bughya*, this task seems to him all the more urgent in that al-Ghazālī himself is one of these counterfeiters.

> 4. AL-GHAZĀLĪ'S INCOHERENCE – Thereafter, although they confess that to make these Ṣābi'an philosophical meanings the things named by these prophetic terms – or by [these terms] which are said to be prophetic – participates of what these philosophizers say, they peremptorily affirm these [same things] in other places or, rather, in [writings] which they consider part of the noblest sciences and knowledges. They even consider them part of the sciences to be withheld from those who are not **[196]** worthy of them (*al-ʿulūm allatī yuḍannu bihā ʿalā ghayr ahlihā*),[30] and part of the concealed gnosis (*al-ʿilm al-maknūn*) which the people deluded about God disavow and which nobody knows but the people [possessing] the gnosis of God. Such [affirmations] are found in many places as, for example, in the *Book of the Distinction* (al-Tafriqa) *between Faith and Crypto-Infidelity*, when it is mentioned that:
>
> ✳ *Unbelief* (kufr) *is to pronounce the Messenger as liar in any of the things which he brought…*
>
> and it is moreover said that:
>
> ✳ *Holding [something] as true [begins with] the examination of*[31] *the information* (khabar) *and really consists in acknowledging the existence of that of whose existence the Messenger informed [us]. Existence, however, has five levels: essential, sensory, imaginative, intellectual and analogous.*
>
> To speak about these two premises, what there is in the first one in the matter of neglect of the truth and inability to [grasp] it, and what there is in the second one in the matter of hostility against the truth and addition to it, is done elsewhere. The object of our concern [here], however, is that [al-Ghazālī] said:
>
> ✳ *As for intellectual existence, its examples are many…*
>
> until he said:

30 Allusion to al-Ghazālī, *al-Maḍnūn bihi ʿalā ghayr ahlihi*, in M. M. Abū l-ʿAlā' (ed.), *al-Quṣūr al-ʿawālī min rasā'il al-imām al-Ghazālī*, 4 vols. (Cairo: Maktabat al-Jandī, 1390/1970), vol. 3, pp. 124–169.

31 ilā: anna **B**

✳ *A second example is [the Prophet's] statement, the prayer and peace be upon him: "God Most High fermented Adam's clay with His Hand for forty mornings"* ⁂

In accordance with the interpretation (*ta'wīl*) of those [philosophizers, al-Ghazālī] considered the Hand, the Pen and the intellect as expressing one same thing, and he considered this [thing] to be what is meant thereby for them, [i.e.] in these terms appearing in the Book and the Sunna.

He said similar things in the book *The Niche of Lights*[32] when he spoke of the niche and the lamp, the glass and the tree, the oil and the fire. He considered the niche to be the sensory spirit, the glass to be the imaginative spirit, the lamp the intellect, the tree the ratiocinative spirit, and the oil the holy prophetic spirit which is peculiar to the Prophets and some of the Friends [of God]. This book is like the origin (*'unṣur*) of the doctrine of the unionists (*ittiḥādī*) who affirm the oneness of existence, although its author was not affirming it but, on the contrary, might pronounce whoever was affirming it an unbeliever.

This being so, in this [book] there is sometimes equivocity (*ijmāl*) and sometimes philosophizing, showing up the objectives pursued by the philosophers (*maqāṣid al-falāsifa*) about the prophetic terms, and interpreting of the latter in accordance with them. [Therein], there is also, sometimes, opposition to what is proven by the Book, **[199]** the Sunna, and the consensus or, rather, sometimes, opposition to what is known by a clear intellect. Because of [all] this and, also, because of what there is in [this book] of matters which are said by them to require what they say, the disavowal of this book and its like by the imams of Islam was so great that [many] chapters were written about this which it would be long to review.

[Al-Ghazālī] divided the book [titled *The Niche of Lights*] into three chapters.

✳ *The first chapter expounds that the real light is God Most High, and that, for others than Him, the term "light" is purely metaphorical, without reality.* – His words go back to [the idea] that "light" has the meaning of "existence." Before him, Avicenna proceeded similarly to that, by making a synthesis between the Law and philosophy – and likewise did the Ismā'īlī esotericists proceed in their book called *The Epistles of the Ikhwān aṣ-Ṣafā'*. After him, Averroes also did so. And likewise for the unionists

32 See al-Ghazālī, *Mishkāt*, pp. 79–81, trans. Gairdner, *Mishkat*, pp. 150–153.

(*ittiḥādī*): they make His appearance and His epiphany in the forms have the meaning of His existing in [these forms].

There would be a lot to say about this and it is mentioned elsewhere. The aim, here, is to expound these things, in what they say, thanks to which it will be known that[33] they follow the philosophizing Ṣābi'ans [**200**] and express these [philosophical] ideas by means of the terms of the Prophets and the Envoys, although it is known by every person having been given science and faith or, rather, by every believer, that what there is in those in the matter of opposition to the Book of God Most High, to His Messengers and to His religion, is graver than what there is in the Jews and the Nazarenes, [even] after the abrogation (*naskh*) [of their religions] and [their] replacing (*tabdīl*) [divine precepts by others].

Thereafter, [al-Ghazālī] said:

✳ *The second chapter expounds the symbolism of the niche, the lamp, the glass, the tree, the oil and the fire. To know this requires, first of all, two cardinal considerations, which afford limitless scope for investigation …*

✳ *The first expounds the secret of symbolisation, its method, and the aspect under which the spiritual realities* (rūḥ) *of the ideas are captured by the moulds of the symbols …*

✳ *The second expounds the degrees of the luminous human spirits, as it is by knowing them that the symbols of the Qur'ān are known.*

✳ *As for the third chapter, it concerns the meaning of [the Prophet's] saying, God pray over him and grant him peace: "God has seventy veils of light and darkness: were He to uncover them, then would the splendours of His face surely consume what His sight perceives." In some of the versions reported, [the number is] "seven hundred" and, in some others, "seventy thousand".*

I say: we have spoken extensively elsewhere about this verse, the name of God "the Light", the veils, [**201**] and what is related to that. We have also spoken about what [al-Ghazālī], Abū 'Abd Allāh [Fakhr ad-Dīn] ar-Rāzī and their like have mentioned about that.[34] We have expounded that this hadith, in these terms, is fallaciously attributed to the Messenger of God […]

We have mentioned the hadiths and the traditions concerning the veils, as well as the words of the ancients and the imams about this. We have also expounded the opposition of the Jahmīs – the philosophizers

33 : (min) B

34 See notably the texts translated in Y. Michot, *Textes N.S. XI*.

and others – and their like to the texts abundantly transmitted about this, as well as their opposition to the clear intellect. **[202]** Nevertheless, someone who does not totally care about following the Envoys and following in their tracks, about being guided by their signposts and their lighthouse, and about seeking light from the niche of their lights, considers the authentic hadith weak and the weak one authentic, the true idea vain and the vain one true and clear. This is similarly found in what is said by the rest of those who come out of the path of [our] first predecessors – the Emigrants, the Helpers, and those who followed them in beneficence – and innovate in these things by which they separate themselves from the way of the ancients of the community, its imams, and the rest of the adherents of the Sunna and the communion (*jamāʿa*), although the latter are the well-guided group, victorious until the rise of the Hour as the Messenger of God, God pray over him and grant him peace, said: "A group of my community will not cease to give their support to the triumph of the truth, without being harmed either by those who will oppose them or by those who will betray them, until the Hour rises."[35]

The author of *The Niche of Lights* speaks in accordance with the way of those [philosophizers] inwardly (*fī l-bāṭin*), whilst [using] the wording of the Book and the Sunna outwardly (*fī ẓ-ẓāhir*). It is however reported that he abjured all this. Also, there are people who contest the attribution of these books to him.

The objective, [here], is to draw the [reader's] attention to what these books opposed to the Book and the Sunna contain in the matter of erring, lest ignorant people be deluded by them and by their ascription to highly regarded [personages].

[Al-Ghazālī] said:

✳ *The first cardinal consideration concerns the secret of symbolisation and its method. Know that the world is two worlds, spiritual and corporeal, or, if you will, say: sensory and intellectual; or again, if you will, say: supernal and inferior.* ⁂

I say: the objective here is not to speak in detail about what these words and their like contain [in the matter of opposition to the Book and the Sunna]. The scholars of the Muslims have indeed expounded, thereabout, things that suffice. **[215]** Elsewhere, we have also said thereabout what God Most High has wanted [us to say].

---

35 See al-Bukhārī, *Ṣaḥīḥ*, *Iʿtiṣām*, *Tawḥīd* (Bulaq, vol. 9, pp. 101, 136); Muslim, *Ṣaḥīḥ*, *Imāra* (Constantinople, vol. 6, pp. 52–53); Ibn Ḥanbal, *Musnad*, vol. 5, pp. 34, 269, 278, 279.

[a.] To say it in short, words like these include vain things, from the viewpoint of the tradition (*naql*). There is for example [al-Ghazālī's] saying that, *in the* Ṣaḥīḥ [of al-Bukhārī, it is written] "God created Adam *in the form of the Merciful*", and his saying that "in His form" is not in the *Ṣaḥīḥ*. Such [affirmations] are most obviously vain. Indeed, the wording which [one reads] in the *Ṣaḥīḥ* in various respects is "in His form". As for the saying "in the form of the Merciful", it is reported from Ibn ʿUmar and there are things to be said about it, which we have mentioned elsewhere, together with what groups of people have generally said about this hadith.[36]

[b. Words like these] also include vain things which are in themselves opposed to the Law and the intellect. There are for example [these statements] which they contain and say that ✳ *one of the angels*, i.e. the agent intellect, is the originator (*mubdiʿ*) of all the creatures that are under it, or that ✳ *the angels* – they call them the "intellects" and the "souls" – originate each other, or that ✳ *the world of observation* is the sensibles whereas *the world of the unseen* is the intelligibles, or ✳ that commenting the Qur'ān is like *interpreting a [dream] vision*, and similar statements which are not among the things **[216]** said by the Muslims, the Jews, and the Nazarenes but, rather, among the sayings of the heretics – the Ṣābi'ans, the philosophers, and the Qarmaṭīs.

[c.] In [words like these] there are also things that belong to the genre of the allusion (*ishāra*) and consideration (*iʿtibār*) which the jurists and the Sufis practice. It is for example the case in his saying that ✳ *the angels do not enter a house in which there is a dog*. When this is considered analogous to the purification of the heart from the vicious mores, this belongs to the genre of the allusions of the Sufis and the analogy of the jurists.

[d.] Some of these things also belong to the genre of corrupt analogy, as when he mentions that ✳ *Moses* was commanded, with the *doffing of his two sandals*,[37] to doff this world and the hereafter, and that ✳ what comes down upon *the hearts* of the people of knowledge is of the kind of the discourse that was spoken to Moses. [To claim] that Moses was spoken in such a manner is vain, the ancients of the community and its imams are agreed on this and it is extensively explained elsewhere.

---

36 On the different versions of this hadith, see D. Gimaret, *Dieu à l'image de l'homme. Les anthropomorphismes de la sunna et leur interprétation par les théologiens* (Paris: Cerf, 1997), pp. 123–136.

37 See Q. *Ṭā Hā*, 20: 12.

> ✳ The great importance attached in this [text] to commanding **[217]** [the proper], prohibiting [the reprehensible], and killing whoever *allows* forbidden things, these are excellent words. What Abū Ḥāmid [al-Ghazālī] says about the science of behaviour (*muʿāmala*), command and prohibition, is of the kind of what is said by his like among the people of Sufism and jurisprudence. As for what he named "the science of unveiling", what he says about it is of [various types]: sometimes he speaks of it with the voice (*ṣawt*) of the adepts of philosophy, sometimes with the voice of the Jahmīs, sometimes with a voice which has the tone of the adepts of hadith and knowledge. Sometimes also he speaks evil of those, and sometimes he speaks of things that are other than that.
>
> What we are saying in this answer concerns only the corrupt nature of the arguments which they have put forward about [the Prophet's] saying "When (*awwal*ᵃ) God created the intellect (*ʿaql*ᵃ) ..." We have expounded the corrupt nature of what they say, from [fifteen] viewpoints.[38]

Ibn Taymiyya has no difficulty recognizing al-Ghazālī's merits. In this Text 4 just translated, he considers for example that Abū Ḥāmid was not a proponent of the doctrine of the unicity of existence (*waḥdat al-wujūd*). He is also ready to believe that he "abjured" his philosophizing esotericism at some point. He even praises as "excellent words" the importance given to commanding good and prohibiting evil in the *Mishkāt*. Despite these qualities, however, al-Ghazālī appears all the more shady and untrustworthy to Ibn Taymiyya in that what he relates to philosophizing in the *Miʿyār*, he not only adopts it elsewhere but considers it the highest form of gnostic knowledge, to be protected from unworthy people, in works like his *Maḍnūn*, *Tafriqa*, and *Mishkāt*.

The pages of the *Tafriqa* which the Damascene theologian quotes indeed show that for al-Ghazālī, the words "Hand of God", "Pen", and "intellect" found in Qurʾānic or prophetic texts (authentic or not) all refer to one same thing, to be understood philosophically. The situation is similar for al-Ghazālī's interpretation of the Light verse (Q. *al-Nūr*, 24: 35) in the *Mishkāt*. In Abū Ḥāmid's interpretation, the niche, glass, lamp, tree and oil all become names for spiritual and intellectual realities belonging to the universe of Avicennan epistemology, noology and prophetology. As for his making "light" a symbol of existence, this is an esotericism which Ibn Taymiyya likens not only to that of the Shaykh ar-Raʾīs, but also to the Ikhwān aṣ-Ṣafāʾ, Averroes and the unionists assimilating God's existence to His epiphany. In sum, the author of the *Mishkāt* "speaks

---

38 Ibn Taymiyya, *Bughya*, pp. 195–217.

in accordance with the way of those [philosophizers] inwardly (*fī l-bāṭin*), whilst [using] the wording of the Book and the Sunna outwardly (*fī ẓ-ẓāhir*)."

Beside its philosophizing esoteric interpretations of scriptural expressions, Ibn Taymiyya has several other motives to criticize the *Mishkāt*. He sees in it "the origin" of the *waḥdat al-wujūd* doctrine although al-Ghazālī himself was not a "unionist." It not only contains ambiguous statements but, also, affirmations that contradict the Qur'ān, the Sunna, the consensus and, even, the "clear intellect"; which explains its widespread disavowal amongst scholars. It quotes a number of unauthentic hadiths or mistaken versions of others. It indulges in allusions of Sufi nature and considerations that are of the type practiced by the jurists or, simply, corrupt analogies. This being so, the Damascene theologian nevertheless spends time presenting the structure of the *Mishkāt* and its main divisions, quotes several pages thereof, makes a number of specific comments and, unsurprisingly, eventually finds himself obliged to remind us of his main objective, i.e. "to draw the [reader's] attention to what these books opposed to the Book and the Sunna contain in the matter of erring, lest ignorant people be deluded by them and by their ascription to highly regarded [personages]." He even declares his intention to return to the hadith of the intellect – the object of the original inquiry – and announces that, from several viewpoints, he will refute the arguments of the philosophizers who have misinterpreted it. It is in these second and eighth viewpoints that he quotes al-Ghazālī's *Jawāhir*.

> 5. THE WORLDS OF OMNIPOTENCE, SOVEREIGNTY AND KINGSHIP – Second viewpoint. These people do not consider the intellects and the souls, whose existence the philosophers establish, as part of the world of creation. Rather, they interpret (*fassara*) the world of creation as [being] the world of the bodies, on the basis of the fact that creating is determining (*taqdīr*) and that the bodies have determined measures (*muqaddarāt*). On the basis of the principle[s] of these philosophers and of those who are agreed with them thereabout, these also say that the intellects and the souls are not bodies. Rather they are, according to them, the world of Command. Just as they say what Abū Ḥāmid [al-Ghazālī] mentions in [various] places about the difference between the world of Kingship (*mulk*), Sovereignty (*malakūt*) and Omnipotence (*jabarūt*). They interpret the world of Kingship as the world of the bodies, the world of Sovereignty as the world of the souls, because they are the inward of the bodies, and the world of Omnipotence as the intellects, because they are not joined to the bodies, nor attached to them [...]
>
> This is why they say that none prostrated to Adam except the terrestrial angels and, by "prostration", they mean the submission of these

powers to man, as is [said] in *The Jewels of the Qur'ān*. [Therein, al-Ghazālī] said:

✳ *As for the [divine] acts, they are a sea of vast limits and whose sides are not reached by [any] inquiry. Rather, in the existence, there is nothing but God and His acts. Every thing other than Him is His act.* ⁂

I say: such words will be judged great, unhesitatingly or absolutely, by someone who does not know the real nature (*ḥaqīqa*) of what the Messenger brought and does not know the real nature of the philosophy to which these words are applied and which is expressed by means of the expressions of the Muslims.

✳ *The Qur'ān deals with the creatures,*[39] *i.e. those that appear to the senses. Now, the noblest of the acts of God is what does not appear to the senses.* – The one saying that means that the Qur'ān does not deal with the latter. In such a [statement] there is diminishing of the value of the Qur'ān, claiming that it deals with the deficient part [of the creation], not the perfect one, and pushing the adepts of heresy to disdain what the Messengers brought. Moreover, it is a clear lie: [even] the kids of the Muslims know that it is a lie about the Qur'ān. In the Qur'ān, there are indeed also, as informations about the unseen (*ghayb*) – the angels and the jinn, the Garden and the Fire, etc. – things that are hidden to no one [...]

✳ *[The noblest acts of God] also include the terrestrial angels in charge of the human kind. They are the ones who prostrated to Adam.* – To pretend that the angels of the heavens and the cherubins did not prostrate to Adam is to say a thing which is the farthest away from the sayings of the Muslims, the Jews and the Nazarenes. The Qur'ān has indeed informed [us] that all the angels prostrated together [...][40] The cherubins, according to their conventional vocabulary (*iṣṭilāḥ*), are the ten intellects [...]

✳ *These [cherubins] do not pay attention to the Adamic beings.* – This statement is among the sayings of the erring philosophers. What is well known among the adherents of the Sunna and the communion is that the Prophets and the Friends [of God] are more eminent than all the angels. [They nevertheless pay attention to the other humans ...]

✳ *[The divine acts] also include the satans who are given power over the human kind. It is they who refrained from prostrating.* – This is also wrong. Of the kind of those none was commanded to prostrate except Iblīs.

39 al-khalq B: al-jalī minhā J *with those [acts of God] that are observable...* The copy of *Jawāhir* used by Ibn Taymiyya is obviously mistaken here. He abridges four lines of al-Ghazālī's text.

40 See Q. *al-Baqara*, 2: 34.

And not one of his descendants was commanded to prostrate to Adam. How would they then be described as having refrained in the manner mentioned? [...]

✳ *[The cherubins are] absorbed in the beauty of the [divine] presence and its majesty.* – What is said there belongs to the genre of the ecstatic outbursts (*ṭāmma*). It belongs to the genre of what some Sufis call "extinction" (*fanāʾ*), i.e. the absorption of the heart in the Real until it is not aware anymore of any other than Him. It is [however] well known, and people are agreed on this, the state of permanence (*baqāʾ*) is more perfect than [that of] extinction, and it is the state of the Prophets, the Envoys, and the angels brought near. It is known that the Messengers are the most eminent of the creatures. Now, they invite the servants [to go] towards God Most High and instruct them, wage *jihād* against them, eat food and walk in the markets. If that state [of absorption] was more perfect, people who have not been sent [as Messengers] would then be more perfect than the Messengers! Such an [idea] goes against the religion of the Muslims, the Jews, and the Nazarenes, but corresponds to the religion of the Ṣābiʾan exaggerators (*ghāliya*) – the philosophizers who give more eminence to the philosopher than to the Prophet and the Messenger – and to the state [228] of the Jahmī unionists who give more eminence to the Friend, or to the seal of the Friends, than to the Messengers. Now, it is well known that this is something vain and unbelief for the Muslims. As for his saying:

✳ *Do not regard as unlikely that, among the servants of God Most High, there be some whom the majesty of God Most High distracts from paying attention to Adam and his descendants.* – This is not an attribute of perfection. On the contrary, "the angels glorify night and day; they flag not."[41] Despite that, they administer, of the affairs of the creatures, what they are commanded to administer. God Most High commanded to the angels to prostrate to Adam and they all prostrated together, except Iblīs [...]

✳ *["God has a white earth in which the course of the sun is thirty days thirty times like the days of this world, replete with creatures who do not know that God Most High is being disobeyed on the earth and do not know that God Most High created Adam and Iblīs." Reported by Ibn ʿAbbās.]* – The hadith which [al-Ghazālī] mentioned on the authority of Ibn ʿAbbās is among the invented, fallacious [traditions]. The people of knowledge are agreed thereon and it is found in none of the reliable hadith books. These words,

41 Q. *al-Anbiyāʾ*, 21: 20.

> or something similar, are only found in a section of[42] *On Thinking* (tafakkur) *and Considering* (iʿtibār) by Ibn Abī d-Dunyā.[43] [231] Also, those [philosophizers] believe, from the viewpoint of cosmography (*ʿilm al-hayʾa*), that this hadith is false.[44]

Ibn Taymiyya's second argument against philosophizing interpretations of the so-called hadith "The first [thing] that God created was the intellect..." underlines a contradiction: how could the intellect have been created as, for these philosophers, intellects and souls do not belong to the world of creation? They indeed restrict the world of creation to bodies and consider that souls and intellect constitute two other specific worlds, respectively the world of Sovereignty (*malakūt*) and that of Omnipotence (*jabarūt*). According to the Damascene theologian, Abū Ḥāmid effectively shares such a tripartite division of the universe and, in the *Jawāhir*, it leads him to make various affirmations that might look "great" to some but are, in reality, grave philosophical distortions of the religion. Ibn Taymiyya reproduces verbatim a number of pages of the *Jawāhir* and pinpoints a few cases of such Ghazālian distortions. They have to do with demeaning the worth of the Qurʾān, misrepresenting the angels' role (including their prostrating to Adam), giving pre-eminence to mystical extinction (*fanāʾ*) over permanence (*baqāʾ*) and care for the world, and denying the superiority and perfection of the Prophets and Messengers. And, icing on the cake, al-Ghazālī has quoted another fallacious hadith...

Interesting as all these particular critiques might be in themselves, they do not go to the heart of Ibn Taymiyya's discontentment with al-Ghazālī, i.e. raise the question of the nature of the latter's exegetical methodology. This is done the next time the Damascene theologian quotes the *Jawāhir* in the *Bughya*, in his eighth viewpoint.

> 6. THE PEN AND THE INTELLECT – Eighth viewpoint. These people have heard, in the hadith, that "The first thing which God created is the Pen." This hadith is well known, unlike the first one. It is reported from the Prophet, God pray over him and grant him peace, by Abū Dāʾūd in his *Sunan*.[45] It is reported from Ibn ʿAbbās and other Companions [...]

42 min: fīhi B

43 Abū Bakr ʿAbd Allāh b. Abī d-Dunyā (d. Baghdād, 281/894), moralist and erudite scholar, tutor of several ʿAbbāsid princes.

44 Ibn Taymiyya, *Bughya*, pp. 218–231.

45 See Abū Dāʾūd, *Sunan*, *Sunna* (ed. ʿAbd al-Ḥamīd, vol. 4, pp. 225–226, no 4700).

Those say that what the philosophers call "the first intellect" is the Pen. This is [found] many times in their words and in the words of the author of *The Jewels of the Qur'ān*. It is of the species of what the Qarmaṭīs say. [277] [Al-Ghazālī] said in *The Jewels*: *Know that the Qur'ān and the Traditions contain many [things] of this kind. Look at his saying, God pray over him and grant him peace: "The heart of the believer is between two of the fingers of the Merciful."* ⁂
⁕ *In sum, know that everything which your understanding would not put up with, the Qur'ān offers it to you in the [same] way that, if in your sleep you were reading the Preserved Tablet with your spirit, this would represent itself to you by means of an appropriate symbol which would need to be interpreted* (taʿbīr). *Know also that exegesis* (ta'wīl) *of [the Qur'ān] proceeds in the same manner as the interpretation [of symbols]*. – End of his words.

These words and their like are of the kind of what the Qarmaṭī philosophers say about what God has informed [us] of concerning the matters of faith in God and the Last Day. They consider that to be parables (*mathal*) given in order to make people understand the Lord, the angels, the return (*maʿād*), etc. It is extensively spoken about them elsewhere.

Because he had studied abundantly what the [philosophers] were saying, and had borrowed a lot from them, the author of *The Jewels [of the Qur'ān]* mixed, in what he said, a lot of what they were saying. He nevertheless called them unbelievers for many of the things about which he was agreeing with them elsewhere. And at the end of what he said, he affirmed peremptorily that what they were saying provided neither knowledge nor certainty (*yaqīn*). He even asserted something like that about what the *kalām* theologians were saying. And the last thing he busied himself with was the study of the *Ṣaḥīḥ*s of al-Bukhārī and Muslim. He died while busy doing so. **[280]**

The objective, here, is only to draw the [reader's] attention to what [the philosophers] have mentioned. Many have indeed been misled (*ightarra*) by this because they had found it in the words of [al-Ghazālī], whose venerability (*ḥurma*), for the Muslims, is not like the venerability of somebody who has not entered into jurisprudence (*fiqh*) and Sufism as he had done.

This is why many were the things said about him by the imams of the [various] schools (*ṭā'ifa*) of jurists and Sufis, like Abū Bakr aṭ-Ṭurṭūshī,[46]

---

46 Abū Bakr Muḥammad b. al-Walīd al-Fihrī ṭ-Ṭurṭūshī (d. in Alexandria, 520/1126), an Andalusian Mālikī jurist who criticized al-Ghazālī in two works: *Risāla ilā ʿAbd Allāh b. al-Muẓaffar* and *Kitāb al-Asrār wa-l-ʿibar*; see M. Fierro, *Opposition to Sufism in al-*

Abū ʿAbd Allāh al-Māzarī l-Maghribī,[47] and other Mālikīs; [281] like Abū l-Ḥasan al-Marghīnānī,[48] Abū l-Bayān al-Qurshī,[49] Abū ʿAmr b. aṣ-Ṣalāḥ,[50] Ibn Shukr,[51] the sons of al-Qushayrī[52] and other Shāfiʿīs; like Abū l-Wafāʾ

Andalus, in F. De Jong & B. Radtke (eds), *Islamic Mysticism Contested: Thirteen Centuries of Controversies and Polemics* (Leiden – Boston – Köln: Brill, 1999), pp. 174–206, at pp. 191; E. L. Ormsby, *Theodicy*, pp. 98–101; K. Garden, *Revival*, pp. 179–182; A. Akasoy, *The al-Ghazālī Conspiracy. Reflections on the Inter-Mediterranean Dimension of Islamic Intellectual History*, in Y. Tzvi Langermann (ed.), *Avicenna and his Legacy. A Golden Age of Science and Philosophy* (Turnhout: Brepols, 2009), pp. 117–142, at pp. 117–118.

47 Two scholars opposed to al-Ghazālī are known as al-Māzarī. One is Abū ʿAbd Allāh Muḥammad b. Abī l-Faraj al-Māzarī, known as adh-Dhakī (d. in Isfahan, 510/1116); see K. Garden, *Al-Māzarī al-Dhakī: Al-Ghazālī's Maghribi Adversary in Nishapur*, in *Journal of Islamic Studies*, 21/1 (Oxford, 2010), pp. 89–107. The other is Abū ʿAbd Allāh Muḥammad b. ʿAlī t-Tamīmī l-Māzarī, known as al-Imām (d. in Mahdiyya, 536/1141), a Sicilian Mālikī traditionist and jurist, author of a refutation of the *Iḥyāʾ* entitled *al-Kashf wa-l-inbāʾ ʿalā l-mutarjam bi-l-Iḥyāʾ*; see M. Asin-Palacios, *Un faqīh siciliano, contradictor de al-Ġazzālī (Abū ʿAbd Allāh de Māzara)*, in *Centenario della nascita di Michele Amari*, 2 vols. (Palermo: Virzì, 1910), vol. 1, pp. 216–244; E. L. Ormsby, *Theodicy*, pp. 98–101; F. Griffel, *Al-Ghazālī's Philosophical Theology* (New York: Oxford University Press, 2009), p. 303, n. 232. Ibn Taymiyya refers here to al-Imām but is also aware of al-Dhakī: in *Darʾ al-taʿāruḍ*, vol. 6, p. 240, he mentions the names of both. I am most grateful to K. Garden for this last reference.

48 Elsewhere, Ibn Taymiyya calls him "the companion (*rafīq*) of Abū Ḥāmid, *Abū Naṣr* al-Marghīnānī" (Ibn Taymiyya, *Nubuwwāt*, p. 82), and "his companion (*rafīq*), *Abū Isḥāq* al-Marghīnānī" (Ibn Taymiyya, *Sharḥ al-ʿAqīdat al-Iṣfahāniyya*, ed. Ḥ. M. Makhlūf (Cairo: Dār al-Kutub al-Islāmiyya, n.d.), p. 132; see Y. Michot, *Reader*, Text VIII). He cannot be identified with the later Ḥanafī jurist Abū l-Ḥasan Burhān ad-Dīn ʿAlī b. Abī Bakr b. ʿAbd al-Jalīl al-Farghānī l-Marghīnānī (d. 593/1197) as proposed by M. R. Sālim in his edition of Ibn Taymiyya's *Kitāb aṣ-Ṣafadiyya*, 2 vols. (Mansura: Dār al-Hady an-Nabawī – Riyadh: Dār al-Faḍīla, 1421/2000), vol. 1, p. 210, n. 2, and M. ad-Duwaysh (ed.), *Bughya*, p. 281, n. 1. A better candidate is Ẓahīr ad-Dīn ʿAlī b. ʿAbd ar-Razzāq Abū Naṣr al-Marghīnānī (d. 506/1112), a Ḥanafī scholar from Khurāsān and disciple of al-Ghazālī; see M. Y. Salāma (ed.), *Ibn Taymiyya. Thubūt an-nubuwwāt ʿaql^an wa-naql^an wa-l-muʿjizāt wa-l-karāmāt* (Cairo: Dār Ibn al-Jawzī, 1427/2006), p. 310, n. 3.

49 Nabaʾ b. Muḥammad Abū l-Bayān al-Qurshī, known as Ibn al-Ḥawrānī, Shāfiʿī Sufi of Damascus (d. 551/1156).

50 Taqī d-Dīn Abū ʿAmr ʿUthmān b. ʿAbd ar-Raḥmān al-Kurdī sh-Shahrazūrī, known as Ibn aṣ-Ṣalāḥ (d. in Damascus, 643/1245). On his criticism of al-Ghazālī, see E. L. Ormsby, *Theodicy*, p. 103, and Y. Michot, *Reader*, Text VIII.

51 Abū l-Ḥasan Aḥmad b. ʿAlī b. Muḥammad b. Shukr al-Andalusī (d. in Fayyum, 640/1242).

52 The two sons of ʿAbd al-Karīm b. Hawāzin Abū l-Qāsim al-Qushayrī (d. 465/1073), the author of *The Epistle* (*ar-Risāla*) are: 1) Abū Naṣr ʿAbd ar-Raḥīm b. ʿAbd al-Karīm, preacher in Baghdād (d. 514/1120); 2) Abū l-Fatḥ ʿAbd Allāh b. ʿAbd al-Karīm (d. 521/1127). In *Nubuwwāt*, p. 82, Ibn Taymiyya quotes anti-Ghazālī verses of Abū Naṣr al-Qushayrī (see Y. Michot, *Reader*, Text IX).

b. ʿAqīl[53] and Abū l-Faraj b. al-Jawzī[54] among the Ḥanbalīs – although these two are closer to the doctrines of the deniers than others among the Ḥanbalīs. [**282**] As for the Ḥanafīs, what they say about [al-Ghazālī] is of another sort, a well-known story having happened to him with them and with the companions of the Shāfiʿīs.[55]

What [al-Ghazālī] has mentioned is vain from many points of view [...]

✳ *Every thing has a definition and a reality which is its spiritual essence* (rūḥ). – Thereby [al-Ghazālī] only means, for example, the fact, for this thing, to be writing, just as he considers the reality of the Pen and its definition to be the fact that it inscribes knowledge. He considers this definition and reality to be existing in the intellect. Now, the vain nature of this is well known, necessarily. Indeed, the existing reality of a substance is not simply its having for attribute some action, [be it] disjoined from it or connected with it. If it was supposed that such an attribute is found in its definition, it would be a difference that would distinguish it from other [things] whilst these other things would remain associated with it in their shared genre. Now, this would prohibit affirming this reality about something else. As for considering [this attribute] alone to be the definition and the reality, this is manifestly vain [...]

✳ *Do not regard as unlikely that, in the Qurʾān, there be allusions* (ishāra) *of this kind.* – If [al-Ghazālī] wants to say that such an allusion provides the meaning of the [Qurʾānic] discourse and what it aims to say (*maqṣūd*), this is a displacement (*taḥrīf*) of the words from their [right] places, and an heretization about the signs of God, an errancy of the kind of that of the Qarmaṭīs and their like amongst the heretics. If he wants to say that, in addition to the fact that a verse indicates the meaning that it indicates, there can be in its wording an allusion to another meaning corresponding to it, this is [proceeding] by analogy (*qiyās*) and consideration (*iʿtibār*).

---

53 Abū l-Wafāʾ ʿAlī b. ʿAqīl b. Muḥammad b. ʿAqīl al-Baghdādī (d. 512/1119), Ḥanbalī jurist; see G. Makdisi, *Ibn ʿAqīl: Religion and Culture in Classical Islam* (Edinburgh: Edinburgh University Press, 1997).

54 Abū l-Faraj ʿAbd ar-Raḥmān b. ʿAlī b. al-Jawzī (d. 597/1200), Ḥanbalī ulema. On Ibn al-Jawzī's criticism of al-Ghazālī, see E. L. Ormsby, *Theodicy*, p. 98.

55 This is probably an allusion to the attacks against al-Ghazālī led by Ḥanafī and Shāfiʿī scholars when he resumed his teaching activities at the Niẓāmiyya school of Naysābūr, in 499/1106 according to K. Garden, 501/1108 according to F. Griffel; see K. Garden, *Coming down from the Mountaintop: Al-Ghazālī's Autobiographical Writings in Context*, in *The Muslim World*, 101/4 (Hartford, October 2011), pp. 581–596, at p. 595; F. Griffel, *Theology*, p. 55. Al-Ghazālī defends himself in *al-Imlāʾ fī ishkālāt* al-Iḥyāʾ.

What [314] the Sufis mean by "allusion" is what the jurists mean by "analogy" and "consideration". For most of the scholars, such a [process] is valid when its conditions are fulfilled. It is nevertheless well known that what [al-Ghazālī] wants to say here is the first thing, which belongs to the kind of things which the Qarmaṭī heretics say.

✳ *"He sends down water from heaven."*[56] – Concerning this saying of the Most High which [al-Ghazālī] quotes, the following shall be said: there is no divergence among the Muslims about the presence of parables (*mathal*) in the Qur'ān, in this verse and in others. It shall even be said that there are therein more than forty parables. It is also well known that the thing used as an image [in a parable] (*mumaththal*) is not itself the thing of which this image is given (*mumaththal bihi*). Rather, it resembles it from the viewpoint of the meaning (*maʿnā*) shared [by both]. This is the case with every analogy (*qiyās*), symbolisation (*tamthīl*), and consideration (*iʿtibār*) [...] Would it be permitted to mean by some words something of which an image is [supposedly] given by them – and not to mean by them the thing itself named by such a wording – without an indication (*dalāla*) to do so[57] that they would offer? It is well known, to do so would be a kind of metaphorical borrowing (*istiʿāra*) and assimilation (*tashbīh*). Now, shall a term be taken to mean such a thing simply for this? If that is allowed, then it will be allowed to be said that [the verse] "And of all things have We taken account in a clear Book (*imām*)"[58] refers to ʿAlī b. Abī Ṭālib and others. And, about "the pearl and the coral,"[59] it will be said that they are al-Ḥasan and al-Ḥusayn, because this one died poisoned and that one died murdered, and other exegeses of the Qarmaṭīs who take a word to mean something else than the thing normally considered to be named by it, simply because of some resemblance between them

---

56 Q. *ar-Raʿd*, 13: 17.

57 I.e. without an indication to mean by these words something of which an image is [supposedly] given by them.

58 Q. *Yā-Sīn*, 36: 12. On the interpretation of this verse as referring to ʿAlī, see also Ibn Taymiyya, *Introduction to the Principles of Tafsir*. Explanation by Shaykh Muḥammad b. Ṣāliḥ al-ʿUthaymīn (Birmingham: Al-Hidaayah Publishing & Distribution Ltd, 2009), p. 136.

59 Q. *ar-Raḥmān*, 55: 22. On the interpretation of "the pearl and the coral" as meaning al-Ḥasan and al-Ḥusayn, see also Ibn Taymiyya, *Introduction*, p. 134. This interpretation is traced back to the imām Jaʿfar aṣ-Ṣādiq by Abū Jaʿfar Muḥammad b. Bābawayh al-Qummī (Shaykh Ṣadūq; d. 381/991); see A. Peiravi & T. J. Peiravi, *A Numeric Classification of Traditions on Characteristics*. Translation of *al-Khisal* of Sheikh Sadooq. Edited by L. Z. Morgan (Qum: Ansariyan Publications, 2008), pp. 128–129.

both, without any indication [from that word to do so] or, even, without this word being used in that second sense in the language. **[316]**
✳ *The Qur'ān offers it to you in the [same] way that, if in your sleep you were reading the Preserved Tablet with your spirit, this would represent itself to you by means of an appropriate symbol which would need to be interpreted* (taʿbīr). – This statement of [al-Ghazālī] implies two corrupt principles that are not among the principles of the Muslims but, on the contrary, among the principles of the erring philosophers.

[The first principle] is that what our Prophet, God pray over him and grant him peace, and other Prophets inform [us] of concerning the matters of the unseen (*ghayb*) belongs solely to the genre of the dreams which people see [...]

The second of these two corrupt principles [is the affirmation that] the spirit of the servant is reading the Preserved Tablet. This is what is said by these Qarmaṭī philosophizers, i.e. that the Preserved Tablet is the agent intellect, or the universal soul, the latter being one of the angels, and that the events of existence are [pre-]inscribed in it; so, when the rational soul is joined to it, [these things] flow upon it. Now, every person who knows what the Messenger brought necessarily knows that what is meant by him by "the Preserved Tablet" is not identical to this. Nor is the Preserved Tablet one of the angels; the Muslims are agreed on this. Rather God has informed [us] that "It is a glorious Qur'ān, in a Preserved Tablet"[60] [...] Moreover, the Preserved Tablet is above the heavens, whereas the soul and the intellect which they mention are joined to the sphere of the moon, under the intellects and the souls that are above it!
✳ *If you have not got the force to bear what is reaching your ear of this sort [of things] as long as a commentary is not traced back to the Companions, blind imitation* (taqlīd) *is prevailing in you.* This shall be said to [al-Ghazālī]: I am not bearing this sort [of things] for the sole reason that I necessarily know that it is vain and that God did not mean that. My rejection of Qarmaṭism in aurally transmitted matters (*samʿiyyāt*) is thus like my rejection of sophistry in intellectual matters. And this is like my rejection of every saying which I necessarily know to be a lie and vain. If something like that sort [of things] was transmitted from one of the Companions and the Followers, I would know that it is fallaciously attributed to them. This is why you find that the Qarmaṭīs transmit this from ʿAlī, peace be upon him, and claim that this esoteric science, **[328]** that goes against

60 Q. *al-Burūj*, 85: 21–22.

> what is known outwardly, is taken from him[61] [...] A lot of this Qarmaṭism has entered into the words of many of the Sufis, just as it has entered into the words of the *kalām* theologians.[62]

Another argument put forward by some people in order to support their claim that the intellect was the first creature is a prophetic tradition reported by Abū Dā'ūd: "The first thing which God created is the Pen." According to them this Pen is undoubtedly an image for the intellect. Ibn Taymiyya devotes his eighth viewpoint to the refutation of this argument. It takes him back to al-Ghazālī's *Jawāhir* because the Pen–intellect assimilation is one of the philosophical interpretations of scriptural terms that the Ḥujjat al-Islam develops in that work. And as al-Ghazālī, in the *Jawāhir*, speaks of the principles which he follows in such exegeses, he now offers Ibn Taymiyya the occasion for a full attack.

Following another long quote from the *Jawāhir*, the Damascene theologian begins with a short overview of the symbolist exegesis favoured, in matters of theology and eschatology, by those whom he calls "the Qarmaṭī philosophers," and with a summary of the complex evolution that eventually led Abū Ḥāmid to burn what he had once worshipped: *falsafa*. He then makes two important remarks. First, he asserts that al-Ghazalī's philosophizing, in that he is a particularly revered personage among Muslims, is all the more dangerous; second – and he seems to add this so as to exculpate himself from finding fault with such a famous scholar – Ibn Taymiyya notes that the Ḥujjat al-Islam has been criticized by many, in each of the four juridical schools, including his own.

After this general introduction, Ibn Taymiyya articulates his refutation of al-Ghazālī's exegetical methodology in relation to five particular statements made in the *Jawāhir*.

He starts by remarking that the Pen–intellect assimilation is based on a logical confusion between the definition and reality of a thing and its attributes. The common element put forward to justify this assimilation has to do with inscribing knowledge, a "spiritual essence (*rūḥ*)" considered by al-Ghazālī to be present in both the Pen and the intellect. For Ibn Taymiyya, there is however more in the concrete reality of a pen, and also of an intellect, than this character, and the Ḥujjat al-Islam is in fact forgetting an important axiom of philosophy: "the existing reality of a substance is not simply its having for attribute some action." The objection is fair and goes directly to the core of the

---

61 On the esoteric doctrines misleadingly attributed to 'Alī according to Ibn Taymiyya, see Y. Michot, *Ibn Taymiyya on Astrology. Annotated Translation of Three Fatwas*, in *Journal of Islamic Studies*, 11/2 (Oxford, May 2000), pp. 147–208, at pp. 178–180.

62 Ibn Taymiyya, *Bughya*, pp. 275–328.

exegetical problem: what kind of proof does one need to provide when claiming that a word does not just mean what it is normally considered to mean, but also has, or even exclusively has, some other, non-literal, inward, esoteric, meaning? *"Ceci n'est pas une pipe,"* as René Magritte would say.

In reference to a second statement from the *Jawāhir*, Ibn Taymiyya has no difficulty accepting al-Ghazālī's affirmation that there are "allusions" (*ishāra*) in the Qur'ān. The only essential question nevertheless is, then, what to do with such allusions. Can they be claimed to mean whatever one wants them to mean or is there a specific procedure leading to understanding them properly? For Ibn Taymiyya, the key to opening non-obvious meanings is to proceed "by analogy (*qiyās*) and consideration (*iʿtibār*)," as done by the jurists or by the Sufis speaking of "allusions." "For most of the scholars," the interpretative process is indeed valid when the conditions of such methodologies are fulfilled. In the case of al-Ghazālī, the truth is, unfortunately, according to the Damascene theologian, that his philosophizing interpretations do not result from valid exegetical methodologies but belong "to the kind of things which the Qarmaṭī heretics say."

Ibn Taymiyya's third point develops and completes his attack on al-Ghazālī's lack of a valid, proper, acceptable, exegetical methodology. Yes, there are parables (*mathal*) in the Qur'ān; their number even exceeds forty. For these parables, as for allusions (*ishāra*), there must however be some valid connection between the signifier and the signified. Analogy, symbolisation, and consideration are appropriate means to establish these valid connections – i.e. to identify the indication provided by the signifier to the signified – whereas metaphorical borrowing (*istiʿāra*) and assimilation (*tashbīh*) are not. This is, for example, why the "clear Book (*imām*)" of surah *Yā-Sīn* – 36, verse 12 cannot be said to refer to ʿAlī b. Abī Ṭālib; nor, on the other hand, can "the pearl and the coral" of surah *ar-Raḥmān* – 55, verse 22 refer to his sons al-Ḥasan and al-Ḥusayn. Sheer imagined resemblances between two things do not amount to the "indication (*dalāla*)" required in order to link them in a valid manner as signifier and additional or alternative signified. What the Damascene theologian is affirming here is, thus, that scriptural exegesis is submitted to the same methodological seriousness required of other religious disciplines: for example, jurisprudence and Sufism. In his *Risālat Aḍḥawiyya*, Avicenna had already criticized *kalām* theologians for not following a clear *qānūn at-taʾwīl*, that is a clear "rule of interpretation," of the revealed text. Ibn Taymiyya commented on that Avicennan work.[63] Though he does not mention it here, it has obviously

63 See Y. Michot, *A Mamlūk Theologian's Commentary*.

influenced his reading of the *Jawāhir*. Indeed, he implicitly blames al-Ghazālī for the absence of a proper *qānūn at-taʾwīl*, calling his interpretations "a displacement (*taḥrīf*) of the words from their [right] places, and a heretization about the signs of God," worthless as Shii inventions "and other exegeses of the Qarmaṭīs."

The fourth passage from the *Jawāhir* highlighted by Ibn Taymiyya relates to one's spirit reading the Preserved Tablet while asleep and having to interpret the symbolic data resulting from this reading. For him, the identification of the Preserved Tablet with the agent intellect simply does not make sense. Religiously speaking, it is another example of unjustifiable, Qarmaṭizing assimilationism. Philosophically speaking, it is self-contradictory because the Preserved Tablet is supposed to be above the heavens, whereas the agent intellect and the universal soul of the Avicennan cosmo-epistemological model are joined to the sphere of the moon. Beyond this, however, the Damascene theologian has an even more serious concern about the whole matter. According to this passage, it would indeed seem that al-Ghazālī finally follows some *qānūn at-taʾwīl*: to approach the Qurʾān as one interprets (*ʿabbara*) the symbols of a dream. This reduction of Prophetic revelation to dreams, and of *taʾwīl* to *taʿbīr*, is nevertheless nothing more than an invalid confusion of genres. Philosophers might consider prophetology and oneirology to be one same discipline. For Muslims, however, Ibn Taymiyya says, this is a "corrupt principle." By advocating such an unsound methodology, Abū Ḥāmid makes his case worse rather than improving it.

In the last comment which he makes on a passage of the *Jawāhir* in his *Bughya*, Ibn Taymiyya becomes very personal. Addressing al-Ghazālī in the first person singular, he asserts that his demand for a valid exegetical methodology and rejection of philosophizing interpretations has nothing to do with "blind imitation" (*taqlīd*) but ensues from a necessary knowledge similar to the one that makes someone reject "sophistry in intellectual matters." Two diametrically opposed understandings of the religion, and of God's purpose through prophetic revelations, are now in full clash: a transparent one, that makes them accessible to everyone, and an esoteric one, sometimes traced back to ʿAlī because attributing it to the other Companions and Followers of the Prophet would automatically look fallacious. As Ibn Taymiyya phrases it, "I necessarily know that it is vain and that God did not mean that."

Later in the *Bughya*, Ibn Taymiyya will return to particular pages of the *Tafriqa* and *Mishkāt*. With this last, passionate, comment on the *Jawāhir*, he has however reached the peak of his refutation of al-Ghazālī's philosophizing exegesis and esotericism. *La messe est dite* and there is no need to proceed further. The way the Damascene theologian develops his refutation might sometimes be surprising and far from precise or clear. The multiplication of repetitions, excursuses and references to things said to have been examined "elsewhere" obviously does not help his readers. In spite of all this, there is undoubtedly a semantic coherence, or even a crescendo of meaningfulness and relevance, in the trajectory which Ibn Taymiyya follows in the *Bughya* to explore and map al-Ghazālī's thought, from the *Miʿyār* to the *Jawāhir*, through the *Tafriqa* and the *Mishkāt*. The limits imparted to the present paper did not allow a comprehensive translation of all Ibn Taymiyya's comments. His castigation of the Ḥujjat al-Islam's incoherence, lack of a sound exegetical rule, and philosophical hijacking of Islamic scriptural sources, is however manifest, and this castigation raises essential questions. Though supposedly al-Ghazālī abandoned all this at some point, written works have their own life and destiny, independently of their author, especially in the case of important scholars like him. Ibn Taymiyya's prophylactic efforts might not have really succeeded in stopping their diffusion in the past, but his calls for caution remain there as guidance for whoever is ready to hear them.

Appendix: Concordance of the Beginning of *Bughyat al-murtād* and Various Ghazālian Works

Bughya	*Miʿyār*
✳ P. 185, l. 1, *wa-lākinnā* – l. 10, *li-l-ism*	P. 284, l. 10, *wa-lākinnā* – l. 19, *li-l-ism*
l. 10, *wa-innamā* – p. 186, l. 15, *wa-l-qadīm*	P. 285, l. 10, *wa-innamā* – l. 19, *wa-l-qadīm*
"Until he says:"	
P. 186, l. 17, *al-ʿaql al-kullī* – l. 18, *ʿindahum*	P. 291, l. 10, *al-ʿaql al-kullī* – l. 11, *ʿindahum*
"He means: the philosophers"	
P. 186, l. 18, *thalātha* – p. 189, l. 8, *wujūdihi*	P. 291, l. 11, *thalātha* – p. 293, l. 2, *wujūdihi*
"Before this, Abū Ḥāmid had also said:"	
P. 189, l. 10, *wa-ammā l-ʿuqūl* – p. 191, l. 6, al-malakiyya ∗	P. 289, l. 5, *wa-ammā l-ʿuqūl* – p. 290, l. 11, al-malakiyya
✳ P. 191, l. 7, *inna nafs* – l. 8, *aṭ-ṭabīʿiyya*	P. 293, l. 1, *wa-nafs* – *aṭ-ṭabīʿiyya*
✳ l. 10, *al-ʿuqūl al-faʿʿāla*	P. 289, l. 5, *al-ʿuqūl al-faʿʿāla*
✳ l. 11, *alladhī* – l. 12, *al-fiʿl*	l. 18, *al-mukhrij* – *al-fiʿl*
✳ P. 192, l. 2, *fī l-mādda*	l. 15, *fī l-mawādd*
✳ l. 5, *lā bi-tajrīd ghayrihi*	l. 16, *lā bi-tajrīd ghayrihi*
✳ l. 10, *al-mutaḥayyiz*	l. 13, *al-mutaḥayyiz*

Bughya	*[Fayṣal] al-tafriqa*
* P. 196, l. 3, *al-kufr* – l. 4, *jā'a bihi*	P. 128, l. 8, *al-kufr* – l. 9, *jā'a bihi* (*Boundaries*, p. 92)
* P. 196, l. 4, *at-taṣdīq* – l. 5, *marātib*	P. 129, l. 12, *at-taṣdīq* – l. 14, *marātib* (*Boundaries*, pp. 93–94)
l. 6, *dhātī* – *shabahī*	l. 15, *dhātī* – *shabahī* (*Boundaries*, p. 94)
* P. 196, l. 10, *wa-ammā l-wujūd* – *kathīra*	P. 133, l. 14, *wa-ammā l-wujūd* – *kathīra* (*Boundaries*, p. 98)
* P. 196, l. 11, *al-mithāl* – p. 198, l. 5, *al-mutakallimūn* *	P. 134, l. 3, *al-mithāl* – p. 135, l. 5, *al-mutakallimūn* (*Boundaries*, pp. 99–100)

Bughya	*Mishkāt*
* P. 199, l. 6, *al-faṣl* – l. 7, *ḥaqīqa lahu*	P. 41, l. 1, *al-faṣl* – l. 3, *ḥaqīqa lahu* (*Mishkat*, p. 79)
* P. 200, l. 5, *al-faṣl* – l. 8, *maḥdūd*	P. 65, l. 1, *al-faṣl* – l. 4, *maḥdūd* (*Mishkat*, p. 121)
* l. 9, *al-awwal* – l. 10, *al-amthila*	l. 5, *aḥaduhumā* – l. 6, *al-amthila* (*Mishkat*, p. 121)
* l. 11, *wa-th-thānī* – l. 12, *al-Qur'ān*	P. 76, l. 11, *al-quṭb ath-thānī* – l. 12, *al-Qur'ān* (*Mishkat*, pp. 143–144)
* l. 13, *wa-ammā l-faṣl* – l. 15, *alf*^{an}	P. 84, l. 1, *al-faṣl* – l. 4, *alf*^{an} (*Mishkat*, p. 157)
* P. 202, l. 15, *al-quṭb al-awwal* – p. 205, l. 3, *al-bashariyya*	P. 65, l. 1, *al-awwal* – p. 67, l. 11, *al-bashariyya* (*Mishkat*, pp. 122–126)
P. 205, l. 3, *fa-ghāyatī* – p. 206, l. 2, *al-ḥaqq*	P. 67, l. 12, *fa-ghāyatī* – p. 68, l. 7, *al-ḥaqq* (*Mishkat*, pp. 126–128)
"Until he says:"	
P. 206, l. 3, *fa-aqūlu* – p. 210, l. 11, *al-qulūb*	P. 69, l. 1, *fa-naqūlu* – p. 72, l. 4, *al-qulūb* (*Mishkat*, pp. 129–136)
"Thereafter he said:"	
P. 210, l. 12, *khātima* – p. 214, l. 12, *ghayrahumā**	P. 73, l.1, *khātima* – p. 75, l. 2, *ghayrahumā* (*Mishkat*, pp. 136–141)
* P. 215, l. 3, *fī ṣ-Ṣaḥīḥ* – l. 4, *ar-Raḥmān*	P. 71, l. 18, *fī l-ḥadīth aṣ-Ṣaḥīḥ* – *ar-Raḥmān* (*Mishkat*, p. 136)
* l. 9, *anna malak*^{an} ... l. 10, *al-makhlūqāt*	?
* l. 10, *anna l-malā'ika* ... l. 11, *ba'ḍ*^{an}	?
* l. 11, *'ālam ash-shahāda* ...	P. 65, l. 17–18, *'ālam ash-shahāda* ... (*Mishkat*, p. 123)
* l. 12, *ta'bīr ar-ru'yā* ...	P. 69, l. 1–2, *at-ta'bīr* ... *ar-ru'yā* ... (*Mishkat*, p. 129)
* P. 216, l. 4, *inna l-malā'ika* ... *kalb*	P. 73, l. 13, *lā yadkhulu* ... *kalb* (*Mishkat*, p. 138)
* l. 7, *Mūsā* ... l. 8, *al-ākhira*	l. 9, *Mūsā* ... l. 10, *al-kawnayn* (*Mishkat*, p. 138)

✳ l. 8, *mā yanzilu*… l. 9, *Mūsā*	P. 69, l. 14, *wa-minhu yanfajiru*… l. 15, *aṭ-ṭūr* (*Mishkat*, p. 131)
✳ l. 10, *taʿẓīm*… p. 217, l. 1, *yubīḥ al-muḥarramāt*	P. 74, l. 4, *al-kāmil*… l. 5, *ilā l-ibāḥa* (*Mishkat*, p. 139)

Bughya	***Jawāhir***
✳ P. 220, l. 9, *wa-ammā l-afʿāl* – p. 221, l. 18, *taʿālā* *	P. 10, l. 17, *wa-ammā l-afʿāl* – p. 12, l. 2, *taʿālā* (*Jewels*, pp. 14–15)
✳ P. 222, l. 4, *inna l-Qurʾān* – l. 5, *li-l-ḥiss*	P. 11, l. 2, *al-Qurʾān* ± l. 5, *li-l-ḥiss* (*Jewels*, p. 14–15)
✳ P. 223, l. 3, *wa-minhā* – l. 4, *li-Ādam*	l. 8, *wa-minhā* – l. 9, *li-Ādam* (*Jewels*, p. 15)
✳ l. 15, *inna awlāʾika* – *al-Ādamiyyīn*	l. 12, *lā iltifāt*^{a} – *al-Ādamiyyīn* (*Jewels*, p. 15)
✳ P. 225, l. 4, *wa-minhā* – l. 5, *as-sujūd*	l. 9, *wa-minhā* – l. 10, *as-sujūd* (*Jewels*, p. 15)
✳ P. 226, l. 5, *mustaghriqūn* – *jalālihā*	l. 13, *li-istighrāqihim* – *jalālihā* (*Jewels*, p. 15)
✳ P. 228, l. 3, *wa-lā tastabʿid* – l. 4, *dhurriyyatihi*	l. 14, *wa-lā tastabʿid* – l. 15, *dhurriyyatihi* (*Jewels*, p. 15)
✳ P. 230, l. 13, […] *Ibn ʿAbbās*	l. 16, *inna li-Llāh* – p. 12, l. 2, *ʿAbbās* (*Jewels*, p. 15)
✳ P. 277, l. 1, *wa-iʿlam* – p. 279, l. 3, *akthar minhu* *	P. 29, l. 9, *wa-iʿlam* – p. 30, l. 17, *akthar minhu* (*Jewels*, pp. 37–39)
✳ P. 279, l. 4, *wa-bi-l-jumla* – l. 7, *at-taʿbīr*	P. 30, l. 17, *wa-bi-l-jumla* – p. 31, l. 3, *at-taʿbīr* (*Jewels*, p. 39)
✳ P. 284, l. 12, *li-kull shayʾ* – *rūḥuhu*	l. 7, *wa-li-kull shayʾ* – l. 8, *rūḥuhu* (*Jewels*, p. 38)
✳ P. 313, l. 12, *lā tastabʿid* – *al-jins*	l. 10, *wa-lā yustabʿadu* – *al-jins* (*Jewels*, p. 39)
✳ P. 314, l. 5, *anzala* – *māʾ*	l. 13, *anzala* – *māʾ* (*Jewels*, p. 39)
✳ P. 316, l. 2, *wa-inna l-Qurʾān* – l. 4, *at-taʿbīr*	P. 31, l. 1, *fa-inna l-Qurʾān* – l. 3, *at-taʿbīr* (*Jewels*, p. 39)
✳ P. 327, l. 11, *in kunta* – l. 12, *ʿalayka*	P. 30, l. 10–11, *wa-in kunta* – l. 12, *ʿalayka* (*Jewels*, p. 39)

CHAPTER 18

Arbitrating between al-Ghazālī and the Philosophers

The Tahāfut *Commentaries in the Ottoman Intellectual Context*

M. Sait Özervarlı

The contribution of classical Ottoman thinkers to Islamic intellectual history is relatively neglected in modern and contemporary studies. With the intention of analyzing the impact of al-Ghazālī and related interactions between philosophical rationality and religious sources, this contribution aims to open a space for Islamic studies within existing Ottomanist scholarship.

Following the emergence of Muslim philosophy (*falsafa*) with al-Kindī (d. ca. 252/866), the relationship between philosophical rationality and sacred doctrine became controversial in the 11th and 12th centuries, when two major thinkers, Abū Ḥāmid al-Ghazālī and Abū l-Walīd Ibn Rushd wrote treatises on the subject, both entitled "The Incoherence" (*tahāfut*): al-Ghazālī's work was *Tahāfut al-falāsifa*, literally "the incoherence of the philosophers," to which Ibn Rushd riposted with *Tahāfut at-tahāfut*, or "the incoherence of '*The Incoherence* [*of the Philosophers*].' After this medieval flare, however, scholars writing on this issue generally skip to the 19th and 20th centuries, when rationalism reemerged as a modernist discourse of Muslim religious writing. I propose, however, that these approaches overlook an important phase of the debate: namely, the literature written by Ottoman scholars (*ʿulamāʾ*) of the fifteenth and sixteenth century. The present study suggests that a close examination of Ottoman philosophical literature, especially commentary texts on the *Tahāfut*, demonstrates that Ottoman works were not just mere repetitions of the previous legacy, but also examples of critical analysis and profound insight. As a part of the Ottoman philosophical context, I will examine the case of *Tahāfut* commentaries written by major Ottoman scholars of the classical period, such as Hocazāde, Ṭūsī, Kemalpaşazāde, and Karabāğī.[1]

1 I will use Turkish characters for spelling the names of Ottoman thinkers, and will keep the usual transliteration when referring to the pre- or non-Ottoman authors as well as Arabic titles.

 | DOI 10.1163/9789004290952_019

The Historical Background of the "Incoherences"

In the eleventh century, al-Ghazālī's (d. 504/1111) well-known work *Tahāfut al-falāsifa* (*Incoherence of the Philosophers*), the first comprehensive critique of the philosophers, marked a turning point in Islamic intellectual history in terms of the relationship between philosophy and the Islamic disciplines.[2] Within the text, al-Ghazālī asserted that the views of the Islamic philosophers were hopelessly contradictory, criticizing their metaphysical doctrines on twenty topics. The *Tahāfut* is often regarded as aimed primarily at Ibn Sīnā, due to extensive quotation from his work; Janssens, however, in his examination of the targets and sources of the book, refutes this, seeing al-Ghazālī's intended object as an open question.[3] Nevertheless, the book was probably intended to combat the school of Ibn Sīnā in general, the members of which were regarded as Muslim peripatetics (*mashshāʾiyyūn*) in philosophical circles and philosophers (*falāsifa* or *ḥukamāʾ*) among the theologians. According to al-Ghazālī, the emanation (*ṣudūr*) theory of the philosophers – which was based on the necessary production of the universe from God's essence, just as the sun produces its light – contradicted the theological doctrine of the world being created by God. Al-Ghazālī was also displeased with their denial of the attributes of God as real entities, with their defense of deterministic causality in the physical world, and with their physiological theories of the human soul. In his criticism, therefore, al-Ghazālī argued that the philosophers were "incoherent," not only in regards to Islamic principles, but also *intra se*, demonstrating clear contradiction between specific details of their logical-philosophical system.[4]

It has been a tradition in the West to consider al-Ghazālī's cannonade a decisive setback for philosophical inquiry in the medieval Islamic world. Indeed, the well-known modernist scholar of Islam Mohammed Arkoun asserts that "Many schools of thought started to be weakened and disappear after the thirteenth century. Philosophy, as inherited from Classical Greece, disappeared after the death of Ibn Rushd (1198), though it survived in Iran

---

2 See al-Ghazālī, *Tahāfut al-falāsifa: The Incoherence of the Philosophers*, ed. and trans. by Michael Marmura, Provo: Brigham Young University Press, 1997.

3 Jules Janssens, "Al-Ghazzali's *Tahafut*: Is it really a rejection of Ibn Sina's Philosophy?" *Journal of Islamic Studies*, 12: 1 (2001), 1–17.

4 See Leor Halevi, "The Theologian's Doubts: Natural Philosophy and the Skeptical Games of Ghazali," *Journal of the History of Ideas*, Volume 63, Number 1 (January 2002), 19–39; cf. also M. Sait Özervarlı, "An Unedited *Kalam* Text by Qadi al-Baydawi: Misbah al-arwah," *İslâm Araştırmaları Dergisi / Turkish Journal of Islamic Studies*, 12 (2004), 75–125, in particular 76.

in the form of theodicy and theosophy."[5] Following this approach, therefore, scholars of Islamic studies, especially in the West, have largely ignored the long period of Ottoman intellectual and religious history, in part due to a widespread presupposition that Islamic civilization declined after the 13th century.[6] Wisnovsky points out, though, that the latest evidence shows "the distortedness of the traditional Western portrayal of al-Ghazālī," which suggests that his critique in the *Tahāfut* "caused the annihilation of philosophical activity in Islamic civilization."[7] In concord with this assertion, some contemporary scholars, including Sabra,[8] Gutas,[9] and Endress,[10] have taken a new approach, highlighting the importance of post-12th century intellectual efforts not only among Shiite scholars, but also in the Sunni Ottoman environment. Indeed, rather than eradicate the philosophical spirit, al-Ghazālī appears to

5 Mohammed Arkoun, *The Unthought in the Contemporary Islamic Thought*, London: Saqi Books, 2002, 13.

6 For example, W. Montgomery Watt characterizes the entire period from 1250 to 1850 as "The Stagnation of philosophical theology." See *Islamic Philosophy and Theology*, Edinburgh: Edinburgh University Press, 1985, 131–41.

7 Roberst Wisnovsky, "One Aspect of the Avicennan Turn in Sunni Theology," *Arabic Sciences and Philosophy*, 14: 1 (March 2004), 65–100, 65.

8 See A. I. Sabra, "Science and Philosophy in Medieval Islamic Theology: The Evidence of the Fourteenth Century," *Zeitschrift für Geschichte der Arabisch-Islamischen Wissenschaften*, 9 (1994), 15–23. Also see Sabra's "The Appropriation and Subsequent Naturalization of Greek Science in Medieval Islam: A Preliminary Statement," *Tradition, Transmission, Transformation*, eds. Jamil Ragep & Sally P. Ragep, Leiden: E. J. Brill, 1996, 21–6.

9 In his book on the classical period, Dimitri Gutas emphasizes the neglect of the post Mongol invasion period: "This period of Arabic philosophy, almost wholly unresearched, may yet one day be recognized as its golden age." See *Greek Thought and Arabic Culture*, London: Routledge, 1998, 172. Gutas also emphasizes that the integration of Avicennian Aristotelianism into Shiite thought was not an exception, the Sunni tradition being equally receptive to philosophy and the sciences, "including during the high centuries of Ottoman civilization"; see ibid., 273.

10 Gerhard Endress, "Reading Avicenna in the Madrasa: Intellectual Geneologies and Chains of Transmission of Philosophy and the Sciences in the Islamic East," *Arabic Theology, Arabic Philosophy: From the Many to the One: Essays in Celebration of Richard M. Frank*, ed. James E. Montgomery, Leuven: Peters, 2006, 408–10. George Saliba, too, referring to the quality of contribution of the late 13th century thinkers in his history of Arabic astronomy, notes that "this level of sophistication in astronomical research was not known in the previous centuries, and its very sophistication and originality should force us to reconsider the general character of this period as a period of decline. It should also stimulate research in other fields in order to ascertain whether a similar sophistication can be established." See George Saliba, *A History of Arabic Astronomy*, New York: New York University Press, 1994, 12.

have paradoxically injected philosophy into the heart of Islamic learning. As such, the Muslim theologians of his time – already in favor of rational methodology and the use of logic – began to examine and refer to the works of the philosophers openly.

Al-Ghazālī's transfusion of philosophical discourse into Islamic disciplines is quite similar to al-Ashʿarī's transmission of Muʿtazilite *kalām* methodology to the Sunni schools. When al-Ghazālī legitimizes Aristotelian logic, for instance, he compares it to chapters dealing with the principles of reasoning or dialectics (*Kitāb an-Naẓar, Kitāb al-Jadal,* or *Madārik al-ʿuqūl*), and suggests that only the intellectually pretentious would hold that logic belonged exclusively to philosophy.[11] As for some of the conclusions of the philosophers, al-Ghazālī's stance is decidedly polemical; rather than just presenting his alternative views, he excoriates his opponents with harsh language. Yet, al-Ghazālī's *Incoherence* and his investigation of philosophy, though critical and in some points severe, nevertheless legitimized the logical-philosophical discourse among *kalām*-theologians. As a result, Muslim theologians operating after al-Ghazālī's career – such as, for example, Fakhr ad-Dīn ar-Rāzī (d. 605/1209) and Sayf ad-Din al-Āmidī (d. 630/1233) indulged in philosophical theories, quoting and discussing the ideas of philosophers in their works. These philosopher-theologians began to devote large sections of their theological books to epistemology, ontology, cosmology, and metaphysics, giving more attention to these philosophical subjects than to the traditional doctrinal issues which they relegated to the end of their books. Consequently, the boundaries between the two fields became almost imperceptible; thus, *kalām* was transformed into a full-scale theoretical discipline.[12]

While al-Ghazālī's *Incoherence* caused a methodological revolution in Sunni Muslim theology, it also brought about a revival in the school of philosophers. Ibn Rushd (d. 594/1198), known in the West as Averroes, wrote a refutation of al-Ghazālī's *Incoherence* entitled *Tahāfut at-Tahāfut* (*Incoherence of the Incoherence*). In his response, Ibn Rushd claimed that al-Ghazālī's arguments, lacking proof and certitude, simply reproduced the old theses of early

11 Al-Ghazālī, *Tahāfut al-falāsifa*, 9.

12 Ibn Khaldūn points out the absorption of philosophy by *kalām* in the late period following Fakhr ad-Dīn ar-Rāzī, expressing that it became impossible to differentiate between *kalām* books and philosophical works. See his *Muqaddima*, Beirut: Dār Iḥyāʾ at-turāth al-ʿArabī, n. d., 466; cf. also A. I. Sabra, "Science and Philosophy in Medieval Islamic Theology: The Evidence of the Fourteenth Century," *Zeitschrift für Geschichte der Arabisch-Islamischen Wissenschaften*, 9 (1994), 11–23.

traditionalist scholars. Ibn Rushd's book dealt with each of al-Ghazālī's twenty discussions, answering each of them separately.[13]

Despite Ibn Rushd's criticism, later theologians continued to absorb philosophy, integrating it with Islamic theological thought. Leaving Shiite intellectual history aside,[14] syntheses between philosophy and religious thought in the Sunni world reached a higher level in the works of the Timurid encyclopeadists and commentators of the fourteenth century, especially in Saʿd ad-Dīn at-Taftazānī (d. 792/1390) and Sayyid Sharīf al-Jurjānī (d. 816/1413). Though these works mainly followed the footsteps of Fakhr ad-Dīn ar-Rāzī and ʿAḍūd ad-Dīn al-Ījī (d. 756/1355), they also had mystical and philosophical content, which will be examined below.

The Ottoman Period and the Re-emergence of the *Tahāfut* Debate

Considering the history above, it becomes clear that two major factors characterized Ottoman involvement with the *Tahāfut*: (1) the post-classical tendency of rapprochement between philosophy and theology, beginning from the 11th century onwards (with the establishment of Niẓāmiyya Madrasas in several Iraqi and Iranian towns by the Seljuqs); and (2) the Anatolian environment, which encouraged interaction between various schools.

Influenced to a large degree by the hermeneutic and linguistic skills of the fourteenth century scholars mentioned above, Ottoman thinkers of the fifteenth and sixteenth centuries energetically engaged the wide spectrum of thought ranging between theology and philosophy. More interestingly, they revived the long forgotten tradition of the *Incoherence* debates.[15]

13 Ibn Rushd, *Tahāfut at-Tahāfut*, ed. Maurice Bouyges, Beyrouth: Imprimerie Catholique, 1930. For a translation see *The Incoherence of the Incoherence*, trans. with introduction and notes by Simon van den Bergh, London: Luzac & co., 1954.

14 See Henry Corbin, *En Islam iranien: aspects spirituels et philosophiques*, Paris: Librarie Gallimard, 1978.

15 Bibliographic sources of Islamic literature report other books on the *Incoherence* written in the pre-Ottoman period, but it is not known whether these books are extant or even whether they are related to the same historical debate; for instance, Ismail Pasha al-Baghdadi attributes an *Incoherence* book to a certain ʿAbū l-Huṣayn (or Haṣan) Qutb ad-Dīn Saʿīd b. ʿAbdallah b. al-Ḥusayn b. Hibatullāh ar-Rāwāndī (d. 573/1178), a Shiite scholar, who lived in the period between al-Ghazālī and Ibn Rushd (See *Īḍāḥ al-maknūn*, vol. 1: 340); cf. also Sayyid Muḥsin al-Amīn, *Aʿyān ash-shīʿa*, Beirut: Dar at-Taʿāruf, 1983, 7: 240; ʿUmar Riḍā Kaḥḥāla, *Muʿjam al-muʾallifīn*, Damascus: Maṭbaʿat at-Taraqqi, 1957, 4: 225.

It is evident that following the decline of the Seljuqs, local emirates in the fifteenth century preserved the existing Islamic cultural heritage, especially in the Eastern regions; this heritage was then transferred to the Ottoman dynasty (est. 1299), which became the main authority of the Muslim world. Even earlier than this, scholars of both Arab and Central Asian/Persian origins, including the famous mystic thinker Jalāl ad-Dīn ar-Rūmī (d. 671/1273), found safe havens in Anatolia (then called *bilād ar-Rūm*) after the Mongols' catastrophic invasion of Persia, Iraq, Syria, and Egypt. Ṣadr ad-Dīn al-Konawī (d. 655/1256), Sirāj ad-Dīn al-Urmawī (d. 681/1283), and Quṭb ad-Dīn ash-Shīrāzī (d. 711/1311) were other influential scholars who taught in the pre-Ottoman Anatolian madrasas. Other well-known figures, such as ʿAbd al-Laṭīf al-Baghdādī (d. 628/1231) and Athīr ad-Dīn al-Abharī (d. 663/1265), contemporaries of al-Urmawī and ash-Shīrāzī, also traveled to Anatolia, each spending a part of their life in various Anatolian towns.[16] Moreover, with the immigration of the mathematician-astronomer Alī Kuşçu to Istanbul in the fifteenth century, the scientific production of Samarqand and its surrounding schools later transferred, in part, to Ottoman lands.[17]

Among the earliest Ottoman scholars are Dāvud-i Kayserī (d. 751/1350), who taught at the oldest Ottoman madrasa in İznik (Nicosia), and Molla Fenārī (d. 834/1431), who studied in Iznik, Aksaray, and Cairo, later becoming the first Grand Mufti (*şeyhulislām*) of Istanbul. Both Kayseri and Fenāri, combining philosophy with theological and mystical thought, demonstrated the traditional roots of Anatolian scholarly culture and represented the eclectic form of Ottoman classical thinking. One should remember that Ottoman scholarly literature, including those works by Kayserī and Fenārī, mostly took the form of reiterating traditional knowledge, largely in the form of commentaries, glosses and sub-glosses (*sharḥ, ḥāshiya, taʿlīqāt*). In the case of the "Incoherences," I will argue that, despite their explicit connections to certain previous texts, it would be unfair to deem these works totally devoid of new thoughts, analyses or insights related to contemporary conditions. Although it is true that some commentaries are indeed unsophisticated and simple, many commentaries on

16 Claude Cahen, *Pre-Ottoman Turkey: A General Survey of Material and Spiritual Culture and History c. 1071–1330*, trans. from French by J. Jones-Williams, New York: Taplinger Publishing Company, 2001, 349–50. See entries in *Türkiye Diyanet Vakfı İslam Ansiklopedisi*, Istanbul: Türkiye Diyanet Vakfı, 1988–: Mahmut Kaya, "Abdüllatif el-Bağdadi" (vol. 1. pp. 254–5) and Abdülkuddus Bingöl, "Ebheri, Esiruddin" (10: 75–6).

17 Alī Kuşçu earlier wrote *Zic-i Ulugh Bey, Risāla fī l-hay'a, Risāla fī l-ḥiṣāb* in Persian, and then rewrote the last two books in Arabic with some additions under the titles of *al-Fatḥiyya* and *al-Muḥammadiyya*. These books were dedicated to Mehmed II.

the *Tahāfut* texts reveal important clarifications and re-interpretations by their authors. Indeed, the authors of classical commentaries argued that commentary writing was one of the ways of approaching philosophy, and therefore, that the commentaries represented an important link in the history of thought.[18]

When it came to the reign of Sultan Mehmed II (r. 1432–1481), the relationship between the three main disciplines of Islamic philosophical thought (i.e., *kalām, falsafa* and *taṣawwuf*) received renewed attention. The Sultan, personally interested in philosophical and scientific issues, began to invite prominent scholars from around the Muslim world to the newly conquered Ottoman capital at Istanbul (formerly Constantinople) to both establish a lively scholarly community and revive Islamic intellectual vigor. He enjoyed the company of scholars, and was keen on organizing debates between preeminent figures regarding controversial topics. The Sultan's ambition was to establish a learning center in his new capital Istanbul, thereby attracting scholars from around the Muslim world as well as from the West, especially from Venice;[19] as such, his efforts could be compared to those of the Abbasid Caliph al-Ma'mūn's *Bayt al-Ḥikma*, and the later Seljuq Vizier Niẓām al-Mulk's well-known *al-Madrasa an-Niẓāmiyya* projects. A number of prominent Muslim scholars, including ʿAlī Kuşçu, ʿAlā' ad-Dīn aṭ-Ṭūsī, and Gurānī, came from Persian and Arab lands in this way.[20] The immigration of these scholars increased the pre-existing interest in debates between theologians and philosophers.

18 Richard Sorabji, "The Ancient Commentators on Aristotle," in *Aristotle Transformed: The Ancient Commentators and Their Influence*, edited by Richard Sorabji, London: Duckworth, 1990, 24–27 of 1–30. There are, in fact, different types of commentaries: some are polemical and critical, some are exegetical, and others are merely word-by-word linguistic explanations for pedagogical purposes, or for ordinary readers. Therefore, not all commentaries are the same; each type needs to be treated separately. Serious commentaries were seen as examples of continuation and expansion of thought, and in some cases as a way to express different ideas in a safe and unthreatening format. However, Ottoman texts were not always commentaries, but also independent treatises on various topics, such as existence/non-existence, necessity/contingency, substances and attributes, and so on.

19 For the intellectual interests of Mehmed II, see Kritovolous, *Tarih-i Sultan Mehmed Han*, trans. Karolīdī, Istanbul: Ahmed İhsan ve Şürekası Matbaacılık, 1328 AH [1912], 16, 182. This biography by Kritovolous was originally written in Greek, but was translated into English as *History of Mehmed the Conqueror*, trans. and ed. by Charles T. Riggs, Princeton: Princeton University Press, 1954. See also Franz Babinger, *Mehmed the Conqueror and His Time*, Princeton, N.J.: Princeton University Press, 1978, 485.

20 Mehmed's own teacher Molla Gurānī was invited and brought from Egypt during the reign of his father, Murad II. Furthermore, Mehmed may have intended to invite Molla

One of the most specific attempts by Mehmed, however, was his commissioning of two of Istanbul's leading scholars – Hocazāde Muṣliḥ ad-Dīn Musṭafā (d. 893/1488) and ʿAlāʾ ad-Dīn ʿAlī ṭ-Ṭūsī (d. 877/1472), two rival scholars of the 15th century – to write books similar to al-Ghazālī's *Tahāfut*. The explicit purpose of this commission was to discuss the opposite theses of al-Ghazālī and the philosophers in a brief yet comprehensive way. Yet, why return to a four-century-old text, such as the *Tahāfut*, instead of more a recent text? Indeed, Ottoman scholars were already commenting on more contemporary works, including the *Sharḥ al-Maqāṣid* of Saʿd al-Din al-Taftazānī and the *Sharḥ al-Mawāqif* of Sayyid Sharīf al-Jurjānī; Ottoman manuscript libraries are full of partial or complete commentaries on the latters' books, including those written by Hocazāde and Ṭūsī. This can be explained by the authority of al-Ghazālī, the attraction of comparative approaches among various schools at that time, and the Sultan's desire to claim the honor of settling a debate which had remained inconclusive for centuries. Perhaps the Sultan wished to negotiate contemporary questions by going back to the beginning of the debate.

In any case, the two rivals applied themselves to the Sultan's task. Hocazāde was a son of a rich family in Bursa who had left a life of comfort to study under the prominent Hızır Bey; Hocazāde soon became Hızır Bey's assistant, and later, an important scholar in Istanbul. Ṭūsī, for his part, had immigrated from Iran during the reign of Mehmed's father, Murād II (r. 1421–1451), and later became a famous teacher in the Ottoman madrasas. Both specialized in rational disciplines such as *kalām* and *falsafa*, each writing several books.[21] Having accepted the Sultan's invitation, each completed his own commentary in about six months, thereupon presenting their projects at the Sublime Porte.[22]

A scholarly committee examined the two books, though there is no mention, in the sources, of the names of its members. Both works were awarded

---

ʿAbd ar-Raḥmān-i Jāmī of Herat and Jalāl ad-Dīn ad-Dawwānī as a part of his scholarly projects in Istanbul, but these plans were never realized (See Babinger, 471–2).

21 On Hocazāde's life and scholarly reputation see Taşköprīzāde Ahmed Efendī, *Shaqāʾiq an-nuʿmāniyya*, ed. Ahmed Suphi Furat, Istanbul: Istanbul Üniversitesi Edebiyat Fakültesi, 1985, 126–39; Mecdi Mehmed Efendī, *Ḥadāʾiq ash-shaqāʾiq*, in *Şekaik-i Nuʿmaniyye Zeyilleri*, faximile edition by Abdülkadir Ozcan, Istanbul: Cagri Yayinlari, 1989, 1: 145–158; ʿAbd al-Ḥayy b. ʿImād al-Ḥanbalī, *Shadharāt adh-dhahab fī akhbār man dhahab*, Beirut: al-Maktab at-Tijārī li-ṭ-Ṭibāʿa, n.d., 7: 354–6. See also Saffet Köse, "Hocazâde Muslihuddin Efendi," *Türkiye Diyanet Vakfi İslam Ansiklopedisi*, Istanbul: Türkiye Diyanet Vakfı, 1988–, 18: 207–9.

22 Taşköprīzīde refers to other examples of scholarly debates that were promoted by the Sultan, for instance between Hocazāde and Molla Zeyrek on the arguments of Divine unity (*tawḥīd*). See Taşköprīzāde, *Shaqāʾiq*, 124–5.

the same honorary subsidy (10,000 *dirhams*), though Hocazāde's book was regarded as relatively superior, providing him an additional gift.[23] According to the reports from Taşköprizāde and Kātib Çelebi, a copy of Hocazāde's *Tahāfut* commentary was presented (during a visit by Ottoman scholar Müeyyedzāde) to the well-known Persian thinker Jalāl ad-Dīn ad-Dawwānī (d. 908/1502), who expressed his satisfaction and admiration after examining it.[24]

The rebirth of the *Tahāfut* in this competition generated a lively discussion in further Ottoman studies of the debate. Şemseddīn Aḥmed b. Kemāl, known as Kemalpaşazāde (d. 941/1534), and Muḥyī d-Dīn Muḥammad b. ʿAlī Karabāğī (d. 942/1535) wrote glosses (*ḥāshiya/haşiye*) on Hocazāde's commentary.[25] All of these works, though written by Ottoman scholars, were, following the scholarly tradition, produced in Arabic. Ḥakīm Şah Muḥammad b. Mubārak (d. 930/1523), invited to Istanbul during the reign of Bāyezid II (r. 1447–1512),

23 For other details on the historical background of the Ottoman *Incoherences* and Ṭūsī's dramatic reaction to his loss of the competition, see Taşköprizāde, *Shaqāʾiq an-Nuʿmāniyya*, 97–100; Mecdi, *Ḥadāʾiq ash-shaqāʾiq*, 1: 118–9; Kātib Çelebī, *Kashf aẓ-ẓunūn*, ed. M. Şerefettin Yaltkaya and Kilislī Rıfat Bilge, Ankara: Milli Eğitim Bakanlığı, 1941, 1: 513. Hocazāde's book was printed during the late Ottoman period, and Ṭūsī's work was published in a good scholarly edition recently: see Khojazāde Muṣliḥ ad-Dīn Muṣṭafā Efendi, *Kitāb Tahāfut al-falāsifa*, Cairo: Al-Maṭbaʿa al-ʿĀlamiyya, 1302 AH; ʿAlāʾ ad-Dīn ʿAlī ṭ-Ṭūsī, *Tahāfut al-falāsifa*, ed. Riḍā Saʿāda, Beirut: Dār al-Fikr al-Lubnānī, 1990. The editor of Ṭūsī's *Tahāfut* also produced a comparative analysis of the book with other *Tahāfuts* in a separate volume: see Riḍā Saʿāda, *Mushkilat aṣ-ṣirāʿ bayna al-falsafa wa-d-dīn min al-Ghazālī wa-Ibn Rushd ilā ṭ-Ṭūsī wa-Khojazāde*, Beirut: Dār al-Fikr al-Lubnānī, 1990. Ṭūsī's work was also translated into Turkish; see ʿAlāʾ ad-Dīn ʿAlī aṭ-Ṭūsī, *Tehâfütü'l-Felâsife* (*Kitâb az-Zuhr*), trans. Recep Duran, Ankara: Kültür Bakanlığı, 1990.

24 Taşköprīzāde, *ash-Shaqāʾiq an-Nuʿmāniyya*, 137; Mecdi, *Hadāʾiq ash-Shaqāʾiq*, 1: 157; Kātib Çelebī, *Kashf aẓ-ẓunūn*, I: 513. *Tahāfut* texts by al-Ghazālī, Ibn Rushd and Hocazāde are compared in terms of their approach to the relationship between philosophy and religion. See Mübahat Türker, *Üç Tehafüt Bakımından Felsefe ve Din Münasebetleri*, Ankara: Türk Tarih Kururmu Basımevi, 1956.

25 Kemalpaşazāde's gloss is still in manuscript and awaits editing, though it has been translated into Turkish up to the fourteenth chapter together with Hocazade's commentary (Kemalpaşazāde, *Tehâfüt Hâşiyesi* [*Haşiya ʿalā Tahāfüt al-falāsifa*], trans. into Turkish Ahmet Arslan, Ankara: Kültür ve Turizm Bakanlığı, 1987). Arslan also analyzed both texts in a separate volume; his assessments are valuable: see Ahmet Arslan, *Haşiye ala't-Tehafüt Tahlili*, Istanbul: Kültür ve Turizm Bakanlığı, 1987. For a manuscript copy of the original text see Süleymaniye Library, Hasan Hüsnü Paşa, MS. no. 1235. Karabāğī's gloss, however, has been published and translated in two separate volumes. See *Taʿlīqa ʿalā sharḥ tahāfut al-falāsifa li-Khojazade*, ed. Abdurrahim Güzel, Kayseri: n.p., 1996; and *Karabaği ve Tehafüt'ü*, trans. with intro. Abdurrahim Güzel, Ankara: Kültür Bakanlığı, 1991.

is mentioned as the author of a *Tahāfut* work on Hocazāde's commentary.[26] Mueyyedzāde ʿAbdurraḥmān Efendī (d. 923/1516) and Yaḥyā Malkarāvī, who is known as Nevʿī Efendī (d. 1008/1599) are also reported to have written similar books,[27] though manuscripts of the *Tahāfut* works of the last three authors have not yet been located. Finally, an 18th century Ottoman scholar Mehmed Emin Üsküdārī (d. 1149/1736) abridged the content of the *Tahāfut*;[28] later in the modern period this paraphrase was translated into Turkish, becoming the focus of further examinations.[29]

A similar genre of literature among Ottoman scholars was literature detailing the difference (*ikhtilāf*) between the views of various traditions of Islamic philosophical thought. These comparisons were mostly between the views and methodologies of the theologians (*mutakallimūn*) and philosophers (*ḥukamāʾ/falāsifa*), but in some cases the approach of the mystical thinkers (*mutaṣawwifa/ṣūfiyya*) was also taken into consideration. The Ottoman commentaries on the *Tahāfut*, although to some extent comparisons, were based mainly on al-Ghazālī's work. The *ikhtilāf* books, however, despite their being influenced by the *Tahāfut* debate, took the disputed issues in a more general sense without explicit reference to al-Ghazālī's text; Athīr ad-Dīn al-Abharī and ʿAbd ar-Raḥmān al-Jāmī's books are examples of the *ikhtilāf* genre.[30] Comparisons in the *ikhtilāf* form continued in production among Ottoman scholars up to the early eighteenth century, when Mestcīzāde Abdullah Efendī (d. 1148/1735) wrote another book of the same nature.[31] Ottoman scholars

26 Kātib Çelebī, *Kashf aẓ-ẓunūn*, 1: 513; Taşköprīzāde, *Shaqāʾiq an-nuʿmāniyya*, 379; Mecdī, *Ḥadāʾiq ash-shaqāʾiq*, 1: 341–2; Kahhāla, *Muʿjam al-muʾallifīn*, 11: 151.

27 See Taşköprīzāde, *Shaqāʾiq an-nuʿmāniyya*, 230–1; Ismail Bāshā al-Baghdadī, *Hadiyyat al-ʿārifīn wa-asmāʾ al-muʾallifīn*, ed. M. Şerefettin Yaltkaya and Kilisli Rıfat Bilge, Ankara: Milli Eğitim Bakanlığı, 1941, 1: 642 and 2: 531; Kaḥḥāla, *Muʿjam al-muʾallifīn*, 6: 223 and 13: 21.

28 A manuscript copy of Üsküdarī's *Talkhīs tahāfut al-hukamāʾ* exists in Hacı Selim Ağa Library, Kemankeş, no. 266. An edition and translation of its text into Turkish has been recently published; see Mehmed Amīn al-Uskudārī, *Talkhīs Tahāfut al-hukamā*, edited and translated by Kâmuran Gökdağ, Istanbul: Türkiye Yazma Eserler Kurumu Başkanlığı Yayınları, 2014.

29 These examinations of the modern period demand further study; I am currently working on them for a forthcoming article.

30 See Al-Abharī, *Risāla mushtamila ʿalā thamanī ʿashara masʾala fī l-kalām waqaʿa fīhā n-nizāʿ bayna al-ḥukamāʾ wa-l-mutakallimīn wa-arbāb al-milal wa-l-adyān*, ed. Huseyin Sarıoğlu, Istanbul: n.p., 1995; al-Jāmī, *ad-Durra al-fākhira* [*fī taḥqīq madhhab aṣ-ṣūfiyya wa-l-mutakallimīn wa-l-ḥukamāʾ al-mutaqaddimīn*], ed. N. L. Heer, A. Musavi Bihbehānī, Tehran: Danishgah-i McGill, 1980/1358.

31 There are many copies of Mestcīzāde's *al-Masālik fī l-khilāfiyyāt bayna al-mutakallimīn wa-l-ḥukamāʾ* in Istanbul's manuscript libraries (e.g., Süleymaniye Library, Hasan Hüsnü

also produced commentaries on influential philosophical textbooks such as *Hidāyat al-ḥikma*,[32] and *Īsāgūjī*.[33] Despite these contributions, however, the existing publications on Islamic philosophical thought focus almost exclusively on the pre-Ottoman period, and the few studies, mainly biographical, that address the Ottoman period in Turkish are in separate pieces that mostly lack a methodological framework.

Questions About the "Incoherence" Commentaries within the Ottoman Scholarly Context

It is interesting that Ottoman *Tahāfut* authors do not mention Ibn Rushd's assault on al-Ghazālī, the *Tahāfut at-Tahāfut*. Rather, Ottoman treatises aim to judge between the views of al-Ghazālī and the views of philosophers in general. Some sources, such as az-Zabīdī[34] and Brockelmann,[35] as well as many modern and contemporary secondary works in Turkish, refer to the Ottoman *Tahāfuts* in the classical period as comparisons between al-Ghazālī's and Ibn Rushd's books;[36] even Louis Gardet, in an encyclopedic entry, describes this

Paşa, MS. No. 1119). Apart from a partial edition by Ülker Öktem in her Ph.D. dissertation (submitted to Ankara University in 1993), the manuscript was very recently edited and released by Seyit Bahcivan, Beyrut and Istanbul: Dār Ṣādir and Maktabat al-Irshād, 2007.

32 *Hidāyat al-ḥikma* (Istanbul: Hacı Muharrem Efendi Matbaası, 1303 AH) includes issues of logic, physics and metaphysics following the Avicennian system of thought; the most popular philosophy book among Ottomans was written by al-Abharī. His *Hidāyat al-ḥikma* was the preferred source of many Ottoman and Shiite commentaries on *falsafa*; see Abdülkuddus Bingöl, "Ebheri, Esiruddin", *Türkiye Diyanet Vakfı Islam Ansiklopedisi*, 10: 76.

33 This is a handbook of logic, a summary of Aristotle's *Organon*. The title was borrowed from Porphyry's *Eisagogē* (lit. "introduction"). Sirāj ad-Dīn al-Urmawī's (d. 682/1283) *Maṭāliʿ al-anwār*, Najm ad-Dīn ʿUmar b. ʿAlī l-Qazwīnī's (d. 693/1294) *Shamsiyya*, and Saʿd ad-Dīn at-Taftazānī's (d. 792/1390) *Tahdhīb al-kalām wa-l-manṭiq* were other logic books that drew the interest of the Ottomans. Regarding commentaries on logic literature in the pre-ottoman and Ottoman periods, see Khaled el-Rouayheb, "Sunni Muslim Scholars on the Status of Logic, 1500–1800," *Islamic Law and Society*, 11: 2 (2004), 213–37.

34 Murtaḍā z-Zabīdī, *Itḥāf as-sāda al-muttaqīn bi-sharḥ asrār Iḥyāʾ ʿulūm ad-dīn*, Cairo: al-Maṭbaʿa al-Maymāniyya, 1311/1893–4, 41.

35 Brockelmann, *Geschichte der arabischen Litteratur*, Leiden: E. J. Brill, 1943, 2: 298, Suppl. 2: 322.

36 Modern Turkish historians of philosophy repeat the same mistake; see for instance Hilmi Ziya Ülken, *Türk Tefekkür Tarihi*, Istanbul, Matbaa-i Ebuzziya, 1934, 1: 134, fn.1; Şemseddin Günaltay, "İslâm Dünyasının İnhitatı Sebebi Selçuk İstilası Mıdır?" *İkinci Türk Tarih*

erstwhile "work of the Turk Khojazade (9th/15th century), which, adopting al-Ghazālī's title, sought to refute the *Tahāfut at-Tahāfut* of Ibn Rushd."[37] A closer look at the content and the introduction of these works shows something else entirely, however: in fact, according to the Ottoman narrators of the story, the purpose of Hocazāde and Ṭūsī's assignment was to arbitrate between al-Ghazālī and the philosophers (*muḥākama bayna al-Ghazālī wa-l-ḥukamā'*), ignoring Ibn Rushd's critique of the same title.

Moreover, there is no mention or quotation of Ibn Rushd in any of those Ottoman *Tahāfut* commentaries;[38] this is remarkable given the fact that Ibn Sīnā, as well as many other theologians and philosophers including Fakhr ad-Dīn ar-Rāzī, Naṣīr ad-Dīn aṭ-Ṭūsī, Sa'd ad-Dīn at-Taftazānī, and Sayyid Sharīf al-Jurjānī, are referenced several times. Also remarkably, though Hocazāde and Ṭūsī were asked to write their books in al-Ghazālī's method or style,[39] each developed new arguments and in some cases disagreed with al-Ghazālī's points. As such, it is clear that the Ottoman *Tahāfuts* by Hocazāde and Ṭūsī, and further commentaries later by others, explore both approaches of the philosophers and al-Ghazālī, taking sides in regards to each question and sometimes disagreeing with both.

As was pointed out earlier, the Ottomans belonged to a period when philosophy and theology were mostly integrated.[40] Since this integration had not yet occurred during the time of al-Ghazālī, it is understandable that some Ottoman scholars were unsatisfied with some of his arguments. Regardless of their disagreement, however, their total neglect of Ibn Rushd's refutation of al-Ghazālī

Kongresi, İstanbul: Devlet Basımevi, 1937, s. 11; A. Adnan Adıvar, *Osmanlı Türklerinde İlim*, Istanbul Remzi Kitabevi, 1970, 47; Ekmeleddin İhsanoğlu, *Büyük Cihad'dan Frenk Fodulluğuna*, Istanbul: İletişim, 1996, 29; Süleyman Hayri Bolay, *Osmanlılarda Düşünce Hayatı ve Felsefe*, Ankara: Akçağ, 2005, 256.

37 Louis Gardet, "'Ilm al-Kalām," *Encyclopedia of Islam* (Second edition), 3: 1149a.

38 These commentaries also do not mention al-Kindī and al-Fārābī, but this is understandable since al-Ghazālī's *Tahāfut* primarily targeted the school and views of Avicenna.

39 *"an anẓura fī r-risāla al-musammāt bi-Tahāfut al-falāsifa allatī allafahā* [...] *al-Ghazālī raḥimahu Allāh, wa-aktuba 'alā uslūbihi...*" (Ṭūsī, *Tahāfut al-falāsifa*, 52–3); *"bi-an umliya kitāb*^{an} *'alā-mithālihā wa-ansuja dībāj*^{an} *'alā minwālihā* (i.e. al-Ghazālī's book, see Hocazade, *Tahāfut al-falāsifa*, 3).

40 See Robert Wisnovsky, "The Nature and Scope of Arabic Philosophical Commentary in Post Classical (ca. 1100–1900 AD) Islamic Intellectual History: Some Preliminary Observations," in Peter Adamson, Han Baltussen and M. W. F. Stone (eds.), *Philosophy, Science and Exegesis in Greek, Arabic and Latin Commentaries*, London: University of London, 2004, vol. 2, pp. 149–91.

seems strange.[41] Were Ottoman thinkers of the 15th century unaware of Ibn Rushd's refutation of al-Ghazālī's *Tahāfut*? Or did they deliberately ignore it as a reaction against his position in Arabic/Muslim philosophy?

In order to discuss these questions, we should begin by analyzing Ibn Rushd's influence and popularity in the history of Islamic thought. It is the general consensus that Ibn Rushd had only a minimal impact on post-12th century Muslim thinkers; rather, his influence appears to have been felt primarily within European philosophical circles in the Christian world.[42] Ibn Rushd's books were banned even in his native region in al-Andalus, and his pure Aristotelian rationalism – compared to Avicenna's eclectic philosophy – was regarded as inconvenient to the wide-ranging dimensions of later Islamic thought. This poor reception, however, does not at all mean that Ibn Rushd was unknown to wider Muslim scholarship; on the contrary, the pre-Ottoman period's most significant thinkers, including the philosophers' most blistering critics, were indeed familiar with Ibn Rushd. Ibn Taymiyya (d. 727/1327), for example, refers to Ibn Rushd in his books quite often, specifically mentioning and extensively citing his *Tahāfut at-Tahāfut* several times.[43] Ibn Khaldūn (d. 809/1406), the well-known historian of Islamic civilization, writes about Ibn Rushd in his *Muqaddima*.[44] We can conclude, therefore, that Ibn Rushd was known to Muslim scholars; as such, his *Tahāfut* against al-Ghazālī must have been extant in intellectual circles prior to the Ottoman period.

It must be pointed out, of course, that Ibn Taymiyya and Ibn Khaldūn were themselves not very popular among Ottoman scholars in the early period. Ibn Taymiyya, a Ḥanbalī/Salafī thinker, was a misfit in the broader Ḥanafī/Maturīdī Ottoman intellectual environment; this intellectual atmosphere, influenced mainly by Central Asian and Persian schools of thought, combined the philosophical, theological, and mystical traditions of Islam. The impact of Ibn Khaldūn, likewise, was felt mostly in the fields of ethical and political philosophy following his "discovery" in the 17th century and subsequent popularity.[45]

---

41 This detail is beside the point and will not be pursued here, but similarly strange is the absence of al-Ghazālī's *Maqāṣid al-falāsifa*, his basic introduction to the views of Muslim philosophers, in Ottoman commentaries; see *Maqāṣid al-falāsifa*, ed. Maḥmūd Bījū, Damascus: Maṭbaʿat aṣ-Ṣabāḥ, 1420/2000. Kātib Çelebī's bibliographic work, again, seems to be the earliest source to refer to it; see *Kashf aẓ-ẓunūn*, II, 1280.

42 Cf. Simon van Den Bergh, *Averroes' Tahāfut al-Tahāfut* (Introduction), xii.

43 Taqī d-Din Ibn Taymiyya, *Darʾ taʿāruḍ al-ʿaql wa-n-naql*, ed. Muḥammad Rashād Sālim, Riyad: Jāmiʿat al-Imām Muḥammad b. Suʿūd, 1979–1983, 1: 162; 2: 397–403; 6: 210–1.

44 Ibn Khaldūn, *Al-Muqaddima*, 491.

45 See Ejder Okumuş, *Osmanlı'nın Gözüyle İbn Haldun*, Istanbul: İz Yayıncılık, 2008.

Rather than draw their lineage through Ibn Khaldūn and Ibn Taymiyya, Ottoman thinkers were, instead, connected to the heritage of Fakhr ad-Dīn ar-Rāzī, on one hand, and Muḥyī d-Dīn Ibn al-ʿArabī (d. 637/1240) on the other. Both ar-Rāzī and Ibn al-ʿArabī (one the renewer of the *kalām* tradition, the other a Sufi theorist) were influenced by al-Ghazālī and Ibn Sīnā. The views of ar-Rāzī were transmitted, as I mentioned earlier, through the reconstructions of Ījī, Taftazānī and Jurjānī, while those of Ibn al-ʿArabī were passed on by ʿAfīf ad-Dīn at-Tilimsānī (d. 690/1291), ʿAbd ar-Razzāq al-Kāshānī (d. 735/1335), and by Ibn al-ʿArabī's student Ṣadr ad-Dīn al-Konawī (d. 661/1263). Moreover, the Illuminationist school of Islamic philosophy established by Suhrawardī (d. 591/1191) and reconstructed by Ṣadr ad-Dīn ash-Shīrāzī, another source of Ottoman thought, was also linked to Ibn Sīnā.

The heavy influence of Ibn Sīnā being transmitted through so many channels, could there be any trace of the views of his foe Ibn Rushd among the Ottomans? Despite the relatively increased awareness of his book in the field of *uṣūl al-fiqh* (*Bidāyat al-mujtahid*), early Ottoman sources do not refer to his philosophical works. Later, in the 17th century, however, the famous bibliography of Kātib Çelebī (d. 1067/1657), *Kashf aẓ-ẓunūn*, contains a citation of Ibn Rushd's *Tahāfut at-Tahāfut*; indeed, at the end of his entry on al-Ghazālī's *Tahāfut al-falāsifa*, in which he describes the work of al-Ghazālī in great detail, Çelebī mentions the refutation of Ibn Rushd, quoting the beginning and the end of Ibn Rushd's text.[46] Compared to the long description of al-Ghazālī's *Tahāfut*, however, Çelebī spares only a few lines for Ibn Rushd, declines comment or evaluation, and moves quickly to commentaries written by Ottomans. Nevertheless, Kātib Çelebī's quotation from *Tahāfut at-Tahāfut*, though sparse, suggests that Ottoman libraries – or at least some Ottoman scholars – had copies. In my own search through Turkish manuscript libraries, I found less than ten traceable copies of *Tahāfut at-Tahāfut*. That this small number could be found among the mountain of copies of al-Ghazālī's *Tahāfut* gives a clear portrait of Ibn Rushd's minimal influence on Ottoman thought, at least in regards to the *Incoherence* debate.[47] Though Ottoman commentaries on al-Ghazālī's *Tahāfut* include some points that parallel Ibn Rushd's counter criticisms, these

46 Kātib Çelebī, *Kashf aẓ-ẓunūn*, 1: 512–3.

47 I located copies of *Tahāfut at-Tahāfut* in the Süleymaniye Library (Laleli 2490, Yeni Cami 734, Şehid Ali Paşa 1582), the Beyazit Library (Veliyüddin Efendi 4024), the Kayseri Raşid Efendi Library (Raşid Efendi 530), the Konya Yusuf Ağa Library (487), and the Giresun Halk Library (1220).

cannot certify an awareness of Ibn Rushd's *Tahāfut* inasmuch as they could have arisen independently, without reference to Ibn Rushd.[48]

If they were only commentaries on al-Ghazālī's *Tahāfut*, to what degree did the Ottoman *Tahāfuts* by Hocazāde and Ṭūsī and their commentators follow al-Ghazālī – that is to say, to what extent did these authors prefer the views of the post-Ghazālī *mutakallimūn* of the 12th through 15th centuries? Here we have evidence of Ottoman reaction, engagement, and elaboration: Hocazāde adds two chapters to al-Ghazālī's original twenty chapters (each chapter discussing a question), introducing a new chapter on the necessary in itself (*mūjib bi-dhātihi*) and dividing the discussion of the Divine attributes into two separate chapters. Kemalpaşazāde commented on Hocazāde's chapters selectively, dealing only with fifteen; Karabāğī, in turn, discussed only twelve chapters. 'Alā' ad-Dīn aṭ-Ṭūsī, however, in his rival work to Hocazāde's, examined the questions in twenty chapters – that is, exactly the same number of chapters as al-Ghazālī; nevertheless, he added general epistemological issues to the fifteenth chapter, which is on the Divine knowledge.

Reading through the texts of Hocazāde and Ṭūsī, both authors acquit themselves of blindly following al-Ghazālī; instead, they claim to base their analysis on evidence, without prejudice to the philosophers.[49] The systematic and categorical Ṭūsī, for instance, promises to defend only what he considers certain

48 Ottoman thinkers who examined and referred to the philosophical works of Ibn Rushd can be found, though they belong to the later period: for example, the 18th-century Ottoman philosopher and translator Yanyavī Es'ad Efendī (d. 1144/1731), who was known as the Third Teacher (*al-Mu'allim ath-thālith*) among the Ottomans, was one of them; see Yanyavī, *at-Ta'līm ath-thālith*, Ragıb Paşa Library, MS. No. 824, fol. 2a. For Yanyavī's references to Ibn Rushd also see M. Sait Özervarlı, "Yanyalı Esad Efendi's Works on Philosophical Texts as Part of the Ottoman Translation Movement in the Early Eighteenth Century," *Europa und die Türkei im 18. Jahrhundert / Europe and Turkey in the 18th Century*, ed. Barbara Schmidt-Haberkamp, Göttingen: V&R Press, Bonn University Press, 2011, 466–467. Furthermore, in the 19th century, Şeykhulislām Mūsa Kāzim (d. 1919) wrote a chapter specifically on Ibn Rushd's objections to al-Ghazālī, though his analysis was not comprehensive. See Mūsa Kāzim, "İbn Rüşd'ün Felsefî Metodu ve İmam Gazzalî ile Bazı Konulardaki Münazarası," in his *Küllīyāt: Dini, İctimai Makaleler*, Istanbul: Evkaf-ı İslamiyye Matbaası, 1326 AH, 139–96.

49 *"fa-wāfaqtu ṭarīqat al-Imām al-Murshid* [i.e., al-Ghazālī] *fī l-aṣl, lākin lā bi-ṭariqat at-taqlīd, bal bi-muqtaḍā t-taḥqīq al-baḥt, aw bi-mā huwa sharīṭat al-munāẓara wa-l-baḥth, fa-inna at-taqlīd fī amthāl hadhā min nidhālat al-jidd wa-safalat al-bakht"* Ṭūsī, *Tahāfut al-falāsifa*, 54. See also: *"inna mā awradnā min al-mubāḥatha wa-l-munāẓara ma' al-falāsifa laysa al-maqṣūd min majmū'ihā l-ḥukm bi-buṭlān maṭālibihim"* (Ṭūsī, ibid., 368); cf. *"bal tanbīh^{an} 'alā l-marām ḥasab mā 'anna lī min ar-rad wa-l-qubūl wa-n-naqd wa-l-ibrām"* (Hocazade, *Tahāfut al-falāsifa*, 4).

and correct; he also pledges to dispute only what is rationally problematic, excusing himself from "bigotry" (*taʿaṣṣub*), or deviation from the "path of fairness" (*jāddat al-inṣāf*). Ṭūsī, moreover, regards such interactive dialogues with the philosophers as both "useful" (*mufīda*) and "quite possible" (*ghayr baʿīda*).[50]

In his introduction, Ṭūsī employs comparatively gentler language towards the philosophers, especially when compared to Hocazāde's; the latter, as will be seen, includes a more pointed critique of al-Ghazālī, sometimes describing al-Ghazālī's arguments as "of no significance" (*laysa bi-shay'*). Kemalpaşazade, for his part, is astonished that Hocazāde's book criticizes al-Ghazālī instead of the philosophers; this astonishment must have prompted Kemalpaşazāde's speculation as to whether Hocazāde wrote his *Tahāfut* commentary in order to criticize the philosophers or, rather, al-Ghazālī himself.[51]

Insofar as al-Ghazālī did not reject all the views of the philosophers but rather highlighted his major criticisms of some of their arguments, Ottoman authors likewise, although they considered themselves close to al-Ghazālī in a philosophical sense, did not feel obliged to merely ape him. Indeed, despite their belonging to al-Ghazālī's tradition of thought, Ottoman commentators criticized some of his arguments; in some cases they even evince views parallel to Ibn Rushd, though they were apparently unaware of his book.[52] They did not, moreover, see it necessary to accept or reject a view as a whole, but rather agreed with some details while criticizing others. For instance, Hocazāde evaluates al-Ghazālī's arguments against illumination (*ṣudūr*) theory regarding the lack of Divine action and Actor. In al-Ghazālī's view, the illumination of the universe, though suggestive of a cause, does not by necessity imply the will of the Actor. Al-Ghazālī rejects necessary causation in the universe and therefore refers to the Divine will between the cause and effect of all physical events. Hocazāde, however, sees the reference to the actor and his will in al-Ghazālī's examples as unnecessary; in normal language, Hocazāde estimates, the causes are considered sufficient for the understanding of actions, and they are not accepted allegorically. Therefore, it is generally accepted that ice makes things cold, fire causes burning, and water obviates thirst, even when the agents behind the actions are not known or seen; according to this view, the illumination of the universe from God does not exclude His being an actor. Ṭūsī, in contrast, supports al-Ghazālī in this regard, emphasizing the importance of the actor

50 Ṭūsī, *Tahāfut al-falāsifa*, 54.

51 Kemalpaşazāde, *Tehâfüt Hâşiyesi*, 511.

52 Cf. Ahmet Arslan, *Hāşiye ala't-Tehafüt Tahlili*, 28, 88.

in the cause-effect chain.[53] Likewise, in some cases disagreements take place among the Ottomans themselves; for instance, in regards to al-Ghazālī's possibility of a distinction in the necessary being of God, Kemalpaşazāde considers Hocazāde's comments incorrect and useless.[54] As such, it is clear that Ottoman scholars took a nuanced approach to al-Ghazālī's work; considering this, this stage of Islamic intellectual history represents not a cessation, but a continuation of the Islamic philosophical heritage.

Comparisons between the Two Commentary Texts

In order to demonstrate this selective approach, I will give a more detailed analysis of Ṭūsī and Hocazāde's treatments of al-Ghazālī's text.

The issue in question is al-Ghazālī's condemnation of what he viewed as the philosophers' most egregious transgressions. Besides his twenty general criticisms of Muslim Peripatetic thinkers, al-Ghazālī also accused the *falāsifa* of disbelief (*kufr*) in three specific matters among all. The subjects of accusation were the eternity of the world in the first chapter, the absence of knowledge of the particulars by God in the thirteenth chapter, and the spiritual resurrection after death in the last twentieth chapter. In the conclusion of his work, al-Ghazālī argues that those views could never be accommodated within Islam in any way; as such, the philosophers holding such opinions must be condemned.[55]

In response, Ibn Rushd denounces al-Ghazālī for not understanding the earlier philosophers correctly and for, in some cases, distorting their intentions. He emphasizes al-Ghazālī's grave responsibility for misleading his readers, claiming that the book ought to be renamed, rather, as the "*Tahāfut Abī*

53 Hocazāde, *Sharḥ Tahāfut al-falāsifa*, 44–7; Kemalpaşazāde, *Tehâfut Hâşiyesi*, 354–9. In addition, Hocazāde disagrees with al-Ghazālī on the issues of color, on the eternity of the world, and on the ability of God to know particulars. Hocazade also criticizes al-Ghazālī for misrepresenting Ibn Sīnā's ideas and rejects the charge of *takfīr* against Ibn Sīnā, which he viewed as unwarranted and extreme (See Mübahat Türker, *Üç Tehafüt Bakımından Felsefe Din Münasebeti*, 386).

54 Kemalpaşazāde, *Tehâfüt Hâşiyesi*, 409; Ahmet Arslan, *Haşiye ala't-Tehafüt Tahlili*, 268–9.

55 Al-Ghazālī, *Tahāfut al-falāsifa*, 230. It is interesting to note that al-Ghazālī in his own lifetime faced a similar accusation of *kufr*. In another work, he complains that a group of jealous opponents accused him of deviating from the path of the predecessors, alleging that any view different from Ash'arism would be the cause of disbelief (See *Fayṣal at-tafriqa bayna al-Islām wa-z-zandaqa*, ed. Samīḥ Dughaym, Beirut: Dār al-Fikr al-Lubnānī, Beirut 1993, 47).

Ḥāmid" (i.e., "The Incoherence of al-Ghazālī"). Despite his energetic defense of the philosophers in general, however, Ibn Rushd does not agree with his predecessors in all particulars, especially when they depart from the Aristotelian position. Therefore, the main goal his *Tahāfut at-Tahāfut* was to demonstrate al-Ghazālī's mangling of the issues rather than to exonerate the views of Ibn Sīnā and the earlier philosophers.[56]

When we examine the Ottoman commentaries, however, it becomes clear that – despite the authors' disagreement with the *falāsifa* and their silence about Ibn Rushd's above criticisms – Ottoman scholars use much gentler language than al-Ghazālī when referring to the philosophers. Ṭūsī, for example, when classifying the views of the philosophers that differ from orthodox Muslim believers (*arbāb ash-sharā'iʿ*), includes most philosophers' views within the sphere of interpretation. Furthermore, according to Ṭūsī, some disagreements between the philosophers and theologians, such as the description of God by the philosophers as substance (*jawhar*) instead of using the term existent by itself (*qā'im bi-nafsih*), are only terminological and nominal (*mā yurjiʿ al-khilāf ilā mujarrad al-iṣṭilāḥ wa-t-tasmiya*). Those are literal (*lafẓī*) disagreements, he says, which have no effect on essential beliefs. Ṭūsī tends to consider al-Ghazālī's accusation of blasphemy as disputable, since the number of different approaches to the allegation documented a lack of unanimity. Although some scholars, in Ṭūsī's view, would see a clear conflict between the views of the philosophers – in the above three matters – and the principles of religion, others would find no clear and certain evidence within the sources of religion.[57]

Hocazāde, in contrast, criticizes some of al-Ghazālī's arguments on the issue of pre-eternity, and emphasizes that the priority of God to the universe in essence neither requires the pre-eternality of both God and the universe nor their origination in time. According to Hocazāde, God's priority to the universe is not through or in time, but through timelessness; the pre-eternity of God does not mean His existence within a time, but a timeless and endless existence that covers an eternal time or is *trans*-time.[58] Kemalpaşazāde, in his gloss on Hacazāde's commentary, refers sympathetically to Ṭūsī's above remarks, suggesting that although people widely accuse the philosophers of blasphemy, condemnation was not universal; their perceptions had been upheld by some great theologians like al-Rāzī. He then quotes a passage of Fakhr ad-Dīn ar-Rāzī's

56 Averroes, *Tahāfut at-Tahāfut* (*The Incoherence of Incoherence*), trans. Simon van den Bergh, Oxford: Oxford University Press, 1934, 1: 9–10, 18, 47, 236, and so on.

57 Ṭūsī, *Tahāfut al-falāsifa*, 61–3.

58 Kemalpaşazāde, *Tehâfüt Hâşiyesi*, 160, 172; Ahmet Arslan, *Haşiye ala't-Tehafüt Tahlili*, 109.

al-Maṭālib al-ʿāliya which is quite similar to Ṭūsī's. According to ar-Rāzī, there are no open statements in the revealed books that explain the origination of the universe in time. The lack of such an open explanation, ar-Rāzī emphasizes, also requires or at least implies that the issue was within the sphere of forgiveness. Following the quotation, Kemalpaşazāde points out that the lack of any statement about the matter in the sacred books was indeed important inasmuch as it made possible to argue against al-Ghazālī's allegation of blasphemy. Kemalpaşazāde is, of course, aware of the counter-argument that religious sources were not limited to the sacred books; they included the prophetic traditions, the *sunna* and *ḥadīth*. As a response, Kemalpaşazāde highlights a principle in theology that any knowledge based on a single tradition is not regarded as completely certain; its rejection, therefore, does not cause blasphemy. He supports his view with a reference to al-Ghazālī's book *Fayṣal at-tafriqa*.[59] This flexibility on the part of the Ottoman authors demonstrates both their relative position regarding al-Ghazālī's accusations and their effort to revise them through linguistic and interpretative methods.

In the eighth chapter of his *Tahāfut*, al-Ghazālī criticizes the philosophers for their view of the essence of God, claiming that the *falāsifa* denied an essence or quiddity (*māhiyya*) for the existence of God due to its simplicity. The presentation of the position of the philosophers by al-Ghazālī becomes the subject of harsh controversy in Ibn Rushd's response to the book. Though this theory about essence and existence found its beginning in the work of al-Fārābī and the early *mutakallimūn*, it was systematized by Ibn Sīnā, from whence it influenced later philosophical and theological Islamic discourse through the Ghazālīan *Tahāfut*. Both early Ashʿarite and Maturidite *mutakallimūn*, for example, while discussing the nature of existence, did not accept the crucial distinction between existence (or being) and essence (or quiddity), the view that was held by al-Fārābī and most of the Muʿtazilites.[60]

59 Kemalpaşazāde, *Tehâfüt Hâşiyesi*, 24–6. For comparisons of these quotes to the original text, see Fakhr ad-Dīn ar-Rāzī, *Al-Maṭālib al-ʿāliya min al-ʿilm al-ilāhī*, ed. Aḥmad Ḥihazī as-Saqqā, Beirut: Dār al-Kitāb al-ʿArabī, 1987, 5: 29, 32; al-Ghazālī, *Fayṣal at-tafriqa*, 77–8.

60 It should be briefly noted that pre-Avicennian *kalām* scholars – in order to distinguish between the divine and temporal categories of existence – divided the existent into two categories: that which is Eternal (*qadīm*) and that which has a beginning (*ḥādith/muḥdath*). Avicenna and the school of philosophers, however, divided existence into necessary existence (*wājib al-wujūd*) and possible/unnecessary (*mumkin al-wujūd*). In the post-Avicennian period of the 11th century the *mutakallimūn* changed direction and came closer to the philosophers. In order to explain the nature of the eternality possessed by God and His attributes, however, al-Ghazālī – influenced by his teacher al-Juwaynī – and his fellow Sunni theologians distanced themselves from the earlier

Ibn Sīnā argues that the existence of a thing must be regarded as an attribute added to its essence, as the essence was the actor or agent of the thing. According to Ibn Sīnā, the First Thing (*al-Awwal*, i.e., God Himself) has no agent, its existence therefore being identical with its essence. This position, in fact, brought together earlier views; unlike the *mutakallimūn*, Ibn Sīnā took a different approach towards possible and necessary existents, especially regarding to the essence-existence relation. For Ibn Sīnā and the philosophers, essence comes first for the possible existents, because our concept formation about things exists without their physical existence. In the Necessary Existent, however, the First cause of possible existents, essence and existent must be the same. Otherwise, like other possible existents, God would need another cause: this would be contrary to His nature and would create an unending chain of causes.[61]

Ibn Sīnā's approach is referred to likewise by al-Ghazālī in his *Maqāṣid al-falāsifa*.[62] However, in the *Tahāfut*, al-Ghazālī presents the idea of identification as the denial of the essence of God, arguing that – contrary to the view of the philosophers – the reality and the essence of God exists. Al-Ghazālī points out that it is irrational to have an existence without essence, since it is its reality that differentiates the existent from other things. Moreover, to negate the essence is to negate the reality, and in the absence of reality, existence cannot be rationally perceived. Therefore, al-Ghazālī asserts, the position of the philosophers actually accepts existence without the existent, a contradiction. If existence without its reality or essence was rational, al-Ghazālī continues, the same must be true for other causal effects (*maʿlūlāt*). Since the philosophers agree about their essence, why not accept this for the First cause? It would be illogical, according to al-Ghazālī, to differentiate between the First necessary existent and other possible existents, both being existents, whether having an essence or not. The lack of essence, he repeats, is the lack of reality, and the lack of reality is nothing other than an empty existence.[63]

---

kalām position. Instead, they employed more philosophical terms, including "impossible of non-existence" (*mustaḥīl al-ʿadam*) and "necessary existence" (*wājib al-wujūd*), though they used these with some hesitation; see al-Juwaynī, *Al-Lumaʿ fī qawāʿid ahl as-sunna wa-l-jamāʿa*, ed. Michel Allard, Beirut: Dār al-Mashriq, 1968, 137; al-Ghazālī, *al-Iqtiṣād fī-l-iʿtiqād*, Beirut: Dār al-Kutub al-ʿIlmiyya, 1403/1983, 20; ibid., *Tahāfut al-falāsifa*, 118–120; al-Pazdawi, *Uṣūl ad-dīn*, ed. Hans Peter Linss, Cairo: Dār Iḥyāʾ al-Kutub al-ʿArabiyya, 1963, 20; Abū l-Muʿīn an-Nasafī, *Tabṣirat al-adilla*, ed. Claude Salāma, Damas: Institut Français de Damas, 1993, 61–2.

61 Ibn Sīnā, *al-Mubāḥathāt*, ed. Muḥsin Bidarfar, Qom: Intisharat-i Bidar, 1992, 279–88.

62 Al-Ghazālī, *Maqāṣid al-falāsifa*, 105–6.

63 Al-Ghazālī, *Tahāfut al-falāsifa*, 118–20.

In his response, however, Ibn Rushd contends that the philosophers did not deny the Divine essence at all; insisting on the fundamental simplicity of God's essence, the *falāsifa* merely reject any separation or combination in God through divisions in His essence and existence. Al-Ghazālī's critique of the philosophers, therefore, was mere sophistry.[64] Theologians after al-Ghazālī such as Fakhr ad-Dīn ar-Rāzī divided existence into "necessary of permanent existence in itself" (*wājib ath-thubūt li-dhātihi*) and "possible existence in itself" (*mumkin al-wujūd li-dhātihi*).[65] Al-Bayḍāwī and his commentator al-Iṣfāhānī – under the influence of Avicennian syntheses – suggested that existence was an addition to essence, neither identical nor part.[66] To both, distinguishing between the Necessary Existent and the temporal reality regarding their essences violates both the communality of the existence and its definition as a shared quality for all beings.

The Ottomans, in turn, saw nothing unusual in using this philosophical division of necessary and temporal existents for their own *Tahāfut* commentaries. On the relation of existence and essence in the Necessary Existent, each Ottoman scholar took a different position. Hocazāde, for his part, focuses on Ibn Sīnā's disputational methods rather than explicitly criticizing his equation of existence and essence in God. Though Hocazāde finds the proofs on this issue insufficient, he at the same time dismisses the philosophers' views and their arguments against Ibn Sīnā. Likewise, though he mentions three opposing arguments made against Ibn Sīnā's view by al-Ghazālī, as-Suhrawardī and ar-Rāzī, Hocazāde expresses his dissatisfaction with their assertions by raising theoretical objections to their assertions. Hocazāde, furthermore, did not see any open contradiction between Ibn Sīnā's position and the principles

---

64 Averroes, *Tahāfut at-Tahāfut*, trans. Simon van den Berg, 1: 236–40. For a further reading on the discussion in the context of contingency, see Taneli Kukkonen, "Possible Worlds in the Tahafut al-tahafut: Averroes on Plenitude and Possibility," *Journal of the History of Philosophy*, Volume 38, Number 3 (July 2000), pp. 329–347; and "Possible Worlds in the Tahafut al-Falasifa: Al-Ghazali on Creation and Contingency," *Journal of the History of Philosophy*, Volume 38, Number 4 (October 2000), pp. 479–502.

65 Fakhr ad-Dīn ar-Rāzī, *Muḥaṣṣal afkār al-mutaqaddimīn wa-l-muta'akhkhirīn min al-ʿulamā'*, Cairo: Maktabat al-Kulliya al-Azhariyya, n.d., 93.

66 Edwin E. Calverley and James w. Pollock (eds. and trans.), *Nature, Man, God in Medieval Islam: 'Abd Allah al-Baydāwī's text Ṭawāliʿ al-anwār min Maṭāliʿ al-anẓār along with Maḥmūd Iṣfahānī's Commentary Maṭāliʿ al-anẓār sharḥ Ṭawāliʿ al-anwār*, Leiden: Brill, 2002, 192.

of Islamic thought, pointing out that some theologians of the later period agreed with Ibn Sīnā on the issue of essence and existence.[67]

Ṭūsī, similarly, chooses to highlight the objections of Fakhr ad-Dīn ar-Rāzī, suggesting that these were not in fact related to the philosophers' actual views. He points out, disparagingly, that ar-Rāzī's argument – based on the assumption that intellectually identifying a commonality among various beings equates them in reality – is simply the product of an overactive imagination, rebuking ar-Rāzī for his negligence. Accepting the separation of God's existence and essence for God, Ṭūsī apologizes for his prolixity. His tarrying in the matter, he explains, was simply caused by a desire to clarify issues and resolve misunderstandings.[68]

Kemalpaşazâde, in contrast, introduces new arguments to refute the claim of the philosophers. According to him, Ibn Sīnā's arguments do not prove the identification of essence and existence in God, but rather show the inclusion of existence into essence as its part. Kemalpaşazâde rejects the argument of an unending chain of causes, asserting that the concept of existence, as well its qualities, are theoretical; they do not necessarily require causes. As such, the identification of essence and existence of God could not be demonstrated.[69]

Karabāğī, however, agrees with Ibn Sīnā and the philosophers on their position of identification, while separating them in the case of possible existents. Karabāğī criticizes his fellow Ottoman Hocazâde of being contradictory in his position; for, while trying to counter Ibn Sīnā, the content of Hocazâde's text nevertheless proves Ibn Sīnā's views. The identification of essence and existence, Karabāğī argues, actually supports the Islamic doctrine of absolute unity of God rather than contradicting it; there is no reason, therefore, to oppose the philosophers and Ibn Sīnā in this regard.[70] In sum, examining the Ottoman texts and their contributions to this long debated case, it becomes clear that the Ottomans reached their own critical and original conclusions.

67 Hocazâde, *Kitāb Tahāfut al-falāsifa*, 68–74; Kemalpaşazâde, *Tehâfut Hâşiyesi*, 462–72. Also see Riḍā Saʿāda, *Mushkilat aṣ-ṣirāʿ bayn al-falsafa wa-d-dīn min al-Ghazālī wa-Ibn Rushd ilā ṭ-Ṭūsī wa-l-Khūjazāde*, Beirut: Dār al-Fikr al-Lubnānī, 1990, 107.

68 Ṭūsī, *Tahāfut al-falāsifa*, 203–7, 215.

69 Kemalpaşazâde, *Tehâfut Hâşiyesi*, 462–82.

70 Karabāğī, *Taʿlīq ʿalā sharḥ tahāfut al-falāsifa li-Khūjazāde*, 161–2.

Conclusion

Ottoman philosophical thought, as traced through the aforementioned *Tahāfut* commentaries, clearly demonstrates active, integrative, and productive Ottoman participation in the context of the Anatolian environment and later Islamic philosophy. Ottoman scholars transplanted Islamic rationality to their own society by engaging, interpreting, critiquing, and re-working pre-Ottoman texts.

This further demonstrates a deep Ottoman familiarity with classical philosophical doctrines and techniques of argumentation. Rather than imitating al-Ghazālī's polemical tone, Ottoman scholars regarded the philosophers in general – and Ibn Sīnā in particular – as simply one side of an on-going debate within Islamic intellectual history. For that reason, Ottoman *Tahāfuts*, though explicitly following the title and the text of al-Ghazālī, nevertheless resemble Fakhr ad-Dīn ar-Rāzī's *Sharḥ al-ishārāt wa-t-tanbīhāt*, which, as we have seen, a philosophical criticism of Avicennian doctrine discreetly disguised as a commentary. As we have also seen, Ottoman authors did not base their efforts on a mere and outright acceptance of al-Ghazālī's views and arguments, but instead made careful distinctions, highlighting weak points and criticizing his assertions when they saw contradictions.

Therefore, Hocazāde, Ṭūsī, and their Ottoman followers seem to employ al-Ghazālī's book only as a textual basis for their views, putting forward different or opposite arguments as reacting philosophers. In each chapter, the Ottoman discussions exceed each topic by focusing on the epistemological details of the subject matter. However, Ottoman authors were not primarily interested in building new philosophical systems or theories, but rather in understanding, expanding, and detailing ideas; this simply debunks the absence of thought: indeed, their philosophical activity – and their interpretation, evaluation, and combination of pre-existing material – contributed to the restoration, vitalization, and transmission of thought to later periods.

Bibliography

1 Works by al-Ghazālī

Ajwibat al-Ghazālī ʿan asʾilat Ibn al-ʿArabī, ed. Muḥammad ʿAbdū, Beirut: Dār al-Kutub al-ʿIlmiyya, 1433/2012.

Ayyuhā l-walad, ed. and translated by Tobias Mayer, *Al-Ghazālī, Letter to a Disciple: Ayyuhā ʾl-Walad*, Cambridge: Islamic Texts Society, 2005.

Bidāyat al-hidāya, printed on the margins of Minhāj al-ʿĀbidīn, Cairo, 1337.

Faḍāʾiḥ al-bāṭiniyya wa-faḍāʾil al-Mustaẓhiriyya, ed. ʿAbd ar-Raḥmān Badawī, Cairo: Ad-Dār al-Qawmiyya, 1383/1964.

Fayṣal at-tafriqa bayn al-islām wa-z-zandaqa, ed. Sulaymān Dunyā, Cairo: ʿIsā l-Bābī l-Ḥalabī, 1381/1961.

"Fayṣal a-tafriqa bayn al-islām wa-z-zandaqa" in: M. M. Abū l-ʿAlāʾ (ed.), *al-Quṣūr al-ʿawālī min rasāʾil al-imām al-Ghazālī*, Cairo: Maktabat al-Jundī, 1390/1970.

Fayṣal a-tafriqa bayn al-islām wa-z-zandaqa, ed. Muḥammad Bījū, Damascus, 1993.

Fayṣal at-tafriqa bayn al-Islām wa-z-zandaqa, ed. Samīḥ Dughaym, Beirut: Dār al-Fikr al-Lubnānī, 1993.

Iḥyāʾ ʿulūm ad-dīn, 5 vols., Beirut: Dār al-Maʿrifa, 1403/1982.

Iḥyāʾ ʿulūm ad-dīn, 5 vols., ed. ʿAbd al-Muʿṭī Amīn Qalʿajī, 2nd edition, Beirut: Dār Ṣādir, 2004.

Iḥyāʾ ʿulūm ad-dīn, 5 vols., Cairo: Al-Maktaba at-Tijāriyya al-Kubrā, n.d.

Iḥyāʾ ʿulūm ad-dīn, 4 vols., Cairo: Lajnat Nashr ath-thaqāfa al-islāmiyya, 1937–1938.

Iḥyāʾ ʿulūm ad-dīn, 5 vols., Cairo: Muʾassasat al-Ḥalabī, 1967–1968.

Iljām al-ʿawāmm ʿan ʿilm al-kalām, ed. Muḥammad M. al-Baghdādī, Beirut: Dār al-Kitāb al-ʿArabī 1406/1985.

Al-Iqtiṣād fī l-iʿtiqād, ed. by Ibrahim Agah Çubukçu and Hüsseyin Atay, Ankara: Nur Matbaasi, 1962.

Al-Iqtiṣād fī l-iʿtiqād, Beirut: Dār al-Kutub al-ʿIlmiyya, 1403/1983.

Jawāhir al-Qurʾān wa-duraruhu, ed. Lijnat Iḥyāʾ at-Turāth al-ʿArabī, 6th edition, Beirut: Dār al-Āfāq al-Jadīda, 1411/1990.

Jawāhir al-Qurʾān, ed. Sālim Shams ad-Dīn, Beirut: Al-Maktaba al-ʿAṣriyya, 2006/1427.

Jawāhir al-Qurʾān wa-duraruhu, ed. Khadīja Muḥammad Kāmil, reviewed by ʿIffat ash-Sharqāwī, Cairo: Dār al-Kutub wa-l-Wathāʾiq al-Qawmiyya, 1432/2011.

Al-Khulāṣa al-musammā [sic] *Khulāṣat al-mukhtaṣar wa-naqāwat al-muʿtaṣar*, ed. Amjad Rashīd, Jeddah: Dār al-Minhāj, 1428/2007.

Kitāb Ādāb tilāwat al-Qurʾān in: *Iḥyāʾ ʿulūm ad-dīn*. Wa-bi-hāmishihi *al-Mughnī ʿan ḥaml al-asfār fī takhrīj mā fī l-iḥyāʾ min akhbār* li-Zayn ad-Dīn Abī l-Faḍl ʿAbd ar-Raḥīm b. al-Ḥusayn al-ʿIrāqī. Wa-bi-dhaylihi *Taʿrīf al-aḥyāʾ bi-faḍāʾil al-Iḥyāʾ*

li-ʿAbd al-Qādir b. Shaykh b. ʿAbdallāh al-ʿAydarūs. Wa-*l-imlāʾ ʿan ishkālāt al-Iḥyāʾ*, Cairo: Dār as-Salām, 2003.

Kitāb al-Arbaʿīn: *Kitāb al-Arbaʿīn fī uṣūl ad-dīn*, ed. Muḥyī d-Dīn Ṣabrī l-Kurdī, Cairo: Al-Maṭbaʿa al-ʿArabiyya, 1344/1925.

Kitāb al-Arbaʿīn: *Kitāb al-Arbaʿīn fī uṣūl ad-dīn*, ed. Muḥammad Muḥammad Jābir, Cairo: Maktabat al-Jundī, 1964.

Kitāb al-Arbaʿīn fī uṣūl ad-dīn. ed. ʿAbd al-Qādir Makrī, Jeddah: Dār al-Minhāj li-n-Nashr wa-t-Tawzīʿ, 2006.

Kitāb Miḥakk an-naẓar fī l-mantiq, ed. Muḥammad Badr ad-Dīn an-Naʿsānī l-Ḥalabī and Muṣṭafā l-Qabbānī d-Dimashqī, Cairo: al-Maṭbaʿa al-Adabiyya, n.d.

Kitāb an-Najāt, ed. Majid Fakhry, Beirut, 1985.

Maʿārij al-quds fī madārij maʿrifat an-nafs, ed. Muḥammad Bījū, Damascus: Dār al-Albāb, 1998.

"Al-Maḍnūn bihi ʿalā ghayr ahlihi" in: M. M. Abū l-ʿAlāʾ (ed.), *al-Quṣūr al-ʿawālī min rasāʾil al-imām al-Ghazālī*, vol. 3, Cairo: Maktabat al-Jundī, 1390/1970.

Makātīb-i fārisī-yi Ghazzālī be-nām-i Fażāʾil al-anām min rasāʾil Ḥujjat al-Islām, ed. ʿAbbās Iqbāl Āshtiyānī, Tehran: Kitābfurūsh-i Ibn Sīnā, 1333/1954.

Maqāṣid al-falāsifa, Cairo, 1936.

Maqāṣid al-falāsifa, ed. Sulaymān Dunyā, Cairo: Dār al-Maʿārif, 1961.

Al-Maqṣad al-asnā fī sharḥ maʿānī asmāʾ Allāh al-ḥusnā, ed. Fadlou Shehadi, Beirut: Dar al-Machreq, 1971; 1982.

Al-Maqṣad al-asnā fī sharḥ maʿānī asmāʾ Allāh al-ḥusnā, anonymous edition, Limasol, 1987.

Al-Maqṣad al-asnā fī sharḥ asmāʾ Allāh al-ḥusnā, Cairo: Maktabat al-Jundī, n.d.

Miʿyār al-ʿIlm fī fann al-mantiq, ed. Muḥyī d-Dīn Ṣabrī l-Kurdī, Cairo: Al-Maṭbaʿa al-ʿArabiyya, 1927.

Miʿyār al-ʿilm, ed. Sulaymān Dunyā, Cairo: Dār al-Maʿārif, 1379/1960.

Miʿyār al-ʿilm fī fann al-manṭiq, ed. M. M. Abū l-ʿAlāʾ, Cairo: Maktabat al-Jandī, 1392/1972.

Miʿyar al-ʿilm, Beirut: Dār al-Kutub al-ʿIlmiyya, 1990.

Mishkāt al-anwār, ed. A. ʿA. ʿAfīfī, Cairo: Dār al-Qawmiyya li-ṭ-Ṭibāʿa wa-n-Nashr, 1383/1964.

Mishkāt al-anwār wa-miṣfāt al-asrār, ed. ʿAbd al-ʿAzīz ʿIzz ad-Dīn as-Sayrawān, Beirut: ʿĀlam al-Kutub, 1407/1986.

Mīzān al-ʿamal, ed. Muḥyī d-dīn Ṣabrī l-Kurdī, Cairo: al-Maṭbaʿa al-ʿArabiyya, 1342/1923.

Mīzān al-ʿamal, Cairo: Maktabat al-Jundī, 1973.

Mīzān al-ʿamal, ed. Aḥmad Shams ad-Dīn, Beirut: Dār al-Kutub al-ʿIlmiyyah, 1989.

Mīzān al-ʿamal, ed. ʿAlī Bū Milḥim, Beirut: Dār wa-Maktabat al-Hilāl, 1995.

Mīzān al-ʿamal, ed. Muḥammad Bījū, Damascus: Dār at-Taqwā, 2008.

Al-Munqidh min aḍ-ḍalāl, Damascus, 1934.

"Al-Munqidh min aḍ-ḍalāl" in: *Majmūʿat rasāʾil al-imām al-Ghazālī*, 7 vols., ed. Aḥmad Shams ad-Dīn, Beirut: Dār al-Kutub al-ʿIlmiyya, 1988 (reprinted 1997).

Al-Munqidh min aḍ-ḍalāl / Erreur et deliverance, ed. Farid Jabre. 3rd ed., Beirut: Commission libanaise pour la traduction des chefs-d'œuvre, 1969.

Al-Munqidh min aḍ-ḍalāl wa-l-mūṣil ilā dhī l-ʿizza wa-l-jalāl, ed. Jamīl Ṣalībā and Kāmil ʿIyād, Beirut: Dār al-Andalus, 1967; 1969; 1981.

Al-Mustaṣfā min ʿilm al-uṣūl, 4 vols., ed. Ḥamza ibn Zuhayr Ḥāfiẓ, Medina: al-Jāmiʿa al-Islāmiyya – Kulliyyat ash-Sharīʿa, 1413/1992–93.

Al-Mustaṣfā min ʿilm al-uṣūl, 2 vols., ed. M. S. al-Ashqar, Beirut: Muʾassasat ar-Risāla, 1417/1997.

Qānūn at-taʾwīl, ed. Muḥammad Zāhid al-Kawtharī, Cairo: Maktab Nashr ath-Thaqāfa al-Islāmiyya, 1359/1940.

Qanūn at-Taʾwīl, ed. M. Bījū, Damascus, 1993.

Al-Qisṭās al-mustaqīm, ed. Victor Chelhot, Beirut: Imprimerie Catholique, 1959.

Al-Qisṭās al-mustaqīm, ed. M. Bījū, Damascus: Al-Maṭbaʿa al-ʿIlmiyya, 1993.

Al-Quṣūr al-ʿawālī min rasāʾil al-imām al-Ghazālī, 4 vols., ed. M. M. Abū l-ʿAlāʾ, Cairo: Maktabat al-Jundī, 1390/1970.

Tahāfut al-falāsifa, ed. Riḍā Saʿāda, Beirut: Dār al-Fikr al-Lubnānī, 1990.

Tahdhīb al-akhlāq, ed. C. Zurayq, Beirut: American University of Beirut Press, 1966.

Al-Wajīz fī fiqh al-Imām ash-Shāfiʿī, 2 volumes, eds. Muʿawwaḍ, ʿAlī and ʿAbd al-Mawjūd, ʿĀdil, Beirut: Dār al-Arqam bin Abī l-Arqam, 1418/1997.

Al-Wajīz fī fiqh madhhab al-Imām ash-Shāfiʿī, ed. Aḥmad Farīd az-Zaydī, Beirut: Dār al-Kutub al-ʿIlmiyya, 1425/2004.

Al-Wasīṭ fī l-madhhab, 7 vols., ed. Aḥmad Maḥmūd Ibrāhīm, Cairo: Dār as-Salām, 1417/1997.

2 Translated Works by al-Ghazālī

Abul Quasem, Muhammad, *The Jewels of the Qurʾān*, Kuala Lumpur: University of Malaysia Press, 1977.

———, *The Recitation and Interpretation of the Qurʾān. Al-Ghazālī's Theory*, London et al.: Routledge and Kegan Paul, 1982 (reprinted 1984).

Abu Risha, Yahya, *Maʿarij al-quds fī madārij maʿrifat an-nafs. On the Soul*, Irbid: Dar Al-Hilal for Translation and Publication, 2001.

Ateş, Ahmed, "Ḥujjat al-ḥaqq wa-qawāṣim al-bāṭiniyya (*The Proof of the Truth and Backbreakers of the Baṭinites*)" in: *İlâhiyat Fakültesi Dergisi* (1954).

Bakhtiar, Laleh, *Jewels of the Quran*, Chicago: Great Books of the Islamic World, 2009.

Brewster, D. P. (trans.), *Al-Ghazali, The Just Balance. A Translation with Introduction and Notes*, Lahore: Sh. Muhammad Ashraf, 1978.

Buchman, David, *The Niche of Lights*. A parallel English-Arabic text translated, introduced, and annotated, Provo and Utah: Brigham Young University Press, 1998.

Burrell, David B. and Daher, Nazih, *The Ninety-Nine Beautiful Names of God* (*Al-Maqṣad al-asnā fī sharḥ asmāʾ Allāh al-ḥusnā*), Cambridge: Islamic Texts Society, 1999.

Davis, Dennis Morgan, *Al-Ghazālī on Divine Essence: a translation from the* Iqtiṣād fī al-Iʿtiqād, PhD. diss., Salt Lake City: The University of Utah press, 2005.

Elschazlī, ʿAbd-Elṣamad ʿAbd-Elḥamīd, *Abū Ḥāmid al-Ghazālī. Das Kriterium des Handelns. Aus dem Arabischen übersetzt, mit einer Einleitung, mit Anmerkungen und Indices herausgegeben*, Darmstadt: Wissenschaftliche Buchgesellschaft, 2006.

Farah, Madelain, *Marriage and Sexuality in Islam: A translation of al-Ghazālī's Book on the Etiquette of Marriage from the* Iḥyāʾ, Salt Lake City: University of Utah Press, 1984.

Faris, Nabih Amin, *Book of Knowledge. Being a Translation with Notes of the* Kitāb al-ʿIlm *of al-Ghazzālī's* Iḥyāʾ ʿulūm al-Dīn, 4th Ed., Lahore: Sh. Muhammad Ashraf, 1974 (reprinted 1979).

Gairdner, W. H. T., *Al-Ghazzali's* Mishkat Al-Anwar (*"The Niche for Lights"*). A translation with introduction, 2nd edition, Lahore: Sh. Muhammad Ashraf, 1952.

Goldenthal, Jacob (trans.), *Mīzān al-ʿamal: Compendium doctrinae ethicae, auctore Al-Gazali Tusensi*, Hebrew translation, Leipzig: Gebhardt & Reisland, 1839.

Goldziher, Ignaz (trans.), *Streitschrift gegen die Batinijja-Sekte*, 2 vols., reprint: Brill: Leiden, 1956.

Gramlich, Richard, *Muḥammad al-Ġazzālīs Lehre von den Stufen der Gottesliebe. Die Bücher 31–36 seines Hauptwerkes eingeleitet, übersetzt und kommentiert*, Wiesbaden: Franz Steiner, 1984.

Malter, Heinrich (ed.), *Die Abhandlung des Abū Ḥamid al-Ġazzāli: Antworten auf Fragen, die an ihn gerichtet wurden*, Frankfurt a. Main.: J. Kaufmann, 1896.

Marmura, Michael E., *Al-Ghazālī. The Incoherence of the Philosophers*: Tahāfut al-falāsifa. A Parallel English-Arabic Text, 2nd edition, Provo: Brigham Young University Press, 2000.

McCarthy, Richard J., *Deliverance from Error: An Annotated Translation of* al-Munkidh min al-ḍalāl *and Other Relevant Works of al-Ghazālī*, Louisville, Kentucky: Fons Vitae, 1980 (reprinted 1999).

———, *Freedom and Fulfillment. An Annotated Translation of Al-Ghazālī's* al-Munqidh min al-Ḍalāl *and Other Relevant Works of al-Ghazālī*, Boston: Twayne Publishers, 1980.

Ormsby, Eric L., *Love, Longing, Intimacy and Contentment: Kitāb al-Maḥabba wa'l-shawq wa'l-uns wa'l-riḍā. Book XXXVI of The Revival of the Religious Sciences*: Iḥyāʾ ʿulūm al-dīn, Cambridge: Islamic Texts Society, 2011.

Renard, John, *Al-Ghazālī*, Kitāb Sharḥ ʿajāʾib al-qalb. *Knowledge of God in Classical Sufism (partial translation)*, New York: Paulist Press, 2004.

Sa'ari, Che Zarrina, *Al-Ghazālī and Intuition: An Analysis, Translation and Text of* al-Risāla al-Laduniyya, Kuala Lumpur: Department of Aqidah and Islamic Thought, 2007.

Stern, M. S., *Kitāb al-Tawba. Al-Ghazzali on Repentance*, New Delhi: Sterling Publishers, 1990.

Watt, William M. (trans.), *Deliverance from Error and the Beginning of Guidance*, Kuala Lumpur: Islamic Book Trust, 2005.

Winter, Timothy J., *Al-Ghazālī on Disciplining the Soul*: Kitāb Riyāḍat al-nafs *and on Breaking the Two Desires*: Kitāb Kasr al-shahwatayn, Cambridge: The Islamic Texts Society, 1995.

3 Works by Other Authors

ʿAbbās, Iḥsān, "Riḥlat Ibn al-ʿArabī ilā l-Mashriq kamā ṣawwarahā Qānūn at-ta'wīl" in: *al-Abḥāth* 21 (1968), 59–91.

Abdel-Kader, Ali Hassan, *The Life, Personality and Writings of al-Junayd*, London: Gibb Memorial Trust, 1976.

Abel, K., "Das Propatheia-Theorem: Ein Beitrag zur stoischen Affektenlehre" in: *Hermes* 111 (1983), 78–97.

Al-Abharī, *Risāla mushtamila ʿalā thamanī ʿashara mas'ala fī l-kalām waqaʿa fīhā an-nizāʿ bayna al-ḥukamā' wa-l-mutakallimīn wa-arbāb al-milal wa-l-adyān*, ed. Huseyin Sarıoğlu, Istanbul: n.p., 1995.

Abrahamov, Binyamin, "Al-Ghazālī's Supreme Way to Know God" in: *Studia Islamica* 77 (1993), 141–68.

———, "Al-Ghazālī's Theory of Causality" in: *Studia Islamica* 67 (1988), 75–98.

———, *Divine Love in Islamic Mysticism: The Teachings of al-Ghazālī and al-Dabbāgh*, London and New York: Routledge, 2003.

———, "Ibn al-ʿArabī's Attitude toward al-Ghazālī" in: Y. Tzvi Langermann (ed.), *Avicenna and His Legacy: A Golden Age of Science and Philosophy*, Turnhout: Brepols Publishers, 2010.

———, "Ibn al-ʿArabī's Theory of Knowledge" in: *Journal of the Muhyiddin Ibn ʿArabī Society* 42 (2007), 9–22.

———, "Ibn Sīnā's Influence on Al-Ghazālī's Non-Philosophical Works" in: *Abr-Nahrain* 29 (1991), 1–17.

———, "Necessary Knowledge in Islamic Theology" in: *British Journal of Middle Eastern Studies* 20 (1993), 20–32.

———, "Review of *Between Mysticism and Philosophy: Sufi Language of Religious Experience in Judah Ha-Levi's* Kuzari by Diana Lobel" in: *Journal of the American Oriental Society* 123 (2003), 244–246.

Abū Dāwūd, *Sunan Abī Dāwūd*, 4 vols., ed. Muḥammad Muḥyī 'd-Dīn ʿAbd al-Ḥamīd, Beirut: Dār al-Kutub al-ʿIlmiyya, n.d.

Abul Quasem, Muhammad, "Al-Ghazālī in Defense of Ṣūfistic Interpretation of the Qurʾān" in: *Islamic Culture* 53 (1979), 63–86.

———, *The Ethics of al-Ghazālī: a Composite Ethics in Islam*, Delmar: Caravan Books, 1978.

Abu Shanab, R. E., "Ghazālī and Aquinas on Causation" in: *Monist* 58 (1974), 140–150.

Abū as-Suʿūd, W., *Iʿjāzāt ḥadītha ʿilmiyya wa-raqamiyya fī l-Qurʾān*, Beirut, 1991.

Abu-Sway, Mustafa, *Al-Ghazzālyy. A Study in Islamic Epistemology*, Kuala Lumpur: Dewan Bahasa dan Pustaka, 1996.

Abu Zayd, Abdu-r-Rahman, Al-Ghazali on Divine Predicates and their Properties, Lahore: Kitab Bhavan, 1970 (reprinted 1974).

Abū Zayd, Naṣr Ḥāmid, *Mafhūm an-naṣṣ. Dirāsa fī ʿulūm al-Qurʾān*, 3rd Ed., Beirut: Al-Markaz ath-Thaqāfī l-ʿArabī, 1996.

———, *An-Naṣṣ, as-sulṭa, al-ḥaqīqa*, 2nd Ed., Beirut: Al-Markaz ath-Thaqāfī l-ʿArabī, 1997.

Acar, Rahim, "Creation: Avicenna's metaphysical account" in: David B. Burrell et al. (ed.), *Creation and the God of Abraham*, Cambridge: Cambridge University Press, 2010, 77–90.

Adamson, Peter, "Before Essence and Existence: al-Kindi's conception of being" in: *Journal of the History of Philosophy* 40 (2002), 297–312.

———, *The Arabic Plotinus: A philosophical study of the 'Theology of Aristotle'*, London: Duckwirth, 2003.

Adang, Camilla, "Islam as the Inborn Religion of Mankind: The Concept of *Fiṭrah* in the Works of Ibn Ḥazm" in: *Al-Qanṭara* 21 (2000), 391–410.

Adıvar, A. Adnan (ed.), *Osmanlı Türklerinde İlim*, Istanbul: Remzi Kitabevi, 1970.

Ahmed, Leila, "Early Islam and the Position of Women: The Problem of Interpretation" in: Nikki Keddie and Beth Baron (eds.), *Women in Middle Eastern History: Shifting Boundaries in Sex and Gender*, New Haven and London: Yale University Press, 1991, 58–73.

———, *Women and Gender in Islam*, New Haven and London: Yale University Press, 1992.

Akasoy, Anna A., "The al-Ghazālī Conspiracy. Reflections on the Inter-Mediterranean Dimension of Islamic Intellectual History" in: Y. Tzvi Langermann (ed.), *Avicenna and his Legacy. A Golden Age of Science and Philosophy*, Turnhout: Brepols Publishers, 2009, 117–142.

Al-Akiti, Muhammad Afifi, "Index to Divisions of al-Ghazālī's Often-Cited Published Works" in: *The Muslim World* 102 (2012), 70–200.

———, "The Good, the Bad, and the Ugly of *Falsafa*: Al-Ghazālī's *Maḍnūn, Tahāfut*, and *Maqāṣid*, with Particular Attention to their *Falsafī* Treatments of God's Knowledge of Temporal Events" in: Y. Tzvi Langermann (ed.), *Avicenna and His Legacy: A Golden Age of Science and Philosophy*, Turnhout: Brepols Publishers, 2009, 51–100.

———, "The Three Properties of Prophethood in Certain Works of Avicenna and al-Ġazālī" in: Jon McGinnis (ed.), *Interpreting Avicenna. Science and Philosophy in Medieval Islam. Proceedings of the Second Conference of the Avicenna Study Group*, Leiden: Brill, 2004, 189–212.

Albertini, Tamara, "Crisis and Certainty of Knowledge in al-Ghazālī (1058–1111) and Descartes (1596–1650)" in: *Philosophy East and West* 55 (2005), 1–14.

Altmann, Alexander, "Moses Narboni's Epistle on *Shiʿur Qomah*" in: Alexander Altmann (trans.), *Jewish Medieval and Renaissance Studies*, Cambridge: Harvard University Press, 1967, 225–288.

Al-Amīn, Sayyid Muḥsin, *Aʿyān ash-shīʿa*, 7 vols., Beirut: Dār at-Taʿāruf, 1983.

Ammann, Ludwig, *Vorbild und Vernunft: Die Regelung von Lachen und Scherzen im mittelalterlichen Islam*, Hildesheim: George Olms, 1993.

Aoyagi, Kaoru, "Transition of Views on Sexuality in Sufism: Al-Makkī, al-Ghazālī and Ibn ʿArabī" in: *The Journal of Japan Association of Middle East Studies* 22 (2006), 1–20.

Arberry, Arthur J., *The Koran Interpreted*, New York: The Macmillan Company, 1955 (reissued 2008).

Aristotle, *De partibus animalium*, ed. Immanuelis Bekkerli, Berolini: Typis Academis, 1829.

———, *De Anima*, with translation, introduction and notes by R. D. Hicks, Cambridge: Cambridge University Press, 1907.

———, *Metaphysics*, 2 vols., translated by W. D. Ross, New York: Oxford University Press, 1924.

———, *Nicomachean Ethics*, translated by W. D. Ross, New York: Oxford University Press, 1961.

———, De anima, *Books II and III*, translated by D. W. Hamlyn, Oxford: Clarendon Press, 1968.

———, *The Complete Works of Aristotle*: The revised Oxford Translation, ed. Jonathan Barnes, Princeton: Princeton University Press, 1984.

Arkoun, Mohammed, *The Unthought in the Contemporary Islamic Thought*, London: Saqi Books, 2002.

Arnzen, Rüdiger (trans.), *Averroes, On Aristotle's "Metaphysics"*, Berlin and New York: Walter de Gruyter, 2010.

———, "The Structure of Mullā Ṣadrā's *al-Ḥikma al-mutaʿāliya fī l-asfār al-ʿAqliyya al-arbaʿa* and his Concepts of First Philosophy and Divine Science" in: *Medioevo* 32 (2007), 199–239.

Arslan, Ahmet (ed.), *Haṭiye ala't-Tehafüt Tahlili*, Istanbul: Kültür ve Turizm Bakanlığı, 1987.

Al-Aʿsam, ʿAbd al-Amīr (ed.), *Al-Faylasūf al-Ghazālī: Iʿādat taqwīm li-munḥanā taṭawwurihi ar-rūhī*, 3rd ed., Beirut: Dār al-Andalus, 1981.

Asin-Palacios, M., "Un faqīh siciliano, contradictor de al-Ġazzālī (Abū ʿAbd Allāh de Māzara)" in: *Centenario della nascita di Michele Amari*, vol. 1, Palermo: Virzì, 1910, 216–244.

ʿAṭṭār, Farīd ad-Dīn, *Manṭiq aṭ-ṭayr*, ed. Ṣādiq Gawharīn, Tehran, 1978.

———, *The Conference of the Birds*. Translated with an introduction by Afkham Darbandi and Dick Davis, London: Penguin Books, 1984.

———, *The Speech of the Birds: Concerning Migration to the Real: The Manṭiqu ṭ-Ṭair*, translated by Peter Avery, Cambridge: The Islamic Texts Society, 1998.

Austin, R. J. W., "The Sophianic Feminine in the Work of Ibn ʿArabi and Rūmi" in: Leonard Lewisohn (ed.), *The Heritage of Sufism*, 2 vols., vol. 2, Oxford: Oneworld, 1999–2003, 233–245.

Avneri, Zvi, "Abner of Burgos" in: Michael Berenbaum and Fred Skolnik (eds.), *Encyclopaedia Judaica*, 16 vols., vol. 1, 2nd ed., Detroit: Macmillan Reference USA, 2007, 264–265.

Avtalion, Joav, *A Comparative Study: Abraham Maimonides'* Kitāb Kifāyat al-ʿābidīn *and Abū Ḥāmid Muḥammad al-Ghazālī's* Iḥyāʾ ʿulūm ad-dīn (*Hebrew*), PhD diss., Ramat Gan: Bar-Ilan University Press, 2011.

Babinger, Franz, *Mehmed the Conqueror and His Time*, Princeton and New Jersey: Princeton University Press, 1978.

Bachillér, A. Rodríguez, *Influencia de la filosofía árabe en el* Pugio *de Raimondo Marti*, Madrid: Casa Hispano-Árabe, 1969.

Badawī, ʿAbd al-Raḥmān, *Arisṭū ʿinda al-ʿArab*, Kuwait: Wakālat al-Maṭbūʿāt, 1978.

———, *Muʾallafāt al-Ghazālī*, 2nd edition, Kuwait: Wikālat al-Maṭbūʿāt, 1977.

Badran, Abū al-Fadl, Muhammad, "... denn die Vernunft ist ein Prophet' – Zweifel bei Abū ʾl-ʿAlāʾ al-Maʿarrī" in: Friedrich Niewöhner and Olaf Pluta (eds.), *Atheismus im Mittelalter und in der Renaissance*, Wiesbaden: Harrassowitz Verlag, 1999, 61–84.

Bahcivan, Seyit (ed.), Mestcīzāde's *al-Masālik fī l-khilāfiyyāt bayna al-mutakallimīn wa-l-ḥukamāʾ*, Beirut and Istanbul: Dār Ṣādir and Maktabat al-Irshād, 2007.

Bakar, Osman, *Classification of Knowledge in Islam: A Study in Islamic Philosophies of Science*, Cambridge: Islamic Texts Society, 1998.

Bargeron, Carol L., *The Concept of Causality in Abu Ḥāmid Muḥammad Al-Ghazālī's* Tahāfut Al-Falāsifah, thesis, Wisconsin: University of Wisconsin-Madison Press, 1978.

Barkai, Ron, "Greek Medical Traditions and Their Impact on Conceptions of Women in the Gynecological Writing in the Middle Ages" in: Yael Azmon (ed.), *A View into the Lives of Women in Jewish Societies*, Jerusalem: The Zalman Shazar Center for Jewish History, 1995, 115–142.

Barlas, Asma, "Women's Reading of the Qur'ān" in: Jane Dammen McAuliffe (ed.), *The Cambridge Companion to the Qur'ān*, Cambridge: Cambridge University Press, 2006, 255–258.

Barnes, Jonathan, *Commentary on Aristotle Posterior Analytics*, Oxford: Clarendon Press, 1993.

Barthes, Roland, *Image-Music-Text*, London: Fontana, 1977.

———, "The Death of the Author" in: Hazard Adams (ed.), *Critical Theory since Plato*, Florida: Harcourt Brace Javanovich, 1971, 1130–1133.

———, "The Structuralist Activity" in: Hazard Adams (ed.), *Critical Theory since Plato*, Florida: Harcourt Brace Javanovich, 1971, 1128–1130.

Baumstark, Anton, *Aristoteles bei den Syrern*, Leipzig: Teubner, 1900.

———, *Geschichte der syrischen Litteratur*, Bonn: Marcus and Weber, 1922.

Bedjan, Paulus (ed.), *Ethicon seu Moralia Gregorii Barhebræi*, ed. Paulus Bedjan, Paris and Leipzig: Harrassowitz, 1898.

——— (ed.), *Gregorii Barhebræi Chronicon syriacum*, Paris: Maisonneuve, 1890.

——— (ed.), *Liber columbæ seu Directorium monachorum Gregorii Barhebræi*, Paris and Leipzig: Harrassowitz, 1898 [= appendix to Bedjan's edition of the *Ethicon*].

——— (ed.), *Nomocanon Gregorii Barhebræi*, Paris and Leipzig: Harrassowitz, 1898.

Beitia, A. Cortaberria, "Les sources arabes de l'*Explanatio simboli* du dominicain catalan Raymond Martin" in: *Mélanges de l'Institut Dominicain d'Études Orientales* 16 (1983), 95–115.

Benkheira, Mohammad H., Giladi, Avner, Mayeur-Jaouen, Catherine and Sublet, Jaqueline (eds.), *La famille en Islam d'après les sources arabes*, Paris: Les Indes Savantes, 2013.

Bergson, Henri, *Le Rire: Essai sur la signification du comique*, Paris: Presses Universitaires de France, 1959.

Berti, Enrico, *L'unità del sapere in Aristotele*, Padua: CEDAM, 1965.

Bertman, Martin A., "Alfarabi and the Concept of Happiness in Medieval Islamic Philosophy" in: *The Islamic Quarterly* 14 (1970), 122–125.

Bertolacci, Amos, "The Doctrine of Material and Formal Causality in the '*Ilāhiyyāt*' of Avicenna's '*Kitāb al-Šifā*'" in: *Quaestio* 2 (2002), 125–154.

Bianquis, Tierry, *La famille arabe médiévale*, Bruxelles: Éditions Complexe, 2005.

Bingöl, Abdülkuddus, "Ebheri, Esiruddin" in: *Türkiye Diyanet Vakfı İslam Ansiklopedisi*, vol. 10, Istanbul: Türkiye Diyanet Vakfı, 1988–, 75–76.

Bland, Kalman (trans.), *The Epistle on the Possibility of Conjunction with the Active Intellect by Ibn Rushd with the Commentary of Moses Narboni*, New York: Jewish Theological Seminary, 1982.

Blum, Georg G., *Die Geschichte der Begegnung christlich-orientalischer Mystik mit der Mystik des Islams*, Wiesbaden: Harrassowitz, 2009.

Blumenthal, David R., *Philosophic Mysticism: Studies in Rational Religion*, Ramat Gan: Bar-Ilan University Press, 2006.

——— (ed.), *The Commentary of R. Ḥōṭer ben Shelōmō to the Thirteen Principles of Maimonides*, Leiden: Brill, 1974.

Böhm, Walter (ed.), *Johannes Philoponus, Grammatikos von Alexandrien (6. Jahrhundert n. Chr.). Ausgewählte Schriften übersetzt, eingeleitet und kommentiert*, München, Paderborn und Wien: Schöningh, 1967.

Bolay, Süleyman Hayri (ed.), *Osmanlılarda Düşünce Hayatı ve Felsefe*, Ankara: Akçağ, 2005.

Bonadeo, Cecilia Martini, "Averroes on the Causality of the First Principle: a Model in Reading 'Metaphysics': Lambda 7, 1072b 4–16" in: Andreas Speer and Lydia Wegener (eds.), *Wissen über Grenzen. Arabisches Wissen und lateinisches Mittelalter* (*Miscellanea Mediaevalia 33*), Berlin and New York: Walter de Gruyter, 2006, 425–437.

Bonner, A., "L'apologètica de Ramon Marti i Ramon Llul devant de l'Islam i del Judaism" in: *Estudi generali* 9 (1989), 171–85.

Bori, Caterina, "Théologie politique et Islam à propos d'Ibn Taymiyya (m. 728/1328) et du sultanat mamelouk" in: *Revue de l'Histoire des Religions* 224 (2007), 5–46.

Bouhdiba, Abdelwahab, *Sexuality in Islam*, London: Routledge and Kegan Paul, 1985.

Bousquet, Georges-Henri, *L'Ethique sexuelle de l'Islam*, Paris: Desclée de Brouwer, 1990.

Bouyges, Maurice, *Essai de chronologie des œuvres de al-Ghazali (Algazel), édité et mis à jour par Michel Allard*, Beirut: Imprimerie Catholique, 1959.

Brock, Sebastian and Mouawad, Ray Jabre in: *Dieu Miséricorde Dieu Amour. Patrimoine Syriaque Colloque VIII*, Antélias: Markaz ad-Dirāsāt wa-l-Abḥāth al-Mashriqiyya, 2002.

Brockelmann, Carl, *Geschichte der arabischen Litteratur*, 2nd edition. 2 vols. Leiden: Brill, 1943–1949. *Supplementbände*, 3 vols., Leiden: Brill, 1937–1942.

Bruns, Paulus Iacobus and Kirsch, Georgius Guilielmus (eds.), *Gregorii Abulpharagii sive Bar-Hebraei Chronicon syriacum*, Leipzig: Boehme, 1789.

——— (eds.), *Gregorii Bar-Hebraei Chronicon syriacum*, Leipzig: Boehme, 1789.

Bucaille, Maurice, *La Bible, le Coran et la science: les Écritures Saintes examinées à la lumière des connaissances modernes*, Paris: Seghers, 1976.

Burnyeat, Myles F., "Aristotle on Learning to be Good" in: Amélie Oksenberg Rorty (ed.), *Essays on Aristotle's Ethics*, Berkeley: University of California Press, 1980, 69–92.

Burrell, David B., "Causality and necessity in Islamic thought" in: Edward Craig (ed.), *Routledge Encyclopedia of Philosophy*, 10 vols., vol. II, London and New York: Routledge, 1998, 241–244.

———, *Faith in Divine Unity and Trust in Divine Providence*, Louisville: Fons Vitae, 2001.

———, "Mulla Sadra on 'Substantial Motion': A Clarification and a Comparison with Thomas Aquinas" in: *Journal of Shi'a Islamic Studies* 2 (2009), 369–386.

———, "The act of creation with its theological consequences" in: David B. Burrell (ed.) et al., *Creation and the God of Abraham*, Cambridge: Cambridge University Press, 2010, 40–52.

Cahen, Claude, *Pre-Ottoman Turkey: A General Survey of Material and Spiritual Culture and History c. 1071–1330*, trans. from French by J. Jones-Williams, New York: Taplinger Publishing Company, 2001.

Calverley, Edwin E. and Pollock, James W. (trans.), *Nature, Man, God in Medieval Islam: 'Abd Allah al-Bayḍāwī's text Ṭawāliʿ al-anwār min Maṭāliʿ al-anẓār along with Maḥmūd Iṣfahānī's Commentary Maṭāliʿ al-anẓār sharḥ Ṭawāliʿ al-anwār*, Leiden: Brill, 2002.

Cardahi, Gabriel (ed.), *Abulfaragii Gregorii Bar-Hebraei mafriani Orientis Kithâbhâ dhiyaunâ seu Liber columbae*, vol. 1, Rome: Academia Lynceorum, 1898.

Chahine, Osman, *Ontologie et théologie chez Avicenne*, Paris: Adrien Maisonneuve, 1962.

Chejne, Anwar G., "Ibn Ḥazm of Cordova on Logic" in: *Journal of the American Oriental Society* 104 (1984), 57–72.

Chittick, William, *The Sufi Path of Knowledge: Ibn al-'Arabi's Metaphysics of Imagination*, New York: State University of New York Press, 1989.

Çiçek, Yuliyos Yeshuʿ (ed.), *Ktobo d-yawno meṭul duboro d-iḥidoye b-karyoto men syome d-abun ṭubtono Mor Grigoriyos mafryono qadisho d-Madnḥo d-metidaʿ Bar 'Ebroyo. Bar Hebraeus's Book of the Dove*, vol. 1, Glane-Losser: Dayro d-Mor Afrem Suryoyo, 1983.

———, *Nomocanon of Bar-Hebraeus*, Glane-Losser: Bar Hebraeus Verlag, 1986.

Cohen, Boaz, "The Classification of the Law in the Mishneh Torah" in: *Jewish Quarterly Review* 25 (1934–5), 519–540.

Colless, Brian (trans.), *The Wisdom of the Pearlers. An Anthology of Syriac Christian Mysticism*, Kalamazoo: Cistercian Publications, 2008.

Colville, Jim (trans.), *Two Andalusian Philosophers: the story of Hayy ibn Yaqzan & The Definitive Statement*, New York: Kegan Paul, 1999.

Corbin, Henry, *En Islam iranien: aspects spirituels et philosophiques*, Paris: Librarie Gallimard, 1978.

———, "Mystique et humour chez Sohravardī" in: Mehdi Mohaghegh and Hermann Landolt (ed.), *Collected Papers on Islamic Philosophy and Mysticism*, Tehran and Montreal: The Institute of Islamic Studies, 1971, 16–38.

Cornell, Rkia, "Early Sūfi Women" in: Leonard Lewisohn (ed.), *The Heritage of Sufism*, Oxford: Oneworld, 1999–2003, 15–70.

Corrigan, Kevin, *Evagrius and Gregory: Mind, Soul and Body in the 4th Century*, Farnham: Ashgate, 2009.

———, "The Organization of the Soul: Some Overlooked Aspects of Interpretation from Plato to Late Antiquity" in: Suzanne Stern-Gillet and Kevin Corrigan (eds.),

Reading Ancient Texts. Volume II: Aristotle and Neoplatonism: Essays in Honour of Denis O'Brien, Leiden: Brill, 2007, 99–113.

Cortaberria, A., "Fuentas árabes del «Pugio fidei» de Ramón Martí: Algazel (1085–1111)" in: *Ciencia Tomista* 112 (1985), 581–96.

Daiber, Hans, "Die Kritik des Ibn Ḥazm an Kindīs Metaphysik" in: *Der Islam* 63 (1986), 284–302.

———, "Griechische Ethik in islamischem Gewande: Das Beispiel von Rāġib al-Iṣfahānī" in: Burkhard Mojsisch and Olaf Pluta (eds.), *Historia Philosophiae Medii Aevi: Studien zur Geschichte der Philosophie des Mittelalters*, 2 vols., vol. 1, Amsterdam: B. R. Grüner Publishing Company, 1991–92, 181–192.

———, *Islamic Thought in the Dialogue of Cultures. A Historical and Bibliographical Survey*, Leiden and Boston: Brill, 2012.

———, "Prophetie und Ethik bei Fārābī (gest. 339/950)" in: Christian Wenin (ed.), *L'homme et son Univers au moyen Âge*, Louvain-la-Neuve: Editions de l'Institut Supérieur de Philosophie, 1986, 729–753.

———, "Qosṭā ibn Lūqā (9. Jh.) über die Einteilung der Wissenschaften" in: *Zeitschrift für die Geschichte der arabisch-islamischen Wissenschaften* 6 (1990), 93–129.

———, "Rationalism in Islam and the Rise of Scientific Thought: The Background of al-Ghazalī's Concept of Causality" in: Hans Daiber, *The Struggle for Knowledge in Islam: Some historical Aspects*, Sarajevo: Kult B, 2004, 67–86.

———, "Rebellion gegen Gott. Formen atheistischen Denkens im frühen Islam" in: Friedrich Niewöhner and Olaf Pluta (eds.), *Atheismus im Mittelalter und in der Renaissance*, Wiesbaden: Harrassowitz Verlag, 1999, 23–44.

———, "Review of *Reason and Tradition* by George F. Hourani" in: *Der Islam* 64 (1987), 299–302.

———, "Science and Technology versus Islam: A Controversy from Renan and Afghānī to Nasr and Needham and its Historical Background" in: *Annals of Japan Association for Middle East Studies* 8 (1993), 169–187.

——— (ed.), *The Islamic Concept of Belief in the 4th/10th Century. Abū l-Laiṯ as-Samarqandī's Commentary on Abū Ḥanīfa (died 150/767)* al-Fiqh al-absaṭ, Introduction, Text and commentary, Tokyo: Institute for the Study of Languages and Cultures of Asia and Africa, 1995.

———, "The Limitations of Knowledge According to Ibn Sīnā. Epistemological and theological aspects and the consequences" in: Matthias Lutz-Bachmann, Alexander Fidora and Pia Antolic-Piper (eds.), *Erkenntnis und Wissenschaft. Probleme der Epistemologie in der Philosophie des Mittelalters*, Berlin: Akademie-Verlag, 2004, 25–34.

Dallal, Ahmad, "Science and the Qur'ān" in: Jane Dammen McAuliffe (ed.), *Encyclopaedia of the Qur'ān*, 6 vols., vol. 4, Leiden: Brill, 2004, 540–558.

D'Alverny, Marie-Thérèse, "Anniyya-Anitas" in: Etienne Gilson (ed.), *Mélanges offerts a Étienne Gilson*, Toronto: Pontifical Institute, 1959, 59–61.

D'Ancona, Cristina, "Platonic and Neoplatonic terminology for being in Arabic Translation" in: *Studia Graeco-Arabica*, The Journal of the Project: *Greek into Arabic Philosophical Concepts and Linguistic Bridges* (available at: http://www.greekintoarabic.eu/uploads/media/SGA_I_2011.pdf).

Ad-Dārimī, ʿAbd Allah ibn ʿAbd al-Raḥmān, *Sunan ad-Dārimī* (available at: http://hadith.al-islam.com/Loader.aspx?pageid=261).

Davidson, Herbert A., *Alfarabi, Avicenna, and Averroes on Intellect. Their Cosmologies, Theories of the Active Intellect, and Theories of Human Intellect*, New York: Oxford University Press, 1992.

———, "Maimonides' *Shemonah Peraqim* and Alfarabi's *Fuṣūl Al-Madanī*" in: *Proceedings of the American Academy for Jewish Research* 31 (1963), 33–50.

———, *Moses Maimonides: the Man and His Works*, Oxford: Oxford University Press, 2005.

———, *Proofs for Eternity, Creation, and the Existence of God in Medieval Islamic and Jewish Philosophy*, New York: Oxford University Press, 1987.

Defter-i kütüpkhaneh-yi Veliyeddin, Istanbul: Dersaadet Maḥmut Bey Maṭbaası, 1303/1885–86.

Descartes, René, "Meditations on First Philosophy" in: *Meditations and Other Metaphysical Writings*, translated by D. Clarke, London and New York: Penguin, 1998.

Dobbs-Weinstein, Idit, "Maimonides' Reticence toward Ibn Sīnā" in: Jules Janssens and Daniel De Smet (eds.), *Avicenna and His Heritage*, Leuven: Leuven University Press, 2002.

Dolabani, Yuḥanon (ed.), *Ktobo d-yawno meṭul duboro d-iḥidoye b-karyoto men syome d-abun ṭubtono Mor Grigoriyos mafryono qadisho d-Madnḥo d-metidaʿ Bar ʿEbroyo*, vol. 1, ʿUmro d-Mor Ḥananyo-Dayr al-Zaʿfarān, 1916.

Druart, Thérèse-Anne, "Al-Ghazālī's concept of the Agent in the *Tahāfut* and in the *Iqtiṣād*: Are people really agents?" in: James E. Montgomery (ed.), *Arabic Theology, Arabic Philosophy: From the Many to the One: Essays in Celebration of Richard M. Frank*, Peeters: Leuven, 2006, 425–440.

Duran, Recep (trans.), *ʿAlāʾ ad-Dīn ʿAlī aṭ-Ṭūsī, Tehâfütü'l-Felâsife (Kitâb az-Zuhr)*, Ankara: Kültür Bakanlığı, 1990.

Dutton, Blake D., "Al-Ghazālī on Possibility and the Critique of Causality" in: *Medieval Philosophy and Theology* 10 (2001), 23–46.

Eagleton, Terry, *Literary Theory: An Introduction*, Oxford: Blackwell, 1983.

Efendi, Khojazāde Muṣliḥ ad-Dīn Muṣṭafā (trans.), *Kitāb Tahāfut al-falāsifa*, Cairo: Al-Maṭbaʿa al-ʿĀlamiyya, 1302 A.H.

Efendī, Mestcīzāde Abdullah, *Hidāyat al-ḥikma*, Istanbul: Hacı Muharrem Efendi Matbaası, 1303H.

Efendi, Şemseddin Ahmed, *Tehâfüt Hâţiyesi* [*Haţiya ʿalā Tahāfüt al-falāsifa*], trans. into Turkish by Ahmet Arslan, Ankara: Kültür ve Turizm Bakanlığı, 1987.

Efendī, Taşköprīzāde Ahmed, *Shaqāʾiq an-nuʿmāniyya*, ed. Ahmed Suphi Furat, Istanbul: Istanbul Üniversitesi Edebiyat Fakültesi, 1985, 126–139.

*EI*² = *Encyclopaedia of Islam*. New Edition. Edited by H. A. R. Gibb et al., 11 vols. Leiden and London: Luzac and Brill, 1954–2003.

EI3 = *Encyclopaedia of Islam, THREE*. Edited by Gudrun Krämer, Denis Matringe, John Nawas, and Everett Rowson. Brill Online 2007–, http://www.encislam.brill.com.

Elias, Norbert, *The Civilizing Process*, Oxford and Cambridge: Blackwell, 1994.

Endress, Gerhard, "Reading Avicenna in the Madrasa: Intellectual Genealogies and Chains of Transmission of Philosophy and the Sciences in the Islamic East" in: James E. Montgomery (ed.), *Arabic Theology, Arabic Philosophy: From the Many to the One: Essays in Celebration of Richard M. Frank*, Leuven: Peters, 2006, 371–422.

Eran, Amira, "Al-Ghazali and Maimonides on the World to Come and Spiritual Pleasures" in: *Jewish Studies Quarterly* 8 (2001), 137–166.

———, *Me-Emunah Tammah le-Emunah Ramah*, Tel-Aviv: Hakibbutz Hameuchad, 1998.

Esudri, Yossi, "R. Abraham Ibn Da'ud and His Philosophical Book *The Exalted Faith*: Miscellanea (Hebrew)" in: Ari Ackerman, Esti Eisenmann, Aviram Ravitsky, and Shmuel Wygoda (eds.), *Adam le-Adam: Studies Presented to Warren Zev Harvey*, forthcoming.

Fakhry, Majid, *Islamic Occasionalism*, London: Allen and Unwin, 1958.

——— (trans.), *The Qur'an: A Modern English Version*, London: Garnet Publishing House, 1997.

Al-Fārābī, Abū Naṣr, *Iḥṣāʾ al-ʿulūm*, ed. ʿUthmān Amīn, Cairo: Maktabat al-Anǧlū l-Miṣriyya, 1968.

———, *Kitāb al-Jamʿ bayna raʾyay al-ḥakīmayn*, ed. Alber Naṣrī Nādir, 3rd Ed., Beirut: Dār al-Mashriq, 1968.

———, *Kitāb Taḥṣīl as-saʿāda*, ed. Jaʿfar Āl Yāsīn, Beirut: Dār al-Andalus, 1401/1981.

———, *Mabādiʾ ārāʾ ahl al-madīna al-fāḍila. On the Perfect State. Revised Text with Introduction, Translation, and Commentary* by Richard Walzer, Oxford: Oxford University Press, 1985.

———, *Mabādiʾ al-falsafa al-qadīma*, Cairo 1328/1910.

Al-Farāhīdī, Al-Khalīl bin Aḥmad, *Kitāb al-ʿAyn*, 8 vols., ed. Mahdī l-Makhzūmī and Ibrāhīm as-Sāmarrāʾī, Beirut: Dār al-Hilāl, n.d.

Fathi, Jean, "The Mystic Story of Childhood from Suhrawardi to Bar 'Ebroyo: The Maphrian's last Syriac work and its Persian model" forthcoming in: *The proceedings of the Second Aleppo Syriac Colloquium: "The Life and Works of Mar Bar Ebroyo (Barhebraeus) +1286" (held at the Syrian Orthodox Archdiocese of Aleppo, 1st–4th July, 2010)*.

Fenton, Paul, "The Literary Legacy of David ben Joshua, Last of the Maimonidean *Negidim*" in: *The Jewish Quarterly Review* 75 (1984–1985), 1–56.

Fidora, Alexander, "Abraham Ibn Daud und Dominicus Gundissalinus: Philosophie und religiöse Toleranz im Toledo des 12. Jahrhunderts" in: Matthias Lutz-Bachmann and Alexander Fidora (*eds.*), *Juden, Christen und Muslime. Religionsdialoge im Mittelalter*, Darmstadt: Wissenschaftliche Buchgesellschaft, 2004, 10–26.

Fierro, M., "Opposition to Sufism in al-Andalus" in: F. De Jong and B. Radtke (eds.), *Islamic Mysticism Contested: Thirteen Centuries of Controversies and Polemics*, Leiden, Boston and Köln: Brill, 1999, 174–206.

Fihrist al-kutub al-ʿarabiyya al-maḥfūẓa bi-l-Kutubkhāna al-Khidīwiyya, 7 vols., Cairo: al-Maṭbaʿa al-ʿUthmāniyya, 1301–1309/1883–1891.

Fontaine, Resianne, "Was Maimonides an Epigone?" in: *Studia Rosenthaliana* 40 (2007–8), 9–26.

Fontaine, T. A. M., *In Defence of Judaism: Abraham Ibn Daud*, Assen and Maastricht: Van Gorcum, 1990.

Forster, Regula, "Auf der Suche nach Gold und Gott. Alchemisten und Fromme im arabischen Mittelalter" in: Almut-Barbara Renger (ed.), *Meister und Schüler in Geschichte und Gegenwart. Von Religionen der Antike bis zur modernen Esoterik*, Göttingen: V&R Unipress 2012, 213–230.

Foucault, Michel, *The History of Sexuality*, 3 vols. New York: Vintage Books, 1990–1992.

Frank, Richard M., *Al-Ghazālī and the Ashʿarite School*, Durham: Duke University Press, 1994.

———, "Al-Ghazālī on *Taqlīd*: Scholars, Theologians and Philosophers" in: *Zeitschrift Für Geschichte Der Arabisch-Islamischen Wissenschaften* 7 (1991/92), 207–252.

———, *Creation and the Cosmic System: Al-Ghazâlî and Avicenna*, Heidelberg: Carl Winter Universitätsverlag, 1992.

———, "The Origin of the Arabic Philosophical Term *anniyya*" in: *Cahiers de Byrsa* 6 (1956), 181–201. (also in: Richard M. Frank, *Philosophy, Theology and Mysticism in Medieval Islam. Texts and Studies on the Development and History of Kalam*, ed. Dimitri Gutas, Burlington: Ashgate Pub Co., 2005, 181–201).

———, "The Structure of Created Causality according to Al-Ašʿarī. An Analysis of the *Kitāb al-Lumaʿ*" in: *Studia Islamica* 25 (1966), 13–75.

Freudenthal, Gad, "The Medieval Astrologization of the Aristotelian Cosmos: From Alexander of Aphrodisias to Averroes" in: *Mélanges de l'Université Saint-Joseph* 59 (2006), 29–68.

Freudenthal, Gideon, "The Philosophical Mysticism of Maimonides and Maimon" in: Idit Dobbs-Weinstein (ed.), *Maimonides and His Heritage*, New York: State University of New York Press, 2009.

Gairdner, William Henry Temple, "Al-Ghazālī's *Mishkāt Al-Anwār* and the Ghazālī-Problem" in: *Der Islam* 5 (1914), 121–153.

Garden, Kenneth, *Al-Ghazālī's Contested Revival*: Iḥyāʾ ʿUlūm al-Dīn *and Its Critics in Khorasan and the Maghrib*. Unpublished PhD dissertation, University of Chicago, 2005.

———, "Al-Māzarī al-Dhakī: Al-Ghazālī's Maghribi Adversary in Nishapur" in: *Journal of Islamic Studies* 21 (2010), 89–107.

———, "Coming Down from the Mountaintop: Al-Ghazālī's Autobiographical Writings in Context" in: *The Muslim World* 101 (2011), 581–596.

———, *The First Islamic Reviver: Abū Ḥāmid al-Ghazālī and his Revival of the Religious Sciences*, Oxford: Oxford University Press, 2013.

Gardet, Louis and Anawati, Marcel M., *Introduction à la théologie musulmane: essai de théologie comparée*, Paris: Libraire J. Vrin, 1948.

Gardet, Louis, *La pensée religieuse d'Avicenne*, Paris: Libraire J. Vrin, 1951.

Gawlick, G., "Rationalismus" in: Joachim Ritter et al. (eds.), *Historisches Wörterbuch der Philosophie*, 13 vols., vol. 8, Darmstadt: Schwabe 1992, 44–47.

Ghazzati, Nathan, "Ghazali, Abu Ḥāmid Mohammed ibn Mohammad al-" in: *Jewish Encyclopedia* (available at: http://www.jewishencyclopedia.com/articles/6650-ghazali-abu-hamid-mohammed-ibn-mohammed-al).

Gianotti, T. J., *Al-Ghazālī's Unspeakable Doctrine of the Soul: Unveiling the Esoteric Psychology and Eschatology of the* Iḥyāʾ, Leiden: Brill, 2001.

Giladi, Avner, "A Short Note on the Possible Origin of the Title *Moreh ha-Nevukhim* (Hebrew)" in: *Tarbiz* 48 (1979), 346–347.

———, "Children of Islam: Concepts of Childhood" in: *Medieval Muslim Society* (1992), 45–60.

———, "Guardianship" in: Jane Dammen McAuliffe (ed.), *Encyclopaedia of the Qurʾān*, 6 vols., vol. 2, Leiden and Boston: Brill, 2002, 373–375.

———, "Herlihy's Theses Revisited: Some Notes on Investment in Children in Medieval Muslim Societies" in: *Journal of Family History* 36 (2011), 235–247.

———, "Islamic Educational Theories in the Middle East: Some Methodological Notes with Special Reference to Al-Ghazālī" in: *Bulletin of the British Society for Middle Eastern Studies* 14 (1988), 3–10.

———, "On the Origins of Two Key Terms in al-Ġazālī's *Iḥyāʾ ʿulūm al-dīn*" in: *Arabica* 36 (1989), 81–93.

Gimaret, Daniel, "Dahrī II (In the Islamic Period)" in: *Encyclopaedia Iranica*, ed. Ehsan Yarshater, 16 vols., vol. 6, California: Costa Mesa, 1993, pp. 588–590.

———, *Dieu à l'image de l'homme. Les anthropomorphismes de la sunna et leur interprétation par les théologiens*, Paris: Cerf, 1997.

———, *La doctrine d'al-Ashari*, Paris: Cerf, 1990.

———, *Une Lecture Muʿtazilite du Coran. Le Tafsīr d'Abū ʿAlī al-Gjubbāʾī (m. 303/915) partiellement reconstitute à partir de ses citateurs*, Louvain-Paris: Peters, 1994.

Girdner, Scott, *Reasoning with Revelation: the significance of the Qur'ānic contextualization of philosophy in al-Ghazālī's* Mishkāt al-Anwār (*The Niche of Lights*), PhD diss., Boston: Boston University Press, 2010.

Goethe, Johann W. von, *West-östlicher Divan* [*Sämtliche Werke nach Epochen seines Schaffens*, vol. 11.1.2], ed. Karl Richter, München: Hanser, 1998.

Goodman, Lenn E., "Morals and Society in Islamic Philosophy" in: Brian Carr (ed.), *Companion Encyclopedia of Asian Philosophy*, London: Routledge, 1997, 1000–1023.

———, "Three Enduring Achievements of Islamic Philosophy" in: B. Khorramshāhī and J. Jahānbakhsh (eds.), *Mohaghegh Nāma. Collected papers presented to Professor Mehdi Mohaghegh*, 2 vols., vol. 2, Tehran: Sinānegār, 2001, 59–89.

Götz, Ignacio L., "The Quest for Certainty: al-Ghazālī and Descartes" in: *Journal of Philosophical Research* 92 (2003), 13–16.

Graeser, Andreas (ed.), *Mathematik und Metaphysik bei Aristoteles*, Bern and Sttutgart: Haupt Verlag, 1987.

Griffel, Frank, *Apostasie und Toleranz im Islam: Die Entwicklung zu al-Ġazālīs Urteil gegen die Philosophie und die Reaktionen der Philosophen*, Leiden: Brill, 2000.

———, "Between al-Ghazālī and Abū l-Barakāt al-Baghdādī: The Dialectical Turn in the Philosophy of Iraq and Iran During the Sixth/Twelfth Century" in: Peter Adamson (ed.), *The Age of Averroes: Arabic Philosophy in the Sixth/Twelfth Century*, London: Warburg Institute, 2011, 45–75.

———, "Al-Ghazālī" in: Edward N. Zalta (ed.), *The Stanford Encyclopedia of Philosophy*, vol. 4, 2007 (available at: http://plato.stanford.edu/entries/al-ghazali/).

———, "Al-Ghazālī's Appropriation of Ibn Sīnā's Views on Causality and the Development of the Science in Islam" in: *Uluslararasi Ibn Sīnā sempozyumu bildiriler*, 22–24 Mayis 2008, 105–115.

———, "Al-Ġazālī's Concept of Prophecy: The Introduction of Avicennan Psychology into Aš'arite Theology" in: *Arabic Sciences and Philosophy* 14 (2004), 101–44.

———, "Al-Ghazālī's Cosmology in the Veil Section of His *Mishkat al-anwār*" in: Y. Tzvi Langermann (ed.), *Avicenna and His Legacy*, Turnhout: Brepols Publishers, 2009, 27–49.

———, "Al-Ghazālī's Use of 'Original Human Disposition' (*Fiṭra*) and its Background in the Teachings of al-Fārābī and Avicenna" in: *The Muslim World* 102 (2011), 1–32.

———, "MS London, British Library, Or. 3126: An Unknown Work by al-Ghazālī on Metaphysics and Philosophical Theology" in: *Journal of Islamic Studies* 17 (2006), 1–42.

———, "Muslim Philosophers' Rationalist Explanation of Muḥammad's Prophecy" in: Jonathan E. Brockopp (ed.), *The Cambridge Companion to Muhammad*, New York: Cambridge University Press, 2010, 158–179.

———, *The Philosophical Theology of al-Ghazālī: A Study of His Life and His Cosmology*, New York: Oxford University Press, 2009.

Günaltay, Şemseddin, "İslâm Dünyasının İnhitatı Sebebi Selçuk İstilası Mıdır?" in: *İkinci Türk Tarih Kongresi*, İstanbul: Devlet Basımevi, 1937.

Gutas, Dimitri, *Avicenna and the Aristotelian Tradition: Introduction to Reading Avicenna's Philosophical Works*, Leiden and New York: Brill, 1988.

———, *Greek Thought and Arabic Culture*, London: Routledge, 1998.

———, "Intellect Without Limits" in: Maria-Candida Pacheco and José F. Meirinhos (eds.), *Intellect et imagination dans la philosophie médiévale*, 3 vols., Turnhout: Brepols Publishers, 2006, vol. 1, 351–72.

Güzel, Abdurrahim (ed.), *Karabaği ve Tehafüt'ü*, Ankara: Kültür Bakanlığı, 1991.

——— (ed.), *Ta'līqa 'alā sharḥ tahāfut al-falāsifa li-Khojazade*, Kayseri: n.p., 1996.

Gwyne, Rosalind W., *Logic, Rhetoric, and Legal Reasoning in the Qur'ān*, London: Routledge Curzon, 2004.

Gyekye, Kwame, "Al-Ghazālī on Causation" in: *Second Order* 2 (1973), 31–39.

Al-Ḥajjāj, Muslim ibn, *Ṣaḥīḥ Muslim*, ed. Abdul Hamid Siddiqi (available at: http://theonlyquran.com/hadith/Sahih-Muslim).

Halevi, Leor, "The Theologian's Doubts: Natural Philosophy and the Skeptical Games of Ghazālī" in: *Journal of the History of Ideas* 63 (2002), 19–39.

Hallaq, Wael B., "Logic, Formal Arguments and Formalization of Arguments in Sunnī Jurisprudence" in: *Arabica* 37 (1990), 315–58.

Halm, David E., *The Origins of Stoic Cosmology*, Columbus, Ohio: Ohio State University Press, 1977.

Al-Ḥanbalī, 'Abd al-Ḥayy b. 'Imād, *Shadharāt adh-dhahab fī akhbār man dhahab*, Beirut: al-Maktab at-Tijārī li-ṭ-Ṭibā'a, n.d.

Al-Ḥaqq, Jalāl, "Al-Ghazālī on Causality, Induction, and Miracles" in: *Al-Tawḥīd* 3 (1986), 55–62.

Harari, Orna, *Knowledge and demonstration. Aristotle's* Posterior Analytics, Dordrecht et al.: Kluwer Academic Publishers, 2004.

Hartmann, Eduard Von, *Geschichte der Metaphysik*, 12 vols., Leipzig: Hermann Haacke, 1899 (reprinted in Darmstadt: Wissenschaftliche Buchgesellschaft, 1969).

Harvey, Steven, "Al-Ghazali and Maimonides and their Books of Knowledge" in: Jay M. Harris (ed.), *Be'erot Yitzhak: Studies in Memory of Isadore Twersky*, Cambridge: Harvard University Press, 2005, 99–117.

———, "Author's Introductions as a Gauge for Monitoring Philosophic Influence: The Case of Alghazali" in: Sara Klein-Braslavy, Binyamin Abrahamov and Joseph Sadan (eds.), *Studies in Jewish and Muslim Thought Presented to Professor Michael Schwarz*, Tel Aviv: Tel Aviv University Press, 2009, 53–66.

———, "Avicenna's Influence on Jewish Thought: Some Reflections" in: Y. Tzvi Langermann (ed.), *Avicenna and his Legacy: A Golden Age of Science and Philosophy*, Turnhout: Brepols Publishers, 2009, 327–340.

———, "Did Maimonides' Letter to Samuel Ibn Tibbon Determine Which Philosophers Would Be Studied by Later Jewish Thinkers?" in: *Jewish Quarterly Review* 83 (1992), 51–70.

———, "Why Did Fourteenth-Century Jews Turn to Al-Ghazali's Account of Natural Science?" in: *Jewish Quarterly Review* 91 (2001), 359–376.

Harvey, Steven and Harvey, Warren Zev, "Rabbi Ḥasdai Crescas's Attitude toward al-Ghazālī (Hebrew, with an English summary)" in: Nahem Ilan (ed.), *The Intertwined Worlds of Islam: Essays in Memory of Hava Lazarus-Yafeh*, Jerusalem: Ben-Zvi Institute, 2002, 191–210.

Harvey, Warren Zev, "Maimonides' Avicennianism" in: *Maimonidean Studies* 5 (2008), 107–119.

———, *Physics and Metaphysics in Ḥasdai Crescas*, Amsterdam: J. C. Gieben, 1998.

Hasse, Dag N., *Avicenna's* De Anima *in the West. The Formation of a Peripatetic Philosophy of the Soul 1160–1300*, London and Turin: The Warburg Institute and Nino Aragno Editore, 2000.

Hayoun, Maurice R., *La Philosophie et la Théologie de Moïse de Narbonne*, Tübingen: J. C. B. Mohr, 1989.

——— (trans.), "L'epître du libre Arbitre de Moïse de Narbonne" in: *Revue des études juives* 141 (1982), 139–167.

Hedwig, Klaus, *Sphaera lucis. Studien zur Intelligibilität des Seienden im Kontext der mittelalterlichen Lichtspekulation*, Münster: Aschendorff, 1980.

Heer, Nicholas L., "Abū Ḥāmid al-Ghazālī's Esoteric Exegesis of the Koran" in: Leonard Lewisohn (ed.), *The Heritage of Sufism*, 2 vols. Vol. 1: *Classical Persian Sufism from its Origin to Rumi (700–1300)*, Oxford: Oneworld, 1999, 235–257.

———, "Al-Ghazali's The Canons of Ta'wil" in: John Renard (ed.), *Windows in the House of Islam: Muslim Sources on the Spirituality and Religious Life*, Berkeley: University of California Press, 1998, 48–54.

———, "Moral Deliberation in al-Ghazālī's *Iḥyāʾ ʿulūm al-dīn*" in: Parviz Morewedge (ed.), *Islamic Philosophy and Mysticism*, Delmar: Caravan Books, 1981.

———, "The Priority of Reason in the Interpretation of Scripture: Ibn Taymīya and the Mutakallimūn" in: Mustansir Mir (ed.), *The Literary Heritage of Classical Islam: Arabic and Islamic Studies in Honor of James A. Bellamy*, Princeton: Darvin Press, 1993, 181–95.

Hein, Christel, *Definition und Einteilung der Philosophie: Von der spätantiken Einleitungsliteratur zur arabischen Enzyklopädie*, Frankfurt am Main: P. Lang, 1985.

Heyde, Johannes E., *Entwertung der Kausalität?*, Stuttgart: Kohlhammer, 1957.

Hodgson, Marshall G., *The Venture of Islam: Conscience and History in a World Civilization*, 3 vols., Chicago and London: The University of Chicago Press, 1974.

Holzman, Gitit, *The Theory of the Intellect and Soul in the Thought of Rabbi Moshe Narboni, Based on his Commentaries on the Writings of Ibn Rushd, Ibn Tufayl, Ibn Bajja and al-Ghazali* (Hebrew), PhD Diss., Jerusalem: Hebrew University Press, 1996.

Hoover, J. R., *Ibn Taymiyya's Theodicy of Perpetual Optimism*, Leiden and Boston: Brill, 2007.

Hourani, George F., "A Revised Chronology of Ghazâlî's Writings" in: *Journal of the American Oriental Society* 104 (1984), 289–302.

———, *Averroes. On the Harmony of Religion and Philosophy. A translation with introduction and notes, of Ibn Rushd's* Kitāb Faṣl al-maqāl, *with its appendix (Ḍamīma) and an extract from* Kitāb al-Kashf ʿan manāhij al-adilla, Leiden: Brill, 1961.

———, "Ghazālī on the Ethics of Action" in: *Journal of the American Oriental Society* 96 (1976), 69–88.

———, *Reason and Tradition in Islamic Ethics*, Cambridge: Cambridge University Press, 1985.

Hübner, Johannes, "Ursache/Wirkung" in: Joachim Ritter et al. (eds.), *Historisches Wörterbuch der Philosophie*, 13 vols., vol. 11, Darmstadt, 2001, 377–384.

Ibn Abī ad-Dunyā, Abū Bakr ʿAbdallāh, *Kitāb al-ʿIyāl*, ed. ʿAbd ar-Raḥmān Khalaf, al-Manṣūra, 1997.

Ibn al-ʿArabī, Abū Bakr, *al-ʿAwāṣim min al-qawāṣim*, ed. ʿAmmār Ṭālibī, Cairo: Maktabat Dār at-turāth, 1997.

———, *Qānūn at-taʾwīl*, ed. Muḥammad Sulaymānī, Beirut: Dār al-Gharb al-Islāmī, 1990.

Ibn al-ʿArabī, Muḥyī d-Dīn, *Al-Futūḥāt al-makkiyya*, 4 vols., ed. Abū ʿAlā al-Afifi, Beirut: Dār al-Kutub al-ʿIlmiyya, 1999.

Ibn Ḥanbal, Aḥmad, *Al-Musnad*, ed. Shuʿayb al-Arnaʾūṭ and ʿĀdil Murshid, 13 vols., Beirut: al-Maktab al-Islāmī, n.d.

Ibn Ḥazm, Abū Muḥammad, *Ar-Radd ʿalā Ibn an-Naghrīla al-yahūdī wa-rasāʾil ukhrā*, ed. Iḥsān ʿAbbās, Cairo, 1960.

Ibn al-ʿIbrī, Abū al-Faraj / Barhebraeus, Gregorius, *Taʾrīkh mukhtaṣar ad-duwal li-l-ʿallāma Ghrīghūriyūs Abī l-Faraj b. Ahrūn aṭ-ṭabīb al-malaṭī al-maʿrūf bi-Ibn al-ʿIbrī (Compendium of the History of the Dynasties)*, ed. Anṭūn Ṣālḥānī, Beirut: Dār ar-Rāʾid al-Lubnānī, 1983.

Ibn Khaldūn, Walī d-Dīn, *Muqaddima*, Beirut: Dār Iḥyāʾ at-turāth al-ʿArabī, n.d.

Ibn Māja, Abū ʿAbdillāh, *as-Sunan*, ed. Hudā Khaṭṭāb, Riad: Dār as-Salām, 2007.

Ibn Rushd, Abū l-Walīd / Averroes, *Aristotelis opera cum Averrois commentariis*, Venetiis, 1562–74.

———, *Al-Kashf ʿan manāhij al-adilla fī ʿaqāʾid al-milla*, ed. Muṣṭafā Ḥanafī, with Introduction and Comments by Muḥammad ʿĀbid al-Jābirī, Beirut: Markaz Dirāsāt al-Waḥda al-ʿArabiyya, 1998.

———, *Kitāb Faṣl al-maqāl with its Appendix (Ḍamīma) and an Extract from Kitāb al-Kashf ʿan manāhij al-adilla*, ed. George F. Hourani, Leiden: Brill, 1959.

———, *Tafsīr mā baʿd aṭ-Ṭabīʿa*, 3 vols., ed. Maurice Bouyges, Beirut: Imprimerie Catholique, 1938.

———, *Tahāfut at-Tahāfut*, ed. Maurice Bouyges, Beirut: Dār al-Mashriq, 1930 (reprinted 3rd Ed., 1992).

———, *Tahāfut at-Tahāfut* (The Incoherence of the Incoherence), 2 vols. Translated by Simon van den Bergh, London: Luzac, 1954 (reprinted: London, 1969).

Ibn Sīnā, Abū ʿAlī, *Ilāhīyāt-i Dānishnāma-yi ʿAlāʾī taṣnīf-i Shaykh-i Raʾīs Abū ʿAlī Sīnā*, ed. Muḥammad Muʿīn, 2nd ed., Hamadan: Dānishgāh-i Bū ʿAlī Sīnā, Tehran: Anjuman-i Āthār wa Mafākhir-i Farhangī, 1383/2004.

———, *Al-Ishārāt wa-t-tanbihāt*, 2 vols., ed. Jacob Forget, Leiden: Brill 1892.

———, *Al-Mubāḥathāt*, ed. Muḥsin Bidarfar, Qom: Intisharat-i Bidar, 1992.

———, *Kitāb an-Najāt*, ed. Majid Fakhry, Beirut, 1982.

———, *Kitāb an-Najāt*, ed. Muḥyiddīn Ṣabrī l-Kurdī, Tehran: Murtazavi, 1346H.

———, *Rasāʾil ash-Shaykh ar-Raʾīs Abū ʿAlī l-Ḥusayn b. ʿAbdallāh b. Sīnā fī asrār al-ḥikmah al-mashriqīyah* (*Traites Mystiques d'Abou ʿAlī Hosain b. ʿAbdallāh b. Sīnā ou d'Avicenna*), 21 (of the Arabic text of *Ḥayy b. Yaqẓān*), ed. with French translation by A. F. Mehren, Leiden: E. J. Brill, 1899.

———, *Tisʿ rasāʾil fī l-ḥikma wa-ṭ-ṭabīʿiyyāt*, al-Qusṭanṭīnīya: Maṭbaʿat al-Ǧawāʾib, 1298/1881.

———, *ʿUyūn al-ḥikma*, ed. ʿAbd ar-Raḥmān Badawī, 2nd Ed., Kuwait and Beirut, 1980.

Ibn Taymiyya, Taqī d-Din, *Bughyat al-murtād fī r-radd ʿalā l-mutafalsifa wa-l-qarāmiṭa wa-l-bāṭiniyya ahl al-ilḥād min al-qāʾilīn bi-l-ḥulūl wa-l-ittiḥād*, ed. M. B. S. ad-Duwaysh, n.p.: Maktabat al-ʿUlūm wa-l-Ḥikam, 1408/1988.

———, *Darʾ taʿāruḍ al-ʿaql wa-n-naql*, 11 vols., ed. Muḥammad Rashād Sālim, Riad: Jāmiʿat al-Imām Muḥammad b. Suʿūd, 1979–1983.

———, *Kitāb an-Nubuwwāt*, Beirut: Dār al-Fikr, n.d.

———, *Ar-Radd alā l-manṭiqiyyīn* (*Refutation of the Logicians*), ed. ʿA. Ṣ. Sh. D. al-Kutubī, Bombay: Qayyimah Press, 1368/1949.

———, *ar-Risāla ṣ-Ṣafadiyya*, 2 vols., Al-Manṣūra: Dār al-Hādī n-Nabawī, Riad: Dār al-Faḍīla, 1421/2000.

———, *Majmūʿ al-fatāwā*, 37 vols., ed. ʿAbd ar-Raḥmān b. Muḥammad b. Qāsim, Medina 1425/2004.

———, *Sharḥ al-ʿAqīda al-Iṣfahāniyya*, ed. Ḥ. M. Makhlūf, Cairo: Dār al-Kutub al-Islāmiyya, n.d.

Ibn Ṭufail, Abū Bakr, *Ḥayy bin Yaqẓān*, ed. Alber Naṣrī Nādir, Beirut: Dār al-Mashriq, 1986.

İhsanoğlu, Ekmeleddin, *Büyük Cihad'dan Frenk Fodulluğuna*, Istanbul: İletişim, 1996.

Ikhwān aṣ-Ṣafāʾ, *Rasāʾil Ikhwān aṣ-Ṣafāʾ*, 4 vols., Beirut: Dār Ṣādir, n.d.

Ilan, Nahem, "Fragments of al-Ghazālī's Theory Related to Speech in the Commentary on Avot by Rabbi Israel Israeli of Toledo (Hebrew)" in: Nehemia Levtzion (ed.), *The Intertwined Worlds of Islam: Essays in Memory of Hava Lazarus-Yafeh*, Jerusalem: Ben-Zvi Institute, 2002, 20–58.

Irwin, Terence, *Aristotle's first principles*, Oxford: Oxford University Press, 1988.

Al-Iṣbahānī, Jāmiʿ al-ʿUlūm al-Bāqūlī ʿAlī bin al-Ḥussain, *Jawāhir al-Qurʾān*, Algiers: Dār al-Jāʾiza, 2012.

Al-Iṣfahānī, ar-Rāghib, *Kitāb al-Dharī'a ilā makārim ash-sharī'a*, ed. Abū l-Yazīd al-'Ajamī, Cairo, 1987.

———, *Kitāb al-Dharī'a ilā makārim ash-sharī'a*, ed. Sayyid Ali Mir Lawhi Falawurjani, Isfahan: University of Isfahan Press, 1997.

———, *Kitāb Mufradāt alfāẓ al-Qur'ān*, ed. Samīḥ 'Āṭif Zayn, Beirut: Dār al-Kitāb al-Lubnānī, 2009.

———, *Tafṣīl an-nash'atayni wa-taḥsīl as-sa'ādatayni*, ed. A. Najjār, Beirut, 1988.

Al-Iskandarī, 'Abd al-Mu'ṭī l-Laḥmī, *Sharḥ manāzil as-sā'irīn*, ed. 'Abd al-Mu'ṭī l-Laḥmī, Cairo, 1954.

Ivry, Alfred L. (trans.), *Averroës Middle Commentary on Aristotle's* De anima, Provo, Utah: Brigham Young University Press 2002.

———, "Moses ben Joshua (Ben Mar David) of Narbonne" in: Cecil Roth (ed.), *Encyclopaedia Judaica*, 16 vols., vol. 12, Jerusalem: Keter Publishing, 1972, 422–423.

———, *Moses of Narbonne*, Ma'amar bi-Shelemut ha-Nefesh (*Treatise on the Perfection of the Soul*), Jerusalem: The Israel Academy of Sciences and Humanities, 1977.

———, "Moses of Narbonne's 'Treatise on the Perfection of the Soul': A Methodological and Conceptual Analysis" in: *The Jewish Quarterly Review* 56 (1967), 293–97.

———, "The Guide and Maimonides' Philosophical Sources" in: Kenneth Seeskin (ed.), *The Cambridge Companion to Maimonides*, Cambridge: Cambridge University Press, 2005, 58–81.

Jabre, Farid, *La Notion De Certitude Selon Ghazali Dans Ses Origines Psychologiques Et Historiques*, Beirut: Université Libanaise, 1958.

Jackson, Sherman A., *On the Boundaries of Theological Tolerance in Islam: Abū Ḥāmid al-Ghazālī's Fayṣal al-Tafriqa Bayna al-Islām wa al-Zandaqa*, Karachi: Oxford University Press, 2002.

Al-Jāhiẓ, 'Amr b. Baḥr, *Kitāb al-Bukhalā'*, Beirut, 1991.

———, *Kitāb al-Ḥayawān*, 8 vols., ed. 'Abd as-Salām Muḥammad Hārūn, Cairo, 1938 (2nd edition Cairo, 1965).

Al-Jāmī, *Ad-Durra al-fākhira [fī taḥqīq madhhab aṣ-ṣūfiyya wa-l-mutakallimīn wa-l-ḥukamā' al-mutaqaddimīn]*, ed. Nicholas L. Heer and Ayatollah Musavi Bihbehānī, Tehran: Danishgah-i McGill, 1358/1980.

Janos, Damien, "Moving the Orbs: Astronomy, Physics and Metaphysics, and the Problem of Celestial Motion According to Ibn Sīnā" in: *Arabic Sciences and Philosophy* 21 (2011), 165–214.

———, "The Greek and Arabic Proclus and al-Fārābī's Theory of Celestial Intellection and its Relation to Creation" in: *Documenti e studi sulla tradizione filosofica medievale* 21(2010), 19–44.

Jansen, J. J., *The Interpretation of the Qur'ān in Modern Egypt*, Leiden: Brill, 1974.

Janssens, Jules, *Avicenna: tussen neoplatonisme en Islam*, PhD thesis, Leuven: Catholic University of Leuven Press, 1984.

———, "Creation and Emanation in Ibn Sīnā" in: *Documenti e studi sulla tradizione filosofica medievale* 8 (1997), 455–477.

———, "Al-Ghazālī and his use of Avicennian texts [XI]" in: Miklós Maróth (ed.), *Problems in Arabic Philosophy*, Pilicsaba: The Avicenna Institute of Middle Eastern Studies, 2003, 37–49.

———, "Al-Ghazālī between philosophy (*falsafah*) and Sufism (*taṣawwuf*): His Complex Attitude in the Marvels of the Heart (*'Aja'ib al-Qalb*) of the *Ihya Ulum al-Din*" in: *The Muslim World* 101 (2011), 614–632.

———, "Al-Ghazālī's *Mīzān al-'Amal*: An Ethical Summa Based on Ibn Sīnā and al-Rāghib al-Iṣfahānī" in: Anna Akasoy and Wim Raven (eds.) *Islamic Thought in the Middle Ages: Studies in Text, Transmission and Translation in Honour of Hans Daiber*, Leiden: Brill, 2008, 123–137.

———, "Al-Ghazālī's *Tahâfut*: Is it really a Rejection of Ibn Sînâ's Philosophy?" in: *Journal of Islamic Studies* 12 (2001), 1–17.

———, "Al-Ghazālī: The Introduction of Peripatetic Syllogistic in Islamic Law (and Kalām)" in: *MIDEO* 28 (2010), 219–233.

———, *Ibn Sīnā and his influence on the Arabic and Latin World*, Aldershot: Ashgate-Variorum, 2006.

———, "The Latin Translation of al-Ġazālī's *Maqāṣid al-Falāsifa*" in: Henrik Lagerlund (ed.), *Encyclopedia of Medieval Philosophy. Philosophy between 500 and 1500*, Heidelberg, London and New York: Springer, 2011, 387–90.

Johnson-Davies, Denys, *Al-Ghazali on the Manners relating to Eating: Book XI of the Revival of the Religious Sciences*, Cambridge: Islamic Texts Society, 2000.

Jomier, J. and Caspar, P., "L'exégèse scientifique du Coran d'après le Cheikh Amîn al-Khûlî" in: *MIDEO* 4 (1957), 269–280.

Al-Juwaynī, Abū l-Ma'ālī, *Al-Luma' fī qawā'id ahl as-sunna wa-l-jamā'a*, ed. Michel Allard, Beirut: Dār al-Mashriq, 1968.

———, *Nihāyat al-Maṭlab; Al-Wasīṭ fī l-madhhab, published with an-Nawawī's commentary (At-Tanqīṭ fī sharḥ al-Wasīṭ) and three other commentaries*. Edited Aḥmad Maḥmūd Ibrāhīm and Muḥammad M. Tāmir, Cairo: Dār as-Salām, 1418/1997.

Kaḥḥāla, 'Umar Riḍā, *Mu'jam al-mu'allifīn*, 15 vols., Damascus: Maṭba'at at-Taraqqī, 1957–1961.

Al-Kalābādhī, Muḥammad ibn Ibrāhīm, *Kitāb at-Ta'arruf li-madhhab ahl at-taṣawwuf*, Beirut, 1980.

Kalin, Ibrahim, "Will, necessity and creation as monistic theophany in the Islamic philosophical tradition" in: David B. Burrell (ed.), *Creation and the God of Abraham*, Cambridge: Cambridge University Press, 2010, 107–132. (Also in: *Ishraq* (2010), 345–367).

Käs, Fabian, *Die Mineralien in der arabischen Pharmakognosie*, 2 vols., Wiesbaden: Harrassowitz, 2010.

Kato, Mizue, "The Meaning of *Tafakkur* in al-Ghazali's Thought" in: *Bulletin of the Society for Near Eastern Studies in Japan* 49 (2006), 150–164.

Al-Kawtharī, Muḥammad Zāhid, *Muqaddimāt al-Imām al-Kawtharī*, Cairo: Dār ath-Thurayyā, 1418/1997.

Kaya, Mahmut, "Abdüllatif el-Bağdadi" in: *Türkiye Diyanet Vakfi İslam Ansiklopedisi*, vol. 1, Istanbul: Türkiye Diyanet Vakfı, 1988–, 254–5.

Kāzim, Mūsa, "İbn Rüşd'ün Felsefî Metodu ve İmam Gazzalî ile Bazı Konulardaki Münazarası" in: Mūsa Kāzim (ed.), *Küllīyāt: Dini, İctimai Makaleler*, Istanbul: Evkaf-ı İslamiyye Matbaası, 1326 AH, 139–96.

Khadra, Hanna, *Le Nomocanon de Bar Hebraeus: son importance juridique entre les sources chrétiennes et les sources musulmanes*, Rome: Pontificia Universitas Lateranensis, 2005.

Kholeif, Fathallah (ed.), *Al-Māturīdī. Book on the unity of God* (Kitāb at-Tawḥīd), Beirut, 1970.

Khoury, Joseph (trans.), *Le Candélabre du sanctuaire de Grégoire Abou'lfaradj dit Barhebraeus, Quatrième Base: de l'Incarnatio*n, Paris: Firmin-Didot, 1964.

Al-Khūlī, Amīn, *Manāhij tajdīd fī n-naḥū wa-l-balāgha wa-t-tafsīr wa-l-adab. Al-Aʿmāl al-kāmila*, 10 vols., Cairo: Al-Hay'a al-Miṣriyya al-ʿĀmma li-l-Kitāb, 1987–1995.

Khusraw, Nāṣir-i, *Jāmiʿ al-ḥikmatayn*, ed. H. Corbin and M. Mo'in, Tehran and Paris, 1953.

Al-Khwārizmī, Rukn ad-Dīn b. al-Malāḥimī, *Tuḥfat al-mutakallimīn fī r-radd ʿalā l-falāsifa*, ed. Hassan Ansari and Wilferd Madelung, Tehran, 2008.

Kim, Sung Ho, "Max Weber" in: Edward N. Zalta (ed.), *The Stanford Encyclopedia of Philosophy*, vol. 5, 2008 (available at: http://plato.stanford.edu/archives/fall2008/entries/weber/).

Al-Kindī, Abū Yaʿqūb b. Isḥāq, *Rasāʾil al-Kindī l-falsafiyya*, 2 vols., ed. Muḥammad ʿAbd al-Hādī Abū Rīda, Cairo: Dār al-Fikr al-ʿArabī, 1950–1953.

Kleinknecht, Angelika, "Al-Qisṭās al-Mustaqīm: Eine Ableitung der Logik aus dem Koran" in: Samuel M. Stern, Albert H. Hourani and Vivian Brown (eds.), *Islamic Philosophy and the Classical Tradition*, Oxford: Cassirer, 1972, 159–87.

Knuuttila, Simo, *Emotions in Ancient and Medieval Philosophy*, Oxford: Oxford University Press, 2004.

Kogan, Barry S., *Averroes and the Metaphysics of Causation*, Albany: State University of New York Press, 1985.

———, "Al-Ghazali and Halevi on Philosophy and the Philosophers" in: John Inglis (ed.), *Medieval Philosophy and the Classical Tradition: In Islam, Judaism and Christianity*, London: Curzon Press, 2002, 54–80.

———, "The Philosophers Al-Ghazālī and Averroes on Necessary Connection and the Problem of the Miraculous" in: Parviz Morewedge (ed.), *Islamic Philosophy and Mysticism*, New York: Caravan Books, 1981, 113–132.

Köse, Saffet, "Hocazâde Muslihuddin Efendi" in: *Türkiye Diyanet Vakfi İslam Ansiklopedisi*, Istanbul: Türkiye Diyanet Vakfı, 1988–, 18.

Kraemer, Joel, "The Influence of Islamic Law on Maimonides: The Case of the Five Qualifications" in: *Te'udah* 10 (1996), 225–44.

Kraus, Paul, "Kitāb al-Akhlāq li-Jalīnūs" in: *Bulletin of the Faculty of Arts of the University of Egypt* 5 (1937), 1–51.

Krawietz, Birgit, "Verstehen Sie Spaß? Ernsthafte Anmerkungen zur schariatrechtlichen Dimensionen des Scherzens" in: Georges Tamer (ed.), *Humor in der arabischen Kultur/Humor in Arabic Culture*, Berlin: Walter de Gruyter, 2009, 29–47.

Kritovoulos, Michael, *History of Mehmed the Conqueror*, translated and edited by Charles T. Riggs, Princeton: Princeton University Press, 1954.

———, *Tarih-i Sultan Mehmed Han*, trans. Karolīdī, Istanbul: Ahmed İhsan ve Şürekası Matbaacılık, 1328/1912.

Kukkonen, Taneli, "Creation and Causation" in: Robert Pasnau (ed.), *Cambridge History of Medieval Philosophy*, Cambridge: Cambridge University Press, 2010, 232–246.

———, "Al-Ghazālī on the Signification of Names" in: *Vivarium* 48 (2010), 55–74.

———, "Al-Ghazālī's Skepticism Revisited" in: Henrik Lagerlund (ed.), *Rethinking the History of Skepticism: the missing medieval background*, Leiden: Brill, 2010, 29–59.

———, "Possible Worlds in the *Tahāfut al-Falāsifa*: Al-Ghazālī on Creation and Contingency" in: *Journal of the History of Philosophy* 38 (2000), 479–502.

———, "Possible Worlds in the *Tahafut al-tahafut*: Averroes on Plenitude and Possibility" in: *Journal of the History of Philosophy* 38 (2000), 329–347.

———, "Receptive to Reality: Al-Ghazālī on the Structure of the Soul" in: *The Muslim World* 102 (2012), 541–561.

———, "The Self as Enemy, the Self as Divine: A Crossroads in the Development of Islamic Anthropology" in: Juha Sihvola and Pauliina Remes (eds.), *The Ancient Philosophy of Self*, Dordrecht: Springer, 2008, 205–224.

Landolt, Hermann, "Ghazālī and 'Religionswissenschaft': Some Notes on the *Mishkāt al-Anwār*" in: *Asiatische Studien* 45 (1991), 19–72.

Langermann, Y. Tzvi, "A Judaeo-Arabic Poem Attributed to Abū Ḥamid al-Ghazālī" in: *Miscelánea de Estudios Arabes y Hebraicos: Sección de Hebreo* 52 (2003), 183–200.

———, "The 'Hebrew Ajwiba' Ascribed to al-Ghazālī: Corpus, Conspectus and Context" in: *The Muslim World* 101 (2011), 680–697.

Lazarus-Yafeh, Hava, "Some Notes on the Term '*Taqlīd*' in the Writings of Al-Ghazzālī" in: Hava Lazarus-Yafeh (ed.), *Studies in al-Ghazzālī*, Jerusalem: Magnes Press of the Hebrew University, 1975, 488–502.

———, *Studies in al-Ghazzālī*, Jerusalem: Magnes Press of the Hebrew University, 1975.

———, "Was Maimonides Influenced by Alghazali?" in: Mordechai Cogan, Barry L. Eichler, and Jeffrey H. (eds.), *TigayTehillah le-Moshe: Biblical and Judaic Studies in Honor of Moshe Greenberg*, Indiana: Eisenbrauns, 1997, 163–193.

Leibson, Gideon, "Parallels between Maimonides and Islamic Law" in: Ira Robinson, Lawrence Kaplan and Julien Bauer (eds.), *The Thought of Moses Maimonides*, Lewiston and New York: Edwin Mellen Press, 1990, 209–48.

Leites, Adrien, "Ghazzāli's Alteration of *ḥadīths*: Processes and Meaning" in: *Oriens* 40 (2012), 133–148.

Lerner, Ralph and Mahdi, Muhsin (eds.), *Medieval Political Philosophy: A Sourcebook*, New York: Glencoe, 1963.

Lizzini, Olga, *Fluxus (fayḍ): Indagine sui fondamenti della metafisica e della fisica di Avicenna*, Bari: Edizioni di Pagina, 2011.

Lloyd, A. C., *The Anatomy of Neoplatonism*, Oxford: Clarendon Press, 1998.

Lobel, Diana, *A Sufi-Jewish Dialogue: philosophy and mysticism in Baḥya Ibn Paqūda's Duties of the Heart*, Philadelphia: University of Pennsylvania Press, 2007.

———, *Between Mysticism and Philosophy: Sufi Language of Religious Experience in Judah Ha-Levi's* Kuzari, Albany: State University of New York Press, 2000.

———, "'Silence Is Praise to You': Maimonides on Negative Theology, Looseness of Expression, and Religious Experience" in: *American Catholic Philosophical Quarterly* 76 (2002), 51–74.

Lohr, Ch., "Logica Algazelis. Introduction and Critical Text" in: *Traditio* 21 (1965), 223–90.

Lorenz, Hendrik, *The Brute Within: Appetitive Desire in Plato and Aristotle*, Oxford: Oxford University Press, 2006.

Losee, John, *Theories of Causality: From Antiquity to the Present*, London: Transaction Publishers, 2011.

MacDonald, Duncan B., "The Life of al-Ghazzālī, with especial references to his religious experience and opinions" in: *Journal of the American Oriental Society* 20 (1899), 71–132.

Madden, Edward H., "Averroes and the Case of the Fiery Furnace" in: Parviz Morewedge (ed.), *Islamic Philosophy and Mysticism*, Delmar: Caravan Books, 1981, 133–150.

Madelung, Wilferd, "Ibn al-Malāḥimī's Refutation of the Philosophers" in: Camilla Adang, Sabine Schmidtke and David Sklare (eds.), *A Common Rationality: Mu'tazilism in Islam and Judaism*, Würzburg: Ergon Verlag, 2007, 331–336.

———, "Al-Ghazālī on Resurrection and the Road to Paradise" in: S. Günther and T. Lawson (eds.), *Roads to Paradise*, Leiden: Brill, forthcoming.

———, "Ar-Rāġib al-Iṣfahānī und die Ethik al-Ġazālīs" in: Richard Gramlich (ed.), *Islamwissenschaftliche Abhandlungen Fritz Meier zum sechzigsten Geburtstag*, Wiesbaden: Franz Steiner Verlag, 1974, 152–63.

Madkour, Ibrahim, *La Place d'Alfarabi dans l'école philosophique musulmane*, Paris: Adrien-Maisonneuve, 1934.

Maius, Angelo, *Scriptorum veterum nova collectio*, Rome: Collegium Urbanum, 1838.

Makdisi, G., *Ibn ʿAqīl: Religion and Culture in Classical Islam*, Edinburgh: Edinburgh University Press, 1997.

Al-Makkī, Muḥammad b. Alī Abū Ṭālib, *Die Nahrung der Herzen*, 4 vols., eingeleitet, übersetzt und kommentiert von Richard Gramlich, Wiesbaden: Franz Steiner Verlag, 1991–1995.

Al-Makkī, Muḥammad b. ʿAlī al-Ḥārithī Abū Ṭālib, *Qūt al-qulūb fī muʿāmalat al-maḥbūb wa-waṣf ṭarīq al-murīd ilā maqām at-tawḥīd*, Cairo: Muṣṭafā l-Bābī l-Ḥalabī, 1961.

Manekin, Chales H., "Divine Will in Maimonides' Later Writings" in: *Maimonidean Studies* 5 (2008), 207–209.

Manrique, M. J. Casas y (ed.), *Ǧāmiʿ al-Ḥaqāʾiq bi-taǧrīd al-ʿalāʾiq: Origen y texto*, Uppsala: Almquist and Wiksell, 1937.

Marʿashlī, Jamāl (ed.), *ʿĀriḍat al-aḥwadhī bi-sharḥ Ṣaḥīḥ at-Tirmidhī*, 14 parts in 8 vols., Beirut: Dār al-Kutub al-ʿIlmiyya, 1997.

March, Joseph M., "En Ramón Martí y la seva 'Explanatio simboli apostolorum'" in: *Anuari de l'Insitut d'estudis Catalans* 2 (1908), 443–496.

Marino, Ada Rosanna, *Confronto tra il Taʾrīḫ muḫtaṣar ad-duwal e il Chonicon Syriacum di Abū l-Faraǧ Ibn al-ʿIbrī (Barebreo)*, Diss., Venezia: Università degli studi di Venezia Cà Foscari, 2002/3.

Marmura, Michael E., "Avicenna and the Division of Sciences in the *Isagogè* of His *Shifāʾ*" in: *Journal for the History of Arabic Science* 4 (1980), 239–251 (reprinted in: Michael E. Marmura, *Probing in Islamic Philosophy: Studies in the Philosophies of Ibn Sina, al-Ghazali and Other Major Muslim Thinkers*, Binghamton: Global Academic Publishing, 2005, 1–15).

———, "Avicenna and the Problem of the Infinite Number of Souls" in: *Mediaeval Studies* 22 (1960), 232–39 (reprinted in: Michael E. Marmura, *Probing in Islamic Philosophy: Studies in the Philosophies of Ibn Sina, al-Ghazali and Other Major Muslim Thinkers*, Binghamton: Global Academic Publishing, 2005, 171–179).

———, "Avicenna's Proof from Contingency for God's Existence in the *Metaphysics* of the *Shifāʾ*" in: *Medieval Studies* 42 (1980), 337–352.

———, "Al-Ghazālī" in: P. Adamson and R. C. Taylor (eds.), *The Cambridge Companion to Arabic Philosophy*, Cambridge: The Cambridge University Press, 2005, 137–154.

———, "Ghazālian Causes and Intermediaries" in: *Journal of the American Oriental Society* 115 (1995), 89–100.

———, "Ghazali and Demonstrative Science" in: *Journal of the History of Philosophy* 3 (1965), 183–204.

———, "Ghazali's Attitude to the Secular Sciences and Logic" in: George F. Hourani (ed.), *Essays on Islamic Philosophy and Science*, Albany: State University of New York Press, 1975, 100–111.

Marmura, Michael E. (trans.), *Ibn Sīnā*, ash-Shifā' al-Ilāhīyāt: *A dual language edition published as The Metaphysics of the Healing*, Provo and Utah: Brigham Young University Press, 2005.

———, *The Conflict over the World's Pre-eternity in the Tahāfuts of Al-Ghazāli and Ibn Rushd*, PhD thesis, Ann Arbor: University of Michigan Press, 1959.

———, "The Metaphysics of Efficient Causality in Avicenna (Ibn Sina)" in: Michael E. Marmura (ed.), *Islamic Theology and Philosophy: Studies in Honor of George F. Hourani*, New York: State University of New York Press, 1984, 172–187.

Maróth, Miklós, "Das System der Wissenschaften bei Ibn Sīnā" in: Burchard Brentjes and Sonja Brentjes (eds.), *Avicenna – Ibn Sina (980–1036)*, 2 vols., Leipzig: B. G. Teubner Verlagsgesellschaft, 1980.

Marzolph, Ulrich, *Arabia ridens*, 2 vols., Frankfurt am Main: Vittorio Klostermann, 1992.

Al-Marzouki, Abu Yaarub, *Le concept de causalité chez Gazali*, Tunis: Éditions Bouslama, 1998.

Matin, Abdul, "The Ghazalian and the Humian Critiques of Causality: a comparison" in: *The Dacca University Studies* 29 (1978), 29–43.

Al-Maydānī, Abū l-Faḍl Aḥmad, *Majmūʿ al-amthāl*, 4 vols., edited and annotated by Jān ʿAbdallah Tūmā, Beirut: Dār Ṣādir, 1422/2002.

Mayer, Toby, "Ibn Sīnā's *'Burhān al-Ṣiddiqīn'*" in: *Journal of Islamic Studies* 12 (2001), 18–39.

McCarthy, Richard J. (trans.), *The Theology of Al-Ashʿarī*, Beirut: Imprimerie Catholique, 1953.

McGinnis, Jon, "Occasionalism, Natural Causation and Science in al-Ghazālī" in: James E. Montgomery (ed.), *Arabic Theology, Arabic Philosophy: From the Many to the One: Essays in Celebration of Richard M.*, Peeters: Leuven, 2006, 441–463.

Meier, Fritz, *Abū Saʿīd-i Abū l-Ḫayr (357–440/967–1049): Wirklichkeit und Legende*, Leiden and Tehran: Brill, 1976.

Menn, Stephen, "The Discourse on the Method and the Tradition of Intellectual Autobiography" in: Jon Miller and Brad Inwood (eds.), *Hellenistic and Early Modern Philosophy*, Cambridge: Cambridge University Press, 2003, 141–191.

Michot, Yahya, "A Mamlūk Theologian's Commentary on Avicenna's *Risāla Aḍḥawiyya*: Being a Translation of a Part of the *Dar' al-Taʿāruḍ* of Ibn Taymiyya, with Introduction, Annotation and Appendices", part 1 in: *Journal of Islamic Studies* 14 (2003), 149–203.

———, "A Mamlūk Theologian's Commentary on Avicenna's *Risāla Aḍḥawiyya*: Being a Translation of a Part of the *Dar' al-Taʿāruḍ* of Ibn Taymiyya, with Introduction, Annotation and Appendices", part 2 in: *Journal of Islamic Studies* 14 (2003), 309–363.

———, "An Important Reader of al-Ghazālī: Ibn Taymiyya" in: *Proceedings of the International al-Ghazālī Symposium, Isparta, May 2011*, Isparta: Süleyman Demirel Üniversitesi, 2012.

———, “From al-Maʾmūn to Ibn Sabʿīn, via Avicenna: Ibn Taymiyya’s Historiography of Falsafa” in: F. Opwis and D. Reisman (eds.), *Islamic Philosophy, Science, Culture, and Religion. Studies in Honor of Dimitri Gutas*, Leiden: Brill, 2012, 453–475.

———, *Ibn Taymiyya. Against Extremisms. Texts translated, annotated and introduced. With a foreword by Bruce B. Lawrence*, Beirut and Paris: Albouraq, 1433/2012.

———, “Ibn Taymiyya on Astrology. Annotated Translation of Three Fatwas” in: *Journal of Islamic Studies* 11 (2000), 147–208.

———, “Ibn Taymiyya’s Commentary on the Creed of al-Ḥallāj” in: Ayman Shihadeh (ed.), *Sufism and Theology*, Edinburgh: Edinburgh University Press, 2007, 123–136.

———, “Ibn Taymiyya’s “New Mardin Fatwa”. Is genetically modified Islam (GMI) carcinogenic?” in: *The Muslim World* 101 (2011), 130–181.

———, “L’autorité, l’individu et la communauté face à la Sharīʿa: quelques pensées d’Ibn Taymiyya” in: *Mélanges de l’Université Saint Joseph* 64 (2013), 261–286.

———, “Misled and Misleading … Yet Central in their Influence: Ibn Taymiyya’s Views on the Ikhwān al-Ṣafāʾ” in: N. El-Bizri (ed.), *The Ikhwān al-Ṣafāʾ and their* Rasāʾil. *An Introduction*, Oxford: Oxford University Press, 2008, 139–179 (Corrected version on www.muslimphilosophy.com).

——— (trans.), *Muslims under Non-Muslim Rule. Ibn Taymiyya on fleeing from sin, kinds of emigration, the status of Mardin (domain of peace/war, domain composite), the conditions for challenging power. Texts translated, annotated and presented in relation to six modern readings of the Mardin fatwa. Foreword by J. Piscatori*, Oxford and London: Interface Publications, 2006.

———, *Textes spirituels d’Ibn Taymiyya (Nouvelle série). XI. Abū Ḥāmid al-Ghazālī & Fakhr al-Dīn al-Rāzī* (available at: www.muslimphilosophy.com, July 2011).

———, “Vanités intellectuelles. L’impasse des rationalismes selon le Rejet de la contradiction d’Ibn Taymiyya” in: *Oriente Moderno* 19 (2000), 597–617. Michot, Yahya, “Vizir « hérétique » mais philosophe d’entre les plus éminents: al-Ṭūsī vu par Ibn Taymiyya” in: *Farhang* 15–16, (2003), 195–227.

Mir, Mustansir, “Humor in the Qur’ān” in: *The Muslim World* 81 (1991), 179–193.

Mitha, Farouk, *Al-Ghazālī and the Ismailis. A Debate on Reason and Authority in Medieval Islam*, London and New York: I.B. Tauris in association with The Institute of Ismaili Studies, 2001.

Moad, Edward Omar, “Al-Ghazali on Power, Causation and Acquisition” in: *Philosophy East and West* 57 (2007), 1–13.

Mohamed, Yasien, “Al-Rāghib al-Iṣfahānī’s Classical Concept of the Intellect” in: *Muslim Educational Quarterly* 13 (1995), 52–61.

———, “ ‘Knowledge and Purification of the Soul’, An Annotated Translation with Introduction of al-Iṣfahānī’s *Kitāb al-Dharīʿa ilā Makārim al-Sharīʿah* (58–76; 89–92)” in: *Journal of Islamic Studies* 9 (1998), 1–34.

———, “The Ethical Philosophy of al-Rāghib al-Iṣfahānī” in: *Journal of Islamic Studies* 6 (1996), 51–75.

Mohamed, Yasien, "The Ethics of Education: Al-Iṣfahānī's *al-Dharīʿa* as a Source of Inspiration for al-Ghazālī's *Mīzān al-ʿAmal*" in: *The Muslim World* 101 (2011), 633–657.

———, "The Metaphor of the Dog in Arabic Literature" in: *Tydskrif vir Letterkunde* 45 (2008), 75–86.

——— (trans.), *The Path to Virtue: The Ethical Philosophy of Al-Rāghib al-Iṣfahānī*, An Annotated Translation with Critical Introduction of *Kitāb al-Dharīʿah ilā Makārim al-Sharīʿah*, Kuala Lumpur: International Institute of Islamic Thought and Civilization, 2006.

———, "The Unifying Thread Intuitive Cognition of the Intellect in al-Fārābī, al-Isfahānī and al-Ghazālī" in: *Journal of Islamic Science* 12 (1996), 27–47.

Mohammadian, Mohammad, "Der oblique Blick. Zum Verhältnis von Philosophie und Religion in den Robā'iyāt von Omar Khayyām" in: Friedrich Niewöhner and Olaf Pluta (eds.), *Atheismus im Mittelalter und in der Renaissance*, Wiesbaden: Harrassowitz Verlag, 1999, 95–114.

Mohammed, Khaleel, "Sex, Sexuality and the family" in: Andrew Rippin (ed.), *The Blackwell Companion to the Qur'ān*, Oxford: Blackwell, 2006, 298–307.

Moldenhauer, Eva (ed.), *Histoire de l'athéisme. Les incroyants dans le monde occidental à nos jours*, Weimar: Böhlaus Nachfolger, 2000.

Montgomery, James, "Al-Jāḥiẓ on Jest and Earnest" in: Georges Tamer (ed.), *Humor in der arabischen Kultur/Humor in Arabic Culture*, Berlin: Walter de Gruyter, 2009, 209–240.

Moore, Keith, *The developing human. Clinically oriented embryology. With Islamic additions: Correlation studies with Qur'ān and ḥadīth*, Jeddah: Dar al-Qiblah for Islamic Literature, 1983.

Moosa, Ebrahim, *Al-Ghazali and the Poetics of Imagination*, Chapel and London: The University of North Carolina Press, 2005.

Morewedge, Parviz (trans.), *The Metaphysics of Avicenna (Ibn Sīnā): A critical translation-commentary and analysis of the fundamental arguments in Avicenna's* Metaphysica *in the* Dānish Nāma-I ʿalā'ī (The Book of Scientific Knowledge), London: Routledge, 1973.

Muckle, J. T. (ed.), *Algazel's Metaphysics. A Medieval Translation*. Toronto: St. Michael's college, 1933.

Al-Muḥāsibī, Abū ʿAbdallāh al-Ḥāriṯ, *Al-ʿaql wa-fahm al-Qurʾān*, ed. Ḥusayn al-Quwwatilī, Beirut, 1982.

Musallam, Basim F., *Sex and Society in Islam: Birth control before the nineteenth century*, Cambridge: Cambridge University Press, 1983.

———, "The Human Embryo in Arabic Scientific and Religious Thought" in: G. R. Dunstan (ed.), *The Human Embryo: Aristotle and the Arabic and European Traditions*, Exeter: University of Exeter Press, 1990, 32–46.

Nabi, Mohammed N., "Criticism of Al-Ghazali on the Theory of Emanation presented by Plotinus and Ibn Sina" in: Mahmudul Haq (ed.), *Reason and Tradition in Islamic Thought*, Aligarh: The Government of India Press, 1992, 116–129.

———, "Theory of Emanation in the Philosophical System of Plotinus and Ibn Sīnā" in: *Islamic Culture* 56 (1982), 233–238.

An-Najjār, Zaghlūl, *Sources of scientific knowledge. The geographical concepts of mountains in the Qur'ān*, Herndon: International Institute of Islamic Thought, 1991.

Najm, Sami M., "The Place and Function of Doubt in the Philosophies of Descartes and Al-Ghazālī" in: *Philosophy East and West* 16 (1966), 133–41.

Nakamura, Kojiro, "Al-Ghazālī, Abu Hamid" in: Edward Craig (ed.), *Routledge Encyclopedia of Philosophy*, 10 vols., vol. 4, London: Routledge, 1998, 61–68.

———, "Imām Ghazālī's cosmology reconsidered with special reference to the concept of *jabarūt*" in: *Studia islamica* 80 (1994), 29–46.

———, "Was Ghazālī an Ash'arite?" in: *Memoirs of the Research Department of the Toyo Bunko* 51 (1993), 1–24.

Nallino, Carlo Alfonso, "Il diritto musulmano nel Nomocanone siriaco cristiano di Barhebraeus" in: *Rivista degli studi orientali* 8 (1921–23), 512–580 (reprinted in: Carlo Alfonso Nallino (ed.), *Raccolta di scritti editi e inediti*, 6 vols., vol. 4, Rome: Istituto per l'Oriente, 1942, 214–300).

An-Nasafī, Abū l-Mu'īn, *Tabṣirat al-adilla*, ed. Claude Salāma, Damascus: Institut Français de Damas, 1993.

Nettler, Ronald L., *Sufi Metaphysics and Qur'ānic Prophets*, Cambridge: The Islamic Texts Society, 2003.

Nicholson, Reynold A. (trans.), *Al-Hujwīrī*, Kashf al-Maḥjūb of al-Hujwīrī: *"The Revelation of the Veiled" An Early Persian Treatise on Sufism*, trans. from the Persian, London: Gibb Memorial Trust, 2000 (rep. of the 1911 edition).

Okumuş, Ejder, *Osmanlı'nın Gözüyle İbn Haldun*, Istanbul: İz Yayıncılık, 2008.

Oliver, Simon, "Trinity, motion and ex nihilo" in: David B. Burrell, Carlo Cogliati, Janet M. Soskice and William R. Stoeger (eds.), *Creation and the God of Abraham*, Cambridge: Cambridge University press, 2010, 133–151.

Ormsby, Eric L., *Between Reason and Revelation: Twin Wisdoms Reconciled*, London: I. B. Tauris, 2012.

———, *Al-Ghazālī: The Revival of Islam*, Oxford: Oneworld Publications, 2008.

———, *Theodicy in Islamic Thought. The Dispute over al-Ghazālī's "Best of all Possible Worlds"* Princeton: Princeton University Press, 1984.

———, "The Taste of Truth: The Structure of Experience in Al-Ghazālī's *Al-Munqidh min al-Ḍalāl*" in: Wael B. Hallaq and Donald P. Little (eds.), *Islamic Studies Presented to Charles J. Adams*, Leiden: Brill, 1991, 133–152.

Ozcan, Abdülkadir, "*Mecdi Mehmed Efendī. Ḥadā'iq ash-shaqā'iq*" in: *Ţekaik-i Nuʿmaniyye Zeyilleri*, Istanbul: Cagri Yayinlari, 1989, 1: 145–158.

Özervarlı, M. Sait, "An Unedited *Kalam* Text by Qadi al-Baydawi: *Misbah al-arwah*" in: *İslâm Araştırmaları Dergisi / Turkish Journal of Islamic Studies* 12 (2004), 75–125.

———, "Yanyalı Esad Efendi's Works on Philosophical Texts as Part of the Ottoman Translation Movement in the Early Eighteenth Century" in: Barbara Schmidt-Haberkamp (ed.), *Europa und die Türkei im 18. Jahrhundert / Europe and Turkey in the 18th Century*, Göttingen: V&R Press, Bonn University Press, 2011, 466–467.

Pambrun, James R., "Creatio ex nihilo and dual causality" in: David B. Burrell et al. (eds.), *Creation and the God of Abraham*, Cambridge: Cambridge University Press, 2010, 192–220.

Al-Pazdawi, 'Alī b. Muḥammad, *Uṣūl ad-dīn*, ed. Hans Peter Linss, Cairo: Dār Iḥyā' al-Kutub al-ʿArabiyya, 1963.

Pellat, Charles, *The Life and Works of Jāḥiẓ*, Berkeley: University of California Press, 1969.

Perler, Dominik and Rudolph, Ulrich, *Occasionalismus. Theorien der Kausalität im arabisch-islamischen und im europäischen Denken*, Göttingen: Vandenhoeck and Ruprecht, 2000.

Peters, F. E., *Aristoteles Arabus. The Oriental Translations and Commentaries on the Aristotelian corpus*. Leiden: Brill, 1968.

Pines, Shlomo (trans.), *Moses Maimonides: The Guide of the Perplexed*, Chicago: University of Chicago Press, 1963.

Plato, *The Dialogues of Plato: The Seventh Letter, ed. and translated by Benjamin Jowett and J. Harward*, Chicago et al.: William Benton, 1952.

Plotini opera, 3 vols., eds. Paul Henry and Hans-Rudolf Schwyzer, Paris and Bruxelles: Oxford University Press, 1959–1964.

Poggi, Vincenzo M., *Un classico della spiritualità Musulmana*, Rome: Libreria dell'Università Gregoriana, 1967.

Pohlenz, Max, *Die Stoa*, 4th ed., Göttingen: Vandenhoeck and Ruprecht, 1970.

Pormann, Peter E. and Savage-Smith, Emilie, *Medieval Islamic Medicine*, Edinburgh: Edinburgh University Press, 2007.

Pourjavady, Nasrollah, *Majmūʿah-ye Falsafī-e Marāghah*, Tehran, 2002.

———, *A Jewish Philosopher of Baghdad: 'Izz al-Dawla ibn Kammūna (d. 683/1284) and His Writings*, ed. Sabine Schmidtke, Leiden: Brill, 2006.

Putnam, Hilary, *Reason, Truth and History*, Cambridge: Cambridge University Press, 1982.

Al-Qushayrī, Abū l-Qāsim ʿAbd al-Karīm, *ar-Risāla al-Qushayriyya*, 2 vols., eds. ʿAbd al-Ḥalīm Maḥmūd and Maḥmūd ibn ash-Sharīf, Cairo: Dār al-Maʿārif, 1994.

Radtke, Bernd (ed.), *At-Tirmidhī, Thalāth muṣannafāt*, Wiesbaden: Franz Steiner Verlag, 1992.

——— (ed.), *Drei Schriften des Theosophen von Tirmid*, Wiesbaden: Franz Steiner Verlag, 1996.

Rahman, Yusuf, "Causality and Occasionalism: A Study of the Theories of the Philosophers Al-Ghazālī and Ibn Rushd" in: *Hamdard Islamicus* 21 (1998), 23–31.

Rapoport, Yossef and Ahmed, Shahab (eds.), *Ibn Taymiyya and his Times*, Karachi: Oxford University Press, 2010.

Ar-Rāzī, Fakhr ad-Dīn, *Maʿālim uṣūl ad-dīn*, ed. Ṭāhā ʿAbd ar-Raʾūf Saʿd, Cairo: al-Maktaba al-Azhariyya li-t-Turāth, 2004.

———, *Al-Maṭālib al-ʿāliya min al-ʿilm al-ilāhī*, 5 vols., ed. Aḥmad Ḥijāzī as-Saqqā, Beirut, 1987.

———, *Muḥaṣṣal afkār al-mutaqaddimīn wa-l-mutaʾakhkhirīn min al-ʿulamāʾ*, Cairo: Maktabat al-Kulliya l-Azhariyya, n.d.

———, *an-Nubuwwāt wa-mā yataʿallaq bihā*, ed. Aḥmad Ḥijāzi as-Saqqā, Cairo: Maktabat al-Kulliyya al-Azhariyya, 1985.

———, *Sharḥ al-ishārāt wa-t-tanbihāt*, 3 vols., Cairo, 1907.

———, *Taʾsīs at-taqdīs*, edited under the title *Asās at-taqdīs*, ed. Muḥyī d-Dīn Ṣabrī l-Kurdī et al., Cairo: Maṭbaʿat Kurdistān al-ʿIlmiyya, 1328 (1910–11).

Reinhart, A. Kevin, *Before Revelation: The Boundaries of Muslim Moral Thought*, Albany: State University of New York Press, 1995.

Reinhardt, Karl, *Kosmos und Sympathie*, München: Beck, 1926.

Richardson, Johanna (ed.), *Edward Fitgerald, Selected Works*, London: Rupert Hart-Davis, 1962.

Rippin, Andrew, "Devil" in: Jane Dammen McAuliffe (ed.), *Encyclopaedia of the Qurʾān*, 6 vols., vol. 1, Brill: Leiden, 2001, 524–28.

Rist, J. M., *Plotinus: The road to reality*, Cambridge: Cambridge University Press, 1977.

Ritter, Hellmut (ed.), *Al-Ašʿarī, Abū-ʾl-Ḥasan ʿAlī Ibn-Ismāʿīl, Kitāb Maqālāt al-islāmīyīn wa-iḫtilāf al-muṣallīn*, Wiesbaden: Steiner Verlag, 1932.

——— (ed.), *The Ocean of the Soul*, Leiden: Brill, 2003.

Ritter, Helmut and Walzer, Richard, "Uno scritto morale inedito di al-Kindî" in: *Memorie Della Reale, Accademia Nazionale Dei Lincei, Classe Di Scienze Morali, Storiche e Filologiche* 8 (1938), 5–63.

Rosemann, Philipp, *Omne agens agit sibi simile: A Repetition of Scholastic Metaphysics*, Leuven: Leuven University Press, 1996.

Rosenthal, Franz, "Die Arabische Autobiographie" in: *Analecta Orientalia* 14 (1937), 1–40.

———, *Humor in Early Islam*, 2nd edition, with an Introduction by Geert Jan van Gelder, Leiden: Brill, 2011.

———, *Knowledge Triumphant. The concept of knowledge in medieval Islam. With an Introduction by Dimitri Gutas*, Leiden: Brill, 2007.

Rosenthal, Franz, "Nineteen" in: *Analecia Biblica* 12 (1959), 304–318.

El-Rouayheb, Khaled, "Sunni Muslim Scholars on the Status of Logic, 1500–1800" in: *Islamic Law and Society* 11 (2004), 213–37.

Rubio, Luciano, *El "Ocasionalismo" de los teologos especulativos del Islam. Su posible influencia en Guillermo de Ockham y en los "ocasionalistas" de la Edad Moderna*, El Escorial: Ediciones Escurialenses, 1987.

Saʿāda, Riḍā, *Mushkilat aṣ-ṣirāʿ bayna al-falsafa wa-d-dīn min al-Ghazālī wa-Ibn Rušd ilā aṭ-Ṭūsī wa Khojazāde*, Beirut: Dār al-Fikr al-Lubnānī, 1990.

Sabra, Abdelhamid I., "Science and Philosophy in Medieval Islamic Theology: The Evidence of the Fourteenth Century" in: *Zeitschrift für Geschichte der Arabisch-Islamischen Wissenschaften* 9 (1994), 11–23.

———, "The Appropriation and Subsequent Naturalization of Greek Science in Medieval Islam: A Preliminary Statement" in: Jamil Ragep and Sally P. Ragep (eds.), *Tradition, Transmission, Transformation*, Leiden: Brill, 1996, 21–26.

Salāma, M. Y. (ed.), *Ibn Taymiyya. Thubūt an-nubuwwāt ʿaqlan wa-naqlan wa-l-muʿjizāt wa-l-karāmāt*, Cairo: Dār Ibn al-Jawzī, 1427/2006.

Salamah, Youhanna, *Séparation et divorce selon l'enseignement de Bar Hebraeus et l'implication oecuménique*, Diss., Ottawa: University of Ottawa Press, 2005.

Salamah-Qudsi, Arin S., "A Lightning Trigger or a Stumbling Block: Mother Images and Roles in Classical Sufism" in: *Oriens* 39 (2011), 199–226.

Saliba, George, *A History of Arabic Astronomy*, New York: New York University Press, 1994.

Sambursky, Samuel, *Physics of the Stoics*, Princeton: Princeton University Press, 1987.

———, *The Physical World of Late Antiquity*, London: Routledge and Kegan Paul, 1962.

Samir, Samir Khalil, "Cheminement mystique d'Ibn al-ʿIbrī (1226–1286)" in: *Proche-Orient Chrétien* 37 (1987), 71–89.

———, "Un récit autobiographique d'Ibn al-ʿIbrī" in: *Dirasat. Lettres & Sciences humaines, Université Libanaise, Faculté de Pédagogie* 15 (1988), 15–51.

Schimmel, Annemarie, *Mystical Dimensions of Islam*, 3rd edition, Chapel Hill: The University of North Carolina Press, 1978.

———, "Reason and Mystical Experience in Sufism" in: Farhad Daftari (ed.), *Intellectual Traditions in Islam*, London and New York: I. B. Tauris in association with The Institute of Ismaili Studies, 2000, 130–145.

Schmidtke, Sabine, *The Theology of al-ʿAllāma al-Ḥillī*, Berlin: Klaus Schwarz, 1991.

Schütte, H.-W., "Atheismus" in: Joachim Ritter et al. (eds.), *Historisches Wörterbuch der Philosophie*, 13 vols., vol. 1, Darmstadt, 1971, 595–599.

Schwarz, Michael (trans.), Maimonides, *Guide of the Perplexed*, Tel-Aviv: Tel-Aviv University Press, 1996.

Sedgwick, Mark, *Against the Modern World: Traditionalism and the Secret Intellectual History of the Twentieth Century*, Oxford: Oxford University Press, 2009.

Sellheim, Rudolph, "Das Lächeln des Propheten" in: *Festschrift A. Jensen*, München: Renner, 1964, 621–30.

Sezgin, Hilal, *Gesammelte Schriften zur arabisch-islamischen Wissenschaftsgeschichte*, Gesammelt, bearbeitet und mit Indices versehen v. Dorothea Girke u. Dieter Bischoff, III, B 1/3, Frankfurt am Main: Institut für Geschichte der Arabisch-Islamischen Wissenschaften an der Johann-Wolfgang-Goethe-Universität, 1984.

Shailat, I. (ed.), *Iggerot ha-Rambam*, 2 vols., Maʿaleh Adumim and Jerusalem: Shailat Publishing, 1995.

Ash-Shāmī, Rizq Yūsuf, "Ibn Taymiyya: Maṣādiruhu wa-manhajuhu fī taḥlīlihā" in: *Journal of the Institute of Arabic Manuscripts* 38 (1994), 183–269.

Shehaby, Nabil, "ʿIlla and Qiyās in Early Islamic Legal Theory" in: *Journal of the American Oriental Society* 102 (1982), 27–46.

Sheilat, Yitzhaq (ed.), *Haqdamot ha-Rambam la-Mishnah*, Jerusalem: Maʿaleh Adumim, 1994.

Sherif, Mohamed A., *Al-Ghazālī's Theory of Virtue*, Albany: State University of New York Press, 1975.

Shihadeh, Ayman, "From al-Ghazālī to al-Rāzī: 6th/12th Century Developments in Muslim Philosophical Theology" in: *Arabic Sciences and Philosophy* 15 (2005), 141–179.

———, "The Mystic and the Sceptic in Fakhr al-Dīn al-Rāzī" in: Ayman Shihadeh (ed.), *Sufism and Theology*, Edinburgh: Edinburgh University Press, 2007, 101–122.

Sinaceur, Mohammed A., "Logique et causalité chez Ghazali" in: *Un trait d'union entre l'orient et l'occident: Al-Ghazzali et Ibn Maimoun*, Rabat: Academie du Royale Maroc, 1986, 173–211.

Siorvanes, Lucas, *Proclus: Neo-Platonic Philosophy and Science*, New Haven and Connecticut: Yale University Press, 1997.

Smith, Margaret, *Al-Ghazālī the Mystic*, London: Luzac, 1944.

———, "The Forerunner of al-Ghazālī" in: *Journal of the Royal Asiatic Society* 68 (1936), 65–78.

Socrates, *Kirchengeschichte*, ed. Günther Christian Hansen, Berlin: Akademie-Verlag, 1995.

Sorabji, Richard, *Emotion and Peace of Mind*, Oxford: Oxford University Press, 2000.

———, "The Ancient Commentators on Aristotle" in: Richard Sorabji (ed.), *Aristotle Transformed: The Ancient Commentators and Their Influence*, London: Duckworth, 1990.

Spectorsky, Susan A., *Women in Classical Islamic Law: A Survey of the Sources*, Leiden and Boston: Brill, 2010.

Spevack, Aaron, *Ghazali on the Principles of Islamic Spirituality: Selections from Forty Foundations of Religion*, Vermont: Jewish Lights Publishing, 2011.

Steinschneider, Moritz, *Die hebräischen Übersetzungen des Mittelalters und die Juden als Dolmetscher*, Berlin: Kommissionsverlag des Bibliographischen Bureaus, 1893.

Stowasser, Barbara Freyer, "The Status of Women in Early Islam" in: Freda Hussain (ed.), *Muslim Women*, New York: St Martin's Press, 1984.

Stroumsa, Sarah, *Maimonides in His World: Portrait of a Mediterranean Thinker*, Princeton: Princeton University Press, 2009.

———, "The Religion of the Freethinkers of Medieval Islam" in: Friedrich Niewöhner and Olaf Pluta (eds.), *Atheismus im Mittelalter und in der Renaissance*, Wiesbaden: Harrassowitz Verlag, 1999, 45–59.

As-Subkī, Taqī d-Din, *Ṭabaqāt ash-shāfiʿiyya al-kubrā*, 10 vols., ed. Maḥmūd M. aṭ-Ṭanāḥī and ʿAbd al-Fattāḥ M. al-Ḥilū, Cairo: ʿĪsā l-Bābī l-Ḥalabī, 1964–1976.

Suwaydān, Ṭāriq, *Iʿjāz al-Qurʾān al-karīm. Min al-iʿjāz al-ʿadadī fī l-Qurʾān*, n.p., n.d.

Sviri, Sara, *The Sufis: An Anthology*, Tel Aviv: Tel Aviv University Press and MAPA, 2008.

———, "Wa-rahbāniyatan ibtadaʿūhā: an Analysis of Traditions Concerning the Origins and Evaluation of Christian Monasticism" in: *Jerusalem Studies in Arabic and Islam* 13 (1990), 195–208.

Szpiech, Ryan, "Hermeneutical Muslims? Islam as Witness in Christian Anti-Judaism" (available at: htpp://cas.uchicago.edu/workshops/westmedcult/files/2010/11/Szpiech-Hermeneutical-Muslims.pdf).

———, "In Search of Ibn Sīnā's 'Oriental Philosophy' in Medieval Castile" in: *Arabic Sciences and Philosophy* 20 (2010), 197–199.

Ṭabarsī, Abū Naṣr b. al-Faḍl, *Makārim al-akhlāq*, Cairo: Maktabat al-Qāhira, n.d.

El-Taher Uraibi, Muhammed Y., *Al-Ghazalis Aporien im Zusammenhang mit dem Kausalproblem*, PhD thesis, Bonn: University of Bonn Press, 1972.

Takahashi, Hidemi, *Aristotelian Meteorology in Syriac: Barhebraeus, Butyrum sapientiae, Books of Mineralogy and Meteorology*, Leiden: Brill, 2004.

———, *Barhebraeus: A Bio-Bibliography*, Piscataway: Gorgias Press, 2005.

———, "Barhebraeus und seine islamischen Quellen. Têgrat têgrātā (Tractatus tractatuum) und Ġazālīs Maqāṣid al-falāsifa" in: Martin Tamcke (ed.), *Syriaca. Zur Geschichte, Theologie, Liturgie und Gegenwartslage der Syrischen Kirchen. 2. Deutsches Syrologen-Symposium (Juli 2000, Wittenberg)*, Münster: LIT, 2002, 147–175

———, "Bemerkungen zum Buch der Blitze (*Ktobo d-zalge*) des Barhebraeus" in: Martin Tamcke and Andreas Heinz (eds.), *Die Suyoye und ihre Umwelt. 4. deutsches Syrologen-Symposium in Trier 2004*, Münster: LIT, 2005, 407–422.

———, "Between Greek and Arabic: The Sciences in Syriac from Severus Sebokht to Barhebraeus" in: Haruo Kobayashi and Mizue Kato (eds.), *Transmission of Sciences: Greek, Syriac, Arabic and Latin*, Tokyo: Waseda University Press, 2010, 16–32.

———, "Observations on Bar ʿEbroyo's Marine Geography" in: *Hugoye: Journal of Syriac Studies* 6 (2003), 77–130.

———, "Simeon of Qalʿa Rumaita, Patriarch Philoxenus Nemrod and Bar ʿebroyo" in: *Hugoye: Journal of Syriac Studies* 4 (2001), 45–91.

Ṭālibī, ʿAmmār, *Ārāʾ Abī Bakr ibn al-ʿArabī l-kalāmiyya*, 2 vols., Algiers: Ash-Sharika al-Waṭaniyya li-n-nashr wa-t-tawzīʿ, 1974.

Tamer, Georges (ed.), *Humor in der arabischen Kultur/Humor in Arabic Culture*, Berlin: Walter de Gruyter, 2009.

———, *Islamische Philosophie und die Krise der Moderne. Das Verhältnis von Leo Strauss zu Alfarabi, Avicenna und Averroes*, Leiden: Brill, 2001.

———, "The Qur'ān and Humor" in: Georges Tamer (ed.), *Humor in der arabischen Kultur/Humor in Arabic Culture*, Berlin: Walter de Gruyter, 2009, 3–28.

———, *Zeit und Gott: Hellenistische Zeitvorstellungen in der altarabischen Dichtung und im Koran*, Berlin: Walter de Gruyter, 2008.

At-Tawḥīdī, Abū Ḥayyān, *Al-Muqābasāt*, ed. Muḥammad Tawfīq Ḥasan, Baghdad: Matbaʿat al-Irshād, 1970.

Taylor, David G., "L'importance des Pères de l'Église dans l'œuvre speculative de Barhebræus" in: *Parole de l'Orient* 33 (2008), 63–85.

Taylor, Richard, *The Liber de causis* (Kalām fī Maḥḍ al-khair): A Study of Medieval Neoplatonism, PhD thesis, Toronto: Toronto University Press, 1981.

Teule, Herman G., "A Christian-Muslim Discussion: The Importance of the Bodily and Spiritual Purity. A Chapter from the Second Memro of Barhebraeus' *Ethicon* on 'The Right Conduct Regarding the Sustenance of the Body'" in: W. J. van Bekkum (ed.), *Syriac Polemics: Studies in Honour of Gerrit Jan Reinink*, Louvain: Peeters, 2007, 193–203.

———, "An important Concept in Muslim and Christian Mysticism: the Remembrance of God – *dhikr Allah – ʿuhdōnō d-Alōhō*" in: Martin Tamcke (ed.), *Gotteserlebnis und Gotteslehre. Christliche und islamische Mystik im Orient*, Wiesbaden: Harrassowitz, 2010, 11–24.

———, "Barhebraeus' *Ethicon*, al-Ghazâlî and Ibn Sînâ" in: *Islamochristiana* 18 (1992), 73–86.

———, "Christian Spiritual Sources in Barhebraeus' *Ethicon* and the Book of the Dove" in: *Journal of Eastern Christian Studies* 60 (2008), 333–354.

——— (trans.), *Ethicon seu Moralia Gregorii Barhebræi*, ed. Paulus Bedjan, Paris and Leipzig: Harrassowitz, 1898. Critical edition and translation of Book 1: Gregory Barhebraeus, *Ethicon. Mēmrā I*, 2 vols., Louvain: Peeters, 1993.

———, "L'amour de Dieu dans l'œuvre de Bar'Ebroyo" in: *Dieu Miséricorde Dieu Amour: Actes du colloque VIII Patrimoine Syriaque*, vol. 1, Antélias: CERO, 2003, 259–275.

———, "La vie dans le monde: perspectives chrétiennes. Une étude de Memrō II de *l'Ethicon* de Grégoire Abū l-Farağ Barhebræus" in: *Parole de l'Orient* 33 (2008), 115–128.

———, "The Perception of the Jerusalem Pilgrimage in Syriac Monastic Circles" in: René Lavenant (ed.), *VI Symposium Syriacum 1992*, Rome: Pontificio Istituto Orientale, 1994, 311–321.

Thiele, Jan, *Kausalität in der muʿtazilitischen Kosmologie. Das Kitāb al-Muʾaṯṯirāt wa-miftāḥ al-muškilāt des Zayditen al-Ḥasan ar-Raṣṣāṣ (st. 584/1188)*, Leiden: Brill, 2011.

Tibawi, Abdel Latif, "Al-Ghazālī's Sojourn in Damascus and Jerusalem" in: *Islamic Quarterly* 9 (1965), 65–122.

———, "Ar-Risālah al-Qudsīyah: Al-Ghazali's Tract on Dogmatic Theology" in: *Islamic Quarterly* 9 (1965), 79–94.

At-Tirmidī, Muḥammad Ibn ʿĪsā (ed.), *Sunan at-Tirmidhī*, Vaduz, Thesaurus Islamicus Foundation, n.d.

Tirosh-Samuelson, Hava, "The Ultimate End of Human Life in Postexpulsion Philosophic Literature" in: Benjamin R. Gampel (ed.), *Crisis and Creativity in the Sephardic World 1391–1648*, New York: Columbia University Press, 1997, 223–254.

Tolan, Jon, "Saracen philosophers secretly deride Islam" in: *Medieval Encounters* 8 (2002), 184–208.

Tornberg, C. J. (ed.), *Codices arabici, persici et turcici Bibliothecae Regia Universitatis Upsaliensis*, Lund: Impensis Reg., 1949.

Travaglia, Pinella, *Magic, Causality and Intentionality: The doctrine of rays in al-Kindī*, Turnhout: Edizioni del Galluzzo, 1999.

Treiger, Alexander, "Al-Ghazali's Classifications of the Sciences and Descriptions of the Highest Theoretical Science" in: *Dîvân. Disiplinlerarasi Çalişmalar Dergisi*, cilt 16 sayı 30 (2011), 1–32.

———, *Inspired Knowledge in Islamic Thought: Al-Ghazālī's Theory of Mystical Cognition and Its Avicennian Foundation*, London: Routledge, 2012.

———, "Monism and Monotheism in al-Ghazālī's *Mishkāt al-Anwār*" in: *Journal of Qur'ānic Studies* 9 (2007), 1–27.

———, *The Science of Divine Disclosure: Al-Ġazālī's Higher Theology and its Philosophical Underpinnings*, PhD diss., New Haven: Yale University Press, 2008.

Tsabari, Erez, *The Hebrew Translations of Mishkāt al-anwār by Abū Ḥāmid al-Ghazālī (Hebrew)*, M.A. thesis, Ramat Gan: Bar-Ilan University Press, 2012.

Türker, Mübahat (ed.), *Üç Tehafüt Bakımından Felsefe ve Din Münasebetleri*, Ankara: Türk Tarih Kururmu Basımevi, 1956.

Twersky, Isadore (ed.), *A Maimonides Reader*, Springfield: Behrman House, 1972.

Ülken, Hilmi Ziya (ed.), *Ibn Sina Risâleleri 1*, Ankara: Türk Tarih Kurumu Basımevi, 1953.

——— (ed.), *Türk Tefekkür Tarihi*, Istanbul: Matbaa-i Ebuzziya, 1934.

Ullmann, Manfred, *Die Natur- und Geheimwissenschaften im Islam*, Leiden: Brill, 1970.

———, *Wörterbuch der klassischen arabischen Sprache*, 2 vols., Endgültiges Literaturverzeichnis zum zweiten Band (Lām) in Band II, Wiesbaden: Harrassowitz, 1970–2009.

Urvoy, Dominique, "La démystification de la religion dans les textes attribués à Ibn al-Muqaffaʿ" in: Friedrich Niewöhner and Olaf Pluta (eds.), *Atheismus im Mittelalter und in der Renaissance*, Wiesbaden: Harrassowitz Verlag, 1999, 85–94.

ʿUthmān, ʿAbd al-Karīm, *Sīrat al-Ghazālī wa-aqwāl al-mutaqaddimīn fīhi*, Damascus: Dār al-Fikr, n.d.

Vajda, Georges, *Recherches sur la philosophie et la kabbale dans la pensée juive du Moyen Age*, Paris: Mouton & Co., 1962.

Van Ess, Josef, *Die Erkenntnislehre des ʿAḍudaddīn al-Īcī*, Wiesbaden: Franz Steiner Verlag, 1966.

———, "Quelques remarques sur le *Munqidh min aḍ-ḍalâl*" in: Abdel-Magid Turki (ed.), *Ghazâlî: La raison et le miracle, Table ronde UNESCO, 9–10 décembre 1985*, Paris: Éditions Maisonneuve et Larose, 1987, 57–68.

———, "The Logical Structure of Islamic Theology" in: Gustav von Grunebaum (ed.), *Logic in Classical Islamic Culture*, Wiesbaden: Harrasowitz, 1970, 21–50.

———, *Theologie und Gesellschaft im 2. und 3. Jahrhundert Hidschra. Eine Geschichte des religiösen Denkens im frühen Islam*, 6 vols., Berlin: Walter de Gruyter, 1991–97.

Van Gelder, Geert Jan, *Close Relationships: Incest and Inbreeding in Classical Arabic Literature*, London and New York: I. B. Tauris, 2005.

———, *Of Dishes and Discourse: Classical Arabic Literary Representations of Food*, Richmond: Curzon, 2000.

Van Leeuwen, Arend Th., *Ghazālī als Apologeet van de Islam*, Leiden: E. Ijdo, 1947.

Van Rompay, Lucas, "Juridical Literature" in: Sebastian P. Brock et al. (eds.), *Gorgias Encyclopedic Dictionary of Syriac Heritage*, Piscataway: Gorgias Press, 2011.

Vuillemin-Diem, G. (ed.) and De Moerbeka, Guillelmi (trans.), *Aristoteles Latinus*, Metaphysica, Leiden, New York and Köln: Brill, 1995.

Walzer, Richard, *Greek into Arabic*, Cambridge and Massachusetts: Harvard University Press, 1962.

Watt, William M., "A Forgery in al-Ghazālī's *Mishkāt*?" in: *Journal of the Royal Asiatic Society of Great Britain and Ireland* (1949), 5–22.

———, *Free Will and Predestination in Early Islam*, London: Luzac, 1948.

———, *Islamic Philosophy and Theology*, Edinburgh: Edinburgh University Press, 1985.

———, *Muslim Intellectual: a Study of al-Ghazālī*, Edinburgh: University Press, 1963.

———, "The Authenticity of Works Attributed to al-Ghazâlî" in: *Journal of the Royal Asiatic Society* (1952), 24–45.

Wehr, Hans (ed.), *Al-Ġazzālī's Buch vom Gottvertrauen: Das 35. Buch des Iḥyāʾ ʿulūm ad-dīn*, Halle (Saale): Nemeyer, 1940.

Weiss, Raymond L. and Butterworth, Charles, *Ethical Writings of Maimonides*, New York: Dover Publications, Inc., 1975.

Weitz, Lev, Ghazālī, *Bar Hebraeus and 'the Good Wife' between Islam and Christianity*, forthcoming.

Wensinck, Arent J., *A Handbook of Early Muhammadan Tradition, Alphabetically Arranged*, Leiden: Brill, 1927.

———, *Bar Hebraeus's Book of the Dove together with Some Chapters from His* Ethikon, Leiden: Brill, 1919.

Wensinck, Arent J., et al. (eds.), *Concordance et indices de la tradition musulmane*, 8 vols., Leiden: Brill, 1936–88.

———, "Ghazālī's *Mishkāt al-Anwār* (Niche of Lights)" in: *Semetische Studien uit de Natatenschaap van Professor Dr. A. J. Wensinck*, Leiden: A. W. Sijthoff's Uitgeversmaatchappi 75, 1933, 183–209.

Whittingham, Martin, *Al-Ghazālī and the Qur'ān: One Book, Many Meanings*, London and New York: Routledge, 2007.

Wiedemann, Eilhard, *Aufsätze zur arabischen Wissenschaftsgeschichte*, Hildesheim and New York: Olms, 1970.

Wilson, N. G. (trans.), *Aelian, Historical Miscellany* [*Varia Historia*], Cambridge: Harvard University Press, 1997.

Wisnovsky, Robert, *Avicenna's Metaphysics in Context*, Ithaca and New York: Cornell University Press, 2003.

———, "One Aspect of the Avicennan Turn in Sunni Theology" in: *Arabic Sciences and Philosophy* 14 (2004), 65–100.

———, "The Nature and Scope of Arabic Philosophical Commentary in Post Classical (ca. 1100–1900 AD) Islamic Intellectual History: Some Preliminary Observations" in: Peter Adamson, Han Baltussen and M. W. F. Stone (eds.), *Philosophy, Science and Exegesis in Greek, Arabic and Latin Commentaries*, 2 vols., vol. 2, London: University of London press, 2004, 149–91.

Wizārat al-Iʿlām, al-Hayʾa al-ʿĀmma li-l-Istiʿlāmāt, Markaz al-Iʿlām wa-t-Taʿlīm wa-l-Iittiṣāl, *Ḥaqāʾiq wa-maʿlūmāt ʿan tanẓīm al-usra*, Cairo, 1990.

Wolfsohn, Julius, *Der Einfluß Ġazali's auf Chisdai Crescas*, Frankfurt am Main: J. Kauffmann, 1905.

Wolfson, Harry A., *Crescas' Critique of Aristotle*, Cambridge and Massachusetts: Harvard University Press, 1929.

———, "Nicolaus of Autrecourt and Ghazālī's Argument Against Causality" in: *Speculum* 44 (1969), 234–238 (reprinted in: Harry A. Wolfson (ed.), *The Philosophy of the Kalam*, Cambridge, Massachusetts and London: Harvard University Press, 1976, 593–600.)

———, *The Philosophy of the Kalam*, Cambridge, Massachusetts and London: Harvard University Press, 1976.

Yaltkaya, Mehmet Ş., "Gazali'nin Te'vil Hakkında Basılmamış Bir Eseri" in: *Darülfünun İlahiyat Fakültesi Macmuası* 4 (1930), 46–58.

Yaltkaya, M. Ţerefettin and Bilge, Kilislī Rıfat, *Kātib Çelebī, Kashf aẓ-ẓunūn*, 2 vols., Ankara: Milli Eğitim Bakanlığı, 1941.

Az-Zabīdī, Murtaḍā, *Itḥāf as-sāda al-muttaqīn bi-sharḥ asrār Iḥyāʾ ʿulūm ad-dīn*, Cairo: al-Maṭbaʿa al-Maymāniyya, 1311/1893–4.

Zaki, Mona M., "Barzakh" in: Jane D. McAuliffe (ed.), *Encyclopaedia of the Qurʾān*, 6 vols., vol. 1, Leiden: Brill, 2001, 204–7.

Az-Zindānī, ʿAbd al-Majīd, *al-Muʿjiza al-ʿilmiyya fī l-Qurʾān wa-s-sunna*, Cairo, n.d.

Zonta, Mauro, "Fonti antiche e medievali della logica ebraica nella Provenza del Trecento" in: *Medioevo: Rivista di storia della filosofia medievale* 23 (1997), 515–594.

———, "The Jewish Mediation in the Transmission of Arabo-Islamic Science and Philosophy to the Latin Middle Ages: Historical Overview and Perspectives of Research" in: Andreas Speer and Lydia Wegener (eds.), *Wissen über Grenzen: Arabisches Wissen und lateinisches Mittelalter*, Berlin: Walter de Gruyter, 2006, 89–105.

Index of Works by al-Ghazālī

Ajwibat al-Ghazālī ʿan asʾilat Ibn al-ʿArabī 92n11
Ayyuhā l-walad 129, 189, 193, 336n37

Bidāyat al-hidāya 127

Faḍāʾiḥ al-bāṭiniyya wa-faḍāʾil al-mustaẓhiriyya 65n62, 68n76, 170n27, 236, 293n15
Fayṣal at-tafriqa bayna l-Islām wa-z-zandaqa 45, 94n15, 96n23, 97, 98, 100n35, 101n41, 109, 110, 111, 112, 115, 118, 119, 268n39, 347n12, 348, 391n55, 393

Ḥujjat al-ḥaqq wa-qawāṣim al-bāṭiniyya 68n76

Iḥyāʾ ʿulūm ad-dīn xi, xii, xv, xvi, 16n91, 17n92, 93, 94, 18n98, 27, 36n5, 39n25, 41, 42, 43, 44n46, 48, 45, 46, 47n60, 49, 52n8, 53, 55, 65n63, 66n66, 68n73, 70, 72n91, 73, 74n101, 75n104, 95n21, 97, 102n41, 107, 108n57, 113, 122, 124n10, 125, 126n19, 21, 22, 23, 127, 128n32, 33, 129n34, 131, 132, 133, 135, 136, 137n54, 138, 141n11, 142n13, 143n17, 144n24, 25, 26, 145n31, 32, 33, 34, 35, 146n37, 38, 41, 147n42, 43, 44, 148n46, 47, 149n50, 51, 52, 53, 54, 150n55, 56, 57, 58, 60, 61, 62, 151n63, 64, 67, 152n68, 69, 70, 71, 153n73, 75, 76, 77, 154n78, 80, 81, 83, 155n84, 85, 88, 89, 156n90, 157n94, 96, 97, 158n98, 100, 159n101, 103, 105, 160n107, 109, 161n110, 112, 162n118, 119, 120, 163n121, 123, 165, 166, 167, 168, 169, 170, 171, 172, 173n37, 174n45, 175n48, 49, 50, 51, 176n52, 53, 54, 55, 56, 177n58, 60, 178n61, 64, 179n72, 73, 74, 181n81, 82, 84, 85, 86, 182, 184, 185, 188, 189, 190, 191, 193, 203n60, 204, 205, 206, 208, 213n10, 222n39, 242n32, 260n23, 265n32, 267n39, 269n42, 270n46, 272n48, 49, 290, 294, 295, 296n25, 297n27, 306, 309, 310, 311, 312, 313, 320n46, 47, 48, 49, 50, 51, 52, 324, 325, 329, 330, 331n14, 15, 337n40, 346n5, 6, 365n47, 366n55, 385n34
  Kitāb Ādāb al-akl 170, 185
  Kitāb Ādāb an-nikāḥ 170, 171, 172, 175, 176, 177, 178n64, 179n73, 180, 181n81, 82, 84, 85, 86, 182n87, 88, 89, 183
  Kitāb Ādāb tilāwat al-Qurʾān 55n16, 65n63, 72n91, 260n23
  Kitāb al-ʿIlm xi n10, 42, 73, 188, 268n39, 295, 320n46
  Kitāb Kasr ash-shahwatayn 167n9, 170, 171, 172, 174, 175n48, 179n72, 180, 183, 185
  Kitāb al-Maḥabba wa-sh-shawq wa-l-uns wa-r-riḍā 74n101, 75n104, 122, 128n32, 132, 312n27, 330n10
  Kitāb Qawāʿid al-ʿaqāʾid 185, 270n46
  Kitāb Riyāḍat an-nafs 167n9, 170n27, 28, 171, 185, 188
  Kitāb aṣ-Ṣabr wa-sh-shukr 27, 46, 47n60, 75n104, 172n34
  Kitāb Sharḥ ʿajāʾib al-qalb xi, 11, 97, 108, 170n27, 185, 209, 227, 267n39, 272n49
  Kitāb at-Tafakkur 43, 173, 185, 310n23
  Kitāb at-Tawba 185, 269n42, 272n49, 330
  Kitāb at-Tawḥīd wa-t-tawakkul 4, 46n58, 185, 265n32, 268n39, 269n42, 272n49

Iljām al-ʿawāmm ʿan ʿilm al-kalām 31, 32n10, 33, 34, 41n32, 97, 98, 111, 349
Al-Iqtiṣād fī l-iʿtiqād 11n58, 25, 26, 31, 68, 133, 269n42, 270n46, 394n60

Jawāhir al-Qurʾān wa-duraruhu xiv, 50–88, 115, 269n42, 347, 348, 349, 360, 361n39, 363, 369, 370, 371, 372

Al-Khulāṣa al-musammā [sic!] khulāṣat al-mukhtaṣar wa-naqāwat al-muʿtaṣar 69, 308n17, 309
Kīmiyāʾ as-saʿāda 52n8
Kitāb al-Arbaʿīn fī uṣūl ad-dīn 15n86, 16n89, 43, 46n57, 53, 138n1, 265n32, 268n39, 269n42, 272n48, 49

Maʿārij al-quds fī madārij maʿrifat an-nafs 193, 268n39 [its authorship is still controversial]
Al-Maḍnūn bi-hi ʿalā ghayri ahlihi 12n68, 69, 29, 30, 32, 33, 70, 71, 192n26, 208n1, 227, 346n6, 354n30, 359
Majmūʿat rasāʾil al-Imām al-Ghazālī 93n14, 199n48, 223n41
Makātīb-i fārisī-yi Ghazzālī be-nām-i Fażāʾil al-anām min rasāʾil Ḥujjat al-Islām 98n29
Maqāṣid al-falāsifa xiii, xvii, xviii, 11n64, 12n68, 23, 24, 28n, 29, 33, 208n1, 265n32, 276, 277, 278, 280, 282, 284, 285, 286, 287, 289, 291, 294, 296, 298, 299, 300, 301, 302, 314, 315, 316, 319, 324, 326, 327, 329n9, 355, 387n41, 394
Al-Maqṣad al-asnā fī sharḥ maʿānī asmāʾ Allāh al-ḥusnā 11, 15n86, 16n89, 43, 53n11, 142n13, 145n32, 148n45, 162n118, 173n37, 260n23, 261n24, 265n32, 268n39, 269n42, 272n48, 49, 332, 343, 344
Miḥakk an-naẓar fī l-manṭiq 69, 192, 242, 342
Mishkāt al-anwār wa-miṣfāt al-asrār xvii, 12, 39, 44, 49, 50n1, 56n25, 98n28, 145n33, 150n60, 233n14, 253–274, 297, 298, 332, 335, 343, 347, 348, 349, 355n, 359, 360, 371, 372, 373, 374
Miʿyār al-ʿilm fī fann al-mantiq xviii, 40, 69, 192, 208n3, 217, 242, 280, 281, 282, 297, 342, 347, 348, 349, 352, 353, 359, 372
Mīzān al-ʿamal xvi, 38n21, 39n26, 40n29, 41, 108n57, 127, 138, 139n5, 6, 142n13, 143n22, 145n31, 32, 34, 35, 146n37, 147n44, 148n46, 149n50, 52, 54, 150n56, 62, 152n70, 153n74, 77, 155n88, 159n102, 104, 106, 160n108, 161n110, 112, 162n116, 170n27, 174n47, 184–206, 207–228, 297, 329, 330, 332, 336, 338n46, 340, 341n59, 343
Al-Munqidh min aḍ-ḍalāl wa-l-mūṣil ilā dhī l-ʿizza wa-l-jalāl xvi, 30, 42n41, 57n28, 65n62, 71n86, 88n155, 104n48, 106, 113, 114, 116, 141n11, 167n13, 190, 191, 198n45, 199n48, 202n57, 204, 207, 208n2, 223n41, 225n44, 229, 230, 231, 232n8, 9, 233n13, 15, 234, 235, 236n19, 20, 21, 239, 240, 241, 249, 251, 252, 267n39, 304, 305, 313, 314, 320n46, 321, 322, 323, 326, 327, 329n9, 332, 333, 334, 335, 336, 337, 338, 339, 340, 344
Al-Mustaṣfā min ʿilm al-uṣūl 27, 29, 30, 52n8, 116, 346n6

Qānūn at-ta ʾwīl xiv, 89–101, 103n46, 105n51, 107n54, 56, 108n58, 109n60, 61, 62, 110n65, 66, 69, 111n70, 112n73, 74, 114, 115, 116n83, 118, 119, 270n46, 370, 371
Al-Qisṭās al-mustaqīm 45, 50, 114, 115, 116, 230, 239, 240, 241, 242, 243, 244n40, 245n41, 42, 43, 44, 45, 46, 246n48, 50, 51, 247, 248, 249, 250, 251, 252, 267n39, 269n42, 44
Al-Quṣūr al-ʿawālī min rasāʾil al-imām al-Ghazālī 70n84, 176, 347n12, 354n30

Ar-Risāla al-laduniyya 12n68
Ar-Risāla al-qudsiyya 68, 269n42

Tahāfut al-falāsifa xiii, xv, xviii, 1n2, 2, 12n68, 13, 14n75, 77, 78, 79, 17n94, 18n101, 24, 25, 26, 27, 29, 30, 31, 33, 34, 68, 71, 106, 109, 122, 133, 134, 158n100, 163n125, 193, 207n, 208n1, 236, 277, 280, 283, 284, 285, 289, 293, 294, 296, 300, 301, 316n44, 321, 326, 329n9, 332, 333, 334, 336, 337, 338, 339, 340, 341, 342, 344, 346n6, 347n11, 375–397

Al-Wajīz fī fiqh madhhab al-Imām ash-Shāfiʿī 307, 308
Al-Wasīṭ fī l-madhhab 69n79, 307, 308

Index of Authors

ʿAbbās, Iḥsān 7n31, 91, 92n11, 98
Abdel-Kader, Ali Hassan 36n6
Abdera, Democritus of 121
ʿAbdū, Muḥammad 92n11
Abel, K. 156n91
Al-Abharī, Athīr ad-Dīn 93n12, 380, 384, 385n32
Abrahamov, Binyamin xiv, 15n86, 16n91, 17n92, 93, 94, 96, 18n98, 101, 41n32, 42n35, 43n44, 45, 44n47, 48 n67, 69, 71, 241, 251n61, 254n4, 256n9, 290, 293, 299n38
Abū l-ʿAlāʾ, M. M. 70n84, 347n12, 348n16, 354n30
Abū Dāwūd, Sulaimān b. al-Ašʿaṯ 102, 126n20, 363, 369
Abū Ḥanīfa, an-Nuʿmān b. Thābit 4, 237
Abū Rīda, Muḥammad ʿAbd al-Hādī 81n132, 150n59
Abu Risha, Yahya 268n39
Abu Shanab, R. E. 2n5
Abū s-Suʿūd, W. 78n117
Abū Zayd, ʿAbdu-r-Raḥmān 11n58, 68n74
Abū Zayd, Naṣr Ḥāmid xi n12, 51n4, 60n43, 65n64, 75n103, 85n145, 87n150
Abul Quasem, Muhammad 50n3, 55n16, 65n63, 72n91, 139n4, 149, 166, 167n9, 171n29, 261n23, 269n42
Abu-Sway, Mustafa 232n8
Acar, Rahim 21n119
Adamson, Peter 8n36, 37, 22n121, 262n25, 288n, 386n40
Adang, Camilla 141n10
Adham, Ibrāhīm b. 173
Adıvar, A. Adnan 386n36
Al-Afghānī, Jamāl ad-Dīn 20
Ahmed, Leila 180n75, 78, 79
Al-ʿAjamī, Abū l-Yazīd 186n1
Al-Akiti, M. Afifi 12n68, 29n8, 70n84, 101n38, 104n50, 138n2, 190n19, 20, 192, 208n1, 227n
Āl Yāsīn, Jaʿfar 84n141
Albalag, Isaac 299
Albertini, Tamara 232n8
ʿAlī, Amjad Rashīd Muḥammad 309n17
Allard, Michel 394n60
Altmann, Alexander 276n5
Al-Āmidī, Sayf ad-Din 378
Amīn, ʿUthmān 81n132
Al-Amīn, Sayyid Muḥsin 379n15
Ammann, Ludwig 126n20, 22, 127n28, 132n43
Anawati, G. C. x n6
Anawati, Marcel M. 81n132
Al-Andalusī, Abū l-Ḥasan Aḥmad b. ʿAlī b. Muḥammad b. Shukr 365n51
Ansari, Hassan 33n12
Al-Anṣārī al-Harawī, Abū Ismāʿīl ʿAbd Allāh b. Muḥammad 37, 353n27, 354
Aphrodisias, Alexander of 9, 14n73
Aquinas, Thomas 2, 10n54, 16, 232n8, 326
Arberry, Arthur J. 3, 61n46, 73n94, 181n83, 283
Arezzo, Bernard of 2
Aristotle 6, 8n44, 16n87, 33, 43, 60n44, 80, 87, 121, 136, 140n9, 142, 144n29, 149n49, 151, 159n103, 163, 170, 190, 218, 222, 223, 231, 243, 244, 245, 246, 256, 260n23, 263n27, 276, 280, 281, 282, 285, 293, 294, 299, 300, 301, 302, 321, 334, 335n34, 35, 337n41, 338, 350, 381n18, 385n33
Arkoun, Mohammed 376, 377n5
Arnaldez, Roger xi n11
Arnzen, Rüdiger 10n54, 335n34
Arslan, Ahmet 383n25, 390n52, 391n54, 392n58
Al-Aʿsam, ʿAbd al-Amīr 95n18, 19
Al-Ashʿarī, Abū l-Ḥasan 5n21, 24, 25, 15n82, 23, 25, 26, 28, 31, 33, 37, 255, 268n42, 378
Al-Ashqar, M. S. 52n8
Āshtiyānī, ʿAbbās Iqbāl 98n29
Asin-Palacios, M. 365n47
Assemanus, Joseph Aloysius 306n9
Atay, Hüsseyin 11n58, 68n74, 268n39
Ateş, Ahmed 68n76
ʿAṭṭār, Farīd ad-Dīn 129, 136
Austin, R. J. W. 180n78
Autrecourt, Nicolaus of 2

Avery, Peter 130n37
Avigdor, Abraham 299
Avneri, Zvi 277n6
Avtalion, Joav 296n25
ʿAyyād, Kāmil 141n11, 167n13, 229n1, 314n38, 320n46, 321n54, 332n19

Babinger, Franz 381n19, 382n20
Bachiller, A. Rodriguez 327n2
Badawī, ʿAbd ar-Raḥmān 53n11, 65n62, 68n76, 82n138, 93n12, 94n16, 95n18, 170n27, 189n11, 260n23
Badran, Muhammad Abū l-Fadl 3n7
Al-Baghdādī, ʿAbd al-Laṭīf 380
Al-Baghdādī, Abū l-Barakāt 288n
Al-Baghdādī, Abū l-Wafāʾ ʿAlī b. ʿAqīl b. Muḥammad 365, 366
Al-Baghdadi, Ismail Pasha 379n15, 384n27
Al-Baghdādī, Muḥammad al-Muʿtaṣim bi-llāh 32n10, 111n72
Bahcivan, Seyit 385n31
Bakar, Osman 81n132
Bakhtiar, Laleh 50n3, 347n14, 349
Baneth, David 289, 290
Al-Bāqillānī, Abū Bakr 15, 91, 98
Bargeron, Carol Lucille 1n2
Barhebraeus / Abū l-Farağ b. al-ʿIbrī xvii, 303–325
Barkai, Ron 182n89
Barlas, Asma 180n77
Barnes, Jonathan 190n17, 231n5, 6, 7, 244n39, 245n44, 246n49
Barthes, Roland 187, 188n5, 6
Baumstark, Anton 314, 315
Al-Bayḍāwī, ʿAbdallah b. ʿUmar 376n4, 395
Bedjan, Paulus 305n6, 306n7, 8, 9, 309n18, 19, 311n24, 26, 312n28, 313n35, 37, 320n46, 321n55
Beitia, A. Cortaberria 328n5
Bellefonds, Y. Linant de 173n36
Benkheira, Mohammed H. 167n12
Bergson, Henri 121, 125
Berti, Enrico 231n7
Bertman, Martin A. 76n110
Bertolacci, Amos 10n54
Bey, Hızır 82
Bianquis, Tierry 167n12
Bidarfar, Muḥsin 394n61
Bihbehānī, A. Musavi 384n30
Bījū, Maḥmūd 93n14, 186n2, 211n, 230n3, 248n56, 268n39, 270n46, 387n41
Bilge, Kilislī Rıfat 383n23, 384n27
Bingöl, Abdülkuddus 380n16, 385n32
Al-Bīrūnī, Abū r-Rayḥān 61n44
Al-Bisṭāmī, Abū Yazīd 213
Bland, Kalman 276n2
Blum, Georg Günter 310n21
Blumenthal, David R. 35n3, 36n4, 296n25
Böhm, Walter 6n29
Bolay, Süleyman Hayri 386n36
Bonadeo, Cecilia Martini 2n4
Bonner, A. 329n9
Bouhdiba, Abdelwahab 174n43, 179, 180n76
Bousquet, Georges-Henri 166n7
Bouyges, Maurice 2n4, 71n86, 94n16, 96n23, 97n26, 189n11, 338n47, 379n13
Brewster, D. P. 50n2
Brock, Sebastian 313n35
Brockelmann, Carl 93, 385
Bruns, Paulus Iacobus 305n6, 306n7
Bryson 139
Bucaille, Maurice 77n116
Buchman, David 12n67, 39n24, 50n1, 56n25, 233n14, 253n, 256n10
Al-Bukhārī, Muḥammad b. Ismāʿīl 100n36, 101n41, 102, 357n, 358, 364
Burnyeat, Myles F. 151n67
Burrell, David B. 2n5, 10n54, 11n59, 60, 61, 62, 63, 64, 65, 12n66, 13n70, 15n86, 16n89, 21n119, 133n47, 260n23
Butterworth, Charles 253n

Cahen, Claude 380n16
Calverley, Edwin E. 395n66
Cardahi, Gabriel 311n26, 313n35, 37
Caspar, P. 77n115
Celebī, Kātib 383, 384n26, 387n41, 388
Chahine, Osman 13n73
Chejne, Anwar G. 40n28
Chelhot, Victor 50n2, 115n81, 248, 267n39
Chittick, William 46n59
Çiçek, Yuliyos Yeshuʿ 306n9, 311n26, 313n35, 37
Clarke, D. 232n10

Cohen, Boaz 295
Colless, Brian 314n37, 322n58
Colville, Jim 254n2
Corbin, Henry 129, 136n53, 379n14
Cornell, Rkia 180n78
Corrigan, Kevin 149n49, 157n93
Crescas, Ḥasdai 288, 289, 299, 300, 301, 302
Çubukçu, Ibrahim Agah 11n58, 68n74, 268n39

D'Ancona, Cristina 262n25
Daher, Nazih 11n59, 60, 61, 62, 63, 64, 65, 12n66, 13n70, 15n86, 16n89, 260n23
Daiber, Hans xiii, xviii, 2n4, 3n5, 3n7, 8, 4n11, 12, 14, 15, 5n21, 6n26, 27, 7n31, 32, 33, 34, 35, 20n109, 111, 21n118, 72n92, 81n132, 87n153, 189
Dallal, Ahmad 78n119
Ad-Daqqāq, Abū ʿAlī 38
Ad-Dārānī, Abū Sulaymān 173
Darbandi, Afkham 130n37
Davidson, Herbert A. 5n22, 6n29, 41n32, 104n47, 105n52, 254n4, 255, 256n9, 262n26, 263n27, 293, 294
Davis, Dennis Morgan 268n39
Davis, Dick 130n37
Ad-Dawwānī, Jalāl ad-Dīn 382n20, 383
De Beaurecueil, S. 353n27
De Vaux, B. Carra 100n34
Descartes, René 232
Ad-Dimashqī, Muṣṭafā l-Qabbānī 69n77
Dobbs-Weinstein, Idit 295n20
Dolabani, Yuḥanon 311n26, 313n35, 37
Druart, Thérèse-Anne 18n101, 158n100
Dughaym, Samīḥ 391n55
Dunyā, Sulaymān 28n, 38n21, 94n15, 127n26, 138n2, 186n2, 265n32, 281n17, 282n22, 316, 336n36, 341n59, 343n71, 73, 347n11
Duran, Recep 383n23
Dutton, Blake D. 14n76
Ad-Duwaysh, Mūsā B. S. 347, 348n15, 365n48

Eagleton, Terry 187n3, 188n6
Efendi, Khojazāde Muṣliḥ ad-Dīn Muṣṭafā 383n23, 25, 386
Efendī, Mecdi Mehmed 382n21
Efendī, Mestcīzāde Abdullah 384
Efendī, Mueyyedzāde ʿAbdurraḥmān 384
Efendī, Taşköprīzāde Ahmed 382n21
Efendī, Yanyavī Esʿad 389n48
Elias, Norbert 171n31
Elschazlī, ʿAbd-Elṣamad ʿAbd-Elḥamīd 127n26, 209n
Endress, Gerhard 377
Eran, Amira 279n12, 291, 292n10, 293, 295
Esudri, Yossi 291n9
Euclides 337n41

Fahd, T. 102n43
Fakhr al-Mulk 54
Fakhry, Majid 2n5, 13n73, 14n74, 76, 78, 79, 16n88, 90, 193n
Falawurjani, Sayyid Ali Mir Lawhi 186n1
Al-Fārābī, Abū Naṣr (Alpharabius) x n6, xi, 8n36, 14n73, 21, 35n3, 76n110, 80, 81, 82n137, 83, 84n141, 87, 104n47, 105n52, 118, 141n12, 186n1, 223, 251, 254n4, 255, 256n9, 261n25, 267, 289, 301, 329n9, 331, 386n38, 393
Farah, Madelain 175n49, 50, 51, 176n52, 53, 54, 55, 56, 177n58, 60, 178n61, 64, 181n81, 84, 85, 86, 182n87, 88, 89
Al-Farāhīdī, Al-Khalīl b. Aḥmad 61n44
Faris, Nabih Amin 73n97, 203n60, 268n39
Al-Fārisī, ʿAbd al-Ghāfir b. Ismāʿīl 168n15
Fathi, Jean 314n39
Fenārī, Molla 380
Fenton, Paul 36n4, 296n25, 297n27
Fidora, Alexander 291n9
Fierro, M. 364n
Fitzgerald, Edward 129, 130
Fontaine, Resianne 291, 292n10
Fontaine, T. A. M. 291n7, 9, 292n10
Forster, Regula 86n146
Foucault, Michel 183
Frank, Richard M. xi n13, 15n84, 86, 16n91, 17n94, 18n97, 42n40, 84n143, 96n23, 117n86, 141, 163n125, 207n, 255n4, 256n9, 260n23, 261n25
Freudenthal, Gideon / Gad 9n49, 35n3
Furat, Ahmed Suphi 382n21

Gairdner, William Henry Temple 50n1, 254n2, 268n41, 347n13, 355n
Galen 106, 139, 140n9, 142n16, 144n30, 145, 147, 150n59, 333, 341

Garden, Kenneth xvi, 54n14, 96n23, 190, 208n2, 346n5, 349n19, 365n46, 47, 366n55
Gardet, Louis 13n73, 35n3, 81n132, 385, 386n37
Gawharīn, Ṣādiq 130n37
Gawlick, G. 1n1
Gellius, Aulus 156
Gersonides 299
Gianotti, T. J. 43n44, 46n56
Giladi, Avner xv, 166n5, 167n9, 10, 12, 171n31, 173n36, 37, 174n41, 43, 178n68, 189, 222, 294
Gimaret, Daniel 4n9, 13n70, 14n78, 65n61, 358n36
Girdner, Scott Michael xvi, 233n14, 255n5, 256n9, 257n11, 260n23, 261n24, 268n42, 270n46, 47, 272n48, 273n50, 297, 303n1
Goethe, Johann Wolfgang von 124
Goldenthal, Jacob 297n28
Goldziher, Ignaz 68n76
Golius, Jacobus 232n8
Goodman, Lenn E. 1n2, 188n8
Götz, Ignacio L. 232n8
Gramlich, Richard 102n41, 133n47, 139n5, 167n11, 331n14
Griffel, Frank xi n13, xix, 1n2, 12n66, 67, 68, 13n73, 14n80, 15n86, 16n89, 91, 18n97, 100, 20n112, 21n113, 116, 22n121, 23n, 26n, 39n22, 43n43, 45n52, 54n12, 91n7, 92n9, 96n24, 97n25, 98n28, 101n37, 38, 39, 104n48, 50, 111n71, 72, 113n76, 77, 78, 117n90, 118n92, 141, 157n96, 207n, 209, 215n20, 251n61, 256n9, 268n41, 285n32, 287n37, 288n, 297n31, 301, 324n61, 335n35, 365n47, 366n55
Günaltay, Şemseddin 385n36
Gundissalinus, Dominicus 277, 291
Gurānī, Molla 381
Gutas, Dimitri 66n66, 81n132, 161n115, 261n25, 377
Guttmann, Julius 289
Güzel, Abdurrahim 383n25
Gwyne, Rosalind W. 240n29
Gyekye, Kwame 1n2

Ḥāfiẓ, Ḥamza b. Zuhayr 116n84
Al-Ḥalabī, Muḥammad Badr ad-Dīn an-Naʿsānī 69n77
Halevi, Judah 277, 288, 289, 290n6, 299, 300
Halevi, Leor 43n43, 233n12, 376n4
Ha-Levi, Moses b. Joseph 296n25
Al-Ḥallāj, Manṣūr 213, 345
Hallaq, Wael B. 247n54
Halm, David E. 9n48
Hamlyn, D. W. 280n16
Ḥanafī, Ḥassan xi n11, 12
Ḥanafī, Muṣṭafā 71n87
Al-Ḥanbalī, ʿAbd al-Ḥayy b. ʿImād 382n21
Hansen, Günther Christian 322n57
Al-Ḥaqq, Jalāl 17n94
Ha-Penini, Jedaiah 299
Harari, Orna 231n7
Hartmann, Eduard von 21n114
Hārūn, ʿAbd as-Salām Muḥammad 4n10, 179n69
Harvey, Steven xvii, 166n5, 206n69, 277n8, 293n15, 294n19, 295n20, 21, 296n26, 297n29, 298n38, 300n42, 301n46, 302n48, 303n1
Harvey, Warren Zev 294n19, 300, 301n46, 302n48
Hasse, Dag N. 104n47
Hayoun, Maurice R. 275n, 277n7
Hedwig, Klaus 8n41
Heer, Nicholas L. 45n52, 85n144, 90n5, 94n16, 101n40, 108n58, 109n60, 61, 62, 110n65, 66, 69, 112n73, 75, 116n83, 118n91, 119n93, 120n96, 138n4
Hein, Christel 81n132
Heyde, Johannes Erich 2n5, 19, 20n108
Hicks, R. D. 87n151
Al-Ḥilū, ʿAbd al-Fattāḥ M. 95n17
Hodgson, Marshall G. 167n14
Holzman, Gitit 275n, 277n8, 278n, 279n10, 11
Hoover, J. R. 345n1
Hourani, George F. 42n42, 53n11, 79n125, 97n26, 117n86, 189n11, 208n3, 251n62
Hübner, Johannes 9n46
Al-Hujwīrī, ʿAlī b. ʿUthmān 37, 38
Hume, David 3
Al-Ḥusaynī, ʿAbdalmuḥin b. Ibrāhīm ix
Ḥuyayy, Ṣafiyya bt 102

Ibn ʿAbbās 362, 363, 374
Ibn ʿAbd al-Hādī 347
Ibn ʿAbd al-Karīm, Abū l-Fatḥ ʿAbd Allāh 365n52

Ibn ʿAbd al-Karīm, Abū Naṣr ʿAbd ar-Raḥīm 365n52
Ibn Abī d-Dunyā, Abū Bakr ʿAbdallāh 181n86, 363
Ibn Abī l-Khayr, Abū Saʿīd 130, 132
Ibn al-ʿArabī, Abū Bakr xiv, 35, 38n20, 91, 92, 94, 95, 96, 97, 98, 99, 100n33, 101, 115, 117, 120, 209n, 215n20
Ibn al-ʿArabī, Muḥyī d-Dīn 46n59, 48, 180, 388
Ibn al-Ḥaddād, Muḥammad 79
Ibn al-Ḥajjāj, Muslim 100n32, 36, 103n45
Ibn al-Ḥakam, Hishām 5, 19
Ibn al-Ḥārith, Bishr 131
Ibn al-Malāḥimī, Rukn ad-Dīn b. al-Malāḥimī al-Khwārazmī 24n2, 33
Ibn al-Mubārak 131
Ibn ʿAmr, Ḍirār 5
Ibn an-Nadīm, Abū l-Farağ 338n47
Ibn ʿAqnin, Joseph 297
Ibn Bāja, Abū Bakr b. aṣ-Ṣāyigh 276, 278
Ibn Da'ūd, Abraham 289, 290, 291, 292, 297
Ibn Ezra, Abraham 297
Ibn Ḥanbal, Aḥmad 26, 58n34, 80n127, 109, 126n20, 357n35
Ibn Ḥasdai, Abraham 297
Ibn Ḥazm, Abū Muḥammad 7, 40n28, 141n10
Ibn ʿIyād, Fuḍayl 131
Ibn Kammūna, Saʿd b. Manṣūr 296n25
Ibn Kaspi, Josef b. Abba Mari 299
Ibn Khaldūn, Walī d-Dīn 378n12, 387, 388
Ibn Māja, Abū ʿAbdillāh 102
Ibn Maymūn, Mūsā (Maimonides) 35n3, 133n48, 166n5, 206n69, 253–259, 261–267, 273, 274, 276, 277, 279, 292–297
Ibn Paquda, Baḥya 262n25, 290
Ibn Qāsim, ʿAbd ar-Raḥmān b. Muḥammad 80n126
Ibn al-Qayyim al-Jawziyya 347
Ibn ar-Rāwandī, Abū l-Ḥasan Aḥmad 233n12
Ibn Rushd, Abū l-Walīd (Averroes) xi, xiii, xvii, 1n2, 2, 9n49, 13n71, 17n94, 20n109, 33, 71, 79n125, 82n137, 89, 104n47, 105n52, 118, 134, 251, 254, 256n9, 275, 276, 278, 279, 280, 281, 284, 287, 288n, 289, 297, 299, 301, 302, 326, 335, 336, 338n47, 48, 342, 346, 355, 359, 375, 376, 378, 379, 383n23, 24, 385, 386, 387, 388, 389, 390, 391, 392, 393, 395
Ibn Sabʿīn, ʿAbd al-Ḥaqq 346n3, 347, 348
Ibn Samajūn, Ḥāmid 60n44
Ibn Shabīb, Muḥammad 4, 5
Ibn Sīnā, Abū ʿAlī (Avicenna) x n6, xi, xii, xiii, xiv, xvii, 1n2, 2, 8, 10, 11, 12n66, 13n73, 15, 16n88, 91, 20, 21, 23, 24, 25, 26, 28, 29, 30, 31, 33, 35n3, 48n69, 51, 60n44, 78, 81, 82, 83, 89, 98n29, 101, 102, 103, 104, 105, 106, 107, 118, 139, 141n12, 142, 148, 151, 161n115, 163n125, 187, 191, 192n24, 26, 202, 204, 205, 207, 208n1, 210, 223, 251, 254n4, 256n9, 259, 260, 261n25, 262n26, 263n26, 27, 266n36, 271, 272, 277, 278, 284, 285, 286, 289, 292, 294, 295n20, 297n31, 298n31, 302, 304, 305n6, 306, 308n15, 315, 316n45, 317, 319, 323, 324, 326, 329n9, 331, 333n24, 334, 335n35, 336, 341n62, 345, 346n3, 355, 359, 365n46, 370, 371, 376, 377n7, 10, 386, 387, 388, 391, 392, 393, 394, 395, 396, 397
Ibn Sīrīn 56
Ibn Taymiyya, Taqī d-Dīn x, xviii, 59n37, 80n126, 89–92, 94, 98, 119, 120, 166n5, 345–350, 352, 353, 359, 360, 361, 363, 365n47, 48, 52, 367n58, 59, 369, 370, 371, 372, 387, 388
Ibn Tibbon, Samuel 292
Ibn Ṭufail, Abū Bakr 60n44, 70, 71n85
Ibn Tūmart 89
Ibn ʿUmar 358
Ibn Waqār, Joseph b. Abraham 296n25, 297n31
Ibrāhīm, Aḥmad Maḥmūd 69n79, 308n17
İhsanoğlu, Ekmeleddin 386n36
Al-Ījī, ʿAḍūd ad-Dīn 379, 388
Ikhwān aṣ-Ṣafāʾ xi, 59n39, 81n132, 82n138, 142, 345, 346n3, 350, 351, 355, 359
Ilan, Nahem 296n25
Irwin, Terence 231n7
Al-Iṣbahānī, Jāmiʿ al-ʿUlūm al-Bāqūlī ʿAlī b. al-Ḥussain 54n11
Al-Iṣfāhānī, Maḥmūd xv, 123, 139n5, 148, 150, 186–210, 395

Al-Iskandarī, ʿAbd al-Muʿṭī l-Laḥmī 37n10
Israeli, Rabbi Israel 296n25
Ivry, Alfred L. xvii, 206n69, 276n3, 4, 279n12, 287n36, 297n30

Jābir, Muḥammad Muḥammad 53n9
Al-Jābirī, Muḥammad ʿĀbid xi n12, 71n87
Jabre, Farid 57n28, 104n48, 254n4, 332n19
Jackson, Sherman A. 128n31, 347n12, 348
Al-Jāḥiẓ, ʿAmr b. Baḥr 4, 5n19, 122, 125, 127, 178, 179, 290
Al-Jāmī, Molla ʿAbd ar-Raḥmān-i 382n20, 384
Janos, Damien 8n36, 14n73
Jansen, J. J. G. 77n115
Janssens, Jules xii n13, xvii, 14n73, 69n77, 139n5, 190, 191n24, 192, 207n, 210n4, 295n20, 301, 303n1, 376
Al-Jawzī, Abū l-Faraj ʿAbd ar-Raḥmān b. ʿAlī b. 366
Johnson-Davies, Denys 126n21, 132n42
Jomier, J. 77n115
Jones-Williams, J. 380n16
Judah, Moses b. 299
Al-Jurjānī, Sayyid Sharīf 379, 382, 386, 388
Al-Juwaynī, Abū l-Maʿālī 23, 91, 98, 394n60

Kaḥḥāla, ʿUmar Riḍā 379n15, 384n26, 27
Al-Kalābādhī, Muḥammad b. Ibrāhīm 36, 37
Kalin, Ibrahim 21n119
Kāmil, Khadīja Muḥammad 50n3, 53n9, 349n19
Karabāğī, Muḥyī d-Dīn Muḥammad b. ʿAlī xviii, 375, 383, 389, 396
Käs, Fabian 61n44
Al-Kāshānī, ʿAbd ar-Razzāq 388
Kato, Mizue 70n83, 321n55
Kaufmann, David 289
Al-Kawtharī, Muḥammad Zāhid 93n14, 97n27, 109n59
Kaya, Mahmut 380n16
Kayserī, Dāvud-i 380
Kāzim, Şeykhulislām Mūsa 389n48
Kemāl, Şemseddīn Aḥmed b. (Kemalpaşazāde) xviii, 93n12, 375, 383, 389, 390, 391, 392, 393, 396
Khadra, Hanna 307, 308n14
Khalaf, ʿAbd al-Raḥmān 181n86
Al-Khālidī, ʿAbdallāh 16n91, 17n92, 93, 18n98
Al-Kharrāz, Abū Saʿīd 36
Al-Khattāb, ʿUmar b. 337n40
Al-Khayyām, Omar 3n7
Kholeif, Fathallah 4n17
Khoury, Joseph 305n5
Al-Khūlī, Amīn 77n115
Khusraw, Nāṣir-i 136
Kierkegaard, Søren 122
Kim, Sung Ho 35n1
Al-Kindī, Abū Yaʿqūb b. Isḥāq 7, 20, 21, 81n132, 150n59, 151, 161n115, 262, 375, 386
Kirsch, Georgius Guilielmus 305n6, 306n7
Kleinknecht, Angelika 243n35
Knuuttila, Simo 151n65, 154n79, 156n91, 157n93
Kogan, Barry S. 2n4, 17n94, 290n6
Al-Konawī, Ṣadr ad-Dīn 380, 388
Konstan, David 154n79
Köse, Saffet 382n21
Kraemer, Joel 296n24
Kraus, Paul 142n16
Krawietz, Birgit 127n27
Kritovolous 381n19
Kukkonen, Taneli xv, 2n5, 22n122, 141n12, 143n23, 148n45, 152n72, 163n125, 233n12, 395n64
Al-Kurdī, Muḥyī-d-Dīn Ṣabrī 53n9, 69n77, 90n5, 108n57, 263n27
Kuşcu, ʿAlī 380, 381
Al-Kutubī, ʿA. Ṣ. Sh. D. 347n9

Landolt, Hermann 12n67, 39n23, 129n36, 256n9, 268n41
Lange, Christian 100n34
Langermann, Y. Tzvi 13n68, 298
Lazarus-Yafeh, Hava 12n67, 68, 40n31, 42n39, 66n66, 83n140, 166n5, 168n16, 17, 169n19, 290n4, 293, 294n17
Leibson, Gideon 296
Leites, Adrien 181n80
Lenk, Timur 124
Lewis, Geoffrey 8n41
Lewisohn, Leonard 165n3
Linss, Hans Peter 394n60
Lloyd, A. C. 8n44, 9n50, 51, 10n52

Llull, Ramon 232n8, 329n9
Lobel, Diana 261n25, 265n32, 266n33, 289, 290
Lohr, Ch. 328n7
López-Farjeat, Luis Xavier xvi, 229
Lorenz, Hendrik 144n29
Losee, John 22n123

Al-Maʿarrī, Abū l-ʿAlāʾ 3n7
MacDonald, Duncan B. 116n86, 141n10
Madden, Edward H. 17n94
Madelung, Wilferd xiii, 24n, 27n, 31n, 33n, 123n6, 139n5, 189, 191, 192, 324n61
Madkour, Ibrahim x n6, 35n3
Magnus, Albertus 2
Magritte, René 370
Mahdi, Muhsin 84n141
Maḥmūd, ʿAbd al-Ḥalīm 172n33, 254n2
Makdisi, George 366n53
Makhir, Jacob b. 297
Makhlūf, Ḥ. M. 365n48
Al-Makhzūmī, Mahdī 61n44
Al-Makkī, Abū Ṭālib Muḥammad b. ʿAlī l-Ḥārithī 12, 37, 129, 139, 167, 172, 174, 184, 191
Makrī, ʿAbd al-Qādir 265n32
Malkarāvī, Yaḥyā (Nevʿī Efendī) 384
Malter, Heinrich 13n68, 69, 298n33
Al-Maʾmūn 346n3, 381
Manekin, Charles H. 293
Manrique, M. J. Casas y 93n13
Marʿashlī, Jamāl 100n33
March, Joseph M. 328n4, 331n16
Al-Marghīnānī, Abū Isḥāq 365n48
Al-Marghīnānī, Abū l-Ḥasan 365
Al-Marghīnānī, Abū Naṣr 365n48
Al-Marghīnānī, Ẓahīr ad-Dīn 365n48
Marino, Ada Rosanna 305n6
Marmura, Michael E. 10n55, 13n71, 72, 14n75, 77, 78, 79, 15, 16n91, 17n94, 22n121, 25n, 66n66, 68n75, 81n132, 109n64, 134n50, 260n23, 262n25, 26, 283n27, 284, 333n24, 341n62, 376n2
Maróth, Miklós 81n132, 191n24
Marti, Raymond xvii, xviii, 326–344
Marzolph, Ulrich 126n19
Al-Marzouki, Abu Yaarub 1n2
Massignon, Louis 189n11
Matin, Abdul 3n6
Al-Māturīdī, Maḥmūd Abū Manṣūr 4, 5, 387
Al-Mawjūd, ʿĀdil ʿAbd 69n79, 308n17
Al-Maydānī, Abū l-Faḍl Aḥmad 60n44
Mayer, Tobias 129n35, 189n14, 263n27
Mayeur-Jaouen, Catherine 167n12
Al-Māzarī, Abū ʿAbd Allāh Muḥammad b. Abī l-Faraj 365n47
Al-Māzarī, Abū ʿAbd Allāh Muḥammad b. ʿAlī t-Tamīmī 365n47
McCarthy, Richard J. 15n82, 42n41, 57n28, 65n62, 117n86, 229n1, 230n2, 3, 231n4, 232n9, 233n13, 15, 234n17, 235n18, 236, 240n25, 26, 27, 28, 243n36, 38, 244, 245, 246n47, 48 50, 51, 247n52, 53, 248n55, 57, 249n58, 59, 250n60, 267n39, 272n49, 294n16, 17
McGinnis, Jon 22n121
Mehmed II 380n17, 381
Mehren, A. F. 266n36
Meier, Fritz 130
Menn, Stephen 208n2
Michot, Yahya xviii, 59n37, 98n28, 345n1, 2, 3, 346n4, 7, 356n34, 365n48, 50, 52, 369n61, 370n
Minois, Georges 3n7
Mir, Mustansir 132n44
Miskawayh, Abū ʿAlī Aḥmad 123, 126n24, 139, 147, 148, 150n59, 161, 167, 188, 189, 190, 191, 205
Mitha, Farouk 54n12, 238n
Moad, Edward Omar 1n2
Moerbeka, Guillelmi de 338n48
Mohamed, Yasien xv, 139n5, 149, 150n59, 186n1, 190n18, 204n64, 210n4
Mohammadian, Mohammad 3n7
Mohammed, Khaleel 170n26
Moldenhauer, Eva 3n7
Montgomery, James E. 127n29
Moosa, Ebrahim 189n15
Morewedge, Parviz 12n66
Motzki, Harald 174n43
Mouawad, Ray Jabre 313n35
Muʿawwaḍ, ʿAlī 69n79, 308n17
Mubārak, Ḥakīm Şah Muḥammad b. 383
Muckle, J. T. 328n6, 8
Muḥammad, Ṭāriq b. ʿAwaḍ Allāh b. ix
Al-Muḥāsibī, Abū ʿAbd Allāh al-Ḥārith 36, 139, 154, 191, 205

Muʿīn, Muḥammad 136n53, 316, 394n60
Murād II 381n20, 382
Musallam, Basim F. 166, 174n43, 177, 178n63, 67, 179n71
Musṭafā, Hocazāde Muṣliḥ ad-Dīn xviii, 375, 382, 383, 384, 386, 389, 390, 391, 392, 395, 396, 397
Al-Mustaẓhir 65n62, 68n76, 236
Al-Mutanabbī, Abū ṭ-Ṭayyib 79

Nabi, Mohammed Noor 2n3, 13n73
Nādir, Alber Naṣrī 60n44, 71n85, 80n129
Najjār, A. 191
An-Najjār, Zaghlūl 78n118
Najm, Sami M. 232n8
Nakamura, Kojiro 2n5, 12n68, 16n91
Nallino, Carlo Alfonso 307, 308
Narboni, Moshe xvii, 275–287, 297n30, 298, 299
An-Nasafī, Abū l-Muʿīn 394n60
Nathan, Isaac b. 298
Nathan, Judah b. Solomon 297n26, 299
Naumkin, V. V. 232n8
An-Naẓẓām xii, 4, 5, 7, 18, 19
Nettler, Ronald L. 35n4
Nicholson, Reynold A. 37n12
Nietzsche, Friedrich 122
Niẓām al-Mulk 381

Oktem, Ülker 385n31
Okumuş, Ejder 387n45
Oliver, Simon 22n119
Ormsby, Eric M. xiv, xv, 21n113, 64n59, 74n101, 88n, 128n32, 33, 131n40, 132n46, 136n52, 53, 137n54, 55, 140n8, 155n87, 165n3, 4, 166n5, 168n14, 16, 18, 169n21, 23, 173n38, 238n, 312n27, 330n10, 346n5, 365n46, 47, 50, 366n54
Özervarlı, M. Sait xviii, 376n4, 389n48

Pambrun, James R. 22n119
Al-Pazdawi, Abū Yusr 394n60
Peiravi, A. 367n59
Peiravi, T. J. 367n59
Pellat, Charles 125n13
Perler, Dominik 2n5
Peters, F. E. 338n47
Philoponus, John 6
Pines, Shlomo 133n48, 258n16, 292, 293
Plato 8, 80, 142n14, 144, 149n49, 170, 188n5, 222, 223, 334, 337n41
Poggi, Vincenzo M. 116n86, 294n17, 332, 333n23
Pohlenz, Max 9n48
Pollock, James W. 395n66
Pormann, Peter E. 131n41
Pourjavady, Reza 13n68, 69, 296n25
Proclus 2, 7, 8n36, 42, 9, 10, 22n120
Ptolemaeus 337n41
Putnam, Hilary 232

Qalʿajī, ʿAbd al-Muʿṭī Amīn xi n10, 55n16, 73n97, 74n101
Al-Qazwīnī, Najm ad-Dīn ʿUmar b. ʿAlī 385n33
Al-Qummī, Abū Jaʿfar Muḥammad b. Bābawayh 367n59
Al-Qurshī, Nabaʾ b. Muḥammad Abū l-Bayān 365
Al-Qushayrī, Abū l-Qāsim ʿAbd al-Karīm 37, 129, 132, 139, 172n33, 365
Al-Quwwatilī, Ḥusayn 36n8

Rābiʿa al-ʿAdawiyya 180
Radtke, Bernd 38n20, 365n46
Rahman, Yusuf 1n2
Ar-Rāshid, Fahd Sālim Khalīl 53n11
Ar-Raṣṣāṣ, al-Ḥasan 12n66
Ar-Rāwāndī, Qutb ad-Dīn Saʿīd b. ʿAbdallah 379n15
Ar-Rāzī, Fakhr ad-Dīn 43n43, 47, 48, 89, 90, 91, 94, 117, 119, 120, 305, 326, 346n7, 356, 378, 379, 386, 388, 392, 393, 395, 396, 397
Reinhardt, Karl 9n48
Reinhart, A. Kevin 29n7
Renan, Ernest 20
Renard, John 267n39
Riggs, Charles T. 381n19
Rippin, Andrew 102n43, 103n45, 170n26
Rist, J. M. 8, 9n48
Ritter, Hellmut 5n21, 24, 25, 132n45, 46, 151n66
Rosemann, Philipp 9n51, 10n52, 53, 55
Rosenthal, Franz 52n6, 66n66, 121n1, 5, 123, 125n18, 195n37, 208n2, 233n14, 239n, 295

El-Rouayheb, Khaled 385n33
Rubio, Luciano 1n2
Rudolph, Ulrich 2n5
Ar-Rūmī, Jalāl ad-Dīn 85n144, 136, 180n78, 380

Sa'ari, Che Zarrina 12n68
Sa'āda, Riḍā 383n23, 396n67
Ṣabbāḥ, Ḥasan-i 238n
Sabra, Abdelhamid I. 377, 378n12
Sa'd, Ṭāḥā 'Abd ar-Ra 'ūf 117n89
Aṣ-Ṣādiq, Ja'far 367n59
Sadooq, Sheikh 367n59
Ṣadrā, Mullā 10n54, 21
Salāma, Claude 394n60
Salāma, M. Y. 365n48
Salamah, Youhanna 308n13
Salamah-Qudsi, Arin Shawkat 170n25
Ṣālḥānī, Anṭūn 305n6
Saliba, George 377n10
Ṣalībā, Jamīl 141n11, 167n13, 229n1, 314n38, 320n46, 321n54, 332n19
Sālim, Muḥammad Rashād 89n1, 345n2, 365n48, 387n43
As-Samarqandī, Abū l-Layth 4
As-Sāmarrā'ī, Ibrāhīm 61n44
As-Saqqā, Aḥmad Ḥijāzi 47n64, 117n89, 393n59
As-Sarrāj, Abū Naṣr 36
As-Sayrawān, 'Abd al-'Azīz 'Izz ad-Dīn 50n1, 335n35
Sambursky, Samuel 6n30, 9n45
Samir, Samir Khalil 314n37
Sarıoğlu, Huseyin 384n30
Savage-Smith, Emilie xviii, 131n41
Schimmel, Annemarie 36n7, 84n142, 169n21, 22, 177n41, 42, 180
Schmidtke, Sabine 117n89, 296n25
Schütte, H.-W. 3n7
Schwarz, Michael 294n16
Sedgwick, Mark 215n17
Sellheim, Rudolph 126n19
Şerafettin, Mehmet 94n16
Ash-Shahrazūrī, Taqī d-Dīn 365n50
Shailat, I. 292n11
Ash-Shāmī, Rizq Yūsuf 346
Shams ad-Dīn, Aḥmad 93n14, 186n2, 191n23, 223n41, 336n36, 341n59, 343n71, 73
Shams ad-Dīn, Sālim 50n3
Ash-Sharīf, Maḥmūd b. 172n33, 232n8
Ash-Sharqawī, 'Iffat 50n3, 349n19
Ash-Shīrāzī, Quṭb ad-Dīn 380
Ash-Shīrāzī, Ṣadr ad-Dīn 388
Shehaby, Nabil 247n54
Shehadi, Fadlou A. 11n59, 60, 61, 62, 63, 64, 65, 12n66, 13n70, 15n86, 16n89, 142n13, 260n23
Sheilat, Yitzhaq 253n
Sherif, Mohamed Ahmed 37n9, 42n38, 45n51, 46n59, 138, 149, 170n28, 189, 207n, 209n
Shihadeh, Ayman 43n43, 47, 48n68, 345n3
As-Sijistānī, Abū Sulaymān al-Manṭiqī 121
Sinaceur, Mohammed Allal 1n2
Siorvanes, Lucas 8n42, 9n48, 10n52, 56, 22n120
Smith, Margaret 75n101, 139n5
Socrates 223, 334, 337n41
Solomon 60n44, 258n15
Sorabji, Richard 157n93, 381n18
Spectorsky, Susan A. 173n36
Spevack, Aaron 53n9
Steinschneider, Moritz 297n26
Stern, M. S. 269n42
Stowasser, Barbara Freyer 180n77
Stroumsa, Sarah 3n7, 293n15
As-Subkī, Tāj ad-Dīn 95, 168n15
Sublet, Jaqueline 167n12
As-Suhrawardī, Shihāb ad-Dīn 314n39, 388, 398
As-Sulamī, Mu'ammar b. 'Abbād 6, 21
Sulaymānī, Muḥammad 96n24
Aṣ-Ṣu'lūkī, Abū Sahl 38
Suwaydān, Ṭāriq 78n117
Sviri, Sara 174n44, 180n78
Szpiech, Ryan 298n31, 326n, 327n2

Aṭ-Ṭabarsī, Abū Naṣr b. al-Faḍl 181n82
At-Taftazānī, Sa'd ad-Dīn 379, 382, 385n33, 386, 388
Takahashi, Hidemi xvii, 206n69, 303n2, 304n4, 308n15, 310n21, 311n25, 315n43, 321n55, 323n
Ṭālibī, 'Ammār 95n20, 216n
Tamer, Georges xiv, 3n8, 82n137, 123, 127n27, 29, 132

Tāmir, Muḥammad Muḥammad 69n79
Aṭ-Ṭanāḥī, Maḥmūd M. 95n17
At-Tawḥīdī, Abū Ḥayyān 121, 122
Taylor, David G. K. 304n3
Taylor, Richard C. 10n56, 11n57, 22n121
Teule, Herman G. B. 305n6, 309n18, 19, 310, 312n28, 29, 320n46, 325
Thiele, Jan 12n66
Tibawi, Abdel Latif 68n73, 269n42
At-Tilimsānī, ʿAfīf ad-Dīn 388
At-Tirmidhī, al-Ḥakīm 38, 58n34, 35, 80n127, 100n33
Tirosh-Samuelson, Hava 299n39
Tolan, Jon 329n9
Travaglia, Pinella 7n31
Treiger, Alexander xii n13, 52n8, 53n11, 66n66, 73n98, 82n139, 161n114, 208n1, 3, 213n10, 215n19, 220, 225, 256n9, 260n23, 324n60
Tsabari, Erez 298
Tuazon, Allen ix
Tūmā, Jān ʿAbdallah 60n44
Türker, Mübahat 383n24, 391n53
Aṭ-Ṭurṭūshī, Abū Bakr Muḥammad b. al-Walīd al-Fihrī 364
Aṭ-Ṭūsī, ʿAlā' ad-Dīn ʿAlī xviii, 375, 381, 382, 383n23, 386, 389, 390, 391, 392, 393, 396, 397
Aṭ-Ṭūsī, Naṣīr ad-Dīn xvii, 303, 304, 306, 319, 345, 346n3, 386
At-Tustarī, Sahl 140n7
Twersky, Isadore 259n19

Ülken, Hilmi Ziya 315n42, 385n36
Ullmann, Manfred 60n44, 86n146
Uraibi, Muhammed Yasin El-Taher 1n2
Al-Urmawī, Sirāj ad-Dīn 380, 385n33
Urvoy, Dominique 3n7
Üsküdārī, Mehmed Emin 384
Al-ʿUthaymīn, Shaykh Muḥammad b. Ṣāliḥ 367n58
Al-ʿUthmān, ʿAbd al-Karīm 168n15

Vajda, Georges 36n4, 296n25, 298n31
Van den Bergh, Simon 2n4, 134n49, 379n13, 387n42, 392n56
Van Ess, Josef 4n18, 5n19, 22, 23, 24, 25, 6n26, 27, 103n44, 135n51, 208n2, 240n29
Van Gelder, Geert Jan 121n1, 123, 166, 171n31
Van Leeuwen, Arend Th. 116n86
Van Rompay, Lucas 307n10
Vuillemin-Diem, G. 338n48

Walzer, Richard x n6, 76n110, 145n36, 151n66
Warner, Levinius 232n8
Al-Wāsiṭī, Muḥammad b. al-Ḥasan 95
Watt, William Montgomery ix n11, 5n25, 166, 189n11, 191n23, 198n45, 199n48, 202n57, 203n60, 204n63, 209n, 241, 242, 254n4, 268n41, 377n6
Weber, Max 35n1
Weiss, Raymond L. 253n
Weitz, Lev 310n21
Wensinck, Arent J. 100n33, 36, 102n42, 174n43, 256n9, 10, 310, 311n26, 312n28, 313n35, 37
Whittingham, Martin 41n32, 45n53, 55, 51n4, 59n39, 66n66, 80n126, 94n16, 95, 96n22, 243n35, 256n9
Wiedemann, Eilhard 16n89
Wilson, Catherine 232n8
Wilson, N. G. 121n2
Winter, Tim J. 160n109, 167n9, 171n29, 30, 31, 174n41, 45, 175n48, 179n72, 188n7
Wisnovsky, Robert 10n55, 377, 386n40
Wolfsohn, Julius 300
Wolfson, Harry Austryn 2n5, 5n24, 14n77, 17n94, 18n99, 300, 301n45, 302n47, 49

Yaltkaya, Mehmet Şerefettin 94n16, 383n23, 384n27

Az-Zabīdī, Murtaḍā 95, 126n23, 385
Az-Zajjāj, Ibrāhīm 53n11
Zaki, Mona M. 100n34
Zakzouk, Hamdi 232n8
Az-Zaydī, Aḥmad Farīd 308n17
Zayed, S. x n6
Zeyrek, Molla 382n22
Az-Zindānī, ʿAbd al-Majīd 78n118
Zonta, Mauro 291n9, 297n30
Zurayq, Constantine K. 126n24, 147n42

Index of Subjects

ʿAdl 170, 174
Anthropomorphism 31, 358
Apatheia 151, 152, 153, 154
Al- ʿAql al-faʿʿāl xiv, 87, 104n47, 276n2, 279, 286
Al-ʿAql bi-l-fiʿl 279, 280, 286, 287, 352, 358, 368, 371
Asceticism 42, 43, 57, 154, 199, 238, 289
Aṣḥāb aṭ-ṭabāʾiʿ / Aṭ-ṭabīʿiyūn 5, 222, 327, 333
Ashʿarite xiv, 1, 11, 13n70, 14, 15, 16n91, 18, 20, 21, 22, 23, 25, 26, 28, 31, 33, 37, 48, 84, 94n14, 96n23, 110, 111, 112, 113, 114, 116, 117, 133, 134, 139, 146n37, 162n118, 207n1, 251, 255, 268n42, 270, 391n55, 393

Bāṭin 45, 51, 52n8, 55, 65, 68, 80n126, 84, 160, 196, 170n27, 229n1, 236, 238, 242, 243, 248, 289, 293n15, 335, 347n8
Birth control 165, 166, 173, 174n43, 176, 177, 178

Cardinal virtues 48, 159, 160, 218
Causality xiii, xiv, 1–22, 25, 26, 42, 72n92, 133, 134, 163, 346n6, 376
Coercion 6, 7
Comedy 122
Complexion 333
Contingency 10n55, 15, 163n125, 263n26, 381n18, 395n64

Dahr 3, 332
Dahriyyūn / Dahrites 3, 4, 5, 332
Desiderative dynamics 140
Divinity 6, 143, 244, 258

Education xi, xv, xvi, 52, 81, 139n5, 151, 166, 171, 178, 186, 187, 188, 189, 192n26, 193, 196, 204, 205, 206, 210n4
Esotericism xviii, 29, 43n44, 45n52, 50, 65, 83, 84, 85n144, 87n150, 88, 236, 238, 242, 345, 351, 355, 359, 360, 368, 369n61, 370, 371
Eternity xii, xiii, 7, 13, 25, 29, 31, 210, 236, 262n25, 293n15, 321, 327, 331, 334, 341, 390n53, 391, 392
European Enlightenment 1

Falsafa xi, xii, xiii, xv, 7, 12n68, 80n126, 81n131, 160, 162n118, 190n19, 208n1, 227n48, 254n2, 269n42, 298n31, 345, 346, 353, 369, 375, 381, 382, 383n23, 385n32, 395n67
Fiqh 4, 23, 40n28, 49, 50, 52n8, 64, 69, 70, 79, 81, 203, 203, 247, 306, 307, 308n17, 351, 359, 364, 370, 388
First Cause xiii, 7, 8n36, 10n54, 15, 16, 20, 22, 394
Fiṭra 44, 141, 144, 145n35, 171
Free Will 5n25, 8, 13n70, 17, 264n28, 277, 293

Gharīza 145

Ḥāl 7, 37, 44, 163, 172, 272
Ḥayawāniyya 121, 122
Hermeneutics xi, xiv, xvii, 45, 49, 50, 51, 52, 56, 58, 65, 66, 74, 83, 84, 87n150, 88, 252, 253, 263, 267, 270n46, 272, 273, 274, 326n, 327n2, 351, 379
Humour 121, 122, 123, 124, 126, 129, 130, 132, 133, 135, 136

Iʿjāz al-Qurʾān 77, 78
Ilāhiyyūn 221, 334
Ilhām 40
ʿIlm xii, xvi, 27, 29, 37, 44, 52, 55, 64, 67, 68, 70, 77, 97, 162, 163, 168, 169, 185, 190, 211, 212, 221, 223, 226, 231, 239, 354, 363
ʿIlm al-muʿāmala 40, 168, 359
ʿIlm al-mukāshafa 40, 169, 184
Intellectualization 35

Jabarūt 25, 28, 212, 360, 363
Jewish philosophy 262n25, 275, 288, 289, 300
Jocularity 125, 126

Kalām 2n5, 5n24, 8n36, 10n56, 14n77, 17n94, 18n99, 26, 29, 30, 31, 32, 33, 37, 41, 49, 50, 68, 69, 70, 79, 81, 97, 102, 110, 111, 139, 182, 204, 207, 234, 239, 240, 250, 261, 263, 264, 267n39, 281, 290, 293, 347, 349, 352, 353, 364, 369, 370, 376, 378, 381, 382, 384n30, 385n33, 386n37, 387, 393n60, 399

Kamāl fiṭrī 145
Al-Khayal 20, 33, 39, 41, 46n59, 86, 87, 99, 103, 107, 109, 157, 161n115, 189n15, 267, 285, 341, 348, 396

Al-Madīna al-fāḍila 87
Maḥabbat Allāh 43, 48
Māhiyya 261, 262n26, 393
Malakūt 360, 363
Marriage xv, 63, 166, 168, 170, 172, 173, 174, 175, 176, 178, 179, 181, 182, 183, 308n13
Metriopatheia 152, 154
Moderation 152, 153, 179
Muʿtazila xiii, 5, 12n66, 20, 21, 25, 26, 28, 33, 36, 65, 84, 89, 264n28, 268, 269, 378, 393

Naẓar xv, 2, 12n66, 19, 20, 22, 114, 122, 125, 129, 351
Necessary Existent 29, 48, 253, 259, 260, 261, 262, 263, 271, 272, 273, 291, 350, 394, 395
Neoplatonic xiii, 1n2, 2, 6, 7, 8n41, 9n49, 10n54, 11, 12, 13, 14n73, 19, 20, 21, 22n121, 43, 50, 262n25, 266
Niẓāmiyya xvi, 26, 96, 97n26, 114, 207, 208, 224, 366n55, 379, 381

Perception ix, 39, 51n5, 56, 57, 76, 78, 85, 86, 87, 107, 142, 143, 144, 149, 151, 156, 168, 176, 257, 258, 259, 261, 265n32, 266, 267, 280, 281, 309n18, 312n29, 317, 339, 392
Pleasure 39, 43, 61, 75, 76, 128, 129, 135, 136, 142, 143, 144, 146, 148, 153, 158, 173n37, 178, 183n91, 202, 211, 213n10, 221, 279, 294, 295, 328n6, 329, 330n10, 331, 333, 334n27, 335, 343, 344, 351
Prime Mover 6, 16
Procreation xv, 170, 174, 183
Propatheia 156

Qaḍāʾ wa-qadar 5n25, 11, 15
Qānūn kullī xiv, 90, 91, 94, 101, 108, 118, 119, 120
Al-Quwwa al-mutakhayyila 107, 279, 285

Rahbāniyya 174
Ar-Raʾīs al-awwal 87
Rationalization xii, 35, 43, 149
Rationalized Spirituality 78
Resurrection xii, xiii, 25, 26, 27, 29, 30, 31, 63, 71n86, 100n36, 101n41, 236, 284, 327, 329n9, 331, 333, 334, 342, 391
Rūḥ 46n56, 56, 58, 59, 78, 88, 95n18, 356, 366, 369, 374

Saʿāda 46n59, 209, 210, 211, 212, 213, 215n18, 216, 217, 218, 219, 220, 221, 222, 223, 224, 225, 226, 227, 228
Satan xiv, 58, 95, 99, 100, 101, 102, 103, 105, 106, 149, 150, 159, 222, 361
Self-realization 189
Sharʿ ix n2, xiv, xvi, 23, 27, 29n7, 30, 37, 40, 41, 42, 45, 46, 48, 50, 60n43, 88, 89, 90, 91, 92, 94, 95, 99, 100, 101, 102, 103, 104, 105, 106, 107, 108, 109, 110, 111, 112, 113, 114, 115, 116, 117, 118, 119, 120, 136n53, 137n55, 169, 181, 230, 231, 236, 239, 240, 241, 242, 243, 244, 249, 250, 251, 252, 255n5, 256n9, 257n11, 260n23, 261n24, 268n42, 270n46, 271, 272, 273, 274, 327, 336n39, 337, 344, 349, 371
Shemonah Peraqim 253, 254, 255, 256, 257, 258n15, 16 and 17, 259n19, 261n25, 262n26, 264n28, 266, 267, 272, 273, 274
Stoic 1n2, 2, 8n41, 44, 9, 22n121, 135n51, 145, 148, 152, 156, 157, 242, 243
Ṣudūr 2n3, 6, 8, 10n54, 13n73, 19, 21, 26, 28, 29, 38, 44, 183, 233, 234, 240, 376, 388, 390
Sufism xi, xii, xiv, xv, xvi, 12, 23, 26, 27, 29, 30, 31, 32, 33, 35, 36, 37, 38, 39, 40, 41, 43, 45n52, 46n59, 47, 48, 49, 50, 51, 53, 55, 56, 57, 64, 70, 73, 76, 77, 79n121, 81, 83, 84, 85n144, 86, 88, 103, 104, 105, 108, 113, 114, 123, 129, 130, 131, 132, 136, 139, 147, 148, 166, 167, 168, 169, 170, 171, 172, 173, 174, 175, 176, 180, 183, 184, 189, 190, 191, 192, 193, 203n60, 204, 205, 206, 207, 208, 209n3, 210, 211, 213, 214, 215, 216, 217, 218, 219, 220, 221, 222, 223, 224, 225, 226, 227, 229n1, 233n14, 234, 236, 238, 239, 241, 242, 251, 262, 265n32, 266, 267n39, 272, 289, 290, 294, 335, 345, 351, 353, 358, 359, 360, 362, 364, 365n49, 367, 369, 370, 384, 388
Syro-Roman Lawbook 307

Tadhakkur 37, 44, 62, 310, 311
Tafakkur xiv, 37, 43, 44, 45, 63, 70n83, 107, 217, 226, 310n23, 363
Tajriba 30, 35, 46, 47, 49, 76, 84n142, 88n155, 113, 114, 116n86, 128, 129, 142, 146, 147, 168, 173n37, 203, 214, 216, 221, 225, 227, 239, 241, 247, 261n24, 25, 262n25, 271, 272, 273, 279, 285, 289, 290n2, 3
Taqlīd ix, xii, 28, 40, 42, 44, 59, 141n12, 205, 222, 224, 286, 368, 371, 389n49
Taṣawwuf xi, xii, xiv, xvi, 17n94, 26, 27, 33, 35, 36, 38n20, 39, 40, 41, 43n44, 44, 45, 46, 47, 48, 49, 53n11, 70, 75n101, 76n108, 77, 83, 84n142, 87, 88, 128, 129n36, 138n4, 161n114, 167, 171, 174, 180, 182, 189, 190, 191, 208n1, 220, 225, 233, 234, 238, 239, 241, 254, 255, 256n9, 261n24, 25, 264n28, 265, 267, 271, 272, 273, 274, 289, 290n2, 3, 4, 309, 310n21, 314, 324n60, 363, 365n46, 379, 380, 384, 387
Tawakkul 36, 46n58, 165, 185, 190
Tawba 43, 158, 190, 269n42
Taʾwīl xiv, 59, 85n145, 89n3, 91, 92, 93, 94, 95, 96n24, 97n25, 27, 98, 99, 100, 101n40, 103n46, 105n51, 107n54, 56, 108n58, 109n60, 61, 62, 110n65, 66, 69, 111, 112n73, 75, 114, 115, 116n83, 118, 119, 120n96, 270n46, 355, 364, 370, 371
Temporales 331, 332, 333, 334, 335, 336
Transcendence 7, 21, 48, 90, 274

Al-ʿulūm al-burhāniyya 41, 219

Wājib al-wujūd 11, 33, 393n60
Waḥdat al-wujūd xviii, 359, 360
Wujūd xiii, xviii, 4, 9n47, 10, 11, 12, 18, 25, 27, 28, 30, 31, 35, 36, 39, 48, 56, 58, 62, 72, 77, 83, 84, 85, 86, 87, 95, 113, 133n48, 134, 144, 149, 153, 156, 170, 172, 176, 187, 212, 213, 222, 225, 232n8, 243, 248, 258, 259, 260, 261n24, 25, 262n26, 263, 265n30, 271, 272, 283, 285, 312, 319, 327n2, 329n9, 330, 331, 333, 334n27, 339, 341n1, 2, 348, 351, 352, 354, 355, 361, 368, 381n18, 381, 392, 393, 394, 395, 396

Yaqīn xvi, 29, 250, 364

Ẓāhir 45, 65n63, 64, 67, 70, 89n3, 101, 108, 111n72, 115, 118, 357, 360

Printed in the United States
By Bookmasters